Essential
Judaism

Essential Judaism

A Complete Guide to Beliefs, Customs, and Rituals

George Robinson

POCKET BOOKS

NEW YORK   LONDON   TORONTO   SYDNEY   SINGAPORE

POCKET BOOKS, a division of Simon & Schuster Inc.
1230 Avenue of the Americas, New York, NY 10020

Library of Congress Cataloging-in-Publication Data

Robinson, George, 1953–
    Essential Judaism: a complete guide to beliefs, customs and rituals / George Robinson.
        p. cm.
    Includes bibliographical references.
    ISBN: 0-671-03480-4
    1. Judaism.   I. Title.
    BM561.R58 2000
    296—dc21   99–055288

First Pocket Books hardcover printing March 2000

10   9   8   7   6   5   4   3   2   1

POCKET and colophon are registered trademarks of
Simon & Schuster Inc.

Printed in the U.S.A.

To Margalit Fox,
Marsha Melnick,
Margaret Moers Wenig—
women of valor.

And for Joel David Robinson and Lenora Miller Robinson—
may their memory be a blessing.

CONTENTS

CHAPTER 3
BIRTH TO DEATH:
A JEWISH LIFE CYCLE   138

CHAPTER 4
613 WAYS:
LIVING A JEWISH LIFE   195

CHAPTER 8
THE PHILOSOPHERS:
THE CONTINUING EVOLUTION
OF JEWISH THOUGHT   404

ACKNOWLEDGMENTS

For me, it all began with Paul Cowan. I never knew him, but when I picked up a copy of his wonderful memoir *An Orphan in History,* a book about his return to Judaism as an adult, it set me off on my own journey. On one level, this book is the culmination of that trip, and I have Cowan to thank. Otherwise I never would have come to be here.

Here, for me, is Beth Am, The People's Temple, a small, sometimes struggling, Reform congregation in Washington Heights. Upper Manhattan was once the home of many thousands of Jewish refugees from the Nazis, elegant and cultivated Austrians, Germans, and Hungarians who had been forced to flee for their lives. But by the time I moved to the Heights, nearly twenty years ago, they were moving out or dying out, and it was hard for a Reform congregation to survive, let alone grow.

But Beth Am has survived and, in the decade I have been a member, grown (albeit slowly). Had I read Cowan but not discovered Beth Am, I might have taken another path to Judaism or even a path away. I was lucky enough to find Beth Am shortly after reading the book and that, as they say, has made all the difference.

Many of the ideas in this volume were first broached at Beth Am. The section on Zionist thought had its genesis in a class I taught in 1997–1998 with Rabbi Margaret Moers Wenig. My thanks go to the four students in that class—Neta Bolzman, David Brent, Joseph Herson, and Benjamin Stix—who helped keep my thinking clear and honest. Likewise, the eight students—Allison Ancowitz, Abraham "Ace" Bouchard, Michael Herson, Elana Leopold, Tina Ritter, Joshua Rotbert, Daniel Saez, and Gabriel Salzman—in the class on Torah that I co-taught with Rabbi Wenig, Gerson Goodman, and Edith Rubino the following year were helpful in ways which they are too young to be aware of yet. The sidebar on Torah cantillation was helped immeasurably by the contributions of Margot Fein. The sections on the divergences among the four streams of American Judaism and the divisions within the Jewish people that emerged with Emancipation were road-tested in an adult education class that Ernest Rubinstein and I taught in

January 1999. The chapter on Jewish Philosophy had its beginnings in an excellent class that Ernie taught a few years earlier, and his gracious assistance in reviewing that chapter was an absolutely essential part of its completion. Many of my own ideas on prayer, the Festivals and the Sabbath were first aired from Beth Am's pulpit or in the spirited discussions that invariably follow Friday night services. It would not be an exaggeration to say that the entire congregation deserves thanks for letting me bend their ears from time to time.

One member of the congregation must get special thanks. When someone asks me, "Who did you write this book for?" I will always think of Connie Heymann. Connie was my "naive informant," a person who isn't an expert in the field but whose intelligence and interest (not to mention patience) made her the perfect reader. She vetted the entire manuscript and made thorough and helpful suggestions and comments throughout. For her many hours of help, I thank her (and her husband John Muller and their charming daughter Katherine Muller) profusely.

I have also been fortunate in having the aid of several expert readers who helped me refine the ideas found here: Michael Michlin, for his work on Chapter 6; Bruce Rosenstock, who reviewed Chapters 5, 7, 9, and 10; and especially Dina Weiner, who reviewed Chapters 1–4 in staggering detail. Needless to say, they are not responsible for any mistakes found in these pages.

I must express special gratitude to Beth Am's extraordinary rabbi. I grew up in the labor movement and Democratic party politics and when my father used the word "rabbi" he sometimes meant a Jewish member of the clergy but equally often was referring to a mentor or protector or just a good friend. Margaret Moers Wenig has been all of those things to me and to the rest of her congregants. "Rabbi" literally means "teacher" or "master," and she has been that as well. Her input in Chapter 1 was invaluable, but she has left her stamp on the author of this book even more than on the book itself. My thanks also to Rabbi Sharon Kleinbaum, one of the people who suggested me as a possible author, and who was an excellent guide to the burgeoning world of gay and lesbian synagogue life.

Marsha Melnick, the head of Roundtable Press, has been considerably more than just a business associate. Marsha has sweated through the long and painful interim between cancellation by another publishing house and eventual revival by Pocket Books with more patience than I could have asked for. She has been generous and supportive and inventive, a tough negotiator, a demanding editor when needed and a loyal friend and colleague at all times.

Many thanks also are due to Nancy Miller and Kimberly Kanner, my editors at Pocket Books, who have seen me adroitly through the minefields of the book publishing experience, and Jill Parsons for diligent, sensitive copy editing.

My family—Barbara Robinson; Marc Robinson; Stacey, Mike, Joanna, Mikey, and Justin Goodman; David and Laura Fox—were always wonderful. I hope they find the end product sufficient justification for my long absences and protracted silences. David Fox, my father-in-law, died as this book was going through the final editing process; he was a dear friend and it is one of my greatest regrets that he will not see the final product.

One of the founding members of Beth Am always told me not to list people I was thanking by name. "You'll forget someone and make an enemy out of a friend," she cautioned. It was sound advice—and I apologize profusely to anyone I have omitted—but there are some friends and colleagues whose help I must acknowledge. They are, in alphabetical order: Deborah Beshaw, Ivan Farkas, and the rest of CIW Team 6 and the staff of the Buddy Program at GMHC; David Feinberg, whose music guided me gently into the spiritual realm; Miriam Frank, Desma Holcomb and Ruth Frank Holcomb; Frank Free, Lea Gavrieli, Sarah Gold; Rob Goldblum and the staff of *Jewish Week;* Ira Hozinsky and Teresa Williams; Jon Kalish, Michael Kimmel, Bob Lamm, Jon Lukomnik, Russell Miller; my friends and colleagues in the New York Independent Film Critics Circle; Harriet Perlmutter; Andy Polin and Rabbi Bruce S. Warshal; the men who gave me my first job in Jewish journalism; Charles Salzberg, Carin Smilk, Mark Sprecher and Jace Weaver. Whether it was help with the book or support during the long hiatus, you were all there when I called.

Finally, a special thank you to the one person who suffered with me through all the difficulties and celebrated the triumphs. My wife, Margalit Fox, has always been a huge help to me professionally; she has the best eye and ear of any reader or editor I know and is utterly fearless and ruthless when necessary. The sixteen months that this book was in cold storage were a difficult time for me personally and professionally, but I never doubted that I had her full support in any way. I am forever in her debt.

A Note to the Reader

Hebrew, Aramaic, and Yiddish—the languages that account for the preponderance of the terminology encountered—are all written using the Hebrew alphabet. Although there are standard transliterations available, I have tried to follow my own ears as much as possible. In particular, I have transliterated the guttural sound usually given as "ch" with the letters "kh" throughout so that readers cannot mistake the pronunciation for a more familiar but incorrect one.

When he revived Hebrew as a modern language, Eliezer Ben-Yehuda chose Sephardic pronunciation over Ashkenazi, with the result that the State of Israel uses the Sephardic and, following their lead, the Reform movement in the United States does the same. That's what I learned, so that's what I've used.

I have translated non-English terms the first time they appear and occasionally thereafter. When in doubt, check the glossary.

Throughout this book I have scrupulously avoided gendered language when referring to the Supreme Being. God is beyond gender, and the use of gendered "God-talk" bothers me for a number of obvious reasons. Consequently, I have not even used words like Lord or King, preferring Adonai (admittedly a Hebrew word meaning "our Lord"—and a gendered one at that) and gender-free English terms.

All dates are given as B.C.E. (Before the Common Era) or C.E. (Common Era). Jews do not recognize Jesus as the Son of God, so *Anno Domini,* that is, "in the year of our Lord," is inappropriate. Besides, as someone pointed out to me recently, how can years be labeled B.C. when the birth of Jesus is generally dated from 4 C.E.?

Introduction

A decade ago, I went to a synagogue for the first time in more than twenty years. I had little idea what I would find there. I knew that I was looking for some sort of identity, of belonging. In my mid-thirties I had decided to seek out the roots I felt were somewhere for me to grasp. I just wasn't sure where. I had political affiliations and connections in abundance, professional organization and union memberships. But I didn't feel connected to my own past much beyond my immediate family.

The synagogue seemed a likely place to look. I was raised in classical Reform Judaism, in a somewhat typical suburban congregation on Long Island. I enjoyed Hebrew school—for a bookish kid with little athletic prowess, it was one more place to excel. I eventually left that synagogue and, for the next two decades, I was a "culinary Jew," as I like to call it—someone whose attachment to Judaism consists of eating bagels and lox and kosher deli. But when I went into another synagogue ten years ago, I wanted to see what it would be like to be a Jew again.

I found that I loved it. Ten years later, I'm an active member of that same synagogue, a trustee, choir member, newsletter editor; I served as president for two years, I lead services often, give occasional sermons, and teach both children's and adult classes.

But a decade ago, I was often baffled by what I saw and heard there. My instinctive reaction was to look for a book that would explain what was going on. I found plenty. There has never been a shortage of books on Judaism, on how to pray, on the festivals, rituals, customs, and folkways; on Jewish history, languages, and leading figures; on Jewish philosophy, ideology, theology, theosophy.

What I couldn't find was one volume that answered *all* my questions, large and small.

What I needed was a book that would explain what to do when the Torah was carried past me during a service, when it was proper to wear a prayer shawl or a skullcap, when to stand up and when to sit down. There are books on prayer that cover those topics. Some may even tell how and where to put up a *mezuzah,* how to keep kosher, how to lead a Passover *seder.* But those books often don't tell *why* to do those things, why Jews do those things. Too often, what is missing is the historical and philosophical underpinnings of Jewish practice.

And there were other questions that *those* books never addressed. Why pray in Hebrew and not, say, Yiddish? Why do Orthodox Jews do one thing and Reform Jews another? Why are Reform synagogues often called "temples," but Orthodox congregations never? How did the tragedies of Jewish history affect the way Jews pray and behave?

I have tried to write a book that will answer all these questions and put the answers into a larger context whenever possible. You are holding it in your hands.

A people's ideas are formed by their history, and vice versa. The interrelationship between events and ideas has always exerted a powerful attraction, and a lot of this book is about that relationship. Given the eventful history of the Jewish people, it would be hard to ignore the connection anyway, but it is of paramount importance to acknowledge the interplay. There are some who would have you believe that Judaism is a transhistorical, immutable system of belief, but that just isn't true.

The greatest discovery I made on my journey back into Judaism was that while I thought I was seeking another "political" identity and community, what I really had been looking for all along was a spiritual community. It has been the search for the ineffable, the mysterious, the . . . well, the holy, to be blunt, that has drawn me ever more deeply into Judaism as an adult. Most people will first encounter Judaism in this form—as a religion—whether by attending a wedding, bar mitzvah ceremony, funeral, a holiday celebration, or just an ordinary service at a synagogue.

So that is where this book begins. The first chapter of *Essential Judaism* covers Jewish prayer: the ideas behind it, the nuts-and-bolts mechanics of praying in a synagogue, the layout of a house of prayer, the role of the rabbi, music, and ritual choreography. From there, the book expands outward over the next three chapters, from the Jewish year to the Jewish life cycle to the ideas that motivate everyday Jewish life. In Chapter 2 you will find a guide to all of the Jewish holidays, how to celebrate them, and when. Chapter 3 takes you from before birth to after death in a Jewish life. Chapter 4 focuses on the idea of the *mitzvah*, which is usually translated as "commandment" but, as you will see, is a richer and more complex phenomenon. The *mitzvot* (plural) are at the center of how Jewish religious thought conceives of the covenantal relationship between God and humanity, and this chapter explains how that relationship permeates every aspect of Jewish life, no matter how mundane.

At the heart of the Jewish experience described in the first four chapters are certain basic sacred texts: the Bible, the Talmud and other rabbinic writings. Chapters 5 and 6 discuss these books: what you will find in them; how they figure in Jewish worship, thought, law, and practice; and how to explore them for yourself. Ultimately, there is no substitute for actually reading these texts, and I hope these two chapters will convince you to do so.

Chapters 7 and 8 bring into play two more aspects of Jewish thought, each of them significant in the evolution of Judaism. Chapter 7 traces the mystical strain within Judaism. Although Jewish mysticism is almost two thousand years old, this area of Jewish thought had been neglected by serious scholarship until the 1930s. Today, however, a great deal is being said and written about Jewish mysticism; it might truthfully be said that we are living in the Golden Age for the study of the subject. Unfortunately, there is as much nonsense as good sense being said on the subject at present; it might be equally truthfully said that we are living in the Age of Dross in the field of Jewish mysticism. In Chapter 7 I try to separate the real gold from the fool's variety.

Jewish philosophy is as old as Jewish mysticism, and has often been held in as deep disrepute. Jewish philosophers have always occupied an ambiguous position in the faith, but the importance of men like Philo, Maimonides, Buber, and Heschel is undeniable. Chapter 8 traces the development of Jewish thought "outside the Tabernacle," so to speak, as seen through the minds of eleven key thinkers, and examines why Jewish religious leaders have had such a difficult relationship with philosophy.

Chapter 9 examines the series of cataclysmic shocks that history dealt the Jews between the advent of Hasidism and the Holocaust. For some fifteen hundred years leading up to the end of the eighteenth century, there was basically one kind of Judaism—what today we call rabbinic Judaism—grounded in the Talmud and other rabbinic writings, with a very specific approach to Jewish law and practice. But with the coming of the Enlightenment in Europe, the position of the Jews in society changed radically and irreversibly as they came to be accepted—often grudgingly and always slowly—as citizens, and that change had a stunning impact on the nature of Judaism. Although this is not a book about Jewish history per se, by its very nature this chapter must deal with a stretch of significant events in Jewish and European history. No introduction to modern Judaism can ignore these events. In order to understand what Judaism is today, one must see how it has changed over the past two hundred years.

But the enormity of the changes the Jewish people underwent in the Enlightenment, the Emancipation, and their aftermath is dwarfed by the nature of the Jewish experience in one-tenth that time at the middle of the twentieth century. Between 1933 and 1948 the place of Jews in the world and in history was altered more radically—and more violently—than in any period ten times as long. I have deliberately chosen *not* to recount the events of the Holocaust or the founding and history of the State of Israel. Until recently, the Judaica section of most bookstores primarily consisted of books on those two subjects. There are many excellent volumes on each topic. (An interested reader would be well advised to start with Howard Sachar's two-volume history of Israel and popular works on the Holocaust by Martin Gilbert, Noah Levin, or Leni Yahil.) I felt it would add nothing to this book to duplicate such material. But there is no gainsaying the magnitude of these events or their impact on Jewish thought. Consequently, the last chapter of *Essential Judaism* concludes by addressing the reaction of the Jewish people to the Holocaust, and the founding of the State of Israel, as well as the interaction of Jewish theology and modern feminism, and the special place of American Jews in the Diaspora.

As this volume took shape I realized that it was more a book about Judaism as a system of belief (mostly, but not always, religious belief) and practices than a book of Jewish history. I have written about history where it has a direct impact on ideas; by its very nature, the final chapter is marked by the events of the Holocaust and Israeli history, but those events are familiar enough that I felt comfortable assuming that readers knew something about them.

One historical constant of Judaism is that, as the old joke goes, when you have two Jews in a room you get three opinions. Moses complains repeatedly to God that the Jews are "a stiff-necked people," fractious, and sometimes downright bad-tempered. Judaism has never been a monolithic entity (although it is only in the past 250 years that it has become as splintered as it is today). This book tries hard to reflect that reality. Generally, I have attempted to present the wide range of interpretations and practices that co-exist under the broad umbrella of Judaism. Undoubtedly, there will be many who will say that such-and-such "isn't authentic Jewish practice." What they mean is, "we don't do that, so anybody who does isn't as Jewish as we are." There are many ways to be an "authentic" Jew. If this book presents traditional practices in greater detail, that's because they are the baseline from which other practices depart. As a Reform Jew veering toward greater observance, I have tried to present all the options fairly.

This topic is vast. If I had thought four years ago about how vast it is, I might never have started to write this book. Certainly I have omitted many subjects—there is little about Jewish literature, the history of the Jewish-American experience, or Jewish art. I have left out some interesting historical figures for lack of space. (I particularly regret the loss of Heinrich Heine, whose sense of rootlessness and alienation anticipates much of modern Jewish literature, from Kafka to Philip Roth.) There just wasn't enough time or space for everything.

Finally, a closing word on why I wrote this book.

For four thousand years the Jewish people have persevered despite persecution and hatred. They have never been more than three percent of the world's population at any time in their history, yet their impact on world civilization is incalculable. They have survived despite great odds and against powerful enemies. As a Jew, I am an inheritor of that history; I feel obligated—proud—to pass it along. If one person who reads this book chooses to follow my path back to Judaism and experiences the joy, serenity, intellectual challenge, and emotional satisfaction that I have received in the decade since I walked into that synagogue, then my labor has been worth it.

CHAPTER I

Service of the Heart:
Prayer and Ritual

THE JEWISH IDEA OF PRAYER

In the beginning, the Jews were a tribe, a band of nomads, probably shepherds. Had they remained merely shepherds, they would have eventually died out, one of many tiny "nations" to be found in the ancient Near East, forgotten by all but the archaeologists.

But the Jews became something more. They were the bearers of a radical new concept, ethical monotheism, and that concept became the basis for a new kind of religion, Judaism. The latter was a religion marked by a new relationship between people and Deity.

Some would say that it was the idea of ethical monotheism that allowed the Jewish people to survive long after more powerful empires had vanished. Perhaps.

Contemporary scholars suggest that—at least at the start—the Hebrews believed in their own god, acknowledging the existence of other people's gods, but they also believed that their god could beat up everyone else's gods. Scripture tends to confirm that view; in Exodus 12:12, Adonai tells Moses, "[A]gainst all the gods of Egypt I will exercise judgments."

Eventually that notion evolved into something quite different, indeed, different from any previous idea of a Supreme Being.

This much seems clear: the idea of a single, omnipotent, omniscient God is a Jewish invention, one that has changed the course of Western (and, therefore, world) history. Let's begin with that concept and the ways in which it marks the Jewish religion. The Jewish idea of the relationship between God and humanity is perhaps nowhere clearer than in Jewish prayer, so it is there that we turn.

In other early belief systems, the ones that we casually denote as "pagan," divine creatures predate the creation of the world and humanity; but these belief systems have creation myths that usually involve the creation of the gods themselves. The opening words of the Hebrew Bible—*Bereshit bara elohim . . . /In the beginning God created . . .*—offer a very different vision. God is a given, a Being who creates out of *tohu v'bohu/the unformed and the void,* chaos and nothingness, a Being who preexists Creation, who was, is, and always will be.

The traditional Jewish liturgy underlines that belief explicitly. *Adon Olam,* the poetic hymn that is part of the morning service and which observant Jews recite every night before sleep, opens with the words, *Adon olam asher malakh beterem kol yitzer nivrah/Eternal Ruler who reigned before any creature had been created.* A few lines later, God is described as ruling "after all is ended," an eternal verity.

At the heart of Jewish prayer is the idea that God listens to prayer, that prayer is part of a dialogue between man and Creator. This idea has its roots in the Hebrew Bible itself, implicit in the statement that man was created *b'tzelem Elohim/in the image of God.*[1] Throughout the Bible, God engages in dialogue with the Forefathers and Foremothers, with the Prophets. The Forefathers and Foremothers of the Hebrew people beseech, praise, offer thanks to the Eternal. They even argue with God; Abraham negotiates over the destruction of Sodom and Gomorrah, finally convincing God to spare the two cities if a mere ten righteous men can be found (Genesis 18).

The incredible variety of prayers in the Jewish liturgy suggests the multiplicitous nature of the relationship between God and humanity. In the course of a single service, we may encounter God the Creator, the Redeemer, the Father, the Judge, Rock of Israel, Shield of Abraham, and many others. Each of these personifications of God implies a different relationship between the Deity and the person praying.[2]

THE NAMES OF GOD

In his revision of Frazer's *The Golden Bough,* Theodor Gaster notes, "In primitive thought, the name of a person is not merely an appelation, but denotes what he is to the world outside of himself—that is, his "outer" as distinguished from his inner being. Thus, the 'name of God' in the Bible is His outward manifestation in the world. . . ." Not surprisingly, given the plethora of divine attributes, God has many Names in the Hebrew Bible and in Jewish liturgy, and those Names are multiplied by the inexactitude of the translator's art.

The Holy One tells Moses, "I revealed Myself to Abraham, to Isaac and to Jacob as El Shaddai, but My Name Adonai I did not make known to them (Exodus 6:3)." In the Bible and the Talmud, God has many more Names: *El/The Strong One, El Shaddai/God Almighty, El Olom/God Everlasting, El Khai/The Living God, El Elyon/God Most High, Elohim/God, Adon/Lord, Adonai/Lord, Adonay Tzivaot/Lord of Hosts, Abir/The Strong, Kedosh Yisroel/Holy One of Israel, Melekh/The Ruler, Tzur Yisroel/Rock of Israel.*

For non-Jews, the most familiar Name derived from the Hebrew Bible is probably Jehovah, a mistransliteration of the four-letter Name, *Yud-Hay-Vav-Hay,* the Tetragrammaton or, in Hebrew, the *Shem Hameforash.* This Name is actually never vocalized in Hebrew—it is too sacred, too powerful. Reading the four-letter Name aloud, a Jew will say "Adonai." (As we will see in Chapter 7, the Jewish mystics believed that the Tetragrammaton had unusual significance attached to it.) The Tetragrammaton is frequently shortened to Yah (*Yud-Hey*), Yahu or Yeho (*Yod-Heh-Vav*), especially when used in combination within names or phrases, as in *Yehoshua* (Joshua, meaning "the Lord is my Salvation"), *Eliyahu* (Elijah, meaning "my God is the Lord"), and *Halleluyah* ("praise the Lord"). A traditionally observant Jew will not vocalize God's other Names outside the context of prayer. Thus, in an Orthodox prayer book or songbook, one will find *Elokeinu* for *Eloheinu/Our God, Adoshem* for *Adonai* or, most commonly, *Hashem/The Name.*

Progressive Jews have brought their own set of concerns and strictures to the naming of the Supreme Being. God has no gender in conventional human terms, but gendered God-talk has historically implied a valorization of God's masculine attributes. Reform, Reconstructionist, and some Conservative *siddurim* will avoid using gendered names for God, discarding Lord or King in favor of Adonai or Ruler.

Many traditionally observant Jews will not write the vernacular equivalent of the sacred names, preferring G–d or L–rd (although other no less traditional Jews deride this practice because these words are English and therefore *not* true names of God). This practice, however, has different roots from the ban on uttering the *Shem Hameforash,* the proscribed sacred Name. Contrary to popular belief, this practice does not come from the commandment not to take God's Name in vain. In Jewish thought, that commandment refers solely to oath-taking, and is a prohibition against swearing by God's Name falsely or frivolously (the word normally translated as "in vain" literally means "for falsehood"). Incidentally, this is why observant Jews serving on juries or testifying in court will affirm rather than swear.

Judaism does not prohibit writing the Name of God per se. But it does prohibit erasing or defacing a Name of God. Consequently, observant Jews avoid writing any Name of God casually because of the risk that the written Name might later be defaced, obliterated, or destroyed accidentally or by one who does not know better. The commandment not to erase or deface the name of God is derived from Deuteronomy 12:3–4. In verse 3, the people are commanded that when they take over the promised land, they should destroy all things related to the idolatrous religions of that region, and should utterly destroy the names of the local deities. Immediately afterwards in verse 4, we are commanded not to do the same to our God. From this, the rabbis inferred that we are commanded not to destroy any holy thing, and not to erase or deface a Name of God. This prohibition applies only to Names that are written in some permanent form. Recent rabbinical decisions have held that typing on a computer is not a permanent form, thus it is not a violation to type God's Name into a computer and then backspace over it or cut and paste it, or copy and delete files with God's Name in them. However, once you print the document out, it becomes "permanent."

In adddition, the prayers found in the *siddur* (prayerbook, derived from the Hebrew word *seder*, meaning "order") fall into several different genres, enriching the dialogue between God and each Jew. Prayers of blessing, supplication, thanksgiving and praise all may appear in the benedictions. In Hebrew liturgy, such a prayer, known as a *b'rakhah/blessing* or in plural form as *b'rakhot*, ends with the formula *Barukh atah Adonai/Blessed are You, Adonai* . . . begins with the same formula followed by words praising God appropriate to the occasion or need. For example, in the Amidah, the standing prayer that is at the center of the liturgy, we pray, *Barukh atah Adonai mekhayei hakol/Blessed are You Lord, who gives life to all.* This is the shortest version of the *b'rakhah* formula, a *khatimah/seal* (pl. *khatimot*) that closes off a section of prayer.

In *b'rakhot* that stand on their own, we add the words *Eloheinu Melekh ha-olam / our God, Ruler of the Universe* to the opening formula. For example, the following blessing occurs in the morning service:

Barukh atah Adonai, Eloheinu Melekh ha-olam, she-asani b'tsalmo.

Blessed are You, Adonai, our God, Ruler of the universe, who has made me in your image.

In *b'rakhot* said before fulfilling a specific *mitzvah / obligation* (see Chapter 4), the formula is expanded further. For example, the blessing for the lighting of Sabbath candles reads:

Barukh atah Adonai Eloheinu Melekh ha-olam, asher kid'shanu b'mitzvotav v'tzivanu l'hadlik ner shel Shabbat.

Blessed are you Adonai our God, Ruler of the Universe, who sanctifies us by Your commandments and commands us to kindle the lights of the Sabbath.

In virtually all *b'rakhot,* there are two interesting paradoxes that reflect key elements in the relationship between God and Jew. First, there is a shift between the opening of the shorter form of the *b'rakhah,* which expresses an intimate personal relationship between God and the one who prays ("Blessed are You, Adonai, our God") and the second part, which bespeaks a cosmic relationship ("Ruler of the Universe").

Second, between the opening ("Blessed are You . . .") and the second part of the *b'rakhah,* the prayer shifts from the second person to the third person ("who sanctifies us . . . and commands us"). This change is not always apparent in the English translation of the blessings because many translators choose to smooth over this apparent "mistake" in grammar, but it is present in virtually all *b'rakhot.* Much has been written about this second shift, this peculiar change in person. Most commentators believe that, like the first change in tone in the formula, it reflects God's dual relationship between intimacy and distance, affection and awe, moving from direct address, "You," to indirect address (implicitly, "the One who commands us").

Judaism has always placed great value on an individual's relationship with and reaction to God. The second-century sage Rabbi Yose says that when the Israelites were given the Law at Sinai, each of them heard a different voice of God, a splendid metaphor for the unique response of each Jew to the traditions of Judaism. Prayer, too, is an individual experience and, as we will see shortly, the state of mind that an individual brings to worship is of enormous importance in Jewish practice.

The relationship between God and man is not only a solitary relationship. Virtually all the *b'rakhot* are written in the first-person plural: "the one who commands *us*." Although it is possible for a Jew to pray alone, Judaism insists on the communal nature of worship, on prayer as an act most fittingly performed in a community. Certain key prayers may only be recited in the presence of a *minyan/quorum* of ten adult Jews. As Dr. Eugene Borowitz, a contemporary Reform theologian, writes:

> Judaism does not think of man abstracted from his relation to mankind. It does appreciate the meaning of the individual in isolation, but holds him, the single one, in unremitting importance, against a background of society and history. For the Jew, man is a social and historical creature. Hence his prayer should properly be a communal, comradely affair. Public worship is a universal human need and, also, a specifically Jewish requirement.
> — "The Individual and the Community in Jewish Prayer," *Gates of Understanding* (New York, 1977)

Praying in a community serves many functions. Rabbi Lawrence Hoffman, a contemporary expert in liturgy, has said that communal worship represents mankind's attempt to impose meaning on a chaotic, arbitrary, and indecipherable universe. Certainly there is great comfort in being surrounded by like-minded worshippers during times of crisis.

Jewish prayer rituals are designed to reinforce that sense of community. Even if a Jew is unable to pray in Hebrew, she can still say "Amen" after hearing a *b'rakhah*. Rabbi Judah writes in a second-century midrash, a homiletic commentary, "He who answers Amen in this world is privileged to answer Amen in the World to Come." To answer "Amen" is to participate in prayer as part of *klal Yisrael/the community of Israel*.

For the individual Jew, communal worship provides the additional satisfaction of being tied into a historical continuity that began with a covenant between God and Abraham, and continues with the world-wide community of Jews. Sociologist William Helmreich, recalling his Orthodox upbringing in Brooklyn, writes:

> Although I might be nothing more than a speck on the map of Jewish history, the shape and location of that map were clear in my mind. I belonged—and every ceremony we performed, every prayer I said, strengthened that image. When I went to a friend's house for Shabbos [the Sabbath] and heard the same melodies, uttered the same benedictions and even ate the same foods, I felt a bond that tied me inseparably to my people.
>
> —*Wake Up, Wake Up, to Do the Work of the Creator* (New York, 1976)

There are more connections made when a Jew prays than even he may realize. Any time a Jew prays, he stands in a spiritual river made up of three tributaries of time.

First, an individual Jew brings a personal history to prayer. Does a certain musical setting of *Adon Olam* have a special meaning for her? Is he saying the Mourner's *Kaddish* for a recently deceased parent? How does she conceive the Creator?

Second, assuming one is praying in a synagogue, that synagogue has its own *minhag*, its own customary ways of doing things. For example, in an Ashkenazi congregation, it is customary for the entire congregation to stand when the Mourners' *Kaddish* is recited; in a Sephardic congregation, only the mourners will stand.

Or, to give another example that is closer to home for me, in all but Reform congregations, the *hakafah,* the procession around the congregation with the Torah scrolls that precedes the reading of the Torah, is standard practice. But in the Reform movement, custom varies. The first time I prayed at my current synagogue, I was utterly baffled by a Torah service that included a *hakafah*. What was I supposed to do when the Torah was carried past me? (You either kiss the Torah, or touch your prayerbook to it and kiss the prayerbook.) Seven years later, I can't imagine a Torah service *without* such a procession. Yet, when I visit another Reform synagogue, that may be precisely what I encounter. It all depends on the *minhag* of that congregation.

Finally, and most important, a Jew prays within an uninterrupted four-thousand-year history of Judaism, of a four-millennium-long covenant between God and the Jews, a history that includes some two thousand years of organized and ordered liturgy.

One unique feature of Jewish worship underlines the importance of that history: study of sacred texts is considered an integral part of the worship. The weekday morning service, for example, includes several passages from the Talmud—not a liturgical text at all, but a compilation of biblical commentary, legal rulings, folktales, and much more—and from the Torah. There is a *b'rakhah* specifically for Torah study. (For that matter, the *Sh'ma,* the second most important prayer in the liturgy, comes from Deuteronomy and is considered recitation of a biblical text rather than prayer. See sidebar "The *Sh'ma,*" p. 33.) The continual poring over familiar texts like Torah—read in its entirety in annual cycles—is meant to lead not only to knowledge, but also to respect and awe for God. One could picture Jewish worship as an ongoing search for spiritual enlightenment, with textual study as one of the key components of that search. The Jews have rightly been called "the People of the Book," for they are intoxicated by words, by text, by study.

The complex web of relationships between the individual Jew, the worship community, and the Jewish people, between past and present, is an essential part of the Jewish experience of communal prayer.

What is striking about Jewish communal prayer is not merely that it presumes an active dialogue between God and the individual. Christianity asserts similar relationships in individual prayer. What sets Judaism (and Islam) apart is that it believes in *direct* discourse with God without benefit of the intervention of clergy, even in a communal prayer setting. Because Judaism is not a religion based on sacraments like communion, which can only be administered by a priesthood, a Jew doesn't need a rabbi to speak to God, even in a formal religious service. Any ten adult Jews (in traditionally observant practice, adult male Jews) can form a *minyan,* a quorum for prayer, and hold a service in a reasonably appropriate place. In fact, one doesn't even need a *minyan* to hold a service (although there are certain prayers that are communal in nature and are, therefore, omitted from a service at which fewer than ten are present).[3]

Any Jew over the age of thirteen can lead a service, can read from the Torah, can give a sermon. In a women's *tefilah/prayer* group, any girl over twelve can perform these tasks. In Reform, Reconstructionist, and many Conservative congregations, women are counted in a *minyan* and can perform any of the functions allotted in a worship service. The leader in a synagogue service is usually called the *shaliakh tzibbur/messenger of the community;* he (or she in many liberal congregations) functions as reader or cantor, leading worship by repeating aloud certain passages of the liturgy, leading hymns, and so on. The *Shulkhan Arukh,* the medieval digest of Jewish laws that is still the guide for Orthodox Jews, lists six qualities required of a *shaliakh tzibbur:* humility, acceptability to the congregation, knowledge of the rules of prayer and proper pronunciation of Hebrew, an agreeable voice, proper dress, and a beard. The last qualification is waived except for the High Holy Days.

Judaism wasn't always so democratic. When Solomon built the First Temple in Jerusalem, only the priests could perform certain rituals, receiving sacrifices and making them. When that Temple was destroyed in 586 B.C.E. and the Jewish people were sent into exile in Babylonia, their leaders had to devise new ways of worshipping God. The Temple was rebuilt after their return to Palestine, but with the second and final destruction of the Temple in 70 C.E., it was no longer possible to bring sacrifices and offerings to God as prescribed in Jewish law. With no Temple, there was no place to perform those specific rites. Rituals freed of sacrifices and offerings no longer require a priestly caste. A worship centered on liturgy, on words, rather than on sacraments (as is the case in, say, Christianity), could be led by laymen. (There is one holdover from the days of the Temple in Jerusalem: the schedule of daily services used today—*shakharit/the morning service, minkhah/the afternoon service, ma'ariv/the evening service*—roughly corresponds to the schedule of sacrifices.)

Thus, the second great innovation of Judaism was, as one Christian theologian put it, the creation of a form of worship that did not involve spilling blood.

THE ROLE OF THE RABBI

For the vast majority of modern practicing Jews ever since (with the notable exception of certain Hasidic communities; see Chapter 7), Judaism is still resolutely nonhierarchical in worship. The distinction between lay leadership and the rabbinate is much narrower in practice and theory than in most Christian denominations.

About the only thing a rabbi can do in front of a congregation that can't be done by an ordinary Jew is sign a marriage license, and that power is not granted by a Jewish body but by the state. A layperson can conduct a a funeral or a *kiddushin/sanctification* ceremony for a wedding. (However, even the most progressive congregations will not permit a layperson to be responsible for performing a wedding; there are too many legal questions, issues like witnesses, the rings, etc., to take the risk.)

That being the case, what exactly does a rabbi do in terms of worship? To some extent, the answer to that question depends on the branch of Judaism to which the congregation belongs, the *minhag* of the congregation, and even its financial situation.

For example, in a prosperous Conservative synagogue, the congregants may expect services to be led by a polished, highly trained cantor, who will *daven* (Yiddish "pray") the entire service, except when there's a *bar mitzvah* and the *bar mitzvah* boy or *bat mitzvah* girl will lead portions of the service. The rabbi may do little more during services than announce page numbers and deliver a sermon (although the latter is no small thing!). A less well-to-do congregation may hire a rabbi who can *daven* well.

In general, in a Reform synagogue the rabbi leads services. For reasons growing out of the evolution of the Reform movement, which had its roots in nineteenth-century Germany and which in its first century tried to emulate the style of neighboring Protestant churches, members of Reform congregations were until recently less likely to learn to lead services, deferring to the rabbinate and cantorate. The result was a Reform lay population that until the past twenty or so years was less educated in liturgy and worship. In recent years, the Union of American Hebrew Congregations, the umbrella organization of Reform synagogues in the United States, and the Central Conference of American Rabbis, the organization representing the Reform rabbinate, have moved to remedy that problem. In smaller congregations that lack a full-time rabbi, congregants are now leading services, trained by a rabbinic aide program.

But even with a more educated lay membership, Reform and Conservative rabbis are still an indispensable part of worship. They are still the most informed in matters of the laws of traditional liturgy, the most educated about what's going on in the Jewish world liturgically, the first to hear when a movement publishes a new prayerbook. And even in an Orthodox synagogue, a congregation in which the average layperson is well qualified to *daven* on his own, it still falls to the rabbi to decide thorny questions of practice.

"The rabbi is necessary as a teacher and as someone to rule on Jewish law, including liturgical questions, but is not needed to lead services," one prominent Reform rabbi told me. "You need someone in the room to make sure that what is done is being done right. There are so many minute details of Jewish law that there has to be someone there who is really learned."

In addition, there are issues of the aesthetics and cultural principles that have to be taken into account in planning worship. "The clergy are still the most educated in planning worship," the rabbi concluded. "Who knows the most about what you have to do to make worship 'work'?"

Regardless of what a rabbi knows or does during worship, he or she cannot intercede with God for the congregation. Ultimately every Jew is responsible for his own conversation with God. And what happens in that dialogue is a matter of great concern in Judaism.

Imagine yourself in conversation with someone you cannot see, someone you have never seen, yet who is omnipresent and omnipotent. Needless to say, left to your own devices, you would probably be rendered speechless, or reduced to a handful of mumbled, stammered commonplaces. The rabbis who began the process of setting the liturgy recognized this problem some two thousand years ago, and the establishment of a fixed order of prayers is the way in which they addressed it.

A Jew needn't invent his own prayers to God (although there is space within the liturgy to do so at points in the *Amidah*). She needn't feel that God's response to her worship will be based on how eloquent or poetic her words are. The words are the same at each of the day's services, the same on each Sabbath, on each festival.[4] An observant Jew who prays every day, three times a day, will undoubtedly have memorized large portions of the liturgy. A knowledgeable Jew can walk into a synagogue anywhere in the world and know where she is in the service. But even an occasional synagogue-goer can pick up a *siddur/prayerbook* and follow the service in Hebrew or in translation.

The great medieval Jewish philosopher and legal scholar Maimonides said that the Torah requires that one pray only once a day. He defined prayer to include, at the least, praise, supplication, and thanks, in that order. Prior to the time of Ezra (fifth century B.C.E.), that is probably what people did. With the Exile after the destruction of the Temple, Hebrew ceased to be the only language spoken by the Jews; as its use became more unnatural for Jews in the Diaspora, it became necessary to establish fixed prayers.

But the rabbis understood that a fixed liturgy was only a starting point. A Jew who relies on a rote knowledge of the *siddur* to speed through his devotions, who prays without feeling—by rote—is not really praying. "Rabbi Eliezer says, 'When someone makes their prayer *kevah/fixed,* their prayer is not prayer' " *(Mishnah Berakhot 4:4).*

The rabbis of the first century C.E., the great sages of the era in which the liturgy began evolving towards its current form, called prayer "service of the heart," and they understood that the heart must be involved in prayer for prayer to reach to the gates of Heaven. "Prayer," they said, "needs *kavanah.*"

What is *kavanah?* Literally translated it means "intention" or "direction." In practice, it refers to the focus and directedness with which one should pray. Referring to the two most important prayers in the Jewish liturgy, Maimonides writes, "The first thing you must do is turn your thoughts away from everything else when you recite the *Shema* or *Amidah.* . . . When you are engaged in the performance of religious duties, have your mind concentrated entirely on what you are doing." *(Guide for the Perplexed,* 3.51). It is written that the pious Jews of old would wait for an hour before reciting the *Amidah,* hoping to develop the appropriate state of mind to speak with God. After all, as Rabbi Eliezer also said in the first century C.E., "When you pray, know before Whom you stand!" Maimonides would add that at the same time one should focus on the content of the words.

Kavanah is undoubtedly responsible for one of the most oft-remarked aspects of Jewish prayer, the swaying to and fro during prayer that one often sees in a synagogue, particularly in an Orthodox congregation. Called *shucklin,* a Yiddish word, this bowing or swaying often grows out of the intensity of feeling experienced by the one praying. The *Zohar,* a key work of Jewish mysticism, says that when a Jew "says one word of Torah, a lamp is kindled and he cannot keep still, but sways to and fro like the flame of a wick." Others attribute this movement to the words of Psalm 35, which says, "All my limbs shall declare, Adonai, who is like

You?" It should be noted that swaying during prayer isn't obligatory; in fact there are rabbinical authorities who oppose it, but the general consensus is that if it is an aid to *kavanah* it is acceptable, if not, then not.

Kavanah is also responsible for another aspect of Orthodox worship that many non-Orthodox Jews find disconcerting: everyone prays at his/her own pace, with little of the service repeated in unison. William Helmreich recalls an experience from his childhood in an Orthodox congregation: "To have said each prayer in unison would have inhibited the freedom of expression that enabled us to pray with fervor. Besides, certain words meant more to different people, and at different times, depending on their mood" (*Wake Up, Wake Up, to Do the Work of the Creator* [New York, 1976]).

Many of the enchanting tales of the Hasidic rabbis of the eighteenth and nineteenth centuries illustrate the supreme importance of *kavanah* in worship. One of the best-known concerns the little boy who came with his father to the Yom Kippur service conducted by the Baal Shem Tov, the founder of Hasidism and one of the great figures of eighteenth-century Judaism. The boy had with him a small flute. As the service drew to its dramatic close and shofar was blown to signal the end of this holiest of days, the little boy pulled out the flute and in his excitement he sounded a note of his own, a shrill piercing sound that brought everything to a halt. His father was mortified and infuriated, but the Baal Shem Tov calmed him, saying, "Until that moment there was some doubt if our prayers would ascend to heaven, but at the sound of that flute, the angels held open the gates and all the prayers entered."

THE BLESSINGS OF DAILY LIFE

Although communal prayer is one of the central tenets of Jewish religious practice, it is no more important than home ritual. There is a wide range of ritual practices that are specifically earmarked for the home, rituals and prayers meant to be performed within the family circle. Home and family are paramount values in Judaism; perhaps that is to be expected from a people whose history has been one of almost constant exile. Along with community and God, family has been one of the mainstays that has enabled the Jewish people to survive, and a people that has been uprooted repeatedly knows the value of home.

Home worship practices range from the lighting of candles and reciting of *kiddush* (a prayer of sanctification over wine) to mark the Sabbath and the festivals, to the building and eating of meals in the *sukkah*, an open-ended decorated booth, during the holiday of *Sukkot*. We will discuss home worship in greater detail elsewhere, but its importance points to another significant aspect of Jewish prayer: its pervasiveness in the daily life of an observant Jew. When a Jew rises in the morning, he thanks God for preserving him through the night. Before a Jew goes to sleep, she prays to God to protect her slumber. A Jew says a *b'rakhah* before eating anything and grace after, a *b'rakhah* over washing his hands upon rising and another for washing hands before a meal, even a *b'rakhah* after using the toilet. There are blessings for different types of food, fragrances, and natural phenomena, for seeing great men sacred or secular. (See sidebar "An Assortment of Blessings" below.)

In short, there is almost no aspect of life for which an observant Jew does not thank and bless the Creator. As a *midrash* observes, almost every moment and action of a Jew's day is charged and regulated by some sort of commandment. In worship, the creation of sacred space and time are of paramount importance, but in Judaism even the everyday has a sacred aspect. The works of the Eternal are all around us, and traditional Jewish practice calls upon us to recognize their ubiquity and to respond appropriately.

AN ASSORTMENT OF BLESSINGS

For the observant Jew, even the most ordinary aspects of life are invested with an aura of wonder, of sanctity. Judaism includes blessings for almost anything one can experience during the day (and the rabbis believed that a Jew should offer at least a hundred *b'rakhot* every day). Here is a selection of blessings for a wide range of occasions and phenomena.

Before eating bread:
Barukh ata Adonai Eloheinu Melekh ha'olam ha-motzi lekhem min ha'aretz/Blessed are You Adonai our God, Ruler of the Universe, who brings forth bread from the earth
Before eating products of wheat, barley, rye, oats, or spelt:
Barukh ata Adonai Eloheinu Melekh ha'olam borei minei mizonot/Blessed are You Adonai our God, Ruler of the Universe, who creates many types of nourishment

Before drinking wine or grape juice:

Barukh ata Adonai Eloheinu Melekh ha'olam borei p'ree ha-gafen/Blessed are You Adonai our God, Ruler of the Universe, who creates the fruit of the vine

Before eating fruit grown on a tree:

Barukh ata Adonai Eloheinu Melekh ha'olam borei p'ree ha-eitz/Blessed are You Adonai our God, Ruler of the Universe, who creates the fruit of the tree

Before eating produce grown in the earth:

Barukh ata Adonai Eloheinu Melekh ha'olam borei p'ree ha-adamah/Blessed are You Adonai our God, Ruler of the Universe, who creates the fruit of the earth

Before eating or drinking any other foods:

Barukh ata Adonai Eloheinu Melekh ha'olam she-hakol ni-hiyeh b'dvaro/Blessed are You Adonai our God, Ruler of the Universe, through Whose word everything came to be

Upon smelling fragrant shrubs, trees, or their flowers:

Barukh ata Adonai Eloheinu Melekh ha'olam borei atzei b'samim/Blessed are You Adonai our God, Ruler of the Universe, who creates fragrant trees

Upon seeing lightning:

Barukh ata Adonai Eloheinu Melekh ha'olam oseh ma'aseh b'reisheet/Blessed are You Adonai our God, Ruler of the Universe, who makes the work of Creation

Upon seeing the ocean:

Barukh ata Adonai Eloheinu Melekh ha'olam she'aseh et ha-yam ha-gadol/Blessed are You Adonai our God, Ruler of the Universe, who made the great sea

Upon seeing exceptionally beautiful people, trees, or fields:

Barukh ata Adonai Eloheinu Melekh ha'olam shekakhah lo ba-olamoh/Blessed are You Adonai our God, Ruler of the Universe, who has such in His universe

Upon seeing exceptionally strange-looking people or animals:

Barukh ata Adonai Eloheinu Melekh ha'olam mishaneh hab'riyot/Blessed are You Adonai our God, Ruler of the Universe, who makes the creatures different

Upon hearing unusually good news that benefits not only oneself but others:

> Barukh   ata   Adonai   Eloheinu   Melekh   ha'olam   ha-tov
> v'hametiv/Blessed are You Adonai our God, Ruler of the Universe, who
> is good and does good
> **Upon hearing unusually bad news:**
> Barukh ata Adonai Eloheinu Melekh ha'olam dayan ha-emet/Blessed
> are You Adonai our God, Ruler of the Universe, the true Judge

THE DAILY SERVICES

There are at least three worship services each day, whether
it is a weekday, *Shabbat/Sabbath,* or a festival day: *shakharit/morning,*
minkhah/afternoon, and *ma'ariv/evening.* (On Shabbat and the Festivals,
there is a fourth service, *musaf/additional,* which immediately follows
the morning service. On Yom Kippur, there is a fifth service, *ne'ilah,* as
we will see in Chapter 2.) The elements of each service, regardless of
time of day or day of the week or year, are fundamentally the same. By
following a typical weekday in the life of a traditionally observant Jew,
we can see how worship is structured and also understand how it has
evolved in the other streams of Judaism: Reform, Conservative, and
Reconstructionist.

BEFORE THE MORNING SERVICE

When a traditionally observant Jew rises in the morning, the first
thing he says is:

*Modeh ani l'fanekha, Melekh khai v'kayam, shekhezarta bi, nishmati
b'khemlah—rabah emunatekhah.*

*Thank you, O God, Living and Eternal Ruler, for having compassionately
returned to within me my soul—abundant is your faithfulness.*

He then washes his hands in the prescribed ritual manner: with his
right hand, he picks up a vessel of water, passes it to his left and pours
water over the right. Then he switches hands and repeats the process.
He does this three times for each hand, then recites:

*Reisheet khokhmah yir'at Adonai, sekhel tov l'khol osekhem, tehilato
omedet la'ad.*

The beginning of wisdom is fear of God—good understanding to all their practitioners; His praise endures forever.

Barukh sheim k'vod malkhuto l'olam va'ed.

Blessed be His Name forever.

This passage is taken from Psalm 111.

A traditionally observant male Jew will now put on a *tallit katan*, a four-cornered undershirt with a set of *tzitzit/fringes* at each of its corners, reciting the following blessing for the wearing of *tzitzit* (see sidebar "*Tallit* and *Tzitzit*" below):

Barukh atah Adonai Eloheinu Melekh ha'olam asher kid'shanu b'mitzvotav v'tzivanu al mitzvat tzitzit.

Blessed are You, Adonai our God, Ruler of the Universe, who has sanctified us and commanded us concerning the tzitzit.

If one is saying the morning blessings at home, it is now time to put on the *tallit/prayer shawl* and, for Orthodox men and those other men and women who do so, to don the *tefillin/phylacteries,* reciting the appropriate blessings and Torah passages regarding the wearing of each ritual object, as prescribed in the *siddur.* (See sidebar "*Tefillin,*" p. 25.) If one begins the day with the morning service at synagogue, these rituals are performed there.

TALLIT AND TZITZIT

The final paragraph of the *Sh'ma* is a passage from Numbers 15:38 instructing the Israelites to wear fringes on any four-cornered garment as a reminder of Adonai's commandments. Male Orthodox Jews, even small boys, will wear an undershirt *(tallit katan/small tallit)* with four corners and fringes *(tzitzit)* from the moment he awakens until he undresses at night. Most Jewish men (and many Jewish women in Conservative, Reconstructionist, Reform, and even some Modern Orthodox congregations) will wear a prayer shawl, a *tallit gadol/large tallit,* at morning services, *musaf,* all day on Yom Kippur (even into the evening), and for minkhah at Tisha b'Av, in recognition of this mitzvah. (The shaliakh tzibur will wear a tallit regardless of time or marital status.)

The tzitzit are tied in a specific way: four threads doubled over, making eight threads; one thread, longer than the others, wound around them and double-knotted, usually with the double knot followed by seven, eight, eleven and finally thirteen windings, leading to a total of five double knots, numbers that have a kabbalistic significance. The tzitzit must be inspected regularly to make sure they are still kosher/legal with no tears or the kind of wear that creates more than eight threads. If there is damage, they must be replaced.

Usually a tallit gadol will have an embroidered neckpiece to indicate where the collar is. The neckpiece is called the atarah/crown and is there, in part, to strengthen the fabric at the point at which it will bear the most strain. To put on a tallit, one holds it spread out in both hands with the neckpiece at the top, then recites the blessing:

Barukh atah Adonai Eloheinu Melekh ha'olam, asher kidshanu b'mitzvotav, v'tzivanu l'hitatef b'tzitzit.

Blessed are You, Adonai our God, Ruler of the Universe, who sanctified us with His commandments, and commanded us to wrap ourselves in tzitzit.

If you have borrowed another congregant's tallit for only a few minutes, it is not necessary to recite the blessing; however, if you are wearing a tallit that belongs to the synagogue and will have it on for an extended period of time—say the length of the morning service—you should recite the blessing. Many worshippers like to cover their heads with the tallit while reciting the blessing, fulfilling the commandment by "wrapping" themselves and taking a moment for quiet meditation on the significance of this commandment. The tallit should be draped over the shoulders, hanging down the front of the body so that the tzitzit lie at the four corners or directions around the person.

Like the priests in the Temple in Jerusalem who wore turbans to mark their awareness of the presence of the Almighty, a Jew who wears a tallit adds a sense of formality and solemnity to prayer. At the same time, wearing a tallit helps one to feel sanctified in the service of God. Putting the tallit over one's head during the Amidah allows a worshipper to experience both the public and private nature of Jewish prayer simultane-ously.

In traditionally observant congregations, it is the *minhag* for many to press the fringes to the eyes and to kiss them three times during the recitation of the last section of the *Sh'ma*, when saying the word *tzitzit*. When the Torah comes past your seat during the *hakafah*, you may extend your *tzitzit* to touch it, then kiss them. When called to the Torah to read the blessings, it is customary in most congregations for you to touch the *tzitzit* to the place in the scroll where the reader will begin, and then to kiss them, and to repeat this gesture when the reader finishes.

TEFILLIN

"You shall bind them as a sign upon your hand and they shall be a sym-bol before your eyes. . . ." So we are told in the *Sh'ma*. For the rabbis of the Talmudic period, this was an injunction from God to wear *tefillin*, small wooden boxes containing parchment scrolls on which the words of four paragraphs from the Torah (Exodus 13:1–10, 11–16; Deuteron-omy 6:4–9, 13–21) are written. The boxes have wider bases and an opening through which leather straps are passed. The Hebrew letter *shin* is written on the boxes; the head strap is tied with a knot in the shape of the letter *daled*, the arm strap with a knot in the shape of the letter *yud*. These three letters spell *Shaddai*, one of the names of God. *Tefillin* can be purchased at most Judaica shops.

Tefillin are worn for the daily morning service in Orthodox and most Conservative synagogues. However, they are not worn on Shabbat or Festivals because keeping the Sabbath and the Festivals is already a sign of God's covenant, so a further reminder is deemed unnecessary. (They are also not worn on the first day of mourning or by a groom on his wedding day.)

The donning of *tefillin* is a somewhat complicated affair; it is recom-mended that the first couple of times you put them on, get the help of an experienced *davener*. After putting on your *tallit*, but while still standing, place the *tefillin* on the muscle of the left forearm so that it is facing your heart and recite the blessing, which concludes *"v'tzivanu l'haniakh tefillin/commanded us to put on* tefillin." Tighten the strap and wind it seven times counterclockwise around the forearm below the elbow. (This is the Ashkenazi custom; in Hasidic and Sephardic *minhag*, you face the knot on the arm away from you and wind clockwise.) Making sure that the black side of the strap is outside, now wind the remainder around the palm of the hand. Now take the head *tefillin* (also called the *shel rosh*) from the bag, unwind the straps, remove the case, and place it upon your head. Before you adjust the straps, recite the blessing (which concludes *"v'tzivanu al mitzvat tefillin/commanded us regarding the mitzvah of* tefillin*"*) and the statement *Barukh shem k'vod malkhuto l'olam va'ed/Blessed is the name of God's glorious sovereignty forever.* Adjust the *shel rosh* so that it is above the forehead, lying above your hairline and centered between the eyes. The knot should be resting at the base of your skull, the straps over each shoulder down the front of your chest. Now unwrap the strap on your hand from your palm, wind it three times around your middle finger. The remainder of the strap is wrapped around the ring finger and then around the palm. While doing this, one recites a passage from Hosea, "I will betroth you to me forever; I will betroth you to me in righteousness and justice, in kindness and mercy; I will betroth you to me in faithfulness, and you shall know Adonai."

Removing the *tefillin* is simply a reversal of putting them on. Unwind the arm strap from your fingers, rewind it about the palm. Remove the *shel rosh* and wrap it up neatly, then unwrap the strap around your palm and forearm and slip it off. Wrap up the *tefillin* neatly and put both away in their bag. It is customary to kiss the *tefillin* when taking them out of the bag and putting them away.

Jewish men are not required to don *tefillin* until they have become *bar mitzvah*. Being allowed to do so at the age of thirteen constitutes a significant rite of passage. William Helmreich recalls, "More than anything else tefillin was the mitzvah that made me feel the significance of my newly acquired status. It was the most tangible evidence that I was now a man."

In the Middle Ages, there was a spirited dispute over the order in which the parchments were to be placed in the *tefillin*, with the great medieval sage Rashi and his grandson, Rabbenu Tam, in strong disagreement. As a result, some Hasidic Jews would wear two sets of *tefillin*, one of Rashi's and another of Rabbenu Tam's, in order to be certain of complying with the commandments.

The wearing of *tefillin*, say the sages, is one commandment that even God observes. Where Jews wear *tefillin* upon whose parchment is written the *Sh'ma*, however, Adonai wears *tefillin* containing the verse from I Chronicles, "And who is like unto Your people Israel, a nation one in the earth."

SHAKHARIT/THE MORNING SERVICE

The first prayer one utters upon entering a synagogue for a morning service, whether it is a weekday, Sabbath, or festival, is *Mah Tovu,* a series of five verses taken from the Bible (Numbers 24:5; Psalms 5:8, 26:8, 95:6, and 69:14). The prayer takes its name from its first verse, *Mah tovu ohalekha Ya'akov mishkenotekha Yisrael/How lovely are your tents O Jacob, your dwelling places O Israel,* and its subject is the feeling of joy and reverence with which one encounters the synagogue. This prayer is generally followed by the blessing for the study of Torah, as Torah study is an integral part of the morning service (and the blessing covers any other Torah study that one may undertake during the remainder of the day).

THE BASIC STRUCTURE OF THE SERVICE

The daily morning service includes all the key elements of the liturgy, so it makes a good outline.

Birkat Hashakhar/Morning Blessings
P'sukei D'zimrah/Songs of Praise
The *Sh'ma* and Its Blessings
   Call to Prayer (the *Barkehu*)
   Yotzer
   Birkat ha-Torah
   The *Sh'ma* (3 paragraphs)
   G'ulah
Amidah/Standing Prayer
   Blessings of Praise
   Blessings of Petition (omitted on Shabbat but replaced by a blessing for the Sabbath)
   Blessings of Thanksgiving
Silent Prayer
*Seder K'riat ha-Torah/*Service for the Reading of the Torah (Monday, Thursday, and *Shabbat*)
   Concluding Prayers
      Aleinu
      Mourner's Kaddish

COVERING THE HEAD

In ancient Near Eastern cultures it was considered a sign of respect to keep one's head covered. With its roots in that part of the world, Judaism adhered to that custom. In Mesopotamia, for example, men of high caste wore some sort of head covering in public at all times; in the period of First Temple until its destruction in 586 B.C.E., priests and other officials of the Temple wore turbans or mitres, probably in imitation of the local custom.

In the Talmud, there were a variety of opinions expressed but, finally, the day was carried by those who believed it impertinent to allow the *Shekhinah*, the female manifestation of God, to see their bare heads below Her.

The debate over men's head covering would continue for several more centuries, but in the Middle Ages the choice was gradually taken away from the Jews. In much of Europe, Christian authorities demanded that Jews wear special hats or hoods that, along with yellow badges that prefigure the Nazi-imposed star of the Holocaust period, identified them as non-Christian.

Since that time, customs regarding head covering have evolved to reflect the history of various Jewish communities. Hence, some Hasidic Jews of Eastern Europe (and their successors in the United States, Western Europe, and Israel) favored the fur-covered round hat called a *shtreimel*. Today, many American Orthodox Jewish men wear black fedoras. The Jews of Central Asia wore turbans, but now are most identified with the brightly colored cylindrical Bukharan skullcaps.

The most familiar manifestation of the custom of covering the head, however, is the flat, round skullcap known in Hebrew as a *kippah* (plural, *kippot*) or in Yiddish as a *yarmulkah*, the head covering of choice for the vast majority of Ashkenazi Jews. Even here, the *minhag* has evolved in different directions: Orthodox men will wear a *kippah* throughout their waking hours; Conservative and Reconstructionist Jews may do the same, but are equally likely to wear it only in synagogue, at meals, or while studying sacred texts; some Reform synagogues actually went so far as to proscribe the wearing of headgear on their premises, but in recent years many Reform congregations have begun offering *kippot* to worshippers (both men and women), and students at Hebrew Union College, the Reform rabbinical seminary, usually are seen wearing *kippot*.

Unlike the *tefillin* and *tallit,* the *kippah* has no intrinsic sanctity, perhaps because wearing it is not prescribed in Torah; consequently, there is no blessing for donning a skullcap (nor is there an extensive literature on the *kippah* comparable to the many books on other Jewish ritual objects). It should also be noted that some Jews, especially those raised in the Hasidic tradition, will cover their heads with the *tallit* during certain important prayers such as the *Amidah.*

Throughout the debate on men's head covering, all the sages were in agreement on one thing: married women must cover their hair. Even in Biblical times, it was considered a brazen violation of the rules of modesty for a married woman to allow anyone but her husband to see her hair. For the Orthodox, this regulation remains in place. Contemporary women's head coverings run the gamut from scarves and snoods to fashionable hats. Hasidic women will, even today, have their heads shaved just prior to the wedding ceremony and will wear a scarf to cover their heads. One other option available to Orthodox women is the *sheitel* (Yiddish), a wig. In all Orthodox, many Conservative, and even some Reform synagogues, women are asked to cover their heads during worship and "chapel caps," small, flat lace equivalents of the *kippah,* are provided for that purpose.

In our contemporary world, a world of men and women traveling through outer space, of fiber-optic cable thinner than a human hair, of DNA testing and the ubiquitous computer, we have perhaps become so jaded that we don't notice the miraculous nature of the everyday. But the morning service is designed to bring the seemingly ordinary to our attention forcefully. At this point in the *shakharit* service, we begin the fifteen blessings called the *nisim b'khol yom,* a series of prayers that thank God for such simple miracles as the ability to distinguish day from night, the strength to rise from our beds, for clothing, freedom, the earth on which we walk, and *am Yisrael/the people Israel.*[5]

Two of these fifteen blessings, however, have engendered considerable controversy both among Jews and non-Jews. In Orthodox prayerbooks, the second of the blessings reads:

Barukh atah Adonai Eloheinu Melekh ha'olam shelo asani goy.

Blessed are You Adonai our God, Ruler of the Universe, for not making me a Gentile.[6]

For men the fourth blessing thanks God for not making them women; for women the text thanks God for "having made me according to His will." In the *ArtScroll Siddur,* one of the most comprehensive of Orthodox *siddurim,* the commentators explain that "The Torah assigns missions to respective groups of people. . . . All such missions carry extra responsibilities and call for the performance of *mitzvos* associated with them. We thank God, therefore, for the challenge of improving His universe in accordance with His will." Men, consequently, thank God for not having made them women so that they are obligated to carry out all commandments that have a designated time for performance, *mitzvot* from which women are excused by traditional Jewish law (on the assumption that their traditional household duties may make it difficult for them to perform them in a timely fashion).

However, the Conservative, Reform, and Reconstructionist movements reject this argument; indeed, all three ordain women as rabbis and cantors and do extensive interfaith work with non-Jewish clergy and laypeople. Their prayerbooks have significantly altered these two *b'rakhot.* In the Conservative-endorsed *Siddur Sim Shalom,* for example, these blessings have been replaced by ones that thank God "for making me a Jew" and "for making me in God's image."

In Orthodox (and in some Conservative) synagogues, the next section of the morning service is a series of Talmudic and Biblical readings, including the story of the Binding of Isaac, the *Akeidah.* This is followed by a lengthy series of readings on the sacrificial offerings that were made in the Temple in Jerusalem during the time it was standing. The great Torah sages of the Diaspora considered the study of these passages to serve as a substitute for the making of the offerings themselves, impossible since the destruction of the Temple.

In the Talmud we are advised, "A person should always praise God first and make his requests afterwards." Thus, the morning service proper begins with a selection of Bible verses and Psalm 30, which introduce the next section of the *siddur,* the *P'sukei d'zimrah/Songs of Praise* (which is known as the *z'mirot/songs* in Sephardic prayerbooks). These are drawn from the Psalms and from I Chronicles 16:8–36. Beginning with the blessing that precedes this series, *Barukh She'amar/Blessed is He who spoke,* it is forbidden to interrupt your prayer with conversation until the conclusion of the *Amidah.* (In an Orthodox congregation, with everyone praying at his own pace, you may find yourself still *davening P'sukei d'zim-*

rah while the reader has moved on to other prayers. If so, it is permissible to respond "amen" where appropriate, and to respond to the *Barekhu* and *Kaddish* as indicated in the prayer book.)

Opening the songs of praise with *Barukh She'amar* is an apt choice; this prayer is a call to praise directed primarily to the role of God as Creator and Initiator. The *Yishtabakh* blessing, which is the last of the *P'sukei d'zim-rah*, concludes this section of the service by proclaiming that the Eternal One shall always be praised. *Yishtabakh* is introduced by another series of biblical verses and Exodus 16, the "Song at the Sea," and followed by a half-*Kaddish,* that is, a *Kaddish* from which the final three verses are omitted, which serves here as a punctuation device, dividing one section of the liturgy from the next. (See sidebar *"Kaddish"* below.)

KADDISH

Kaddish is a prayer that should be familiar to even nonobservant Jews. Because it is the prayer for mourners in one of its several forms, it is one prayer that almost everyone has heard at some point in their lives. More than that, it occurs several times in some version during the course of most worship services.

The prayer is a hymn of praise to Adonai, calling for the establishment of God's sovereignty. Written in Aramaic, it really exists in four variants: the *Khatsi Kaddish/half-Kaddish;* the whole *Kaddish; Kaddish de-Rabanan/Kaddish for the Teachers;* and the Mourner's *Kaddish.*

The half-*Kaddish* contains the first two verses of the prayer, and is used to separate sections of the service. The whole *Kaddish* is recited by the *hazan/cantor* immediately following the repetition of the *Amidah. Kaddish for the Teachers* adds an entire verse to the whole *Kaddish,* a prayer "for Israel, our teachers and their disciples, and for all who study Torah." It is recited at the end of study sessions and in Orthodox and many Conservative congregations after passages of the worship service that are drawn from the rabbinic literature.

The recitation of the Mourner's *Kaddish* allows the bereaved to lead the community in praising God. Everyone responds with the lines *Y'hei sh'mei rabah m'vorakh le'olam va'ed/May God's great name be blessed forever.* The prayer was written in Aramaic because that was the common language of the Jewish world when it was composed, and it is imperative that any Jew be able to say it. Being able to restore one's faith in God after the experience of losing a loved one is an essential part of the grieving process for a person of faith; saying *Kaddish* is a moving part of that process. At the same time, it is a way of honoring the deceased by praising Adonai in their name.

When saying the whole *Kaddish* and the Mourner's *Kaddish*, it is customary on reciting the final lines *(Oseh shalom bim'romav, hu ya'aseh shalom aleinu v'al kol Yisrael/May the One who causes peace to reign in Heaven let peace descend on us and on all Israel)* to take three steps backward before uttering the words, bowing first to the left on *oseh shalom*, then to the right on *hu ya'aseh aleinu*, and finally forward on *aleinu v'al kol Yisrael*. This choreography is designed to replicate the etiquette of taking leave of a sovereign.

In the medieval mystical text the *Zohar* it is written, "All sacred acts require summoning." With that in mind, the rabbis placed next the *Barekhu*, a summons to worship by the *shaliakh tzibur,* who bows at the waist and solemnly intones, *"Barekhu et Adonai hamevorakh/Bless Adonai, Who is blessed,"* to which the congregation responds, bowing, *"Barukh Adonai hamevorakh l'olam va-ed/Blessed is Adonai, Who is blessed forever and ever."* The *shaliakh tzibur* then repeats that response, so that he is included with the congregation in that blessing of God. Some fifteen hundred years ago, in some Jewish communities, services actually began with the *Barekhu;* it truly was a call to prayer, much like the cry of the muezzin that alerts Muslims that it is time to pray. The liturgy that now precedes it began to accumulate as early as the second century C.E. (When fewer than ten are present—i.e., in the absence of a prayer quorum, called a *minyan*—the *Barekhu* is omitted; if a *minyan* is not present, the gathering does not constitute public prayer but rather private worship, and so a call to prayer is unnecessary.)

The *Barekhu* is the beginning of the *Sh'ma* and its blessings. This series of prayers is among the central elements in the liturgy of every service. More than that, the paragraphs of the *Sh'ma* are derived from Deuteronomy, so they constitute Torah study. The service cannot move directly into the *Sh'ma* itself without some proper preparation. For that reason, one now says the blessing *Yotzer/Giver of light,* which thanks God for the gift of light and the ongoing miracle of Creation and follows it with *Ahavah Rabbah,* a *b'rakhah* that thanks God for the gift of the *mitzvot* and Torah and pledges to follow its precepts.

THE *SH'MA*

It is the first prayer a Jewish child learns; the last thing an observant Jew says before sleep each night; the last prayer a Jew says before death; and, in a religion noticeably devoid of statements of creed, a religion that has no catechism, it is as close as you can come to a Jewish statement of essential faith.

> *Sh'ma yisrael Adonai Eloheinu Adonai ekhad.*
>
> *Hear, O Israel, our God Adonai is one.*

This is the part of the prayer that almost every Jew knows but, in fact, there is considerably more to it than that one sentence, important though that sentence is. In fact, the *Sh'ma* is three paragraphs long, including not only this essential statement of God's uniqueness but also sections of Deuteronomy (6:4–9, 11:13–21) and Numbers (15:37–41) that prescribe some of the most important elements of Jewish ritual, including instructions on when to recite the *Sh'ma*.

The full text of the prayer instructs us to recite these words "when we lie down and when we rise up," and to wear them upon our heart and as a sign between our eyes, to inscribe them "upon doorposts of your house and upon your gates." On the basis of these instructions, the rabbis devised the schedule of reciting the *Sh'ma* congregationally twice daily, at the morning and evening services, and in bed just before sleep, the idea of wearing *tefillin* at the morning service and placing a *mezuzah* on the doorways to Jewish homes (See sidebar "Mezuzah," p. 51). In addition, the final paragraph prescribes the wearing of *tzitzit*, the ceremonial fringes on four-cornered garments.

The other element of the *Sh'ma* that amplifies its importance in Jewish theology is that the middle section, drawn from Deuteronomy 11:31–21 adds the concept of reward and punishment, a concept that is one of the cornerstones of ethical monotheism: there's more to this than just believing in one Supreme Being, you also have to behave properly.

Given the prayer's importance, it should come as no surprise that the rabbis ask for the utmost in concentration when it is said. Many Jews cover their eyes with their right hand while saying the opening two lines of the prayer, the better to concentrate on God's oneness, as one prayer book has it. Maimonides writes, "One who reads the *Sh'ma* and does not concentrate his mind while reciting the verse 'Hear, O Israel, our God Adonai is One,' has not fulfilled his liturgical duty."

The second line of the prayer,

Barukh shem k'vod malkhuto l'olam va'ed.

Blessed be the name of God's glorious kingdom forever.

is said in an undertone except on Yom Kippur. There are several explanations for this in the rabbinic literature. Perhaps the most poetic is the notion that Moses heard the angels singing this line to God when he reached the peak of Mt. Sinai; since he "stole" it from the angels, we can only recite it *sotto voce* until we atone for our sins on Yom Kippur and are, briefly, as pure as the angels.

Although it is usually thought of as a statement of monotheism, the *Sh'ma* is convincingly read as an affirmation of God's uniqueness and unity, that the Creator is not only one and not many, but wholly Other, different from anything in the Creation. Some Hasidic thinkers go even farther, suggesting that there is nothing but God, that the whole universe exists only within God.

After these two *b'rakhot* we recite the two most important passages in Jewish liturgy, the *Sh'ma* and the *Amidah*. (See sidebars on p. 33 and below.) There is a blessing that falls between the *Sh'ma* and the *Amidah* creating a thematic bridge between them. The *Sh'ma* concludes with the declaration that God took us out of Egypt; the *Amidah* opens with a blessing that asserts God's ability to redeem us in the future. Between them is a blessing that refers to the redemption from Israel and the miracle of the parting of the Reed Sea (familiarly but incorrectly translated as the Red Sea). Thus, God has saved us in the past and we believe in and invoke the power of the Almighty to save us in the future.

THE *AMIDAH*

The rabbis thought the *Amidah*, the standing prayer, so important that they originally called it *ha-Tefillah/The Prayer*.

In its fullest version, nineteen blessings in all, it states some of the most basic assumptions of the Jewish faith. It is also called the *Shemoneh*

Esrei/Eighteen Benedictions, a name that dates from before the addition of the nineteenth benediction when the text was standardized.

In traditionally observant congregations, the *Amidah* is said silently by the congregation, and repeated by the *hazan* in the morning and afternoon (in the presence of a *minyan*), with the congregation answering "amen" after each of the blessings. The prayer is recited at all three daily services in its full version. On Shabbat the first three and last three blessings are recited, with a middle blessing added in place of the intermediate blessings (for a total of seven); the middle blessing differs depending on which Shabbat service is being *davened*.

The first three blessings are known as *Shevakh/Praise*, and consist of *Avot/Patriarchs*, *Gevurot/Mighty Deeds*, and *Kedushat ha-Shem/Holiness of God's Name*. The final three blessings are known collectively as *Hoda'ah/Thanks*, and consist of *Avodah/Temple Service*, *Hoda'ah/Thanksgiving*, and *Birkat Shalom/Blessing for Peace*. The intervening weekday blessings are: *Da'at/Insight* (also called *Binah*), *Teshuvah/Repentance*, *Selikhah/Forgiveness*, *Ge'ulah/Redemption*, *Refu'ah/Healing*, *Birkat ha-Shanim/Season Blessing*, *Kibutz Galuyot/Ingathering of Exiles*, *Hashavat Mishpat/Justice* (also called *Din*), *Birkat ha-Minim/Against Heretics*, *Al ha-Tzadikim/For the Righteous*, *Binyan Yerushalayim/Rebuilding Jerusalem*, *Mashiakh/Messiah*, and *Kabalat Tefillah/Acceptance of Prayer*. Because these middle blessings are prayers of supplication, they are omitted on the Sabbath and Festivals; the replacement is *Kedushat ha-Yom/Holiness of the Day*, a blessing that is specific to the day of worship.

It is customary to recite the *Amidah* while facing towards Jerusalem. (If you are in Jerusalem, you are supposed to face the Old City; if you are in the Old City, you face the Temple Mount, site of the Temple.) One is supposed to articulate each word when praying the silent *Amidah*, with one's feet planted together as a sign of respect (and to be parallel to the angels, who have only one foot, as per Isaiah 6). At the beginning of the prayer, a worshipper is supposed to take three steps forward, as if approaching the Throne; at the end of the prayer, one takes three steps back. In the opening benediction, "*Avot*," the worshippers bend at the knees at the word *Barukh/Blessed*, bow the head at *atah/are you*, and straighten up at *Adonai*. This is done at the beginning and the end of "*Avot*" and is repeated in the next-to-last benediction, at the opening words *Modim*, and at *V'khol ha-khayim*, which concludes the blessing.

No conversations are permitted during the praying of the *Amidah.* Indeed, the Talmud cautions, "One should not say the *Tefillah* while immersed in sadness or idleness or laughter or light talk or frivolity, but only in the joy of the performance of the *mitzvot.*" (*Berakhot 31a*)

For many centuries, the morning service ended here, the worshippers dispersed and went about their daily rounds. But with the passage of time and the addition of many individual devotions, the service began to expand to include other prayers and today the *Amidah* is followed by a confession of sins; a petition for grace and forgiveness called the *Takhanun* (which is omitted during all festivals); a Torah reading on Mondays, Thursdays, and Festivals that concludes with the first *aliyah* (the calling of a congregant to read the blessings for the reading of the Torah) of the following Sabbath's Torah reading; the recitation of Psalm 145, which is part of another song of praise to Adonai called *Ashrei—Uva l'Tzion* (verses from Chronicles, a song of supplication that is omitted on festivals); a full *Kaddish; Aleinu* (which we will examine momentarily); and the Mourner's *Kaddish.*

Aleinu is the prayer which closes every service. It is followed only by the Mourners' *Kaddish* and, in most synagogues, a closing hymn. The *Aleinu* is a firm proclamation of God's sovereignty, an exploration, as it were, of God the Ruler of all. Like the *Barekhu, Aleinu's* recitation is accompanied by a small piece of choreography: when reciting the words

Va'anakhnu kor'im umishtakhavim u'modim,
lifnei Melekh malkhei ham'lokhim ha-Kadosh barukh Hu.

We bend our knees, bow and acknowledge our thanks to
the King who reigns over kings, the Holy One, Who is blessed.

worshippers bend their knees at *kor'im* and then bow from the waist at *umishtakhavim,* rising again at *lifnei Melekh.*

Aleinu is a prayer that has caused considerable trouble for Jews in the past. In the year 1400, an apostate Jew started the rumor that the passage that said that other peoples "bow down to vanity . . . and pray to a god that cannot save" was a slander specifically aimed at Christians, and French and German authorities demanded the removal of that section. In 1703 Prussian authorities demanded that *Aleinu* be removed from the liturgy and posted sentinels to make sure that it was not recited. After several more run-ins with authorities in Germany, the offending passage was deleted from *Aleinu* in Ashkenazi worship, although it is still found in Sephardic *siddurim* and has been restored to many Orthodox Ashkenazi prayer books.[7]

Although Conservative, Reform, and Reconstructionist services end with the Mourner's *Kaddish,* in most Orthodox congregations it is followed by the recitation of the Psalm of the day. In the Temple in Jerusalem, the Levites, the priestly class, would recite a Psalm chosen for its appropriateness to the day of the week. As a memorial to the Temple, Orthodox Jews continue that practice. On Sundays, they recite Psalm 24; on Mondays Psalm 48; on Tuesdays Psalm 82; on Wednesdays Psalm 94—95:3; on Thursdays Psalm 81; and on Fridays Psalm 93. (The Psalm for Saturday is 92, but Saturday is also the Sabbath and an entirely different set of rules regulating liturgy comes into effect, as we shall see shortly.) Finally, there is a series of readings of psalms and other Bible verses after the conclusion of the *Shakharit* service, of which Orthodox Jews may avail themselves.

MINKHAH/THE AFTERNOON SERVICE

Minkhah is the shortest service of the day. Its name is derived from the meal offering that was made at midday in the Temple in Jerusalem. The order of the service is quite simple. It opens with Psalm 145 (often called *Ashrei*), which is followed by half-*Kaddish;* the *Amidah;* on those days on which it is prescribed, the penitential prayer called *Takhanun; Aleinu;* and concludes with the Mourner's *Kaddish.* The *Sh'ma* is not said, as the service doesn't fall at one of the times specified for its recitation in Deuteronomy 6:7. On the Sabbath, the Torah is read but the *Haftarah,* the reading from the Prophets, is omitted. In addition, on fast days, there is a Torah reading (two sections of Exodus, 32:11—14 and 34:1—10) and a *Haftarah* (Isaiah 55:6—56:8). *Minkhah* can be prayed no earlier than a half hour after midday, and no later than sunset. In many congregations, *Minkhah* will be prayed as late as can be permitted so that the service may segue conveniently into *Ma'ariv/The Evening Service.*

MA'ARIV/THE EVENING SERVICE

The *Ma'ariv* service derives its more commonly used name from one of its opening prayers in which we thank God *"ha-ma'ariv arivim/Who brings on the evening."* The service is occasionally called *Arvit/evening,* and occurs shortly after sundown.

Ma'ariv is the only one of the three daily services that doesn't correspond to the schedule of offerings in the Temple in Jerusalem. In fact, because the *Amidah* was considered the equivalent of a sacrificial offering, for many years (until roughly the ninth century C.E.) the standing prayer was omitted from the evening service. Gradually it was introduced into the service and is now an integral part of the *Ma'ariv* liturgy. The *Amidah* is still not repeated by the *shaliakh tzibur* at *Ma'ariv* in a traditional congregation.

After an opening confessional prayer *(Vehu Rakhum/For God is merciful),* the prayer leader will intone the *Barekhu* and the congregation responds.

The *Sh'ma* is preceded by two benedictions, as opposed to only one in the morning. The first of these has as its theme God's role as the bringer of evening, the second God's redemption of Israel from slavery in Egypt. The *Sh'ma* and its blessings are followed in the evening by two more benedictions. The first of these is *Emet v'emunah/True and faithful,* which appropriately describes our reliance on God through the night (as opposed to *emet veyatziv/true and steadfast,* which is said in the morning), and leads into the hymn *Mi khamokha/Who is like You?* This blessing is followed by *Hashkiveinu,* a particularly poignant prayer in which the congregation asks that God watch over them as they sleep, guarding them from harm, an apt theme for an evening worship service. The remainder of the service consists of the *Amidah* and the Mourner's *Kaddish.*

But before a Jew goes to sleep, there is one last private prayer to offer, the "bedtime" *Sh'ma.* After offering forgiveness to anyone who has wronged us during the preceding day, and asking that our words find favor with God, we pray for protection from harm during sleep, including bad dreams. Then the *Sh'ma* is said, including the first paragraph from Deuteronomy 6:5–9 and a series of Psalms extolling God's role as protector, followed by *Hashkiveinu,* and the threefold Priestly Benediction:

Yiv'verekhekhah v'yishm'rekhah

May God bless you and guard you

Ya'er Adonai panav eilekhah v'khumekhah

May God show you favor and be gracious to you

Yisah Adonai panav eilekhah va-yasem l'khah shalom

May God show you kindness and grant you peace.

Finally, *Adon Olam* is recited, with its final verse: *"I place my spirit within His care, when I wake as when I sleep / God is with me, I shall not fear, body and spirit are within his care."* Thus, a Jew ends the day the same way it began, by offering praise to God as a Protector and Creator without limits.

THE SHABBAT SERVICES

KABBALAT SHABBAT / WELCOMING THE SABBATH AND *MA'ARIV*

As the sun disappears on Friday evening, Shabbat begins. Indeed, Jewish holidays also begin with sunset. Why?

The answer is startlingly simple. In the first verses of *Bereshit / Genesis*, God creates light and "there was evening and morning, the first day." (Genesis 1:5) The rabbis reasoned that if the Torah, the product of divine revelation, said that the first day began with evening, that must have been God's intention, for "days" to begin at sunset.

So when the sky is streaked with the fading Friday sunlight, in Jewish homes around the world, candles are lit, *b'rakhot* are said, and Shabbat is welcomed. And in synagogues, the Friday *ma'ariv* service begins with a series of hymns, Psalms, and blessings collectively known as *Kabalat Shabbat / Welcoming the Sabbath*.

In Orthodox congregations, *Kabbalat Shabbat* consists of Psalms 95 through 99, Psalm 29, the hymn *L'khah Dodi / Come my beloved*, Psalms 92 and 93, a lengthy reading from the Talmud passages governing the Sabbath, placed here to separate *Kabbalat Shabbat* from *Ma'ariv*, and both the Mourner's *Kaddish* and *Kaddish de-Rabanan,* a *Kaddish* said after learning in a group, in honor of our teachers. In Conservative, Reform, and Reconstructionist services, the Talmud passages and the two versions of *Kaddish* may be omitted, often replaced by a half-*Kaddish* that separates the *Kabbalat Shabbat* from the *Ma'ariv* service proper.

Shabbat is a time of joy, and the six Psalms that make up the bulk of the *Kabbalat Shabbat* are celebratory, corresponding to the six days of creation; but it is *L'kha Dodi* that many feel is the true centerpiece of this portion of the Shabbat evening service. In the sixteenth century, the small town of Safed, located in the mountains of Galilee in northern Israel, was a center of Jewish mysticism. Solomon ben Moses HaLevi Alkabets was one of the many mystics who lived and studied there. On Friday nights, Alkabets and his colleagues would dress in white like bridegrooms and joyously dance and march through the fields outside town to greet the Sabbath, which is depicted in both Talmud and in mystical texts as a bride and queen. Around 1540, Alkabets, a poet, composed a beautiful ode to the Sabbath Bride, *L'kha Dodi,* urging Jews to greet the Sabbath and extolling her virtues. The poem quickly became an eagerly awaited part of the Friday night service, adapted by German Ashkenazim within less than a hundred years. Today, with more than two thousand musical settings of Alkabets's Hebrew text, it is recited or sung in virtually every synagogue in the world as the Sabbath is ushered in. In many congregations, when the final verse is sung and the words "Enter, O Bride," are said, the worshippers will turn to the entrance of the sanctuary and bow in honor of the Sabbath Queen. (Incidentally, the initial letter of each of the first eight verses of *L'kha Dodi* form an anacrostic spelling of Alkabets's name, one example of the linguistic cleverness of a poem that is full of biblical allusions, puns, and wordplay.)

After *Kabbalat Shabbat,* the basic shape of the Sabbath evening service closely resembles that of its weekday counterpart, up to the recitation of the *Amidah,* with the *Barekhu,* the *Sh'ma,* and the *b'rakhot* that precede and follow it. Just prior to the recitation of the *Amidah,* however, worshippers recite an injunction to keep the Sabbath, known as *V'shamru.* Moreover, the Sabbath version of the *Amidah* is considerably shorter than the daily version. On a day of joy, a day that reaffirms the covenant between God and the Jewish people, the rabbis thought it rude to ask for special favors. Hence the middle blessings of the *Amidah,* the blessings of supplication, are omitted. The Sabbath *Amidah* consists of the first three and last three blessings of the daily prayer, with a middle blessing that thanks God for the institution of the Sabbath. The middle blessing includes the biblical verses that refer to God's creation of the Sabbath, in order to fulfill the rabbinic understanding of the command to "remember the Sabbath Day," which appears in the Ten Commandments (Exodus 20). The rabbis interpreted this verse to include the necessity for verbal testimony to the holiness of the Sabbath, which is done twice on Friday night, during the *Amidah* and again during *Kiddush*, each time with the same verse from Genesis. At the end of the Sabbath *Amidah,* a short prayer, "the essence of [the] *Tefillah,*" called *Magein Avot / Shield of Our Fathers,* is read.

Although some members of a congregation will have already made *kiddush* over wine at home before coming to the evening service (or will do so upon returning home afterwards), at this point in the liturgy the prayer leader will recite the *kiddush* again. The historical evidence is unclear as to which came first, the home ceremony or the communal one. However, the rationale behind the duplication is believed to have its roots in the early days of the synagogue as an institution, when it doubled as a temporary place of lodging for traveling Jews; being on the road and away from home, they could count on making *Kiddush* and having a sip of Sabbath wine in the synagogue. The rabbis saw no reason to eliminate either recitation of the prayer and, indeed, in our busy workaday world of the late twentieth century, for many Jews *kiddush* in the synagogue is the only one they will have a chance to experience on a given Friday night.

With *kiddush* completed, the evening service moves quickly to its conclusion, with *Aleinu* and the Mourner's *Kaddish,* and a final hymn, usually one of the many settings of the hymns *Adon Olam* or *Yigdal,* a hymn based on Maimonides' Thirteen Articles of Faith.

SHAKHARIT / MUSAF

It is Shabbat, a day of rest. There is no rush on Saturday morning to finish *davening,* to head off to work or school. With that in mind, the rabbis who helped structure the *siddur* knew that they could make the Shabbat morning service a longer one. Indeed, in addition to the morning service, they included a *Musaf / Additional* service, a parallel to the additional sacrifice offered on Shabbat and the Festivals in the Temple in Jerusalem.

Shabbat morning begins with *Yigdal* and follows the weekday morning service up to the *P'sukei d'zimrah,* omitting the blessing for the wearing of *tefillin* (which are not worn on Shabbat, see sidebar "Tefillin," p. 25). It is during this sequence of Psalms that we find the first addition specifically for Shabbat, *Nishmat Kol Khai / The Souls of All the Living,* which thanks God for his beneficence toward humanity, acknowledging man's inability to adequately praise the Creator.

P'sukei d'zimrah is followed by a half-*Kaddish* which separates it from the Call to Worship and the *Sh'ma* and its blessings. The Shabbat version of this section of the morning service is somewhat more elaborate than its weekday equivalent.

The Shabbat *Amidah* is, as noted elsewhere, shorter than the daily version, with the middle section and its prayers of supplication omitted and a middle blessing for the Sabbath interpolated in their place. What follows, *Seder K'riat ha-Torah / Service for the Reading of the Torah,* is the highlight of the Shabbat morning service.

Each week a section of the Torah, the first five books of the Hebrew Bible, is read in synagogue. Over the course of a single year, the entire Torah will be read, one *parasha / portion* (also called a *sidra*) per week. (See also Chapter 5.) But the reading of the Torah on Shabbat is not only study, even though study is a central feature of Jewish worship. The *Seder K'riat ha-Torah* is also a chance for worshippers to delight in, take pride in, and rejoice in the giving of the Torah and the honor of having been chosen to receive it.

The congregants rise and the prayer leader or leaders go to the *Aron ha-Kodesh / Holy Ark.* The entire body of worshippers chant or sing the verses from Numbers in which Moses spoke as the Ark of the Covenant moved forward, then a verse from Isaiah, "*Ki mi-tzion tetsei Torah, ud'var Adonai mi-Yerushalyim / From out of Zion Torah shall go forth, and the word of Adonai from Jerusalem.*" The cantor or reader takes the *Sefer Torah / Scroll of the Law* from the Ark (in Reform and some Conservative shuls, he will hand it to the congregant who has been chosen for the honor of carrying the scroll that morning). Everyone echoes the cantor's recitation of the *Sh'ma,* and as the Torah is carried around the room (the *hakafah,* mentioned earlier), hymns to the greatness of Adonai are sung, while congregants bow to or kiss the *Sefer Torah* as it passes by.

The scroll is returned to the *amudah,* the reading table at the front of the congregation, and the worshippers are seated. The *gabbai,* a layperson who assists the prayer leader during the Torah reading, calls each of seven congregants to the Torah; each congregant will recite blessings before and after the reading of the Torah, and the *ba'al kri'at/one who reads* will chant the Torah portion for the week. In a traditionally observant congregation, the first person to be given an *aliyah* (literally, a "going up" to the Torah, the honor of coming up and reading the blessings) will be a *Kohen,* the second a *Levi,* descendants of the ancient priestly castes, and the remaining five "Israelites." The custom is to reserve *aliyot* (the plural form of *aliyah*) for congregants observing a *yahrzeit* (the anniversary of the death of a close family member), and for guests and visiting scholars. *Mi sheberakh* blessings for sick members of the congregation and their families, for the person given the *aliyah,* especially on special occasions like a wedding or a significant anniversary, or in a traditional *shul,* for the naming of a baby girl, are offered by the *gabbai* or the leader after the reading of the Torah (either after each *aliyah* or at the conclusion of the reading, depending on the *minhag* of the congregation).

In a traditionally observant congregation, an eighth member will be called to the *bimah/pulpit* for an *aliyah* after the completion of the reading of the entire *parashah*; called the *maftir/concluder,* he reads the same blessing over the Torah and the *ba'al kri'ah* will repeat the last verses of the *parashah*. Then two more congregants are called up, one of whom—the *magbiah*—holds the scroll overhead (called *hagbah*), turning so that the entire congregation can see several panels of the Torah; as he turns, they chant a verse of Deuteronomy that declares, "This is the Torah that Moses placed before the Children of Israel by the command of Adonai." The other congregant, the *golel,* then dresses the Torah in its mantle and ornamentation, called *gelilah*. The *maftir* then reads from a section of the Prophets, called the *Haftarah,* preceded and followed by the blessings for the reading of the *Haftarah* passage.

With another series of benedictions, the *Sefer Torah* is now returned to the Ark, with the congregation singing *Eitz Khayim,* "[The Torah] is a tree of life to those who hold fast to it. . . ."

In traditionally observant congregations, the *Musaf/Additional* service follows the Torah reading for Shabbat mornings, with a half-*Kaddish* separating them. In the Temple in Jerusalem, there were additional sacrifices prescribed for Shabbat afternoons; *Musaf* is designed to correspond to those offerings.

MINKHAH AND *HAVDALAH*

The afternoon service for Shabbat opens with *Ashrei* and follows it with the prayer *Uva l'Tzion* and a half-*Kaddish* and a somewhat shortened Torah service. The *Amidah* for the Shabbat *Minkhah* service comes next, again an *Amidah* with only seven blessings. One of these blessings on Shabbat and *Musaf* is a repetition of the *Kedushah* proclaiming God's holiness. The cantor chants a full *Kaddish* and the congregation recites *Aleinu,* which is followed by the Mourner's *Kaddish*.

By now, the Sabbath is almost concluded. The evening service is a regular *Ma'ariv* service for a weekday, with one significant addition. For those observing the end of the Sabbath in the synagogue, as the sun sets, *Havdalah* is recited. *Havdalah* is a series of prayers, blessings, and rituals which are usually performed at home but are also observed in the synagogue; the name of the ritual comes from one of its key blessings, thanking God for separating the sacred from the ordinary. (The *Havdalah* blessing is also inserted into the Saturday *ma'ariv Amidah*.)

This lovely ritual begins with the lighting of an intricately braided two-wicked *Havdalah* candle which the leader holds in one hand. In the other she holds an ornate spice box, containing a mixture of aromatic spices. A cup of wine is poured to overflowing. The leader then recites blessings for the wine, the spices (which are then passed among the worshippers for them to smell), the light of fire (she will gaze at her fingernails to see the fire's reflection in them), and for the separation of "holy and secular, light and dark, Israel and the [other] nations, Shabbat and the six days of labor." The leader drinks from the cup of wine and extinguishes the candle in it. The Sabbath is over. Sacred time has been suspended and the real world crowds in on us once again.

FESTIVAL SERVICES

By and large, the Festival services follow the structure of their weekday and Shabbat counterparts. Of course, each holiday service has features unique to its liturgy, but we will consider those in the chapter on the festivals.

However, the Festival services include a few prayers that can be found in almost every holiday observance. For each holiday, there is a prayer, parallel to the place *V'shamru* occupies in the Shabbat service, announcing the festival itself: on the three Pilgrimage Festivals (Sukkot, Pesakh, and Shavuot), *Vayidaber Moshe;* on Rosh Hashanah, *Tiku ba-Khodesh shofar;* and on Yom Kippur, *Ki va-Yom Hazeh.* On the three Pilgrimage Festivals, the middle blessing of the *Amidah, Kedushat ha-Yom,* is composed of five verses referring to the special qualities of the day. During *Seder Kri'at ha-Torah* on a Festival morning, the hymn *Adonai, Adonai,* from Exodus 34:6–7 which enumerates the qualities of God's mercy, is added.

But the most significant addition to the Festival liturgy occurs just after the morning *Amidah,* immediately prior to the Torah service. Called by one commentator "the classical expression of joyful thanksgiving for divine redemption," *Hallel* is one of the crowning moments of a Festival service and is a time for singing with extra joy. In its full form, *Hallel* consists of Psalms 113 through 118. (When recited on the first night of Pesakh, this version is also called *Hallel ha-Mitzri/the Egyptian Hallel.*) *Khatsi Hallel/the half-Hallel* omits the first eleven verses of Psalms 115 and 116. Finally, *Hallel ha-Gadol/the Great Hallel* consists of Psalm 136, and is recited on Shabbat and Festival mornings as part of *P'sukei d'zimrah.*

The rules determining which *Hallel* is recited are straightforward and derive from the era of the Temple in Jerusalem. Shabbat, Rosh Hashanah, Yom Kippur, and Purim are holidays for which no pilgrimage to the Temple was made; therefore, *Hallel* is not recited on those days. On the first day of Pesakh and all the days of Sukkot and Shavuot, a pilgrimage to Jerusalem and offerings at the Temple were customary, so on those holidays the full-*Hallel* is recited. In addition, the full-*Hallel* is recited as part of the observances of Hanukah and of the modern festival days, Yom Haatzma-ut (Israeli Independence Day) and Yom Yerushalayim (the anniversary of the reunification of Jerusalem). (Actually, there are some Orthodox authorities who object to the recitation of the full-*Hallel* on the latter two days because it implies that they are of equal holiness to Hanukah.) Finally, the half-*Hallel* is recited on the remaining days of Pesakh and on Rosh Khodesh (the New Moon, marking the beginning of a new month in the Jewish calendar).

Hallel is recited while standing. In Ashkenazi congregations, it is preceded by a blessing in recognition of the "reading of *Hallel.*" By contrast, in Sephardic congregations the blessing is in recogition of "the completion of *Hallel,*" and is therefore omitted when a half-*Hallel* is recited.

With a few minor alterations for the specific holidays, the Festivals are concluded with *Havdalah,* just as the Sabbath is.

THE SYNAGOGUE

Although the origin of the synagogue as an institution is uncertain, most experts believe that its roots lie in the Babylonian exile, after the destruction of the First Temple in 586 B.C.E. (see p. 15). Over time, the phrase "small sanctuary" was applied to these places of worship, a phrase that is often also applied to the Jewish home. The word "synagogue" itself comes from the Greek, meaning assembly or gathering. Although there is no equivalent word in Hebrew, there are several phrases that have been used to characterize the institution in its various forms, *Bet Midrash/House of Study, Bet Tefillah/House of Prayer,* and *Bet Knesset/House of Assembly.* The Yiddish word *shul* is often used as well.

Whatever its genesis, it is obvious that the destruction of the Second Temple and the dispersion of the Jews hastened the growth of the synagogue as an institution. Although there may have been as many as four hundred synagogues in Jerusalem at the time of the Second Temple (according to the Jerusalem Talmud), the necessity for a place of worship in the Diaspora undoubtedly spurred synagogue-building even more rapidly. Where else could Jews go to assemble and to pray? As we have seen, prayer was considered a substitute for the offerings that had been brought at the Temple, and the basic structure of worship evolved out of the schedule of sacrifices made at the Temple.

The essential structure of the synagogue today reflects the physical structure of the Temple as well. At the front of the sanctuary space is the *Aron Kodesh/Holy Ark,* containing the *Sifrei Torah/Torah scrolls.* Hanging over it is the *Ner Tamid/Eternal Light,* a visual equivalent of the eternal light of Torah, prescribed by God to Aaron and his sons in Exodus 27:20–22. The *bimah* corresponds to the pulpit used by the priests to preside over sacrifices.

The shift from sacrifices to prayers fundamentally changed the nature of Jewish worship, making it a democratic and individual affair. Still, the synagogue is seen as a holy place in which gossip and idle chatter are discouraged, and eating and sleeping are proscribed.

The modern American synagogue has developed far beyond the relatively modest buildings of the ancient world and the austere gathering places of the Middle Ages. Today, the synagogue building will usually include not only a sanctuary in which services are held (or more than one sanctuary in some cases). It will also house classrooms, offices, social halls, auditoriums, and even recreational facilities. As Mordecai Kaplan, the American theologian who inspired the Reconstructionist movement, envisioned it, the synagogue has become a center for the Jewish community, a role it had had in the Middle Ages as well.

In an Orthodox synagogue today one will find separate seating for men and women, with a curtain, screen, or wall, called a *mekhitzah,* between the sections. The *bimah* will be located in the center of the sanctuary, usually surrounded on all four sides by congregants, with everyone facing the same way in most Ashkenazi *shuls,* or with three sides facing the *bimah* but not away from the Ark in Sephardic congregations. By contrast, gender-segregated seating has been abolished in the synagogues of the other denominations; in Reform synagogues, the *bimah* is generally found at the front of the sanctuary, usually raised above the seating floor, placed in front of the Ark. (Reform synagogues will also have a piano and/or organ and, occasionally, a choir loft.)

LITURGICAL MUSIC

Jews have always used music as part of their worship. When the Egyptian army was destroyed at the Reed Sea, Miriam "took a timbrel [something like a tambourine] in her hand," to accompany the song of exultation that the Israelites sang, "And all the women went out after her with timbrels and dances." The Psalms invoke musical instruments at many points, most notably in Psalm 150, which is recited as part of the *Birkat ha-Shakhar/the morning blessings:* "Praise God with lyre and harp . . . with drum and dance . . . with organ and flute . . . with clanging cymbals . . . with resonant trumpets." And David, one of the greatest of the Israelite kings, is depicted as a musician of skill who utilized his gifts to sing the praises of Adonai.

In the First and Second Temples, the Levites engaged in both vocal and instrumental music, although it is impossible for us to reconstruct what it sounded like. The liturgy of the First Temple apparently consisted primarily of Psalms, which were sung chorally. According to the Mishnah, the Second Temple had a choir of twelve Levites and an orchestra. But after the destruction of the Temple, the synagogue service replaced the offerings and instrumental music was banished in mourning for the fall of the Temple, leaving only vocal music as part of worship. Given the text-based nature of Jewish prayer and the idea of prayer as a conversation with God, it seems appropriate that prayer set to music should be primarily vocal in nature. However, because it was believed that the sound of a woman's voice was an incitement to sexual indecency, only men sang in the synagogue services. Finally, playing musical instruments during the Sabbath service would be a violation of the ban on work during the Sabbath.

As the synagogue service became standardized, new poetic prayers called *piyutim* were incorporated; these were composed and performed by singers called *paytanim,* and may have even included congregational parts. Such poet-performers may have been forerunners of the modern *hazan/cantor,* a *sheli'akh tzibur* with a trained voice who not only can lead the congregation in prayer but can do so musically. The position became a permanent one shortly before the Middle Ages, as the liturgy grew more complex and knowledge of Hebrew declined among the laity.

It was in the medieval period, under the influence of its Arab neighbors, that Jewish liturgical music enjoyed a period of rapid development. A dominant figure like Morenu HaRav Jacob ha-Levi ben Moses (1365–1427), known as the Maharil, achieved influence as both a rabbinical leader and a *hazan,* creating musical standards that Ashkenazi Jews would continue to sing for more than five hundred years, cautioning those who would come after him to respect local musical traditions. He also became known as the source of a body of tunes said to derive "mi-Sinai/from Sinai," a group of melodies that became the heart of Ashkenazi liturgical music.

The Sephardic musical tradition of the period owes much to the influence of nearby Arab populations in Spain, Portugal, and North Africa. Songs written in Ladino, a Judeo-Spanish, were often included in liturgy and many of them live on today.

The development of Jewish liturgical music after the Middle Ages in some respects mirrors the development of non-Jewish music, with Salomone di Rossi, an Italian Jew from Mantua, publishing a series of polyphonic compositions, the style of the period, for use in the synagogue in 1622, and Baroque-influenced compositions turning up in synagogues some fifty years later.

However, it was the Reform movement that pushed the liturgical music boundaries the farthest, adding organ accompaniment and trained choirs to nineteenth-century German worship. Compositions dating from this period by Solomon Sulzer are still in use in Reform congregations today (his setting of the *Sh'ma* will be familiar), and strike an occasionally uneasy balance between Ashkenazi cantorial style and German Protestant hymn.

Although they eschewed instrumental accompaniment, the early leaders of the Hasidic movement were firm believers in the power of music. Influenced by the mystical writings of Isaac Luria (1534–1572), the Baal Shem Tov, founder of Hasidism, and his followers believed that music was divinely inspired, and spirited singing of *zemirot / table songs* at the Shabbat dinner table remains a distinctive feature of Hasidic ritual to this day. The Hasidim are particularly drawn to wordless tunes, called *niggunim,* to which they ascribe great spiritual powers. There is a vast library of *niggunim,* many of them composed by the Hasidic rabbis themselves.

In the early decades of the twentieth century, spurred no doubt by the new and rapidly advancing technologies of phonograph, radio, and motion pictures, we entered a veritable golden era of cantorial singing, marked by the emergence of such virtually operatic virtuosi as Joseph Rosenblatt, Mordechai Herschmann, and David Brod. Rosenblatt, legend has it, was offered a contract to join the Metropolitan Opera, and hearing records he made in the 1920s it's not hard to believe the story.

The only problem with these powerhouse voices is that one could hardly sing along with them. There was the distinct danger that prayer would become performance and congregation would be reduced to audience, a danger that was amplified in the United States by the use of professional choirs and the ever-diminishing knowledge of Hebrew among Reform Jews.

The growth of day schools and camp programs for children and the rise of the folk music movement in the early 1960s may have helped to short-circuit that development. Youth-group veteran teens brought new songs and a new approach to their synagogues with results that might have been less brilliant than the cantorial genius of a Rosenblatt but which were a lot easier to pass on to the average congregant.

At the same time—and spurred by the same impetus—we have seen the emergence of new voices and composers, folksinger-performers like Debbie Friedman, neo-Hasidic performer-rabbis like the late Shlomo Carlebach, and many others who have taken to heart the injunction of the Torah, "Let us sing to God a new song."

HOME RITUALS

The synagogue is one of the two centers of Jewish life. The home is the other. Through all the sacred texts of Judaism, the home and the family have been the heart of Jewish life.

As we have seen, an observant Jew begins the day and ends it with prayer. Meals are accompanied by prayer and concluded with it. Even practices like *Havdalah* and candle-lighting for Shabbat and the Festivals are more often practiced at home than in the synagogue. Other key elements of Jewish life—virtually all the life-cycle events from birth to death, the observation of dietary laws, the important *mitzvah* of extending hospitality to the wayfaring stranger—are home-centered. Indeed, one could pray all the weekday services without leaving the house if necessity demanded (with the notable exception of *Seder Kri'at ha-Torah*, which requires a *minyan*).

The home worship experience par excellence, though, is the Shabbat evening meal. Candles are lit and blessed. *Kiddush* is said:

Vayehi erev, veyhi voker, yom ha-shishi. Veyekhulu hashamayim veha-aretz vekhol tz'va'am, veyekhal Elohim bayom hash'vi'i melakhto asher asah; vayishbot vayom hash'vi'i mikol melakhto asher asa. Va-yevareikh Elohim et yom hash'vi'i v'yekadeish otoh, ki vo shavat mikol melakhto asher barah Elohim la'asot.

There was evening and there was morning, a sixth day. Now the heavens and the earth were completed and all their host. On the seventh day, God completed all the work of creation. God blessed the seventh day and set it apart. For on the seventh day, God rested from all the work of creation.

Barukh atah Adonai Eloheinu Melekh ha-olam, borei p'ri ha-gafen.

Blessed are You, Adonai our God, Ruler of the Universe, who brings forth the fruit of the vine.

Barukh atah Adonai Eloheinu Melekh ha-olam, asher kid'shanu b'mitzvotav veratzah vanu kod'sho b'ahavah u'veratson hinkhilanu, zikaron l'ma'asei v'reishit. Ki hu yom tekhilah l'mikaeh kodesh zekher litsiat Mitzrayim. Ki vanu vekhartah veotanu kidashtah mikol ha'amim, veshabat kodshekhah beahavah u'veratson hinkhaltanu. Barukh atah Adonai, mekadeish ha-shabat.

Blessed are You, Adonai our God, Ruler of the Universe, who sanctified us with mitzvot *and takes delight in us. In God's love and favor the Almighty has made the holy Sabbath our heritage, as a reminder of the work of creation. It is the first among our holy days, and a reminder of the Exodus from Egypt. O God, You have chosen us and set us apart from all peoples, and in love and favor have you given us the Sabbath as a sacred inheritance. Blessed is Adonai, for the Sabbath and its holiness.*

In some homes, parents say a blessing over their children, encouraging them to be " like Ephraim and Manasseh . . . Sarah, Rebecca, Rachel, and Leah," and offering the traditional threefold Priestly Blessing: "May Adonai bless you and keep you; may the light of God's countenance shine upon you; may Adonai show you favor and grant you peace."

A husband will sing to his wife *Eishet Khayil / A Woman of Valor,* an ode derived from Proverbs 31 that the Kabbalists used to sing to the Sabbath Queen. Two *khalot / braided loaves of bread* will be eaten and after a warm family meal, the Grace after Eating will be said and Shabbat *z'mirot / songs* may be sung.

The nexus of Shabbat and family life brings to the fore two of the most important elements of Jewish continuity. It is often said, "As much as the Jews kept the Sabbath, the Sabbath kept the Jews." And the family remains, even today in this era of assimilation, a principal site of Jewish identity, passed from fathers and mothers to their children.

MEZUZAH

"And you shall write them on the doorposts of your house and on your gates."   —Deuteronomy 6:9

Thus is it commanded to the Jews in the passage of Torah that is said every day as the *Sh'ma.* This commandment is the reason for one of the most visible of Jewish ritual objects, the *mezuzah,* a small case affixed to the right-hand doorpost of a Jewish home, containing a parchment scroll on which is written the passage from Deuteronomy governing this commandment.

The *mezuzah* is attached to the upper part of the doorpost, in a slant-ing position. The choice of the diagonal placement is a compromise resulting from another disagreement between Rashi and his grandson, Rabbenu Tam; Rashi argued that the *mezuzah* should be placed verti-cally, while his grandson held out for the horizontal.

Every doorway in a Jewish home which fulfills certain conditions should have a *mezuzah* and:

- the room into which it enters must be at least four cubits (two yards) square, and must have a ceiling;
- the doorway must be at least forty inches high and sixteen inches wide, must have doorposts on either side and a lintel, as well as doors that open and close, although even a doorway without a door should have a *mezuzah* affixed;
- the doorway must be for ordinary dwelling, for human dwelling and "dignified" dwelling (a toilet or bathroom, for example, does not have a *mezuzah* affixed);
- the dwelling must be a permanent one; and
- gateways leading to a Jewish home, if they are tall enough and have a lintel and doorposts, should also have a *mezuzah*.

The blessing for putting up a *mezuzah* is

Barukh atah Adonai Eloheinu Melekh ha'olam
asher kid'shanu b'mitzvotav vitzivanu lik'boa mezuzah

Blessed are You Adonai our God, Ruler of the Universe,
who sanctified us by the commandments and has commanded us
to affix a mezuzah.

Generally one says the blessing before putting the *mezuzah* on the main door to the house, then puts up the rest of the *mezuzot* immediately after.

Many Jews will touch the *mezuzah* with their hand when leaving or entering the house as a way of expressing their fulfillment of the com-mandment and of expressing gratitude to the Almighty.

THE EVOLUTION OF THE PRAYER BOOK

Group public prayer in Judaism probably dates from the early days of the Second Temple, around 400 B.C.E. These early prayer services, which were held in addition to, and possibly in conjunction with, sacrifices and offerings, are believed to have included the *Sh'ma,* some Psalms, and, in lieu of sacrifices at certain times, Torah readings.

Many of the practices that we associate with Jewish worship today date far back to this period. Ezra is believed to have begun the reading of Torah in a public square in Jerusalem over four hundred years B.C.E. Regular readings would take place on Mondays and Thursdays, the market days during which men and women would gather to trade and sell; today, the weekday morning services at which Torah is read still take place on Mondays and Thursdays. Many of the prayers that we still read today date from this period.

The liturgy of this time was almost entirely oral. A reader—the forerunner of the rabbis and *shelichim* (plural of *shaliakh*) *tzibur* of today—would recite the service from memory, with the congregants responding "Amen" at the appropriate places. There was a rigid division between the written law of Torah which, as Rabbi Judah ben Nakhamani cautioned, "you are not at liberty to say by heart," and the orally transmitted words of prayer, which "you are not at liberty to recite from writing."

But the arrival of the Roman imperialists in the second and third century C.E. led to massive oppression of the Jews, and the rabbis feared for the future of the liturgy as it became increasingly difficult to hold public worship services and to pass on prayers and hymns orally. Reluctantly the rabbis agreed to permit the writing down of liturgy. At first, according to some historians, handwritten prayer books were available to prayer leaders on Yom Kippur and other fast days; these services were longer and more complicated, hence harder to memorize. Gradually the practice extended to the other services as well.

Although synagogue service was established in something resembling its present form by the time of the destruction of the Second Temple in 70 C.E., the first actual prayer book was not compiled until the ninth century. The work of the great Babylonian scholar Amran Gaon, the volume bears his name, *Seder Rav Amran Gaon.* Rav Amran was asked to create this volume in the ninth century by Spanish Jews; the result was a collection of prayers for the entire year and a guide to the *halakhah,* the regulations, that governed them. The volume even included a section outlining the life-cycle events. For the first time in Jewish history, there was a benchmark for worship against which a community could measure its *minhag.* Rabbi Lawrence Hoffman has observed, "[Amran's] commentary could . . . accurately be described as a condensation of Talmudic teaching for a community that did not exactly know what the Talmud said on the subject of prayer."

The need for such a commentary was the direct result of the Diaspora, the exile and dispersion of the Jewish community that came in the wake of the destruction of the Second Temple in Jerusalem in 70 C.E. Scattered throughout the known world, with no central authority to which they could turn and no central place to which to make pilgrimages, Jewish communities were forced to appeal to those scholars whose achievements they recognized, as the Spanish Jews would do with Rav Amran.

The Arabic-speaking Jews of Egypt were faced with a similar dilemma in the tenth century. They turned to one of the great Jewish thinkers of the period, Rav Saadiah Gaon. (He was not related to Amran; Gaon is a term of respect, not a surname.) The result was a *siddur* designed for use by the ordinary worshipper, unlike Amran Gaon's which was intended for community leaders.

The first "true" prayer book as we know it was compiled in eleventh-century France by Rabbi Simkhah ben Samuel, a student of the great Rashi. In addition to the prayers of the daily services, the book, called the *Makhzor*[8] *Vitry/Prayer Cycle for Vitry,* also included a Pesakh *Hagadah,* prayers for *Simkhat Torah,* and extensive commentaries.

It was in the medieval period that a division in liturgical practice between Ashkenazi (originally German and German-speaking) and Sephardic (originally Spanish and Spanish-speaking) Jews began to evolve. This split actually dates back to the time of Amran, as the Babylonian and Palestinian rabbis developed different liturgies that would eventually take the shape of their Ashkenazic and Sephardic successors, respectively. The primary difference between them was in the inclusion of *piyutim,* poetic prayers usually of Sephardic origin, in the Sephardic liturgy. In many cases, the difference was in the actual wording of prayers that is retained to this day.[9]

The importance of the advent of printing was not lost on the Jews of

Europe. Within a few years of Gutenberg's invention of movable type, printed prayer books were circulating. Among the incunabula (books printed prior to 1500) one finds many *siddurim,* primarily Spanish and Italian. Jews became very active in the printing business after 1500 and Hebrew printing enjoyed a lively boom.

As we have seen, the liturgy came into its present form through a process of accretion, of accumulation, with new prayers, poems, and hymns being added over a period of some two thousand years. Until the nineteenth century, no one had challenged this process or its result. But several events took place in Europe in the early part of the century that would lead to a radical disruption of this process, changing the shape of Judaism forever.

THE RISE OF DENOMINATIONS

REFORM JUDAISM

The rise of the Enlightenment in Europe with its flood of new ideas like tolerance, democracy, and the equality of man before the law made the climate for Jews in the Christian West a little less uncomfortable. The triumphant march of Napoleon's armies across the continent meant the forceable importation of the French Revolution's trio "Liberty, Equality, Fraternity," into previously inhospitable locales. Napoleon was a firm supporter of the emancipation of Europe's Jews, another idea that he imposed on the countries he conquered.

The ideas of the Enlightenment had their own impact on Jewish thought as well. As we will see in several later chapters, Judaism experienced its own Enlightenment, called the *Haskalah;* one of the first and most influential thinkers to emerge from that period was the German philosopher Moses Mendelssohn (1729–1786). (Incidentally, his grandson was the composer Felix Mendelssohn, who was baptized as a Christian.) Although Mendelssohn himself never ceased to be an Orthodox Jew, his writings and thought had an incalculable impact on a group of German Jews who were rethinking the relationship between Judaism and modernity. Mendelssohn was a formidable advocate of the idea that Jews could live as free and equal citizens, that the ideas of Judaism could be understood in a rationalist context.

The Jews of the *Haskalah* were coming out from behind the ghetto walls, seemingly forever. It was in that atmosphere that Israel Jacobson built and opened a new synagogue in Seesen, Westphalia, in 1810. When French occupying troops left Westphalia, Jacobson followed suit, moving his pulpit to Berlin in 1815. Three years later another congregation was established in Hamburg, using its own revised *siddur*.

Emancipation had meant an end to the special judicial power of local rabbis and Jewish community leaders who had served as political officials as well at the behest of absolutist Christian monarchs. As a result, Jacobson and the reformers in Hamburg could challenge the rule of the Orthodox rabbinate with impunity.

What did the early practitioners of Reform Judaism, as they called their new version of the old religion, believe and why did they enrage the Orthodox rabbinate?

First, they encouraged prayer in the local vernacular rather than in Hebrew, a way of diminishing the difference between them and their non-Jewish neighbors. Sermons were delivered in German, which traditional rabbis denounced as a violation of Jewish tradition. In 1832 Leopold Zunz, a scholar of considerable attainments, demonstrated that sermons in the local tongue were, in fact, the norm before the establishment of the ghettos in the late Middle Ages.

Second, men like Jacobson believed that their mission was to bring Judaism into line with modern thought, a mission that they took into the schools and seminaries. The "new" Jewish thinking held that rabbinical training should not be limited just to Talmud and Torah.

Jacobson and another prominent German Reform rabbi who would follow him, Abraham Geiger, came to believe that Judaism was an evolving process of belief, not a fixed set of historically mandated rules and regulations. The center of Judaism was the idea of ethical monotheism; now that Jews were no longer confined in literal and metaphorical ghettos, they needed to shift the focus of their liturgy away from nationalistic ideas like a return to Zion or the restoration of the Temple and animal sacrifice. They no longer needed to pray in Hebrew or to completely abstain from certain behaviors on Shabbat.

As Reform Judaism evolved in Europe and the United States in the nineteenth century, its practice came to resemble liberal German Protestantism. Services were conducted almost entirely in the local tongue, with minimal Hebrew. Prayers were led by a rabbi, spoken in unison, often responsively with the rabbi; no more of the "indecorous" free-form of Orthodox worship. Organ music was introduced. The new music composed for Reform worship bore a striking resemblance to German Protestant hymns. (A key model of "decorum" for the German Reform congregations was the behavior of their Sephardic neighbors.) In England, Reform rabbis were even called "Reverend" and "ministers." Some Classical Reform congregations even went so far as holding their Shabbat services on Sundays.

The United States proved the most fertile ground for Reform Judaism. An egalitarian and tolerant society almost from its birth (in theory, if not always in practice), America lacked the infrastructure of a long-standing Orthodox tradition like Western Europe's. Rabbi Isaac Mayer Wise, an immigrant from Bohemia, pioneered a specifically American brand of Judaism, one that would reconcile the variety of practices coming out of Europe. In 1857 Wise authored a new prayer book, *Minhag America,* and tried to devise a Jewish practice that would be suited to the New World.

Ironically, Wise found himself opposed by another German transplant, Rabbi David Einhorn, who was more concerned with reform of ritual practices than with finding an American voice for Jewish worship. In direct response to *Minhag America,* Einhorn devised his own prayer book, *Olat Tamid,* written mostly in German and omitting prayers for the restoration of animal sacrifice in the Temple, the return to Zion, and the resurrection of the dead. A controversy ensued over just how much and what kind of reform was needed. Eventually, after a series of conferences, the various Reform rabbis met in 1873 to establish the Union of American Hebrew Congregations (UAHC), which remains the umbrella organization of Reform Judaism in America to this day. The Union's first priority was to establish its own rabbinical seminary, Hebrew Union College, in 1875 in Cincinnati. In 1885 a rabbinical conference headed by Wise but dominated by Kaufman Kohler, Einhorn's son-in-law, issued the "Pittsburgh Platform," a document that made a clear break between Reform Judaism and the *halakhic* past. (For the texts of all major platforms released by U.S. denominations, see Appendix 1.) The UAHC would adopt *The Union Prayer Book* in 1895, a *siddur* that drew heavily on Einhorn's model.

The new Judaism that Classical Reform advocated featured several telling changes. The *bimah* was moved from the center of the sanctuary to the front and was elevated, a change that was indicative of the

"Protestantization" of the role of the rabbi. The rabbi's weekly sermon was now given greater weight in the worship service, all the more so since once-a-week worship gradually became the norm rather than the exception. Where the *Amidah* had been the key prayer in the service, a prayer for which the congregation respectfully stood, Reform liturgy shifted its attention to the *Sh'ma,* a less particularistic prayer.

The turn-of-the-century Reform leadership hadn't reckoned on the tides of history. With the rise of Fascism in Europe and the accompanying tide of anti-Semitic atrocities around the world in the 1930s, the United States experienced an influx of Eastern European Jews who felt little affinity with Classical Reform. There was a growing sense of dissatisfaction with the Pittsburgh Platform within the Central Conference of American Rabbis (CCAR), the Reform movement's rabbinical organization. In 1937 the CCAR adopted the Columbus Platform; it represented an adjustment towards a somewhat more traditional Judaism. For example, while not calling for a renewed belief in the return to Zion, it did urge all Jews to recognize an obligation to aid in the building of Palestine as a Jewish homeland.

The Reform movement enjoyed explosive growth in the post–World War II years, the product of a post-Holocaust return to Judaism and the suburbanization of American Jewry with its concomitant financial prosperity. Between 1940 and 1980, the number of Reform congregations in the United States doubled. Hebrew Union College added New York, Los Angeles, and Jerusalem campuses, ordained women for the first time in 1975, and ordained its first Israeli student in 1980.

The most significant trend within the Reform movement in the past two decades, spurred by the then president of the UAHC, Rabbi Alexander Schindler, was a swing back towards more traditional observance in many key areas (accompanied by a new support for Zionism, once low on the Reform agenda). In the newest version of the movement's prayer book, *Gates of Prayer* (1975), and its High Holy Day prayer book, *Gates of Repentance* (1978), many of the prayers that had been omitted from the *Union Prayer Book* were restored. It should be noted that this new emphasis has gone hand-in-hand with the Classical Reform concern with a "prophetic" Judaism that is based firmly in action for social justice. Thus, more Hebrew was introduced into services at the same time that the *siddur* was being rewritten to include gender-neutral God-language.

Additionally, the UAHC and CCAR have encouraged more personal observance outside the confines of the synagogue. Under Schindler, the Reform movement has moved in a direction that encourages a greater emphasis on spirituality and has even broached the possibility of restoring many traditional practices without sacrificing its commitment to social action.

CONSERVATIVE JUDAISM

Zacharias Frankel had seen at first hand what Reform Judaism would mean for liturgy and worship. Frankel was head of the Jewish Theological Seminary in Breslau at the same time that Abraham Geiger was serving as rabbi in that city. Frankel was anything but happy with what had transpired. A gifted scholar, he was dissatisfied with Orthodoxy's rejection of scientific study of sacred texts; for the Orthodox, the Torah and Talmud were the products of divine revelation, so a philological analysis of them was anathema. At the same time, Frankel was unhappy with the budding Reform movement's rejection of Jewish nationalism and its willingness to discard *mitzvot* of which it didn't approve.

What was needed, he reasoned, was a third way, a middle-ground approach that didn't reject *halakhah* but wasn't a slave to it. Judaism, he asserted, was not the ahistorical product of revelation at Sinai; it had evolved over time. Yet its traditions were worthy of preservation, and Jewish nationalistic impulses had to be respected, particularly in an age when new nation-states were forming all the time to accommodate the longings of other peoples.

Frankel's thoughts on this matter undoubtedly came to a head when he stormed out of a conference dominated by the young Reform movement in 1845. He argued that changes in liturgy and worship practice shouldn't be made simply to conform to the mores of the day. He offered instead what he called "Positive Historical Judaism." Within eleven years of his completion of his tenure at the seminary in Breslau in 1875, his ideas would find a permanent home in the United States.

A group of scholars and rabbis of traditional bent who were dismayed by the Pittsburgh Platform decided to establish their own Jewish Theological Seminary (JTS), this one in New York City. Initially, led by Sabato Morais, they had hoped to unite all the traditionalist elements in American Judaism in opposition to the rising tide of Reform. Perhaps they cast their net a bit too wide to accommodate such a disparate group of men; whatever the reason, the seminary faltered, struggling along until 1902, when Rabbi Solomon Schechter took over.

Schechter succeeded where his predecessors had not. JTS became a home of distinguished scholars and a training ground for a body of new rabbis and cantors who espoused what he called "historical" Judaism, a name it would eventually shed in exchange for Conservative Judaism. Like Morais before him, Schechter hoped to make the Conservative umbrella big enough to encompass a wide range of observant Jews and, in fact, to this day there is a broad spectrum of degrees of observance within Conservative Judaism.

The movement was a perfect answer to the needs and changing demographics of the American Jewish community. The new wave of Eastern European Jews arriving on the East Coast found the German Jews who constituted the bulk of the Reform movement too unwelcoming, but looked at Orthodoxy as a hangover from the world of pogroms and poverty that they had left behind. In the Conservative movement, they found a home that offered "authenticity" leavened by a modern, intellectual approach to faith. In the years after World War II, the Conservative movement enjoyed unprecedented growth and became—and remains today—the largest branch of American Judaism.

That success was not without its price.

Under the chancellorship of Gerson D. Cohen, JTS moved to more progressive positions on some key issues, dragging the lay leadership of the movement along. In 1955, the Rabbinical Assembly, the Conservative equivalent of the CCAR, allowed women to come to the *bimah* to read Torah. In 1973, women were to be counted toward a *minyan* and, in 1983, JTS admitted its first female students to both its rabbinical and cantorial programs. At a time when Orthodox Judaism in the United States was undergoing its own divisions, these changes in the Conservative movement created a left-right split and in the past decade some pro-feminist Modern Orthodox and the "right" wing of Conservative Judaism have pulled together in a small way. The result has been a new movement, the Union for Traditional Judaism, which established its own rabbinical seminary in Westchester in the mid-1990s.

Ironically, as Reform rabbis and lay leaders moved to embrace Zionism and Jewish nationhood and restored many rituals and prayers to their practice, the lines between Reform and Conservative have blurred somewhat. In Israel, both the Reform and Conservative movements have had to fight, usually together, for acceptance in the face of staunch opposition from the ultra-Orthodox rabbis who control the state-religious nexus that includes the religious courts. At present, both movements remain small in the Jewish homeland, in startling contrast to their widespread membership in the United States and, to a slightly lesser extent, Great Britain (where Reform synagogues are called Liberal and Conservative synagogues are labeled Traditional).

RECONSTRUCTIONISM

Although the Reform and Conservative movements have enjoyed their greatest success in the United States, each was born in Germany in the mid nineteenth century. Reconstructionism, by contrast, can honestly claim to be the only major stream of American Judaism to have come into existence in the United States. Indeed, the movement is little known outside America, although its influence in American Jewish thought vastly outweighs its small size (approximately three percent of affiliated American Jews belong to Reconstructionist congregations).

Its founder, Rabbi Mordechai Kaplan, is a figure who bridges every one of the four streams of American Judaism. Born in 1881, he was educated and began his career as an Orthodox rabbi. Becoming dissatisfied with Orthodoxy, he went on to a teaching position at Jewish Theological Seminary which he would hold for fifty-four years while also serving as the rabbi at the Society for the Advancement of Judaism, a synagogue he founded in 1922 in New York City. Kaplan had a tremendous influence on the thinking of the post–World War II Reform movement and, of course, fathered Reconstructionism.

Ironically, as his biographer, Mel Scult has said, "Kaplan never intended to start a new movement within American Judaism. He wanted to shift the emphasis within the Conservative movement," to reconstruct what he saw as a religion that was not meeting the needs of American Jews.

For Kaplan, Judaism was not merely a religion or a nationality. It is, rather, an evolving religious civilization, a body of customs and folkways, history, language, and culture, a sense of attachment to Israel, an ethical worldview, all of which are informed and unified by a set of religious beliefs. Thus, the *mitzvot* are seen as part of an ethnography, a set of customs that have changed in the past and which can be changed again, as each new generation brings its intelligence and experience to bear on them. The sacred texts, he said, are not the product of divine revelation but are the creation of the Jewish people. As such they represent four thousand years of Jewish aspirations towards God.

On the organizational level, Reconstructionism is the most democratic of all four movements of American Judaism. Reconstructionist rabbis are taught to strive for a breakdown of the hierarchical relationship between rabbinate and laity that exists even in the egalitarian world of Jewish worship. The synagogue is seen as a Jewish community center fulfilling a multitude of communal needs; indeed, it was Kaplan who first devised the idea of the Jewish Community Center (JCC), now a common feature of the Jewish-American landscape. And even more than Reform, Reconstructionism is deeply committed to gender equality. The *bat mitzvah* ceremony for twelve-year-old girls was created by Kaplan, and his daughter was the first young woman ever to go through it; Reconstructionist Rabbinical College (RRC) has been ordaining women since it opened its doors in 1967.

In terms of theology, Kaplan and his successors pushed the envelope even further than Reform in some important ways. Because Reconstructionism emerged from the Conservative movement and retained an attachment to many traditional practices—dietary laws, a considerable amount of Hebrew in the liturgy, men in *yarmulkes* (the Yiddish word for *kippot/skullcaps*—Reconstructionist practice *looks* like Conservative practice. But the Reconstructionist *siddur, Kol Haneshama,* is as gender-free as *Gates of Prayer,* and the movement rejects the concept of the Jews as the Chosen People (see sidebar, p. 73) and the idea of a personal Messiah. Indeed, in 1945 when the Reconstructionist *Sabbath Prayer Book* was published in the United States, a group of Orthodox rabbis condemned it and held a public burning of copies.

The reach of Kaplan's ideas far exceeds the size of the movement he helped begin. Today, the *bat mitzvah* is a common feature of Reform and Conservative synagogue life, the synagogue as community center is the norm in those movements, and the *havurah,* the small prayer group as a self-sustaining organization, has been an integral part of the growth of Reconstructionism (and has helped revitalize the Conservative movement as well).

Intriguingly, the Reconstructionist movement has undergone a small transformation not unlike the one shaking up Reform Judaism. Where Kaplan devised a rationalist, intellectual version of Judaism, some of his successors, many of them current and former faculty members at RRC, have turned their sights back to the mystical side of Jewish thought, to the early Hasidic masters and spirituality.

MODERN ORTHODOX

Before the *Haskalah,* there was no such thing as "Orthodox" Judaism. There were only Jews, non-Jews, and apostates. Although there were many different strains within Jewish liturgy and practice, every version of Judaism that was practiced in, say, 1600 would be instantly recognizable to a modern Jew as "Orthodox." But with tne Enlightenment and the beginnings of Reform and the movements that came after it (and the rise, particularly in the United States, of another new phenomenon: the "secular" Jew), Orthodoxy was no longer the only kind of Judaism, it was merely one of several kinds of Judaism. Of course, the Orthodox didn't see it that way and, even now, many of them still believe that their way is the only legitimate carrier of Jewish identity and tradition.

With the advent of Reform Judaism, traditionally observant Jews characterized themselves as "Orthodox" for the first time. To their way of thinking, Reform Judaism was a betrayal of the very nature of Judaism, a direct affront to divine revelation by its rejection of *halakhah* in the form of dietary laws, dress, and the entire infrastructure of the liturgy. Conservative Judaism was no less inauthentic with its concern with scientific analysis of sacred texts and historical development of *halakhah.*

There were two ways to react to the forces of modernity that had spawned these new movements. One could withdraw from contact with the modern world and the non-Jewish world as much as possible, which is what much of the East European Jewish community did (aided immeasurably by the brutal anti-Semitism of the Polish and Russian regimes for whom emancipation of the Jews was utterly inconceivable). Or one could make some kind of reluctant peace with this new world, incorporating the values of modernity that were compatible with traditional Judaism.

The latter line of thought led to what is commonly known in the United States as Modern Orthodox (as distinct from "ultra-Orthodox" as some call it, or "Torah-true" as it proclaims itself) Judaism. Unlike the other streams within Judaism, what separates Modern Orthodoxy from other paths of traditional belief is not rooted in liturgy or ritual practice. Rather, the aspects of Modern Orthodoxy that diverge from its ultra-Orthodox counterparts almost all concern the relationship between Orthodox Jews and the rest of society, including other Jews.

Generally, the Modern Orthodox believe in participation in the general culture of society; Yeshiva University, the foremost academic product of the movement, offers a full complement of academic courses. Modern Orthodox rabbis will participate in cross-denominational Jewish organizations with other, non-Orthodox rabbis. The Modern Orthodox are actively pro-Zionist, unlike many ultra-Orthodox groups who believe that there can only be a Jewish State when the Messianic Era comes. And, finally, Modern Orthodox interpretations of *halakhah*, while still adhering to the basic structures of Jewish religious-legal thought, are slightly more flexible than those of their predecessors.

BA'AL TESHUVAH

The growing interest in spirituality in the United States has led to a relatively new phenomenon among American Jews, that of the *ba'al teshuvah* (pl. *ba'alei teshuvah*). This Hebrew term, which might be literally translated as "one who has returned," refers to a previously nonreligious or unaffiliated Jew who chooses to become traditionally observant. Orthodox synagogues have been making a special effort in recent years to attract these young men and women, often educated urban professionals, who are seeking a return to what they perceive as their religious roots. (Incidentally, in a somewhat tongue-in-cheek piece of slang, some Orthodox Jews will distinguish between B.T.s and F.F.B.s—*Frum/tradi-tionally "observant" From Birth*.)

In recent years, the Modern Orthodox have found themselves under extraordinary pressure from the right. The ultra-Orthodox communities enjoy certain clear demographic and social advantages: they have large families, discourage any interest in secular activities, and have been successful in establishing their own network of educational and social institutions. One result of this pressure has been the division that led to some pro-feminist Modern Orthodox joining with right-wing Conservatives to form the Union for Traditional Judaism. This is ironic, since it was the ordination of women as rabbis and cantors that drove them out of the Conservative Movement. It is too soon to tell in what direction events will take Modern Orthodox Judaism, a movement whose future is at present uncertain. But other forces, right out of today's headlines, are shaking up Jewish worship from the opposite direction.

HAVURAH

Living in an open and pluralistic society, American Jews are as influenced by the events of their time as anyone. The best example of how that influence can make itself felt in the sphere of ritual and worship is the birth in the late '60s of the *havurah* movement. Many young Jewish men and women raised in Conservative congregations were experiencing a disillusionment with the large and often impersonal synagogues of suburban America, a perhaps inevitable by-product of the movement's rapid post– World War II growth. As a natural outgrowth of the politics and counterculture of the '60s, these young people attempted to create a new format for their worship, one that would accommodate their fervor, their seriousness, and their need for a more intimate religious experience.

The first of *havurot* (fellowships) was founded in Denver in 1967; it was a small and knowledgeable group of Jews who came together to worship collectively without the need of a rabbi or cantor. The next year, another *havurah,* this one structured more like a commune, was founded in the Boston suburb of Somerville; unlike the Denver group, the members of the Somerville *havurah* not only worshipped together, but lived together as well.

More recently, *havurot* have also been established within larger mainstream liberal congregations, usually with a considerable amount of autonomy granted by the larger parent body.

What made the *havurah* movement significant was not only that it enabled potentially alienated young Jews to find an outlet for their spiritual needs within Judaism at a time when many were experimenting with Eastern religions, cult groups, and other spiritual disciplines, but equally important, it became a birthing ground for many prominent Jewish intellectuals who emerged from *havurot* in the late 1970s and the 1980s to preach a newly revitalized Jewish spirituality. Influential books like the three *Jewish Catalogs* compiled by Michael and Sharon Strassfeld, and Paul Cowan's *An Orphan in History* came from the movement.

Danny Siegel, who co-edited the first *Jewish Catalog,* is a prominent figure in the Jewish Renewal Movement. *Havurot* continue to proliferate and grow in the American Jewish community, providing an outlet for those who seek a family-like setting in which to explore Judaism.

JEWISH RENEWAL MOVEMENT

Despite the claims of anti-Semites that Jews are clannish and keep to themselves, the history of Judaism in the Diaspora is a study in how to assimilate outside cultural and political forces. This is nowhere more apparent today than in the burgeoning Jewish Renewal Movement.

Not yet a distinct stream within American Judaism but definitely growing in its influence on the four movements, Jewish Renewal draws elements from all four streams but the most important influence on it comes from Hasidism, with its strong attachment to Jewish mysticism. Jewish Renewal can be clearly seen as a response to New Age thinkers and the growing number of Westerners (particularly Jews) who have experimented with Sufism, Buddhism, and other Eastern spiritual disciplines, as well as the rise of women's and gay liberation movements in the '70s and '80s.

On their website (www.aleph.org), Jewish Renewal describe themselves as "rooted in a midrashic response to Torah, drawing on ancient wisdom without getting stuck in it." Drawing on a wide range of Jewish thought—the mysticism of Kabbalah, the Neo-Hasidism espoused by figures as disparate as Martin Buber and Shlomo Carlebach, the intimacy of the *havurot,* the commitment to Social Action of the Reform movement—as well as elements of "the insights of contemporary ecology, feminism, and participatory democracy," Jewish Renewal looks very much like a hybrid of '60s radical activism, the early days of the Hasidic movement, and a New Age revival meeting. Even the activists of Jewish Renewal themselves will gladly tell you that they are a work-in-progress, but the appeal of the movement both within conventional Jewish circles and without is undeniable.

GAY AND LESBIAN SYNAGOGUES

It took an interesting confluence of political events to create a desire for gay and lesbian synagogues in America. Of course, the Stonewall riots that gave birth to the gay liberation movement in 1969 were an essential catalyst. But no less important was the equally visible and vocal (if somewhat less organized) Jewish pride movement that grew out of the Israeli victory in the Six-Day War in 1967 and Jewish involvement in the Civil Rights movement. The first gay and lesbian synagogue in the United States (and probably in the entire world) was founded in the fall of 1972. Beit Chayim Chadashim (BCC), located in Los Angeles and inspired by the non-denominational gay Christian group, the Metropolitan Community Church, was the first small ripple in what quickly became a good-sized wave.

Today there are over a dozen gay and lesbian synagogues operating on a full-time basis in the United States, located in cities that have significant Jewish populations. Not surprisingly, the largest one, Congregation Beth Simchat Torah—with over a thousand members—is located in New York, home of the planet's largest Jewish community (and one of its largest and most visible gay and lesbian communities as well). Another mark of the growth of these congregations is that they even have their own umbrella organization, The World Congress of Gay and Lesbian Jewish Organizations, which was founded in 1980.

The reaction of the mainstream liberal congregations has changed over time. When BCC applied to the Reform movement's Union of American Hebrew Congregations shortly after it opened its doors, the application was rejected, but five years later the Angelenos were welcomed into the UAHC. Six of the nation's gay and lesbian congregations are now affiliated with the UAHC; the Atlanta-based Bet Haverim is a member of the Reconstructionist movement's umbrella organization.

When you walk into a service at CBST, as the New York synagogue is casually known, you might be "surprised at how traditional the congregation is," says Rabbi Sharon Kleinbaum, the congregation's spiritual leader. "There are things in our worship that might strike people as different. We have a special prayer for AIDS, for example. And we are a young congregation, with a young median age, but [because of the epidemic] we carry an enormous death load around."

Would there still be a need for gay and lesbian congregations if there were a greater acceptance of such Jews in the "mainstream" *shuls?* "That's the $64,000 question," Kleinbaum replies. "We support mainstream congregations that do outreach to gays and lesbians. That's fantastic. But the reality is that it's going to be a very rare non-gay congregation that will provide social life for single gay people—it's different for couples, but for a young gay or lesbian Jew, how do you have a critical mass so that they can meet each other and find partners?"

There is a second issue that comes into play as well, Kleinbaum says. "A non-gay congregation just isn't going to be a setting where gay and lesbian issues can be a priority."

For the foreseeable future, she concludes, there will be a need for both gay/lesbian and non-gay synagogues. Still, she is optimistic about the future of gay and lesbian Jews. "It's an exciting time," Rabbi Kleinbaum says.

WOMEN'S PRAYER GROUPS

As women took a more active and visible role in Reform and Conservative Judaism (they had always had such a role in the Reconstructionist movement), it was inevitable that their Orthodox sisters would follow suit in their own fashion. When the progressive denominations began ordaining rabbis and cantors, it seemed highly unlikely that even the most liberally inclined Modern Orthodox institutions would do the same. But Modern Orthodox women were experiencing comparable stirrings of their own.

Those stirrings took the form of women's *tefillah/prayer* groups, the first of which were established in the mid-1970s. Women gather on their own, in private homes and in synagogues, generally once a month, on Shabbat or *Rosh Khodesh;* they pray, read Torah, and often celebrate rites of passage specific to women, including the naming of newborn girls and *bat mitzvah* ceremonies.

Since the beginning, the groups have treaded carefully in the minefield of Jewish law. They do not recite *Kaddish* or the *Barekhu,* both of which require a *minyan* of ten men in an Orthodox setting (many Conservative congregations and all Reform and Reconstructionist congregations count women toward a *minyan*). Still, the women's *tefillah* groups have met with resistance and controversy in the Orthodox world.

From almost the outset of the movement's existence, the women's groups received an endorsement from Rabbi Avi Weiss, the spiritual leader of the Riverside Hebrew Institute (Bronx, N.Y.) and a controversial figure in his own right for his political activism on Jewish issues. Weiss was one of the only Orthodox rabbis to offer women the use of his synagogue and to support them from the pulpit at a time when few others would take such a public stand. Rabbi Saul Berman, then at Lincoln Square Synagogue in Manhattan, also expressed his support in public. In 1985, the controversy surrounding the groups, which had been quietly brewing in Modern Orthodox circles, burst into public view when a group of five rabbis affiliated with Yeshiva University, the flagship of Modern Orthodox education and home of the movement's prestigious rabbinical school, issued a *responsa*—a *halakhic* ruling—prohibiting organized women's prayer groups in any form. Weiss responded by publishing a reply in support of the women.

The women's own response was swift and decisive: they formed an organization to support one another's work, the Women's Tefillah Network. Since then, the growth of the organization has been slow but steady. In 1989, the Network's members numbered sixteen groups; in 1997 there were forty-four affiliated prayer groups. The organization's growth should continue; when a rabbinical council in Queens, N.Y., issued a ruling that year against the prayer groups, it spurred even more interest among Orthodox women.

What purpose do these groups serve? Bat Sheva Marcus, chair of the Women's Tefillah Network and executive director of the Union for Traditional Judaism, observes that the prayer groups fill an important educational function, "and the more we women learn the more curious we become and the more connected we feel." At a time when the Modern Orthodox community is being squeezed from the right by the ultra-Orthodox and the left by the Conservative and Traditional movements, it is imperative that its women feel more connected if it is to survive. As Marcus wrote in the magazine *Sh'ma,* "The women's *tefillah* groups become a greenhouse where this learning and growing can take place in a safe environment."

Women's *tefillah* groups are now turning up all over the world, even in Jewish schools. There are at least four in Israel at this writing, including one at Dror High School, which is the only group in the entire world that meets every day.

SHUL ETIQUETTE

It's your first time in a synagogue. Well, maybe it's your first time in a synagogue since your *bar mitzvah* ceremony, a long time ago. Should you wear a *kippah*? A *tallit*? When do you stand? The person next to you is bowing from the waist, should you be doing that? When you come in the usher asks you if you would like an *aliyah;* what do you say? Many Orthodox *shuls* don't have ushers; now what happens?

The first time you walk into an unfamiliar synagogue can be a daunting experience, even for the most veteran *davener*. Although there are many constants to the worship service, each congregation has its own *minhag / custom,* known only to its long-time members. To some extent, you needn't worry about such *minhagim*—you won't be expected to know things that only a member might know—but there are basic customs common to almost every synagogue service.

What follows can hardly be an exhaustive list, but here are a few things to be aware of when you go into a Jewish worship service:

1. Other than on the High Holy Days (and even then only in some synagogues), there is seldom assigned seating in a *shul*. Take a vacant seat anywhere. If seats are being held for special guests of the congregation (family of the *bat mitzvah* or guest speaker, for example), or if you have managed to sit in one of the rare assigned seats in a congregation, you may be asked to move. Do so casually and quietly.

2. In an Orthodox synagogue, men and women will not be seated together. Women will be seated behind (or alongside, depending on the layout of the sanctuary) the *mekhitzah*, the screen between the two sections, or they may be seated upstairs. Both men and women will be asked to cover their heads, men with *kippot,* women with a lace chapel cap. If you are a man and it is a morning service, you will be offered a *tallit;* it is certainly your choice whether you wear one, but the custom in Ashkenazi congregations is for only married men to do so. Should you need to use the restroom, **do not** take the *tallit* in with you; hooks will be provided outside the door. (If you take the *tallit* off for such an eventuality, you needn't recite the blessing for wearing it before putting it back on. Once a day is enough.)

3. In a Conservative congregation, men and women generally are permitted to sit together. Headcovering and *tallit* guidelines are the same as for Orthodox. In many progressive Conservative synagogues, women may wear *tallitot* and *kippot,* too. That's a personal choice.

4. In Reform and Reconstructionist synagogues, seating is **never** gender-segregated. In all Reconstructionist and most Reform congregations, headcovering is optional but is a nice gesture (more for men
than women, though); *tallitot* are optional. In a few classical Reform
congregations, *kippot* are actively discouraged.

If you are uncertain whether to wear headcovering or a prayer shawl,
look at the people in the pews when you come in. If that doesn't
provide an answer, ask the usher. If there is a basket of *kippot* and
another of chapel caps near the entrance to the sanctuary, you may rest
assured that you have, at the very least, the option of wearing one.
Regardless of the denomination of the synagogue, you should dress
tastefully, preferably jacket and tie for men. Women going to an
Orthodox (or more traditionally inclined Conservative) *shul* should not
wear pants, short sleeves, or skirts that end above the mid-calf. In general, respectful good taste should be your guide, but on your first visit
to an unfamiliar congregation, it is probably better to err on the side of
caution.

One of the major fears of every first-time synagogue-goer is getting
lost in the text of the service. When you enter the sanctuary, the usher
will probably hand you a prayer book and possibly a *khumash* (a volume
containing the Torah in its entirety and the *haftarah* readings). Generally, she will be glad to show you where in the *siddur* to begin; if not,
ask. Failing that, you can always ask your neighbor.

As for the choreography of worship—the bowing, bending, standing,
and sitting—many prayer books will include this information in their
text. (Contemporary Orthodox *siddurim* like the *ArtScroll Siddur,* or the
Conservative *Siddur Sim Shalom,* often give copious explanations of what
you are supposed to be doing at any given moment.) You can always try
to follow your neighbor. It wouldn't hurt, before you go to a service,
to take a look at one of the beginners' guides like Rabbi Hayim Donin's
To Pray as a Jew, or even the first chapter of the present book.

When the Ark is opened and the Torah lifted, you should stand.
When the Torah passes you during the processional, you may touch the
fringes of your *tallit* to it, then kiss them. If you are not wearing a *tallit,*
do the same thing with your prayer book or even your fingertips.

If you are offered an *aliyah* and don't feel comfortable enough with the
Hebrew blessings for the reading of the Torah, feel free to politely decline.

However, it is the job of the *gabbai* to help you and there will usually be a transliteration of the blessings on the *bimah,* so try it if you can.

If you should accept the honor, when you are called to the Torah (by your Hebrew name), walk quickly and quietly to the *bimah* by the shortest possible route. Generally you will stand on the right of the person reading Torah; the person reading from the Torah will point to the place where she is going to begin, you will touch it with the fringes of your prayer shawl, then kiss the fringes. (If you are not wearing a *tallit,* you can either use the fringes of the reader's prayer shawl or your *siddur.* **Do not** touch the Torah scroll; the oil from your skin is bad for the parchment, and it is bad form to do so.) Then, holding the handles of the Torah, you recite the *Barekhu;* the congregation gives the traditional response, which you repeat, bowing at *Borukh Adonai ham'vorakh* and straightening up at *l'olam va-ed;* then you recite the Torah blessing. The reader will then take over; when she is finished, you repeat the process, touching the *tzitzit* to the point at which the passage finishes. Then you will recite the concluding Torah blessing and shake hands with everyone on the *bimah;* in a Reform synagogue, you quickly and quietly resume your seat, elsewhere you stand to the left of the Torah reader during the next *aliyah.*

As you return to your seat, people may offer you a hearty *"Yasher koakh,"* which roughly means "may your power be increased," a nice Jewish way of saying "job well done." The appropriate response is *"Barukh ti-hiyeh,"* which roughly means "may you be blessed." It is always appropriate and welcome to tell a participant in the service *"Yasher koakh."* On the other hand, it is almost never appropriate to applaud— and no photography, please.

Bringing children to synagogue is a complicated matter. On the one hand, children are indisputably the future of the Jewish people and the earlier they realize how important the synagogue experience is to their parents, the better. Children's programs enrich the life of a worship community and are fun besides. And many synagogues will have special services or arrangements for kids.

On the other hand, some common sense should be observed in the interests of decorum and the seriousness of worship. Long and solemn adult services—the High Holy Days are a good example—are not a good way to start your kids off in Jewish worship. Toddlers and preschoolers may not be ready for an entire evening in quiet company;

know your child's endurance levels and the signs that they have reached the outer limits. If you have an infant or toddler who is clearly either running out of gas, or is in need of a change, or food and drink, quietly take the child out of the sanctuary and do whatever is necessary.

With slightly older children, look for a synagogue that is child-friendly, one that runs youth programs on a regular basis. Ask other parents what their experiences have been. And, by all means, bring children to services. The best time to bring them is for services that are long on music, pageantry, and storytelling—Hanukah, Simkhat Torah, Sukkot, Pesakh, and, most of all, Purim are great times to introduce your child to the joys of Judaism.

Finally, a general observation on the issue of *shul* etiquette: if you are polite and not overtly disruptive, exercise common sense and good taste, there is no *faux pas* so egregious that it is unforgivable. Any rabbi will tell you that the most important aspect of prayer for you to focus on in any worship is not whether you bowed from the waist or the knees, but whether you spoke to the Eternal with real *kavanah*. And that's what you should be focusing on in synagogue.

THE CHOSEN PEOPLE?

The Jews are often called "the Chosen People," not the least of all by themselves. God, they say, selected them from among all the nations of the world. But what does that mean? Do Jews consider themselves to be morally superior to the rest of humanity on the basis of that Choice?

There are two *midrashim/parables* about the Choosing that illustrate nicely the ambivalence that the Jews have always felt towards their Chosen-ness. In one, God shops the Torah around to other nations. One group asks, "What's in it?" and God replies, "Thou shalt not steal." "Well, that's how we make our living. Not interested." Another people ask what the Torah contains and God tells them, "Thou shalt not kill." "We're a nation of warriors, we can't do that, sorry." Finally, God asks the Hebrews and they agree to accept the Torah.

Another *midrash* says that God lifted Mount Sinai into the air, suspended it over the heads of the Israelites, and told them that if they did not accept the Torah, he would drop the mountain on them. Some choice.

The Jews were not Chosen for their superiority but for their willingness to follow God's laws. The Jews were Chosen because they dared not refuse. Either way, the worldview these two stories propound is one in which being Chosen is a responsibility and a burden. In Deuteronomy 7:7, God tells the Israelites that they were not Chosen because they were *greater* among the nations but because they were *small*, the least of the nations.

Judaism teaches that our "Chosen-ness" does not mean that non-Jews cannot experience a profound relationship with the Eternal. It does not dehumanize non-Jews. And if the Jews are Chosen, it is a status that is available to anyone who agrees to accept the strictures that accompany Jewishness.

This is not to say that there aren't Jews—religious Jews—who are uncomfortable with the idea of Chosen-ness, who reject it in the name of universalism. Mordecai Kaplan, the founder of Reconstructionism, found the idea abhorrent, and the Reconstructionist prayer book is unique among *siddurim* in its editing out any passage affirming Jewish Chosen-ness.

On the other hand, there is Rabbi Arthur Hertzberg, who wrote, "God says, I chose you not because you are more numerous or more powerful, and not because you are morally, spiritually, or intellectually superior. You are not. I chose you out of my unknowable will."

NOTES

1. This phrase has important implications for Jewish belief beyond the conception of God's relationship to humanity. If all people are created in God's image, then it follows that the relationship to God is not limited to Jews alone. In fact, many non-Jews in the Bible are seen as true worshippers of God, including Noah and Jethro, Moses's father-in-law. One needn't accept the Jewish faith to be "saved."

2. At the same time, there is a strong strain within Jewish thought that rejects the use of anthropomorphic language to describe God. Maimonides, for example, says that we can only describe God in negative terms: God is not corporeal, etc. Or as another Jewish thinker put it, "If I could describe God, I would *be* God."

3. In traditionally observant women's *tefillah*/*prayer* groups (see p. 68), the worshippers do not count themselves as a *minyan* and hold services without reciting the communal prayers.

4. *Gates of Prayer*, the Reform movement's prayer book, actually offers several versions of each service, but even these follow the basic structure of the traditional liturgy.

5. Although there are prayers for the well-being of the State of Israel in modern *siddurim*, the reference to "the people Israel" that is a recurring motif in Jewish texts gener-

ally refers to the entire Jewish people—descended from Jacob, renamed Israel by God—rather than Israel, the modern nation-state.

6. The rabbinic Hebrew and Yiddish usage of the word *goy* refers specifically to any non-Jew (often in a pejorative tone in Yiddish usage). The Hebrew word, however, is a generic term for any nation, the plural *goyim*. Hence the often-sung verse from Isaiah, *Lo yisa goy el goy kherev* is translated, "Let no nation lift up sword against another nation."

7. The distinction between Ashkenazi and Sephardi is one with its roots in the history of the Diaspora. Sephardic Jews are those who settled first in Spain and were subsequently dispersed throughout the Mediterranean basin, as well as the Netherlands, England, and the Iberian colonies in the New World. Ashkenazi Jews had their roots in Germany and Eastern Europe.

8. A *Makhzor* is a compilation of a cycle of prayers, usually for a specific festival. Today the word is usually applied to the prayer book for the High Holy Days. The distinction between *siddurim* and *makhzorim* is Ashkenazic in origin and relatively recent.

9. One intriguing paradox emerges in the Sephardi/Ashkenazi split. Although the Hasidic movement has its roots in eighteenth-century Poland and later Russia, both Ashkenazi regions, the Hasidic liturgy is drawn partially from the Sephardic; this is a reflection of the tremendous importance for the Hasidim of the school of mysticism that originated in sixteenth-century Palestine with the teachings of Isaac Luria, a Sephardic Jew. What the Hasidim *daven* is called *nusakh sepharad* and is based in part on the Spanish-derived Sephardic liturgy. However, it is more closely related to the Ashkenazic liturgy than to that used by the Sephardic Jews of Arab countries.

CHAPTER 2

Rejoice in Your Festivals: The Jewish Year

SACRED TIME—THE JEWISH CALENDAR

Prayer and ritual in Judaism are in part about the creation of sacred space, as we saw in the previous chapter. When we pray, wherever we pray, that place, however mundane, is transformed—if only briefly—into sacred space. This basic principle helped the Jewish religion to survive the two thousand years of exile and dispersion that followed the destruction of the Second Temple in 70 C.E.

But holiness in space is a concept found in many other religions before and after the beginnings of Judaism. For pagans, polytheists, and pantheists, the concept of a place or natural phenomenon imbued with holiness is a common one. Sacred trees, sacred mountains, sacred animals are all found in a wealth of religious traditions.

What set the Jews apart was a gradual shifting of focus from the holiness of space to the holiness of time, "from things to events," as the late philosopher Abraham Heschel puts it. If an object is sacred to Jews, it is so only because of a conscious act of man, not because of a status conferred upon it by a deity. Think back to the previous chapter: the synagogue is not inherently holy, it is only holy because—and when—we pray in it. You can say more or less the same prayers in your own home.

No, it is the when and not the where of prayer that counts the most in Judaism. Judaism is a religion—indeed, the first religion and, by and large, the only religion—that sanctifies time over space. So when we talk about the Jewish year, the cycle of holiday observances that a typical Jew engages in annually, we are coming to the heart of Jewish belief, to the way that Judaism separates the sacred from the mundane (as the *Havdalah* service puts it).

One of the first and most obvious ways in which Judaism takes its practitioners outside the realm of mundane time, earthly time, is by regulating its ritual time in a radically different way from most other belief systems (although both the derivative Christian and Islamic ritual calendars have some, but not all, of the same features). The Jewish calendar itself is unconventional, seemingly a holdover from a pre-scientific era in which men and women watched the sky in wonder and fear, trying to understand the cycles of nature that affected them in a direct way, bringing rain or dew for their crops or drought and deprivation.

The Jewish calendar is a lunar calendar, based on a twelve-month year, regulated by the cycles of the moon, unlike our secular (and solar) calendar, which is based on the movement of the earth around the sun. A Hebrew month begins with the new moon, an event which is even celebrated as *Rosh Khodesh/Head (beginning) of the month*. (See sidebar "Rosh Khodesh" below; for a list of the Hebrew months, see sidebar "The Jewish Calendar," p. 78.) Each of the twelve Hebrew months is either 29 or 30 days long, so each year is only 354 days in duration. Obviously, this creates a significant discrepancy between the lunar and solar calendars. In order to make up the difference, the Jewish calendar adds an additional month (Adar II) in the spring seven times in each nineteen years.[1] (The Islamic calendar, also a lunar calendar, does not include a leap year, with the result that key holidays like Ramadan fall at different times every year. The Christian calendar recognizes some holidays—most prominently Easter—as "moveable feasts," but others, like Christmas for example, are fixed.)

ROSH KHODESH

Rosh Khodesh literally means "head of the month," and refers to celebration of the new moon, which marks the beginning of a new month in the Jewish calendar. During the period of the First Temple, Rosh Khodesh was a major event. There were special sacrifices, feasts, and a day off from work. Sometime after the end of the Babylonian exile, at the end of the sixth century B.C.E., it was reduced to a minor holiday, not unlike the intermediate days of Sukkot and Pesakh. Eventually, it lost even that status and, today, is recognized by some additions to the liturgy, including a prayer for the new month, a half-*Hallel*, a special Torah reading, and a special *maftir* reading of the passage in Numbers 28 describing the sacrifices held in the Temple on Rosh Khodesh.

Traditionally, the coming of the new month was regarded as a propitious time for self-examination, a time for atonement. The sixteenth-century kabbalists of Safed even introduced a fast day, called *Yom Kippur Katan/the Little Day of Atonement,* on which they fasted on the eve of the new moon until the afternoon service. This practice never gained much favor and although there are individuals who still observe it and a few congregations in which special penitential prayers are read in the morning service in recognition of the day, this fast has essentially disappeared.

In recent years, with the rise of women's *tefillah/prayer* groups, Rosh Khodesh has taken on a new sheen. Traditionally, Rosh Khodesh was observed by women in the home by not cleaning, et cetera. Today, Jewish feminists have reclaimed the holiday and observe it as a day of special significance for Jewish women. It is undoubtedly too soon to tell if this observance will resonate sufficiently in Jewish communities to have a longer life than *Yom Kippur Katan,* but creative women rabbis, cantors, and laypeople are devising many attractive new rituals and liturgies in recognition of Rosh Khodesh.

THE JEWISH CALENDAR

MONTH	NUMBER OF DAYS	SPECIAL DAYS
Spring		
Nisan	30	15—First day of Pesakh
		27—Yom ha-Shoah
Iyar	29	5—Yom ha-Atzma'ut
		18—Lag b'Omer
		28—Yom Yerushalayim
Summer		
Sivan	30	6—Shavuot (first day)
Tammuz	29	17—Fast of 17 Tammuz
Av	30	9—Tisha b'Av
Elul	29	

Autumn		
Tishri	30	1—Rosh Hashanah
		3—Fast of Gedaliah
		10—Yom Kippur
		15—Sukkot (First Day)
		22—Shemini Atzeret
		23—Simkhat Torah
Kheshvan	29 or 30	
Winter		
Kislev	29 or 30	25—Hanukah (First Day)
Tevet	29	10—Fast of 10 Tevet
Shevat	30	15—Tu bi-Shevat
Adar	29 (30 in leap year)	13—Fast of Esther
		14—Purim
Adar II	(29 in leap year)	14—Purim (leap year only)

In the time of the Temple in Jerusalem (the First Temple was destroyed in 586 B.C.E., the Second Temple, built in 538 B.C.E. was razed in 70 C.E.), communication over long distances was problematic. It was imperative, if all Jewish communities were to celebrate at the same time, that everyone know when the new moon occurred, since the date of a festival would be based on when the first of the month fell. (For example, *Pesakh/Passover* falls on 15 Nisan; if you know when Nisan begins, you need only count the days to know when Pesakh begins. But you have to know when the new moon is in order to do that.) Until 358 C.E., when Rabbi Hillel II introduced a permanent fixed calendar, it was up to the Sanhedrin, the governing body of rabbis in Jerusalem, to decide when the new moon fell, based on eyewitness testimony. They in turn would send a signal to a man on a neighboring hilltop who would light a signal fire; another fire would be lit on a nearby hilltop and so on, until a chain of signal fires was flickering through the known Jewish world, telling the Jews that the new month had begun.

This was, needless to say, an inexact system. The rabbis of the Sanhedrin worried that communities outside the Holy Land would not know the exact date on which to celebrate a festival. In response to this problem, they instituted a second day for each festival in the Diaspora so that there could be no mistake. This second day is preserved in the practice of Orthodox and Conservative Jews in the Diaspora of celebrating a second day of major holidays. In Israel and the Reform movement, only one day of each festival is observed.[2]

Why have the Jews retained this awkward, downright perverse calendrical system? Surely this throwback to a time before scientific astronomical instruments is too impractical, too outmoded to remain in use. Perhaps.

But having a second, ritual calendar, one that is markedly different from the one that governs our secular lives, forces us to think in a deliberate manner about the coming of the holidays, sets them apart in a practical way that we experience directly and unmistakably. In short, it creates a sacred time that is distinct from the ordinary time we experience in our offices, on the bus, while shopping for dinner. It does so by making us turn our minds back to pre-industrial rhythms, to the rhythms imposed on us by nature, by the cycle of the seasons and the movement of the moon around the earth. We are taken out of the harrowing tempo of modern life, however briefly, to reflect on our covenantal relationship with God and God's creation.

And that is anything but perverse. On the contrary, it is the governing principal behind Jewish observance.

THE FESTIVALS

The holidays and the Sabbath are the logical outcome of this approach to setting aside sacred time. They offer us moments out of ordinary time in which we are instructed, encouraged to exult, to rejoice. In Deuteronomy 16:14–15, the Israelites are instructed, "You shall rejoice in your festivals and shall be altogether joyful." In the Talmud, it is written: "Rejoicing on a festival is a religious duty." The first-century sage Rabbi Eliezer said, "[One] has nothing else to do on a festival, only either to eat and drink or to sit and study."

Work is forbidden on the Sabbath and the major festivals. The major festivals consist of the three "Pilgimage Festivals," Pesakh (Passover), Shavuot (Pentecost), and Sukkot (Booths), and the High Holy Days, Rosh Hashanah (New Year) and Yom Kippur (the Day of Atonement). On the festivals, the only exception to the prohibition against work is that one is permitted to do work that enhances the enjoyment of the festival, for example, cooking. Work that can be done before the festival without impairing the quality of the food should not be delayed until the festival. For example, it would not be permissible to grind wheat to make bread for the festival. On the other hand, contemporary rabbis have ruled that it *is* permissible to grind coffee beans by hand, because fresh ground coffee tastes better and therefore adds to one's enjoyment of a *yom tov/holiday* (literally "a good day"). But one is not permitted to prepare food during a holiday for use after the holiday.

As we will see momentarily, the prohibition against working on *Shabbat/the Sabbath* is much stricter. The reason for the difference can be found in the Torah. In Leviticus 23:3 the Jews are enjoined to "do no manner of work" on Shabbat; four verses later, they are told that on the festivals "you shall do no manner of servile work," in other words, work as an employee, bondsman, or slave.

SHABBAT

In the Torah it is written, "On the seventh day God finished the work . . . and ceased from all the work . . . and God blessed the seventh day and declared it holy, because on it God ceased from all the work of creation . . ." (Genesis 2:2–3)

Most people reading that passage find it a bit of a shock. "On the seventh day God finished the work. . . ." But what did God create on the seventh day? Didn't God "cease . . . from all the work of creation" on the seventh day? What God created on the seventh day, the ancient rabbis tell us, was . . . rest.

The Hebrew word used here is *menuhah,* and "rest" is an inadequate translation. To say that *Shabbat Menuhah* means a "Sabbath of rest" only tells half the story. In the Shabbat liturgy we are given a more complete, many layered understanding of the word. It is, the *Minkhah/afternoon* service tells us, "a rest of love freely given, a rest of truth and sincerity, a rest in peace and tranquility, in quietude and safety." Yet, at the same time, it is a rest yoked in the same breath to "holiness." And inextricably linked to that concept is the fact that this rest comes from the Almighty and exists so that we might glorify God's name, to bring holiness to God.

Shabbat is the only Jewish holiday whose timing does not depend on the calendar at all—seven days are seven days, regardless of the phases of the moon. Like the Creation itself, it is beyond human influence. And its observance, in turn, informs the way most of the other holidays are celebrated.

The Sabbath is the only day of observance mentioned in the Ten Commandments. In the first version of the Decalogue we are enjoined to "Remember the Sabbath day and keep it holy" (Exodus 20:8); in the second version, we are told to "observe" the Sabbath (Deuteronomy 5:12). What more compelling evidence can one find for the paramount importance of this day?

But not to work? An enforced rest? The rabbis who began to codify Jewish law *(halakhah)* during the time of the Second Temple specified thirty-nine categories of prohibited activities—and objects associated with those activities are *muktzeh*/literally, *set aside*—based on the activities that were involved in the building of the Tabernacle as described in the Tanakh, the Hebrew Bible. (For a complete list, see sidebar below.) One should not handle a hammer or money. One should not rearrange the books on a shelf. What sort of holiday is this?

THE THIRTY-NINE CATEGORIES OF FORBIDDEN WORK

The Talmud establishes thirty-nine categories of work forbidden on the Sabbath. Ostensibly, these categories were based on the description of the building of the Ark of the Covenant found in the Torah. (From these categories, the rabbis derived numerous other subcategories; they also would add prohibitions of their own in order to protect the Sabbath from desecration.)

A. Agricultural work
  1. Plowing the land
  2. Sowing seeds on the land
  3. Cutting or harvesting crops
  4. Binding or gathering crops

(The next four categories each involve separating the useful from the useless.)

  5. Threshing
  6. Winnowing
  7. Selecting

8. Sifting
9. Grinding
10. Kneading
11. Baking

B. Working with clothing/fabric
   12. Shearing
   13. Bleaching
   14. Carding
   15. Dyeing
   16. Spinning
   17. Inserting thread into a loom
   18. Weaving
   19. Taking off a finished product from a loom
   20. Separating threads
   21. Tying a (permanent) knot
   22. Untying a knot (in order to re-tie it)
   23. Sewing
   24. Tearing

C. Working with leather or parchment; writing
   25. Catching game/hunting
   26. Slaughtering
   27. Skinning or flaying
   28. Tanning
   29. Scraping
   30. Marking out (e.g., in preparation for cutting)
   31. Cutting
   32. Writing
   33. Erasing (for the sake of writing again)

D. Construction work
   34. Building
   35. Demolishing (for the sake of building)
   36. A final hammer blow—any act that completes or makes usable a finished product

E. Working with fire
   37. Kindling

> 38. Extinguishing (when done for a positive purpose, as in the manu-
> facture of charcoal)
> 39. Carrying—from the public domain to the private or vice versa

We are commanded in the Torah "Six days shall you labor and do all your work." To abstain from labor on the seventh day is, as Abraham Joshua Heschel says in his magnificent little book *The Sabbath: Its Meaning for Modern Man,* "not a depreciation but an affirmation of labor, a divine exaltation of its dignity." We are suddenly lifted out of the process of time, removed from the world of natural and social change. Instead of creating the world anew, we are at one with the world created.

We are not beasts of burden. We should not live to work. We should not be chained to routine. Shabbat unchains us. As Heschel states,

> To set one day a week for freedom, a day on which we do not use the instruments which have been so easily turned into weapons of destruction, a day for being with ourselves, a day of detachment from the vulgar, of independence of external obligations, a day on which we stop worshipping the idols of technical civilization, a day on which we use no money, a day of armistice in the economic struggle with our fellow men and the forces of nature—is there any institution that holds out a greater hope for [humanity's] progress than the Sabbath? (p. 28)

Shabbat is meant to be a day of peace, *Shabbat shalom,* the peace of the Sabbath. It offers us a chance for peace with nature, with society, and with ourselves. The prohibitions on work are designed to make us stop—if only for one day of the week—our relentless efforts to tame, to conquer, to subdue the earth and everything on it. The prohibition against making fire is also said by the rabbis to mean that one should not kindle the fires of controversy against one's fellow humans. And, finally, the Sabbath offers us a moment of quiet, of serenity, of self-transcendence, a moment that allows us to seek and perhaps achieve some kind of internal peace.

Shabbat is also a time of joy, of good food and wine (even if the food preparation must be done beforehand). Judaism is most decidedly not an ascetic religion. It is no accident that it is considered a *mitzvah* (loosely, a commandment; but see Chapter 4 for a more detailed explanation) to have sexual relations with your spouse on the Sabbath.

The concept of *oneg shabbat / joy in the Sabbath* is so crucial that any sadness is banished. Fast days are postponed a day if they should fall on Shabbat (except for Yom Kippur). Active mourning is expressly forbidden on the Sabbath. Funerals are put off until Sunday and mourners do not sit *shivah* on Shabbat. (See the section "Death and Mourning," in Chapter 3, p. 184.) Indeed, the only time they can leave their homes during the week of mourning is to come to synagogue for the Sabbath observance. On Friday night, they sit outside the sanctuary during *Kabbalat Shabbat / Welcoming the Sabbath,* entering after *L'kha Dodi* has been sung; worshippers greet them with the words, "May God console you among the other mourners of Zion and Jerusalem."

In the post-biblical literature the Sabbath is depicted in two related guises, as a bride *(kallah)* and as a queen *(malkah).* These two personifications of the day can tell us a bit more about how we are to understand this unusual—indeed, unique—religious holiday.

There is a Midrash (a rabbinic commentary in parable form) about *Shabbat ha-Kallah / the Sabbath Bride.* When God created the days of the week, each of them was given a mate—Sunday had Monday, Tuesday had Wednesday, and Thursday had Friday. Only the Sabbath was alone. The Sabbath pointed this out to God, whose answer was to give it to the people Israel as their mate, a bride. (Interestingly, in Hebrew the days are numbered rather than named, with one exception, Shabbat, providing more evidence of how this "bride" stands out from the rest of the week.)

Why a bride? As Samuel Dresner, a contemporary Conservative rabbi, points out, "The symbol of a bride is love, devotion, and joy—an inward feeling." One prepares for the Sabbath with all the fervor and yearning with which one prepares for a bride.

Shabbat ha-Malkah / the Sabbath Queen evokes different feelings. If the Sabbath Bride may be said to represent the "remember" part of the Decalogue's commandments regarding the Sabbath, the Sabbath Queen represents "observe." She is the stern avatar of the laws governing the day. The Sabbath, Dresner writes, "cannot be observed haphazardly." One does not achieve the peace of the Sabbath without observing the rules that lead to that rest. A Jew "makes" Shabbat; it doesn't just come at the end of the week.

Both of these facets of Shabbat are essential to a full realization of the day. A Sabbath without the Bride would be a cold, lifeless recitation of rules and prayers with nothing motivating them but rote and subjugation to a higher will. A Sabbath without the Queen would be without substance or focus, short-lived good feelings with nothing to show for them. The Jewish observance of the Sabbath is an attempt to find an appropriate balance between these two aspects of the day.

An example of that balance: The rabbis of the Gaonic period (sixth to twelfth centuries) cautioned: "There is nothing more important, according to the Torah, than to preserve human life. . . . Even when there is the slightest possibility that a life may be at stake one may disregard every prohibition of the law." This doctrine, called *pikuakh nefesh/saving a soul* applies to the laws governing Shabbat and the festivals; a doctor must act to save another person, even though it means she is "working" on the Sabbath. A sick person may not fast if it threatens his life.

But the Sabbath was designed to be "a delight," as our liturgy tells us. It is a time when families and friends gather together for meals, songs, and stories. The Friday night rituals of candle lighting, making *kiddush* (blessing the wine for the holiday), and *ha-Motzi/blessing the bread* are followed the next day by the tradition of the *se'udah sh'lishit/third meal,* on Shabbat afternoon, another festive gathering, often accompanied by Torah study and lively discussion, and finished off with more singing of *z'mirot/songs.* Even as the Sabbath ends, there is a tradition that allows us to extend the pleasure, the *melaveh malkah/farewell to the Queen,* when Jews gather to reluctantly bid goodbye to the Sabbath after *Havdalah,* with more songs, food, and wine.

As Heschel observes, the Sabbath is the one day on the Jewish calendar for which there are no appurtenances necessary to partake of its holiness—no *shofar* to blow as on Rosh Hashanah, no "four species" to wave as on Sukkot, no *matzah,* no *tefillin,* not even the Tabernacle. Just a group of Jews and the Sabbath, all holiness in itself.

On the other hand, there are many Shabbat customs and traditions that enrich the celebration of this day.

On *Erev Shabbat/the eve of the Sabbath,* as the Sabbath approaches, all must be made ready. One should not still be preparing by late Friday afternoon. The house should be cleaned and an elaborate and festive meal prepared, with guests invited. Traditionally observant Hasidic men will go to the *mikveh/ritual bath* to immerse and purify themselves physically and spiritually for the Sabbath.

The Shabbat candles—at least two, although in families with children there may be additional ones for each child—should be lit eighteen minutes before sunset (although, intriguingly, in Jerusalem Shabbat starts forty minutes before sunset), and the blessing said:

> *Barukh atah Adonai Eloheinu Melekh ha-olam*
> *asher kid'shanu b'mitzvotav v'tzivanu l'hadklik ner shel Shabbat.*
>
> *Blessed are You Adonai our God, Ruler of the Universe, who sanctified us with Your commandments and commanded us to kindle the lights of the Sabbath.*

Although this has traditionally been considered a *mitzvah* that should be performed by a woman, the obligation actually rests with the entire household, both men and women, and a leader of the family should light candles, regardless of gender. With eyes covered,[3] that family member then recites the blessing over the candles. The holiday has begun.

William Helmreich, a sociologist who was raised in an Orthodox family, evokes the *Shabbatot* of his childhood in the following passage, in which he lovingly recounts what would happen next in his home:

> There was something exquisite in [the candle-lighting] ceremony. One could sense in it the quiet of the approaching Sabbath, which above all meant rest and closeness to God. The house was silent; no radio could be played, no telephone answered, no light turned on or off, for any use of electricity was considered work. The candles would eventually burn themselves out, and our home would be darkened and serene.
> —*Wake Up, Wake Up, to Do the Work of the Creator,* pp. 4–5

There should be wine for *kiddush* and two loaves of *khallah,* the braid-shaped bread that is traditional on the Sabbath, which are kept covered until the blessing over the bread is pronounced. The two loaves are in recognition of the double portion of manna that fell in the wilderness the day before Shabbat so that the Israelites wouldn't have to gather it on the day of rest. Similarly, the plate below the *khallot* and the cover over them represent the layers of dew which rested above and below the manna and kept it fresh. After *kiddush,* the loaves are uncovered. Before they can be eaten, there must be the ritual washing of hands (see Chapter 1, p. 22). From the time the blessing for the washing of hands is spoken until the *khallah* is eaten, there should be silence—except for the pronouncement of the blessing over the bread—so that the continuity between these acts is undisturbed. It is also said that Sabbath angels come to visit each Jewish home on Friday night, bringing the blessing of peace for the duration of the Sabbath. It is to those angels that we sing *Shalom Aleichem / Welcome, ministering angels,* one of the most familiar and beloved of Shabbat songs.

Shabbat is one of the most companionable of days. After the morning service, worshippers gather for *kiddush,* often sponsored by a member of the congregation who has a *simkha / joyous event* to celebrate. At the very least, wine and a little cake are served, but often a more elaborate and festive repast is offered, just short of a full meal. Lunch after worship will be another feast, with the same sequence of *kiddush,* hand washing, and *motzi,* the blessing over the bread, experienced at dinner the previous night. In the late afternoon, there will be a *se'udah sh'lishit / third meal,* eaten in conjunction with Torah discussion after the afternoon service. This is a light meal, which may be eaten at home or at the synagogue, often accompanied by soft, sad music to underline our reluctance to see the Sabbath end. The day has already been sanctified, so there is no *kiddush.* Finally, when three stars have appeared in the sky, usually about an hour after the time of the previous night's candle lighting, Shabbat is over and we "make" *Havdalah* (See Chapter 1, p. 44).

On the Sabbath, legend has it, each of us acquires an extra soul, a *neshama yeterah,* the better to savor the day. Indeed, the reason we smell the pungent spices of the *Havdalah* ritual is to revive us after our extra soul has departed. Finally, it is said that the Sabbath is a taste from God of *olam ha-bah / the World to Come,* of paradise, a time in which it will always be Shabbat.

It is significant that a Jewish conception of paradise centers not on place but on time, a Messianic Age when all time will be sacred.

SPECIAL SABBATHS

There are several Sabbaths that have special names, either because of when they fall in the Jewish calendar in relation to festivals or because of the Torah or *haftarah* reading that is prescribed for that Shabbat. The following is a list of them, explaining their content and significance.

Shabbat Mevarekhim. The Sabbath of Blessing, the Sabbath preceding the new moon (except for the month of Tishri, with its many important holidays). In addition to the usual liturgy and Torah readings for the given Shabbat, the prayer for the new month is read, along with *Yehi Ratson*, the prayer asking God to protect the people from disasters and affliction.

Shabbat Makhar Khodesh. Falls on the eve of the new moon. In addition to the prayers for the new moon recited on Shabbat Mevarekhim, there is a special *haftarah*, I Samuel 20:18–42, which describes the covenant between Jonathan and David, made on the eve of Rosh Khodesh.

Shabbat Rosh Khodesh. The Sabbath of the new moon falls on Rosh Khodesh itself. *Hallel* is recited after the morning service and there is a substitution in the *Musaf Amidah*, with the prayer *Atah Yatsartah* replacing *Tikantah Shabbat*. An additional Torah reading is prescribed, Numbers 28:9–15, and the *haftarah* is taken from Isaiah 66:1–24, concluding with a repetition of verse twenty-three.

Shabbat Shuvah. The Sabbath of Return is the Shabbat that falls between Rosh Hashanah and Yom Kippur, during the Ten Days of Repentance. It is customary for the rabbi to speak on the subject of repentance. The special *haftarot* are Hosea 14:2–10, Joel 2:15–27 in Ashkenazi congregations; Hosea 14:2–10, Micah 7:18–20 in Sephardic. Diaspora Ashkenazi congregations will also read the Micah passage before the Joel passage.

Shabbat Khol ha-Moed Sukkot. The Sabbath that falls during the intermediate days of Sukkot is marked by the recitation of *Hallel* and the reading of *Kohelet/Ecclesiastes* in the morning. The Torah reading is from Exodus 33:12–34:26, with a *maftir* portion, Numbers 29. The *haftarah* is Ezekiel 38:18–39:16.

Shabbat Bereishit. The Sabbath of Beginning or the Sabbath of Genesis is the first Shabbat after Simkhat Torah and marks the opening of the annual cycle of Torah readings once again with Genesis 1:1–6:8.

In a traditionally observant congregation, the member chosen on Simkhat Torah as *Khatan Bereishit* will get a special *aliyah* and will provide a special *se'udah/festive meal* or *kiddush* to which all worshippers will be invited after the morning service.

Shabbat Hanukah. Falls during Hanukah (and because the festival lasts eight days, on rare occasions will fall on both the first and last days). *Hallel* is recited after the morning service. In addition to the regular *parshah*, Numbers 7:1–17 is read as *maftir*. If Shabbat also falls on the eighth day of Hanukah, the weekly portion is Genesis 41:1–44:17, the *maftir* is 7:54–8:4. If *Shabbat Hanukah* falls on Rosh Khodesh, Numbers 28:9–15 is read before the *maftir*. The *haftarot* are, respectively, Zechariah 2:14–4:7, I Kings 7:40–50, and Isaiah 66:1–24.

Shabbat Shirah. The Shabbat of the Song occurs when the Torah portion for the week is *Beshalakh*, 13:17–17:16. This *parsha* includes *Shirat ha-Yam*, the "Song at the Sea" (Exodus 15:1–18), sung by Moses, Miriam, and the Israelites when the Egyptians were finally vanquished at the sea. This passage is read with a different, more melodic line. In many congregations, special religious poems will be read as part of the liturgy. In Ashkenazi congregations the *haftarah* is Judges 4:4–5:31; in Sephardic congregations it is Judges 5:1–31. *Shirat ha-Yam* is also read on the seventh day of Passover.

Four Spring Shabbatot. The *Arba Parshiyot/Four Portions* are read on four special Sabbaths during the spring. The first two of these occur before Purim, the second pair after. In addition to the weekly Torah portion for each of these Sabbaths a *maftir* is read from a second *sefer torah*. (If one of these Sabbaths falls on Rosh Khodesh, an additional reading, Numbers 28:9–15 is read.) On all four of these days many congregations will read special religious poems as part of their liturgy. The four Sabbaths include:

1. *Shabbat Shekalim*. The Sabbath of the Shekel Tax is so named because it coincides with Rosh Khodesh Adar (or Adar II in a leap year), the date on which a tax of shekels was mandated to be paid before Nisan. The *maftir*, Exodus 30:11–16, deals with this tax. Ashkenazi congregations read II Kings 12:1–17, Sephardic congregations II Kings 11:17–12:17, as the *haftarah*.
2. *Shabbat Zakhor*. The Sabbath of Remembrance falls before Purim and is so named because the *maftir*, Deuteronomy 25:17–19,

calls on the Jews to "remember what Amalek did to you." Haman is traditionally called a descendant of Amalek, the sworn enemies of Jews for all eternity. The *haftarah* for this Sabbath is I Samuel 15:2–34 in Ashkenazi congregations; Sephardic congregations read the same passage but begin with verse 15:1.

3. *Shabbat Parah.* The Sabbath of the Red Heifer, which takes its name from the animal whose ashes were used for ritual purification, a rite that is described in the *maftir*, Numbers 19:1–22. It is read to commemorate the use of this rite to purify the impure before Pesakh so that they could participate in the pascal sacrifice. The *haftarah* is Ezekiel 36:16–38. (Sephardic congregations finish at 36:36.)

4. *Shabbat ha-Khodesh.* The Sabbath of the Month takes its name from the opening words of the *maftir*, Exodus 12:1–20, which gives the laws governing Passover. This Sabbath precedes or coincides with Rosh Khodesh Nisan, the month in which the festival falls. The *haftarah* is Ezekiel 45:16–46:18. (Sephardic congregations finish at 46:15.)

Shabbat ha-Gadol. The Great Shabbat falls immediately before Pesakh. Traditionally rabbis give a sermon about the holiday. At the afternoon service, portions of the *Hagadah* are read. The *haftarah* is Malachai 3:4–24, concluding with a repetition of verse 23.

Shabbat Khol ha-Moed Pesakh. On the Sabbath for the intermediate days of Passover *Hallel* and *Shir ha-Shirim/Song of Songs* are recited after the morning service. The Torah portions are Exodus 33:12–34:26 and a *maftir*, Numbers 28:19–25. The *haftarah* is Ezekiel 37:1–14. (Some congregations start the *haftarah* at 36:37.)

Shabbat Khazon. The Sabbath of the Vision takes its name from the *haftarah*, Isaiah 1:1–27, in which Isaiah predicts the punishments that will befall Israel. It is traditional to avoid social visiting; congregants wear plain clothes rather than dressing up for Sabbath; the Ark may even be covered by a black curtain. The *haftarah* is chanted to the Lamentations tune used on Tisha b'Av.

Shabbat Nakhamu. The Sabbath of Comfort falls on the Shabbat after Tisha b'Av and takes its name from the *haftarah*, Isaiah 40:1–26, in which Isaiah offers a vision of the final redemption of Israel. The Torah portion for this week is Deuteronomy 3:23–7:11, which includes the Ten

Commandments and the first paragraph of the *Sh'ma*, so it too offers consolation, reaffirming God's covenant with the Jewish people.

THE HIGH HOLY DAYS

The Jewish religious year draws to a close as autumn approaches. The period of mourning for the destruction of the Temple that culminates in midsummer with the fast day of Tisha b'Av (see this chapter, p. 131), has ended and the final month begins. It is a time for *teshuvah*.[4]

ELUL, A MONTH OF *TESHUVAH*

Most books on Judaism translate *teshuvah* as "repentance." That is certainly a key element in the concept, but its literal meaning, "turning," captures another aspect of the process of *teshuvah*. To make *teshuvah* is to turn inward in self-evaluation, to turn back to look on one's deeds of the previous year, to re<u>turn</u> to God.

There are no fast days or festivals in the month of Elul. There is nothing to distract us from a month of "returning" and forgiveness, a month of asking for Divine mercy. Each day of the month we recite Psalm 27 in the synagogue, asking God not to turn away from us, to hear our voices and "be gracious . . . and answer us." In Orthodox and some Conservative synagogues, the *shofar/ram's horn* is sounded after the morning service on each of the twenty-nine days of the month. *Selikhot/Penitential prayers* are recited, calling upon the people Israel to return to God and perhaps (as Rav Abraham Kook has said) to one's true self.

We are making a mental and spiritual preparation for *Yamim Nora'im/the Days of Awe*, the two most powerful days of the Jewish religious year, *Rosh Hashanah/New Year* and *Yom Kippur/the Day of Atonement*. In the *Mishnah*, the compilation of rabbinic law that is at the heart of the Talmud, it is written that all mankind will pass before the throne of God on Rosh Hashanah like a flock of sheep; on that day our fates for the coming year are written, and on Yom Kippur they are sealed.[5]

ROSH HASHANAH

Literally meaning the "head of the year," Rosh Hashanah falls on 1 Tishri (usually in September) and marks the beginning of a period both solemn and joyous. On the one hand, this festival is *Yom ha-Zikaron/the Day of Remembrance*. But it is also the *Yom ha-Teru'ah/the Day of the Shofar Blast* and the "Birthday of the World," the day on which, Jewish lore has it, God created mankind and we symbolically re-enthrone him, an event that calls for an appropriate amount of celebration.

Adding to the mingled feelings is the transformation that comes over the synagogue. The usual fittings—the curtain of the Ark (called the *parokhet*), the mantles over the Torah scrolls, the covering on the reader's table, even the robes worn by the Reform or Conservative rabbi and cantor—have been put aside and in their place are bright white ones. White is the color of purity, of God's cleansing us from sin, a color of festivity. On Yom Kippur, a traditionally observant Jew will wear a white *kittel,* a robe with a multilayered symbolic meaning—it is a white *kittel* in which an Orthodox Jew is buried, but one also wears a *kittel* on Pesakh (p. 118) as a symbol of freedom, and the cantor will wear one on Rosh Hashanah, Hoshanah Rabbah (p. 107), and Shemini Atzeret (page 108), days on which we seek forgiveness.

For the next ten days—Rosh Hashanah, the Ten Days of Repentance, and Yom Kippur—our thoughts turn to mortality, sin, and repentance, and a hoped-for redemption. At midnight on the Saturday before Rosh Hashanah Jews around the world attend *Selikhot* services; setting the tone for the days that follow, a key element of these services is the recitation of the thirteen divine attributes of God's mercy. *Selikhot* (penitential prayers) will be said before dawn each day until Rosh Hashanah.

Rosh Hashanah begins at sundown with candle lighting, synagogue services, *kiddush,* and a festive meal. In addition to the blessing for the lighting of the candles, the *Shehekheyanu* blessing is recited:

Barukh atah Adonai Eloheinu Melekh ha-olam shehekheyanu, v'kiyimanu, v'higiyanu laz'man hazeh.

Blessed are You Adonai our God, Ruler of the Universe, who has given us life, sustained us, and allowed us to reach this day.

(*Shehekheyanu* is a prayer that is recited for almost any special, long-awaited occasion, from holidays to *bar mitzvah* ceremonies. The pleasure of saying this blessing is considered so profound that observant Jews will don a piece of new clothing at the beginnning of Shabbat just so they can recite it.)

After *kiddush,* family members may dip their bread for *motzi* in honey, and after a brief prayer asking for "a good and sweet year," a slice of apple dipped in honey may be eaten. (Although we eat *khallah* at Rosh Hashanah, as on Shabbat, the loaves are either round, to symbolize a good, well-rounded year, or in the shape of a ladder, to signify directing one's year towards the Eternal One. The loaves may also have raisins in them, for a "sweet" year.) Fish is often a central element in this meal, a symbol of fertility. Those who celebrate a second day of Rosh Hashanah—everyone but Reform Jews in the United States—typically will eat a new fruit of the season at dinner on that day, in order to be able to say *Shehekheyanu* again.

The liturgy for the two High Holy Days is structurally the same as that of the other festivals (see Chapter 1, pp. 44–45), but there are considerable and significant additions. First and foremost, all the melodies are unique to the Days of Awe. Indeed, there is a "High Holy Day melody" that runs through both services almost obsessively. Even the melody to which the Torah is chanted is special.

The most awe-inspiring moment in the liturgy for both of these holidays undoubtedly is the *Unitaneh Tokef/Let Us Relate the Power (of This Day)*, a tenth-century *piyut/religious prayer* that recounts the judgment of God as we pass before the Throne: "Who shall live and who shall die, who shall see ripe age and who shall not, who shall perish by fire and who by water. . . ." The God to whom we pray on the Days of Awe is not a cruel or vengeful God. Although on Rosh Hashanah, we are put on trial for our actions of the previous year, to be sentenced on Yom Kippur, as the liturgy says, "It is not the death of sinners that God seeks but that they should repent." As the end of *Unitaneh Tokef* reminds us, "Repentance, prayer, and charity temper judgment's severe decree."

On both days we ask for mercy, intoning the beautiful *piyut Avinu Malkeinu/Our Parent, Our Ruler:* "Be merciful and answer us, we of little merit. Deal with us with love and kindness and help us." (Significantly, when Rosh Hashanah falls on Shabbat, this prayer is omitted. One does not supplicate on the Sabbath, another indication of the primacy of Shabbat among all Jewish observance.)

The blowing of the *shofar* is another highlight of Rosh Hashanah, coming right after the Torah service. In fact, this is the oldest part of the observance of this festival, the element that is prescribed in the Torah in Numbers 29:1. The *shofar* is usually translated as "a ram's horn" and usually is fashioned from that animal, but the horn of a goat, antelope, or gazelle also is acceptable. (A bull's horn is not acceptable, however, because of its harkening back to the Golden Calf with which the Israelites sinned at Sinai.)

The *shofar*'s calls are linked to the three concepts of God's sovereignty *(malkhuyot)*, God's merciful remembrance *(zikhronot)*, and the *shofar*'s evocation of revelation and the eventual coming of the Messianic age *(shofarot)*. Before the *Amidah,* the *shofar* is blown thirty times. After each of the three blessings added to the *Amidah* for the three concepts, the horn is blown ten times. Finally, when the service ends the *shofar* is blown forty times, for a total of a hundred.

After the *Musaf* service, traditionally observant Jews will go to a nearby body of flowing water for a ritual known as *Tashlikh/casting away* (of sins). They will take from their pockets bread crumbs symbolizing their sins of the previous year and cast them into the water, reciting psalms. This penitential act was developed in the thirteenth century and is still practiced by many Jews today. It affords an opportunity for quiet reflection in pleasant company.

DAYS OF REPENTANCE

The ten days that begin with Rosh Hashanah and continue through Yom Kippur are also known as *Aseret Y'mei Teshuvah/the Ten Days of Repentance*. It is now that God is judging mankind. While the completely righteous are immediately inscribed in the Book of Life, and the completely evil in the Book of Death, for the majority of us judgment is pending until the Day of Atonement.

To that end, we are encouraged to engage in acts of *teshuvah, tefillah, tzedekah/repentance, prayer, charity*. Traditionally, Jews will ask their friends, family, and colleagues to forgive them for transgressions they may have committed in the previous year. God may pardon our transgressions against the Eternal, but only a person who has been sinned against may forgive the one who traduced her. *Selikhot* prayers are read before the morning service and *Avinu Malkeinu* is recited after the *Amidah*.

The concept of "sin" in Judaism is not quite the same as in Christianity. The word used to denote sin, *kheit,* comes from archery and means a shot that falls short of the mark, or to fall from the path. Hence, those sins that we repent at this time of year are a failure to live up to our potential, a failure to fulfill one's obligations. The key to *teshuvah* is not merely to acknowledge these failings but, wherever possible, to undo them, to confess the sin aloud to the one we have sinned against, to ask forgiveness, and to pledge not to repeat the transgression.

During this period, it is also customary to visit the grave of close relatives, particularly parents, before Yom Kippur. This custom is undoubtedly related to the commandment in the Decalogue to "honor one's father and mother."

The Sabbath that falls between the Days of Awe is called *Shabbat Shuvah/the Sabbath of Repentance (or Returning)*. At this service it is probable that one will hear a sermon on the theme of repentance. Indeed, even before it became the custom for a rabbi to sermonize regularly, this Shabbat was marked by a sermon, often given by a leader of the Jewish community, exhorting Jews to repent.

The day before Yom Kippur is a sort of minor festival day in its own right. We will fast the next day, but today we are encouraged to feast. The *se'udah mafseket/final meal* is a joyous one. In the Talmud, in the tractate *Berakhot,* it is written: "Whoever eats and drinks on the ninth of Tishri, the Torah considers it as if he had fasted both on the ninth and tenth."

Some Orthodox Jews still observe the custom of *kaparot/expiation of sins* on the day before Yom Kippur. In this rite, a live chicken is waved over the heads of family members while a prayer for redemption is intoned. The chicken is then slaughtered and the meat given to charity. More recently, the tradition has been altered by some so that money for charity is tied in a handkerchief and waved instead of the chicken.

As evening approaches and with it Yom Kippur, many observant men will go to the *mikveh/ritual bath* for purification. By *Minkhah* they may have already donned their symbolic white clothing. They will have recited the *Vidui/Confession of Sins* and given *tzedekah/charity* one more time. Just before the holiday actually begins, most will light memorial candles for departed family members. On this most solemn of fast days it is forbidden to wear leather shoes. One does not ask forgiveness while wearing the skin of another of the Creator's creatures. Before leaving for synagogue, slippers or cloth shoes will be donned by the entire family. After the lighting of the festival candles, they go to synagogue and the most holy day of the Jewish year begins.

YOM KIPPUR

Shabbat Shabbaton / The Sabbath of Sabbaths. The White Sabbath. These names for the Day of Atonement give some indication of how holy, how special this day is for Jews throughout the world. It is the only fast day which is never postponed for Shabbat. It is the only day on which one wears a *tallit / prayer shawl* for all services, even for the evening service that begins the holiday. For many nonobservant Jews this is the only day of the year on which they go to synagogue.

Yom Kippur takes its tone from the passage in Leviticus 16:30–31 mandating its observance: "[I]t shall be a statute forever for you: in the seventh month, on the tenth day of the month, you shall afflict your souls and shall do no manner of work, the home born nor the stranger that sojourns among you. For on this day shall atonement be made for you, to cleanse you; from all your sins before Adonai you shall be cleansed."

All males over the age of thirteen and females over the age of twelve are obliged to observe the fast. However, sick people not only may, but are required to take their medicines and, on advice of rabbi or doctor, those whose health would be injured by fasting are forbidden to do so. As on Shabbat, the doctrine of *pikuach nefesh* takes precedence over other rules. As the story goes, Rabbi Hayim Soloveitchik, a famous nineteenth-century rabbi, was once asked why he was so lenient about letting sick people eat and drink on Yom Kippur; he replied, "On the contrary—I'm not lenient—I'm very strict when it comes to saving lives."

The fast serves several purposes. First, and most obviously, it is a penance for our wrongdoing, a symbol of sacrifice that underlines our sense of remorse in God's eyes. Second, it is a display of self-discipline, a sign (perhaps to ourselves most of all) that we can control our appetites in all things. Third, the fast should help us to focus on the spiritual rather than the material, thinking not of business or food or drink, but of God and the sacred. We fast as if for one day we are angels, purely spiritual in nature. Finally, some have argued, fasting is a way of awakening compassion in ourselves, making us experience for a single day the hunger that so many live with constantly.

In addition to abstention from food and drink and the wearing of leather shoes, Jews are not permitted to have sexual relations, wear cosmetics and lotions, or to wash any part of the body other than the fingers and eyes on Yom Kippur.

There are five services held over the course of the entire holiday, beginning with an evening service, usually referred to as *Kol Nidre/All Vows* after the prayer that marks its opening, perhaps the most famous in all of Jewish liturgy. The following day, there are *Shakharit/Morning, Musaf/Additional,* and *Minkhah* services, the last of which includes a *Yizkor/Memorial* service. These feature some important expansions of the usual festival services, particularly the inclusion of a Torah service in *Minkhah.* Finally, ending the holiday is the *Ne'ilah/Concluding* service. Each of the services includes an extended version of the *Amidah,* as well as *Ashamnu/We have transgressed,*[6] a catalog of sins, the *Vidui Rabbah/Confession of Sins,* and *Avinu Malkeinu/Our Father, Our King* (although the latter is omitted by Askhenazi Jews when Yom Kippur falls on a Sabbath). Significantly, the confessional prayers are written in the first person plural; our sins are collective and we are responsible for our neighbors' as well as for our own.

Before *Kol Nidre,* it is proclaimed that at this time it is permissible to pray with sinners. On Yom Kippur, no one should be excluded or feel estranged from the community, no matter how grave his or her transgressions. And the community must acknowledge that, after all, we are all sinners.

Kol Nidre takes its title from the opening words of a declaration made in Aramaic (a Semitic language closely related to Hebrew, in which many prayers in the liturgy are written), a statement that all the vows, obligations, promises, and oaths made during the previous year, whether unintentionally, impulsively, or under duress, are null and void. The music to which this legal document is set—it is not actually a prayer—is dark and brooding. The full text is chanted three times (usually with each repetition increasing in volume and intensity), in accordance with ancient Jewish legal practice. The effect is an overwhelmingly powerful beginning to the evening service and to Yom Kippur.

In the Middle Ages, as already troubled relations between Jewish and Christian communities deteriorated throughout Europe, *Kol Nidre* was pointed to by anti-Semites as proof that a Jew's word to a non-Jew was worthless, that Jews engaged in sharp business practice as a matter of religious training. In fact, this is a deliberate distortion of the meaning of *Kol Nidre*, which refers solely to promises of a religious nature. However, well into the 19th century, anti-Semites would continue to peddle this lie.

What *Kol Nidre* really is about is the shortcomings of humankind. It is an admission of our failures to live up to the promises we have made to Adonai and ourselves as well as to others over the course of the year, an admission that is an important first step towards the self-improvement that *teshuvah* requires. It is not God's intention that we start the New Year already behind in our obligations.

In the first century of Reform Judaism, from 1844 to 1961, *Kol Nidre* was omitted from Reform *machzor,* disparaged as a throwback to ancient times; it was usually replaced with Psalm 103 or Psalm 130 or a hymn, "O Day of the Lord." However, the inimitable and irreplaceable power of *Kol Nidre* was eventually recognized by the Reform movement and it has been restored in Reform synagogues.

The daytime services for Yom Kippur include two significant elements unique to the holiday. Unlike Shabbat *Musaf,* the Yom Kippur *Musaf* service is a significant and dramatic one, highlighted by the *Avodah* service, a vivid description of the activities of the High Priest on Yom Kippur as it was observed in the Temple in Jerusalem two thousand years earlier. In traditionally observant synagogues, worshippers will prostrate themselves on four separate occasions during this service, kneeling, then doubling over to touch their heads to the floor as the *hazan/cantor* describes the moment in the ancient service in which the High Priest would utter to himself the secret name of Adonai, the *Shem Hameforash*. The congregation then answers aloud, *Barukh sheim k'vod malkhuto l'olam va'ed/Blessed be the Name of God's Sovereignty forever*.

Adding to the intensity of *Musaf* on Yom Kippur is a passage, *Eleh Ezkerah/These I Remember,* that enumerates the martyrdom of the ten second-century Torah sages who defied the Romans and were executed.

The *haftarah* for Yom Kippur *Minkhah* is the Book of Jonah, raising the pertinent questions, "Is repentance truly possible?" and "Is it available to all peoples?" and answering them with an emphatic affirmative.

Ordinarily, as we will see in the remainder of this chapter, *Minkhah* would be the closing service of a holiday. But Yom Kippur is not an ordinary holiday, and there is one service yet to take place.

Twilight is falling, soon the stars will be out, and the holiest day of the year will be over. In Sephardic congregations (and some Ashkenazi), the hymn *El Nora Alilah* is sung, imploring God to hear our pleas once more as the gates of heaven begin to close; it is imperative that our confessions, our prayers, our hopes reach them before they close. The Ark is opened and will remain open for the entire final service, *Ne'ilah/Locking* (the Gates of Heaven). In many congregations, all the worshippers will stand throughout *Ne'ilah*. They implore the Almighty once more to accept their repentance and to seal them in the Book of Life. The service rises to an emotional crescendo with the chanting of *Avinu Malkeinu* and the congregational recitation of the *Sh'ma*. Only on Yom Kippur will Jews say aloud the line from that prayer usually spoken in an undertone: *Barukh sheim k'vod malkhuto l'olam va-ed/Blessed be the Name of God's Sovereignty forever.* This is the last time it will be said aloud until next Yom Kippur and it is repeated three times. The congregation concludes by repeating seven times, *Adonai hu ha-Elohim/Adonai is God!* The shofar sounds once more, a tremendous, extended blast, the congregants sing, *L'shanah ha-ba'ah bi-Yerusha-layim/Next year in Jerusalem,* and the day has ended.

There will be a brief *Ma'ariv* service and *Havdalah,* usually followed by a modest snack to break the fast, and then worshippers rush home to a festive meal, often with guests.

Although this is a day of solemnity, with so much seemingly hanging in the balance, Yom Kippur is not a sad day. It must be experienced to be understood. Over the course of a full day of worship, a congregation develops a feeling of community that surpasses anything else they encounter over the course of the year. This sense of closeness adds to the already singular emotional intensity of the holiday. But Jews face their Creator with the knowledge that God is merciful. Jews are urged to "seek out God when the Almighty is near." On Yom Kippur, the Creator is closest and most open to our prayers, so the day is a joyous one for most congregations. As the sun fades and twilight beckons, there is an electric sense throughout the sanctuary that prayers are heard and, perhaps, answered. It is a feeling that one has completed a task and that, for a moment at least, one has been cleansed.

SUKKOT

Even before he has broken the fast of Yom Kippur, a traditionally observant Jew takes a hammer in his hand and drives a few nails, the first (largely symbolic) blows in the building of a *sukkah/booth or hut*. The building of such a booth is prescribed in the Torah, wherein it is written, "On the fifteenth day of the seventh month shall be the Feast of Booths [Sukkot], seven days for Adonai. . . . For seven days you shall dwell in booths; every citizen of Israel shall dwell in booths so that your generations will know that I made the children of Israel dwell in booths when I brought them out of the land of Egypt." (Leviticus 23:33–44)

Sukkot is one of the three "Pilgrim Festivals," along with Pesakh and Shavuot, holidays for which Jews would make pilgrimages to the Temple in Jerusalem, bringing offerings, in this case from the fall harvest. (In contemporary practice, each of the Pilgrim Festivals includes a *Yizkor [Memorial]* service as part of its liturgy.) Even today, falling five days after Yom Kippur, in the midst of autumn, Sukkot retains its significance as a harvest holiday, a sort of Jewish equivalent of the American Thanksgiving (even to the extent that many Jews will use the overflowing cornucopia as a visual symbol, the same as Thanksgiving).

Thus Sukkot, like many other festivals (particularly its springtime counterparts, Pesakh and Shavuot), is intimately linked not only to Jewish history (here, the Exodus from Egypt and the wanderings in the wilderness) but also to the agricultural cycle that is such an important part of life in Israel. Two of the four names by which the holiday is known reflect that duality: *Khag ha-Asif/Festival of the Ingathering* (of crops) and *Khag ha-Sukkot/Festival of Booths*. Sukkot is also known by two other names that suggest another aspect of the holiday: *Khag/The Festival,* and *Zeman Simkhateinu/Season of Rejoicing.* Lasting nine days (for observant Jews in the Diaspora) or eight days (for Jews in Israel and most Reform Jews in the Diaspora), Sukkot is the longest and most joyous of the festivals. (Like one other multi-day holiday, Pesakh, the intermediate days of Sukkot are called *Khol ha-Moed;* work is permitted on those days and the liturgy prayed is a mixture of weekday and festival elements.) As we will see later in the chapter, Sukkot is so long and joyous that it actually includes two other festivals, Shemini Atzeret and Simkhat Torah.

As the name *Khag/The Festival* suggests, there was probably a time when Sukkot was the principal Jewish holiday. Allotted significant discussion in the Tanakh (the Hebrew Bible), it is not only a harvest holiday and a remembrance of the Exodus and the years in the wilderness; Sukkot was also the time of a festival of water-drawing in ancient Israel, *Simkhat Bet ha-Sho-evah;* at this time, prayers for rain were uttered and libations were poured over the altar at the Temple by way of underlining the necessity that those prayers be answered. With the fall of the Second Temple and the dispersion of Jews throughout the world, leading to a downgrading of agriculture as a Jewish livelihood, Sukkot lost its primacy. Yet it retained its largely agricultural symbolism (although the water-drawing ceremonies are generally no longer observed outside of Israel), from the building and maintenance of the *sukkah* to the "four species," the other ritual objects associated with the festival.

THE *SUKKAH*

The *sukkah* is a ritual object that is endowed with an intricate and richly interlocking network of meanings and associations. On the most obvious level, it is by design a temporary shelter and, thus, a reminder of the hardships endured in forty years of wandering in the wilderness and, by extension, of two millennia lived in the exile of the Diaspora. Living in the *sukkah,* the late Rabbi Menachem Schneerson pointed out, allows a Jew to be literally surrounded by, enveloped in, a *mitzvah.*

At the same time, as is the case with other *mitzvot* that require material objects (the *tashmishei mitzvah/objects used for a mitzvah*), the building and use of the *sukkah* establishes a firm link between the spiritual and material worlds. This connection is made explicit in the *halakhah/religious law* that specifies that one must be able to look through the roof of the *sukkah* at night and see the stars.

Building and decorating the *sukkah* is one of the great family endeavors of the Jewish holidays, a joyous act of preparation (perhaps, as some commentators have suggested, the physical counterpart to the spiritual groundwork done in Elul) for a joyous celebration. (See "Building the *Sukkah*" on p. 103.) Many Jews will make a party of *sukkah*-building and decorating, inviting friends and neighbors to help out. In doing so, all are fulfilling another obligation, *hiddur mitzvah/beautifying a mitzvah.* Decorations adorning the *sukkah* may range from carpeting the interior to stringing greens, bright paper rings, or popcorn on the walls both inside and out.

BUILDING THE *SUKKAH*

The laws governing the construction of the *sukkah* are highly specific and are found primarily in the Talmud tractate called *Sukkah*. Briefly summarized, the principal rules are as follows:

Dimensions: The *sukkah* must be big enough for "the head and majority" of the body of one adult, as well as a table on which to eat. Hence, it should be at least seven *tefokhim*/handbreaths (approx. 28 inches) by seven *tefokhim*, with its covering at least ten *tefokhim* (approx. 40 inches) above the ground. The walls must start within at least three *tefokhim* (approx. 11 inches) of the ground. There is no maximum size, but the *sukkah* may not be more than 20 cubits (approx. 30 feet) high for then it would be too large for the eye to take in.

Walls: The walls should be strong enough to withstand normal winds. Therefore it is permissible to tie wall materials to the framework. The *sukkah* must have at least three walls. Any materials may be used for the walls; in my synagogue we use tarpaulins bought several years ago specifically for this purpose. But the materials used in building the *sukkah* cannot be used for mundane purposes during the holiday, a restriction that underlines the idea that they are consecrated to heaven for the duration of the holiday. In medieval German Jewish communities, it was the custom to have bonfires as part of the celebration of the end of the holiday, fueled by the materials from which the *sukkot* had been constructed.

Roofing: Called the *s'khakh*, the roof covering is to be added only after the walls have been built. It should be made of cut vegetation, but edible fruit should not be left hanging from its branches. The roofing should be dense enough to protect the better part of the interior from the sun by day, although not so dense as to completely block a heavy rainfall, and thin enough that the stars are visible by night. The *s'khakh* shouldn't be wider than 4 *tefokhim* (approx. 14 inches), as a more substantial roof would imply permanence.

Although the biblical injunction is for Jews to live in the *sukkah* for the duration of the holiday, most modern Jews will take this to mean that they should eat all (or at least some) of their meals in the booth. (Of course, sleeping out in the *sukkah* is a great adventure for kids and, weather and bedtimes permitting, should be encouraged.[7]) Certainly, the commandment for adult males to eat their meals within the *sukkah* is strictly regarded by traditionally observant Jews. Women are exempted from that commandment (because it is a time-governed *mitzvah;* see Chapter 4), as are children, the elderly, and the sick. However, God does not demand of Jews that they risk their health to carry out *mitzvot.* If a heavy rainfall occurs, the commandment to eat and live within the *sukkah* is suspended. Most observant Jews will try to at least make *kiddush* in the *sukkah* and to eat a small morsel, a *k'zayit* (defined as being the size of an olive), in the *sukkah* before the weather renders it impossible.

As we have seen, Judaism is very much a religion of community and of communal worship, and one is strictly enjoined not to rejoice alone. As we atone communally on Yom Kippur, we rejoice communally on Sukkot. Jews are urged to invite friends, family, even strangers less fortunate than they, to join them in the *sukkah.*

The rules of hospitality are nowhere more apparent than in the custom of inviting *ushpizin/honored guests* to partake of the shelter of the *sukkah.* The *ushpizin* are not conventional flesh-and-blood guests. Rather, they are the seven great patriarchal figures of biblical history: Avraham, Yitzchak, Ya'akov, Yosef, Moshe, Aharon, and King David. In the *Zohar,* the great medieval mystical work, it is written that these seven great men come to share Sukkot with us. For followers of the Lubavitcher Rebbe, their numbers are doubled by the presence of seven great leaders of Hasidism: the Baal Shem Tov, the Maggid of Mezeritch, the Alter Rebbe, the Mitteler Rebbe, the *Tzemach Tzedek,* the Rebbe Maharash, and the Rebbe Rashab. Hasidic Jews believe that on each of the seven days, the influence of one of the *ushpizin* is felt; on the first day, Avraham and the Baal Shem Tov, and so on through the entire holiday. For non-Orthodox Jews, the list of esteemed visitors is often enlarged to include the great matriarchs—Sarah, Miriam, Rachel, Leah—and other great figures from Jewish and world history.

Ultimately, the *sukkah* is a multi-faceted symbol. Like many of the items specific to this holiday, it links Jews back to their agricultural roots, offering a scaled-down version of the sort of temporary shelters that farmers and shepherds built for themselves near their fields and flocks to eliminate the need for a laborious trip home for a midday meal. But at the same time, the *sukkah* reminds us of our reliance on the will of God in a hostile world. The *sukkah* is open to the elements, temporary, insubstantial; in short, it provides little real shelter. Ultimately, we must look up through the roof of the *sukkah,* through the leafy covering overhead to heaven, when seeking true shelter. More than that, for those of us outside *Eretz Yisroel / the Land of Israel,* it is a reminder of our transient status in the Diaspora.

THE FOUR SPECIES

Just as it specifies the construction and use of the *sukkah,* Leviticus also instructs Jews in the necessity of the so-called Four Species. The Torah commands, "You shall take on the first day the fruit of goodly trees, branches of palms, and boughs of thick trees, and willows of the brook, and you shall rejoice before Adonai your God for seven days" (Lev. 23:40). The call for the palm and willow branches is clear enough; the rabbis of the Talmudic period decided that the command regarding the two unspecified species—"fruit of goodly trees, . . . and boughs of thick trees"—should be fulfilled by taking a citron, a yellow, lemon-like fruit called the *etrog* in Hebrew, and sprigs of myrtle, respectively.

Taken as a complete set, the Four Species are known in Hebrew as the *etrog* and the *lulav,* which consists of a closed frond from a date palm, two branches of willow, and three sprigs of myrtle. The elements of the *lulav* are bound together with strips of palm leaves, the myrtle on the right side, the willows on the left.

Seeking a nice *lulav* and *etrog* is another one of the rituals that comes with this holiday. The shrewd shopper will check out all the *lulavim* and *etrogim* at his neighborhood Judaica shops. She will travel down to the Jewish marketplaces of the Lower East Side or the Orthodox neighborhoods of Brooklyn, or a comparable area of her own town, looking through for the brightest, prettiest *etrog,* the straightest *lulav.* The *etrog* must have its *pitom,* the small nub of stalk where it was attached to the branch on which it grew, intact; otherwise it is *possul / invalid.* (There are, however, some that are grown without a stalk and don't need a *pitom.* If you are unsure, ask the seller for advice.)

As the Torah passage indicates, the ritual "taking" of the *etrog* and *lulav* occurs on the first morning of Sukkot, and each of the mornings after. Although many observant Jews will perform this *mitzvah* in their own *sukkah* each morning of the holiday, at *shul* it is done after the recital of the *Amidah*. Each worshipper takes up the *lulav* in her right hand, the *etrog* in the left with the *pitom* pointing downward. Each now recites the blessing of the *lulav*:

> *Barukh atah Adonai Eloheinu Melekh ha-olam asher kid'shanu b'mitzvotav vitzivanu al n'tilat lulav.*
>
> *Blessed are You, Adonai our God, Ruler of the Universe, who makes us holy through the commandments and commands us concerning the [lifting of the] lulav.*

This is followed by the *Shehekheyanu*. Now the worshippers turn the *etrog* around so that the *pitom* faces upward, bring their left hands together with their right so that all four species are together. They stretch their arms outward in front of them (to the east) and shake the Four Species three times, pulling their hands in toward their bodies between each shake. Still facing east, they now stretch their arms to the right, over their shoulders behind them, to the left, towards the sky and then towards the earth, each time shaking the Four Species as before. (The reason for the turning of the *etrog* before the lifting is simple: the *mitzvah* is to lift them together, so having the *etrog* "upside down" keeps you from performing the *mitzvah* inadvertently before saying the blessing.)

What is the meaning of this strange ritual known as *bentshing/blessing lulav*? Again, the agricultural symbolism is obvious. But what about the six directions and the four species?

The six directions—east, west, north, south, the earth and the sky—represent the omnipresence of God, the six directions of the Universe itself, and the ingathering of the winds and rain for which we pray. The Four Species are associated with the wind and water and come from different areas of *eretz Yisroel*.

The Four Species are often said to represent the four types of Jew. The *etrog*, which has both smell and taste, is the ideal Jew, one who studies Torah and performs *mitzvot*. The palm has good-tasting fruit but not fragrance; it is like a Jew who studies Torah but performs no good deeds. The myrtle has a good fragrance, but no taste; it resembles a

Jew who does good deeds, but doesn't study Torah. And the willow, which has neither taste nor fragrance, is like a Jew who neither studies nor keeps the *mitzvot*. All four of these Jews are necessary to the sustaining of the people Israel, an essential part of the Jewish community, even the unbelieving nonpracticing one. When they are united, each makes up for the shortcomings of the others.

Immediately after the shaking of the *lulav, Hallel* is recited. The *lulav* and *etrog* are also shaken during *Hallel,* at *hod l'Adonai ki tov* when the congregation praises God with the cantor, and at *ana Adonai hoshea na,* when they pray to God to be saved. The only day of the holiday on which we do not *bentsh lulav* is, not surprisingly, Shabbat.

On the Sabbath that occurs during Sukkot, *Shabbat Khol ha-Moed Sukkot,* we read the first of the five *megillot / scrolls,* the five books of the Tanakh that are associated with festival days. For Sukkot, the book read is *Kohelet / Ecclesiastes,* a coolly detached rumination on the natural cycle and man's brief span within it. As we will see momentarily, it is an apt choice.

HOSHANAH RABBAH / THE GREAT HOSANNAH

On each of the first six days of Sukkot (except on Shabbat) during the morning service the congregation makes a processional circuit—a *hakafah*—around the reader's table, carrying their *lulavim* and *etrogim.* During this procession, they recite one stanza of the *Hoshanot,* a series of prayers that begin *Ana Adonai, hoshia na / Please Adonai, save us!*

But on the seventh day, called Hoshanah Rabbah / The Great Hosannah, the congregants will make seven *hakafot* around the reader's table, each time chanting a different stanza of the *Hoshanot.* After the circuits are completed, the Four Species are laid down and the worshippers take up five bunched willow branches—called *hoshanah*—and at the end of the recitation of the *Hoshanot* they beat them five times against the ground until some of the leaves come off.

From the time of the Middle Ages, Hoshanah Rabbah took on a special weight, gradually becoming a virtual extension of Yom Kippur, the very last day on which one can seek forgiveness for the previous year's transgressions. According to one folk belief, on this day notes fell from Heaven declaring the fate of each individual on earth. On one level, the falling willow leaves may be read as symbolic of those heavenly notes.

(The Yiddish greeting from one Jew to another on Hoshanah Rabbah is a reference to that folk belief: *"A gute kvitl/A good note [to you]."*) Among Ashkenazi congregations, the solemnity of this day's worship is underlined by the use of the High Holiday melodies in the first part of the service, up to the *Barekhu.*

The falling leaves of the beaten willow branches have another significance, one that points back to the agricultural element of Sukkot and the two holidays that close out its nine days of rejoicing, Shemini Atzeret and Simkhat Torah. The falling willow leaves convey to God man's reliance on rain, which only the Creator can provide. Like the Water-Drawing Festival, the falling willow leaves are a graphic reminder of the fragile agrarian nature of life in Israel, a semi-fertile land bounded by desert.

More than that, the symbolism of the falling leaves as a reminder of the falling rain link the holiday to the larger rhythms of the natural cycle of the year. The leaves fall, the rain comes, new buds will grow where the leaves once were, and new leaves will open soon.

SHEMINI ATZERET

Nowhere is the connection of humanity to the natural cycle of the year made more manifest than in the most important additions to the liturgy on *Shemini Atzeret/the Eighth Day of Assembly,* the eighth day of Sukkot, but also a festival unto itself. The observance of Shemini Atzeret, which falls on 22 Tishri, is commanded in Leviticus 23:36, "On the eighth day [of Sukkot] you shall observe a holy occasion. . . . It is a solemn gathering [*atzeret*]; you shall not work at your occupations." (We know from the liturgy that it is a separate festival because we recite *Ya'aleh v'Yavo* during the *Amidah,* and *kiddush* is followed by the *Shehekheyanu* blessing, neither of which would be included if it were merely another day of Sukkot.)

There are two specific ties between Shemini Atzeret and the changes in the natural world. First, the Prayer for Rain is chanted during the *Musaf Amidah,* a prayer reminding God of the faithfulness of the Patriarchs and imploring the Eternal One "do not withhold water." In traditionally observant congregations the Ark is opened before the Prayer for Rain is recited so that the Torah scrolls are visible witnesses to the prayer and, in Ashkenazi congregations, the prayer leader wears the white robes of the High Holidays.

Second, from Shemini Atzeret a line is added to the *Amidah*, the phrase which concludes the Prayer for Rain, *"mashiv ha-ruakh u-morid ha-gashem/who causes the wind to blow and the rain to fall."* This line, which follows the words *rav l-hoshia/great is your saving power*, will be recited in the *Amidah* every day until the first day of Pesakh.

Shemini Atzeret also is a key moment in another parallel annual cycle, the reading of the Torah. As the contemporary rabbi and scholar Arthur Waskow suggests, this is a holiday that anticipates the coming of winter, a turning inward, so it is entirely appropriate that we end the reading of the fifth book of the Torah with the moving passage in which Moses dies (in Israel and in Reform congregations in the Diaspora, where the holiday is essentially merged into Simkhat Torah). It is a doubly appropriate reading, because Shemini Atzeret is also marked by a *Yizkor* service.

For some Jewish thinkers, Shemini Atzeret is redolent of a waning autumn, linking it directly back to the solemnity and power of Yom Kippur. The great eighteenth-century Hasidic rabbi Shneur Zalman of Liadi, the founder of Habad Hasidism, once said, "Shemini Atzeret is the tea essence." Asked to explain that cryptic remark, one of his followers said, "To make tea essence, you boil a large quantity of tea leaves for a long time until you get a highly concentrated brew. Then when you want a cup of tea, you mix a small amount of the tea essence with hot water. We trembled before the majesty of God on Rosh Hashanah, we did *teshuvah* on Yom Kippur, we rejoiced on Sukkot. Now, on Shemini Atzeret, we boil it all down into a strong tea essence to supply us throughout the year—until next Rosh Hashanah!" ("A Weekly Review," distributed by Habad-Lubavitch in Cyberspace)

SIMKHAT TORAH

In Israel and among Reform congregations in the Diaspora, Shemini Atzeret is combined with *Simkhat Torah/Rejoicing of the Torah*. The final day of Sukkot will be marked with an evening service using the Shemini Atzeret liturgy, and includes a *Yizkor* service. In Orthodox and most Conservative synagogues in the Diaspora, Simkhat Torah will not be celebrated until the day after Shemini Atzeret, making Sukkot a nine-day-long observance.

Regardless of when it is observed, Simkhat Torah is, as its name implies, an occasion overflowing with joy, a giddy, almost delirious and sometimes bibulous celebration of the completion of another year's reading of the Torah.

Simkhat Torah is actually a relatively new holiday by Jewish standards, a mere thousand years old. There is no indication that the festival was celebrated before the ninth century C.E. Indeed, up to that point, the majority of the Jewish world read the Torah in a three-year cycle rather than on the familiar annual schedule used today. (For more on Torah, see Chapter 5.) In the Middle Ages, the holiday observance focused more on the end of Sukkot than on the Torah readings, with public bonfires in which the remnants of dismantled *sukkot* were consumed.

Today, however, Simkhat Torah festivities center on the reading of the Torah. A congregation will make seven *hakafot* at the beginning of *seder kri'at ha-Torah,* carrying all of the scrolls of the Law that they own, chanting an acrostic prayer similar to the *ana Adonai hoshea na* passage of *Hallel.* Each *hakafah* will be followed by raucous singing and dancing with the scrolls. The children of the community participate eagerly, marching with the adults, carrying little flags or miniature Torah scrolls of their own.

After the seventh *hakafah,* the first of the day's two Torah passages is chanted. (Many congregations read Torah at night on this holiday, regardless of whether they will hold a morning service the next day. In congregations in which the holiday is celebrated at night, this will be the only time all year at which the Torah reading occurs as part of the evening service.) Deuteronomy 33–34 is the story of the death of Moses, the end of the Five Books of Moses. In the morning service, the passage will be divided up in such a way that everyone can be called for an *aliyah* (pl. *"aliyot"*), the honor of reciting the blessings for reading Torah. In progressive synagogues, *aliyot* will be given to "all the adult males," "all the first-born," "all the . . . ," whatever categories the rabbi or *gabbai* (a layperson who assists the rabbi and cantor during services) can devise to include everyone. In some synagogues, many scrolls will be read from simultaneously; in others, passages will be repeated over and over until everyone has had a chance to recite the blessings for the reading of the Torah. And in all congregations, one *aliyah* will be reserved for *kol ha-ne'arim/all the youngsters,* with all the children coming to the *bimah* to recite the blessings, while four adults hold up a *tallit* over the children, a canopy that combines love and tradition.

The *aliyah* for the last section of the passage from Deuteronomy is reserved as a special honor, called the *khatan Torah/bridegroom of the Torah.* And the first *aliyah* over the next section—the beginning of Genesis—is called the *khatan Bereshit/bridegroom of the Beginning.* When the final section of Deuteronomy is completed, the custom is for the congregation to chant, *"Khazak, khazak, v'nit hazeik/Be strong, be strong, and let us strengthen one another."* This chant (which is then repeated by the reader) is offered every time a book of the Torah is completed in synagogue, but it seems to carry an additional fervor on Simkhat Torah.

The symbolic significance of the holiday is unmistakable. To be immersed in Torah is a joyous thing for a Jew, something worthy of celebration. More than that, we do not stop our study of Torah simply because we have completed a single reading of it; like the cycles of nature, the reading of Torah will go on as long as there are Jews to read it. Finally, it is the custom not to end a Torah portion on a sad note. There is no escaping the fact of Moses's death, but we go immediately from this reminder of our own mortality to the Creation anew. (This principle of continuity is underlined by the *haftarah,* the prophetic reading, for Simkhat Torah, Joshua 1, in which Joshua takes up the reins of leadership from Moses.)

Simkhat Torah is a time of joyous public displays. There literally is dancing in the streets of Jewish communities, a spectacle well worth seeing in the Hasidic sections of Brooklyn or on Manhattan's Upper West Side, or in the Orthodox neighborhoods of Jerusalem. For some the holiday is a splendid opportunity to overindulge, leading outstanding rabbinical authorities like the Khafetz Khayim to caution that it is not appropriate to drink to excess on this day. (That kind of celebration, as we will see shortly, should be saved for Purim, when it is a *commandment* to get drunk!)

HANUKAH

HISTORICAL ROOTS

Until the advent of the *Haskalah,* the Jewish Enlightenment of the nineteenth century, and the first stirrings of acceptance by non-Jews of their Jewish neighbors, Hanukah was a minor festival (in spite of its length of eight days). When Jews found themselves coexisting in relative peace with their Christian neighbors in post—World War II America and Europe, this mid-winter holiday (which begins on 25 Kislev) became a sort of Jewish counterpart to Christmas, if only as a marketing ploy, and took on a new importance. In Israel the holiday has taken on an added symbolism, becoming a celebration of Jewish military prowess and national rebirth.

That development is ironic, to say the least. Hanukah is a celebration of the Maccabees, Jewish warriors who fought a lengthy civil war in defiance of hellenization, the first great assimilationist trend in Jewish history. Between 165 and 163 B.C.E. the Maccabees struggled to recapture Jerusalem and to reclaim the Temple for the Jewish people. Even after they successfully liberated Jerusalem from its hellenized Syrian occupiers, the Maccabees, led by Judah Maccabee, would continue to fight for many more years, until they drove the Syrians from ancient Israel and reasserted Jewish sovereignty.

During the Syrian occupation of Jerusalem, the Temple was defiled by pagan sacrifices, on direct orders from the Syrian ruler, Antiochus Epiphanes. Those actions were the direct outcome of the stated Syrian policy of hellenizing all of Palestine and eliminating the practice of the Jewish religion. When the Maccabees (literally, the Hammers) retook Jerusalem, they demolished the now polluted altar of the Temple and built a new one. They discarded the defiled ritual objects and replaced them.

They even found a small quantity of consecrated oil for use in the sacred lamps, but not nearly enough to use for the eight days of celebration and rededication. The priests needed to wait until new pure oil could be produced and delivered to the Temple for the rededication. Reluctantly, the story goes, the priests lit the oil for the first day's worship. Miraculously, the next day there was enough for the second day's services. And so it continued until the entire eight days of worship had been observed, with one day's worth of oil lasting the entire time. It is in honor of this miracle that Hanukah is observed with the lighting of the festival candles over the eight days of the holiday. (One particularly poignant *midrash* says that the real miracle that we commemorate is not that the oil lasted; what was truly miraculous was the faith of the priests who knew they didn't have enough oil for eight days but who lit the lamps each day, trusting that God would provide.) There is a wonderful irony in the idea of celebrating a "holiday of lights" at the darkest time of the calendar year.

Why did the Maccabees celebrate an eight-day festival in the middle of the winter? It is generally believed that the guerrilla fighters had been unable to observe Sukkot during their two years of life under-cover, and the holiday they made on their return to Jerusalem was a sort of belated Sukkot. Regardless, the tradition of eight days of Hanukah lights has lasted to the present. As such, it is Judaism's first post-biblical holiday, one not found in the Tanakh. The story of the Maccabees is related in the Apocrypha, a series of noncanonical texts.

HOME OBSERVANCE

Today, Hanukah is a home-oriented holiday. There are only two sig-nificant additions to the liturgy prayed in addition to *Hallel*. The prayer *al-Hanisim* is added to the *Amidah* and *Birkat ha-Mazon / Grace after meals;* it commemorates the heroism of the Maccabees and thanks Adonai for "the deliverance of our ancestors in other days and in our time." The hymn *Maoz Tzur / Rock of Ages* (not to be confused with the Christian hymn of the same name), a thirteenth-century composition, is sung as well, whether at home or synagogue. Finally, Hanukah is the only holi-day on which there are eight consecutive days of Torah readings taken from the story of the dedication of the Tabernacle.

The principal observance of Hanukah takes place in the home. The central event of each evening of the holiday is the lighting of the Hanukah candles. These are placed in a candelabrum with nine candle-holders, called a *hanukiyah*. (Strictly speaking, a *menorah* found in the synagogue has only seven candles. Most people call their Hanukah can-delabrum a *menorah* anyway.) Ancient *hanukiyot* found by archaeologists in Israel burned oil, often with a single lamp whose flames were designed to form the shape of the Star of David with its six points. However, the post-Talmudic *hanukiyah* must have its candles in a row, with each flame separate and distinct from the others so that each can be seen. In addition to the eight candles representing each of the eight days of the festival, there is a place for a ninth candle, usually set apart and/or above the others, the *shamash / servant,* which is used to kindle the other candles each night.

The Hanukah candles are lit immediately after dark, with the notable exception of Friday nights, when they are lit before the Shabbat candles. The candles are placed in their holders from right to left, then lit from left to right, so that the latest addition is placed last but lit first. The candles should burn for at least half an hour, and should be placed so that they are conspicuous from outside the house (although the Talmud says that if their presence will provoke danger, they may be kept out of sight, a concession to the potential for anti-Semitic violence, one assumes). In Israel, the *hanukiyot* are placed in special glass boxes outside. When the candles have been lit, one recites the blessing for the lighting of the candles:

Barukh atah Adonai Eloheinu Melekh ha-olam asher kid'shanu b'mitzvotav v'tzivanu l'hadklik ner shel Hanukah.

Blessed are You, Adonai our God, Ruler of the Universe, Who sanctified us with Your commandments and commanded us to kindle the lights of Hanukah.

This is followed by a blessing thanking God for the many wonders performed on our behalf:

Barukh atah Adonai Eloheinu Melekh ha-olam sheh'asah nisim l'avoteinu ba-yamim ha-heim u'vaz'man hazeh.

Blessed are You, Adonai our God, Ruler of the Universe, who performed miracles for our ancestors in ancient times and in our days.

On the first night of the holiday only, *Shehekheyanu* is then recited. In Ashkenazi tradition, the recital of the blessings is followed by singing *Maoz Tzur;* Sephardic Jews follow the blessings with Psalm 30.

In many families, each family member will have his or her own *hanukiyah* and will light candles and recite the blessings each night. Hanukah is an excellent holiday to encourage the participation of children (although, obviously, one should take precautions with younger children where matches and open flames are concerned). Even before the days of assimilation and Jewish life in an openly pluralistic society like the United States, children would get small gifts of money, so-called Hanukah *gelt* (Yiddish, meaning Hanukah money). For many families, Hanukah is an occasion for parties, singing, and games. The giving of more elaborate gifts at Hanukah, particularly to children, is a custom of much more recent vintage, an attempt to compete with the commercialization of Christmas.

The best-known Hanukah game is *dreidl/spinning top* (also known as *s'vivon* in Hebrew), a gambling game played with a four-sided top. On each side of the *dreidl* is a Hebrew letter: *nun, gimmel, hey, shin.* These letters are an acronym for the words *"nes gadol hayah sham/a great miracle happened there."* (In Israel, the *shin* is replaced with a *pay,* standing for *po/here.*) Usually, the players gamble for nuts, chocolate, or pennies; each player antes into the pot, then takes a turn spinning the *dreidl.* If the *nun,* which stands for *nits*—"nothing" in Yiddish—comes up, nothing happens. If the spinner gets *gimmel, ganz,* or "everything," she takes the entire pot. *Hey, halb*—"half" in Yiddish—the spinner gets half the pot, and a *shin* for *shtell arein,* "put some in," means the player must pay into the pot. You play until everyone has been bankrupted except for one player, who is the winner.

The other cherished element of Hanukah is *latkes,* the fried potato pancakes that Ashkenazi Jews eat when celebrating the holiday. Made from grated potatoes and sliced onions, fried in oil (in honor of the sacred lamps), they are usually served with applesauce and should be eaten while still hot from the skillet. Cheese is another food often associated with Hanukah, supposedly because the Maccabees were inspired by Judith, who killed the evil Holofernes by lulling him into a stupor with a heavy meal of cheese and wine before decapitating him.

TU B'SHEVAT

Tu b'Shevat, called the "New Year of the Trees," falls at a seemingly incongruous time of year. The fifteenth day of Shevat is mid-winter for North American Jews and the last thing on their minds is, well, Arbor Day. However, if you think in terms of *Eretz Yisroel,* the timing of the holiday makes more sense. The climate in Israel is milder, essentially a Mediterranean climate, and by mid-February, the almond trees are beginning to bloom. It is still the rainy season, so the process of redemption begins at the turning point towards hope.

In fact, the date of the holiday actually correlates to the cutoff point for assessing the tithe levied on fruit grown in the orchards as practiced in ancient Israel (sort of a farmer's equivalent of an American's April 15). Any fruit grown before Tu b'Shevat would have counted towards the previous year's totals, any fruit grown after towards the coming year's. Tu b'Shevat's date also links it to two more prominent agrarian festivals of the Jewish year, Sukkot and Pesakh, both of which begin on the fifteenth of the month.

Tu b'Shevat is a minor festival whose provenance dates only to the time of the Second Temple. However, the kabbalists who clustered around the great fifteenth-century mystic Isaac Luria of Safed placed great weight on the holiday, creating new festivities, gatherings at which hymns were sung, fruit (particularly carob) was eaten, and four cups of wine were taken (as in the Passover *seder*). Many Sephardic communities still engage in these Tu b'Shevat rites.

With the advent of the environmental movement and the focus of modern Israelis on the greening of their nation, Tu b'Shevat has taken on more importance in the last fifty years. In Israel schoolchildren will go out to plant new trees on this day. Diaspora Jews will try to partake of as many as possible of the seven fruits and grains cited in Deuteronomy 8:8 as native to the Holy Land: "wheat, barley, vines, figs, pomegranates, olive trees, and (date) honey." Many ecology-minded Jews have created new Tu b'Shevat *seders* and have followed in the footsteps of Luria and his fellow mystics in extolling this holiday's importance.

PURIM

Purim might be loosely but fairly described as the Jewish answer to Mardi Gras or Carnival. It comes at the same time of year (15 Adar, 15 Adar II in leap years), late February or March. It involves dressing in costume (often in drag), riotous behavior, excessive drinking, and making lots of noise. Of course, the theological underpinnings of the holiday are radically different from its Christian counterparts.

Actually, Purim's theological underpinnings are just a shade tenuous. The events that purportedly inspired the holiday are recounted in the Book of Esther, one of only two books of the Tanakh that never mentions the name of God. (The other is Song of Songs.) And the holiday's roots are probably somewhat more profane; many cultures have a spring holiday that calls for a bacchanalian release of pent-up energy, a welcome explosion of hilarity after the long winter.

At the heart of Purim is the story of Esther, a beautiful and smart Jewish woman who, with the help of her uncle Mordecai, averts the destruction of the Jews by marrying King Ahashverus of Persia and thwarting the evil designs of Haman, one of the royal councillors and a rabid anti-Semite. In the end, Haman, his ten sons, and thousands of his followers are executed, and Esther and Ahashverus live happily ever after, with Mordecai as a chief adviser and the Jews once more safely at peace.

Purim literally means "lots," a name that is derived from Haman's casting of lots to determine the day for his proposed massacre of the Jews. Needless to say, a celebration of his failure calls for great joy and merriment. In the synagogue, the reading of *Megillat Esther/the Scroll of Esther* is met with cheering and shouting. Congregants are supposed to drown out the mention of Haman's name (as in the biblical injunction to blot out Amalek, the sworn enemies of Judaism whose treachery is denounced in the previous week's Torah portion on Shabbat Zachor, "the Sabbath of Remembrance"). At the same time, Jews are supposed to get drunk enough that they cannot distinguish between "Blessed be Mordecai" and "Cursed be Haman," so the proceedings get pretty wild. Adults and children alike come to services in costumes, dressed as Esther, Mordecai, and other figures, carrying *groggers/noisemakers* traditionally made of wood (but usually replaced today with a metal variant on the New Year's Eve noisemaker), pots and pans to beat on, and the occasional semi-illicit bottle. Many synagogues will offer a *Purimspiel/ Purim play* and even a Purim rabbi who delivers a mock-serious sermon, called a Purim Torah, in the Talmudic style. (In fact, the original European *Purimspiel*s of the late Middle Ages were the first example of Yiddish theater.)

Like many Jewish holidays, Purim is associated with a particular food, the little triangular pastries called *hamantaschen/Haman's pockets*. Filled with prunes, apricots, or poppy seeds, these tasty little items are one of the highlights of the holiday. They take their name from the triangular hat and pockets allegedly worn by Haman.

As joyous as the holiday is, it is also a time for serious reflection on the duties of a Jew towards her community, particularly in a post-Holocaust world. The day before the holiday is a minor fast day, the Fast of Esther, timed to coincide with Esther's own fast on the day during which she decided to tell Ahashverus that she is a Jew and to avert the massacre of her people. One of the primary obligations of Purim, beyond the revelry, is to make donations to the poor. One should give money to at least two needy people or good causes, send gifts of food or drink, called *shalakh mones* (Yiddish), to friends. And, finally, one should have a Purim *seudah/festive meal,* with family and friends sharing in the joy of the holiday.

Purim is a minor festival, albeit a much beloved one. It is permissible to work on the holiday (although one may be too hungover to do so).

PESAKH

EXILE AND HOME

It could be said with some accuracy that the tension between home and exile is central to the Jewish experience. From God's first instruction to Avram, *"Lekh lekha"/"Go forth on the road,"* to the modern Diaspora, to be a Jew has meant to be a transient, in search of home. To be at home nowhere and everywhere, always to be seeking a return to the Promised Land, to *Eretz Yisroel/the Land of Israel,* even now, nearly fifty years after the founding of the modern State of Israel.

Nowhere is that tension between exile and home more palpable than in the celebration of *Pesakh/Passover.* The central event of that holiday — the *seder*—is a joyous dinner at home. Yet we try to bring strangers to our Pesakh table (or anyone who does not have a *seder* of their own to attend), a reminder that "you were strangers in Egypt." And the evening ends with the pledge, *"L'Shanah ha-ba'ah bi-Yerushalayim/Next year in Jerusalem!"*

The central event of the *seder* is the recounting of the Exodus from Egypt, a liberation from slavery that leads directly to forty years of wandering in the wilderness but which finally ends in Canaan, in Israel. Yet one cannot help remembering as the story is retold, the two Temples that were destroyed in Jerusalem, the renewed wandering of the Jewish people, the centuries of tragedy and, finally, the promise not yet redeemed.

We are instructed repeatedly in our daily liturgy to remember that we were strangers[8] and then slaves in Egypt, freed from captivity not by our own efforts, but by the hand of the Almighty. And that injunction to remember is fulfilled in its most dramatic and complete form at this time of year. The twin antinomies, slavery/freedom, exile/home, are constantly before us in the observance of Pesakh, embodied in virtually every symbol of this festival.

THE BREAD OF AFFLICTION

Consider, for example, the duality of *matzah/unleavened bread* and *khametz/leavening*. The role of the *matzah* in this holiday is important enough that one of its names is *Khag ha-Matzah/Festival of Unleavened Bread.*

When the Israelites were allowed to leave Egypt—after God had visited ten plagues on the Egyptians, culminating in the death of the first-born sons—they were given little time to prepare. They did not even have time to wait for the yeast to rise in their bread dough; so they made unleavened bread to take on their journey into the unknowns of wilderness and freedom.

In commemoration of this series of events, Jews forego the eating of all forms of *khametz,* which is taken to mean wheat, barley, rye, spelt, and oats or any combination thereof that expands in contact with water, for the duration of the holiday (seven days in Israel and for many Reform Jews in the Diaspora; eight days for all others). More than that, they are instructed to clean their houses of all *khametz.* (Ashkenazi Jews have traditionally included in this prohibition rice and legumes, but Sephardic Jews do not.)

One must not only abstain from eating leaven, one must not own any leaven; any leaven kept during the holiday is prohibited from use even after Passover has finished. Prior to Passover, a Jew will "sell" all of her *khametz* to a non-Jewish friend or neighbor. All utensils that have had contact with *khametz* must either be cleansed in a prescribed fashion (generally by boiling), or if they are porous and therefore have absorbed *khametz* in such a way that they cannot be cleaned of it, must be put away. Hence the need for two extra sets of dishes (meat and dairy) for Passover in Orthodox households that can afford them.

Before dinner on the night before Pesakh (13–14 Nisan) a tradition-ally observant Jew will begin the *bedikat khametz/search for leaven,* a lengthy process done by candlelight and preceded by a blessing ". . . *asher kid'shanu b'mitzvotav v'tzivanu biur khametz/. . . who has sanctified us by the commandments and commanded us to remove the leaven.*" The search, which is conducted in silence, will always turn up at least ten pieces of bread, placed around the house by pre-arrangement so that the *b'rakha* is not said for nothing and the *mitzvah* of burning the last pieces can be observed the next morning. The *khametz* is swept into a bag with a feather and then the feather, the bag, and its contents are burned the following morning. In Jerusalem on *erev Pesakh* morning you can smell the smoke of burning *khametz* everywhere, and every neighborhood has a bonfire into which you can throw your own *khametz*.

The symbolism of this ritual is unmistakable. The solemn mysteriousness of a silent search, conducted by the flickering light of a candle (or flashlight, not as evocative but much more efficient), underlines the importance of a break with the past, with the ties to Egypt and slavery. As long as there is *khametz* in our homes, there is Egypt in our hearts. Then we are like the obstreperous Jews who whined to Moses in the desert that they missed the fleshpots of Egypt.

The *matzah,* the unleavened bread that Jews eat during the holiday, is at once a symbol of both freedom and, at the same time, of slavery. On the one hand, as Exodus 12:39 says, the Israelites "baked unleavened cakes of dough which they brought forth from Egypt . . . for they had been driven out of Egypt and could not delay. . . ." But the *matzah* is also called *lekhem oni/bread of affliction,* in both Deuteronomy 16:3 and in the *Hagadah,* the book from which we conduct the *seder* on the first two nights of the holiday.

Rabbi Menachem Schneerson, the late Lubavitcher Rebbe, has written that the basic theme of Pesakh is that it "enables us to undergo a personal exodus from Egypt by transcending our individual limits." By eating the *matzah,* he says, we internalize—quite literally—this experience. *Matzah* is the "bread of affliction," the bread of the poor, of people humble and without arrogance. By contrast, Schneerson adds, leavening "becomes bloated as it rises, symbolizes self-inflated egotism and pride." As such, one might say that the *khametz* is a physical embodiment of the inclination to evil *(yetzer ha-rah).*

THE *SEDER*

The entire *seder* is similarly heavy with meaning. The word *seder* literally means "order" and the *seder* is nothing if not orderly. At the center of the table is the *seder* plate, which holds a hard-boiled egg, a roasted bone, *maror/bitter herbs* (usually horseradish), *kharoset* (a mixture of chopped apples, nuts, cinnamon, wine, and in some recipes honey), *karpas/greens* (usually parsley or watercress), and a small cup or saucer of salt water. In addition, there is a plate holding three *matzahs*, covered with a cloth. Everyone at the table will have a *Haggadah/the Telling*, the book containing the special liturgy for the evening meal.

Essentially, the evening has fourteen elements, which occur in a prescribed order:

1. *Kadesh:* The *seder* opens with the recitation of the festival *kiddush* over a glass of wine. Everyone drinks their first of four glasses of wine.

2. *Urkhatz:* The ritual washing of the hands, as in the hand-washing before eating bread (see Chapter 1, p. 22), but with the blessing omitted.

3. *Karpas:* The leafy greens are dipped in the salt water and, after the blessing for *karpas* is recited, they are eaten.

4. *Yakhatz:* The middle *matzah* from the center of the table is broken in half. One portion will be hidden for the *afikoman*, to be eaten at the very end of the meal. The tradition is for the host to hide it and for the children to search for it, ransoming it back to the leader at the end of the meal. (In some families, the tradition is reversed, with the children hiding the *afikoman*, and the parents searching.)

5. *Maggid:* The first part of the *Haggadah* is now read. This section of the *seder* includes the Four Questions (see p. 123), the list of the ten plagues, the story of the Exodus, an explanation of the significance of the Paschal lamb, *matzah, maror*, the first part of *Hallel*, and second and third glasses of wine.

6. *Rakhtsah:* Again the hands are washed, this time with the blessing recited.

7. *Motzi Matzah:* The *matzah* is eaten, with a blessing for eating unleav-

ened bread. The blessing serves the same purpose as the blessing for eating bread in a non-Passover meal; it signals the beginning of the meal proper.

8. *Maror:* The bitter herb is dipped in the *kharoset* and eaten, with an appropriate blessing.

9. *Korekh:* A sandwich of bitter herb and *kharoset* on *matzah* is eaten, as was the custom in the time of Hillel (first century B.C.E.) to eat the Paschal sacrifice together with the *matzah* and *maror*.

10. *Shukhan Orekh:* Dinner is served and eaten, a full and festive meal.

11. *Tsafun:* The *afikoman,* representing the Paschal sacrifice, is ransomed and eaten, officially ending the meal. After this no more food should be eaten.

12. *Barekh: Birkat ha-Mazon / Grace after meals* is recited.

13. *Hallel:* The remainder of the *Hallel* psalms are recited.

14. *Nirtzah:* The celebration is "accepted," and those assembled declare, "Next year in Jerusalem." In Jerusalem, they say, *"L'shana ha-ba'ah bi-Yerushalayim ha-benuyah / Next year in a Jerusalem rebuilt."* This is followed by spirited singing of Pesakh songs like *Adir Hu, Khad Gadya / An Only Kid,* and *Ekhad Mi Yode'a / Who Knows One?*

A *seder* is a joyous occasion, a gathering of family and friends that should include not only the recitation of the *Haggadah,* but a spirited discussion with many questions and debate of the meaning of the holiday. With a large meal, the entire evening can last into the early hours of the morning and, in an Orthodox household, the meal itself may not be served until well past midnight.

THE MEANING OF THE *SEDER*

But what does it all mean? Of course, the *Haggadah* itself is largely occupied with explaining the significance of the elements of the *seder,* and their relevance to the agricultural aspects of a major spring festival are self-evident (the greens for the arrival of spring, the egg a symbol of fertility and renewal, the roasted bone a reference to the Paschal sacrifice at the Temple). After all, Pesakh is also known as *Khag ha-Aviv/Festival of Spring*. But the historical/religious aspects are worth some further exploration, bringing us back to the themes of slavery and freedom, exile and home, once more.

Certainly the symbolic nature of the *maror* and the salt water are obvious—the bitterness of slavery and the tears of the Israelites. The *kharoset* relates to the mortar from which the Jewish slaves made bricks for the Pharaoh's storehouse cities, and the shankbone echoes the Paschal lambs' blood with which Israelites marked the lintels of their doorways, signaling their presence to the Angel of Death so that he would not take their first-born (but would *pass over*). But it is equally significant that we are asked in a small way to experience them again at Pesakh and at every Pesakh. The *Haggadah* is very explicit about this: one is to retell the story of the Exodus as if he, too, had been liberated from slavery in Egypt. Indeed, this idea is conveyed emphatically at several points in the text, echoing the words of the *Sh'ma*, "I am Adonai your God, who brought you out of Egypt to be your God," words that we repeat each day.

In the same prayer, we are instructed to teach the word "to your children," or as the phrase goes that recurs throughout Jewish liturgy, *"l'dor va-dor"/"from generation to generation."* Hence the enormous importance of children in Pesakh observance.

The Four Questions are asked by the youngest child at the table. Colloquially known as *Ma nishtana* from their opening words "how different," the questions deal with the eating of *matzah, maror,* and *karpas,* and the practice of eating the Pesakh meal while reclining. By asking these questions, the youngest child allows an adult at the table to explain each of these practices and thereby to fulfill the obligation to tell the story to one's children.

THE FOUR QUESTIONS

Mah nish'tanah ha-lailah ha-zeh mikol ha-lailot?/Why is this night different from all other nights?

Sheb'khol ha-lailot anu okhlin, khametz u-matzah. Ha-lailah ha-zeh kulo matzah./On all other nights we eat either leavened or unleavened bread. But on this night we eat only matzah.

Sheb'khol ha-lailot anu okhlin sha'ar y'rakot. Ha-lailah ha-zeh maror./On all other nights we eat other kinds of vegetables, but on this night we eat bitter herbs.

Sheb'khol ha-lailot ain onu matbilin, afilu pa'am akhat. Ha-laila ha-zeh shtei p'amim./On all other nights we do not dip [our vegetables] even once, but on this night we dip twice.

Sheb'khol ha-lailot anu okhlin, bein yosh'vin u'vein m'subin. Ha-laila ha-zeh kulanu m'subin./On all other nights we eat either sitting up or reclining, but on this night we all recline.

Likewise, the *Haggadah* tells the parable of the Four Sons, each representing one of the types of personality to whom we must impart the story of the Exodus, the wise child, the simple child, the wicked child, and the child who is unable to ask. And the entire ritual of the *afikoman* is clearly designed to keep the kids interested until after dinner has been finished.

The number four recurs throughout the *seder*. In addition to the Four Questions and the Four Sons, we drink four glasses of wine. The four glasses of wine are said to represent the four nations that drove the Jews into exile, the Chaldeans, the Medes, the Greeks, and the Romans, or the four national characteristics that the Jews retained in slavery that allowed them to survive captivity in Egypt—they kept their Hebrew names; did not lose touch with their own language; maintained their ethical standards; and did not inform on one another. Perhaps the most compelling explanation, however, is that the four glasses of wine represent the four promises God made to the Israelites in Exodus 6: "I will liberate you. . . . I will deliver you. . . . I will redeem you. . . . I will take you to me as a people."

The strongest evidence for this interpretation is the custom of reserving a glass of wine at the table for the prophet Elijah, whose return to earth will herald the coming of the Messianic Age, a time of peace and prosperity for all. We sing of his greatness, *Eliahu ha-Navi/Elijah the Prophet*, while holding the door to our homes open for him to partake of our Pesakh hospitality. As such, the hope of his coming is nothing less than an expression of our belief in the Creator's promise of a final redemption and of *olam ha-bah/the World to Come*. This fifth cup of wine corresponds to the fifth promise of Exodus, "*v'heveiti. . . ./and I will bring you to the land which I promised your fathers*."

Pesakh is one of the most home-oriented of Jewish holidays. In the synagogue, there are few changes in the actual text of the liturgy. Generally, it follows the standard practice of festival services, adding *Hallel,* *Ya'aleh v'Yavo,* and a *Yizkor* service in Ashkenazi congregations on the last day. One additional prayer that is unique to the holiday is the *Tefillat Tal/Prayer for Dew,* which is recited before *Musaf* on the first day. Like the Prayer for Rain, it calls on God to remember the needs of a people who live on the land and need water to survive. The special *megillah* read on the Shabbat which falls during the holiday is the Song of Songs, no doubt chosen for its spirited invocation of spring. The intermediate days of the festival, *Khol ha-Moed,* are subject to the same rules as the intermediate days of Sukkot. The final day of the festival is treated as a full holiday.[9]

The great sixteenth-century rabbi, Yehudah Loewe of Prague, known as the Maharal, wrote that the Exodus marked a fundamental change in the nature of the Jewish people, that through the liberation from Egypt they acquired the nature of free men and women, a nature that has not changed over centuries, despite all the suffering and captivity subsequently inflicted on them. Thus it may be truly said that God takes us out of Egypt each day, just as our liturgy tells us.

COUNTING THE OMER

From the second night of Pesakh to Shavuot, the next festival, there are exactly fifty days, seven full weeks linked by a ritual called *S'firat ha-Omer/Counting the Omer* (named for an offering brought to the priests at the Temple in Jerusalem at this time of year). In a sense, then, Pesakh is not only a festival itself but the first part of a lengthy observance that runs through Shavuot, a progression from the liberation from Egypt through the revelation at Sinai. For that reason alone, the Omer period has importance.

Beginning on the second night of Pesakh during the *Ma'ariv/evening service,* the leader will rise and announce that she is "prepared to perform the positive commandment concerning the counting of the Omer." She then recites the blessing for counting the Omer and announces the day and the number of weeks and days thus far elapsed.

In the time of the Temple, Jews were instructed to bring a small harvest offering of grain to the priests on the second day of Pesakh, called the Omer offering. From that day, as instructed in Leviticus 23:9, "you shall count seven weeks," up to Shavuot. The Temple is long since gone, and for the most part Jews have ceased to live on farmland. But still we count the Omer according to a prescribed ritual. Why?

Maimonides, one of the greatest of Jewish sages, says that the reason for counting the Omer is to express the eagerness of the Jewish people, freed from bondage in Egypt, to receive the Torah at Sinai, an eagerness that we want to relive. More than that, the Omer period serves as a bridge between the celebration of freedom at Pesakh and the celebration of law at Shavuot, a link between two concepts that Jewish thought sees as essential to one another.

For historical reasons that are at best uncertain (but probably having to do with a plague that, coinciding with the Omer period, struck and killed 24,000 students of Rabbi Akiba's period during the Bar Kokhba revolt against Rome in the 130s C.E.), this is considered a period of semi-mourning and sadness. Traditionally observant Jews will not get their hair cut or shave; marriages are not held during this seven-week period, and public festivities are avoided. (Although no one actually mourns for the entire Omer period—Jews observe either the period from the second night of Passover until Lag b'Omer or from Rosh Khodesh Sivan until Shavuot—marriages are not held in respect for both customs.)

However, there is one day of respite from the mournful Omer period, the thirty-third day of the counting, Lag b'Omer. Lag b'Omer is a minor holiday of obscure origins, celebrated with picnics and bonfires. There are several rather unsatisfying explanations for its existence; the one most often cited states that the plague that afflicted Akiva's students lifted on this day. In Israel the holiday is particularly identified with the great mystic Simeon Bar Yokhai (second century C.E.), allegedly marking the day of his death; Hasids and Sephardim travel to Meron, his birthplace. If they have three-year-old sons, they will give them their first haircuts at Meron on this day.

SHAVUOT

It seems ironic that the sole account of Shavuot in the Torah—the very document whose giving to the Hebrew people the festival celebrates—refers only to the agricultural basis of the holiday. And it is doubly ironic, because Shavuot is the only major festival mandated in the Torah solely on an agricultural basis, despite the keystone importance of the giving of the Law. (The name *Shavuot* means "weeks," a reference to the fact that the holiday marks the conclusion of the counting of the seven weeks of the Omer period.[10])

In Exodus 23:19, the Jews are commanded, "The choice first fruits of your soil you shall bring to the house of Adonai," after the counting of the Omer. In the time of the Temple, farmers would mark in the early spring which of their fruits and grains were heading for early maturity; as spring turned into summer, they would bring them to Jerusalem as an offering. Consequently, one of the names of this festival is *Khag ha-Bikkurim/Festival of First Fruits.* Offerings of first fruits were accepted at the Temple from Shavuot through Hanukah, although it was considered praiseworthy to bring them before Sukkot.

Today outside Israel there are few vestiges of the agricultural beginnings of Shavuot, although in Israel it is a significant festival on secular *kibbutzim.* The custom of decorating the synagogue with flowers and plants, the practice of marking the holiday with a dairy (i.e., vegetarian) meal, and the inclusion of the *megillah* of Ruth in the service are the primary reminders of its agrarian provenance.

But Ruth's story sounds another theme, one more relevant to the celebration of Shavuot by modern Jews. When her husband dies, Ruth elects to stay with Naomi, her mother-in-law, telling her "your people will be my people," binding herself willingly to the people Israel. Ruth's story is one of commitment to the Jewish people freely made and to the covenant with God that is the core of the Jewish religion and experience. Shavuot celebrates the most important moment in that covenant: the giving of the Torah to Moses and its acceptance by the Jews at Sinai.

There are many *midrashim,* explanatory stories, glosses on holy texts, that account for the uniqueness of the Jews, but it is clear from all of them that the acceptance of the Ten Commandments and the Torah that contains them is at the heart of any concept of Jewish uniqueness and historical mission. If ethical monotheism is the central concept of Judaism, Torah is the center of ethical monotheism, and almost everything Jews believe proceeds from Torah directly or indirectly.

Not surprisingly, Shavuot has come to be dedicated to the idea of Torah study and Jewish education. One custom that traditional Jews still observe is an all-night study session held on the first evening of the festival, called *tikkun leil Shavuot.* This custom, which had its beginnings in the community of kabbalists centered around sixteenth-century Safed, is designed to prepare Jews for "receiving" the Torah again on Shavuot.

In keeping with the theme of Jewish education, Shavuot has traditionally been the time when many Conservative and Orthodox Hebrew high schools marked graduation. The newest observance associated with the holiday is the Reform movement's Confirmation ceremony, reaffirming the participation of high school–age teens in Judaism and Jewish scholarship. It is also at this holiday that many congregations of all denominations consecrate their younger Hebrew school students, urging them to study their tradition and live in it.

Liturgically, the major additions for Shavuot, besides the other festival prayers, a *Yizkor* service, and the reading of Ruth, are the *Akdamut* prayer, which is recited at the morning service in Ashkenazi congregations. *Akdamut* is a forty-four-verse acrostic that glosses the Ten Commandments while offering praise to God and the Creation. Sephardic congregations read a special *ketubah/marriage contract,* in recognition of the "marriage" of God and the Jewish people that receives its consummation with the giving of the Torah.

YOM HA-SHOAH, YOM HA-ATZMA'UT, YOM HA-ZIKARON, AND YOM YERUSHALAYIM

The last sixty years have been unusually turbulent ones for the Jewish people. The addition of several new holidays to a calendar that had remained essentially unchanged for a millennium is dramatic testimony to how much this century has affected them, for better and worse.

The first of these four new holidays, *Yom ha-Shoah/the Day of [commemorating] the Holocaust,* was established by an act of the Israeli Parliament, the Knesset, in 1951. Although the choice of date—27 Nisan, only five days after Passover—caused some initial controversy, it has gradually achieved acceptance. Designed as a day on which the six million Jews murdered by the Nazis could be properly memorialized (in the absence of a true *yahrzeit,* given that we cannot know when they died as individuals), the day is marked by a wide range of observances. In many synagogues, six *yahrzeit* candles are lit to commemorate the six million; *Kaddish* is said, speakers or films on the *Shoah* appear. Gradually, special liturgies are being developed by innovative rabbis, cantors, and concerned laypeople. In Israel a siren is sounded and there is an official torch-lighting ceremony at Yad Vashem, the Holocaust memorial and museum, with music and speeches. However, the ultra-Orthodox community has resisted the creation of this holiday and generally considers the minor fast day *Asarah b'Tevet/the Tenth of Tevet* to be the universal *yahrzeit* for those who were murdered by the Nazis.

The other observances all relate to the State of Israel and have had the most impact there. *Yom ha-Atzma'ut/Israeli Independence Day* falls on 5 Iyar, a week after Yom ha-Shoah, and celebrates the end of the British Mandate and the Declaration of Independence by Israel on May 14, 1948. If the holiday falls on Shabbat, it is celebrated on the previous Wednesday night and Thursday. Although it is a day of parades and parties in Israel, it is understandably somewhat less observed in the Diaspora. But many congregations take the opportunity to sing Israeli songs and to have speakers or a sermon regarding the current state of the Jewish homeland. Many also recite the "Prayer for the State of Israel," composed by Israel's chief rabbi in the 1950s. (Most Modern Orthodox congregations recite this prayer every Shabbat. There is also a special prayer for soldiers serving in the Israel Defense Forces that is said every Shabbat in Israel.)

In Israel the day before Yom ha-Atzma'ut is *Yom ha-Zikaron/the Day of Remembrance,* an equivalent of the American holidays of Memorial Day and Veterans Day, commemorating the nation's war casualties. No native Israeli (and few *olim/immigrants*) has been untouched by losses over the many years of hostilities between Israel and its neighbors. A day of mourning in Israel, it is marked by sirens sounding all over the country at 11 a.m., signaling two minutes of silence. In addition to a communal and official memorial at the Mt. Herzl military cemetery, there is also a torch-lighting ceremony at the *Kotel* (the Western Wall of the ancient Temple), and a general pilgrimage to cemeteries throughout the country.

Yom Yerushalayim/Jerusalem Day is the newest holiday on the Israeli calendar. Observed on 28 Iyar, it celebrates the reunification of Jerusalem on June 7, 1967, as a result of Israeli military successes in the Six-Day War. The single holiest city in Jewish tradition, mentioned over 500 times in the Tanakh, it had been divided as a result of the aftermath of the War of Independence in 1948, with the half of the Old City that included the Western Wall, the only remaining portion of the

Temple, in Jordanian hands. When it was retaken by Israeli troops in 1967, it marked the first time in nearly two thousand years that the city was unified under a Jewish government. A politically charged day, Yom Yerushalayim is more likely to be celebrated by the religious and political right-wings than by supporters of the peace movement, for whom the occupation of East Jerusalem and the other Occupied Territories is seen as an obstacle to a settlement.

MINOR FAST DAYS

There are four "minor" fast days practiced by traditionally observant Jews, fasts that last only from sunrise to sunset. Unlike Yom Kippur and Tisha b'Av, these days are not marked by additional prohibitions against sexual relations, bathing, shaving, or wearing leather.

Tzom Gedaliah/The Fast of Gedaliah falls on 3 Tishri, the day after Rosh Hashanah. Gedaliah was the first and only Jewish governor under Babylonian rule. When he was assassinated on Rosh Hashanah by a Jew hired by Ammonites, rivals to the Israelites, the remaining Jewish loyalists fled to Egypt. Nebuchadnezzar, the Babylonian king, interpreted their flight as a confession of guilt and exiled the remainder of the Jewish population in Babylonia. Consquently, the kingdom of Judah collapsed and Gedaliah's assassination is considered the death knell for Jewish sovereignty in this period.

Asarah b'Tevet/The Tenth of Tevet marks the day on which Nebuchadnezzar's armies began the siege of Jerusalem that led eventually to the destruction of the First Temple. As such, it may be said to commemorate the first great national tragedy to befall the Jews. This day is also designated by many Orthodox rabbis as the universal *yahrzeit* for those who died in the *Shoah*.

Ta'anit Esther/The Fast of Esther falls on 13 Adar, the day before Purim, and is linked to Esther's own fast undertaken with all the Jews of Shushan the night before she decided to reveal to Ahashverus Haman's plot.

Shivah Asar be-Tammuz/The 17th of Tammuz is the day on which the Babylonians first breached the walls of Jerusalem in 586 B.C.E. It is also the day in legend on which Moses shattered the first set of tablets containing the Ten Commandments when he found the Israelites dancing around the Golden Calf.

This fast day also inaugurates a period of public morning called the

"Three Weeks," leading up to Tisha b'Av. During this period, observant Jews may not get married. Ashkenazi practice also bars getting one's hair cut and shaving. Sephardic *minhag/custom* prohibits those activities from the first of Av only. It is also prohibited to perform any action that would call for reciting *Shehekhayanu,* such as wearing new clothes or eating the first fruit of the season. Ashkenazim also refrain from eating meat or drinking wine from the first of Av, Sephardim from the Sunday before Tisha b'Av. On each of the Sabbaths that falls during the Three Weeks, a special *haftarah* is read, the *Telata de-Poranuta/the Three of Calamity,* dark prophecies from Jeremiah 1 and 2 and Isaiah 1, alluding to the destruction that will befall Israel.

TISHA B'AV

Only two fast days in the entire Jewish calendar begin on the evening of the holiday and last over twenty-four hours. It is indicative of the seriousness of *Tisha b'Av/the Ninth of Av* that it is bracketed with Yom Kippur as the second such fast day. Moreover, while other fast days connected with the destruction of the First Temple in 586 B.C.E. (see section "Minor Fast Days," p. 130) were suspended when the Temple was rebuilt after the Babylonian exile, Tisha b'Av was not. Even while the Second Temple stood, Tisha b'Av was observed as a solemn day of mourning. (As noted above, it is a mark of the importance of Shabbat that Tisha b'Av does not take precedence over it. If the holiday falls on Shabbat, observance begins after sundown Saturday night.)

Tisha b'Av is quite simply the saddest day in the Jewish calendar. By custom it is said that both the First and Second Temples were destroyed on this day. Although there is strong historical evidence that the Second Temple was actually destroyed by the Romans on 10 Av 70 C.E., the destruction began on the ninth and a rabbinic ruling of the post-Temple period held that later tragedies may be said to have occurred on the same date. Thus, it is also said that the Romans crushed the nationalistic Bar Kokhba rebellion at Betar on Tisha b'Av 135 C.E.

No rabbinic dictum was necessary for later calamities that fell on Tisha b'Av. In 1190, the entire Jewish population of York, England, was massacred on that day, the victims of the first known example of the infamous "blood libel," the claim that Jews used the blood of Christian children as part of their religious rites. On Tisha b'Av 1290, King

Edward I signed the order banishing all Jews from England. Although the last Jews left Spain in 1492 four days before it went into effect, the expulsion order of King Ferdinand and Queen Isabella set a deadline of Tisha b'Av for their final departure. And on Tisha b'Av 1942 the Nazis began deportations from Warsaw to the death camp at Treblinka (apparently by design).

So by a hideous series of historical coincidences (or, as a traditionally observant Jew might argue, by the design of the Almighty), this midsummer day has seen some of the darkest moments in Jewish history.

None of them are darker than the destruction of the two Temples in Jerusalem. The fall of the First Temple initiated the lengthy Babylonian exile. But the destruction of the Second Temple had even more disastrous and longer-lasting repercussions for the Jews, marking the end of Jewish sovereignty and the beginning of the Diaspora. It could be truthfully said that every pogrom, every anti-Semitic atrocity, up to and including the Holocaust, that occurred between 70 C.E. and the founding of the State of Israel in 1948 was the direct result of the fall of the Second Temple.

It is with good reason, then, that Tisha b'Av is a Jewish holiday unlike any other. On the eve of Tisha b'Av, observant Jews eat a frugal last meal, consisting usually of an egg and lentils, before their fast (unlike Yom Kippur); some Sephardim even dip the egg in ashes to emphasize the tragic nature of this day. Eating, drinking, bathing, shaving, sexual relations, and the wearing of leather shoes are prohibited on Tisha b'Av. Going to work and even Torah study are proscribed as well.

The synagogue wears a face of mourning. The curtain is removed from the Ark, the cloth removed from the *bimah*. The lights are dimmed. Chairs or pews are upended. Congregants sit on the floor or on low stools. They do not greet one another. Neither *tallit* nor *tefillin* are worn at the morning service. (They will be donned—on this day alone—at the afternoon service, then removed before *Ma'ariv*.)

The *megillah Eikhah/Lamentations* is read at the evening service for Tisha b'Av, chanted in a plaintive, melancholy *nusakh* that is used only on this day and for the *haftarah* on the Sabbath before this holiday. Ashkenazi congregations also chant *kinot*, a series of elegiac poems that, like Lamentations, focus on the destruction of the Temple and the scattering of the Jewish people. Many congregations add songs and readings appropriate to the spirit of the day, including many more recently composed *kinot* written in commemoration of the *Shoah*.

And yet Tisha b'Av is not a day without hope. The prophet Zechariah has said that the day will come — when the Messiah arrives — that all our previous fasting days will become days of rejoicing (Zechariah 8:19). The rabbis of the Talmudic period believed that *Moshiach/the Messiah* will be born on Tisha b'Av, coming to make good on God's promise of a final redemption of the Jewish people and the world.

SPECIAL READINGS FOR THE FESTIVALS

THE FIVE *MEGILLOT*

The five *megillot/scrolls* are books of the Hebrew Bible that are associated with specific holidays of the Jewish calendar, read in conjunction with the observance of those holidays.

Sukkot: *Kohelet/Ecclesiastes*
Purim: *Esther*
Pesakh: *Shir ha-Shirim/Song of Songs*
Shavuot: *Ruth*
Tisha b'Av: *Eikhah/Lamentations*

In addition, there are prescribed Torah and *haftarah* readings for each of the festivals. (The readings listed below apply in traditionally observant Ashkenazi communities; readings in Reform and Sephardi synagogues may differ.)

Rosh Hashanah

First Day:	Genesis 21:1–34, Numbers 29:1–6
Haftarah:	I Samuel 1:1–2:10
Second Day:	Genesis 22:1–24, Numbers 29:1–6
Haftarah:	Jeremiah 31: 2–20

Yom Kippur

Morning:	Leviticus 16:1–34, Numbers 29:7–11
Haftarah:	Isaiah 57:14–58:14

Afternoon: Leviticus 18:1–30
  Haftarah: Book of Jonah, Micah 7:18–20

Sukkot

First Day: Leviticus 22:26–23:44,   Numbers 29:12–16
  Haftarah: Zechariah 14:1–21
Second Day: Same as first day
  Haftarah: I Kings 8:2–21
First day Khol ha-Moed: Numbers 29:17–25
Second day Khol ha-Moed: Numbers 29:20–28
Third day Khol ha-Moed: Numbers 29:23–31
Fourth day Khol ha-Moed: Numbers 29:26–34
Shabbat Khol ha-Moed: Exodus   33:12–34:26   and
                                    Numbers 29:17–25, 23–29, or
                                    26–31, depending on whether it
                                    is first, third, or fourth day of
                                    Khol ha-Moed
  Haftarah: Ezekiel 38:18–39:16
Hoshanah Rabbah: Numbers 29:26–34

Shemini Atzeret

Torah: Deuteronomy 14:22–16:17, Numbers 29:35–30:1
  Haftarah: I Kings 8:54–66

Simkhat Torah

Torah: Deuteronomy 33:1–34:12, Genesis 1:1–2:3,
               Numbers 29:35–30:1
  Haftarah: Joshua 1:1–18

Hanukah

First day: Numbers 7:1–17
Second day: Numbers 7:18–29
Third day: Numbers 7:24–35
Fourth day: Numbers 7:30–41
Fifth day: Numbers 7:36–47

Sixth day:	Numbers 7:42–47
Seventh day:	Numbers 7:48–59 (If Rosh Khodesh: Numbers 7:48–53)
Eighth day:	Numbers 7:54–8:4
Hanukah on Rosh Khodesh:	Numbers 28:1–15, plus appropriate reading for sixth or seventh day
Shabbat Hanukah:	Regular Shabbat reading, plus reading for day of Hanukah on which it falls
Haftarah:	Zechariah 2:14–4:7
Second Shabbat of Hanukah:	Regular Shabbat reading (always *Miketz*, Genesis 41:1–44:17), plus Numbers 7:54–8:4
Haftarah:	I Kings 7:40–50
Shabbat Rosh Khodesh:	Regular Shabbat reading, Numbers 28:1–15, plus reading for day of Hanukah on which it falls

Purim

Torah: Exodus 17:8–16

Pesakh

First day:	Exodus 12:21–51, Numbers 28:16–25
Haftarah:	Joshua 5:2–6:1
Second day:	Leviticus 22:26–23:44, Numbers 28:16–25
Haftarah:	Kings 23:1–9, 21–25
Shabbat Khol ha-Moed Pesakh:	Exodus 33:12–34:26, Numbers 28:19–25
Haftarah:	Ezekiel 37:1–14
Seventh day:	Exodus 13:17–15:26, Numbers 28:19–25
Eighth day:	Deuteronomy 15:19–16:17 (if on Sabbath, 14:22–16:17)
Haftarah:	Isaiah 10:32–12:6

Shavuot

First day:	Exodus 19:1–20:23, Numbers 28:26–31
Haftarah:	Ezekiel 1:1–28, 3:12
Second day:	Deuteronomy 15:19–16:17 (if on Sabbath 14:22–16:17)
Haftarah:	Habakuk 2:20–3:19

Yom Ha-Atzma'ut

Torah:	Deuteronomy 7:12–8:18
Haftarah:	Isaiah 10:32–12:6

Tisha b'Av

Morning:	Deuteronomy 4:25–40
Haftarah:	Jeremiah 8:13–9:23
Afternoon:	Exodus 32:11–14, 34:1–10
Haftarah:	Isaiah 55:6–56:8

Readings are the same on other fast days as well.

NOTES

1. Leap years fall in the years 3, 6, 8, 11, 14, 17, and 19 of the cycle. The next leap year will be 5760 (1999–2000).

2. The rabbis had still another thorny issue to deal with: how to prevent Yom Kippur, the most solemn of holy days, from falling on a Friday or a Sunday, which would play havoc with Sabbath observance. Similarly, they did not want Hoshanah Rabah to fall on the Sabbath. Their solution to this problem was to declare that the first day of Rosh Hashanah, the New Year, could not fall on a Sunday, Wednesday, or Friday.

3. The most common explanation for the custom of covering one's eyes when lighting the Shabbat candles is an interesting one. It is customary to say a blessing before performing the act for which it is said. However, to say the blessing over the candles would usher in Shabbat, and it is forbidden to light a fire on the Sabbath. By lighting the fire and closing one's eyes, we are performing the "legal fiction" that the blessing actually precedes the lighting; we open our eyes and, well, the candles are lit.

4. Judaism has four separate calendars, each with its own New Year's celebration, which is why Rosh Hashanah, the "Jewish New Year," actually falls in the seventh month, Tishri. The rabbis of the Mishnah (approximately the third century C.E.) designated a New Year for kings (i.e., a civil calendar) that came on 1 Nisan, the first month of the Hebrew calendar; a New Year for trees (which we celebrate as Tu b'Shevat; see p. 115);

a New Year for tithing cattle, which fell on 1 Elul; and Rosh Hashanah, the religious New Year, which falls on 1 Tishri.

5. Beginning in Elul, Jews greet one another *"L'shanah tovah tikateivu v'teikhateimu/May you be inscribed and sealed [in the Book of Life] for a good year."* However, because it is believed that the righteous are immediately inscribed in the Book of Life, after Rosh Hashanah this greeting is dropped; after all, you wouldn't want to cast doubts on someone's righteousness. Instead, one says *"L'shanah tovah tikhateimu/May you be sealed for a good year."* If you're in doubt, you can simply say, *"L'shanah tovah/A good year."* Similarly, Yiddish speakers may simply wish one another *"A gute yohr/A good year"* or *"Tzetze yohr/A sweet year."* Incidentally, while we're on the subject of greetings, on a holiday, it is proper to say, *"Gut Yontif/Good holiday,"* a Yiddish phrase, or in Hebrew, *"Khag sameakh/A happy festival."*

6. During the recital of the *Ashamnu* and the *Vidui* many Jews will pull their *talliesim* (plural of *tallit*) over their heads, and beat their chests with their fists as a form of gentle self-scourging. The Khafetz Khayim, that astute Orthodox rabbi, noted this latter habit and responded, "God does not forgive the sins of one who smites his heart, but he pardons those whose hearts smite them."

7. Before they were evacuated to Israel, Ethiopian Jews lived year-round in huts. Therefore, they didn't observe the *mitzvah* of living in the *sukkah* during this festival.

8. As on other festivals, hospitality to the stranger is given great importance at Pesakh. More than that, in the month before the holiday, Jewish communities collect *maos hittim/money for wheat,* money to be used to help the poor of the community to pay for the necessities of the festival. Remember, again, that it is a *mitzvah* to enjoy the festivals, one that should not be missed even due to lack of the wherewithal.

9. There is a minor festival, *Pesakh Sheni/Second Passover,* which takes place on 14 Iyar, one month later, for those who were unable to observe Pesakh due to ritual impurity, usually caused by contact with the dead.

10. Shavuot falls on the fiftieth day after the second night of Pesakh, the completion of the counting of the Omer. As such, it is the only Jewish festival that does not have a fixed date on the Hebrew calendar, although that is no longer important now that we know when the new moon falls and are not reliant on the Sanhedrin to mark that event (see sidebar "The Jewish Calendar," p. 78).

CHAPTER 3

Birth to Death:
A Jewish Life Cycle

Our lives are bounded by enigmas, by the mysteries of birth and death. The Talmud says that there are two moments in a human life over which one has no control, the moment in which one is born and the moment at which one dies. In between those two moments shrouded in uncertainty, a Jew will experience many Sabbaths, many festivals, many new moons, a lifetime of sacred time. But the moments he will experience most directly, no less sacred, are the events that mark an individual lifetime, from birth to death (and perhaps beyond). Judaism has its own way of recognizing and commemorating those moments.

The family unit is at the heart of each of these moments. Judaism places tremendous stress on the importance of the family and every significant rite of passage involves the family in some fundamental way. The home shares pride of place with the synagogue as a central institution of the faith. Indeed, both are characterized by the Torah sages as *mikdash me'at / a small (minor) sanctuary*. From the placing of the *mezuzah* on the doorway to the lighting of Sabbath candles, making of *kiddush* and sharing of meals, the Jewish home is a site of observance equal in importance to any in the religion.

Keep in mind the historical context in which the home and the synagogue both rose to new prominence in Jewish practice: the destruction of the Temple in Jerusalem in 586 B.C.E. and an enforced exile in Babylon. Where else would the values of the faith be handed down besides the family? Indeed, as anyone acquainted even distantly with the work of Sholem Aleichem (if only from having seen the sugar-coated *Fiddler on the Roof*) knows, the Jewish home is the place where children, adolescents, and even young adults receive their most important training in *yiddishkeit* (a Yiddish word that one might translate roughly as "Jewishness," which the Orthodox take to mean the specifically religious aspects of Jewishness). It is in the family, in the home, that the principal celebrations of life-cycle events take place in Judaism. If in recent years the home no longer has been as central as the synagogue in Jewish-American life as the carrier of Jewish values for generations to come, that is merely a reflection of the changes in American society that have affected every family, Jewish and non-Jewish alike.

BIRTH

God's first commandment to humankind is "Be fruitful and multiply" (Genesis 1:28). In fact, although the sages of the Talmud encouraged couples to bear children, they felt that a man—and the commandment was given to Adam in Genesis—had discharged his duties in that department if he had given birth to at least a son and a daughter according to Hillel or, in the rulings of the stricter rabbinic authorities of the time, two sons.[1]

Judaism has always considered children to be a gift, a blessing from the Creator. In Genesis 17:16, Adonai tells Abraham, "I will bless [Sarah]. Indeed, I will give her a son by you." Conversely, barrenness was seen as a curse.

Although the pain of childbirth was supposedly the punishment visited on Eve and her successors for her transgression in the Garden of Eden (Genesis 1:16), the Torah recognized—and the rabbis who wrote the Talmud acknowledged in greater detail—the dangers inherent in childbirth in ancient times. Midwives were often present at births, and their role in preserving the Jewish people was celebrated (see Exodus 1:17–21). Moreover, women were allowed, even encouraged, to accept medications to alleviate their pain.

One indication of the rabbinical recognition of the dangers to the mother in childbirth is the explicit statement that the principle of *pikuakh nefesh / saving a soul (life)* applies in most cases in which the life of the mother is threatened. The life of the mother takes precedence over that of the unborn infant in all cases. Only when the child's head has emerged from the birth canal is it considered alive; at that point the life of the child takes precedence. All necessary measures may be taken on Shabbat to save the life of the mother. Moreover, for the first three days after the child's birth, the mother's life is still considered to be in mortal danger and, if a doctor or other health practitioner deems it necessary, the Sabbath may be violated to protect her.

Many of the beliefs that governed childbirth in the Talmudic period were based on misapprehensions about the birth process. Thus, the rabbis believed (like their Greek neighbors) that while a seven-month-old fetus would survive a premature birth, an eight-month-old would not. A first-born child delivered by the cesarean method would not be entitled to the legal rights and duties that ordinarily befell a first-born under Jewish law, nor would any other child born to that woman. (See "Pidyon Ha-Ben," p. 151.)

Similarly, a woman who had given birth was considered "unclean" under the laws governing purity and impurity (see Chapter 4, "Sexuality," p. 244); after giving birth to a male child, she was considered to be impure for seven days, a female child, fourteen days. For the thirty-three days after the seven-day period (sixty-six after a female child), she was not permitted to enter the Temple in Jerusalem or to handle sacred objects. When the prescribed period was over, she would bring a burnt offering and a sin offering to the Temple. Today, traditionally observant Jews consider a new mother in the same category in terms of the laws of purity as one who is menstruating; after the prescribed period, she is purified by immersion in the *mikveh / ritual bath*.

Even today in Ashkenazi congregations, a new mother will come up to the Torah when she is able and *bentsch gomel,* that is, recite the blessing for one who has survived a life-threatening experience:

Barukh atah Adonai Eloheinu Melekh ha-olam, ha-gomel l'khayavim tovot, she-g'malani kol tov.

Blessed are You Adonai our God, Ruler of the Universe, who graciously bestows favor on the undeserving, even as You have bestowed favor on me.

One may still see a red ribbon or piece of yarn hanging from a baby's crib in a Jewish home even now. This talisman is a holdover from medieval Jewry, from a time in which the survival of newborns was a very iffy proposition. Family and friends would gather each night to pray that evil spirits would not take the child. Amulets were hung over the crib. The chief enemy of babies was Lilith, a female demon (according to one *midrash,* the true first woman, created before Eve). As in other cultures, the color red, with its association with blood, was seen as life-giving. (The rabbis, of course, considered such superstitious behavior as little short of idolatry.)

One of the more appealing practices celebrating the birth of a child is the planting of a tree to mark that auspicious event. For a son, the family would plant a cedar, for a daughter a pine or a cypress. When the children were old enough to marry, the wood for their bridal canopy would be taken from the tree planted for their birth. Today, many Jewish families pay homage to this old custom by having a tree planted in Israel in honor of a newborn. One suspects that Israeli officials look rather askance at families coming to *Eretz Yisroel* to chop down "their" trees for a bridal canopy.

A superstition common to both some Jews and many other peoples is that one doesn't announce the name—doesn't even discuss it—of an expected child until after it is born, preferably until after it is given a baby-naming ceremony in the synagogue (part of the rites of circumcision for boys, a ceremony unto itself for girls). One doesn't encourage the "evil eye" by making the name public until it has been conferred officially.

Perhaps we no longer believe that "like his name, so he is" (I Samuel 25:25), but the custom of naming Jewish children for relatives clearly suggests that the power to name still carries an impressive charge (and a sobering responsibility, one would hope). Among Ashkenazi Jews, it is customary to name a child for a deceased relative, often a grandparent, rendering honor to a beloved and departed family member and, one hopes, passing on some of that person's good traits.[2] Sephardic Jews, on the other hand, name the child for a living relative, again often a grandparent, but their selection is motivated by the same reasons.

Generally in the Diaspora non-Orthodox Jews have given their children a "conventional" name for purposes of civil birth records and daily use, and a Hebrew name for religious records and uses. However, Jewish naming practices seem to have changed in recent years. With the advent of the State of Israel, the American fascination with exploring one's family roots, and the turn toward more traditional manifestations of Jewish spirituality in the Reform movement, more couples are giving their children names from the Bible. Certainly there are plenty of those to go around; there are some 2,800 personal names in the Hebrew Bible, about five percent of which are in common use today. Methuselah, anyone?

It is considered especially praiseworthy to bestow a Hebrew name upon a Jewish child as a way of preserving the Jewish heritage. A *midrash* states emphatically that one of the reasons that the Jews were deemed by God to be worthy of liberation from slavery was that they retained their Hebrew names despite four centuries of living in Egypt. On the other hand, the custom of giving both a Hebrew name and a non-Hebrew name also has biblical roots; Esther is also Hadassah (Esther 2:7) and Daniel is also called Belteshazzar (Daniel 1:7).

Regardless of a child's non-Hebrew name, if she has one, the name by which she will be called to the Torah, married, and buried as a Jew, will consist of a Hebrew first name, followed by *bat/daughter of* or *ben/son of* and the Hebrew name of the father. In non-Orthodox settings, the mother's Hebrew name will also be included. An Orthodox Jew who is a descendant of the Priestly or Levitical castes will add Ha-Kohen or HaLevi, respectively. To choose an obvious example, when I am called for an *aliyah* in my synagogue, it is by my Hebrew name, "Gedaliah ben Yoel," George, son of Joel. And I was named for my maternal great-grandfather, who was also named George.

No matter how they are named or for whom, this much is sure for all newborns: in the eyes of Judaism, they are born without sin, blameless. For, as we say in the morning blessings, "The soul you have given me, Adonai, is a pure one."

ABORTION

As may be surmised from its attitudes toward birth, Judaism does not accept the Catholic notion that life begins at conception. At the same time, however, even the most politically progressive movements in American Judaism reject the idea of abortion "on demand." Within the various streams of Judaism, a range of positions may be found on this heated issue, but none of them could be said to partake of the extreme ends of the abortion debate.

The roots of the Jewish position on abortion can be found in a passage of Exodus 21. In verse 22, it is said that if two men fight and hurt a woman who is pregnant, causing her to miscarry, the man responsible will be fined. Rabbinical authorities took this to mean that a fetus could not be considered alive; if it were, the miscreant would be liable for the death penalty, having taken a human life.

When does a fetus become recognized as a human being with rights of its own? Traditionally, when the head of a newborn has emerged from the birth canal, Jewish law considers it to have the status of a full human being.

Even today, the most stringent of Orthodox rabbis will insist on an abortion in a case in which the life of the mother is endangered under the doctrine of *pikuakh nefesh,* saving a life. Indeed, many Orthodox rabbis extend this principle to take into account damage to the pregnant woman's psychological state in the case of a severely deformed fetus.

At the same time, though, rabbinic authorities recognize the fetus as "a potential human life." It has been noted that the doctrine of *pikuakh nefesh* has been applied to permit the violation of the Sabbath to save an unborn fetus and therefore—as at least one contemporary rabbi, I. Y. Unterman, has argued—it follows that abortion is akin to murder. However, even Rabbi Unterman concedes that there are circumstances under which abortion must be permitted.

Even the most lenient of rabbis have been reluctant to approve of abortion. The argument offered by feminists that the decision to abort derives from a woman's right to control her own body does not convince the rabbinate. Jewish tradition holds that our bodies are, as one rabbinical authority puts it, "bailments," simply on loan from God, to whom they really belong. Hence, the CCAr, the Reform rabbinate, takes the position that "if there is serious danger to the health of the mother or child," abortion should be permitted, but "we do not encourage abortion, nor favor it for trivial reasons."

ADOPTION

Jewish law on adoption is sketchy for the simple reason that it doesn't regard children as property and therefore can't really assimilate the notion of transferring "title." However, the Talmud says, "He who raises someone else's child is regarded as if he had actually brought him into the world physically." Although Jewish law may not comment extensively on adoption, the practice is clearly accepted and even applauded. Indeed, Jewish law allows for situations in which a child may be removed from a home situation in which the natural parent(s) are a threat to the child's well-being.

Many of the laws and customs that govern adoption grow logically out of the initial premise, that one does not take title to children as one would chattel. Thus, the relationship between an adopted child and its natural parents is irrevocable. A child who is a Levite or a Kohen does not forfeit this status when adopted; conversely, a child who is adopted by a Levite or a Kohen does not take on his adopted father's status, and a child of a non-Jewish mother who is adopted by a Jewish family must undergo conversion to be considered a Jew. If a child is the first-born of its natural mother, a *Pidyon ha-Ben* should be held, regardless of the status of the adoptive parents (but it will be their responsibility to see that the ceremony takes place).

For the conversion of a non-Jewish child, immersion in the *mikveh* is necessary for a girl, also a *brit milah* for a boy. If the boy was circumcised before, the *mohel* need only take a drop of blood from the point of circumcision. Girls are named in a ceremony at the synagogue, boys during the *brit milah*. However, Reform and Reconstructionist Jews in America recognize the Jewishness of a child who is raised in a Jewish home with Jewish education, celebration and identification, regardless of the status of the birth mother. (This is an issue fraught with emotion [see sidebar "Who Is a Jew?" p. 177] and Israeli Reform rabbis have chosen not to recognize patrilineal descent because of its potential divisiveness.)

MAMZERUT

Illegitimacy confers considerably less stigma on children in Jewish law than in most other societies. A *mamzer/bastard* is the offspring of a marriage forbidden under Jewish law due to family relationships (see sidebar "Prohibited Marriages," p. 169), between a *mamzer* and a non-*mamzer*, or the child of an adulterous or incestuous union. A child born out of wedlock is not considered illegitimate, and bears no stigma at all.

Moreover, Judaism is solicitous of the feelings of such children, reasoning that they are not responsible for their condition. A *midrash* says that the Eternal One personally takes pity on them, saying, "I will comfort them in future life."

The Talmudic sages ruled that a *mamzer* may only marry another *mamzer*. But they also ruled that the bar to any other marriage is only in effect if illegitimacy can be proven. The mere suspicion of illegitimacy is not sufficient. Even the claim of illegitimacy by the parents themselves is not sufficient.

Except for the rarely enforced bar on marriage, a *mamzer* is treated the same as any other Jew; the *mamzer* is obligated to respect the commandments, and is allowed to accept *bar mitzvah*, and to be called to the Torah.

Most cases of *mamzerut/illegitimacy* under Jewish law today occur in situations in which a woman remarried without a *get*. In the eyes of the Orthodox and most Conservative Jews, she is still legally married to her first husband. However, a consensus of the Conservative movement currently believes that in this area the laws of *mamzerut* are inoperative; no one has been keeping track of the births produced by such second marriages, so only an extensive and highly intrusive investigation would make it possible to accurately ascertain the status of a couple a generation or two later (the sort of investigation that the Talmud itself proscribes). The liberal rabbi assumes legitimacy. Orthodox rabbis will investigate as much as feasible.

The Orthodox rabbinate in Israel will not perform marriages between a *mamzer* and a regular Jew if they are aware of some of the cases of *mamzerut*. The largest category of *mamzerim*, the children of Reform or Conservative couples who did not get a religious divorce, cannot marry in Israel. However, the Orthodox rabbis have come up with an ingenious solution to this problem: if they do not accept the *halakhic* legitimacy of a Reform or Conservative wedding, then they don't need to require a *halakhic* divorce. This ruling has solved most questions of *mamzerut*.

BRIT MILAH

Circumcision is probably the best-known indication of Jewishness in a male (if not the most immediately visible!). It is also one of the oldest and most widely followed of Jewish ritual practices. Although circumcision is also an important element of Islam, a common practice in many other belief-systems, and more the medical standard in the industrial West today, it is still most closely associated with Judaism.

For Jews, circumcision has its beginnings in Genesis 17. The Eternal One speaks to Abraham, now ninety-nine, and tells him to circumcise himself and the male members of his household (slaves and manservants included), as "the covenant between Me and you and your offspring to follow. . . . Every male among you shall be circumcised." Abraham does as he is instructed, circumcising himself and his thirteen-year-old son Ishmael.[3]

The first-century Jewish philosopher Philo believed that the rationale for circumcision was twofold: hygienic because it promoted cleanliness, and moral because it was a constant reminder to men of the need to control their sexual urges. Eleven centuries later, Maimonides speculated that it served as a curb on lustful appetites.

Although it is common practice today for Jews and non-Jews alike, there is little evidence that circumcision serves any medical purpose. Nor are the arguments of Philo and Maimonides particularly convincing. What makes circumcision important is its larger symbolic resonance, as a *brit/covenant,* a linking of a newly born Jew to a four-thousand-year-long history, a sign of the relationship between Jews and God. Like many other *mitzvot* (as we shall see in Chapter 4), circumcision can be explained by a variety of not very convincing rationales, but ultimately it is a *mitzvah* one performs for its own sake as a subordination of oneself to a larger entity; whether that entity is the Almighty or a sense of historical community and continuity will depend on the nature of one's beliefs, but this is one of the few practices on which almost all Jews are in agreement.[4] To not circumcise one's son is to cut him off from the Jewish people, in Jewish law and symbolically. Indeed, this is a covenant of such importance that the Torah tells us that Moses himself was nearly subject to a penalty of death because he was late in circumcising his son (Exodus 4).

The *brit milah/covenant of circumcision* (colloquially known as a *bris,* the Ashkenazi pronunciation of *brit*) takes place on the eighth day from the day a boy is born. For instance, if a baby is born on a Monday, the *brit milah* would take place the following Monday. Of course, the Jewish ritual day begins at sunset, so a baby born on a Monday night would have his *brit* on Tuesday.

In Ashkenazi Orthodox households the Friday evening immediately after the birth of a son is a time for gathering after dinner for a custom called *Shalom Zachor* (literally, "the peace to the male"). This somewhat unusual name has two possible explanations: a) *shalom/peace* refers to the Sabbath, *zachor/male* to the newborn; or b) that a woman suffering from the pain of childbirth may feel anger toward her husband but when the child finally emerges, peace is restored to the home. Regardless of the etymology, it is a festive event. Friends come to visit, light refreshments are served. Someone will offer a *d'vrei Torah,* a gloss on the weekly Torah portion, and songs are sung. Chickpeas are always a part of that repast, as in a house of mourning. While in the womb, folklore has it, the baby learns all of Torah, but forgets it at birth, a cause for mourning. Also, a chickpea is circular and the circle is symbolic of the continuity of life.

On the eighth day the actual circumcision will be performed by a *mohel* (a *moil* in the more common Yiddish pronunciation). He is trained in the ritual of circumcision according to the rules prescribed in the *Shulkhan Arukh* (the sixteenth-century book in which Rabbi Joseph Caro codified the laws governing Jewish practice), and modern surgical hygiene. Recently, the non-Orthodox movements have begun certifying as *mohels* both male and female physicians who have undergone training in the theology, history and liturgy of the brit, and an increasing number of Orthodox *mohelim* are also board-certified doctors. The *mohel* will examine the baby to certify that he is healthy enough to undergo the procedure (unless a doctor has decided he cannot). If he is not, it can be postponed to a later date. As usual in matters of physical health, Judaism takes a cautious approach, and *mohelim* are generally more strict on this issue than doctors.

A *brit milah* is one of those rare Jewish rituals that can—in fact, must—be performed on a Sabbath or festival, even Yom Kippur; eight days is eight days. However, if the *brit milah* is postponed because of the baby's health, the rescheduled event cannot take place on the Sabbath or a festival; if you're not going to do it on the eighth day, it's no longer sufficiently imperative that you *have* to do it on Shabbat.

A *brit milah* always takes place during the day, usually in the morning, in the home. The *mohel* will lead the ceremony, which is brief. It is preferable to have a *minyan* present, but not essential; a *brit* can be performed by the *mohel* with no one but the father present.

The child is taken from his mother by the godmother (*kwaterin,* from the German) who presents him to the *sandek,* the honored person who will hold the infant during the ceremony. The boy may have been given a small piece of gauze soaked in wine to suck on to lessen the pain and to help him sleep. The *sandek* takes the child into the room in which the circumcision will be performed and hands him to the *kwater/godfather*. (These positions are ones of honor, conferred on relatives or close family friends, often a couple trying to conceive so that some mystical benefit from doing this *mitzvah* will accrue to them.) The *kwater*, in turn, places the infant on the *kisei shel Eliyahu/Chair of Elijah*. (The Chair of Elijah is symbolic of the presence of that important prophet, who railed against the Jews for forsaking the ritual of circumcision; today, by the use of the Chair of Elijah, he is present at every *brit* as a mute witness to the maintenance of the covenant.) Any chair may be used, but it should be placed next to the chair to be occupied by the *sandek,* and left there unmoved for three days after the ceremony (a holdover from the days when it was believed that the first three days after circumcision were a perilous time for the infant).

The baby is handed to his father who puts him in the lap of the *sandek*. The father may hand the ritual knife (the *izamel*) to the *mohel* as part of the ritual, a symbolic acknowledgment of his responsibility for the *brit*.

Before the *mohel* actually begins cutting, he recites the blessing for circumcision, then the father of the child recites the blessing:

Barukh atah Adonai Eloheinu Melekh ha-olam, asher kid'shanu b'mitzvotav v'tzivanu l'hakhniso bivrito shel Avraham avinu.

Blessed are You, Adonai our God, Ruler of the Universe, who has sanctified us with Your commandments and commanded us to bring him into the covenant of Abraham, our father.

The guests present will answer "Amen." Then they offer a second blessing:

K'sheim she-nikhnas labrit, ken yikaneis l'Torah, u-l'khupah u-l'ma-asim tovim.

As he entered the covenant, may he enter into the study of Torah, into marriage and into the doing of good deeds.

The procedure itself is very brief. The *mohel* uses a *magein/shield* to protect the glans and guide the knife. He may use a silver probe to loosen the foreskin before beginning. There are three phases to the procedure: *meelah,* the actual removal of the foreskin; *periah,* the tearing of the genital membrane underneath the foreskin back to the corona; and *m'tzitzah / suction,* the removal of blood and cleaning of the affected area. In ancient tradition, the *mohel* would actually suck the blood away; this was believed to have a disinfectant effect. By the nineteenth century, with the advent of the germ theory of illness, Jews realized that it actually had the opposite effect. Today, a *mohel* will probably utilize a glass tube and a cotton swab. The *mohel* will put a sterile bandage on the incision and then the boy is dressed.

After the procedure, *kiddush* is recited and the baby is given his Hebrew name. Often the father and mother will offer a few words about the significance of the name they have chosen. Finally, as is the case after most joyous *mitzvot,* the family will offer a *se'udat mitzvot,* a festive meal in honor of the fulfillment of the covenant.

In modern America, most hospitals routinely circumcise newborn boys, and the Reform movement has reluctantly agreed to accept circumcisions performed by surgeons with a rabbi present. However, as writer Anita Diamant points out in *Living a Jewish Life,* a hospital circumcision is a cold thing, a surgical procedure—no more, no less—in which the baby may be strapped to a board to immobilize him, and left alone afterward.

One common form of anti-Semitic persecution in Jewish history has been the prohibition of circumcision. Antiochus Epiphanes, the Greek king who was the target of the Maccabees' revolt forbade it. So did the Roman emperors who governed Palestine in the second century C.E. The *brit milah* survived not because it served a medical purpose but because it was a mark, literally written on the flesh of all male Jews, of the covenant between God and Abraham.

BRIT HABAT—THE BABY-NAMING CEREMONY

If the *brit milah* is one of the oldest of Jewish customs, the *brit habat/*literally, *covenant of the daughter* is one of the newest, so new that there is no set ritual practice to speak of.[5] The ceremony has its roots in the rising tide of American feminism of the 1970s, a societal change that did not leave Judaism untouched. Many Jews were understandably upset that there was no ritual comparable to the *brit milah* to welcome a newborn girl.[6]

Jewish tradition has always held that women were explicitly included in the covenant with God. When Moses enumerates those who have been present for the Revelation at Sinai, he specifically includes women, children, and even the strangers who dwelt with the Hebrews (Deuteronomy 29:9–14), and just as definitely includes women as well as men when he outlines the dire fate that will befall those who turn their backs on the covenant.

Hence, it is entirely appropriate that the arrival of a new daughter should be cause for a celebration of her entering the *brit* as a Jewish child. There are numerous Sephardic traditions of just such celebrations. One such event is the *seder zeved habat/celebration of the gift of a daughter*. Among Spanish Jewish families it was the custom to hold a special party for the mother's recovery. And in Ashkenazi as well as Sephardic congregations, it is traditional to hold a baby-naming ceremony for a newborn girl during the Torah service immediately following birth, with a special *mi sheberakh* blessing for mother and child.

There is no set liturgy for the *brit habat*. But there are elements common to most of the various ceremonies that people are enacting for this joyous occasion. Whether performed in the home or the synagogue, eight days after birth or thirty, the celebrations contain some echoes of the *brit milah* but also some new traditions-in-the-making. Usually the service opens with the infant being brought into the room to a call of *B'rucha habah/Blessed is she who enters*. There will be prayers and readings by the parents and, usually, the rabbi. *Kiddush* may be made; there will certainly be a blessing for wine and a festive drink. Parents who want to find some physical expression of their affection and joy may wash the little girl's feet and hands, with an appropriate blessing. The parents will usually recite *Shehekheyanu*. In traditionally observant families there may be a party or *kiddush* at which the naming may occur; such an event may include a little speech by the parents explaining the name.

The *minhag/custom* for this celebration is still forming, but in many liberal congregations it is becoming a customary event, and the time is not too distant when a more formal liturgy will probably begin to take shape. After all, the *brit milah* ceremony only achieved its current shape in the Middle Ages after about a half-millennium of development. But, then, girls do mature faster than boys.

PIDYON HA-BEN

Judaism places great emphasis on the first products of natural processes. Shavuot not only celebrates the giving of the Torah but also the presentation of the first fruits. First things belong to God. "For every firstborn among the Israelites, man as well as beast is Mine," Adonai says in Numbers 8:17. Thus, the Israelites would offer even their own firstborn sons at the Temple. Of course, God did not want the lives of the firstborn, although the Canaanites actually *did* sacrifice their firstborn sons, a practice that is denounced in the Bible. Rather, the new father would offer a payment of five shekels to a priest of the Temple by way of redeeming the child, or one might donate some of the child's time for work in the Temple when he was older.

Among traditionally observant Jews, this practice is honored in a ceremony called *Pidyon Ha-Ben/Redemption of the Firstborn,* held thirty-one days after the child's birth.[7] (If the thirty-first day falls on Shabbat or a festival, it is held after *Havdalah.*) For many Orthodox families, this is an occasion for a major celebration, with friends and family in attendance, wine, food, and a *d'rash,* a talk on the week's Torah portion, or some other inspirational talk.

Not every firstborn son must be redeemed. The distinguishing characteristic of the firstborn son in terms of Jewish law is that he "opens up the womb"; consequently, a child delivered by cesarean section is not redeemed, nor is the first son who is not a firstborn child, or a firstborn son who has been preceded by a stillbirth or a miscarriage that occurs later than the third month.

In addition, a firstborn son who is a Levite is not redeemed. The reason for this exception goes all the way back to the Exodus from Egypt. Originally, the firstborn males were to serve as assistants to the priests in the Temple, but when the Israelites committed the sin of the Golden Calf, it was the Levites who distinguished themselves before Moses and the Almighty by not participating and by punishing the wrongdoers. As a result, they were given the privilege of working in the Temple with the *Kohanim,* the priestly caste. As a result, Levites hold a special place in the Temple service (in traditionally observant families and congregations).

It is the father's obligation to redeem the first son, although if he is unable to do so in person, he may delegate that responsibility. The father goes before a *kohen,* carrying his son on a silver tray, announcing that this is the firstborn of the child's mother, usually quoting the verse from Numbers that outlines the duty of redeeming the boy. The *kohen* then asks if he prefers to give him the son or to redeem him for five shekels. The father says he will redeem the boy, then gives the *kohen* five silver coins. (*Kohanim* generally keep silver coins on hand specifically for this ritual. The Bank of Israel now mints shekel silver pieces for just this purpose.) The father will recite the blessing for *pidyon ha-ben* and *Shehekheyanu,* then hands the coins to the *kohen.* The *kohen* passes the coins over the child's head, reciting the following formula:

> This [the money] is in place of that [the child]. This is excused on account of that. May it be that this son has entered into life, into Torah, and into fear of God. May it be [God's] will that just as he has entered into redemption, so may he enter into Torah, into marriage, and into good deeds.

The *kohen* completes the ritual with the Priestly Blessing.

The rite of *pidyon ha-ben* is generally not observed by Reform Jews. On the other hand, unlike the *brit milah,* there is nothing inherently gender-specific about the ceremony, and today many liberal Jews— Conservative and Reconstructionist and even a few Reform—will perform it for a firstborn child regardless of gender.

PARENT AND CHILD

The relationship between parent and child in Judaism is an intricate dance of responsibilities and obligations. In the Bible, the Talmud, and subsequent works of Jewish law and ethics, this relationship is defined and refined in myriad ways.

For example, although the Bible says that the children will suffer for their parents' sins "unto the third and fourth generation" (Exodus 20:5), the rabbis of the Talmud softened this by saying that it was intended to refer only to those children who followed in the wickedness of their parents. Similarly, although the Bible calls for the death of a rebellious son (Deuteronomy 21:18–21), the rabbis say that the intention was not to literally bring about the execution of the son but to express the extreme distaste with which such behavior was to be regarded. Such are the strong emotions evoked in Jewish thought by the interplay of parent and child.

Each of the parents is allotted a role in the raising of children, according to the classic Jewish literature, although legal obligations rest primarily with the father. A father is enjoined to educate his children in Judaism, to teach them right from wrong, to redeem the firstborn, to have his male offspring circumcised. He is instructed to teach his children to swim and to teach his son a trade, "otherwise it will be as if he had taught him to be a thief," as one Talmudic sage puts it. He is not legally obligated to see to his daughter's wedding under Jewish law, but he is required to provide her with clothing and the means to make herself marriageable. Likewise, he is required to find a wife for his son.

A mother's obligations in a traditionally observant Jewish household are somewhat less specifically spelled out, in part because the sages always believed that a mother would, by her nature, be more concerned with her children's upbringing and well-being. She is obligated to breastfeed her child unless the father can afford to hire a wet nurse (although today she may be permitted to use formula). She is generally held responsible for the teaching of domestic duties to her daughters and with instilling in them a knowledge of Judaism.

For all the vagueness with which the Talmudic rabbis delineated the mother's role in the Jewish home, clearly she is at its center. Richard Llewellyn says of his Welsh family in *How Green Was My Valley,* "If my father was the head of the family, my mother was its heart." So, too, in the Jewish home. It is the mother with whom the children had the most direct day-to-day contact. As an old Jewish proverb has it, "God could not be everywhere, so mothers were created."

The obligations of children toward their parents are clearly among the most important in all of Judaism. After all, the commandment to "honor your father and mother," is in the Decalogue, and is repeated in various forms elsewhere in the Bible. Children are instructed to honor and to revere their parents, and the responsibilities that attach to those verbs are spelled out quite explicitly. Talmud teaches that to honor one's parents, a child should provide food, drink, clothing, and transportation for parents; to show them respect, one must not sit in their chair, interrupt them, or take the other side in a dispute. Of course, most of these obligations devolve on adult children and become salient only as parents age, but Jewish thought does not absolve younger children of their obligations. And these obligations extend beyond the grave; one should say *Kaddish* for dead parents and mark the anniversary of their deaths. To honor one's parents is to honor God. On the other hand, if a parent counsels her child to violate Jewish law, it is permissible—indeed, expected—that the child will disregard that counsel.

Intriguingly, nowhere in the literature does it say that a child must *love* her parents. The rabbis assumed that parents would love their children, but did not expect or insist that that love be returned. Still, they urged the principle of *shalom bayit/peace in the home;* domestic harmony is greatly valued in Jewish law and thought. By and large, they hoped that such harmony would be achieved through the working out of the dance of mutual responsibilities and through the observation of *mitzvot* and the rituals of the Jewish year.

JEWISH EDUCATION

The Hebrew word used for the concept of education is *khinukh*. The word translates not only as education but also as consecration and, in its use to denote education, means not learning a trade but training for life itself. The distinction is a significant one.

The Jews are often called the "People of the Book"; although the name refers to the centrality of Torah to Jewish thought and life, it also gives an accurate picture of the Jewish home. Whether Reform, Reconstructionist, Conservative, or Orthodox, many Jewish-American families fill their homes with volumes of Jewish lore, history, and religious thought. It is also in the home that a child first encounters the rituals of the Jewish faith.

It is no accident that the Talmud says that it is a parent's responsibility to see that children are raised and educated in Judaism. Jewish education begins in the home. But when?

In Jewish homes in which religion plays a part, children are exposed to prayer at an early age, regardless of the level of observance in the family. From a *halakhic* standpoint, a child's education is supposed to begin at three, and one should teach a child at the least to say the simpler *b'rakhot* then. The Mishnah says that boys are to begin the study of Torah at age five, Mishnah at age ten, and Talmud at fifteen. (Through the medieval period and, in most Jewish communities well into the nineteenth century, girls were given no formal schooling, but were instructed in Judaism by their mothers. Needless to say, this is no longer the case, even in the most rigorously ultra-Orthodox community.)

A child's initiation into Judaism generally will begin very early. Even the very young can be taught to recite the *Sh'ma,* as the Torah instructs, "You shall teach it . . . unto your children." In four separate places in the Torah, God says that it is a father's responsibility to recount for his offspring the story of the Exodus from Egypt. As we have seen in the discussion of Pesakh, retelling this story for the benefit of the children is central to the *seder.*

For many children the first exposure to organized Jewish worship will take place at services designed specifically for youngsters; using a somewhat simplified liturgy, these services are usually marked by a dialogue between the rabbi and the children. Although the children's service as an institution is unknown in Israel, it is one of the more useful innovations of the Diaspora, spurred in large part by the Reform movement, which first experimented with shortened prayer services for children in the mid-nineteenth century. Eventually, the idea was adopted by Conservative and even Orthodox congregations as well.

The educational system that Judaism offers to its young has its roots in the first century B.C.E., when Rabbi Simeon ben Shetakh established the first schools and ordered parents to send their children to them. But it was in the first century C.E. that Rabbi Joseph ben Gamla, the High Priest of the Second Temple in Jerusalem until its destruction in 70 C.E., arranged for towns to have their own teachers with the result that education became a community function rather than a family one exclusively. (These may have been the first such community-sponsored schools in the history of Western civilization.) Until then, fathers taught sons as their fathers had taught them, but a boy without a father had no way to learn. As a result, from the period of the fall of the Second Temple until the *Haskalah* in the nineteenth century, most male Jews received at least some schooling and the rate of literacy among Jewish men was considerably higher than in the general population.

It should be noted, however, that for many of these young men the sole subject of their education was the sacred texts of Judaism. This was not always the case. The Spanish Jews of the medieval period were highly educated in both sacred and secular subjects and many of the great minds of the medieval period were educated Jews like Maimonides, who was not only a rigorous neo-Aristotelian philosopher but a trained physician as well. On the other hand, in much of the world, whether the Jewish schools regarded secular learning as useful or not, non-Jewish majorities produced laws prohibiting Jews from engaging in secular study.

Our image of the day-to-day life of a young boy in a *kheyder*, literally "a room," but used to refer to the small one-room schoolhouses in which most Jewish boys were educated in the villages of Eastern Europe, is shaped primarily by our reading of popular authors like Sholem Aleichem. We are told of dark, dank schoolrooms presided over by an impecunious *melamed/Hebrew teacher*, sharp-tongued and quick to whack the knuckles of a slow student with a ruler. Of course, there is no more or less truth to that picture of rural education in the eighteenth- and nineteenth-century *shtetl* (Yiddish word of a small Jewish village; pl. *shtetlakh*) than there is to the picture of rural education in nineteenth-century Middle America given in *Tom Sawyer*.

The *kheyder* was not a school in the sense that we know it. A student might progress from one teacher to another as he grew older and even might eventually go on to a yeshiva to study sacred texts when he reached his teens. However, most of these boys would enter the labor market with minimal education (although probably more than their Polish or Russian counterparts of the era). In larger communities, a *Talmud Torah* (literally "study of Torah"), an organized school, might exist but again its focus would be almost exclusively on Talmud, Torah, and other Jewish texts. It would only be in the nineteenth century that the yeshiva, an organized school with a series of grades through which students progressed, began to flourish in Eastern Europe.

By contrast, with the rise of the *Haskalah* in Western Europe and the emancipation of Jewish populations a more common phenomenon, Jewish children in Western Europe increasingly found themselves in schools that combined religious and secular studies. As Jews were permitted to enter public schools in Western Europe and North America, religious education became supplementary to rather than privileged over secular studies. Jewish children might only receive religious training one or two afternoons a week, after public school, or on Sundays.

For the sons of the Orthodox in America, however, things were very different. They were educated in yeshivot (plural of yeshiva) in which secular classes were offered only because the state compelled it. Yet the yeshivot were not there to train rabbis. They were designed to ingrain a love of Jewish learning, so that the study of Talmud would be a lifelong adventure, and the Talmudic frame of reference would be a reflex.

For a long time, Jewish-American day schools would remain an Orthodox phenomenon exclusively. In the period after World War II, however, the Conservative movement came to believe that day schools were a necessary part of transmitting Jewish values and commitment to its children and it began establishing its own network of Solomon Schechter schools. In recent years, even the Reform movement, which has been wary of the separatism implied in the creation of exclusively Jewish day schools in pluralist America, has changed its position and begun to create Reform counterparts to the Schechter schools and the Orthodox *Torah U-Mesorah* program.

Jewish education for girls is a relatively recent development. From its outset, Reform Judaism rejected discrimination on the basis of gender and offered its female offspring the same educational opportunities available to boys. However, it was only in the twentieth century that the other streams of Judaism began to follow suit. Today, even Orthodox girls receive classroom training in Judaism at all levels of education. There is still a division within Orthodox ranks over the appropriateness of teaching Talmud to girls; in Modern Orthodox and Lubavitch Hasidic schools, this is now the practice, but in other traditional schools it is not.

BAR / BAT MITZVAH

Let's get one thing straight right away. *Bar mitzvah* means "son of the commandment." (*Bar* is the Aramaic term for son.) *Bat mitzvah* means "daughter of the commandment." No one gets *"bar mitzvahed"* or *"bat mitzvahed."* That would be like saying you were "sonned" or "daughtered." Or maybe "commandmented."

When I turned 13, I "became" a *bar mitzvah*.

This is not an idle piece of grammatical nitpicking. In fact, it goes to the heart of the meaning of the terms *bar* and *bat mitzvah*. A boy achieves that status by the mere fact of having turned thirteen, a girl by turning twelve. No more, no less. No special ceremony is necessary to be a *bar mitzvah;* all you have to do is reach the right age.

That said, it is necessary to acknowledge that, in fact, this is a momentous event in the life of a Jewish boy or girl and well worthy of celebration. The designated ages are the ones at which a Jew is considered by Jewish law to be able and ready to fulfill the *mitzvot,* the central tenets of the Jewish religion. Not only ready and able but obligated to do so. In the eyes of religious law, he is no longer a minor but an adult both permitted to enjoy the religious privileges and responsible for the religious transgressions he may commit. In essence, he is now a full-fledged recipient of the religious heritage of the Jewish people and member of the community.

The *bar mitzvah* ceremony has taken on its current importance only in the past hundred or so years. Its origins are unclear; it is mentioned in neither the Tanakh nor the Talmud (although the term *bar mitzvah* does occur in the Talmud, referring only to one who observes the commandments). In fact, there is no evidence of the *bar mitzvah* ceremony before 1400. However, the Talmud does specify that adolescence for a male child begins at thirteen years and one day.

In its earliest versions, the *bar mitzvah* ceremony consisted of a boy wearing *tefillin* for the first time and receiving his first *aliyah,* perhaps even reading from the Torah scroll. In Western Europe, a thirteen-year-old would say the blessing for the reading of the Torah, would chant *maftir,* and also the *haftarah.* Gradually other Jewish communities came to regard that set of responsibilities as the standard. After his son had completed the second Torah blessing, the boy's father would recite the *Barukh she-petarni,* a prayer in which he acknowledged his son's new status and asked to be absolved of responsibility for any of the boy's future sins.

Over time, the *bar mitzvah* ceremony became more elaborate, with the boy chanting not only *maftir* but the entire Torah portion. The event was moved from a weekday morning service to Shabbat, although it can take place on Monday or Thursday, the other days on which Torah is read in synagogue. Some boys would lead the *Kabbalat Shabbat* the night before. More would deliver a *d'rash* on the week's portion on Saturday morning. The family-sponsored *kiddush* grew in size from a modest offering to the congregation for the Third Sabbath Meal into the occasionally excessive celebration it is today.

Rabbi Mordecai Kaplan, visionary as usual, found the exclusion of girls from this rite of passage troublesome, to say the least. In response he promoted the *bat mitzvah* ceremony; in 1922 his daughter Judith became the first girl to undergo the ceremony. For many years in most Conservative congregations the *bat mitzvah* ceremony took place on Friday night, with the girl reading from the *haftarah*. Today, the ceremony has evolved to the point that it is indistinguishable from its male counterpart. Even many Modern Orthodox congregations now perform *b'not mitzvah* (the plural of *bat mitzvah*), albeit significantly different from those one sees in Reform, Reconstructionist, and Conservative synagogues.

CONFIRMATION

Confirmation is a practice devised by the early Reform movement, originally designed to supplant the *bar mitzvah* ceremony. First introduced by one of the movement's pioneers, Rabbi Israel Jacobson, in his German congregation in 1810, it originally bore more than a faint resemblance to German Protestant rites of passage. *Bar Mitzvah* proved a hardier ritual than the early Reformers had realized, gradually enjoying a resurgence in Reform congregations until, today, it is the more important event of the two.

The difference between *bar mitzvah* and confirmation is more than just the difference between a thirteen-year-old boy or girl and a high school student. *Bar mitzvah* is a celebration of individual achievement and a family affair; but it also marks the recognition of a passage that is not chosen. Confirmation is a celebration of and by the community, a group ceremony whose primary content is intellectual and spiritual, marking an acceptance and affirmation of one's Jewishness.

The Confirmation ceremony takes place as part of the Shavuot service. The confirmands in a Conservative congregation are called *b'nei Torah* and *b'not Torah,* sons and daughters of the Torah. There is no set liturgy for this event, but the young men and women are encouraged to participate actively in the planning and performance of the festival service as a mark of their commitment to Judaism.

ENGAGEMENT AND MARRIAGE

THE JEWISH VIEW OF MARRIAGE

It is no accident that the term for the marriage ceremony in Hebrew is *kiddushin / sanctification*. Marriage is viewed by Judaism as a sacred act, also an imperative one. In the time of the Temple, the High Priest was not permitted to conduct the Yom Kippur rites if he was unmarried. The sages who wrote and compiled the Talmud were invariably married men. The Talmud states explicitly that one of the duties of a father is to see his son to the altar and to provide enough material support that his daughter will be marriageable. Even God is "married" to the Jewish people; in Hosea 2:21, Adonai says, "I will betroth you unto Me forever." Similarly, we greet the Sabbath as a bride. Such is the power and holiness of marriage in Jewish thought.

Marriage as an institution is as much the creation of God as anything in the Torah. "It is not good for man to be alone," the Creator says of Adam in Genesis 2:18 before creating Eve as his companion. By investing marriage with a Divine origin, Judaism gives it even greater weight and sanctity.

At the same time, marriage is a legal, contractual agreement. Traditionally, the marriage contract represents the agreement of a woman to give up a portion of her legal autonomy in return for a promise of financial support and other rights that she receives from a man. A Jewish marriage contract *(ketubah)* is made between two autonomous entities, man and woman; but there is a *quid pro quo* here, an arrangement negotiated between equals—to an extent.

The Mishnah quotes Torah to the effect that a man "acquires" a wife, but the Talmud glosses the Mishnah, making it clear that a wife is not property. The husband will be the contracting party, the one who executes the contract. But it becomes effective only when the wife accepts it. (For a more detailed discussion of the contract itself, see sidebar "The *Ketubah*," p. 161.) Even in an arranged marriage between minors, the girl always had the right to refuse to accept her putative fiancé.

Jewish men are obligated by the Talmud and the marriage contract to provide their wives with food; clothing; medical care; conjugal relations; ransom if she is kidnapped; suitable burial if she dies first, or support from his estate and the right to live in his house if he dies first; a fund for the support of his daughters until they marry if he dies before that event; a sum of money mandated in the *ketubah;* and that same sum to her sons in addition to whatever they inherit if she dies before her husband.

Jewish women, in turn, are obligated by the Talmud to provide earnings from her labor (if any); any ownerless object she finds while out of the house; profits from her capital, but only for purposes of the household (and not including the capital itself); and the right to inherit her estate. Jewish law has always permitted women to own property and to enter into contracts, even after marriage. Additionally, it explicitly proscribes husbands from beating their wives, forcing them to have sex, or restricting their free movement.

These dual obligations may seem insignificant to some today, but as a foundation stone on which the Jewish marriage was built two thousand years ago, they constituted an impressively progressive beginning. Even today, at least on paper, from the most *frum/strictly observant* to the most Reform, Jewish marriage laws are designed to protect the rights of wives. (Divorce, as we will see in the next section of this chapter, can be a rather different story.)

THE *KETUBAH*

Long before there was an organized feminist movement, Jewish law made some tentative moves towards protecting the rights of married women. As far back as the Book of Exodus and continuing through the Talmud, certain rights and obligations incumbent on husbands were spelled out explicitly. But the document that protected those rights the most thoroughly, indeed, the oldest surviving institutionalization of a woman's marriage and divorce rights, is the *ketubah,* the marriage certificate that is signed and handed to the bride during a Jewish wedding ceremony. The obligations outlined in the *ketubah* (literally, "the writing") are statutory and therefore binding under Jewish law.

The oldest known example of a *ketubah* dates back to the fifth century B.C.E.; its terms are not significantly different from those to be found in a contemporary Orthodox wedding certificate.

A traditional *ketubah* will usually include the following provisions:

- A provision for the maintenance of the wife after divorce, to be paid in a lump sum; the amount is supposed to be equivalent to the amount needed to support her for one year.

- The value of the property the bride brings to the marriage; the husband may enjoy the income accrued from this property, but in a divorce he must repay the principal.
- An additional amount pledged by the husband, the *"tosefet ketubah/additional ketubah."*
- A woman's *ketubah* acts as a lien on her husband's property, a mortgage, as it were, assuring her ability to collect in the event of his death or their divorce.

In recent years, rabbis have begun supplying couples with a "plain-English" summation of the obligations of the husband.

The Talmud states explicitly that the purpose of the *ketubah* was to make sure that "it should not be easy for a husband to divorce his wife," a protection that is necessary under Jewish law since only the husband can initiate a divorce.

Beginning sometime in the tenth or eleventh century, it became common for *ketubot* (the plural) to be executed in beautifully illuminated versions, often decorated with biblical verses that were appropriate to the nature of the occasion. Different schools of illumination developed reflecting the artistic bent of the Diaspora communities in which they were designed. Since the 1960s, there has been something of a renaissance of the hand-painted *ketubah*, with many couples hanging their *ketubot* in the home as a work of art with a highly personal emotional significance.

The Conservative movement has in recent years introduced a passage into their *ketubot* in which both husband and wife agree to accept the decision of the *bet din*, the rabbinical court, in matters regarding divorce. The Reform movement has replaced the traditional *ketubah* with a more modern "egalitarian" version, focusing more on the interpersonal obligations of marriage and less on the financial and legal ones. Given the history of the document as the first real assertion of a woman's rights in marriage, that seems an eminently logical and just development within Reform tradition.

ENGAGEMENT

Today, arranged marriages put together by a *shadkhan/matchmaker* are a rarity in all but ultra-Orthodox families. Even in those families, though, the parents ultimately have no authority to force a marriage, nor do they have the right to veto their children's choice of spouse. There are still, however, some marriages that are prohibited by Jewish law, usually for reasons of consanguinity. (See sidebar "Prohibited Marriages," p. 169.)

Among ultra-Orthodox Jews the custom of bestowing a dowry (*nadan* in Hebrew) is still observed. It often takes the form today of the *kest,* a promise to support the new son-in-law while he studies at the yeshiva. Even in previous centuries a great scholar or the scion of an important rabbinical line was considered a greater catch than a rich ignoramus; the *kest* is one of the more benevolent fruits of that attitude.

Jewish engagements are like anyone else's; they can last a week, or they can last several years. (You may be old enough to remember Milton Berle's running jokes about his sister's several-decades-long engagement.) Among Orthodox Jews, however, engagements are short; once the decision has been made, and an engagement document signed, there is no reason to delay a *simkha/joyous event* and, given that Orthodox couples will have no physical contact before the marriage, it also seems the considerate thing to do for young people.

The choice of a wedding date is bit thornier for Jews than for non-Jews. Even in Reform Judaism, one does not get married on certain days. Among the proscribed days are Shabbat, the festivals, the High Holy Days, and the Ten Days of Repentance. In addition, more traditionally observant Jews will not get married during the Omer period (except on Lag b'Omer or, in Zionist circles, Yom Ha'atzma'ut or Yom Yerushalayim), the Three Weeks mourning period, or any major or minor fast day. Additionally, because an Orthodox man is forbidden to come in contact with his wife when she is menstruating, Orthodox couples will try to time a wedding to her menstrual cycle.

BEFORE THE CEREMONY

The Shabbat before the wedding both Orthodox and non-Orthodox Jewish couples will enjoy a ritual called the *aufruf,* a Yiddish word that means "calling up." The groom (and in non-Orthodox congregations usually the bride as well) is called to the Torah for an *aliyah.* After he has completed the second of the blessings for the reading of the Torah, he will be pelted from all sides by candy, symbolic of the congregation's wishes for a sweet future for the couple. (In Israel they throw candy at *bar mitzvah* ceremonies as well.)

The day before the wedding, a traditionally observant bride will visit the *mikveh/ritual bath* to immerse herself. In the *shtetlakh*, she would often be accompanied to the door by *klezmorim*, the itinerant musicians that could be found all over Eastern Europe and hired for just such events.

On the day of an Orthodox wedding, just before the ceremony itself, the *ketubah* is signed by two witnesses. This is followed by a *t'nayim/conditions*, a legal contract between the parents agreeing that their children will be married; after the *t'nayim* is read aloud, the two mothers will break a dish, a symbol of the irreversible nature of the decision that has been made. (Since the engagement document was written to be difficult to abrogate if the couple changed their minds, this ceremony is now held off until the day of the wedding, but in the past it may have been done in advance, when the engagement was announced.)

Now the groom is escorted from the room by a phalanx of male friends who sing to him, walking backwards before him, "clearing the way" for him to go to his bride for the *bedeken*, a Yiddish word that literally means "bedecking." He is taken to the room where the bride is waiting and there he lowers her bridal veil over her face.

In non-Orthodox weddings, few of these rituals are observed except for the signing of the *ketubah*. Instead, we proceed to the wedding itself.

THE WEDDING CEREMONY

The groom at a Jewish wedding may wear a *tallit*, depending on the custom of the community; in an Orthodox wedding, he will usually also wear a *kittel*, a white robe that he will wear from then on at Yom Kippur, at the Pesakh *seder*, and, eventually, to his own burial. In Ashkenazi tradition, the *tallit* will be his first, a gift from his bride. The groom will take his place first, the bride stands to his right.

Jewish wedding ceremonies essentially have two parts, the *kiddushin* (here, the betrothal) and the *nisu'in/nuptials*. The first part designates for the community that the *kallah/bride* and *khatan/groom* are for one another only; the second gives them to one another. Ten centuries ago, these were two separate ceremonies, often with as much as a year between them, but today they are one continuous event.

A Jewish wedding begins with the parents of both bride and groom leading their children to the *khupah/marriage canopy*. The *khupah* can be no more than a *talit* supported by four poles held by friends of the couple, or it may be a more elaborate embroidered cloth. There is no "giving away" of the bride; she is not the property of her father, and the wedding unites not just individuals but two families. Usually, this processional will be accompanied by music, sometimes by members of the wedding party leading the way with candles. The *khupah* symbolizes the couple's new home, open to the community in which they will be included and which they will want to include. A *minyan* must be present.

When they have come under the *khupah,* the bride will circle the groom either three or seven times (depending on the community's *minhag*). Some communities have abandoned this ritual because of its suggestions of female subservience to the husband. Others, conversely, have the groom repeat the ritual, or have each circle the other while they hold hands.

Now the rabbi (or whoever is conducting the ceremony[8]) introduces the couple to the guests, then recites a prayer asking for God's blessing on their union, *Mi Adir*. As is the custom at so many joyous occasions, a blessing is said over a glass of wine, as is a special blessing for the *nisui'in/nuptials,* after which the bride and groom drink wine together.

The groom places the wedding ring on his bride's finger, reciting:

"Harai at mekudeshet li, b'taba-at zu, k'dat Moshe v'Yisroel."

"Be sanctified to me with this ring, according to the laws of Moses and Israel."

In some modern ceremonies, she will do the same. Her acceptance of the ring constitutes her consenting to become his wife; two qualified witnesses are required for this part of the ceremony. Jews traditionally have eschewed all but the most simple of wedding rings. A ring with a stone or other gaudy ornamentation calls attention to its value, and raises the possibility of fraud. Only gold marked with its weight in karats is used for the same reason. The ring must belong solely to the groom. If the ring is a family heirloom, it must be "purchased" by the groom with a token sum. (Today, particularly at liberal Jewish weddings, the bride may also present the groom with a ring.)

This is the point at which the two halves of the ceremony were joined in the eleventh century. Usually the break between them is demarcated by a reading of the *ketubah*. Often the rabbi will make a short speech and members of the wedding will offer personal prayers, songs, poems, etc.

The second half of the ceremony, the *nisu'in,* begins with the recital of the *sheva b'rakhot / seven blessings.* The blessings, prescribed in the Talmud, are for:

- wine

- Creation

- the creation of humanity

- the creation of the human ability to reproduce

- the future joy of Zion and her children

- the joy of the bride and groom

- love, kinship, peace, friendship, and the sound of happy wedding couples in a restored Jerusalem

Only two of the blessings relate to marriage, but taken together, they serve to place the joy of the wedding in the larger context of Jewish history and belief, from Eden to the Messianic future and the promise of a return to Zion.

There is one part of the Jewish wedding ceremony that everyone, even non-Jews, seems to be familiar with, and it comes now: the groom is handed a glass (or a lightbulb or plate) covered in a white cloth; he places it on the ground and steps on it with his right heel, shattering it. There are several reasons given for this custom. The most common explanation is that the breaking of the glass reminds us of the destruction of the Temple, a sign of mourning; often the verse, "If I forget thee, O Jerusalem," will be recited or sung before the glass is broken. Some suggest that it is a superstition designed to allay the jealousies of evil spirits. Another possible explanation is an anthropological one, that it symbolizes the taking of the bride's virginity, which will follow not long after the wedding ceremony.

Regardless of the reason, the sound of the glass breaking triggers a rising wave of shouts of *Mazel tov / Good luck!* and music. In Orthodox tradition, the men who led the groom to the *bedeken* will now lead the couple back down the aisle; they are given a few minutes together in *yikhud / seclusion*. *Yikhud* is a legal requirement to the marriage, symbolizing its consummation. A wedding dinner traditionally follows, no matter what branch of Judaism is involved, preceded by the appropriate blessings. In traditionally observant families and congregations, the *sheva b'rakhot* will be repeated as part of *Birkat ha-Mazon / Grace After Meals*.

While other Jewish couples may follow their wedding with a honeymoon, the Orthodox newlyweds will spend the next week being feted at the homes of friends. These festive meals, and the week following the wedding in which they take place, are also called the *sheva b'rakhot*, and the blessings will be repeated in *Birkat ha-Mazon / Grace After Meals* at each of those meals.

LEVIRATE MARRIAGE

In ancient times when the survival of children could not be taken for granted, and the continuance of a family line was largely a matter of luck, the death of a man before he fathered children was considered a particularly unfortunate loss to the community and the family. The Torah declares marriage between a woman and brother-in-law to be incestuous except when her husband has died under precisely those circumstances. Then, in the interest of keeping the family name and line intact, she is required to marry the brother. Such a marriage is called *yibum* in Hebrew, or levirate marriage (from *levir*, the Latin for husband's brother).

Despite the biblical nature of this law, the rabbis of the Talmud were manifestly uncomfortable with the notion of such a union, particularly if it were only for religious purposes. To them it smacked of incest, regardless of its legal roots. As a result, rabbinic law requires the surviving brother to release his sister-in-law to marry someone else. The ceremony governing this release is called *khalitzah*, and must be conducted by a *bet din*.

Today, only the Orthodox recognize levirate marriage and the need for *khalitzah*.

INTERMARRIAGE

Intermarriage is a painful subject for Jews. When the 1990 National Population Survey conducted by the UJA-Federation of Jewish Philanthropies showed a fifty-two percent intermarriage rate, accompanied by a steady decline in the number of such families that raised their children as Jews, alarm bells went off all over Jewish communities in the United States. For a moment, let us put aside the issues in Jewish law that are raised by intermarriage—and there are several—to concentrate on the issue that concerns Jews in their gut, the question of Jewish continuity in North America.

Jewish history is a long string of socio-political traumas inflicted on Jewish communities from outside. Whether one buys into the idea expressed by some ultra-Orthodox rabbis that the destruction of the two Temples in Jerusalem, mass murder of Jews in Western Europe during the Crusades, pogroms against the Jews in Eastern Europe over a three-hundred-year period and, finally, the *Shoah,* are divine punishment against us for not following Torah, there is no question that our continued existence in this world has always been at risk.

Yet we have survived for four thousand years, survived where dozens of "greater" civilizations, empires, have disappeared—the Persians, Greeks, Romans, Macedonians, Babylonians, Mongols each had their moment on the world stage, then faded back into the history books. But the Jews persevered and survived.

How ironic, then, if the force that finally destroys this four-millennium-old heritage were to be the greater freedom and acceptance that we have won in pluralistic societies like America and Canada, if an inattentiveness to our own traditions is what finally causes them to wither away.

Will this happen? Hard to say, but it appears to most Jewish activists to be the choice the Jewish communities of North America are facing.

Very few American rabbis will officiate at interfaith ceremonies. Couples who find themselves unable to obtain a rabbi to perform their wedding should be cognizant of Jewish law governing such a union. A Jewish wedding is a legal, contractual event. As we have seen in this chapter, when a bride accepts the ring from her groom, she is acknowledging acceptance of a contract binding under Jewish law. If only one of the parties is bound by Jewish law, how can the marriage have legal standing under that law?

The major function of marriage in the eyes of Jewish law is to establish and promulgate Jewish homes and families. If children born to non-Jewish mothers are not Jewish under Jewish law, if recent surveys show that the children of mixed marriages seldom identify themselves as Jews (regardless of which parent was Jewish), one can understand the unwillingness of rabbis to perform such ceremonies.

Still, within the Reform movement, there are qualms and misgivings about the blanket refusal to solemnize intermarriages. There are rabbis who will perform such weddings if the couple agree to raise their children as Jews, to create a Jewish home. (There are also rabbis who will perform a wedding if the couple are not planning to have children.) There are some who argue that to turn such couples away is to send the message that Judaism isn't interested in retaining them in the faith. And the Reform movement recently took the further step of recognizing patrilineal descent in cases of mixed marriage in which the children have been raised in the Jewish faith. The wider implications of that decision are being much discussed (see sidebar "Who Is a Jew?" p. 177).

Of course, if the non-Jewish spouse in an intermarriage is prepared to convert to Judaism, he or she will find full acceptance in any Jewish community. A marriage between a Jew-by-birth and a Jew-by-choice is a marriage between two Jews, not an intermarriage.

PROHIBITED MARRIAGES

There are numerous marriages that are prohibited by biblical law and Talmudic law. Many of these prohibitions are also found in civil law. The following table of prohibited marriages enumerates those proscriptions that are recognized by all branches of Judaism.

PROHIBITED DUE TO DEGREE OF CONSANGUINITY:
1. Mother, grandmother (both paternal and maternal)
2. Daughter
3. Granddaughter; son's or daughter's granddaughter
4. Sister and half-sister
5. Father's sister; grandfather's sister
6. Mother's sister; grandmother's sister

PROHIBITED DUE TO DEGREE OF AFFINITY:

Through one's own marriage:

7. Wife's mother; wife's grandmother; wife's stepmother (not prohibited but considered objectionable)
8. Wife's daughter (stepdaughter)
9. Wife's granddaughter
10. Wife's sister (during wife's lifetime, in case of divorce)

Through marriage of near–blood relation:

11. Father's wife (stepmother); father's or mother's stepmother
12. Father's brother's wife; mother's brother's wife; father's uterine brother's wife
13. Son's wife; grandson's or great-grandson's wife
14. Brother's wife (except in case of levirate marriage)

Traditionally observant Jews are bound by a further set of prohibitions. They are not permitted to marry under the following circumstances:

1. A man may not marry a woman who has not received a *get* and therefore is not divorced under Jewish law.
2. A *kohen* is forbidden to marry a divorcee, a proselyte, a woman known to be promiscuous, the offspring of a forbidden marriage between a *kohen* and any woman falling into one of the forbidden categories, or a woman released through *khalitzah*.

DIVORCE

Given the sanctity with which it approaches marriage, it is no surprise that Judaism considers divorce a grave step. As it says in the Talmud, "When a man puts aside the wife of his youth, even the very altar weeps." But Judaism is nothing if not realistic and recognized from its earliest days that divorce would happen; although marriage is *kiddushin/holy,* a deeply unhappy marriage is not holy. "[T]he law of divorce is given for the peace of [humanity] and the unity of the family," says one contemporary Orthodox scholar. "Those who divorce when they must, bring good upon themselves, not evil."

Divorce has always been possible in Judaism, but it has had a legal character so that it cannot be entered into lightly. It is regarded as a last resort whose invocation is nothing less than tragic. In Malachi 2:14—

16, the eponymous prophet declares, "For I hate divorce, says Adonai, the God of Israel." He characterizes it as an act of treachery, a betrayal of the covenant between husband and wife.

That said, it must be noted that in Jewish law it is the husband's exclusive prerogative to divorce. The divorce decree must be given in writing, a *sefer keritut,* literally, a "book of cutting off," referred to in the Talmud as a *get.* The husband must deliver it into his wife's hand.

In their establishment of the grounds for divorce, the rabbis of the Mishnaic period (first century B.C.E.) disagreed. As was often the case in disputes over the interpretation of Jewish law, the School of Shammai took a narrow, strict view, counterposed by the more lenient School of Hillel. The followers of Shammai argued that the passage that said a man could divorce his wife only if "he finds some unseemly quality" in her, specifically and solely meant, in cases of marital infidelity. But the School of Hillel read this passage more broadly, arguing that a wife could be divorced for displeasing him even by an act as trivial as burning the soup. As was usually the case, the School of Hillel won out; Hillel's argument was, in fact, probably designed to protect the rights of the wife, making it possible for a divorced woman to remarry without someone assuming that her first marriage had ended because of some truly spectacular misconduct on her part.

Regardless, Jewish law favored the husband in divorce proceedings from its inception. The Mishnah was not utterly devoid of solicitude for wives; a man who "is afflicted with boils or a bad odor, or who works with malodorous material" could be compelled to grant his wife a divorce. As the Talmud reinterpreted Mishnah, the rabbis redressed the imbalance somewhat further. A number of circumstances were established under which the rabbinical court could compel the husband to grant a divorce: if a wife remained barren after ten years of marriage; if a husband contracted a "loathsome" disease; if a husband refused to or proved unable to support his wife; if a husband refused to have sex with his wife; if a husband was a wife-beater, even after having been warned by the court to stop.

A further improvement (at least in Ashkenazi communities) occurred around 1000, when Rabbenu Gershom issued a *takanah,* a rabbinical enactment, stating that a wife could not be divorced without her consent. For all intents and purposes, divorce now could only be the product of an agreement between both spouses. About 150 years later, Rabbi Jacob Tam issued a *takanah* that provided for some narrow exceptions in emergencies. For instance, if a woman left the Jewish faith and therefore could ignore a summons to appear before a rabbinical court, the husband would be allowed to deposit a *get* before the court without her approval.

The process by which a Jewish divorce is granted is a relatively simple one (particularly when compared to civil divorce in some states). A *bet din,* literally "house of judgment," a rabbinical court consisting of three rabbis competent in the laws governing marriage and divorce, must be convened. A *sofer/scribe* and two witnesses should be present. They must be disinterested parties (and practicing Jews). Members of the *bet din* may serve as witnesses if no one else is available. If a civil divorce has already been granted, the rabbinical court will accept that the two parties are amenable to the divorce and will not inquire into the grounds or the financial settlement.

The manner in which the rabbis approach a divorce is meticulous in the extreme. The rabbi will ascertain with great precision the names of the individuals divorcing—including nicknames—so that no one could possibly misconstrue the people meant. The description of the location at which the divorce occurred is also treated with precision. The river on which the city is situated is included in the document (since more than one city could have the same name) and divorces cannot be executed in cities where this detail is not clear.

The rabbis will interview both husband and wife to ascertain that each consents of his/her free will to the divorce. In the Diaspora, the participation of a Jew in such a court is purely voluntary; only in Israel does the (Orthodox) rabbinate actually control matters of marriage and divorce. If the divorce is granted, the *sofer* draws up the *get,* a document in Hebrew, hand-lettered like a column from the Torah. There is no "form" *get;* each one is unique to the proceeding, a way of discouraging thoughtless divorce. Once the proceedings, which take about 90 minutes, are completed and the document has been delivered to the wife, either by the husband or a messenger of his appointment (which may include a member of the *bet din*), one of the rabbis will tear the *get,* thereby indicating that it has been used and cannot ever be used again. The wife is prohibited from marrying for ninety days, ostensibly a way of insuring that if she remarries and becomes pregnant immediately there can be no question of the paternity of the child.

Although the complexities of the process were designed to protect women, in practice it hasn't always worked out that way. In recent years a controversy has emerged concerning women whose husbands are either unwilling or unable to seek a *get*. For example, a husband who cannot be found—either due to a death to which there aren't at least two (male) witnesses or for which no corpse can be produced, or by his own devious means—cannot be compelled to grant a divorce. In the past, an Orthodox Jew who went off to war would grant his wife a provisional divorce in case he were to die without leaving a corpse and without witnesses, but when millions of Jews disappeared in the inferno of the Holocaust, no one had the time or foreknowledge to take such a precaution. As a result, after World War II the rabbis who governed marriage and divorce in Israel were forced by threats of mass suicide to make a blanket exception to the law.

Still, the problem of the Orthodox *agunah*—the "chained" woman, unable to obtain a *get* and therefore unable to remarry under Jewish law—will not go away. The Conservative movement found a solution that satisfied its rabbinate, inserting a clause into the *ketubah* that states that a husband who disappears for a period of several years and does not communicate with his wife for that time means for her to be divorced from him. The Reform movement follows a Talmudic principle, *dina demalkhuta dina/the law of the land is the law,* which states that in such matters secular law obtains. Consequently, a couple that seeks and receives a civil divorce is divorced in the eyes of the Reform rabbinate.

The Orthodox have rejected both these solutions. Their rabbis will not consider a change in the traditional form of the *ketubah,* and an Orthodox Jew must have a *get* in order to remarry. Moreover, the *get* must come from an Orthodox *bet din* or it is not acceptable to them. A child born to a woman who remarries after a divorce not sanctioned by an Orthodox *bet din* will be considered a *mamzer,* illegitimate. (See sidebar "Mamzerut," p. 144.) Ironically, because under *halakhah,* the strict interpretation of Jewish law, a man may have more than one wife, the same principle would not apply to the children of a remarried man. Recently, some Orthodox rabbis have required a prenuptial agreement that calls for hefty fines in cases like those before they will perform a marriage. In Israel, a recalcitrant husband may find himself in prison or stripped of his passport. But the problem of the *agunot* persists.

The question of the status of children of remarried Jews is one that has come up very infrequently. But the plight of the *agunah* has other ramifications, much more painful and destructive. A husband can decide—for whatever reason—that he will not grant his wife a divorce under any circumstances; he can virtually blackmail her, extort from her all the rights that would be guaranteed to her in the *ketubah,* and still refuse to obtain a *get*. He can simply refuse to show up at the *bet din*. She remains trapped in her status as an *agunah,* unable to remarry.

Orthodox rabbinate in the United States and Israel have only begun to deal with this problem in the last few years. Traditionally, a *bet din* was empowered to use any means necessary in such a case, up to and including physical coercion, to make the man actually say "I want to divorce my wife." In practice that has not been the case, particularly in Israel where Jewish marriage and divorce are governed by the rabbinical courts exclusively. It is a situation that continues to evolve even as I write this sentence.

CONVERSION TO JUDAISM

Most people are familiar with Judaism's history as a religion that does not actively proselytize, does not seek out converts. However, it wasn't always that way. Abraham opened the flaps of his tent and welcomed the stranger, telling him of Adonai, the one true God, and urging him to put aside idolatry and polytheism. While he was speaking to the men, his wife Sarah would speak to the women.

Abraham and Sarah provided an example that Jesus and his followers took to heart quite successfully. At the time of his death, Jesus could number 120 among his group; in the year 312 C.E., Constantine the Great, head of the Roman Empire, would convert to Christianity. The year after his conversion, Constantine issued an edict of tolerance recognizing Christianity as one of the official religions of the empire, thereby putting it on an even legal footing with Judaism. Effectively this edict accelerated the spread of Christianity in Palestine. Coupled with the devastation undergone by the Jewish community there in the previous century, the result was that the Jews found themselves increasingly marginalized within what had once been their own country.

When Christianity was proclaimed the official faith of the Roman

Empire in 315 C.E., proselytizing by the Jews was forbidden on pain of death to both the convert and the one who converted him. Jews would be allowed to circumcise their own sons, but it would be illegal to circumcise non-Jews. In this way, the Romans hoped to eliminate proselytization on behalf of Judaism. With the ascendancy of a Christian emperor to the throne in Rome, the imperial battle against proselytizing for Judaism would take on increasing ardor and even violence. In 339 C.E. Constantius II prohibited the marriage of non-Jewish women to Jewish men and forbade Jews to purchase non-Jewish slaves. A ban was issued on the building of new synagogues in Palestine and it was made increasingly difficult to repair existing ones. In 353 C.E. it was decreed that non-Jews who converted to Judaism would forfeit all their goods to the State. The bans on circumcision were restated numerous times with increasingly harsh penalties until it was decreed that one who circumcised a non-Jew did so on pain of death.

Islam took a similarly dim view of Jewish conversion efforts. Proselytizing for Judaism came to a halt, and until recent discussions among contemporary rabbis (see sidebar "Should Judaism Proselytize?" p. 179), that had been the situation for the past thousand-plus years. Even so, many men and women chose to embrace Judaism despite having been raised in another faith or no religion at all. There are historical records of many large-scale conversions, the most famous being the mass conversion of the Central Asian tribe, the Khazars, in the eighth century.

Judaism looks with favor on those who do convert. The Bible speaks of the *ger/stranger* in your gates as a special class of people. The rabbis of the Talmud spoke of two types of *ger*, the *ger tzedek*, the convert to Judaism, and the *ger toshav*, those non-Jews who lived among the Jews and accepted the seven tenets of the Noahide laws, the essential religious duties of humanity as prescribed in Torah. It is said in Jewish lore that there will be a reward in the World to Come for the righteous of all nations, and those who follow the Noahide laws (see sidebar "The Noahide Laws," p. 177) are considered to be among them. Indeed, for that reason, Jews have felt less of a pressing need to seek converts; we don't believe that only "believers can be saved."

Traditionally, rabbis have initially tried to discourage a non-Jew who asks to convert. On the most obvious level, it may have been dangerous, even life-threatening, to offer to help such a person become a Jew. At the same time, though, attempts to dissuade them serve another purpose, to make them re-examine their decision, not to take it lightly. A candidate for conversion must be warned of the possibility of persecution and of the rigors of accepting the *mitzvot*. With such knowledge placed before him, a potential convert who stays the course will be someone who is genuinely eager to become a Jew. In general, along that line of thought, rabbis will be reluctant to convert someone who is doing so only because their prospective spouse is Jewish or for some perceived material benefit. A would-be convert must be sincerely committed to the Jewish faith and its tenets.

The process leading to conversion begins with a period of study. Orthodox and Conservative converts are urged to spend some time living under the strictures that govern the life of a traditionally observant Jew. The level of commitment required of a convert will be the same as that expected of a Jew by birth; a Reform rabbi will expect a convert to live up to the same standard of practice as a Reform Jew, a Reconstructionist rabbi that of a Reconstructionist, and so on. Rabbis of all denominations of Judaism will require study of Jewish history, lore, and religious practice. The Orthodox rabbinate, which is more stringent regarding the level of observance of its converts, refuses to recognize conversions performed by anyone other than the Orthodox. This decision has had larger ramifications for Jewish unity, particularly as regards Israeli citizenship. (See sidebar "Who Is a Jew?," p. 177.)

When the rabbi has determined that the convert is sincerely motivated and has achieved a satisfactory level of Jewish knowledge and practice, she will go before a *bet din* which will interview her to ascertain her level of understanding and acceptance of the *mitzvot* and other facets of the religion. A male convert will undergo circumcision; if he is already circumcized, he undergoes a symbolic pinprick at the place of the circumcision. (Reconstructionist rabbis and Reform rabbis in the Diaspora consider this optional.) Finally, both male and female converts undergo immersion in the *mikveh*. The new convert is given a Hebrew name, ———— *ben* or *bat Avraham Avinu / son* or *daughter of Abraham Our Father*. Once the conversion is completed, if the convert should opt out of Judaism for a time, she is still considered a Jew for purposes of religious law and, returning, would not need to undergo a second conversion process.

Virtually the only restrictions on a convert are that she cannot marry a *kohen* and he cannot be anointed king. The latter, needless to say, is not an issue that will arise anytime soon, and the former has no weight with Reform or Reconstructionist Jews who have discarded the priestly caste designations as being inapplicable after the destruction of the Temple. Other than those two strictures, the convert is a full-fledged Jew. She is welcomed as one who has begun life over again. Any of the privileges, rights, and responsibilities that a Jew by birth has are the same for a "Jew by choice." Maimonides said that he should even pray "our God and God of our fathers," because he has "come under the wings of the Divine Presence [where] there is no difference between us—all the miracles done for us were done for him too!" And the rabbis were emphatic in denouncing any Jew who considered a convert anything less than a fully empowered member of the Jewish people. In a major midrashic commentary on Torah, the *Tanhuma,* it is written, "The stranger who yields himself to the divine commands is dearer to God even than Israel at Sinai, for he comes without the constraining terror of thunder and lightning and voluntarily submits himself to be one with the Holy One."

THE NOAHIDE LAWS

In God's covenant with Noah in the aftermath of the Flood, the Creator extracts certain promises from Noah. The seven precepts to which he agrees are now called "the Noahide laws." In the Torah, non-Jews are encouraged to follow these guidelines. They are:

1. Do not murder.
2. Do not steal.
3. Do not worship false gods.
4. Do not practice sexual immorality.
5. Do not eat the limb of an animal before it is killed.
6. Do not curse God.
7. Set up courts and bring offenders to justice.

WHO IS A JEW?

As we will see in subsequent chapters, before the *Haskalah,* the Jewish Enlightenment, there were only two kinds of Jews, those that we would today call traditionally observant and apostates. But in the modern world, with different streams of Judaism, the possibility of assimilation, and the apparent threat of intermarriage, things are not so simple.

Consider this statistic. There are an estimated 220,000 children in the United States born to non-Jewish women married to Jewish men. Under *halakhah*, Jewish religious law, those children are not Jews. But in 1983, the Reform movement broke with its more traditional colleagues and declared that such children—if their parents raise them with a Jewish identity—are in fact Jewish. The rumblings from this decision were loud and insistent, but as Rabbi Joseph Telushkin has dryly observed, the practical difference it made is minimal since Orthodox rabbis wouldn't recognize the formal conversion of these children if it were performed by a Reform rabbi. In theory, though, one result of the Reform re-definition of Jewish identity could be that non-Reform Jews would be forced to do some serious genealogical research before they could feel comfortable marrying a Reform Jew.

In fact, as the CCAR points out in a responsum on the subject of patrilineal and matrilineal descent, the rabbinic tradition is not as clear-cut as the contemporary Orthodox rabbis would have it. In fact, rabbinic tradition is *patrilineal* when it comes to descent of the priesthood; a *kohen*'s son is a *kohen*, regardless of who his mother is. In the biblical period, until the time of Ezra, patrilineality was the rule of the day.

But the question of patrilineal vs. matrilineal descent is not the real focus of the heated debate on the question generally known as "Who is a Jew?" It is an important piece of the background to that battle but does not bear on it directly.

It is in Israel that the question of who actually is Jewish becomes a vexed one. Under Israel's Law of Return, passed by the Knesset, Israel's parliament, in 1950, anyone who is a Jew, a spouse or relative of a Jew "has the right to come [to Israel]" as an immigrant. Passed not too long after the Holocaust, when the memories of the death camps and the displaced persons camps were still agonizingly fresh, the Law of Return seemed a logical component of building a Jewish state.

So there is no question of denying the right to make *aliyah*, that is, to come to Israel and become a citizen. The question, rather, is whether such people will be listed with the Ministry of the Interior as Jews, whether their identification cards will say that they are Jewish. Given that the Orthodox rabbinate will not perform a wedding between a Jew and a non-Jew and that there is no such thing as a civil marriage in Israel as of this writing, one can see possible problems. (However, civil marriages and Reform and Conservative marriages performed outside of Israel are recognized by the Ministry of the Interior.)

For anyone whose mother was Jewish, the question is moot. Your mother was a Jew? Then you're a Jew. The Reform movement's 1983 decision complicates matters considerably for American Jews born in mixed marriages.

And what about converts? It is on the issue of conversion that the shaky Israeli ship of state has run aground repeatedly. The Orthodox rabbis who control religious matters in Israel refuse to recognize the validity of conversions performed by Conservative or Reform rabbis. So the real crux of the matter is not so much "who is a Jew" as "who is a [real] rabbi?" The vast majority of Jews in the Diaspora are Conservative, Reform, or non-observant; American Jews in particular find it objectionable to be asked to support a Jewish state that doesn't recognize the validity of their rabbinate.

The battle over the legitimacy of the progressive movements in Israel has continued in other areas. For the moment the "Who Is a Jew?" question is seen as too explosive for any Israeli prime minister to concede to the Orthodox point of view, no matter how badly his governing coalition might need the votes of the religious parties. Moreover, a commitment to ensure the status quo was made at the founding of the Jewish State, a commitment that no prime minister is likely to abrogate. "Status quo" was not defined until now; with the growing power of the religious parties, the new militancy of the secular Israeli community, and the heated input from both sides coming from Diaspora Jewry, the issue has become supercharged. It remains to be seen if that will be the case in the future.

SHOULD JUDAISM PROSELYTIZE?

About eighteen years ago, Rabbi Alexander Schindler, then the president of the Union of American Hebrew Congregations, the umbrella group of Reform Judaism in North America, urged Jews to go out and actively seek converts. When he repeated that call in 1993, it triggered a small firestorm within the American Jewish community (not excepting the Reform movement itself). When a prominent Conservative rabbi, Harold Schulweiss, echoed that call in October 1996, the debate was joined in full force.

Both Schindler and Schulweiss invoked the missionary practices of Abraham and Sarah in their urging, as the latter put it, to create "a national or international Jewish movement to educate, invite, and embrace non-Jews into the fold." Schulweiss went on to point out that converting the non-Jewish spouses of intermarriage is one of the surest ways of promoting strong Jewish identity in their children. Today, only one out of fourteen non-Jewish spouses in an intermarriage converts to Judaism.

So what's the big deal? Although most people think that Judaism has *traditionally* been a nonproselytizing faith, that development is comparatively recent and more the product of lethal pressure from non-Jewish governments. And at a time when deeply troubling questions about the future of North American Jewry are in the air . . . But it is precisely those questions of Jewish continuity and survival that opponents of Jewish proselytizing cite when the subject comes up.

William LeBeau, dean of the rabbinical school at the Conservative movement's Jewish Theological Seminary, stated the issue bluntly in a story written by Tom Tugend for the Jewish Telegraphic Agency in November 1996: "We have to decide whether to use our limited resources and energy on reaching non-Jews or within the Jewish community."

LEAVING THE FOLD

John Kenneth Galbraith once wrote wryly that being a Reform Democrat was like being in the High Episcopal Church: "Once you've taken communion, you're stuck for life." Judaism conceives of Jewish identity as even more binding. Even if you become an apostate, you're an apostate Jew.

Apostasy is common in Jewish history. But excommunication, actually being cut off from the tribe, is rare. In fact, there are provisions in the Talmud for an escalating series of punishments to those who transgress against the community (and it is specifically for sins against the community that these were designed), although the harshest, *kherem/banning*, hasn't been invoked with any degree of authority since the seventeenth century.

The mildest form of punishment, *nezifah/rebuke*, lasted only one day when enacted in Babylonia, a full week in Palestine. The recipient of such an edict was forced to retire to his house for the period, to consider his failing without benefit of contact with the rest of the community. After he had expressed his regrets, he was allowed to resume his normal place in Jewish society.

Nidui/banishment was much more serious, and usually lasted thirty days. The person so punished was treated as a genuine pariah; his family behaved as if in mourning and were not allowed to attend services. His children could be denied circumcision or permission to attend Jewish schools during the period of the punishment. (The contemporary Orthodox community has begun using *nidui* in response to recalcitrant husbands who refuse to grant a divorce to their wives.)

The final and most serious form of excommunication is *kherem*. During the Middle Ages, when the Jewish communities in Europe and North Africa were under extreme pressure from church, mosque, and royal court, their survival appeared to depend on complete conformity and compliance from within. With that attitude foremost in their minds, the rabbis had no other means of enforcement at their disposal for the most serious breaches except *kherem*. The penalties enacted last an indefinite time and essentially cut off the one penalized from the entire Jewish community. When Rabbenu Gershom issued his *takanot* against polygamy and divorcing a woman against her will, it was the threat of *kherem* that made it possible for the community to enforce them. Later, the Sephardic community of Amsterdam would ban Uriel Acosta and Baruch Spinoza (see Chapter 8, pp. 424–28). But the profligate use of *kherem* by medieval rabbinic authorities, combined with the growing assimilation of Jews in the modern world, took the sting out of the edict and it fell out of use.

ILLNESS

Sickness is an inevitable, if regrettable, part of life for all of us. Early cultures believed that illness was caused by bad spirits and demons, a view of the human body that early Judaism accepted. As we have seen, even today there are vestigial traces of that belief in practices such as the hanging of red ribbons from a newborn child's crib. Among the Orthodox it is common practice to change one's name during serious illness—often to Chaim or Chavah, both of which mean "life" or Raphael, which means "God heals"—to fool the Angel of Death, or as a form of prayer.

Even so, Judaism has seldom accepted the notion that illness comes from God and must be accepted as the will of the Almighty. On the contrary, Jews have traditionally been drawn to the healing professions, believing that we have a right, indeed a responsibility to intervene on behalf of the sick. It is not an accident that a great Jewish philosopher like Maimonides was also a physician of renowned skill.

One of the most important principals in Judaism is *pikuakh nefesh,* the preservation of life. In the interest of protecting another human life, it is permissible even to violate the Sabbath. The life of a mother endangered in childbirth takes precedence over that of the unborn child because of the principal of *pikuakh nefesh.* A person whose health is at risk is not only encouraged not to fast on Yom Kippur, but ordered to eat. In one of the most famous examples of the importance of the preservation of human life, Rabbi Israel Lipkin, known as the Great Salanter, founder of the Musar movement and a tremendously pious Orthodox rabbi, when told that because of the plague endangering his city no one should risk fasting for the Day of Atonement, not only ordered the city's Jews to eat on that day but actually stood at the *bimah* with two other rabbis and ate a roll in front of his entire congregation.

It is considered a great *mitzvah* to visit the sick. This commandment, *bikur kholim/visiting the sick,* brings with it eternal reward. The Talmud considers it one of the ten basic *mitzvot* for which one is rewarded in the World to Come. "A person who visits the sick helps them to recover," it says. In many Jewish communities there are *bikur kholim* societies, created for the explicit purpose of making sure that an isolated Jew, confined either to a hospital or home by illness, is not alone.

AGING

Like illness, aging is an inevitable part of life. However, unlike illness, aging is not thought to be a burden. The Bible considers longevity to be a great blessing—old age is a reward for honoring one's parents, for obeying the Torah. The Talmud defines an elder as one who has reached the age of sixty-one and says that at seventy-one one has attained "gray-haired old age."

Traditionally, Judaism has invested its elders with great authority, earned by dint of wisdom and experience. In Leviticus 19:32, the

Israelites are instructed to "rise before the aged and show deference to the old." At the same time Jewish law makes allowances for a certain loss of physical powers. It is permitted to soak *matzah* in water so that an older family member may eat it at the *seder*. The old were exempted from traveling to Jerusalem for the Pilgrim Festivals during the time the Temple stood. An older Jew who needs a cane in order to walk may carry it with her on the Sabbath.

Care for the elderly has always been a hallmark of Jewish communal life. Long before the establishment of myriad old-age homes and programs funded by such philanthropic organizations as the United Jewish Appeal, those older Jews who had no surviving family could look forward to being cared for by the larger community. Caring for the elderly is seen as a logical and necessary extension of the commandment to honor one's parents.

In recent years, with the advent of oral history programs and the rising interest in spirituality among progressive Jews, concern for the elderly has taken another turn. Although the loss of the extended family of several generations living under one roof has made it more difficult to draw on the wisdom and influence of our elders, people like Rabbi Zalman Schachter-Shalomi have created programs in "spiritual eldering." Schachter-Shalomi, the founder of the Jewish Renewal movement, has pioneered a series of seminars designed to train older Jews and others in spiritual pursuits like meditation, with an eye towards harnessing their experiences and allowing them to pass those life-experiences on to younger men and women in the community. As he has written, "[T]he resource of our elders is too precious to lose by not working to develop a process that will best serve to bring them 'From Aging to Sage-ing.' "

ETHICAL WILLS

It is a *mitzvah* in Judaism to prepare an ethical will, called a *tzava'ah*, as a way of passing on moral instruction to one's children. A uniquely Jewish literary genre, rabbinic literature is full of such documents, and they make for moving and edifying reading. In the Talmud tractate *Ketubot*, Rabbi Judah the Prince calls his sons to him as he lays dying. They gather around his bed and he offers them this teaching:

"Take care that you show proper respect to your mother. The light shall continue to burn in its usual place; the table shall be laid in its usual place; my bed shall be spread in its usual place."

Many of the prominent men in Jewish history left similar, if more detailed ethical wills, including the great minds of the medieval period, Maimonides, Nachmanides, Judah Ibn Tibbon, and Rabbi Judah ha-Khasid, as did the Vilna Gaon. For a fascinating collection of such documents and a brief history of the genre, see *Jewish Ethical Wills,* edited by Israel Abrahams (Jewish Publication Society, Philadelphia, 1976).

DEATH AND MOURNING

DEFIANCE AND ACCEPTANCE

Eventually the time comes when no amount of prayer, no changing of names, can avert the inevitable. Judaism views death with a mixture of defiance and acceptance. It is considered praiseworthy to fight off the end with all of one's might. Life is cherished and preserved, longevity is a blessing, and premature death a tragedy. The prophet Isaiah declares that eventually "God will destroy death forever."

Yet, at the same time, death is seen as a necessary thing. When a loved one dies, family members recite

Barukh atah Adonai, Dayan ha-emet

Blessed are you Adonai, the true Judge,

a prayer that reveals an acceptance of the decrees of the Almighty. There is even a *midrash* that says that when God completed the work of creation and said it was "very good," he was referring to the creation of death itself, the final piece in the puzzle of existence.

DYING

Needless to say, Judaism views the process of dying with great sobriety. A dying person should not be left alone. It is a *mitzvah* to be present for her at the very end. Death is seen as an ultimate atonement for all sins. Although Judaism has no formal deathbed sacrament and does not demand a final confession, it is customary, particularly among traditionally observant Jews, to recite the *vidui*, a deathbed confession. When informing a dying person that they should consider a final confession, we are strongly enjoined not to frighten them or to cause them to abandon hope. It is a source of merit that a dying Jew's last words be the Sh'ma.

A *goses* is a person on the brink of death. Such a person is considered to still be living. The verbal instructions of a *goses* are legally binding, even a deathbed change of last will and testament. Jewish law opposes euthanasia or physician-assisted suicide (see sidebar "Right to Die? Euthanasia and Assisted Suicide" below), and it is forbidden to manipulate a *goses* in a manner that would speed up the dying process. On the other hand, it is permitted to remove an external obstacle that is preventing death. Some rabbis have even held that it is permissible to pray for the death of a terminally ill patient who is suffering greatly.

In the days before modern medical technology made it possible to prolong life under the most dire of circumstances, the Talmud decreed that a person who had ceased breathing was dead by Jewish law. Today, of course, many men and women are resuscitated after breathing has stopped; the cessation of brain activity is generally considered the mark of death. However, some Orthodox rabbis would consider a person who is still breathing unaided to be living, regardless of the electrical status of the upper brain.

One who commits suicide is abhorred by Judaism as one who has denied the life given him by God. Although Judaism is very lenient in determining suicide as a cause of death (because a suicide cannot be buried in a Jewish cemetery with full funeral rites and because the stigma attached to suicide in some communities may still be visited on surviving family members), the faith is unequivocal in its disapproval. Likewise, those who knowingly undermine their own health—substance abusers, smokers, compulsive overeaters—are considered to be committing suicide, albeit slowly.

RIGHT TO DIE?
EUTHANASIA AND ASSISTED SUICIDE

It remains to be seen how many issues on which Reform and Orthodox rabbis will agree, but one major debate in American society has engendered near-unanimity from official spokespersons for the movements (despite a tiny minority of dissenters in the rabbinate). Every branch of American Judaism has emphatically stated its opposition to physician-assisted suicide and legalized euthanasia. In doing so, they are merely following the dictates of two thousand years of Jewish law.

Jewish law is quite explicit in its rejection of suicide. Life belongs to God alone. Your body is, to put it crudely, a loaner. The rabbis even extended this prohibition on self-destruction to prohibit the execution of a criminal in a capital case in which his own confession was the only evidence against him.

Human life is sacred, inviolable up until the last moment. There is no distinction made in Jewish law between one who is dying (a *goses*) and anyone else. Each of us is created in the image of God. Thus, the one who kills a *goses* is guilty of murder in the eyes of Jewish authorities.

It may be pointed out that the prohibition against suicide in Judaism is not absolute. A Jew is actually *obligated* to accept death rather than commit murder, idolatry, or incest. A martyr dies *kiddush Hashem/sanctifying the Holy Name*. Some have noted that the rabbis have traditionally been very lenient in ascribing a disturbed mental state to those who commit suicide under other circumstances, but that is precisely because suicide is stigmatized.

Rabbinic authorities are hardly deaf to the cries of those who suffer as death approaches. Jewish history is replete with the screams of its martyred rabbis, murdered by oppressors. But, as Rabbi Yitzkhok Breitowitz, a contemporary Orthodox authority, has written, "While we cannot personally condemn those who in the midst of unbearable pain and suffering take their own lives, we cannot encourage, condone, or participate in such an act."

Asked for a responsum on care for the terminally ill, a committee of Reform rabbis wrote:

> Our duty to the sick is to heal them or, when this is no longer possible, to care for them; it is not to kill them. The sick, the terminally ill, have a right to expect compassion from us, for such flows from the repect we ought to display to ourselves and to others as children of God. But they are not entitled to ask that we take their lives, and should they make that request, we are not entitled to grant it. For when we define "compassion" so as to include the killing of human beings, we have transgressed the most elemental

of Jewish moral standards and the most basic teachings of the Jewish tradition as we understand it.

What, then, does the Jewish tradition permit us to do for the dying? There are two permissible ways for Jews to express their compassion for those suffering in the edge of death. The first is by measures aimed at the relief of pain (even if such measures, such as the administering of morphine, may ultimately shorten life). Pain itself is "a disease," as the Reform rabbis put it in their responsum, and its relief is a legitimate medical objective.

The second is by cessation of unnecessary medical treatment for the terminally ill. The Reform group offers as an example the case of a cancer patient who "would accept radiation and/or chemotherapy so long as according to informed medical judgment these offer a reasonable prospect of curing, reversing, or controlling the cancer. Once this prospect has disappeared and the therapies can serve only to increase suffering by prolonging the patient's inevitable death from the disease, they are no longer to be regarded as *medicine* [emphasis in the original] and may therefore be withdrawn." To prolong a patient's agony beyond all hope of cure is no longer *pikuakh nefesh* or healing, and it fulfills no commandment known in Jewish law.

PREPARATIONS FOR BURIAL

Death is the final decree of the Great Judge, the equalizer that returns us all to dust. Everything in Jewish funeral and mourning practice is pointed towards this understanding of the final passage. When death finally comes, the eyes and mouth are closed, traditionally by the firstborn son. The body is covered with a sheet to maintain its dignity. The corpse is not to be left alone from now until burial. A *shomer/guard* will stay at its side, reading Psalms. Among the Orthodox, the immediate family tear their clothing, a custom known as *k'riah/tearing;* the torn garments will be worn throughout the seven-day mourning period known as *shivah.* Among Liberal Jews the equivalent practice is the wearing on the lapel of a small black ribbon which is torn.

Now the *khevrah kadishah* may enter the scene. Literally "holy society," they are the burial society that is found in any Jewish community of substantial size, a group of volunteers (or sometimes professionals) whose duty it is to prepare a corpse for interment. This is one of the greatest of *mitzvot,* because it is one that the recipient will never be able to return in kind. Members of the *khevrah kadishah* will wash the corpse in warm water, cut the hair and nails (if that is the custom of the community), and wrap it in a white linen shroud. Males will also be wrapped in their *tallit,* but the *tzitzit* will be cut, signifying that this Jew is no longer required to perform the *mitzvot.* (In Jerusalem, the earth itself is considered a *tallit,* and the corpse will only be wrapped in a shroud.)

Outside the United States, traditionally observant Jews will be buried in nothing more than these garments. American laws mandate the use of a casket. The casket used should be a simple wood box, made without nails; nothing must be done to impede the return of the body to the earth. Jewish practice abjures embalming, which slows this process; above-ground interment, which renders it all but impossible; and cremation, which shows disregard for the body created "in the image of God" and harkens back to the pagan practices of earlier non-Jewish civilizations. The plainness and simplicity of Jewish burial arrangements are designed as a reminder that in the face of death all are equal.

In the Diaspora, a small bag of earth from Israel may be placed under the head of the deceased. The Orthodox believe that when the dead are resurrected after the coming of the Messiah, those buried in the earth of *Eretz Yisroel* will be revived first. The Talmud also speaks of the atoning powers of the soil of the Holy Land.

BURIAL

It is Jewish practice to bury the dead within twenty-four hours of death if possible. Allowances are made when close relatives have to travel long distances, and for prominent figures for whom a large public funeral is in order. Burial may not take place on Shabbat or on the festivals.

Before burial, it is customary to hold a service, usually at the funeral home chapel. Although there is no set liturgy for such a service, it will often include Psalm 23, the memorial prayer *El Maleh Rakhamim/God Full of Compassion,* the Mourner's *Kaddish,* and a eulogy. (Often *Kaddish* and *El Maleh Rakhamim* will be recited at the ceremony at the graveside.)

Participating in the burial of the dead is a *mitzvah,* so for the funeral of a Jew it is hoped that as many participants as possible will themselves be Jewish, even the gravediggers. Escorting the dead is one of the basic acts of *gemilut khasadim/humanitarian concern,* for which Jews are rewarded in the World to Come; one is obligated to accompany the casket on foot at least part of the way into the cemetery.

One part of the actual burial that some people find disturbing is the practice of having each person present at the graveside, beginning with the immediate family, take a shovel and place three shovelsful of dirt in the grave. In fact, this ritual may be seen as one more aspect of Jewish acceptance of death as an inevitable and necessary event, an act of resignation that makes it impossible for the family and friends to deny the reality of a loved one's final departure. It is also an act that honors the dead; one has actively taken part in their burial, rather than leaving it to others. Generally, the participants will not pass the shovel on after they have finished but will plant it back in the ground; one should not "pass death on."

It is the custom among observant Jews to wash their hands before leaving the cemetery. Contact with a corpse makes one *tamei met/ritually impure* under Jewish law. This applies even to one who walks into a cemetery. Members of the *khevrah kadishah* who perform the ritual washing of a corpse also will wash their hands immediately after they have finished. In the time of the Temple in Jerusalem, there was a special ritual of purification in which those who were *tamei met* were cleansed by the High Priest, who would sprinkle on them a mixture of pure spring water and the ashes of a red heifer (See Numbers 19:14–22).

Until the actual burial, the focus of the rituals has been on honoring the deceased. Now attention shifts to comforting the mourners.

MOURNING

From the moment of death until the actual burial, the mourners have been in *aninut/the first stage of the mourning process.* Their attention has been focused on the necessities of the funeral. An *onen,* one who is in *aninut,* is exempted from the positive *mitzvot* such as wearing *tefillin,* reciting *b'rakhot,* even from praying. Similarly, an *onen* may not engage in activities that give pleasure, such as attending a *simkha.*

It is customary on the completion of the funeral services to return to the home of the deceased's family for a meal that traditionally consists of bread and a hard-boiled egg. As it does in the Pesakh *seder,* the hard-boiled egg symbolizes fertility, the renewal of life in the face of death as the continuation of the natural cycle. Chickpeas and bagels may be served; like the egg they are circular, suggesting the never-ending cycle of life, death, and life. The mourners are not expected to prepare this meal; friends will do it for them.

This begins the second stage of the mourning process, *shivah,* which takes its Hebrew name from the length it lasts, seven days. In a traditionally observant household, mirrors will be covered, removed, or turned to the wall; it is debatable whether the reason for this is religious, a denial of human vanity in the face of death, or more primitive, a fear of the reflection as a projection of the human soul that can be snatched by the spirit of the recently deceased. As on Yom Kippur and Tisha b'Av, mourners do not wear leather shoes during the *shivah* period and, as on Tisha b'Av, one sits on low stools, boxes, or the floor. The mourners are forbidden to shave, bathe, go to work, study Torah (except for passages relating to mourning), engage in conjugal relations, extend greetings, get haircuts, do their laundry, or wear freshly laundered clothes. (Notice the similarity of these prohibitions to those concerning communal days of mourning like Tisha b'Av.)

This is the time when it is customary to pay condolence calls on a mourning family. Now is the time when a community comes together to help a family remember their departed loved one, bringing food so that they needn't be distracted by mundane tasks like cooking. The traditional greeting to a mourner is

"Ha-Makom yinakhem otkha b'tokh sh'ahr avalei Tzion v'Yerushalayim."

"May the Almighty comfort you among the mourners of Zion and Jerusalem."

Customarily the first day of mourning is reserved for family and close friends. It is a *mitzvah* to help mourners to make a *minyan* so that they can pray at home; it is particularly important for them to be in a *minyan* at this time because it is necessary to have a *minyan* to say *Kaddish.*

Shivah is suspended for the Sabbath. *Oneg shabbat/joy of the Sabbath* takes precedence over mourning. However, it is customary for a mourner to sit outside the sanctuary during *Kabbalat Shabbat;* when she enters after *L'kha Dodi,* she is greeted by the congregation with the words, *"Ha-Makom yinakhem otkha b'tokh sh'ahr avalei Tzion v'Yerushalayim."*

Shivah ends on the morning of the seventh day after death. It is customary for a close friend to come in the morning that day to say the customary greeting and escort the mourner outside for the first time in a week. In Israel, the mourner will usually go to the graveside on this day.

Judaism recognizes that one does not cease mourning for a loved one after a week. The mourning period continues through the thirtieth day, a time of reduced restrictions called *sheloshim/thirty.* Men should not shave and no mourner should have their hair cut. Mourning for spouses, children, and siblings ends officially after thirty days. Mourning for a parent, however, is considered to continue for eleven months. Traditionally observant Jews will not get a haircut or shave until friends "urge" them to. During *sheloshim* one does not attend festive gatherings; when mourning for a parent, this restriction is carried through the eleven-month period. Those who are mourning parents are given priority in leading services in the synagogue, and it is a great *mitzvah* to do so at this time.

Mourners traditionally say *Kaddish* for a loved one for eleven months following their death. The reason for this odd figure is that in the Talmud it is written that the truly evil spend a full year after their deaths undergoing the tortures of *Gehenim,* the closest thing Jews have to Hell, and it is unlikely that any of us considers a loved one to be *that* wicked; therefore one says *Kaddish* for eleven months to avoid the implication that the deceased may have been evil. However, the *Shulkhan Arukh* also says that if you *know* your parents aren't wicked then it is permissible to say *Kaddish* for a full year (although nobody does).

UNVEILING AND *YAHRZEIT*

Although the custom in Israel is to erect a tombstone at the end of *sheloshim,* among American Jews the *minhag/custom* is to wait until a full year from death. At this time, the family of the deceased will hold an "unveiling." There is no set liturgy for this event, but it will usually include another eulogy or speech remembering the deceased, recitation of Psalm 23, *El Maleh Rakhamim*, and *Kaddish*. The tombstone will be covered with a white linen cloth which is removed at some point during the ceremony.

The anniversary of a close relative's death is called the *yahrzeit,* a Yiddish word whose literal meaning is "time of year." This is a time when it is particularly praiseworthy for the family members of the deceased to lead services or at least to take an *aliyah* and say *Kaddish*. It is also traditional to light a memorial candle, which burns for twenty-four hours, in the home. Some Ashkenazi Jews will also fast on the *yahrzeit* of a parent or grandparent.

THE AFTERLIFE

Contrary to the popular misconception, Jewish thought does not reject the idea of a life after death. The Torah is rather vague on the specifics of such an existence. The Bible does refer to *sheol/the grave* as the place to which the dead go, but it is unclear whether this involves more than mere burial. Jacob tells his sons that the apparent death of Joseph will send him to *sheol* in mourning; Korakh and his followers are sent there.

Belief in the resurrection of the dead, a key element in traditionally observant Judaism's vision of the Messianic age, dates from the period of the Pharisees, and may be an outgrowth of Greek or Persian influence. While the Pharisees accepted the idea of resurrection, the Saduccees rejected it emphatically. According to at least one Jewish historian, Louis Jacobs, the idea of resurrection of the dead gained its first currency at the time of the Maccabees, around the second century B.C.E., a period of great suffering for the Jews. In the face of such trauma, the old ideas of reward of good and punishment of evil seemed untenable, but the notion of another life after death promised a final, cosmic justice.

It is in the Hellenistic period (around the beginning of the common era) that the term *olam ha-bah/the world to come* first gained currency. The Mishnah explicitly states that corporeal resurrection will be a part of the World to Come, except for one "who says there is no resurrection of the dead." And in Orthodox and some Conservative prayer books, the *Amidah* includes a benediction to "Adonai who gives life to the dead." The rabbis of the Talmud debated quite heatedly over what would happen to those who were neither truly righteous nor utterly wicked—in other words, the vast majority of us. Unsurprisingly, there was no one definitive answer.

The same may be said of the idea of the afterlife as it evolved during the Medieval period and after. The great Jewish mystics of the time and their neo-Platonic and neo-Aristotelian counterparts all believed in some variation on the resurrection of the dead, but were in disagreement on what form that would take. There is even, among the Jewish mystics of that period, a notion of reincarnation through the transmigration of souls.

Whatever form it may take, there clearly is a consistent strain of thought in Judaism that posits the soul as immortal and one part of an integrated unit of mind, body, and soul; most observant Jews believe in eventual resurrection in some form (although the idea of the immortality of the soul is not dependent on bodily resurrection in Jewish thought). Still, Jewish thought generally emphasizes our actions in this world, *olam ha-zeh,* and not in the next, *olam ha-bah.* The one certain form of life after death is the deeds we do while we are here. As we will see in the next chapter, the afterlife is less central to Judaism than ethical behavior in this life.

NOTES

1. Of course, in a society that valued male offspring before female, as the ancient Israelites did, he could find himself producing many daughters before he had a son! Because they believe that women are exempt from many *mitzvot* and actually barred from some, Orthodox Jews still strive for at least one male child. In ultra-Orthodox communities, only a male child can recite *Kaddish* for his dead father; a female would not be counted toward a *minyan,* without which the Mourner's *Kaddish* cannot be recited. For the streams of Judaism that believe in gender equality—Reform, Reconstructionist, and most Conservative—this is not an issue. More than that, the rabbis believed that in order to fulfill the commandment to "be fruitful and multiply," one had to produce at least one male and one female child; after all, without one of each gender the human race could not be sustained.

2. The custom of naming Jewish children after departed relatives has an ancient lineage, having been traced as far back as the sixth century B.C.E. to the Egyptian Jewish community of the period.

3. As Ishmael is considered the founding patriarch of the Arab nation, this explains the Islamic practice of not circumcising boys until they are thirteen.

4. But not *all* Jews. In 1990 *Tikkun,* a liberal Jewish magazine, ran an article by Lisa Braver Moss, a Jewish mother, calling into question the practice and triggering a spirited debate in that journal's pages. In classroom papers and chapel sermons at Hebrew Union College in recent years, Reform rabbis have expressed a desire to see the practice of *brit milah* reconsidered. (There is also an extremely secular group in Israel who have gone so far as to petition the Supreme Court to have the practice declared illegal.)

5. It is so new that there isn't even complete agreement on what to call it: covenant ceremonies for a newborn daughter are also known as *simchat bat / joy of the daughter, brit khaim / convenant of life, brit bat Zion / covenant of the daughters of Zion, brit Sarah / covenant of Sarah,* and several other names based on specific practices such as immersion in the *mikveh.* There is a parallel Sephardic traditional ceremony for the birth of a baby girl called a *zeved habat.*

6. Judaism most emphatically rejects the generally discredited practice of female circumcision. The primary purpose of the clitorectomy and related surgical procedures is to deprive a woman of sexual pleasure and, in extreme cases, to make it impossible for her to lose her virginity prior to marriage. While Judaism believes that sex should take place within marriage, it also firmly believes that sexual activity should be pleasurable and that female pleasure is every bit as important as male. As we will see in Chapter 4, Jewish law is adamant on this last point.

7. Like most people of their time, the sages of the Talmud believed that an infant was only fully viable after it had lived thirty days.

8. A rabbi officiates at a wedding as both a religious authority and a civil one, an officer of the state. Religiously speaking there is no reason someone other than a rabbi can't officiate at a *kiddushin,* although they couldn't sign a marriage license, lacking the civil authority to do so.

CHAPTER 4

613 Ways:
Living a Jewish Life

Judaism is like a three-legged stool. Upholding it are three kinds of sacredness: sacred space, sacred time, and sacred humanity. In the previous chapter, we saw one aspect of how Judaism creates a holiness of the individual through the consecration of certain life-cycle events. For all but truly secular Jews—and maybe even for them, as we will see shortly—there are daily rituals that make the holiness of the individual more than just a sometime thing. Rather, that holiness is as deeply ingrained in quotidian acts of an observant Jew as breathing.

At the heart of Jewish law are two passages from Torah; the first, a phrase from Genesis 1:27 that states that God created male and female *"b'tselem Elohim/in the image of God";* the second, from Leviticus 19, in which God says to the people Israel, "You shall be holy for I, Adonai your God, am holy." If one is made in the image of the Almighty, it follows that one should behave in the manner of the Holy One, to do honor to that image, and to render thanks unto the One who made us. "What does Adonai your God require of you but to . . . walk in God's ways, to love and serve Adonai . . . with all your heart . . . [and] to keep the commandments and the statutes?" (Deuteronomy 10:12–13)

These interlocking concepts are central to Jewish theology and even to most secular Jewish ideologies: we have been created in the image of God and commanded to be holy, to walk in the ways of the Creator, *imitatio dei,* as the Latin says. "The fact that it has been revealed to us that we are made in [God's] image gives us the incentive to unfold the image and in so doing to imitate God," wrote Martin Buber earlier in this century in his book *Israel and the World.*

This is a tall order, to imitate God. What does it mean to imitate God? Should we destroy evil cities, as Adonai destroyed the earth with the Flood? Or should we create the world anew? Actually, Judaism gives a pretty complete series of answers to the basic question of what it would mean to live one's life in God's way. Indeed, for those who are traditionally observant, the answer to the question is given so thoroughly that it governs their every waking minute (and even may intrude into their sleep).

The answer is found in the Torah itself, the first five books of the Hebrew Bible, and is elaborated in thousands of pages of Talmudic and post-Talmudic rabbinical writings: There are 613 ways to imitate God, the 613 *mitzvot*.

THE *MITZVOT*

What are *mitzvot* (sing. *mitzvah*)? The word is usually translated as "commandment," but it also has come to mean "good deed" colloquially. But good deed (as in, "It would be a *mitzvah* for you to visit your Aunt Shirley") misses the core of the concept by a long way. Arthur Lelyveld, a contemporary Reform rabbi, has written, "The word *Mitzvah,* writ large and uttered reverently, means an act which I perform because God requires it of me."

A *mitzvah* is an act having a religious significance, commanded to humanity by God through the medium of the Torah, and defined by the Talmud as being of biblical origin (a *mitzvah d'oraita / commandment from Torah*).

But 613 *mitzvot?* That many? Where did that number come from?

In the third century C.E. Rabbi Simlai stated that there are 613 commandments given by God in the Torah—365 negative commandments and 248 positive commandments. These numbers, Simlai explained, had a significance of their own: 365 "thou shalt nots" correspond to the number of days in a (solar) year, while the 248 "thou shalts" equalled the supposed number of organs in the human body. Many Jews refer to the totality as *taryag mitzvot, taryag* being a word derived from the numerical value of 613 in Hebrew letters. (See sidebar *"Gematria:* Making the Letters Add Up," p. 197.)

GEMATRIA: MAKING THE LETTERS ADD UP

Gematria, a word that is actually derived from the Greek word *geometria,* refers to a sort of Hebrew numerology. Each of the twenty-two letters of the Hebrew alphabet is assigned a numerical value; the values of the letters in a word are then added together to arrive at the word's numerical significance. The assignment of numerical values is not arbitrary; in Hebrew the letters are usually used to denote numbers. Look at any modern edition of the Torah and you will see the chapter and verse numbers are indicated by the use of letters. (See chart on p. 198.)

Gematria is one of thirty-two different systems of scriptural interpretation applied to the Torah in the Talmud and in *midrash.* The results can be interesting, if not always convincing. For example, when the famine hits Canaan in Genesis, Jacob tells his sons to "go down" to Egypt to buy grain. The Hebrew verb used is *redu* and its numerical value is 210; the sages took this to mean that the Israelites would stay in Egypt for 210 years.

Gematria was also used to calculate the inscriptions to be placed on amulets to ward off spells and curses. Needless to say, many authorities were uncomfortable with such uses and there was a tendency in some circles to discourage those who would take *gematria* too seriously.

However, even those Jews who are completely ignorant of the larger significance and more arcane uses of *gematria* probably partake of it in a small way: the numerical value of the word *khai/life* is eighteen, and it is customary when making donations to Jewish causes, or giving gifts for a *bar* or *bat mitzvah,* to do so in multiples of that number.

Over the last two thousand years, rabbis and sages have devised many systems for grasping the systematic nature of the *taryag mitzvot.* The great Jewish thinkers have always been prone to dialectical thinking so most analyses of the *mitzvot* have treated them as dualities.

Positive and negative commandments. Positive commandments consist of duties to be performed such as wearing *tefillin* or putting up a *mezuzah,* celebrating the festivals, giving to the poor.

Negative commandments are prohibitions. Do not place a stumbling block before the blind. You shall not eat unclean animals. Have no other gods before Adonai.

NAME	BOOK	CURSIVE	NUMBER
Aleph	א	IC	1
Bet	ב	ꞓ	2
Gimel	ג	౽	3
Dalet	ד	౩	4
He	ה	౩	5
Vav	ו	I	6
Zayin	ז	ꞓ	7
Khet	ח	ɳ	8
Tet	ט	౪	9
Yud	י	౨	10
Kaf	כ	౩	20
Lamed	ל	ꞓ	30
Mem	מ	N	40
Nun	נ	౪	50
Samekh	ס	O	60
Ayin	ע	౩	70
Pei	פ	౭	80
Tzadi	צ	3	90
Kof	ק	౭	100
Resh	ר	౩	200
Sin	ש	e	300
Tav	ת	౪	400

Between God and humanity or between people. The Torah distinguishes between obligations to God *(mitzvot bein adam la-Makom/obligations between humanity and the Almighty)* such as prayer or sacrifices, and commandments that govern relations among people *(mitzvot bein adam le-khavero/obligations between a person and comrades),* concerning subjects like liability in accidents or the charging of interest in lending

Khukim* and *mishpatim. The *mishpatim* are rationally derived rules governing behavior; it is bad to covet another's goods because such behavior sows seeds of strife between us. By contrast the *khukim* may seem arbitrary, even irrational: why should we wear *tefillin* or abstain from mixing meat and dairy dishes? Because God has so ordained it.

Timebound and timeless. Some *mitzvot* are time-dependent. One does not eat *matzah* at Rosh Hashanah or wear *tefillin* at the *ma'ariv* service. Others are not time-dependent. There is never a "wrong" time to give help to the poor.

Traditionally observant Jews have held that women are excused from the time-bound *mitzvot*. The reasoning was that women's domestic responsibilities (nursing in particular) are so enormous and time-consuming that it would be unfair to further burden them with an additional set of obligations that must be fulfilled at a designated time. However, virtually all rabbinical commentators have said that a woman may observe such *mitzvot*. Indeed, in the eyes of many of the sages, such voluntary observance confers great merit on she who performs the *mitzvot*.

While women can choose to observe timebound *mitzvot* as individuals, custom has determined which ones all women—as a collective entity—have taken on. As a result of the widespread nature of such customs, these optional *mitzvot* have, increasingly, taken on the force of obligation. For example, women are now obligated to hear the shofar blown, but praying three times a day remains optional for them. (Some *mitzvot* that appear to be timebound, though, are also considered obligatory for women. Participating in a *seder* at Pesakh and hearing the reading of the *megillah* on Purim are two examples; in each case, female Jews were saved as well as males, so they share in the *mitzvah* of thanking God for their salvation.)

Light and heavy. When the rabbis of the Talmudic period began to codify the *mitzvot* around the beginning of the Common Era, they distinguished between a *mitzvah kalah / light mitzvah* and a *mitzvah khamurah / heavy mitzvah*. Clearly, when you have 613 rules, some are more urgent, more significant, than others.

For example, as noted in Chapter 2, the principle of *pikuakh nefesh*, of saving a life, takes precedence over virtually all other *mitzvot*. However, there are three exceptions, negative command-ments of such importance that they, in turn, take precedence over the principle of life-saving: adultery, idolatry, and murder. Rather than commit any of these three offenses, a Jew is expected to give up his or her life. (See sidebar *"Pikuakh Nefesh:* To Save a Life" below.)

PIKUAKH NEFESH: TO SAVE A LIFE

How can we account for the primacy of *pikuakh nefesh*, the obligation to save a life? There are two interlinked answers to this question. Of course, in saving a human life, we are saving one who was made in the image of God.

But the Talmud offers another answer, in the tractate *Sanhedrin:*

The reason that Adam was created alone is to teach you that who-ever destroys a single human being is considered by the Torah as if he had destroyed the entire world; and whoever keeps a single human alive is considered by the Torah as if he had kept the entire world alive.

In addition to these categories, there are other ways of classifying the *mitzvot*. For example, according to the Khafetz Khayim (1838–1933) there are 26 commandments that are incumbent specifically on Jews living in the land of Israel but not on those living in the Diaspora. (Per-haps that seems like a small number compared to 613, but it helps to recall that many of the *mitzvot* that were in force when the Temple existed in Jerusalem can no longer be fulfilled. It has been estimated by some commentators that with the destruction of the Temple, only 270 of the *taryag mitzvot* are still in effect, a mere forty-four percent, a figure that gives an indication of the centrality of the Temple and its intricate framework of sacrifices and priestly duties in ancient Israel.)

WHO'S COUNTING?

In the seventeen centuries since Rabbi Simlai first proclaimed the figure of 613 *mitzvot*, there have been many sages who have enumerated the commandments. The first codification, written in the ninth century, was the *Halakhot Gedolot/Great Laws,* authored by Rabbi Simeon Kariya. In this volume, 350 negative commandments are listed first, in order of the severity of punishment for their violations, followed by 182 general positive commandments, an additional 18 incumbent on priests, and, finally, 65 communal *mitzvot* that apply in specific contingencies. Maimonides wrote a volume on the commandments—*Sefer Ha-Mitzvot/Book of the Commandments*—that serves as an introduction to his 1165 magnum opus, the *Mishneh Torah,* a compendious code of the law that is still recognized as an important sourcebook. About a hundred years later in Barcelona, Rabbi Aaron HaLevi compiled the *Sefer Ha-Khinnukh/Book of Education,* a volume that offered not only a distillation of the 613 commandments, but an attempt to trace their roots in Jewish ethics and religious thought. The Khafetz Khayim's *Sefer Ha-Mitzvot Ha-Kitzur/Concise Book of the Commandments,* his last completed book, was published in 1931. There are numerous other compilations in this vein; these are only a few of the best-known volumes.

Each of these distinguished sages presents a different taxonomy of the *taryag mitzvot* and arranges them according to his own system. For example, the *Khinnukh* (as it is known) lists the commandments in the order in which they appear in the Torah, so that they may be studied in tandem with the weekly *sidrah/portion.* Maimonides divides the positive commandments into ten categories of his devising. The Khafetz Khayim finds an additional 23 positive commandments to add to Maimonides' list of 60. (For a complete listing, see sidebar, "The 613 *Mitzvot* [According to Maimonides]," p. 202.)

THE 613 *MITZVOT* (ACCORDING TO MAIMONIDES)

In his *Sefer Ha-Mitzvot*, Maimonides enumerates the 613 commandments that he finds in the Torah. Below is his list of the 248 positive commandments and the 365 negative commandments.

248 Positive Commandments

P 1   Believing in God

P 2   Believing in the Unity of God

P 3   Loving God

P 4   Fearing God

P 5   Worshipping God

P 6   Cleaving to God

P 7   Taking an oath by God's Name

P 8   Walking in God's ways

P 9   Sanctifying God's Name

P 10   Reading the *Sh'ma* twice daily

P 11   Studying and teaching Torah

P 12   Wearing *tefillin* of the head

P 13   Wearing *tefillin* of the hand

P 14   To make *Tzitzit*

P 15   To affix a *Mezuzah*

P 16   *Hakhel* during Sukkot

P 17   A king should write a Torah

P 18   Everyone should write a Torah

P 19   Grace after meals

P 20   Building a Sanctuary for God

P 21   Revering the *Beit Hamikdash*/The Temple

P 22   Guarding the *Mikdash*

P 23   Levitical services in the *Mikdash*

P 24   Ablutions of the *Kohanim*

P 25   Kindling the lamps by the *Kohanim*

P 26   *Kohanim* blessing Israel

P 27   The offering of the Showbread

P 28   Burning the Incense

P 29   The perpetual fire on the Altar

P 30   Removing the ashes from the Altar

P 31   Removing *tameh* (ritually impure persons) from the camp

P 32   Honoring the *Kohanim*

P 33   The Priestly garments

P 34   *Kohanim* bearing the Ark on their shoulders

P 35   The oil of the Anointment

P 36   *Kohanim* ministering in watches

P 37   *Kohanim* defiling themselves for deceased relatives

P 38   *Kohein Gadol* should only marry a virgin

P 39   Daily Burnt Offerings

P 40   *Kohein Gadol's* daily Meal Offering

P 41   The Shabbat Additional Offering

P 42   The New Moon Additional Offering

P 43   The Pesakh Additional Offering

P 44   The Meal Offering of the *Omer*

P 45   The Shavuot Additional Offering

P 46   Bring Two Loaves on Shavuot

P 47   The Rosh Hashanah Additional Offering

P 48   The Yom Kippur Additional Offering

P 49   The Service of Yom Kippur

P 50   The Sukkot Offering

P 51   The Shemini Atzeret Additional Offering

P 52   The three annual pilgrimages

P 53   Appearing before Adonai during the Festivals

P 54   Rejoicing on the Festivals

P 55   Slaughtering the Pesakh Offering

P 56   Eating the Pesakh Offering

P 57   Slaughtering the *Pesakh Sheini* (Second Pesakh) Offering

P 58   Eating the *Pesakh Sheini* Offering

P 59   Blowing the trumpets in the Sanctuary

P 60   Minimum age of cattle to be offered

P 61   Offering only unblemished sacrifices

P 62   Bringing salt with every offering

P 63   The Burnt-Offering

P 64   The Sin-Offering

P 65   The Guilt-Offering

P 66   The Peace-Offering

P 67   The Meal-Offering

P 68   Offerings of a Court that has erred

P 69   The Fixed Sin-Offering

P 70   The Suspensive Guilt-Offering

P 71   The Unconditional Guilt-Offering

P 72   The Offering of a Higher or Lower Value

P 73   Making confession

P 74   Offering brought by a *zav* (man with a discharge)

P 75   Offering brought by a *zavah* (woman with a discharge)

P 76   Offering of a woman after childbirth

P 77   Offering brought by a leper

P 78   Tithe of Cattle

P 79   Sanctifying the Firstborn

P 80   Redeeming the Firstborn

P 81   Redeeming the firstling of a donkey

P 82   Breaking the neck of the firstling of a donkey

P 83   Bringing due offerings on the first festival

P 84   All offerings to be brought to the Sanctuary

P 85   Bring all offerings due from outside *Eretz Yisroel* to Sanctuary

P 86   Redeeming blemished offerings

P 87   Holiness of substituted offerings

P 88   *Kohanim* eat the residue of the Meal Offerings

P 89   *Kohanim* eat the meat of the Consecrated Offerings

P 90   To burn Consecrated Offerings that have become *tameh*

P 91   To burn the remnant of the Consecrated Offerings

P 92   The *Nazir* (an ascetic who has dedicated himself to Adonai)
        letting his hair grow

P 93   *Nazirite* obligations on completion of vow

P 94   All oral submissions to be fulfilled

P 95   Revocation of vows

P 96   Defilement through carcasses of animals

P 97   Defilement through carcasses of eight creeping creatures

P 98   Defilement of food and drink

P 99   *Tum'ah* (impurity) of a menstruant

P 100   *Tum'ah* of a woman after childbirth

P 101   *Tum'ah* of a leper

P 102   Garments contaminated by leprosy

P 103   A leprous house

P 104   *Tum'ah* of a *zav* (man with a discharge)

P 105   *Tum'ah* of semen

P 106   *Tum'ah* of a *zavah* (woman with a discharge)

P 107   *Tum'ah* of a corpse
P 108   The law of the water of sprinkling
P 109   Immersing in a *mikveh*
P 110   Cleansing from leprosy
P 111   A leper must shave his head
P 112   The leper must be made distinguishable
P 113   Ashes of the Red Heifer (a rite described in Numbers 19)
P 114   Valuation of a person
P 115   Valuation of beasts
P 116   Valuation of houses
P 117   Valuation of fields
P 118   Restitution for sacrilege
P 119   The fruits of the fourth-year planting
P 120   To leave the corners of your fields for the poor to harvest
P 121   To leave gleanings for the poor
P 122   To leave the forgotten sheaf for the poor
P 123   To leave defective grape clusters for the poor
P 124   To leave grape gleanings for the poor
P 125   To bring First fruits to the Sanctuary
P 126   To set aside the great Heave-offering
P 127   To set aside the first tithe
P 128   To set aside the second tithe
P 129   The Levites' tithe for the *Kohanim*
P 130   To set aside the poor-man's tithe in the third and sixth year
P 131   The avowal of the tithe
P 132   Recital on bringing the First fruits
P 133   To set aside the *khallah* for the *Kohein*
P 134   Renouncing as ownerless produce of the Sabbatical year
P 135   Resting the land on the Sabbatical year
P 136   Sanctifying the Jubilee year
P 137   Blowing the *Shofar* in the Jubilee year
P 138   Reversion of the land in the Jubilee year
P 139   Redemption of property in a walled city
P 140   Counting the years till the Jubilee year
P 141   Canceling monetary claims in the Sabbatical year
P 142   Exacting debts from idolators
P 143   The *Kohein's* due in the slaughter of every clean animal
P 144   The first of the fleece to be given to the *Kohein*

P 145   Devoted thing to God and the *Kohein*

P 146   Slaughtering animals before eating them

P 147   Covering the blood of slain birds and animals

P 148   Releasing the mother before taking the nest

P 149   Searching for the prescribed signs in cattle and animals

P 150   Searching for the prescribed signs in birds

P 151   Searching for the prescribed signs in grasshoppers

P 152   Searching for the prescribed signs in fishes

P 153   Determining the New Moon

P 154   Resting on Shabbat

P 155   Proclaiming the sanctity of Shabbat

P 156   Removal of *chametz* on Pesakh

P 157   Recounting Exodus from Egypt on first night of Pesakh

P 158   Eating *Matzah* on the first night of Pesakh

P 159   Resting on the first day of Pesakh

P 160   Resting on the seventh day of Pesakh

P 161   Counting the *Omer*

P 162   Resting on Shavuot

P 163   Resting on Rosh Hashanah

P 164   Fasting on Yom Kippur

P 165   Resting on Yom Kippur

P 166   Resting on the first day of Sukkot

P 167   Resting on Shemini Atzeret

P 168   Dwelling in a *Sukkah* for seven days

P 169   Taking a *Lulav* on Sukkot

P 170   Hearing a *Shofar* on Rosh Hashanah

P 171   Giving half a *shekel* annually

P 172   Heeding the Prophets

P 173   Appointing a King

P 174   Obeying the Great Court

P 175   Abiding by a majority decision

P 176   Appointing Judges and Officers of the Court

P 177   Treating litigants equally before the law

P 178   Testifying in Court

P 179   Inquiring into the testimony of witnesses

P 180   Condemning witnesses who testify falsely

P 181   *Eglah Arufah* (ceremony for breaking the neck of a calf when a corpse is found outside the city)

P 182   Establishing six Cities of Refuge

P 183   Assigning cities to the *Levi'im*

P 184   Building fences on roof
           Removing sources of danger from our dwellings

P 185   Destroying all idol-worship

P 186   The law of the apostate city

P 187   The law of the Seven Nations

P 188   The extinction of the seed of Amalek (a nation that committed a
           sneak attack on the Israelites in the Wilderness; God made
           Moses and his followers pledge to wipe them out)

P 189   Remembering the nefarious deeds of Amalek

P 190   The law of the non-obligatory war

P 191   Appoint a *Kohein* to speak to the people going to war, and
           Send back any man unfit for battle

P 192   Preparing a place beyond the camp

P 193   Including a digging tool among war implements

P 194   A robber to restore the stolen article

P 195   To give charity

P 196   Lavishing gifts on a Hebrew bondman on his freedom

P 197   Lending money to the poor

P 198   Lending money to the heathen with interest

P 199   Restoring a pledge to a needy owner

P 200   Paying wages on time

P 201   An employee is allowed to eat the produce he's working in

P 202   Unloading a tired animal

P 203   Assisting the owner in loading his burden

P 204   Returning lost property to its owner

P 205   Rebuking the sinner

P 206   Loving our fellow Jew

P 207   Loving the convert

P 208   The law of weights and measures

P 209   Honoring scholars

P 210   Honoring parents

P 211   Fearing parents

P 212   Be fruitful and multiply

P 213   The law of marriage

P 214   Bridegroom devotes himself to his wife for one year

P 215   Circumcising one's son

P 216   Law of the Levirate Marriage

P 217   Law of *khalitzah* (see sidebar "Levirate Marriage," p. 167)

P 218   A violator must marry the maiden he has violated

P 219   The law of the defamer of his bride

P 220   The law of the seducer

P 221   The law of the captive woman

P 222   The law of divorce

P 223   The law of a suspected adultress

P 224   Whipping transgressors of certain commandments

P 225   The law of unintentional manslaughter

P 226   Beheading transgressors of certain commandments

P 227   Strangling transgressors of certain commandments

P 228   Burning transgressors of certain commandments

P 229   Stoning transgressors of certain commandments

P 230   Hanging after execution, transgressors of certain commandments

P 231   Burial on the day of execution

P 232   The law of the Hebrew bondman

P 233   Hebrew bondmaid to be married by her master or his son

P 234   Redemption of a Hebrew bondmaid

P 235   The law of a Canaanite bondman

P 236   Penalty of inflicting injury

P 237   The law of injuries caused by an ox

P 238   The law of injuries caused by a pit

P 239   The law of theft

P 240   The law of damage caused by a beast

P 241   The law of damage caused by a fire

P 242   The law of an unpaid bailee

P 243   The law of a paid bailee

P 244   The law of a borrower

P 245   The law of buying and selling

P 246   The law of litigants

P 247   Saving the life of the pursued

P 248   The law of inheritance

365 Negative Commandments

N 1   Not believing in any other God

N 2   Not to make images for the purpose of worship

N 3   Not to make an idol (even for others) to worship

N 4   Not to make idolatrous figures of human beings

N 5   Not to bow down to an idol

N 6   Not to worship idols

N 7   Not to hand over any children to Moloch

N 8   Not to practice sorcery of the *ov*

N 9   Not to practice sorcery of the *yidde'oni*

N 10   Not to study idolatrous practices

N 11   Not to erect a pillar which people will assemble to honor

N 12   Not to make figured stones on which to prostrate ourselves

N 13   Not to plant *ashera* (trees ritually planted by idolators near a place of pagan worship) in the Sanctuary

N 14   Not to swear by an idol

N 15   Not to divert people to idolatry

N 16   Not to try to pursuade an Israelite to worship idols

N 17   Not to love someone who seeks to mislead you to idols

N 18   Not to relax one's aversion to the misleader

N 19   Not to save the life of a misleader

N 20   Not to plead for the misleader

N 21   Not to suppress evidence unfavorable to the misleader

N 22   To derive no benefit from ornaments which have adorned an idol

N 23   Not rebuilding an apostate city

N 24   Not deriving benefit from property of an apostate city

N 25   Not increasing wealth from anything connected with idolatry

N 26   Not prophesying in the name of an idol

N 27   Not prophesying falsely

N 28   Not to listen to the prophesy made in the name of an idol

N 29   Not fearing or refraining from killing a false prophet

N 30   Not adopting the habits and customs of unbelievers

N 31   Not practicing divination

N 32   Not regulating one's conduct by the stars

N 33   Not practicing the art of the soothsayer

N 34   Not practicing sorcery

N 35   Not practicing the art of the charmer

N 36   Not consulting a necromancer who uses the *ov*

N 37   Not consulting a sorcerer who uses the *yodo'a*

N 38   Not to seek information from the dead

N 39   Women not to wear men's clothes or adornments in order to pass as men

N 40   Men not wearing women's clothes or adornments in order to pass as women

N 41   Not imprinting any marks on our bodies

N 42   Not wearing *Shatnez* (mixture of wool and linen)

N 43   Not shaving the temples of the head

N 44   Not shaving the beard

N 45   Not making cuttings in our flesh

N 46   Not settling in the land of Egypt

N 47   Not to follow one's heart or eyes into evil

N 48   Not to make a covenant with the Seven Nations of Canaan

N 49   Not to spare the life of the Seven Nations

N 50   Not to show mercy to idolators

N 51   Not to allow idolators to settle in our land

N 52   Not to intermarry with a heretic

N 53   Not to intermarry with a male from Ammon or Mo'av

N 54   Not to exclude the descendants of Esav

N 55   Not to exclude the descendants of Egyptians (after four generations)

N 56   Not offering peace to Ammon and Mo'av

N 57   Not destroying fruit trees in time of siege

N 58   Not fearing heretics in time of war

N 59   Not forgetting what Amalek did to us

N 60   Not blaspheming the Great Name

N 61   Not violating a *sh'vu'at bittui* (oath of utterance)

N 62   Not swearing a *sh'vu'at shav* (vain oath)

N 63   Not profaning the Name of God

N 64   Not testing His promises and warnings

N 65   Not to break down houses of worship or to destroy holy books

N 66   Not leaving the body of an executed criminal hanging overnight

N 67   Not to interrupt the watch over the Sanctuary

N 68   *Kohein Gadol* (High Priest) may not enter Holy of Holies at any but prescribed times

N 69   *Kohein* with blemish not to enter Sanctuary from Altar inwards

N 70   *Kohein* with a blemish not to minister in the Sanctuary

N 71   *Kohein* with a temporary blemish not to minister in Sanctuary

N 72   Levites and *Kohanim* not to perform each other's allotted services

N 73   Not to be intoxicated when entering Sanctuary

        Not to be intoxicated when giving a decision on Torah law

N 74   *Zar* (non-*Kohein*) not to minister in Sanctuary

N 75   *Kohein Tamei* (a priest who is impure) not to minister in Sanctuary

N 76   *Kohein* who is *tevul yom* (lowest level of temporary impurity), not to minister in Sanctuary

N 77   *Tameh* person not to enter any part of Sanctuary

N 78   *Tameh* person not to enter camp of Levites

N 79   Not to build an Altar of stones which were cut by iron

N 80   Not to ascend the Altar by steps

N 81   Not to extinguish the Altar fire

N 82   Not to offer any sacrifice whatever on the Golden Altar (other than the incense at prescribed times)

N 83   Not to make oil like the Oil of Annointment

N 84   Not to anoint anyone with special oil except *Kohein Gadol* and King

N 85   Not to make incense like that used in Sanctuary

N 86   Not to remove the staves from their rings in the Ark

N 87   Not to remove the Breastplate from the Ephod

N 88   Not to tear the edge of the *Kohein Gadol's* robe

N 89   Not to offer sacrifices outside the Sanctuary Court

N 90   Not to slaughter holy offerings outside the Sanctuary Court

N 91   Not to dedicate a blemished animal to be offered on the Altar

N 92   Not to slaughter a blemished animal as a *korban* (sacrifice)

N 93   Not to dash the blood of a blemished beast on the Altar

N 94   Not to burn the sacrificial portions of blemished beast on Altar

N 95   Not to sacrifice a beast with a temporary blemish

N 96   Not to offer a blemished sacrifice of a gentile

N 97   Not to cause an offering to become blemished

N 98   Not to offer leaven or honey upon the Altar

N 99   Not to offer a sacrifice without salt

N 100   Not to offer on Altar the "hire of a harlot" or "price of a dog"

N 101   Not to slaughter the mother and her young on the same day

N 102   Not to put olive oil on the meal-offering of a sinner

N 103   Not to put frankincense on the meal-offering of a sinner

N 104   Not to mingle olive oil with meal-offering of suspected adultress

N 105   Not to put frankincense on meal-offering of suspected adultress

N 106   Not to change a beast that has been consecrated as an offering

N 107   Not to change one's holy offering for another

N 108   Not to redeem the firstling (of a clean beast)

N 109   Not to sell the tithe of cattle

N 110   Not to sell devoted property

N 111   Not to redeem devoted land without specific statement of purpose

N 112   Not to sever the head of the bird of Sin-offering during *melikah*

N 113   Not to do any work with a dedicated beast

N 114   Not to shear a dedicated beast

N 115   Not to slaughter the *Korban Pesakh* (offering of the Paschal Lamb) while *khametz* in our possession

N 116   Not to leave any sacrificial portions of *Korban Pesakh* overnight

N 117   Not to allow meat of *Korban Pesakh* to remain till morning

N 118   Not to allow meat of 14 Nisan Festival Offering to remain till day three

N 119   Not to allow meat of *Pesakh Sheini* offering to remain till morning

N 120   Not to allow meat of thanksgiving offering to remain till morning

N 121   Not to break any bones of Pesakh offering

N 122   Not to break any bones of *Pesakh Sheini* offering

N 123   Not to remove Pesakh offering from where it is eaten

N 124   Not to bake the residue of a meal offering with leaven

N 125   Not to eat the Pesakh offering boiled or raw

N 126   Not to allow a *ger toshav* (resident non-Jew) to eat the Pesakh offering

N 127   An uncircumcised person may not eat the Pesakh offering

N 128   Not to allow an apostate Israelite to eat the Pesakh offering

N 129   *Tameh* person may not eat hallowed food

N 130   Not to eat meat of consecrated offerings which have become *tameh*

N 131   Not eating *notar* (a part of the sacrifice that is left over beyond allotted time)

N 132   Not eating *piggul* (a sacrifice brought with improper intentions)

N 133   A *zar* may not eat *terumah* (an offering to the *Kohanim*)

N 134   A *Kohein's* tenant or hired servant may not eat *terumah*

N 135   An uncircumcised *Kohein* may not eat *terumah*

N 136   *Tameh Kohein* may not eat *terumah*

N 137   A *khalalah* may not eat holy food

N 138   Not to eat the meal-offering of a *Kohein*

N 139   Not to eat Sin-offering meat whose blood was brought into Sanctuary

N 140   Not to eat the invalidated consecrated offerings

N 141   Not to eat unredeemed second tithe of corn outside *Yerushalayim*

N 142   Not to consume unredeemed second tithe of wine outside *Yerushalayim*

N 143   Not to consume unredeemed second tithe of oil outside *Yerushalayim*

N 144   Not to eat an unblemished firstling outside *Yerushalayim*

N 145   Not to eat sin-offering and guilt-offering outside Sanctuary court

N 146   Not to eat the meat of a burnt offering

N 147   Not to eat lesser holy offerings before blood dashed on Altar

N 148   A *zar* not to eat the most holy offerings

N 149   *Kohein* not to eat first fruits outside *Yerushalayim*

N 150   Not eating an unredeemed *tameh* second tithe, even in *Yerushalayim*

N 151   Not eating the second tithe in mourning

N 152   Not to spend second tithe redemption money, except on food and drink

N 153   Not eating *tevel* (produce heave-offering and tithes not taken)

N 154   Not altering the prescribed order of harvest tithing

N 155   Not to delay payment of vows

N 156   Not to appear in Sanctuary on festival without sacrifice

N 157   Not to infringe on any oral obligation, even if without an oath

N 158   *Kohein* may not marry a *zonah*

N 159   *Kohein* may not marry a *khalalah*

N 160   *Kohein* may not marry a divorcee

N 161   *Kohein Gadol* may not marry a widow

N 162   *Kohein Gadol* may not have relations with a widow

N 163   *Kohein* with disheveled hair may not enter the Sanctuary

N 164   *Kohein* wearing rent garments may not enter Sanctuary

N 165   Ministering *Kohanim* may not leave the Sanctuary

N 166   Common *Kohein* may not defile himself for dead (except for prescribed family members)

N 167   *Kohein Gadol* may not be under one roof with dead body

N 168   *Kohein Gadol* may not defile himself for any dead person
N 169   Levites may not take a share of the land
N 170   Levites may not share in the spoil of conquest of the land
N 171   Not to tear out hair for the dead
N 172   Not to eat any unclean animal
N 173   Not to eat any unclean fish
N 174   Not to eat any unclean fowl
N 175   Not to eat any swarming winged insect
N 176   Not to eat anything which swarms on the earth
N 177   Not to eat any creeping thing that breeds in decayed matter
N 178   Not to eat living creatures that breed in seeds or fruit
N 179   Not to eat any swarming thing
N 180   Not to eat any animal which is a *nevelah*
N 181   Not to eat an animal which is a *treifah*
N 182   Not to eat a limb of a living animal
N 183   Not to eat the *gid hanasheh* (sinew of the thigh-vein)
N 184   Not to eat blood
N 185   Not to eat the subdermal fat of a clean animal
N 186   Not to cook meat in milk
N 187   Not to eat meat cooked in milk
N 188   Not to eat the flesh of a stoned ox
N 189   Not to eat bread made from grain of new crop (before appropriate sacrifice is brought)
N 190   Not to eat roasted grain of the new crop (before appropriate sacrifice is brought)
N 191   Not to eat fresh ears of grain (before appropriate sacrifice is brought)
N 192   Not to eat *orlah* (the fruit of a tree borne during the first three years after its planting)
N 193   Not to eat *kilai hakerem* (produce of mixed breeds and mixed fields)
N 194   Not to drink *yayin nesach* (libation wine for idol worship)
N 195   No eating or drinking to excess
N 196   Not to eat on Yom Kippur
N 197   Not to eat *khametz* on Pesakh
N 198   Not to eat an admixture of *khametz* on Pesakh
N 199   Not to eat *khametz* on the afternoon of 14 Nisan
N 200   No *khametz* may be seen in our homes during Pesakh

N 201   Not to possess *khametz* during Pesakh

N 202   A *Nazir* may not drink wine

N 203   A *Nazir* may not eat fresh grapes

N 204   A *Nazir* may not eat dried grapes

N 205   A *Nazir* may not eat grape kernels

N 206   A *Nazir* may not eat grape husks

N 207   A *Nazir* may not render himself *tameh* for the dead

N 208   A *Nazir* may not render himself *tameh* by entering house with corpse

N 209   A *Nazir* may not shave

N 210   Not to reap all harvest without leaving a corner for the poor

N 211   Not to gather ears of corn that fell during harvesting

N 212   Not to gather the whole produce of vineyard at vintage time

N 213   Not to gather single fallen grapes during the vintage

N 214   Not to return for a forgotten sheaf

N 215   Not to sow *kilayim* (diverse kinds of seed in one field)

N 216   Not to sow grain or vegetables in a vineyard

N 217   Not to mate animals of different species

N 218   Not to work with two different kinds of animals yoked together

N 219   Not preventing a beast from eating the produce where working

N 220   Not to cultivate the soil in the seventh year

N 221   Not to prune the trees in the seventh year

N 222   Not to reap a self-grown plant in the seventh year as in ordinary year

N 223   Not to gather self-grown fruit in the seventh year as in ordinary year

N 224   Not to cultivate the soil in the Jubilee year

N 225   Not to reap the aftergrowths of Jubilee year as in ordinary year

N 226   Not to gather fruit in Jubilee year as in ordinary year

N 227   Not to sell out holdings in *Eretz Yisroel* in perpetuity

N 228   Not to sell the open lands of the Levites

N 229   Not to forsake the Levites

N 230   Not to demand payment of debts after *Shemitah* year

N 231   Not to withold a loan to be canceled by the *Shemitah* year

N 232   Failing to give charity to our needy brethren

N 233   Not sending a Hebrew bondman away empty-handed

N 234   Not demanding payment from a debtor known unable to pay

N 235	Not lending at interest
N 236	Not borrowing at interest
N 237	Not participating in a loan at interest
N 238	Not oppressing an employee by delaying payment of his wages
N 239	Not taking a pledge from a debtor by force
N 240	Not keeping a needed pledge from its owner
N 241	Not taking a pledge from a widow
N 242	Not taking food utensils in pledge
N 243	Not abducting an Israelite
N 244	Not stealing money
N 245	Not committing robbery
N 246	Not fraudulently altering land boundaries
N 247	Not usurping our debts
N 248	Not repudiating our debts
N 249	Not to swear falsely in repudiating our debts
N 250	Not wronging one another in business
N 251	Not wronging one another by speech
N 252	Not wronging a proselyte by speech
N 253	Not wronging a proselyte in business
N 254	Not handing over a fugitive bondman
N 255	Not wronging a fugitive bondman
N 256	Not dealing harshly with orphans and widows
N 257	Not employing a Hebrew bondman in degrading tasks
N 258	Not selling a Hebrew bondman by public auction
N 259	Not having a Hebrew bondman do unnecessary work
N 260	Not allowing a heathen to mistreat a Hebrew bondman
N 261	Not selling a Hebrew bondmaid
N 262	Not to afflict one's wife or espoused Hebrew bondmaid by diminishing food, raiment, or conjugal rights
N 263	Not selling a captive woman
N 264	Not enslaving a captive woman
N 265	Not planning to acquire someone else's property
N 266	Not coveting another's belongings
N 267	A hired laborer not eating growing crops
N 268	A hired laborer not putting of the harvest in his own vessel
N 269	Not ignoring lost property

N 270	Not leaving a person who is trapped under his burden
N 271	Not cheating in measurements and weights
N 272	Not keeping false weights and measures
N 273	Judge not to commit unrighteousness
N 274	Judge not to accept gifts from litigants
N 275	Judge not to favor a litigant
N 276	Judge not to avoid just judgment through fear of a wicked person
N 277	Judge not to decide in favor of a poor man, out of pity
N 278	Judge not to pervert justice against person of evil repute
N 279	Judge not to pity one who has killed or caused loss of limb
N 280	Judge not to pervert justice due to proselytes or orphans
N 281	Judge not to listen to one litigant in absence of the other
N 282	A court may not convict by a majority of one in a capital case
N 283	A judge may not rely on the opinion of a fellow judge or may not argue for conviction after favoring acquittal
N 284	Not appointing an unlearned judge
N 285	Not bearing false witness
N 286	Judge not to receive a wicked man's testimony
N 287	Judge not to receive testimony from litigant's relatives
N 288	Not to convict on the testimony of a single witness
N 289	Not to murder a human being
N 290	No capital punishment based on circumstantial evidence
N 291	A witness not acting as an advocate
N 292	Not killing a murderer without trial
N 293	Not sparing the life of a pursuer
N 294	Not punishing a person for a sin committed under duress
N 295	Not accepting ransom from an unwitting murderer
N 296	Not accepting a ransom from a willful murderer
N 297	Not neglecting to save the life of an Israelite in danger
N 298	Not leaving obstacles on public or private domain
N 299	Not giving misleading advice
N 300	Not inflicting excessive corporal punishment
N 301	Not to bear tales
N 302	Not to hate another Jew
N 303	Not to put another to shame
N 304	Not to take vengeance on another
N 305	Not to bear a grudge

N 306	Not to take the entire bird's nest (mother and young)
N 307	Not to shave the scall (scaly matter or encrustation on surface of skin)
N 308	Not to cut or cauterize signs of leprosy
N 309	Not ploughing a valley where *Eglah Arufah* was done
N 310	Not permitting a sorcerer to live
N 311	Not taking bridegroom from home during first year
N 312	Not to differ from a majority (composed) of traditional authorities
N 313	Not to add to the Written or Oral Law
N 314	Not to detract from the Written or Oral Law
N 315	Not detracting from the Written or Oral law
N 316	Not to curse a ruler
N 317	Not to curse any Israelite
N 318	Not cursing parents
N 319	Not smiting parents
N 320	Not to work on Shabbat
N 321	Not to go beyond city limits on Shabbat
N 322	Not to punish on Shabbat
N 323	Not to work on the first day of Pesakh
N 324	Not to work on the seventh day of Pesakh
N 325	Not to work on Atzeret
N 326	Not to work on Rosh Hashanah
N 327	Not to work on the first day of Sukkot
N 328	Not to work on Shemini Atzeret
N 329	Not to work on Yom Kippur
N 330	Not to have (sexual) relations with one's mother
N 331	Not to have relations with one's father's wife
N 332	Not to have relations with one's sister
N 333	Not to have relations with daughter of father's wife if sister
N 334	Not to have relations with one's son's daughter
N 335	Not to have relations with one's daughter's daughter
N 336	Not to have relations with one's daughter
N 337	Not to have relations with a woman and her daughter
N 338	Not to have relations with a woman and her son's daughter
N 339	Not to have relations with a woman and her daughter's daughter
N 340	Not to have relations with one's father's sister
N 341	Not to have relations with one's mother's sister
N 342	Not to have relations with wife of father's brother

N 343	Not to have relations with one's son's wife
N 344	Not to have relations with brother's wife
N 345	Not to have relations with sister of wife (during her lifetime)
N 346	Not to have relations with a menstruant
N 347	Not to have relations with another man's wife
N 348	Men may not lie with beasts
N 349	Women may not lie with beasts
N 350	A man may not lie carnally with another man
N 351	A man may not lie carnally with his father
N 352	A man may not lie carnally with his father's brother
N 353	Not to be intimate with a kinswoman
N 354	A *mamzer* may not have relations with a Jewess
N 355	Not to be promiscuous
N 356	Not remarrying one's divorced wife after she has remarried
N 357	Not having relations with woman subject to Levirate marriage
N 358	Not divorcing woman he has raped and been compelled to marry
N 359	Not divorcing a woman after falsely bringing evil name on her
N 360	Man incapable of procreation not to marry a Jewess
N 361	Not to castrate a man or beast
N 362	Not appointing a non-Israelite-born king
N 363	A king not owning many horses
N 364	A king not taking many wives
N 365	A king not amassing great personal wealth

WHY OBSERVE?

This concern, bordering on obsession, with the commandments is one of the earmarks not only of traditional Judaism, but of its progressive branches as well. As we will see shortly, each of the post-Orthodox denominations defines itself in large part by its relationship to the *mitzvot* and the laws that govern them. Abraham Joshua Heschel explains this centrality of the *mitzvot* brilliantly, contrasting their central place in Jewish thought with the much less important role of ceremonies:

Ceremonies, whether in the form of things or in the form of actions, are required by custom and convention; *mitzvot* are required by Torah. Ceremonies are relevant to man; *mitzvot* are relevant to God. Ceremonies are folkways; *mitzvot* are ways to God. Ceremonies are expressions of the human mind; what they express and their power to express depend on a mental act of man; their significance is gone when man ceases to be responsive to them. Ceremonies are like the moon, they have no light of their own. *Mitzvot,* on the other hand, are expressions or inter-pretations of the will of God. While they are meaningful to man, the source of their meaning is not in the understanding of man but in the love of God. Ceremonies are created for the purpose of *sig-nifying; mitzvot* were given for the purpose of *sanctifying.* Their function: to refine, ennoble, to sanctify man. They confer holiness upon us, whether or not we know exactly what they signify.

—"Toward an Understanding of Halacha,"
Moral Grandeur and Spiritual Audacity

Heschel cuts to the heart of another important question: why observe the *mitzvot?* For him it is an existential question. To act in the right way is "to refine, ennoble, to sanctify" humanity. We "confer holi-ness" upon ourselves by expressing our love—our trust, given that we may not even know what these acts mean—of God. In that statement Heschel echoes the words of the Rav, who seventeen hundred years earlier said that the purpose of the *mitzvot* was "to refine humanity."

Of course, other commentators have offered different explanations. In the Torah, the rationale is blunt, almost brutal: humanity is to follow the commandments or it will suffer divine punishment. In Chapters 11 and 28 of Deuteronomy the threat is made explicitly. Indeed, in the full-length version of the *Sh'ma,* recited twice a day by traditionally observant Jews, God promises "I will favor your land with rain at the proper season," for remembering the *mitzvot,* but if they are forsaken, "the anger of God will be aroused." (Deuteronomy 11:13–21)

The punishment/reward schema is certainly an element that comes into play in Jewish thought, particularly in understanding the nature of the covenant between God and the forefathers, and in the writings of the Orthodox rabbinate past and present. After all, there is a *midrash* that says that when God asked the Israelites if they would accept the commandments, the Almighty held Mount Sinai in mid-air over their heads and made the choice even easier: "Say yes, or I drop the mountain on you." The Talmud says that one "who performs one *mitzvah* receives good things."

But even in the precincts of contemporary Orthodox thinkers, this strain of thought is a minor one. In the *Pirkei Avot,* the tractate of Mishnah most directly concerned with ethics, it is written, "Be as eager to perform an easy *mitzvah* as a hard one, for you do not know their merits. . . ." In other words, the *mitzvah* should be thought of as an end in itself. There are even those who read the passage from the *Sh'ma* as a parable with an ecological bent: if you do not observe the commandments that govern the just treatment of the land, of the earth, it will become impossible for you to reap the bounty of the planet, you will get acid rain instead of rain for your crops, etc.

In the Hebrew Bible there are passages that suggest other, ethically based reasons for observing the *mitzvot.* Thus, in Psalm 19 it is written, "The commandments of Adonai are just, rejoicing the heart; the teaching of God is lucid, bringing light to the eyes." Elsewhere in the Bible it is said that by following the commandments, the Jews do honor to God, expressing their love for the Creator's teachings.

Subsequent commentators have provided a profusion of reasons for observing the *mitzvot.* Saadiah Gaon, the ninth-century sage, says that the commandments promote a state of bliss by giving a person entry to the good life, a reward for compliance granted by God's kindness. Maimonides says that the commandments are not arbitrary, as some claim, but were given for humanity's benefit: "The general object of the commandments is twofold, the well-being of the soul and the well-being of the body. They fulfill those functions by teaching people right opinions and promoting proper social relations."

David Polish, a contemporary Reform rabbi, offers a very different but intriguing thesis. He argues that "the observance of the *mitzvot* reflects a Jewish conception of history," by placing those who follow them in the stream of Jewish history, harkening back to the events that the practices themselves evoke, "historic experiences in which the Jewish people sought to apprehend God's nature and His will."

David Wolpe, a contemporary Conservative rabbi, takes another perspective. He notes that if the text of the Bible is not Divine revelation—a premise about which modern liberal (i.e., non-Orthodox) Jews have a great deal of uncertainty—then where is the obligation to observe the *mitzvot?* For if the Bible is not the Revealed Word of God, it must be in whole or in part a human product. "In other words—if God did not say it, why do it?" he asks. His answer is that the obligation stems "from relationship," that Judaism is, as he adroitly puts it, "the language we speak to each other, to history, but most especially, to God." The *mitzvot,* then, should be seen as a symbolic expression of our ongoing relationship with the Creator.

There are those Torah scholars who argue that one does the *mitzvot* because God so commanded, no other reason is necessary. Certainly, there are *mitzvot* whose rationale is unclear to us, and there have always been two schools of thought on these commandments, divided between those who seek a reason behind a *mitzvah* and those who abjure such a search.

Perhaps the latter are more in tune with one of the key themes in the consideration of *mitzvot* in the literature, an emphasis on the *doing,* the observance, more than on intention. In this respect—the valorization of act over intent—Judaism may be said to be unique among the world's major religions. Judaism is, as Bernard Raskas, a contemporary Conservative rabbi, has called it, "a hands-on religion," one in which every Jew is afforded the same opportunity for participation. It is not an accident, Torah commentators say, that when the commandments were given at Sinai, the Israelites told Moses, "We will do and we will hear." Do first, hear after. As Bar Kapparah, a third-century rabbi says, "Greater are the good deeds of the righteous men than all the creation of heaven and earth."

The stress placed on act over intent is not universally valorized. As we saw in Chapter 1, *kavanah/intention* is of enormous importance in prayer. The Khafetz Khayim remarks despairingly of the many *mitzvot* that "slip through our fingers" for lack of intent. But many rabbis would probably concur with their colleague Shmuel Boteach, director of the L'Chaim Society of Oxford University, who recently wrote:

> [W]hen it comes to the perfection of the world outside us, our motivation is wholly unimportant. This is the reason why Judaism insists that one must do a good deed even for the wrong reasons. If a businessman or woman gives a million pounds to an orphanage because they wish to be knighted, although they might not be construed as singularly humanitarian after their good deed, their actions have brought the world so much closer to redemption and

for this they deserve our respect and admiration and never our scorn. . . .

In Jewish thought man's first obligation is to make the world a better place. . . . This is why all people must do good deeds even if it is for misguided or selfish purposes.

At the same time, though, the *mitzvot,* by their very pervasiveness, their focus on the quotidian, are designed to place before us at every point in the day our obligation to "be holy" as God is holy. Thus, our intentions are not to be dismissed completely from a consideration of performing *mitzvot.* But it is a keystone of Jewish belief, as the words of the Israelites at Sinai remind us, that one can only come to understand the *mitzvot* by doing them, by imitating God.

MIND, BODY, AND SOUL

Judaism as a system (to the extent that it can be characterized as such) is based on the idea that human beings are a unity of mind, body, and soul, what Rabbi Eliezer Berkowitz calls a "biopsychic" entity. If one accepts this notion, this strikingly anti-Cartesian rejection of the mind-body split, then much of what constitutes Jewish ethical thought follows logically, almost inexorably. If mind, body, and soul are one— and are created *b'tselem Elohim/in the image of God*—then it is wrong to abuse the body. But it is also wrong to abstain from certain ordained pleasures. If mind, body, and soul are one, created in the image of God, then it is imperative that one follow a sexual ethic that places a premium on certain forms of "modesty" and "purity," because what you do with your body reflects and inflects what is in your mind. If mind, body, and soul are one, then there is an integral relationship between what we think of as worship, ethics, and social action.

So it is in Judaism: to worship God one must perform not only the obligatory "religious" rituals, one must also behave ethically towards other humans, and work for justice in the world. The *mitzvot* include not only when and how to celebrate the festivals and Shabbat, but also how to behave in a business relationship, and how to pursue the larger social good. Being a "good Jew" involves much more than *davening* three times a day and showing up in the synagogue on all the holidays.

The world is imperfect, unredeemed, damaged. The task of humankind is *tikkun olam/to repair the world,* as Rabbi Boteach said. (As we will see in Chapter 7, for the Jewish mystics, this phrase has a special meaning.) One may believe, as traditionally observant Jews do, that this entails a strict adherence to the *mitzvot* in order to bring *Moshiakh/the Messiah.* One may believe, as do Jews of all stripes, that it is within us to aspire to the perfection of the world envisioned in that messianic vision through a variety of means. For liberal Jews, that may include the *mitzvot* or not. But almost all Jews—even the vast majority of secular ones—would agree with Rabbi Jacob Z. Lauterbach, who wrote in 1913 that Judaism "aims to accomplish the ethical and religious perfection of [humanity]." The only question is how?

HALAKHAH: MITZVOT INTO LAW

Since the days of the Talmud, the answer to the question "How do we follow the *mitzvot?*" has been *"halakhah." Halakhah* is the branch of rabbinical literature that outlines the laws of Jewish religious and ethical behavior, how to observe the *mitzvot,* and, in turn, virtually every aspect of daily life for traditionally observant Jews. *Halakhah* takes its name from the Hebrew verb *halakh/walk; halakhah* might be described as the path down which observant Jews are guided by some two thousand years of rabbinical wisdom as they walk through this life.

The roots of *halakhah* are in the Torah, in the 613 *mitzvot,* but the branches of this sturdy tree of Jewish jurisprudence extend from the Talmudic period through the Middle Ages and into this morning's headlines. To understand the process by which the *mitzvot* gave rise to a vast body of legal literature, one must trace the history of *halakhah* briefly. (We will examine some of this same history in much greater detail in Chapter 6.)

In the beginning, if you'll pardon the expression, was the Written Law, *Torah She'bi-khetav,* the Torah as we think of it, the Five Books of Moses. The traditional explanation says that God dictated all of Torah to Moses. Also called *Torah min ha-shamayim/Torah from Heaven,* this was Revealed Truth. But many of the details of how to apply this Truth are missing from the Pentateuch. For example, we are instructed to marry and permitted to divorce, but not told how to go about either.

The sages of the Talmud held that there was a second set of laws, *Torah She'bi-al'peh/the Oral Law,* also given to Moses at Sinai and transmitted by word of mouth from generation to generation. As it says in the opening words of *Pirke Avot:* "Moses received Torah from Sinai and transmitted it to Joshua; Joshua to the Elders; the Elders to the Prophets; and the Prophets to the Men of the Great Assembly." Of course, the rabbis of the Talmud commented, one cannot hand over a written text without some explanation, so we were given the Oral Law as well.

Over the next eight centuries, from about 200 B.C.E. to 600 C.E., the rabbis would expound on the Oral Law, interpreting scripture by two methods that, when compiled, would become what we know as the Talmud (and related texts). One of these methods, *Midrash Agadah,* doesn't concern us at the moment; addressing questions of biblical narrative, it consists of homilies and folktales by which the sages would offer lessons in Jewish ethics and religious practice. (When someone refers to *"midrash"* what they usually are thinking of is *agadah,* as distinct from *halakhah.*)

The rabbis' method for interpreting legal Scripture is *Midrash Halakhah.* This is the basis of rabbinic Judaism, the historical successor to biblical Judaism.

The rabbis saw Scripture as the basis for a major category of *halakhah, d'oraita/from the Torah.* Within *d'oraita,* there are three possibilities: *halakhah* that derives logically from a scriptural verse, such as the prohibition against eating pork; *halakhah* derived from the interpretation of a verse or verses according to prescribed methods (see sidebar "Thirteen Ways of Looking at Torah," p. 314), such as the rules prohibiting the eating of milk and meat that were cooked together; finally, *halakhah l'Mosheh mi-Sinai/halakhah from Moses at Sinai,* strongly held traditions that the rabbis believed were Mosaic in origin and, hence, part of the original *Torah she'bi-al'peh.* Often the rabbis would cite a verse as an *aide-memoire* (called an *asmakhta,* Aramaic for an object joined to another object) in such a case. The rabbis believed that all *d'oraitot* were Sinaitic in derivation; modern scholars and liberal Jews would argue that even these are rabbinic in origin.

In fact, the rabbis did see themselves as a source of *halakhah,* but of a different category. Such *halakhah* were called *d'rabanan/from the rabbis.* The *Pirke Avot* warned, "Build a hedge around the Torah," and the rabbis responded accordingly, issuing prohibitions called *gezerot* (*gezerah* in the singular). *Gezerot* were prohibitions against behaviors that seemingly contravened the *mitzvot* or could lead to transgressions. For example, the rabbis prohibited horseback riding on Shabbat, because one might violate the Sabbath by breaking off a switch to strike the horse.

There are seven positive *mitzvot* that are derived from the Talmud rather than the Torah. These *mitzvot de-rabanan* / mitzvot *from the rabbis* include: (1) washing one's hands before a meal; (2) lighting candles for Shabbat; (3) reciting *Hallel* on a festival; (4) lighting candles for Hanukah; (5) reading the Scroll of Esther at Purim; (6) making an *eruv,* a marked-off area in which it is permissible to carry on Shabbat; and (7) reciting *b'rakhot* before experiencing material pleasures, such as eating or smelling a fragrant plant.

In the *b'rakhot* we say that God commanded us to do these things, even though they are clearly derived from the rabbis; the rabbis derived their authority from the Bible.

With the passing of time, the interpretations of the law by the sages became even weightier, more extensive and detailed than the Written Law.

By the time of the *tannaim,* the rabbinical authorities of the period of Judah Ha-Nasi (approximately 170–220 C.E.), the sheer volume of oral rulings had become so unwieldy that the rabbis reluctantly assented to their recording. The resulting text is the Mishnah, the first compilation of the Oral Law, compiled by Judah Ha-Nasi, Judah the Prince. Mishnah is written in a very compressed style; interpretation and expansion of that text was necessary. In addition, there were other *tannaitic* texts with which it had to be harmonized. And there were also new questions arising from the exigencies of daily life in exile. These materials would be compiled and codified under the name *Gemara*. Taken together, Mishnah and Gemara are what we now know as the Talmud.

The world has changed significantly in the past 1800 years, and Jewish law has had to address those changes. No code of law, no matter how ingenious, can possibly anticipate every problem that will come before its judges, particularly if it is going to be of any practical use for an extended period of time. The Talmudic sages realized that simple fact and made allowances for rabbis in subsequent centuries to issue rulings of their own, called *takanot* (*takanah* in the singular). The establishment of the *ketubah* as the marriage contract for a Jewish union is an example of a *takanah* most Jews are familiar with, although it is unlikely they know that it is, in fact, a *takanah*. The *takanot* are rulings designed to promote the public welfare and religious practice.

As we will see in Chapter 6, the Talmud is not an organized code of law but a compendium that is seemingly haphazard in its organization. Add to its structure the growing body of *gezerot, takanot,* and customs, and the average Jew was faced with an impenetrable wall of chaotic verbiage and *minhagim.* As early as the eighth century C.E., rabbis recognized the need for some kind of manageable codification of the *halakhah.* Saadiah Gaon's ninth-century *siddur* was one example of this process, offering not only the texts of prayers but the rules governing them. Maimonides' *Mishneh Torah* is one of the most complete and systematic, but the book of Jewish law considered most authoritative by Orthodox Jews today is the *Shulkhan Arukh / Set Table,* written in the sixteenth century by Joseph Caro. (See sidebar "Joseph Caro and the *Shulkhan Arukh,*" below.)

JOSEPH CARO AND THE *SHULKHAN ARUKH*

Even the most observant Jew in the world couldn't keep all 613 *mitzvot* and the myriad laws governing them in his head. To sift through the Five Books of Moses and the countless thousands of pages of Talmudic and other rabbinic literature containing this material would be an onerous task for even the most erudite Jewish scholar. Where does a traditionally observant Jew go to get the answer to a question regarding the *mitzvot* in a quick and easily digested form?

Rabbi Joseph Ben Ephraim Caro (1488–1575) created a book that has served precisely that purpose in one form or another for the past four centuries. Caro, a Jew from the Iberian Peninsula, had written a massive tome, *Bet Yosef,* between 1522 and 1554, a commentary on Jacob ben Asher's *Arba Turim* that attempted to trace every law in the Talmud, its history and development. When he had completed this multivolume work, he decided to write a digest version for use by younger students. The result, the *Shulkhan Arukh/Set Table,* has become the authoritative volume on *mitzvot,* accepted as such by Orthodox Jews around the world.

As great as Caro's achievement was, it was not without flaws. As a Sephardic Jew, he was unfamiliar with the differing *minhagim/customs* of his Ashkenazic brothers and sisters. A sixteenth-century Polish rabbi, Moses Isserles, wrote a commentary, the *Mapah/Tablecloth,* which codified Ashkenazi *halakhic* writings in a manner designed to be compatible with Caro's work, and today is found as notes in the *Shulkhan Arukh.*

Like the *Turim* that inspired its own model, the *Shulkhan Arukh* is divided into four sections: *Orakh Khayim,* a compendium of the ritual obligations of daily life that includes areas such as waking, sleeping, prayer, blessings, the Sabbath, and festivals; *Yoreh Deah,* which deals primarily with the dietary laws and ritual laws governing mourning, char- ity, vows, etc.; *Even Ha-Ezer,* which covers the laws of marriage and divorce; and *Khoshen Mishpat,* which deals with Jewish civil law in the Diaspora.

Even the *Shulkhan Arukh* is too unwieldy for everyday use. There have been many digests of Caro's book prepared and published in the past. The one most commonly used today probably is the *Kitzur Shulkhan Arukh/Digest of the Shulkhan Arukh,* compiled by Rabbi Solomon Ganzfried early in this century.

Today, the *Tur,* the *Shulkhan Arukh,* and the *Kitzur* include only those *mitzvot* that can be performed in the present day. They omit those obliga- tions that relate to the Temple.

But what of the problems that arise today, questions that a four-hundred-year-old law text cannot possibly answer? Is turning on an electric appliance permissible on the Sabbath? Can an observant Jew eat a tomato that has been genetically altered with chromosomes from a pig? Is a brain-dead patient breathing with a respirator still alive?[1] The vehicle for addressing the ongoing problems of modern Jewish life is *teshuvot/responsa.* Writing in response to specific questions of *halakhah,* contemporary rabbis will engage in discussion and debate—on the basis of relevant Talmudic texts, the medieval commentaries on those texts, and relevant precedents—in an effort to solve these puzzles and others that have arisen in the Jewish community, ranging from the role of women in services to the place of *halakhah* in the State of Israel.

Judaism is not hierarchical in structure. Since the destruction of the Second Temple there has been no Great Assembly, no Sanhedrin, no body of sages with vested authority to make laws. Judaism has no Pope, no College of Cardinals, no Archbishop of Canterbury. What gives a ruling the authority to make it stick today? The *tannaim* would point to Deuteronomy.

Today, to some extent, the esteem in which the rabbi who issues the *teshuvah* is held will affect how much weight a ruling carries in the community.

Generally, when considering the validity of a rabbinical ruling, the older ruling takes precedence. After all, the further back in history you go, the closer you are to Sinai and the Ultimate Authority. Subsequent scholars are bound by previous ones; however, where the earlier authorities disagree, the later authority is the guiding one within a given time period—for example, Talmudic, *rishonim* (medieval), *acharonim* (early modern).

Despite all the rules governing the *halakhic* process, there is still considerable leeway for individual intepretation. A community still can, if it chooses, exhibit some flexibility in *halakhah,* and there is a degree of pluralism within even the most Orthodox community.

Even so, it was inevitable that someone would come along and ask what gave a rabbi the authority to issue a ruling in the name of God at all.[2] Such voices would be heard quickly and insistently.

OPPONENTS OF *HALAKHAH*

THE SADDUCEES AND THE KARAITES

Throughout the nearly two millennia in which the process of accretion that is *halakhah* took place, there have been those within the Jewish community who rejected the authority of the rabbis, the validity of *halakhah,* or both. The first such group, the Sadducees, rejected the idea of the "life to come," and the concept of future reward and punishment calculated on the basis of how well one kept the *mitzvot.* The Sadducees came to the forefront in the third century B.C.E., but with the destruction of the Second Temple in 70 C.E. the Sadducees faded from Jewish life.

One might argue convincingly that the most successful opponents of *halakhah* were the early Christians who were, after all, a Jewish sect opposed to what they perceived as the rigid legalism of rabbinic Judaism. The route they took, apostasy and the founding of a new religion, anticipated the path onto which a handful of men like Spinoza were forced.

In the eighth century C.E. another group driven by opposition to the Oral Law came forward, the Karaites. The Karaites preached a literal interpretation of the Written Law and rejected the very idea of Oral Law. They also rejected rabbinical innovations. For example, the rabbis interpreted the biblical proscription against burning a fire on Shabbat (Exodus 35:3) to mean that one could not *light* a fire on Shabbat, but that it was permissible to use one that had been lit before the Sabbath; the Karaites, however, interpreted the verse literally and eschewed the use of fire on Shabbat completely. Although they found fertile ground for their ideas in the Middle East, they were met with fierce opposition within the community, led by Saadiah Gaon, and by the twelfth century had effectively ceased to have any influence in the Jewish world, except for small pockets in the Crimea. They continued to exist as a schismatic sect and small Karaite communities can still be found today in Israel and elsewhere.

REFORM JUDAISM

In the period between the height of Karaite activity and the nineteenth century, other individual opponents of *halakhah* appeared briefly. But the most significant and lasting challenge to rabbinical authority and *halakhah* arose in the nineteenth century with the emergence of Reform Judaism and, subsequently, the evolution of the Conservative and Reconstructionist movements.

Reform Judaism has its roots in nineteenth-century Germany and the *Haskalah,* the Jewish Enlightenment. Within the Reform movement in its earliest days, there were two approaches to *halakhah*. Rabbi Abraham Geiger enunciated one of these two positions, calling for the reform of *halakhic* procedure and practice and for a scientific use of tradition; what he had in mind was a gradual evolutionary process whereby *halakhah* would be brought into line with contemporary realities. By contrast, Rabbi Samuel Holdheim rejected the Oral Law outright as "the rigid hand of the Talmud."

Despite the presence of these two rabbis on the ramparts, the Reform movement was largely led by laymen, albeit unusually well-informed laymen by modern standards. In the early years of Reform Judaism in America, the movement's rejection of *halakhah* was explicit, deliberate, and forthright. In the 1885 Pittsburgh Platform, the founding document of American Reform, the position is stated explicitly:

"We accept as binding only the moral laws and maintain only such ceremonies as elevate and sanctify our lives, but reject all such as are not adapted to the views and habits of modern civilization." Reform rabbis and lay leaders rejected the dietary laws, the existence of a priestly caste, and codes of dress and of sexual and family purity.

But that was over a hundred years ago. In time, the Reform movement's position has evolved in several directions, most of them leading back—sometimes tentatively, sometimes enthusiastically—towards tradition. For example, at Hebrew Union College-Jewish Institute of Religion, the Reform seminary in New York City, the kitchen is strictly kosher. Moreover, the vast majority of students at HUC-JIR wear *kippot*. Reform is by its very nature a pluralistic movement (and, as such, clearly a response to the American situation); as a result, there are few norms and standards to which all member congregations are held.[3] Thus, one can find congregations in which most if not all men (and many women) wear *kippot* during services and, to the contrary, a few congregations in which the wearing of *kippot* is explicitly prohibited!

Reform Judaism has always been a response to *halakhic* guidelines, if only to reject the conventional Orthodox ones. In a growing literature of *responsa,* the Reform rabbinate has been staking out its own *halakhic* turf, so to speak. On the one hand, Reform continues to reject the authority of such Orthodox texts as the *Shulkhan Arukh* and the right of the rabbinate to issue normative rulings that would be binding on congregations and individual Jews. On the other hand, the very existence of Reform *responsa,* going back to the earliest days of the movement, suggests that the relation between Reform Judaism and *halakhah* is more complicated and less adversarial than originally thought.

Writing about Reform *responsa,* Dr. Peter J. Haas predicted in 1987, "Reform practice will not become less diverse, but more so." He adds, "What will hold matters together is not so much a common *minhag* [custom], but a common sense that whatever we do must be grounded in the literature of our common heritage, just as was true in the early Middle Ages." For the Reform Jew, individual conscience, often guided by a four-thousand-year-old heritage, informs ethical decisions. Thus, *halakhah* still is not Revealed Truth, yet neither is it to be dismissed any longer.

CONSERVATIVE JUDAISM

The Reform movement's position didn't satisfy the rabbis who founded the Conservative movement. They joined the Reform rabbinate in rejecting the idea that the Written Law was the literal work of God, the Oral Law an extension of Divine Revelation; they consider the Written Law to be Divine teaching, but transmitted by humans; unlike Reform Jews, they still adhere to *halakhah* as they understand it, treating the Oral Law as the authoritative source for *halakhah*. What sets Conservative Jews apart from their Orthodox counterparts is that although they accept the centrality of *halakhah* to Jewish decision-making in matters of ethics and religious practice, they view *halakhah* as an historical phenomenon, capable of adjusting to meet changing realities imposed by sociology, economics, politics, science, and technology.

If the Oral Law is the authoritative source for *halakhah* in the eyes of a Conservative rabbi, it is so only because it is part of an ongoing search for truth and a Divine message. Each generation must find the contemporary relevance of *halakhah* for itself. Hence, the Conservative movement chose to join with Reform and Reconstructionist Jews in ordaining women as rabbis and cantors.

Essentially, what sets the Conservatives apart from Orthodox Jews in *halakhic* matters is their willingness to consider the influence of history. They point out that *halakhah* has been subject to change throughout history.

The overwhelming majority of Conservative rabbis would undoubtedly reject some of what they would deem the more extreme positions taken by the Reform and Reconstructionist movements. Although *halakhah* should respond to contemporary pressures, they would say, the law should not be changed arbitrarily. Within the Conservative movement, such changes are made only after extensive debate in appropriate forums and a final decision by the Law Committee of the Rabbinical Assembly, the governing body of the Conservative rabbinate.

RECONSTRUCTIONISM

The Reconstructionist position on the role of *halakhah* may be best characterized by one of the most famous formulations of the movement's founder, Rabbi Mordecai Kaplan, who said, "The past has a vote, not a veto." In Kaplan's explanation of Judaism as "a civilization," he rejected the "supernaturalism" that conceived of the Written and Oral Law as Divinely revealed or inspired. Rather, he wrote in 1963, the Torah is "the expression of ancient Israel's attempt to base its life on a declaration of dependence on God, and on a constitution which embodies the laws according to which God expected ancient Israel to live."

Since the Giving of the Law at Sinai, however, Judaism has evolved as a civilization, a panoply of historical developments, folkways and culture, ethics and politics. "Due to the evolutionary character of Judaism," Kaplan explained, "its declaration and its constitution have undergone considerable change." Some of the 613 *mitzvot* are no longer binding as a result of such changes.

From a Reconstructionist viewpoint, the criteria that determine which *mitzvot* are still applicable, he concluded, are "the extent to which a commandment contributes to (a) self-identification with the Jewish people and its civilization and (b) the attainment of the twofold goal of individual and collective maturity." Commandments that do not meet those criteria he dismissed as "archaic." The role of women in Reconstructionism is a good example of how this two-pronged test plays out in practice; Kaplan's own daughter Judith was the first young woman ever to have a *bat mitzvah* ceremony (in 1922), and the Reconstructionist Rabbinical College was the first seminary to admit women as rabbinical students. For Kaplan and his followers, the prohibition on calling women to the Torah and on allowing women to serve as rabbis clearly failed the criteria he had set forth for *mitzvot*.

Ironically, because its roots were in the Conservative movement, Reconstructionist practice is at least superficially more traditional than that of Reform. Reconstructionists are more likely to observe the dietary laws, to wear *kippot,* and to have *mezuzot* on their doorways. But the theological and ethical underpinnings of those choices are based in the Kaplanian concern with the historical continuity of the Jewish people and their civilization.

REACTIONS WITHIN ORTHODOXY

Needless to say, as the influence of Reform and its successors spread, the position of many within Orthodoxy hardened. Many journalists and observers of the Jewish communal world have commented on the growing marginalization of the Modern Orthodox within the American Jewish community as they find themselves under increasing pressure from a yeshiva-trained ultra-Orthodox rabbinate.[4]

Still, there are some voices within even the most conservative (lowercase *c*) branches of Judaism that are dismayed at what they perceive as an obsession with *halakhah*. In a 1996 essay, Shmuel Boteach, a Lubavitch-trained rabbi and the head of the L'Chaim Society at Oxford University, argues that the extreme positions taken by many within the Orthodox community are nothing less than the erection of *halakhah* as a kind of idol, deifying Jewish law at the expense of God.

> [W]e speak today of *halakhah* as if it were a deity, an end in itself. Worse so, we are even seeing how the *halakhah* is being used to prevent Jews from coming closer to their Father in heaven. If we always followed the criteria that the purpose of *halakhah* is to establish a bond between God and man, then we would not make tragic mistakes that allow the *halakhah* to become a fence which isolates wayward Jews from the Creator. A case in point: How could an Orthodox congregation possibly prevent a Reform Jew, or a Jew who drives on Shabbos, from getting an *aliyah?* Shouldn't the *halakhah* facilitate greater observance on the part of all Jews so that they can recite a blessing on God's eternal Law and enjoy divine communion?
>
> —"Has *Halakhah* Become a Foreign God?"

Perhaps the answer to Rabbi Boteach's anguished question can be found within the pages of the Talmud itself, wherein Jews are cautioned, "Live by the commandments; do not die by them."

THE *MITZVOT* IN DAILY LIFE

We have seen how Judaism arrived at the *mitzvot* and how the *mitzvot* in turn led to the concept of *halakhah*. But how do these abstract concepts and processes work in real life, and how do they set Judaism apart in practice from other faiths? What are the practical applications of these broad principles?

GEMILUT KHASADIM / ACTS OF LOVINGKINDNESS

In the Mishnah, it is written that the world rests on three things, *Torah,* *avodah/worship,* and *gemilut khasadim.* Elsewhere in the Talmud it is said that the prerequisite to being a truly pious individual is a good heart. A Jew is expected to exert herself on behalf of others whenever possible. On more than a dozen separate occasions in the Torah, we are enjoined to love the stranger, "for you were strangers in the Land of Egypt."

Gemilut khasadim takes many forms. It is an important *mitzvah* to visit and comfort the sick *(bikkur kholim).* Family and close friends are expected to call as soon as they hear of someone's illness. Others should wait at least three days, but should visit. It is an important *mitzvah* to comfort the bereaved; it is no less commanded that you rejoice with the bride and groom. It is a religious obligation to extend the hospitality of one's home and table to those who need it, an obligation that takes on added weight during the festivals. It is imperative on Jews that they take any expense and trouble needed to save the life of a neighbor; in Leviticus 19, as part of God's injunction to the Israelites to be holy, we are warned, "You shall not stand idly by the blood of your neighbor." One is expected to praise the virtues of others, as you would have them praise yours, to return lost objects to their rightful owners, and to protect the property of others from loss, theft, or damage. Moreover, the obligations of *gemilut khasadim* extend even to relations with idolators.

Underlying all of these *mitzvot* in the area of *gemilut khasadim* is the instruction God gives elsewhere in Leviticus 19: "You shall love your neighbor as yourself." Rabbi Simlai observes that the Torah begins with an act of *khesed/kindness* in Genesis 2:21, when God clothes Adam and Eve, and ends with an act of *khesed,* when Moses is buried in the valley in the land of Moab. As Rabbi Hillel famously told the cynic who demanded that the sage teach him all of Torah while he stood on one foot, "That which is hateful to you do not do unto your neighbor. The rest is commentary."

THE EVIL TONGUE: *LASHON HARA*

Lashon hara/evil speech is one of the most serious of the negative commandments. Carrying gossip, whether true or false, spreading slander—these are specifically and strongly prohibited in the Torah. In Leviticus

19:16 it is written, "You shall not spread slanderous tales among your people."

The degree of severity of the violation ranges from the mildest (gossip) to the most serious (the deliberate spreading of falsehoods with the intention of injuring someone). The rabbis of the Talmudic period felt that slander was an even more egregious violation than such capital crimes as murder, adultery, and incest; in that opinion they were giving voice to their own understanding of the enormous power of the word.

The most comprehensive discussion of *lashon hara* is a book by the twentieth-century rabbi Israel Meir Cohen; indeed, it is probably his most famous book, the one from which he literally got his name: *Khafetz Khayim (Desiring Life)*. That book, in turn, received its title from Psalms 34:13–4: "Which man desires life, who loves days of seeing good? Guard your tongue from evil and your lips from speaking deceit."

TZEDAKAH/DOING JUSTICE

Within the realm of *gemilut khasadim* there is a special category, *Tzedakah,* which has its own set of imperatives. *Tzedakah* is loosely translated as "charity," but that is a misrepresentation of the concept. The Hebrew has its root in another word, *tzedek/justice*. In the Torah we are strongly enjoined, *"Tzedek, tzedek, tirdof/Justice, justice thou shalt pursue."* Rabbinical commentators have said that the repetition of the word justice is designed to underline the importance of the command. *Tzedakah* is not charity given out of *caritas,* in the Christian understanding of those words; it is given as an act of redress, as part of the process of seeking a just world.

How does *Tzedakah* differ from *gemilut khasadim?* Actually, the Talmud says that the latter is the greater deed in three ways: charity can only be performed with one's money, but acts of lovingkindness require one's body, time, *or* money; charity is only for the poor, but one can perform *gemilut khasadim* for everyone; and charity can only be given to the living, but *gemilut khasadim* is for the living and the dead (as in the *mitzvot* associated with burial).

Even so, we are enjoined explicitly to give *Tzedakah,* particularly just before the Sabbath and the festivals. The Torah tells us, "You shall surely open your hand to the poor and the destitute of your land." Elsewhere it is said that Israel will be redeemed by its acts of charity. And in the

Book of Proverbs we are told, "The doing of righteousness and justice is preferable to Adonai than the sacrificial offering."

How important is *Tzedakah?* The *haftarah* for Yom Kippur morning, the holiest day of the year, comes from Isaiah 58:1–14. God cries out to the Israelites, "Is this the fast that I look for? A day of self-affliction? . . . Is it not to share your bread with the hungry, and to bring the homeless poor into your house?" Charity, you may recall from the High Holiday liturgy, is one of the three things that can cancel God's decree of punishment in the year to come.

How we give *Tzedakah* is as important as what we give. "Do not humiliate a beggar," the Talmud warns us. "God is beside him." Rabbi Eleazar said, "The reward that is paid for giving charity is directly related to the kindness with which it is given." Deuteronomy 15:10 cautions, "Your heart shall not be grieved when you give."

Everyone is required to give *Tzedakah* according to her means. Even the poorest Jews, those who need help themselves, are expected to put aside something from what they receive in order to give *Tzedakah.* But that poor Jew's tiny donation is as great as the large donation of the wealthiest. (If making a donation would impair the impecunious Jew's ability to sustain himself, he is absolved from giving. Remember the doctrine of *pikuakh nefesh*—he must not endanger his life to perform this *mitzvah.*) It is forbidden to turn away a poor person empty-handed, but if one truly cannot give, a Jew is expected at least to offer words of comfort.

How much should one give? Judaism, like many subsequent faiths, believes in tithing, that is, in giving one-tenth of one's income for *Tzedakah.* The Talmud also warns against giving more than a fifth of one's income, thereby incurring the danger of ending up destitute and in need of *Tzedakah.*

There are other ways of giving *Tzedakah* besides the straight donation of money. (Maimonides enumerated a "ladder" of *Tzedakah* with eight degrees of charity on it. See sidebar "The Ladder of Charity" below.)

THE LADDER OF CHARITY

Maimonides wrote extensively on the obligation to aid the poor. In one of his works, he offers the following list of the eight degrees of charity:

1. The lowest level of charity is to give grudgingly.

2. The seventh level of charity is to give cheerfully but less than one should.

3. The sixth level of charity is when one gives directly to the poor, but only after being asked.

4. The fifth level of charity is to give directly to the poor without being asked.

5. The fourth level of charity is to give indirectly, with the giver not knowing the identity of the recipient but the recipient knowing the giver.

6. The third level of charity is to give indirectly with the recipient not knowing the identity of the giver but the giver knowing the recipient.

7. The second level of charity is to give indirectly with neither recipient nor giver knowing the identity of one another. (Thus, it is especially praiseworthy to give to a communal charity fund.)

8. The highest level of charity is to help a person *before* they become impoverished, whether by offering a gift in a dignified manner, extending a loan, offering a job, or helping them begin a business of their own.

Supporting one's children after they have reached the age at which they are deemed capable of self-support, supporting one's parents, donating money to an individual who wishes to study Torah—all these are called meritorious.

Along these same lines, the Jewish community has a long tradition of establishing philanthropic organizations, ranging from burial societies to organizations like the Hebrew Loan Society, which gives interest-free loans to the needy, from funds to provide hospitality to wayfaring strangers to the traditional Passover funds to buy *matzah* and wine for poor Jews. Every town in which there is a Jewish community is required *halakhically* to have a charity fund that can disburse monies that cover a week's needs of a poor family.

Judaism also is concerned with the conduct of those who receive *Tzedakah*. They are enjoined not to become dependent on others. The Talmudic sages urged even the scholar to take on menial labor rather than become a burden to the community, and many of them were laborers themselves.

ETHICS AND JUSTICE

Judaism's emphasis on action before faith is of a piece with its concern with *olam ha-zeh,* the real world of the here and now. As we have already seen, the focus of the *mitzvot* is not exclusively on the relationship between human beings and the Creator; the relationship between human beings is of equal importance.

Nowhere is this more apparent than in the stress placed on ethical behavior in the *mitzvot,* a stress that goes beyond *gemilut khasadim.* The prophet Micah says that what is required of humanity is "to act justly, love mercy, and walk humbly with your God," and the order in which he lists those essential behaviors is significant.

Among the injunctions governing interpersonal conduct, the *mishpatim,* one finds strictures against murder, theft, corruption, jealousy, and deceptive business practices. There are prohibitions against oppression of the non-Jew, against perjury, bribery, and the taking of revenge.

Even the rules of war laid down in the Torah are more humane than those practiced by other ancient cultures (if the evidence of *The Iliad* is to be believed). Although there is to be universal male conscription, the Torah explicitly exempts those who have recently built a house but not had time to dedicate it, any man who has become betrothed but has not had time to marry his fiancée, and the newly married. In fact, those who are frightened are specifically exempt from service as well, on the assumption that their fear might spread in the ranks. The laws of war (enumerated in Deuteronomy 20 and 21) also spell out the conduct expected of Jewish troops in victory: rape of captive women is forbidden; women captives must be given proper time to mourn their dead, then they must either be taken as wives or set free. Elsewhere, it is strictly forbidden to destroy the trees of a captured city.

Other societies in the Middle East contemporaneous with the ancient Israelites had some of the same ethical strictures, particularly the bans on murder, theft, incest, and adultery. However, in none of these were the concern with one's fellow man and the thirst for justice given the same centrality in interpersonal ethics. Even a casual reading of the prophets shows that the overall command to act justly, to act *imitatio dei,* is at the heart of the conduct of not only individual Jews but of the society as a whole.

There are many misconceptions about Jewish ethical teachings, especially in three specific areas.

Laws Governing Loans

Thanks in no small part to *The Merchant of Venice* (although that is another issue for another time), the image of the Jew as unscrupulous moneylender has come down through history—from Shylock demanding his pound of flesh, through Ezra Pound's insidious "usura" cantos, Jewish moneylenders have been shown charging extortionate interest rates.

In fact, the roots of Jewish lending are to be found in *Tzedakah,* in charitable works. Loans were to be given as a form of charity, not for gain. Jews were specifically prohibited from lending to other Jews "on interest." The poor were not to be condemned for an inability to repay a loan. Loans could consist not only of money but also of goods and utensils.

There were ethical considerations underlying these strictures. Such a loan was considered a form of *Tzedakah,* indeed, one of the highest forms because, as Maimonides points out in his *Mishneh Torah,* "a person who assists the poor man by providing him with . . . a loan [is] placing him in a situation where he can dispense with other people's aid."

All Jews are obligated to give such free loans, regardless of gender or class. Even those whose livelihood comes from lending are obliged to make free loans to the poor.

This said, it should be noted that the *halakhah* regarding free loans apply only to loans made to other Jews. It is permissible to make loans with interest to non-Jews. Clearly, this policy is discriminatory. To some extent, it is the result of living in an agrarian society in which one's neighbors (likely to be fellow Jews) would seek a loan to tide them over until the next harvest; by comparison, the non-Jew might well be an itinerant merchant who needed the loan purely for business reasons.

Moreover, there are several *halakhic* rulings that mitigate it. Rabbi Isaac Abrabanel, a fifteenth-century commentator, says that the acceptance of interest from non-Jews does not apply to Christians or Moslems, because their faith systems stem from Judaism originally and therefore share a common ethical basis. Likewise, the medieval commentator Rabbi David Kimkhi (known as the Radak) says that a non-Jew who has shown consideration for Jews is to be treated with the same consideration as a Jew when he borrows.

Clearly, the roots of the discrimination between loans to Jews and to non-Jews are to be found, first, in the often violent tensions between Jew and non-Jew, particularly before the Emancipation resulted in the increased integration of Jews into non-Jewish societies and, second, in the more extreme strictures against idolators and polytheists that are present throughout *halakhah* dictating relationships with non-Jews.

That said, it should be pointed out that the Torah, the Talmud, and subsequent commentators all specifically single out usurious practices for disapproval.

Capital Punishment

Genesis 9:6 states: "Whoever sheds man's blood, by man shall his blood be shed." Proponents of capital punishment have derived their position from this Torah passage and from other passages in which death is ordered for one who kills.[5] How do we resolve the apparent contradiction between the death sentence and the doctrine of *pikuakh nefesh/saving a life* and the ban on vengeance?

The sages of the Talmud were very uncomfortable with the idea of capital punishment. In *Pirkei Avot* it is said that a court that put a man to death once every seven years should be considered excessively bloodthirsty; one of the sages quoted in *Avot,* Rav Eleazar ben Azariah, went further, saying a bloodthirsty court was one that issued a death decree once every *seventy* years. Rabbis Akiba and Tarfon responded that had they been in a court with the power to issue the death penalty, no one would have been put to death.

The Oral Law makes it very difficult, virtually impossible, to execute someone for murder. In order for the death penalty to apply, two witnesses must have seen the perpetrator about to commit the crime and warned him of the potential penalty. The perpetrator must then acknowledge that he is aware of the illegality of his act and its consequences. The witnesses must see the actual murder; circumstantial evidence was not admissible in such cases. A capital case could only be heard by a panel of twenty-three judges, but such a panel could only be convened when the Temple was standing. Even then, although a majority of one for acquittal would mean the defendant was found not guilty, a majority of two was needed to convict. Finally, in a case in which the judges voted unanimously for conviction, there still could be no execution; in the legal system of the time, the judges served as both prosecuting and defending attorneys, so if a unanimous decision came down from the court it was considered as if the defendant had not been provided with counsel. As a result, the death penalty was never used, although lengthy prison sentences were often given when guilt could be established. (It is interesting to note that the State of Israel does not have the death penalty in murder cases. The only criminal ever executed in Israel was Adolf Eichmann; the state does reserve the right to use the death penalty in cases of crimes against humanity.)

"An Eye for an Eye"

The passage of Exodus in which the principle of "an eye for an eye" (known in Near Eastern history as the *lex talionis*) occurs is one of the most controversial in the Bible. Jesus explicitly denies its validity. Others have pointed to it as an example of the vengeful nature of justice in the Hebrew Bible. Many liberal Jews are uncomfortable with the message it sends. Or does it send that message?

In discussing this passage, the Talmud specifically states that it is monetary compensation that is to be sought for an injury inflicted, rather than a comparable wound. Some detractors look upon this interpretation as after-the-fact amelioration.

However, at least one recent commentator, Dr. Avigdor Bonchek, offers another view, one that views this passage of Torah in a startlingly new light. Dr. Bonchek (who is both a rabbi and a clinical psychologist) notes that in a contiguous passage discussing a man who is injured in a quarrel, the law demands a cash payment for "the loss of his time" until he is fully healed (Exodus 21:18–19). But in the passage in which the "eye for an eye" statement occurs, Exodus 21:22–25, the reference is clearly to an accidentally incurred injury: "And if men strive and hurt a woman with child so that she have a miscarriage. . . ."

This juxtaposition, he notes, would be odd enough—the accidental injury leading to a more severe penalty than the deliberate one. But if one refers to the Hebrew, a very different meaning becomes apparent. The passage reads, "But if there be harm then you shall give soul for soul, eye for eye, tooth for tooth, hand for hand, burn for burn, wound for wound, bruise for bruise." First, Bonchek notes, the logical wording would be "take soul for soul," etc., but the Hebrew clearly says "give." This diction suggests compensation. What seals the case for him, though, is the use of the Hebrew word *takhat;* this word appears many times in the Torah, he explains, "always with the meaning 'in place of' or 'on account of,' and never 'as identical substitution for.'" Consequently, he reasons, the meaning of the passage is that recompense must be *given in place of* the injured organ.

Seen in this light, it would appear that the ancient Israelite understanding of the *lex talionis* is considerably less savage than its counterpart in other Near Eastern societies of the time. This is not to suggest that Jewish law in these circumstances was somehow morally superior to that of its contemporaries. However, it is important to understand the drive towards a justice that could be applied meaningfully to real-world situations.

TIKKUN OLAM/REPAIRING THE WORLD

It is clearly the duty of every Jew to seek justice. In a world unredeemed, a world that is damaged, it is the job of every Jew to participate in *tikkun olam/repair of the world.* In areas of social justice, social action, Judaism has set itself clear mandates. "You shall do what is right and good," we are told in Deuteronomy 6:18.

To that end, one's professional conduct is as closely regulated as one's private conduct. Jewish law strives to enact fairness in business dealings between buyers and sellers. The rabbis prohibited the making of excess profits through the setting of excessive prices. The Torah banned the giving of short measures and the use of rigged weights. Hoarding of produce to drive up prices was forbidden, as was the use of fraudulent business practices.

Both Torah and Talmud are uneqivocal in their stance on labor. It is forbidden to delay paying a workman his wages, and a worker is entitled to fair pay for his work. The Talmud recognizes the right of workers to organize unions.

Even the rights of animals are safeguarded under Jewish law. The rabbis prohibited hunting for sport and pastimes that inflicted pain on animals. The Talmud explicitly states, "Man must provide for those animals he has domesticated and must not cause them any unnecessary pain." One is even enjoined to rest animals on the Sabbath.

Jewish law is predicated on our understanding that we are God's partners in creation, that we alone can repair the unredeemed world. The only way that we can do this is through moral behavior. It is no accident that in the secular world Jews have usually been in the forefront of movements for social change and social justice. For many secular Jews, social action is what connects them to their Jewish identity. For all Jews, it is nothing less than what our tradition demands of us.

SEXUALITY

Like almost all the other major world religions, Judaism has a complex set of laws governing human sexuality. However, in one major respect, the Jewish attitude toward sexuality is unique: it wholeheartedly approves of sex and of sexual pleasure. Not sex as an unfortunate but necessary way of continuing the species, but sex as a holy experience, a *mitzvah*. From that starting point, all of the other Jewish laws regarding sexual behavior may be seen as a direct outgrowth.[6]

The thirteenth-century sage Nachmanides wrote, "Intercourse is a holy and pure thing when done in an appropriate way, in an appropriate time, and with appropriate intention. . . . We believe that God created all things in accordance with His wisdom. . . . If our sexual organs are a disgrace, how could it happen that God created something shameful or ugly?"

Pleasure, like our sexual organs, is a gift from the Creator. The Talmud specifically states that "a person will be held accountable to God for refusing to enjoy those pleasures that are permitted." Maimonides calls such a person a sinner. So celibacy and self-denial are not on the Jewish agenda.

However, free love doesn't make it either. Nor do prostitution, rape, incest, or bestiality. Sex should not involve the exploitation, coercion, or subjugation of another person.

Traditional Judaism believes in sex and sexual pleasure as an important part of marriage. A husband is supposed to make sure that his wife enjoys sexual intercourse. It is indicative of how holy sex within marriage is considered that it is a *mitzvah* to have intercourse on the Sabbath.

Because the human being is a "biopsychic being," as Rabbi Eliezer

Berkovits puts it, it is essential that sex integrates both the bodily urges and the emotions, that it should "personalize the impersonal," he explains. The sexual act should come out of a genuinely interpersonal exchange for it to be a true *mitzvah*. Sexual intercourse and conversation, someone once said, are the only two human activities that cannot be done alone. What Judaism demands is that an emotional commitment be a concomitant part of the sexual act so that it doesn't become an impersonal, mechanical, animal thing. Hence the emphasis on marriage as a prerequisite to sexual intercourse, and the prohibition on illicit sexual activity.

The rabbis were not fools. They were married men themselves with their own urges. Maimonides writes, one suspects with a sigh on his lips, "No prohibition in all the Torah is as difficult to keep as that of forbidden unions and illicit sexual relations."

The sexual urge is closely linked to the *yetzer hara/evil impulse*, the urge to do evil that exists in all of us. Yet the rabbis knew that the evil impulse, created by God, had its useful side too. In sex, the *yetzer hara* takes the form of what we know as the libido; a *midrash* says that without the *yetzer hara* man would never build a house, marry, nor beget children. Clearly, the *yetzer hara* as it manifests itself in sexuality, is a source of powerful energy and drives, many of them creative (and procreative). Some translate *yetzer* as "ego," an acknowledgment that it is not, of itself, either bad or good.

However, even within marriage, the Torah calls for certain restraints on sexual intercourse. The laws governing *tohorat mishpakhah/family purity* regulate sexual relations between husband and wife. The *halakhah* of *taharat mishpakhah* proscribes intercourse during the five days of the wife's menstrual period and for seven "clean" days after. It is customary in traditionally observant homes for the couple to refrain from any physical contact at all, even sleeping in the same bed. This separation is called *niddah*, and its laws are so complex and important that an entire tractate of the Talmud is dedicated to the subject of family purity.

According to some sources, it is the possibility that a woman is an *ishah niddah*, that is, a woman separated by *niddah*, that has led to the practice among very Orthodox men of not shaking hands with a woman when introduced and to the prohibition on mixed dancing among the observant. Similarly, an Orthodox husband will abstain from public displays of affection with his wife to protect her privacy—no one can tell if she is an *ishah niddah* at a given moment if the couple doesn't touch in public as a matter of course.

The Torah does not say that menstruation is dirty or that a menstruating woman is unclean. However, a menstruating woman is considered ritually impure because she is losing bodily fluids and a potential life.

At the completion of the full twelve days (eleven in Conservative observance), the woman immerses herself in the *mikveh/ritual bath*. Many couples say that the enforced separation makes their reunion on the twelfth night all the more satisfying, and such couples invariably celebrate by making love after the wife returns from the *mikveh*.

THE *MIKVEH*

The ritual bath or *mikveh* is one of the oldest institutions in the Jewish community. Archaeologists have unearthed *mikva-ot* in Jerusalem thought to date back to the time of the Temple, as well as others at Masada and even in private homes. In the Diaspora, every Jewish community tried to have its own *mikveh*. In modern Israel, virtually every town has one.

The *halakhic* requirements for the building of the *mikveh* are strict. The water must come either from an underground source such as a spring, or rainwater, melted snow, or ice. Spring water is considered purifying when it is flowing or moving, but in a *mikveh* that uses rainwater the water must be stationary. In either case, the water cannot be collected by a human agency; it must fall into either a built-in or hewn-out pool or bath. The pipes through which it then passes on its way to the *mikveh* must be free of cavities in which water can collect; such conduit piping must be made of earthenware, stone, concrete, cement, asbestos, or plastic, none of which are materials that would attract sources of impurity in the biblical sense.

The dimensions of the *mikveh* are also specified. Translated into modern measurements, the *mikveh* must have a capacity of at least 201 gallons. Of course, a rabbinical supervisor is necessary in the building and running of the *mikveh*.

Mikva-ot are always attached to public bathing facilities. Before you enter the *mikveh* it is imperative that you wash thoroughly. Immersion in the *mikveh* is only valid if not a speck of dirt comes between you and the waters. However, you are not supposed to bathe immediately after immersion in the *mikveh*.

The *mikveh* is not only used by women completing a period of *niddah*. Proselytes undergo immersion as the symbolic completion of their conversion studies and a part of their entry into Judaism. Many Jews undergo immersion on the eve of Yom Kippur and just before the Sabbath. The *mikveh* is also used for purification of glass utensils for purposes of *kashrut*.

Herein lies one of the explanations for this *mitzvah*. By encouraging a couple to exercise restraint, to set aside their passion for a period of nearly two weeks out of every month, *taharat mishpakhah* makes the times they are together that much more special, confers a holiness on the *mitzvah* of conjugal relations. It also lessens the chance of boredom setting in. The Talmud is quite explicit on this issue, saying, "The husband becomes over-familiar with his wife and tired of her, thus the Torah prohibited her to him so that she may remain as beloved to him as she was on her wedding day."

It is possible that the rabbis had something else in mind as well. Women are usually most fertile in the middle of the menstrual cycle. Twelve days of abstention means that a couple is likely to have sex on those days on which she is likely to conceive. The result is, as Rabbi Wayne Dosick says, "Jewish birth control—in reverse."

KASHRUT/DIETARY LAWS

Up to this point, we have been primarily examining *mitzvot* that have an apparently rational basis, *mitzvot* whose purpose should be obvious to anyone. Moreover, these are largely *mitzvot bei adam le-khavero*/*mitzvot between humans*. However, there is a large body of Jewish law that admittedly is harder to explain in such terms. One area of Jewish law and ritual that is probably the most familiar example of this category and the most problematical for many contemporary Jews is the dietary laws.

Professor Menachem Marc Kellner, a contemporary commentator, refers to Judaism as "a religion of pots and pans in the eyes of those who derogate its concern with actions." Undoubtedly, it was the laws that govern *kashrut*, the Jewish dietary laws, that he had in mind when he offered that phrase.

The laws of *kashrut* are—literally—laws of pots and pans. Also laws of silverware, glassware, refrigeration, sinks, and dishwashers. Not to mention meat, fish, poultry, cheese, milk, and yogurt. Indeed, the laws of *kashrut* even have implications for objects that we don't normally associate with food at all.

The average American—indeed, the average American Jew—may look at a bottle of soda and say, "Why is this labeled kosher? What could be kosher or not kosher about a bottle of soda?" The average American Jew who doesn't observe the dietary laws knows that she isn't supposed to mix meat (*fleishig* in Yiddish) and dairy (*milchig* in Yiddish). But what is *pareve*? And why two sets of dishes, two sinks, even two ovens? The average American Jew knows he isn't supposed to eat pork, shrimp, or lobster. But what about goat? venison? locusts?

KOSHER AND *TREIF*

The term *treif,* commonly used to indicate a food that is not permitted, is a Yiddish variant on the biblical word *trefah,* which actually refers to any meat that has not been killed according to the laws of *kashrut*. The word *kosher* actually means "fit" or "proper" according to Jewish law. If the fringes on my *tallit* are not intact, it's not a *kosher tallit* and I have to get them replaced. If there is a mistake in the writing in the *sefer Torah,* it's not a *kosher* scroll. But how does that apply to food?

In Leviticus 11 and Deuteronomy 14:2–21, God tells the Israelites that there are certain categories of food that they should and should not eat:

- Among land animals, only animals that have cloven hooves and chew their own cud are permitted. Thus, the camel, the pig, the hare, and the rock badger are prohibited, but cows and goats are permissible.

- Among fish (actually sea creatures), only those that have both scales and fins can be eaten. Crustaceans, mollusks, and sharks, for example, are prohibited.

- Among birds, although no characteristics are enumerated, the Torah lists twenty-four species that are prohibited. Most of them appear to be birds of prey or carrion-eaters like the vulture, the hawk, the owl, the ostrich, and others. The permitted birds are chicken, turkey, goose, duck, and dove.

- Among amphibians and insects, anything that crawls on its belly is prohibited, as are "winged swarming things," lizards and rodents, and locusts.

- Needless to say, the products of non-kosher animals are themselves non-kosher. No camel's milk, no vulture eggs. The notable exception to this rule is that one can eat honey from bees—according to the Torah, the real source of the honey is the flowers from which the bees take pollen.

The Torah refers to all permissible creatures as *tahor/clean* and the banned ones as *tamei/unclean*.

The Torah prohibits the eating of any animal that has died a natural death. In addition, meat animals that are *tahor* must be slaughtered according to the rules of *shekhitah/ritual slaughtering*. (*Shekhitah* does not apply to fish, only to meat and fowl.) In keeping with the *mitzvot* protecting animals from unnecessary suffering, an animal killed by *shekhitah* is dispatched with a quick cutting of the throat that severs the trachea, esophagus, vagus nerves, carotid arteries, and jugular vein in a split second. The animal dies almost instantly and with no pain. Finally, all the blood must be drained from meat before it can be certified as kosher. This can be done by either of two methods, soaking and salting, or broiling on a grill. Incidentally, all raw liver must be broiled; it doesn't come "kashered," that is, in compliance with the dietary laws.

But *shekhitah* has a second purpose, one that takes us back to the ban on eating the flesh of animals that died a natural death. This method of killing makes it possible for the *shokhet/ritual slaughterer* to drain the carcass of its blood. It is forbidden by the Torah to eat the blood of an animal. The *shokhet*, incidentally, is more than just a kosher butcher; he must be knowledgeable in the laws governing *shekhitah* as well as those concerning the condition of an animal's organs. An animal with damaged or diseased organs is *trefah*.

MEAT AND DAIRY

The prohibition against mixing meat and dairy has a rather more tenuous origin in Written Law than the ban on eating *tamei* and *trefah*, which are stated quite explicitly. The passage from which it is derived occurs in Exodus 23:19 and reads, "The first of the first fruits of thy ground thou shalt bring to the house of Adonai thy God; thou shalt not seethe [or boil] a kid in its mother's milk." This passage is repeated verbatim in Exodus 34:26; the second half occurs once more in Deuteronomy 14:21. From this sentence the rabbis of the Talmudic period interpolated the proscription on the mixing of meat and dairy. The Oral Law extended the definition of meat to include fowl as well.

From this slender base, the sages erected a considerable edifice of dietary laws. Meat, meat fats, products containing meat fats or other meat ingredients are considered *fleishig* (*basar* in Hebrew)[7]; milk, milk fats, products containing milk derivatives are considered *milchig* (*halav* in Hebrew). Products that contain neither milk nor meat are considered neutral, called *pareve* in Yiddish or *stam* in Hebrew. This category includes everything that is grown in the soil, from fruits and vegetables to coffee, sugar and spices, all kosher fish, eggs, and chemically produced goods. *Pareve* foods may be eaten with either meat or dairy.

The rules against mixing meat and dairy do not stop with dishes that combine the two. It is not permissible to use the same vessel to cook meat and dairy dishes, even if you do so at different times; a vessel that has been used to cook meat may absorb minute amounts of the meat and likewise for a dish used to cook dairy. Consequently, in a traditionally observant household, there will be separate pots, pans, and dishes for meat and for dairy; some houses will include a second sink and even a second refrigerator (although that is more likely in a kosher restaurant or caterer).

After eating a meat meal, an observant Jew must wait between three and six hours before she can eat dairy. This waiting period is designed to allow the fatty residue on the palate and meat particles trapped between the teeth to dissipate. However, after a dairy meal this waiting period is not considered necessary as the fatty materials do not cling to the palate in the same way. (The exception is hard cheeses, fragments of which may become lodged in the teeth.) One may eat meat at lunch and dairy at dinner, but there should be a decent interval between, and the exact nature of that interval is culturally determined. Dutch Jews, for example, may wait only one hour after eating one category of food before being permitted to eat the other.

The problems of maintaining a kosher kitchen have gotten both easier and harder with the advent of modern technology. On the one hand, the increased availability of truly non-dairy substitutes for butter, milk, and cream has afforded kosher cooks a wider range of possibilities. On the other hand, the ingredients that go into prepared foods are getting more arcane all the time. For example, one of the most bizarre problems to arise recently in the field of *kashrut* is the discovery that certain food dyes are composed of the crushed carapaces of beetles, and therefore are *tamei,* as are any foods that use them. But you wouldn't know that from reading the list of ingredients on the label.

Which brings us to the kosher soda bottle and, in a roundabout way, to the question of kosher certification.

What could be unkosher about a bottle of soda? Suppose the bottling plant workers were having a ham-and-Swiss sandwich for lunch and ate next to the assembly line. Of course, that example is a bit outlandish, but in the complexities of modern industrial food manufacturing, stranger things have happened. What kind of lubricant is used in the bottling machine? If it's petroleum-based, there shouldn't be a problem, but what if it is derived from a food product?

Before a company can proclaim its products to be kosher, they must be certified by a qualified rabbi (invariably Orthodox). There are over 400 different bodies in the United States alone that grant a *heksher,* the insignia that guarantees that a product is kosher. Kosher certification has become a big business in the United States as more people seek out kosher foods. Seventh-Day Adventists and Moslems observe similar dietary restrictions and know they are safe eating kosher; health-conscious shoppers know that kosher certification is a theoretical guarantee that the food was produced under the most sanitary of conditions.

BUYING KOSHER

If a product has been certified as kosher, the certifying body will give permission for the manufacturer to put an insignia, a *heksher,* on the package, indicating who has certified it as meeting the standards of *kashrut.* The most common symbol is a capital *U* inside a circle—the OU that stands for the Union of Orthodox Jewish Congregations, an umbrella organization of Modern Orthodox congregations, which is the largest certifying body in America. Poultry will bear a *plumba,* a small metal tag indicating that it has been certified kosher.

There are literally hundreds of certifying groups in the United States and Canada alone, each with its own distinctive *heksher*. For a current guide to kosher products, check at www.koshermall.com/indxagen.htm.

In New York State, a restaurant or food shop that is kosher must post a certificate from the certifying body (or rabbi) responsible for ascertaining its status in a visible place. Wherever you live, if you find such a certificate posted, you are probably on safe ground.

(For further information, please see Appendix 5, the Orthodox Union primer on *kashrut*.)

KOSHER WINE

Because wine is the product of vines, growing from the earth, one might assume that if it is pure it needn't be certified kosher. However, wine is unique among fruit products, no doubt because of its ritual importance in Jewish practice. Because ancient pagans used wine in their rituals as well, it was necessary for Jews to supervise every aspect of the winemaking process, from the growing of the grapes through the bottling and shipping.

Today, only wines whose production has been supervised by an observant Jew at all stages—planting, harvesting, winemaking, barreling, bottling—can be certified as kosher. Traditionally observant Jews may even insist that wine be poured by a Jew.

Today, an increasing number of Jewish families are choosing to observe *kashrut*, including many Reform Jews. They are faced with a wide range of options. Of course, one can observe strict *kashrut*, eating only foods that have a *heksher* and that have been prepared in a kosher kitchen. Others observe "biblical *kashrut*," abstaining from those foods the Torah calls *tamei*, still others take that one step farther and eat only kosher meat. Some combine "biblical *kashrut*" with the separation of milk and meat. These days some Jews have chosen vegetarianism altogether, which moots the point. For many of them, this is a *Jewish* choice, expressing a commitment to the sanctity of animal life.

Why keep kosher? What is the rationale for this complicated set of *mitzvot*?

It has been argued that the animals that are *tamei* are bottom-feeders, like shrimp and clams; carrion-eaters, like the vulture; or just plain filthy, like the pig. Therefore, some reason, *kashrut* is a matter of health. Are the eating habits of goats appreciably more sanitary than that of pigs? Unlikely. In the modern world of government meat inspections, at least in principle, our foods are safe to eat; you are probably as likely to get salmonella from eating chicken or eggs as you are trichinosis from pork. So the health argument isn't convincing today.

An explanation by Edward L. Greenstein is intellectually more compelling. Greenstein says that the animals that one is permitted to eat are those that are herbivorous and which "fall within the categories that God created in the beginning: those that graze on the land, those that wing in the air, and those that flap in the sea." Prohibited animals combine characteristics across those categories; for example, the lobster "walks" in the sea, the pig does not chew its cud (so it doesn't "graze"). Such animals are a sort of affront to God's taxonomy.

Some commentators have suggested that the prohibition on "seething a kid in its mother's milk" is another example of the Torah's concern with the humane treatment of animals.[8] That doesn't explain the extensive set of rules regarding the mixing of meat and dairy dishes. What does a cream in your coffee after a steak at lunch have in common with this passage of Torah?

In fact, for the observant Jew, such explanations are not even necessary. One can search for the reasons[9]; it is an important part of reading the Law and may give us the feeling that we are drawing near to the Eternal. But the observant Jew accepts the arbitrary nature of some commandments as the way things are. Why? Because God wants us to.

If that answer doesn't satisfy, consider this one. For a Jew who keeps kosher, every meal, every snack, every shopping trip forces her to consider the nature of what she is eating, the how and the why of it. And the consciousness that creates goes far beyond the "how many calories, how many grams of fat" of the compulsive dieter. A *kashrut*-observing Jew is brought face-to-face with his belief in the Almighty every time he lifts a fork to his mouth or puts a box of cereal in his shopping cart. To achieve that complete sense of connectedness to the Holy, an extra set of dishes seems a small price to pay.

Ultimately, this consciousness of the presence of the Ineffable is achieved by separating the world into the pure and impure, the sacred and the ordinary. The division between *kosher* and *treif,* the separations of *niddah* are like the *Havdalah* blessing that closes each Shabbat. We acknowledge that God has divided the world in all these many ways and we imitate those divisions by observing these *mitzvot*. And in doing so, we set ourselves apart as a holy people.

TAKING *KHALLAH*

When most people hear the word *khallah*, they think of the braided loaves served on Shabbat. In fact, the name derives from a *mitzvah* that accompanies the baking of these loaves. When the Temple still stood in Jerusalem, one made an offering to the High Priest, as commanded in Numbers 15:7–21. This offering, the *khallah*, consisted of one-twenty-fourth of the "dough of the householder" or one-forty-eighth of the "dough of the baker." With the Temple long since destroyed and no High Priest in attendance, we now burn the dough-offering. When making a *khallah*, before kneading the dough, the baker will take from each batch (a batch being at least 2 pounds, 10 ounces) an olive-sized piece and burn it, while reciting the blessing:

Barukh atah Adonai, Eloheinu Melekh ha-olam, asher kidshanu b'mitzvotav v'tzivanu l'hafrees khallah min ha-isah.

Blessed are You Adonai, our God, Ruler of the Universe, who sanctified us with Your commandments and commanded us to separate khallah *from dough.*

MATCH BUT DON'T MIX: *SHA'ATNEZ*

In Leviticus 19:19 Jews are forbidden to mix wool and linen or to mix other species of seeds. They are also prohibited from mating different species of animals and from yoking them together (behind a plow, for example). It takes no great imagination to understand the prohibitions regarding animals; it would be cruel to yoke together animals that greatly differ in size and strength, since one of them is going to get dragged along, perhaps even choked.

But the other ban is mystifying. Rashi, the great medieval Bible commentator, admits that he cannot find an explanation for it. Still, even today Orthodox Jews will submit garments to a *sha'atnez* test to make sure that they do not contain this forbidden mixture of wool and linen.

Edward L. Greenstein, former professor of Bible at Jewish Theological Seminary now teaching at Tel Aviv University, offers a possible answer. In the initial act of creation, God established categories, classes of things, species. He cites Joseph Bekhor Shor, the twelfth-century Bible commentator and a student of Rashi's, who suggested a ban on all hybrids, "Do not sow your orchard with two kinds [of seed], lest the sum of the seed which you have sown and the produce of the orchard become consecrated." In short, by combining or cross-breeding species, humans usurp the act of creation by making something that the first Creator didn't.

NOTES

1. The quick answer to these questions: simply put, turning on an electrical appliance is considered in the same realm as lighting a fire, so it is prohibited on the Sabbath; because it is not visible to the human eye, pig's DNA used in gene-splicing is not considered *treif/non-kosher*, under a Talmudic principle rather like the Anglo-American *de minimis non curat lex/the law takes no notice of trifles;* where there is no brain activity, life is considered over (although this last issue is a source of considerable disagreement).

2. The answer to this question—who authorized a rabbi to issue rulings—is a simple one—the rabbi before him (or her). Rabbis are ordained in a ceremony called *s'mikhah/laying on of hands*. The original authority is Moses, who vested that authority in Joshua, as stated in the opening sentences of *Pirke Avot*. Each subsequent generation has received that authority by the laying on of hands, an explicit conferring of authority upon the next generation of the rabbinate. During the Roman occupation of Palestine, the chain was broken. Rabbi Akiba was the last to grant actual *s'mikhah*. What is done today in liberal Judaism is purely symbolic. If all the rabbis in Israel agree, *s'mikhah* may be granted; the only person ever to receive this honor was Joseph Caro (which is why the *Shulkhan Arukh* carries such extraordinary weight in Orthodox circles).

3. Despite its detractors, the Union of American Hebrew Congregations, the governing body of Reform Judaism in the United States, does hold its member congregations to certain standards. They rejected an application for membership submitted by a "humanistic" congregation in Cincinnati whose services rejected all mention of God to the extent that the *Sh'ma* was actually omitted from their liturgy.

4. Ironically, one of the primary tenets of Modern Orthodoxy, that one can and should balance secular and religious studies, is a source of the movement's marginalization. The most promising scholars to emerge from Modern Orthodox institutions like Yeshiva University are pursuing careers in the secular world, in everything from the sciences to business and politics. As a result, even YU's faculty has taken on a more ultra-Orthodox flavor; after all, it's the ultra-Orthodox *yeshivot* that are turning out most of the Orthodox rabbinate today.

5. It is significant to note that God does not kill Cain as punishment for the murder of Abel.

6. This positive attitude is circumscribed by an important proviso: traditionally, Judaism valorizes sex between a man and woman who are married to one another. To find a sex-friendly attitude towards gay and lesbian relationships, one must look to the Reform and Reconstructionist movements.

7. To offer one example of the interpretations that result from the inclusion of by-products and meat-derived elements, there has been considerable debate in the Orthodox community over the use of gelatin, since it uses meat by-products in its manufacture.

8. On the other hand, the twelfth-century Bible commentator Joseph Bekhor Shor argued that the entire passage has been misunderstood. He wrote that the word translated as "seethe" or "boil" actually means "to ripen or become mature." Taken in tandem with the first part of the sentence, about offering first fruits as a sacrifice to Adonai, he says, the correct reading of the sentence is that you will not allow a kid to *mature* from its mother's milk but will offer it to God while it is still young.

9. In one of the most convincing arguments, Maimonides holds that the observance of *kashrut* serves as a kind of discipline that "accustoms us to restrain both the growth of desire and the disposition to consider the pleasure of eating and drinking as the end of man's existence."

CHAPTER 5

In the Beginning:
The Hebrew Bible

THE TANAKH

The Jews are often called "the People of the Book." The Bible is *the* Book. Other books are as important; indeed, among the Orthodox, the Talmud is more closely studied than the Bible. But everything in Jewish law and lore, belief and worship, proceeds from the Bible, especially from the first five books of the Bible, the Torah, the Five Books of Moses. The first five books of the Bible are also known as the Pentateuch, a word derived from the Greek meaning "five pieces," and the *Khumash* (pl. *khumashim*), derived from the Hebrew word for five.

The Bible is a book with many names, as befits a work that is protean in form and cosmic in scope. In the rabbinic literature, it is referred to as *Ha-Sefarim/the books,* a name that echoes its English name, derived from the Greek *ta biblia/the books.* From ancient Israel through the medieval period, Jews would also call it *Sifrei Ha-Kodesh/the Holy Books* or *Kitvei Ha-Kodesh/the Holy Writings.* Today, it is commonly called the *Tanakh,* an acronym derived from the Hebrew initials of each of its three parts, as Jews divide the book: *Torah, Nevi'im/the Prophets,* and *Ketuvim/the Writings.* Occasionally it is called the *Mikra/Proclamation,* because it is read aloud in public in the synagogue.

One thing Jews most definitely do *not* call it is "the Old Testament," an appellation applied by Christians in distinction from their Scriptures, "the New Testament." Such a label implies that the Hebrew Bible has been superseded by its Christian successor; in fact, the doctrine that

Christianity has rendered Judaism obsolete is called "supersessionism," and is a source of considerable controversy in interfaith circles.[1]

As the name "Hebrew Bible" would indicate, the Tanakh is written almost entirely in Hebrew. There are a few passages in Aramaic, a Semitic language commonly spoken in the Middle East in the period of its composition. (Aramaic was, in fact, the everyday language of Jews in the period of the Babylonian Exile.) Such passages are few in number: two words in Genesis 31:47, the verse Jeremiah 10:11, sections of the books of Daniel (2:46–7:25) and Ezra (4:8–6:18 and 7:12–26).

THE BOOKS OF THE HEBREW BIBLE

Torah (Five Books of Moses; Khumash, Pentateuch)
  *Bereishit/*Genesis
  *Shemot/*Exodus
  *Vayikra/*Leviticus
  *Bamidbar/*Numbers
  *Devarim/*Deuteronomy

Nevi'im (Prophets)
  Nevi'im rishonim (Former Prophets)
    *Yehoshua/*Joshua
    *Shof'tim/*Judges
    *Shmuel Aleph/*I Samuel
    *Shmuel Bet/*II Samuel
    *Melakhim Aleph/*I Kings
    *Melakhim Bet/*II Kings

  Nevi'im akharonim (Latter Prophets)
    *Yish'yahu/*Isaiah
    *Yirmiyahu/*Jeremiah
    *Yehezkel/*Ezekiel

  The Twelve Minor Prophets
    *Hoshea/*Hosea
    *Yoel/*Joel
    *Amos/*Amos
    *Obadyah/*Obadiah
    *Yonah/*Jonah
    *Mikah/*Micah

*Nakhum/*Nahum
*Habakuk/*Habakkuk
*Zefanyah/*Zephaniah
*Haggai/*Haggai
*Zekaryah/*Zechariah
*Malakhai/*Malachai

Ketuvim (The Writings)
  *Tehillim/*Psalms
  *Mishleh/*Proverbs
  *Iyob/*Job
  *Five Megillot/*Scrolls
    *Shir ha-Shirim/*Song of Songs
    *Rut/*Ruth
    *Eikhah/*Lamentations
    *Kohelet/*Ecclesiastes
    *Ester/*Esther
  *Danyel/*Daniel
  *Ezra/*Ezra
  *Nehemyah/*Nehemiah
  *Dibrei Hayamim Aleph/*I Chronicles
  *Dibrei Hayamim Bet/*II Chronicles

In all, the Tanakh has thirty-nine books (counting the twelve minor prophets as a book apiece rather than a single book, and two books for each of the subdivided texts—Kings, Chronicles, etc.). The division of the Bible into books dates from at least the time of the Greek translation, the Septuagint, roughly the third century B.C.E. The exact form of the canon—the institutionalization of the Hebrew Bible's contents—took place about five hundred years later. (See sidebar "The Apocrypha and Pseudepigrapha" below.) The verse and chapter breakdowns derive from the Vulgate, the Latin translation of the Bible, and are first found in a thirteenth-century manuscript.[2]

THE APOCRYPHA AND PSEUDEPIGRAPHA

The Tanakh was assembled gradually, over several centuries. The earliest writings may date back as far as the eleventh century B.C.E., while the latest ones probably were written as much as eight hundred years later. But sometime around 100 C.E., the rabbis recognized that they would have to determine which of the many books of sacred and religious writings were to be included in the Tanakh, given the imprimatur of the sages, and declared holy. The canonization of the Hebrew Bible was essentially carried out by the school of Talmudic sages at Yavneh. Once the canon was established, no further books were to be added.

The books that fell outside the canon and which were therefore omitted from the Hebrew Bible are of two types, the Apocrypha ("hidden books") and the Pseudepigrapha (books written by someone other than the author to whom they were ascribed). The books from both groups date from the period between the composition of the Tanakh and the New Testament, probably between 300 B.C.E. and 100 C.E.

The Apocrypha include books that are part of the Greek translation of the Bible, the Septuagint. As such, they are a part of the canon of the Bibles of the Greek Orthodox and Roman Catholic churches. Among the books in this group are the four books of the Maccabees (including the story of Hanukah), Tobit, Judith, Baruch, The Wisdom of Solomon, Jubilees, the Sibylline Books, and others. These books were written in a variety of languages, including Hebrew, Aramaic, and Greek.

Since Talmudic scholars did not accept them in the canon, these books were preserved only in Christian churches or in the libraries of the Dead Sea sect, those famous scrolls found in the cave at Qumran, with the exception of the book Ben Sira, which is quoted in the Talmud.

Because they are part of the Catholic and Greek Orthodox canon, the number of books in the Apocrypha is frozen. By contrast, the Pseudepigrapha keep growing all the time. The texts discovered at Qumran, the so-called Dead Sea Scrolls, include many new books.

WHAT IS IN THE HEBREW BIBLE?

The Hebrew Bible can be defined in many, often overlapping ways. As its names suggest, it is a book of *torah/instruction,* of prophecy, and of holy writings of several types. Within its pages, we find law codes, genealogies, histories, cosmology, folktales, poetry, proverbs, prayers, and more. It even includes a description (in the book of Ezra) of its own editing. Indeed, on one level the Bible is a masterpiece of intertextuality, a book that contains its own commentaries; you cannot understand the impassioned tones of the book of Jeremiah without recourse to Deuteronomy, nor the complex legalisms of Deuteronomy without a reading of Leviticus (or Genesis, for that matter).

At the heart of the Tanakh are certain concepts that are basic to the nature of Judaism, some of which we have already encountered: Judaism as a covenant faith, based on a covenant between the Jews and the Creator; a cycle of transgression, exile, and redemption; the unity of God that is the basis for ethical monotheism with its system of reward and punishment.

The contemporary Bible scholar Jon D. Levenson conceives of the Hebrew Bible as a set of polarities: Sinai, the mountain at which the Covenant is forged between the Almighty and Moses on behalf of the Jewish people; and Zion, the site of the Temple, the place of home-coming, of the ingathering of exiles that will precede the coming of the Messianic Age. In these two loci we find the embodiment (and in the Voice that thunders from the mountain, the sound) of the major themes of the Tanakh.

The biblical history of the Jews consists of a series of covenants made by God with Adam, Noah, Abraham, Jacob, Moses, David, followed by transgressions by humanity resulting in expulsions by God and periods of exile, leading eventually to some sort of redemption and God's for-giveness. Consider these sequences that occur in the Bible:

- God gives Adam dominion over the creations in the Garden (implied by the task of naming) and gives him Eve as a partner; the transgres-sion of the eating of the Fruit of the Tree of Knowledge of Good and Evil; expulsion from the Garden; a new covenant—"be fruitful and multiply and subdue the earth";

- God's covenant with Noah—"I will not destroy humanity again"— humans build the Tower of Babel; God scatters them over the face of the earth and confounds their languages; God seeks out Abram and establishes a relationship with him (leading to a covenant);

- God gives Moses the Ten Commandments on Sinai; the Israelites build the Golden Calf; God decides that this generation of Israelites will wander in the wilderness for forty years; God lets the next gen-eration enter Canaan.

There are many more similar series, from the wandering of Cain after he murders his brother, to Jacob's departure after he tricks his father into giving him the blessing meant for Esau. The cycle culminates in the destruction of the First Temple and the Babylonian Exile, which ends with the return of the Hebrews to Palestine and the erection of the Second Temple. Finally, after the destruction of the Second Temple, the Jews are scattered over the face of the earth once more, awaiting the ingathering of the exiles, a return to Israel, and the coming of the Messianic Age, an ultimate redemption of humanity and fulfillment of God's promises.

Throughout the Bible, two facets of God are emphasized, mercy and justice. The rabbis ask repeatedly how it is possible for these two seemingly opposed qualities to co-exist. The answer lies in God's unwillingness to extend a final judgment on human failings. Yes, God destroys humanity with the Flood, but the Creator also preserves some of Creation on the Ark. Yes, Moses, Joshua, and their loyal followers kill many who worshipped the Golden Calf, but Aaron and the women are left alive. Yes, David is punished for his transgressions by not being allowed to build the Temple, but his son Solomon completes that task and the Davidic kingship is guaranteed by the Almighty. Repeatedly, God tempers justice, potentially cruel and usually swift, with mercy.

How are we to read this Book? Although there is strong evidence in recent archaeological finds for the historical actuality of many passages of the Bible, the authors had no notion of objective historical writing as we know it. Instead, they saw themselves as conveying a higher truth, a transcendent truth.

Therein lies one answer to the question. One can take the words of the Tanakh as Revealed Truth, as do Orthodox Jews, words dictated by God to Moses on Sinai. One can adopt the position of the liberal streams of Judaism, that the Bible is the product of humans but divinely inspired. Or you can treat it as a great work of literature, created by anonymous authors and editors out of variegated materials that included Near Eastern legal documents and myths from the Fertile Crescent.

The one thing that we cannot do is to ignore it. There has been no book in the history of the West that has done more to shape the ideologies, theologies, and other belief systems by which we live. For better and worse, the Hebrew Bible has served not only as the founding myth of Judaism but also as the base from which Christianity and Islam evolved. There is no major Western religion that does not owe its existence in some way to the Hebrew Bible.

One final word on reading the Bible: it is tempting but inappropriate to apply contemporary standards of morality and behavior to this text willy-nilly. Clearly, there is a dissonance between our sensibilities and those of the Tanakh, a dissonance that rings loud and often. Particularly as articulated by the liberal denominations of Judaism, a Jew's responsibility is to find a way of reconciling that clash, of finding an ethic based in Scripture that we can live with, neither placing a grid of modernity over an ancient text nor trying to adopt wholesale ancient sensibilities to modern life. (Indeed, this task is one that even the Orthodox contend with in their use of Talmud, as we will see in Chapter 6.)

Professor Joel Rosenberg offers the following astute observation on the tendency of contemporary readers to dismiss biblical passages that are found guilty of "isms" like sexism or nationalism:

> Every biblical story has a silent content that belies these tidy categories, and even in so simple and straightforward a narrative as the recounting of the serpent's temptation of the woman, we can find multiple and possibly contradictory meanings. While there's always the possibility that we're overinterpreting, we can still incur the alternative danger of prematurely choosing a single "correct" reading—which, in its own way, is a form of overinterpretation as well. We must remain imaginatively alive to all possibilities, while reserving definitive judgments until we gain a cumulative impression of many texts.
>
> —"Biblical Narrative," *Back to the Sources: Reading the Classic Jewish Texts,* ed. by Barry Holtz

One could even go further and say, as another contemporary commentator, Michael Fishbane, does that the "capacity of the Bible to incorporate multiple structures of reality" is a part of what makes it a sacred text. Such a structure of openness makes reductive readings foolish indeed.

THE TORAH

This is the starting point, the cornerstone upon which Judaism was built. The rest, as Hillel says in another context, is commentary.

The Torah is—in the most common usage of the word—the first five books of the Bible, called Pentateuch, *Khumash,* or the Five Books of Moses because legend ascribes their authorship to him. (For another view, see the section "Who Wrote the Hebrew Bible?" on p. 306.)

The Torah consists of:

1. Genesis/*Bereishit,* also called *Sefer Ha-Yetzirah/the Book of Creation*[3]

2. Exodus/*Shemot,* also called *Sefer Ha-Ge'ulah/the Book of Redemption*

3. Leviticus/*Vayikra,* also called *Torah Kohanim/Instructions of the Priests*

4. Numbers/*Bamidbar,* also called *Khumash Ha-Pekudim/the Book of the Censuses*

5. Deuteronomy/*Devarim,* also called *Mishneh Torah/the Repetition of the Torah.*

The Hebrew names of each book are derived from the first word of the texts: *Bereishit/Beginning, Shemot/Names, Vayikra/And He Called, Bamidbar/In the Wilderness, Devarim/Words.* The commonly used names (Genesis, etc.) are derived from Greek, and reflect the content of the books. Genesis is a book of the origins of Creation and humanity, Exodus the story of the departure of the Jews from bondage in Egypt, Leviticus a compendium of laws, Numbers for the most part an enumeration of the Israelites and their families, Deuteronomy (from the Greek word for two or twice) a repetition of the laws enumerated in the previous three books.

The word *torah* comes from the Hebrew root *yorah/teach.* Although it is often translated as "laws" and includes a lot of material that could be called legal in nature, it would be more accurate to call the Torah "Instruction" or "Teachings." Jews often refer to "the Torah" when they are discussing a specific section of the Pentateuch covering a single topic, as in the "Torah of the Nazirite." Conversely, the term is often used to encompass not only the first five books of the Bible, but the entire Tanakh and the Oral Law as well. (However, when the term appears in this book, it refers to the Five Books of Moses, unless otherwise stated.)

The Torah's five books offer a continuous narrative, beginning with Creation and continuing all the way up to the death of Moses just before the Jews enter Canaan. (As we shall see shortly, the book of Joshua picks up the story immediately after, and the next several books of the Prophets continue the chronology.)

THE *PARASHIYOT* AND THE *HAFTAROT*

The public reading of the Torah dates from the time of Ezra (approximately 444 B.C.E.), although Deuteronomy was apparently read aloud to the Israelites during the reign of Josiah, some two hundred years earlier. The ritual of reading from a portion of the scroll each week during Shabbat, Monday, and Thursday morning services is of a later vintage. (Monday and Thursday were chosen because they were market days in Jerusalem and, therefore, the services were well-attended by farmers and merchants from outlying areas.) The Palestinian custom was to read the entire book in three-year cycles, the Babylonian custom in one-year cycles. Eventually, the Babylonian custom prevailed.

The division of the Torah into *parashiyot* obviously dates from the time in which the weekly reading became the norm among Babylonian Jews. The division of the scroll into weekly portions followed a few guidelines. When the book of the Torah ends, that is the end of the Torah portion as well. A Torah portion never ends on a sad or depressing note (one more reason why we proceed directly from the end of Deuteronomy, with Moses's death, directly to the beginning of Genesis and the next *parashah*, on Simkhat Torah). The portions take their names (which they, in turn, usually confer upon the Sabbath on which they are read) from the first Hebrew word of the reading.

Among Sephardic Jews, these portions are known as *parashiyot* (sing. *parashah*). Ashkenazim use this term to refer to the seven divisions of the weekly portion into *aliyot;* they use the term *sidrot* (sing. *sidrah*) for the weekly portion. However, many Jews today use these terms virtually interchangeably.

The establishment of the *Haftarot,* the readings from the Prophets that take place after the reading of the *sidrah* for the week in the Torah service, probably took place before the destruction of the Second Temple.

The readings have their roots in the anti-Semitic persecutions of the second century B.C.E., when the Syrian monarch Antiochus Ephiphanes (the one the Maccabees rebelled against) banned the public reading or study of Torah. In response to this edict, the sages instituted the reading of passages of the *Nevi'im* that had a thematic relationship to the week's Torah portion. Even today, there is a link, often tenuous but undeniably there, between the *sidrah* and the *haftarah* for the week.

It is not known when or by whom the readings that we use today were chosen. Every book of the Prophets is used for the *haftarot*, except Nahum, Zephaniah, and Haggai.

The following are the fifty-four *sidrot* and the *haftarot* that accompany them.

TORAH PORTION	TORAH		HAFTAROT
Bereishit	Genesis	1:1 – 6:8	Isaiah 42:5 – 43:10 (42:5 – 21 [Sephardic *Haftarah*])
Noakh	"	6:9 – 11:32	Isaiah 54:1 – 55:5 (54:1 – 10)
Lekh Lekha	"	12:1 – 17:27	Isaiah 40:27 – 41:16
Vayerah	"	18:1 – 22:24	II Kings 4:1 – 37 (4:1 – 23)
Khayeh Sarah	"	23:1 – 25:18	I Kings 1:1 – 31
Toledot	"	25:18 – 28:9	Malachi 1:1 – 2:7
Vayetzeh	"	28:10 – 32:3	Hosea 12:13 – 14:10; 14:7 or Micah 7:18 (11:7 – 12:12)
Vayishlakh	"	32:4 – 36:43	Hosea 11:7 – 12:12 (Obadiah 1:1 – 21)
Vayeshav	"	37:1 – 40:23	Amos 2:6 – 3:8
Miketz	"	41:1 – 44:17	I Kings 3:15 – 4:1
Vayigash	"	44:18 – 47:27	Ezekiel 37:15 – 28
Vayekhi	"	47:28 – 50:26	I Kings 2:1 – 12
Shemot	Exodus	1:1 – 6:1	Isaiah 27:6 – 28:13; 29:22, 23 (Jeremiah 1:1 – 2:3)
Va'era	"	6:2 – 9:35	Ezekiel 28:25 – 29:21
Bo	"	10:1 – 13:16	Jeremiah 46:13 – 28
Beshalakh	"	13:17 – 17:16	Judges 4:4 – 5:31 (5:1 – 31)
Yitro	"	18:1 – 20:26	Isaiah 6:1 – 7:6; 9:5, 6 (6:1 – 13)
Mishpatim	"	21:1 – 24:18	Jeremiah 34:8 – 22; 33:25, 26

Terumah	"	25:1 – 27:19	I Kings 5:26 – 6:13
Tetzaveh	"	27:20 – 30:10	Ezekiel 43:10 – 27
Ki Tisah	"	30:11 – 34:35	I Kings 18:1 – 39 (18:20 – 39)
Vayakel	"	35:1 – 38:20	I Kings 7:40 – 50 (7:13 – 26)
Pekudei	"	38:21 – 40:38	I Kings 7:51 – 8:21 (7:40 – 50)
Vayikrah	Leviticus	1:1 – 5:26	Isaiah 43:21 – 44:23
Tzav	"	6:1 – 8:36	Jeremiah 7:21 – 8:3; 9:22, 23
Shemini	"	9:1 – 11:47	II Samuel 6:1 – 7:17 (6:1 – 19)
Tazriah	"	12:1 – 13:59	II Kings 4:42 – 5:19
M'tsorah	"	14:1 – 15:33	II Kings 7:3 – 20
Akharei Mot	"	16:1 – 18:30	Ezekiel 22:1 – 19 (22:1 – 16)
K'doshim	"	19:1 – 20:27	Amos 9:7 – 15
			(Ezekiel 20:2 – 20)
Emor	"	21:1 – 24:33	Ezekiel 44:15 – 31
Behar	"	25:1 – 26:2	Jeremiah 32:6 – 27
Bekhukotai	"	26:3 – 27:34	Jeremiah 16:19 – 17:14
Bemidbar	Numbers	1:1 – 4:20	Hosea 2:1 – 22
Naso	"	4:21 – 7:89	Judges 13:2 – 25
B'ha'alotekhah	"	8:1 – 12:26	Zechariah 2:14 – 4:7
Shelakh	"	13:1 – 15:41	Joshua 2:1 – 24
Korakh	"	16:1 – 18:32	I Samuel 11:14 – 12:22
Khukat	"	19:1 – 22:1	Judges 11:1 – 33
Balak	"	22:2 – 25:9	Micah 5:6 – 6:8
Pinkhas	"	25:10 – 30:1	I Kings 18:46 – 19:21
Matot	"	30:2 – 32:42	Jeremiah 1:1 – 2:3
Ma'asei	"	33:1 – 36:13	Jeremiah 2:4 – 28, 3:4
			(Jeremiah 2:4 – 28, 4:1, 2)
Devarim	Deuteronomy	1:1 – 3:22	Isaiah 1:1 – 27
Va-etkhanan	"	3:23 – 7:11	Isaiah 40:1 – 26
Ekev	"	7:12 – 11:25	Isaiah 49:14 – 51:3
Re'eh	"	11:26 – 16:17	Isaiah 54:11 – 55:5
Shoftim	"	16:18 – 21:9	Isaiah 51:12 – 52:12
Ki Tetseh	"	21:10 – 25:19	Isaiah 54:1 – 10
Ki Tavo	"	26:1 – 29:8	Isaiah 60:1 – 22
Nitzavim	"	29:9 – 30:20	Isaiah 61:10 – 63:9
Vayelekh	"	31:1 – 30	Isaiah 55:6 – 56:8
Ha'azinu	"	32:1 – 52	II Samuel 22:1 – 51
Zot Ha-B'rakhah	"	33:1 – 34:12	Joshua 1:1 – 18 (1:1 – 9)

GENESIS/*BEREISHIT*

The first book of the Bible, *Bereishit,* consists of 50 chapters, containing 1,534 verses. Read in the synagogue today, it is divided into 12 *parashiyot;* when it was read in Palestine in the time of the Second Temple on a three-year cycle, there were 43 separate sections.

Bereishit begins with the creation of the world by God, from *tohu v'bohu,* chaos and nothingness. God calls for light, separates the darkness from the light creating day and night, creates the "great waters," separates land from sea, and eventually fills the earth with creatures— fowl, fish, land animals, and finally man and woman. In fact, *Bereishit* tells the story of the creation twice, with significant differences between the two versions (including a discrepancy between the creation of Eve from Adam's rib in the version in 2:21–2 and her creation simultaneous with Adam in 1:27).

Almost immediately after the creation of humans, problems begin. Eve is tempted by the serpent and violates God's explicit orders, eating the fruit of the Tree of Knowledge of Good and Evil and encouraging Adam to do likewise. They are expelled from the Garden of Eden. Eve bears children, Cain and Abel, and eventually Cain kills his brother and is condemned to wander the earth. After several more generations, God decides that humanity was a bad idea and resolves to obliterate man and woman from the face of the earth, save for Noah and his family. Noah and his kin are saved and with them are an assortment of the animals as well. Eventually, after the flood waters have subsided, Noah will offer a sacrifice to God, who promises never to repeat this mass extermination. However, it is not long before humans again test God's patience, building the Tower of Babel. The Almighty responds this time by scattering them across the face of the earth and confounding their language; they will now speak in many tongues and be unintelligible to one another.

All of this is but a lengthy prelude to the main story of *Bereishit,* the story of the Patriarchs and Matriarchs who founded the Hebrew people: Abraham and Sarah, Isaac and Rebekah, Jacob, Leah, and Rachel, Joseph and his brothers. Each of these stories pivots on a covenant between the Creator and the Patriarch of his generation, each involves wandering and exile ending in redemption and, finally, a gentle but poignant death. In at least two key cases, central figures are given new names by Adonai, indicating the transformation that their covenant requires.

God's first words to Abram (his name when we first meet him) are "*Lekh lekha/Go forth*." Thus the first of the Patriarchs is sent out into a hostile world with the message that there is only one Deity. God gives an aging Abram and Sarai a son, a token of the promise to make Abram's seed as numerous as the stars in the sky. Yet neither as Abram nor as Abraham is the Patriarch a docile servant of the Almighty. Rather, when God resolves to destroy the cities on the plain, Sodom and Gomorrah, Abraham argues unbendingly for their salvation and, only after he is unable to find even ten righteous men and women within them does he wearily accede to God's decision.

Abraham/Abram is not presented as a perfect man. None of the Patriarchs are. His behavior in the matter of his concubine Hagar and her son by him, Ishmael, whom he sends into the desert at Sarah's behest, is clearly wrong. If it were not, why would the messenger of God save Hagar and Ishmael when they are dying of thirst in the wilderness, an unstated but clear rebuke to Abraham's expulsion of her?

And, in light of his resistance to the destruction of Sodom and Gomorrah, Abraham seems all too willing to follow orders and sacrifice Isaac, his son, on Mount Moriah. And yet . . . the story of the *akeidah/the binding* of Isaac is a good example of how complicated the undercurrents and outcome of biblical narrative can be, of why it is dangerous to jump to seemingly obvious conclusions based on a contemporary understanding of an ancient text.

Perhaps Abraham trusts in God, trusts that the Almighty will not let his son die. God has promised to make Abraham's descendants a great nation; Abraham must believe in the covenant and surely God will not take Isaac. If this is to be a test of faith, then the test goes both ways. God tests Abraham's willingness to follow a divine commandment to the very brink. Abraham tests God's willingness to avert further shedding of human blood—this time innocent blood—and to keep the covenant.

One could go on speculating about the *Akeidah* for literally hundreds of pages. There is a wealth of literature devoted to this episode, rabbinic and post-rabbinic. For the moment, though, I will offer only one other note: at the outset of the *sidra/weekly Torah portion* (see sidebar "The *Parashiyot* and the *Haftarot*," p. 265) that immediately follows the

Akeidah, Sarah dies. Some commentators have said that she died from the shock of hearing what had nearly happened on Mount Moriah. Perhaps we may view that as a punishment for her husband who himself will not live much longer.

Isaac is the least defined, the most passive of the Patriarchs. In his key moments in *Bereishit,* the *Akeidah,* and Jacob's deception leading to his receiving the blessing meant for his older brother, he is acted upon, not active. Alone among the Patriarchs, Isaac doesn't even choose his own wife; his father's servant does it for him. We know more about Rebekah, his wife, her desire for children, the pain of her childbirth, her favoring of the younger of her twin sons, Jacob, over the elder, Esau. Isaac seems to exist primarily to be deceived by Jacob into giving over the blessing owed the firstborn.

Two nations struggle to be born in Rebekah's womb, Israel and Edom, represented by her sons Jacob and Esau, respectively. Eventually the bookish younger son Jacob, "a man of the tents," will supplant his older brother Esau, "a man of the fields," by bargaining for the latter's birthright and taking advantage of their aged father's failing eyesight to secure the blessing intended for the firstborn. Then, afraid of his older brother's understandable wrath, Jacob will go to Beersheva. On the road, he encounters and wrestles with a mysterious being who turns out to be a messenger of God. As the morning light begins to glimmer on the horizon, the messenger defeats him by dislocating his hip, then rewards him with a new name, Israel, and a restatement of the covenant that Adonai had made with his grandfather. In Beersheva, Jacob will meet and fall in love with Rachel. He will labor for seven years for his prospective father-in-law Laban, only to be tricked into marrying her older sister, Leah. After another seven years' labor for Laban, he will finally marry the younger sister as well.

The ethics of Jacob's behavior toward his father and brother are troubling to modern sensibilities, to put it mildly. To our eyes, it looks like Jacob has in essence perpetrated a fraud upon his own father to secure a blessing not rightly his, and held his brother to an absurd bargain to obtain a birthright he doesn't deserve. The sages of the rabbinic period had no such problems. To them, Jacob was clearly the son favored by Adonai, the one who studied Torah (although it hadn't been written yet!), the one whose line would become the Israelite people. There are numerous *midrashic* texts that describe Esau variously as an idolator and killer, one who disdained his birthright and the responsibilities of the convenant.

Such ex post facto explanations do not satisfy modern readers; they smack of special pleading. But there is another fact to consider. Jacob suffers the most of any of the Patriarchs for his legacy. If he purchases the birthright cheaply and the blessing illicitly, he pays for them soon after with the coin of physical pain, fear for his life, some fifteen years as a fugitive, indentured servitude, a shattered family, and death in exile. It is worth noting that, as Professor Joel Rosenberg points out, punishment from God in the Torah almost never comes immediately after the transgression (with the notable exceptions, I would add, of Adam and Eve in the Garden and Lot's wife); rather, it may befall the malefactor much later, perhaps even in a later generation.

The story of the disruption of Jacob's family, the tale of Joseph and his brothers, is the most extended narrative in the book of Genesis, being told over four *sidrot*. Joseph has a knack for interpreting dreams, his own and those of others, a skill that gets him in trouble with his brothers but gets him out of Pharaoh's prison in Egypt.

The root of Joseph's conflict with his brothers lies in his status as Jacob's favorite son. (Given the troubles that he went through with his own brother and parents, one would think Jacob would know better, but this is a recurring theme throughout the Torah.) His brothers fake his death and sell him to a passing slave caravan. He ends up in Egypt where, after a series of misadventures, his mastery of dream interpretation raises him to the status of the Pharaoh's principle advisor. His ingenuity in the face of a lengthy famine helps Pharaoh consolidate his hold over Egypt, and indirectly brings him face to face with his brothers once more. After tormenting them with accusations of theft (with planted evidence to back him up), he finally reveals himself to them, they bring the aged Jacob to Egypt reuniting the family, and they all live happily ever after in Egypt, more or less.

Or at least until a new Pharaoh arises "who knew not Joseph." But that is the story of the next four books.

EXODUS/*SHEMOT*

The second book of the Bible is Exodus, known in Hebrew as *Shemot/Names* for its opening sentence, "These are the names of. . . ."

The book consists of 40 chapters containing 1,209 verses. It is divided into 11 *sidrot;* in ancient Palestine, when it was read as part of the triennial cycle, it consisted of 33 (or according to some sources 29) portions.

The events that are related in Exodus are reputed to have taken place over 129 years, from the death of Joseph to the building of the Ark that will house the tablets of the Ten Commandments. Although the action is a continuation of the story told in Genesis, which culminated in the death of Joseph, Exodus really introduces a whole new storyline, one which will occupy the remainder of the Torah: the story of Moses, the liberation of the Jews from bondage in Egypt, and their wanderings in the wilderness, ending with the death of Moses just before the Israelites enter Canaan, the Promised Land.

Although the laws that will govern Judaism, the building blocks of rabbinic Judaism, are found in the next three books, the central experience of Jewish history, the experience of slavery in Egypt and Divine liberation occurs in Exodus. We are repeatedly enjoined to remember "that you were slaves in Egypt," in the Torah, in the Talmud, in the daily liturgy.

When the book opens, Joseph has been dead for some time and a new Pharaoh has become skittish at the sight of so many Jews in his nation. The Jews are enslaved, forced to build the great storehouse cities of Pithom and Ramses, forced to make bricks without straw. Yet no amount of hard labor seems to stem the growth of the Jewish population. Finally, Pharaoh decrees the death of all firstborn male Jews, but he is foiled by the courage and cunning of the Jewish midwives, who hide the newborn baby boys. One of these endangered Jewish infants is Moses, who is placed by his mother in a basket (described by an unusual Hebrew word, *tavat,* essentially the same one used to describe the Ark in which Noah saves the animals and his family), and set adrift on the Nile. Pharaoh's daughter finds the baby and raises him as an Egyptian prince.

But Moses is an unusual Egyptian prince. When he witnesses a taskmaster mercilessly beating a Jewish slave, he kills the miscreant. There are witnesses and he is forced to flee. Living in exile as a shepherd, he comes upon a burning bush, from which emanates the voice of Adonai, who dispatches him back to Egypt with his brother Aaron to entreat Pharaoh to free the Jews.

Thus begins the classic struggle between an oppressing power and an oppressed minority whose primary weapon is moral authority. Of course, here moral authority takes the form of the wrath of the Almighty. Despite a series of nine plagues, Pharaoh refuses to let the Jews go. Only with the tenth and most devastating plague, the death of the Egyptian firstborn—an echo of and reply to Pharaoh's insidious plot against the Jewish firstborn—does he finally relent. Even then, he changes his mind once more and pursues them to the Reed Sea, where God finally destroys not only Pharaoh but his entire army as well.

Led and sustained in the wilderness by God, the Israelites come to Mount Sinai, where amidst thunder and lightning Moses receives the Ten Commandments, the Decalogue. Moses, in direct dialogue with God, actually receives the entire 613 commandments, many of which are recounted in Exodus. He is on the mountain for forty days and nights (the same length of time that the rains fell during the Flood, an example of the internal echoes one finds throughout the Tanakh). The impatient Israelites implore Aaron to give them a god they can see and touch, a tangible deity. The result is the incident of the Golden Calf. Moses comes back down as the people are dancing before the statue, hurls the Tablets of the Law to the ground in a fury, and with the help of loyal followers from his tribe, Levi, destroys the idol and kills three thousand of those worshipping it. God tells Moses to fashion new tablets, which he does. The remainder of the book is spent in a laborious detailing of the building of the *mishkan,* the elaborate sanctuary that houses the Tablets of the Law.

The Moses who emerges from this book is a fully rounded figure. He is quick-tempered (a trait that will have severe repercussions for him later), painfully shy and self-conscious about his slowness of speech, reluctant to take on a task he initially feels is beyond him. Yet he is the chosen one of Adonai, the only human ever allowed to glimpse the Almighty, even from the back.

LEVITICUS / *VAYIKRA*

Leviticus is the third book of the Bible, known in Hebrew as *Vayikra/And He Called,* for its opening word. The book contains 27 chapters and 859 verses. It is divided into 10 *sidrot;* in the time of the Second Temple when the reading of the Torah was held in the triennial cycle, it was divided into 25 sections.

The bulk of this book consists of the many laws that are a substantial part of the 613 *mitzvot*. In addition, in Chapter 19 there is a passage usually referred to as the "holiness code," the all-important passage, discussed here in Chapter 4, in which God tells the Hebrews that because "I am holy, you shall be holy."

Leviticus essentially is a continuation of the laws that Moses began to enumerate at the end of Exodus. Its focus is mainly on matters of ritual and ethics, covering such topics as sacrifices, the installation of the priests, states of ritual impurity, the observation of Yom Kippur, and the system of vows and tithes.

NUMBERS/ *BAMIDBAR*

Numbers is the fourth book of the Bible, known in Hebrew as *Bamidbar/In the Wilderness,* from its opening word. The book contains 36 chapters and 1,288 verses. For the weekly readings of Torah, it is divided into 10 *sidrot;* in the triennial cycle, it had 32 sections.

Numbers opens with Moses, on orders from God, taking another census of the Israelites. It is now the second year that they have been in the wilderness. Adonai breaks them down into tribes, setting aside the Levites as servants of God. There follows an enumeration of more laws, including the procedures to be observed by the priestly caste, the *kohanim,* who will descend from the line of Aaron.

At this point in the narrative, things begin to boil up again; as Moses says at more than one point in the four books detailing the Exodus, this is a "stiff-necked people." This time, the arguing is over the manna, food from the sky provided to the Israelites by God. They yearn for a return to the fleshpots of Egypt, to eating meat. God, who apparently is almost as annoyed as Moses, says he will give them quail to eat "until it comes out of your noses." He also tells Moses to appoint a council of seventy elders to take some of the burdens of leadership off his shoulders. Miriam and Aaron, his sister and brother, become part of the problem as well, complaining about Moses's non-Hebrew wife; as a punishment for spreading slander, Miriam is visited with a form of leprosy. Moses intercedes on her behalf and she is healed.

There is still more rebellion within this book, with spies sent to Canaan returning to upset the people with tales of giant warriors who will destroy the Israelites, and a Levite nobleman named Korakh challenging Moses's leadership. God realizes that the Israelites still have the mindset of slaves and decides that of the adults, only Caleb and Joshua, the only two members of the reconnaissance party to dispute the report about the prowess of Canaanite warriors, will be allowed to enter the Promised Land. As for Korakh, he is swallowed by the earth.

There is further trouble, involving the Moabites and their king Balak, who unsuccessfully tries to send Balaam, a sorcerer, to curse the Hebrews. But the most important event in the second half of Numbers is that God informs Moses that, because of a fit of temper in which he smote a rock with his staff—rather than speaking to the staff as God commanded—to bring forth water, that he will not be allowed to go into the Promised Land either.

DEUTERONOMY/*DEVARIM*

Deuteronomy is the fifth and final book of the Torah, known in Hebrew as *Devarim/Words* for the first important word in its Hebrew text. Because it consists largely of Moses's repetition of the laws commanded by Adonai in the previous books, its Greek name is *Deuteronomion* (i.e., "second law"); hence its common name Deuteronomy. The book contains 34 chapters and 955 verses. It is divided into 11 *sidrot* for purposes of the weekly Torah reading; in the three-year cycle, it was broken into 27 sections.

The entire contents of Deuteronomy, but for the last few verses, detail an address to the Hebrew people by Moses. In the course of this address, his farewell, he reminds them of the foundations of their faith, their covenant with Adonai, the Ten Commandments, and other fundamentals of Judaism such as the *Sh'ma*. He tells them that they have a choice between blessing and curse, life and death, and that they should choose Adonai and live.

Finally, after detailing more of the laws, Moses bids the Twelve Tribes farewell. He ascends Mount Nebo so that he may see the Promised Land, even though he cannot enter it, and dies there.

Why repeat and embroider so much of the legal material we have encountered already? The answer is embedded in the entire structure of the Torah and in a question that the rabbis of the Talmud took up: why begin the Torah with the Creation and not with, say, the Ten Commandments? By beginning with Creation, the Torah establishes at the outset God's legitimacy as sovereign over the world and all that is in it. We see from the outset that God has created and controls everything from the tiniest insect to the greatest of nations. Consequently, for the Hebrews to have a comparable legitimacy in the conquest of the Promised Land, they must accept God and the *mitzvot*. By maintaining their covenant with the Creator, they earn a right to Canaan and the fulfillment of the promise of a people as numerous as the stars in the sky. The bulk of Deuteronomy consists of Moses exhorting them to eschew idolatry and to keep the laws of ritual purity, so that they may be worthy of the legacy he is leaving them, the Covenant and the Promised Land. The repetition of the commandments in Deuter-onomy—coming just before the Hebrews enter the Promised Land—is designed to emphasize the connection that is the Covenant: observe the *mitzvot* and receive this fertile land for your own.

BIBLICAL MEASUREMENTS

There are numerous weights and measures given in the Bible that have little meaning for us today. Here is a list of some of the most commonly used terms and their approximate modern equivalents.

Measures of Distance
  Digit = .79 inch
  Palm = 3.18 inches
  Span = 5.53 inches
  Cubit = 19.05 inches
  Reed = 114.31 inches

Measures of Volume (dry and liquid)
  log = 0.3 liters
  kav = 1.2 liters
  omer = 2.2 liters
  hin = 3.6 liters
  se'ah = 7.3 liters
  efah = 22 liters
  letekh = 110 liters
  homer = 220 liters

The most basic weight unit is the *shekel*, which actually gets its name from the Hebrew word meaning "to weigh," *shakal*. The largest unit of weight in the Bible is the *kikar/talent*. The weights themselves were made of stone and are often referred to as "stones." Based on a passage in Exodus 38:25–6, experts have offered the following calculations:

603,550 half-*shekels* = 300,000 + 1,775 *shekels*
300,000 *shekels* = 100 talents
3,000 *shekels* = 1 talent

In addition, the *gerah* is one-twentieth of a *shekel*, the *minah* about 50 *shekels*.

MAKING THE TEXT SING: CANTILLATION

Torah was never meant to be merely read. Almost from the very beginning, it was chanted, sung. In most synagogues, the public reading is done by the rabbi or the *baal koreh* or *baal kr'iah/master of the reading*, a layperson trained in cantillation, liturgical chanting.

The Torah scrolls are written in "unpointed" Hebrew, that is, without vowels, punctuation marks, or any indication of the melodies to which the text is chanted. In the post-Talmudic period, systems of notation were developed from previously oral traditions; the notation system, called *t'amim* (sing. *ta'am*), served three purposes. First, it showed the reader how to accent the words; second, it divided the verses correctly; and finally, it transmitted to the reader the melodic patterns used in chanting the text. The most important system of *t'amim* was developed by the Masoretes of Tiberias in the ninth and tenth centuries C.E. The Masoretic text became recognized as the standard version of the Hebrew Bible, including the cantillation marks it included.

Given that a Torah scroll is written with neither punctuation, vowel markings, nor *t'amim*, how does a person preparing to read Torah learn the *sidra?* Generally, a prospective *ba'al koreh* will work with a *tikkun la-korim*, a printed book that gives both the unpointed version found in the *sefer Torah* and the Masoretic version with all its markings in parallel columns. *Ba'aleh koreh* generally will practice with the Masoretic text until they are so familiar with it that the contents of the unpointed version will be readable to them. In earlier times, a *somekh/prompter* would help out with an elaborate series of hand signals indicating the appropriate cantillation. Today, the prompter will usually stand by the *ba'al koreh* and correct any errors that would change the meaning of the text.

Although the *t'amim* are used throughout the world, the tunes they represent differ from community to community. Thus, the *nusakh/musical mode* used to chant Torah and *haftarah* in the South Arab Peninsula, one of the oldest systems of cantillation in Judaism, differs significantly from the one used in North Africa. There are eight major musical traditions: Southern Arab Peninsula, Middle Eastern, Near Eastern, North African, Italian, Sephardic, Western European Ashkenzi, Eastern European Ashkenazi. Within each of these eight modes, one can find many regional variations as well. Moreover, there are different musical modes within each of the main traditions for specific holidays and different books of the Bible. For example, each of the *Five Megillot* has its own *trop* or melody. The "Song of the Sea," the passage of poetry that the Israelite women sing after the miracle of the Reed Sea, has a distinctive *trop*, as does the reading of the Ten Commandments. There is a separate and unique *trop* for the reading of the Torah on the High Holy Days as well. Finally, the *haftarah* is chanted to a melody of its own, with the reader working from the Masoretic text.

TORAH COMES FIRST

How can we account for the primacy of Torah? Why does Judaism place so much emphasis on the first five books, seemingly at the expense of the remainder of the Tanakh?

There is a historical explanation for this state for affairs. When the priest Ezra returned to Judah around 458 B.C.E., after the end of the Babylonian exile, he carried with him two important documents, the "*torah* of Moses" and a letter from the Persian emperor giving him political authority, which he shared with Nehemiah, the governor of Judah. To announce the centralization of political and religious power in Judah and the Temple of Jerusalem, Ezra called a public gathering of the Jews and read aloud to them the Scroll, which historians believe contained the entire Torah, the Five Books of Moses. The reading was followed by a ceremony in which the Jews publicly reiterated their commitment to Adonai, as written in the Torah. Political power now rested in the hands of the priests, led by Ezra. Thus began the custom of the public reading of the Torah, which evolved gradually into the weekly Torah reading that takes place in synagogues around the world today.

But there are other, simpler reasons why Torah takes precedence over the other two sections of the Hebrew Bible. First, even if one doubts or openly rejects the historical actuality of the Torah, these five books tell the story of the very foundations of Judaism itself, as Judaism chooses to understand it. From the Patriarchs through the Exodus to the border of *Eretz Yisroel,* the journey of Torah is the journey of the Jewish people to nationhood, their founding myth and raison d'être— the covenants with God.

More than that, Torah encompasses the 613 *mitzvot,* the defining cornerstone on which the edifice that is rabbinic Judaism will rest. To the extent that Judaism is a religion based on action and ritual—on the Infinite made concrete through daily observance—permeating every waking moment of a religious Jew's day, these books (particularly Leviticus, Numbers, and Deuteronomy) are the basis of belief. Even a Jew whose observance is less stringent—even a secular Jew— acknowledges that basis, if only by choosing *not* to follow the *mitzvot.*

THE *NEVI'IM* / THE PROPHETS

The first books of the Prophets, the *Nevi'im,* essentially constitute a continuation of the history outlined in the Torah. Thus the narrative continues seamlessly from the death of Moses at the end of Deuteronomy directly into the conquest of Canaan, the Promised Land, by Moses's successor Joshua. (The synagogue service tacitly recognizes that narrative continuity by using Joshua 1:1–18 as the *haftarah* reading for the final *sidrah, Zot Ha-B'rakhah.*) In fact, some biblical scholars refer to the Torah with Joshua as the Hexateuch, "six pieces." Professor David Noel Freedman takes this annexation one step further, suggesting that the first four books of the *Nevi'im* could just as easily be grouped with the Torah under the rubric "the Primary History."

JOSHUA

With the death of Moses, Joshua assumes command and leads the descendants of the twelve sons of Jacob into the land of Canaan, where by force of arms (and with the help of God) they conquer the land and make it their home.

The book of Joshua includes two of the most famous episodes in the Bible, the walls of Jericho falling at the blast of a shofar, and Joshua commanding the sun to stand still in the sky during the battle of Gibeon. The book concludes with Joshua's instruction to the Israelites to put aside "strange gods," and his death and burial.

Although the book of Joshua bears the name of a great military and religious leader, the real hero of this tale of the Jews' conquest of Canaan is the Almighty, who makes the Twelve Tribes' victories possible. Archaeologists are somewhat divided on the historical accuracy of this version of the story, although there is evidence to back some of the specifics. It is likely that the actual conquest of the land of Canaan by the Hebrews was a more gradual process and involved such unmilitary maneuvers as settlement and intermarriage with native tribes.

Whether the biblical account of the taking of Canaan is substantially correct or, as some believe, the process was more protracted and less violent, depending on sheer doggedness as much as valor and Divine intervention, the result is a significant threshold in Jewish history—as Jacob Neusner says, not an end to Jewish history but a beginning. For the first time in their brief existence the Hebrews—now Israelites—have a homeland. Their self-chosen nomadism is at an end.

JUDGES

Judges, the second volume of the *Nevi'im,* is a continuation of the history of ancient Israel. The Bible credits Joshua with the military victories that gave the Hebrews—now Israelites—Canaan. But it also makes it clear that the credit for consolidation and pacification of the Canaanite land under the Twelve Tribes belongs largely to the men and women called the *shof'tim/judges*. These tribal leaders are not judges as we understand the term; while their duties may have encompassed adjudication, there is scant evidence of that in the book of Tanakh that bears their name. Their primary function appears to have been military leadership, although Deborah, Eli, and Samuel are also prophets.

With Joshua's death, the Judges are confronted almost immediately with exactly the dilemma of which Joshua had warned. Some of the Israelites are tempted by the worshippers of Baal with the result that

God no longer will insure the military success of the Hebrews' tribal armies. The Judges are shown in sequence leading their tribes in war, striving to control their part of the Holy Land.

Among the most striking passages in this book are the Song of Deborah, a female Judge and one of the best of the lot; the assassination of the enemy general Sisera by Jael, another righteous and courageous woman; and the appointment by God of Gideon to the military leadership of the Israelite armies. Gideon turns down the offer of a kingship, saying that only God can rule over the Israelites, but as we will see shortly, the Hebrews want an earthly king as well. But the most famous episode in this book undoubtedly is the story of Samson, the scourge of the Philistines, a Nazirite whose strength resides in his long hair and devotion to God, and Delilah, who seduces him and robs him of his strength and eyesight.

The book of Judges is important not only for continuing to elaborate on the ongoing theme of the Israelites' temptation to wickedness but also as a source of historical information on a difficult and formative period in the development of the Jewish state in Canaan. Canaan is like a bridge between great empires—the Egyptian, Assyrian, Persian, Babylonian, and Roman. Each in their turn will sweep across that bridge with catastrophic consequences for its inhabitants. As Belgium is to Germany, so Canaan was to all of the great armies of the Mediterranean, a passageway of no great value in itself, but indispensable as a thoroughfare leading to further conquests. It was the misfortune of the Israelites to have made their first home in the path of military history. And they would pay for that misfortune repeatedly, in stories that are recounted in Tanakh and in history long after.

I AND II SAMUEL

Originally the book of Samuel was a single volume. However, both the Greek translation, the Septuagint, and the Latin translation, the Vulgate, broke it into two books and the printed Hebrew Bible dating from early in the sixteenth century picked up that custom.[4]

Samuel is the last of the Judges, a prophet who led Israel through the transition to a monarchy. Like Isaac, Jacob, and Esau before him, Samuel is the son of a "barren" woman, Hannah, whose entreaties to God result in the birth of a special child. Like Samson, he is raised as a

Nazirite, consecrated to God from birth. Like Isaac, his own two sons cause him no end of grief; Joel and Abijah are also Judges, but their unfair rulings and increasing threats from the Philistines create so much unrest among the Israelites that the clamoring for a king finally becomes too great to bear and Samuel, with God's acceptance, reluctantly complies.

Although Samuel warns them that a temporal king will deflect them from their proper loyalty to the Eternal Ruler to whom fealty is rightly due, he reluctantly chooses Saul as the first king of Israel, anointing him as Adonai's chosen one. Previously Saul had enjoyed some success in holding the Israelites together against the Ammonites, another obstreperous neighboring group. That display of military prowess had suggested him as the logical choice for the kingship, although even against the Ammonites he had been unable to secure the help of a united Israel.

Against the Philistines Saul has less luck. At the battle of Michmash a large part of his army deserts and only a ruse by his son, Jonathan, averts total disaster. It will take the emergence of a greater hero to pull the Israelite forces together. The unlikely hero is a shepherd boy named David.

The legend, among the best known in the Bible, is that David electrifies the Israelites with his defeat of the Philistine giant Goliath, killing him with a stone from his slingshot. From an historical point of view the story may not hold up, but this much is clear: David enjoyed a meteoric rise in both military success and popularity, and Saul feels threatened by him.

At first Saul contrives to embrace the boy hero. David and Jonathan become close friends, and Saul marries the young warrior to his daughter Michal, and proclaims him a favorite of the royal court. But Saul's political tact is quickly overcome by his jealousy, fueled by the sound of crowds chanting, "Saul has slain his thousands, but David [has slain] his tens of thousands." Fear of the younger man becomes an idée fixe for the monarch and he makes repeated unsuccessful attempts to have David killed.

Saul has lived up to Samuel's worst nightmares, disobeying both the prophet and Adonai. In his worst offense, he allows the king of the Amalekites, sworn enemies of the Jews, to survive after being explicitly told to do otherwise, solely for mercenary reasons. David is driven from the court and begins fighting a desperate guerrilla action just to survive. Samuel informs Saul of the prophecy that his throne will be taken away from him, then anoints the young shepherd David in secret. Finally, the matter is settled by the Philistines, who overrun Saul's forces at Gilboa. Saul runs on his sword rather than be captured. With David's victory, the ruling Davidic line is established with God's promise that it will last forever.

The second book of Samuel focuses on the reign of David, his many triumphs and missteps and his relationship with God and the prophet Nathan. It is Nathan who calls him to account after the famous incident in which the ruler sends Uriah to his death in battle because he covets Batshevah, Uriah's wife. As in the first book of Samuel, we see the role of the prophets as one of moral watchdogs over the powerful, God's representatives to the people Israel. This role will develop more fully throughout the remaining books of the *Nevi'im*.

David emerges in the Bible as an extraordinary leader, an amalgam of many disparate qualities—warrior, statesman, poet, and musician. Not only does he successfully unite the Israelite people, establish the city of Jerusalem as their capital, and lay the plans for the Temple, he is also the founder of a kingly line that will extend for several centuries, perhaps the longest-lived of any in Western civilization.

I AND II KINGS

Like the two books of Samuel before it and Chronicles after, Kings was originally a single book but was divided in two in the Septuagint and Vulgate versions, with the printed Hebrew Bible of the late Renaissance adopting that structure. With its chronicle of the rise and fall of the Davidic line, Kings completes the Primary History.

This story begins in triumph, with a moving retelling of the last days of David and the ascension to the throne of his chosen son, Solomon. Solomon, whose wisdom is proverbial, builds the Temple in Jerusalem and completes the final consolidation of power. But by doing so he sows the seeds of the downfall of ancient Israel; by locating the central government and the Temple in the north while heavily taxing everyone, Solomon ignites the political resentments that will split Israel in two after his death.

Subsequent to Solomon's death, the kingdom will become divided between Judah (consisting of the tribes of Judah and Benjamin) in the south and the larger nation of Israel in the north (comprising the other ten tribes). From this point on, the story of the Israelites is one of strife, straying from God and, finally of destruction, with the Assyrians eventually overrunning the northern kingdom of Israel and dispersing the survivors.

The Ten Tribes of the north "vanish" as legend has it—giving birth to the notion of the "ten lost tribes of Israel." In the thirty-seven hundred years since the fall of Israel, the label of the ten lost tribes has been applied to everyone from the Ethiopian Jews to Native Americans, from the Cochin Jews of India to the Yemenite Jews. In reality, there is no evidence of ten lost tribes. The Israelites of the north were assimilated into the Canaanite society into which they freely and readily intermarried, spurred by the example of monarchs like Ahab. Moreover, the population of the northern kingdom was badly depleted by the lengthy war in which the Assyrians conquered it, and the typical policy of the period of putting able-bodied male captives to the sword and placing large percentages of the remaining population into some form of slavery.

Only the tribe of Judah is left intact, a vassal state of the Assyrians ruled over by Hezekiah. Its inhabitants are known as the Judeans, ultimately as the Jews.

The other central theme of Kings is the need to centralize worship (despite the building of the Temple). With Josiah, the seventh king of Judah, this long-anticipated event, predicted as far back as Deuteronomy, will finally take place. Despite that achievement, one for which Josiah is much praised, the transgressions of the Jews against Adonai are great and the remaining books of the Prophets consist largely of warnings issued to them, in vain.

Interestingly, the key element of Josiah's religious reforms is the discovery by a priest named Kilkiah of "a scroll of the Torah." Josiah hears the scroll read and decides to reassert the covenant with Adonai, throwing down the statue of a golden bull that was erected by one of his predecessors at Beth-El.

ISAIAH

The first book of the Latter Prophets (so-called because they come after the final four books of the Primary History, also called the Former

Prophets) is the book of Isaiah. The book is reputed to be the work of Isaiah, son of Amoz (although modern Bible scholars believe it to be the work of at least two and possibly three authors).

Isaiah's prophecies begin in the period between the war between Aram and Israel (735 B.C.E.), an event that weakened both nations so much that they ended up under Assyrian rule, and the near-capture of Jerusalem by the Assyrians some fifteen years later, which Isaiah says is averted only because King Hezekiah turns to God for help. This section is followed by a series of prophecies of consolation (which are read as *haftarot* in the weeks surrounding Tisha b'Av). The remainder of the book focuses on the rebuilding of the Temple, the restoration of a new Jerusalem, and the destruction by God of idol-worshippers.

Isaiah's prophecies include the prediction of the coming of the Messianic Age, passages that have drawn considerable attention from Christian Bible scholars. He predicts that the day will come when both Jew and non-Jew alike will worship God. His messages, both of consolation and of denunciation, are of such lasting power that fifteen of the fifty-four *haftarot* are drawn from this book.

JEREMIAH

The book of Jeremiah is the second book of the Latter Prophets. It includes both the biography and prophecies of Jeremiah, a prophet who lived in the seventh and sixth centuries B.C.E. Jeremiah was fortunate enough to have a loyal scribe, Baruch, serving him. As a result, we know a bit more about him than most of the other prophets and his oracles were recorded from his own dictation. In fact, his oracles, which had been given in oral form, were recorded specifically because he had incurred the wrath of King Jehoiakim. When he presented the ruler with a scroll of his oracles denouncing the king for his transgressions, Jehoiakim destroyed the scroll. Jeremiah dictated it once again to Baruch, adding further oracles to its content.

Jeremiah was called to prophesy in 626 B.C.E., while still a young man. Born in the village of Anathoth, northeast of Jerusalem, he lived most of his life in Jerusalem, where he prophesied for over four decades. He offered the Jews a specifically political message as well as a moral one: submit to Babylonian rule and learn from your captivity. It was an unpopular message, as was his religious one, that the people and their leaders, both temporal and spiritual, were wicked, and that all, even other prophets, were guilty of lying and hypocrisy. His life was threatened on several occasions, but he lived to see the bulk of the population of Judah exiled to Babylonia. After the assassination of Gedaliah, the last Jewish governor of Israel, Jeremiah fled to Egypt, where he apparently lived out the remainder of his life.

EZEKIEL

While Jeremiah was left in Judah by the Babylonian conquerors, Ezekiel was taken to Babylonia in captivity in 597 B.C.E. along with most of the Jews. It was in exile that he had his vision of the chariot of God and was declared a prophet. The book that bears his name is an outline of his prophecies.

Ezekiel begins his prophecies by denouncing Judah and Jerusalem for their wickedness. He exhorts the Jews in exile to return to the worship of God. His prophecies include oracles of doom against many of the nations who were enemies of Israel, as well as prophecies of consolation, and, most strikingly, of the restoration of the Temple and Israel.

Ezekiel's imagery is dense, almost hallucinatory in its intensity and strangeness, from the wheel of the chariot carrying away the prophet Elijah (a central topic of early Jewish mysticism) to the valley of dry bones. The Talmudic sages who finalized the canon of the Bible found his book one of the most troublesome, filled with divergences from Torah. Yet it is also considered one of the most holy of the prophetic books, containing as it does the prophecy of the restoration of the Temple.

THE TWELVE MINOR PROPHETS

The remainder of the *Nevi'im* is devoted to the books of the twelve prophets designated as "minor," a reflection not of their importance but of the length of the books.

Hosea is the first of the books of the minor prophets. An eighth century B.C.E. prophet, he prophesied during the reigns of Uzziah, Jotham, Ahaz, and Hezekiah in Israel, and Jereboam II and Menahem, kings of Judah. He warns the Ten Tribes of the north of the fate that will befall them, warns against alliances with foreign, i.e., idolatrous, powers, and is the first prophet to explicitly state that it is forbidden to worship Adonai at multiple altars in the manner of idolators. The Talmud extols his virtues, saying that although he prophesied at the same time as Isaiah, Amos, and Micah, Hosea was the greatest of the four.

There is no known biographical data about the prophet **Joel,** but his prophecies center entirely on Jerusalem and Judah. Modern scholars believe the book was written during the period of Persian dominance of Judah, after the rebuilding of the Temple in 515 B.C.E. Joel prophesies a plague of locusts attacking the people of Judah, and calls for their repentance, then promises a great Day of Adonai that will include the judgment of the nations and the deliverance of Israel.

Before he was called upon to prophesy to the people of the northern kingdom, **Amos** was a Judean fruit-grower and rancher. In his book, he invokes the concept of *galut/exile* for the first time, and warns the people Israel that their devotions to God are meaningless if they are not accompanied by just behavior. The book of Amos has particular resonance for those concerned with social action as a component of Jewish practice and has therefore had a lasting influence on the Reform movement. Amos is a great humanist, proclaiming a God who will not countenance the exploitation of the poor and oppressed.

There is a *midrash* that says that **Obadiah** was a convert to Judaism who preached the downfall of his own pagan nation, but there is no way of knowing if that story is true. Indeed, very little is known of this prophet, whose book is the shortest in the entire Tanakh, with one chapter of twenty-one verses. Obadiah preaches a Judgment Day prophecy and the downfall of the Edomites (descendants of Esau).

Jonah is perhaps the most famous of the minor prophets, known for his sojourn in the belly of a "great fish," the result of his trying to avoid his duties as a prophet. When called to preach to the inhabitants of Nineveh, he tries to escape Adonai but ultimately must carry out his job. Eventually, he preaches to them, they repent, and God shows them mercy, to Jonah's great disgust. The book of Jonah is unique among the prophetic books; it does not include any of Jonah's prophecies but is, rather, a short story of sorts. It is read as the *haftarah* on Yom Kippur afternoon.

Micah is a contemporary of Hosea and Isaiah, according to the Talmud. He is the first to prophesy the destruction of Jerusalem, and his prophecy so moved King Hezekiah that the monarch prayed to Adonai and won the city a reprieve. The book of Micah also contains one of the most famous formulas for righteous behavior in all the Tanakh: "[D]o justice, love mercy, and walk humbly with your God."

Nahum apparently preached in the kingdom of Judah. The destruction of Nineveh by the Babylonians and Medes in 612 B.C.E. seems to have taken place in his lifetime, in the aftermath of his having prophesied it.

Habakkuk was a contemporary of Nahum's and like him was an inhabitant of the southern kingdom. The book of his prophecies falls into two parts, a narrative of five prophecies about injustice in the world, and a psalm extolling God's deeds.

Zephaniah was a descendant of King Hezekiah of Judah. That means that he was a distant relative of Josiah (who reigned from 640– 608 B.C.E.), the monarch whose society he excoriated in his oracles. His vision of the Day of Judgment is particularly ferocious, and he predicts that the surviving remnant of Judah will represent an ingathering of exiles, a society of justice and humane behavior.

Haggai experienced prophetic revelations during the second year of the reign of Darius of Persia, approximately 520 B.C.E. Those revelations, which are the content of the book that bears his name, are concerned mainly with the building of the Second Temple. He also predicts the end of the Persian empire, shattered by a civil war.

The book of **Zechariah** is the longest of the twelve books of the Minor Prophets. Like Haggai, he first prophesied in the second year of the reign of Darius, 520 B.C.E. His book is usually grouped with the books of Haggai and Malachi as prophecies in the aftermath of the Babylonian Exile. Like Haggai, he urges the now impoverished Hebrews to rebuild the Temple and bring on the Messianic age.

The book of **Malachi** is the last of the books of the *Nevi'im*. The penultimate verse is repeated at the end in order not to have the book conclude on a negative note. Malachi is the first prophet to suggest the importance of the prophet Elijah as a forerunner of the Messiah. Malachi is a contemporary of Haggai and Zechariah and the Talmud states that when these three men died, prophecy died with them.

THE ROLE OF THE PROPHETS

Prophecy predates the men we think of as the Prophets. When Moses assembles the seventy elders of Israel in the Tent of Meeting, two men stand outside and offer prophecies, Eldad and Medad, arousing the annoyance of Joshua. But Moses rebukes his lieutenant, "I wish every man and woman of this nation were a prophet."

The prophets of the *Nevi'im* are seldom as graciously received. Jehoiakim wants to have the prophet Uriah executed after he predicts the monarch's downfall; Uriah flees to Egypt, but Jehoiakim has men bring him back and he kills the prophet himself. Jeremiah is imprisoned twice and on another occasion is saved from death at the hands of a mob only by a miracle.

As Haim Cohn, deputy president emeritus of the Israeli Supreme Court, dryly notes, "A person who uses freedom of speech to propound unacceptable views or sharp criticism, or an angry protest, always assumes the risk of persecution, besmirchment, and punishment. . . ." But the prophets also represent a line of critical thinking that can be found throughout Jewish history, men and women willing to call to account those in power who strayed from the teachings of Torah. Although the rabbis of the Talmud say that prophecy ends with the death of Malachi, Haggai and Zechariah, there has been no shortage since them of such truth-tellers.

THE *KETUVIM*/THE WRITINGS

The last section of the Hebrew Bible is a sort of *omnium gatherum*, a grab bag of various kinds of writings, hence its name, *Ketuvim/the Writings*. It is also known by its Greek name, the Hagiographa ("Holy Writings"). Within these fourteen books (thirteen if you count both books of Chronicles as one), one can find wisdom literature such as Proverbs, songs of praise to God, a love song, historical writing, and even a thriller of sorts. Some of these books of the Bible have liturgical significance; the five books known as the Five *Megillot/Scrolls* are read in the synagogue on specific holidays, and the Psalms are found throughout the *siddur/prayerbook*. (See sidebars "Special Readings for the Festivals," p. 133, and "Reading the Psalms," p. 290.)

TEHILLIM/THE PSALMS

The first book of the *Ketuvim* is a series of songs of praise to God, the Psalms. The longest book in the Hebrew Bible, it contains 150 Psalms in 2,527 verses.[5] The Psalms fall basically into three groups, hymns of praise to God, elegies, and didactic poems. The hymns celebrate God as Creator and Redeemer. The laments, conversely, bemoan God's absence. The didactic poems are of many types, ranging from meditations on Torah to brief encapsulations of the history of Israel.

Jewish tradition says that King David composed the Psalms (except for those clearly attributed to another author) and/or edited the book. Modern scholarship recognizes an early date for many of them, but it is generally believed that the editing of the Book of Psalms took place after the Babylonian Exile, hence, well past the death of David.

The Psalms have always played a significant part in the Jewish liturgy. Orthodox Jews recite *Tehillim* every day (see sidebar "Reading the Psalms" below). The *Kabbalat Shabbat* portion of the Friday night service consists primarily of Psalms 29, 92, 93, and 95–99. The most famous of the Psalms of David, Psalm 23 ("Adonai is my shepherd, I shall not want. . . .") is an integral part of any Jewish (or Christian) funeral service.

READING THE PSALMS

For the traditionally observant Jew, reading the Psalms has great significance. Many Jews will read the entire *Tehillim/Psalms* each week, others each month. Here are recommended reading schedules that they usually follow.

Weekly

Sunday	Psalms	1–29
Monday	"	30–50
Tuesday	"	51–72
Wednesday	"	73–89
Thursday	"	90–106
Friday	"	107–119
Shabbat	"	120–150

Monthly (dates based on the Hebrew calendar)

1	Psalms	1 – 9	2	Psalms	10 – 17	3	Psalms	18 – 22
4	"	23 – 28	5	"	29 – 34	6	"	35 – 38
7	"	39 – 43	8	"	44 – 48	9	"	49 – 54
10	"	55 – 59	11	"	60 – 65	12	"	66 – 68
13	"	69 – 71	14	"	72 – 76	15	"	77 – 78
16	"	79 – 82	17	"	83 – 87	18	"	88 – 89
19	"	90 – 96	20	"	97 – 103	21	"	104 – 105
22	"	106 – 107	23	"	108 – 112	24	"	113 – 118
25	"	119:1 – 96	26	"	119:97 – 176	27	"	120 – 134
28	"	135 – 139	29	"	140 – 144	30	"	145 – 150

In months with only twenty-nine days, Psalms 145–150 are recited on the twenty-ninth day.

Many Orthodox *siddurim* also specify special Psalm readings for specific *Shabbatot* and for other special days such as *Khol Hamoed Sukkot* or *Pesakh*.

Finally, it is the custom to read Psalms for those who are ill. Among the traditionally observant, many Psalms are considered appropriate for this purpose, including 6, 9, 20, 13, 16, 17, 18, 22, 23, 30, 31, 32, 33, 37, 38, 39, 41, 49, 55, 56, 69, 86, 88, 89, 90, 91, 102, 103, 104, 107, 116, 118, 142, 143, and 148. In addition, some will read verses whose initial letters spell the patient's Hebrew name. Many will use Psalm 119 for this purpose, because it contains twenty-two sets of eight verses, in alphabetical order in Hebrew.

PROVERBS

The book of Proverbs is an excellent example of an ancient genre, "wisdom literature," literature that celebrates wise behavior and moral conduct and offers proverbs and sayings designed to guide the reader on the right path. Traditionally, the composition of the book of Proverbs is assigned to Solomon except for two of the book's thirty-one chapters, which are attributed to Agur and the mother of King Lemuel, respectively. The Talmud also assigns to Solomon the authorship of Song of Songs and Ecclesiastes, saying that he wrote the earnest love poetry of the Song of Songs while a young man, the maxims of Proverbs in middle age, and the pithy and cynical sayings of Ecclesiastes as an old man. However, modern scholarship suggests that this collection of sayings actually was composed over several hundred years.

The final section of the book of Proverbs, beginning with 31:10, is an acrostic poem in praise of the *"eishet khayil/woman of valor,"* which is often recited by husbands to their wives on Shabbat evening.

JOB

Throughout the Bible there are episodes in which God intervenes in the affairs of humanity, sometimes to uphold the Hebrews, sometimes to punish them. The question is inevitable and inescapable, therefore: if the hand of God can be discerned in the workings of human history, why do the righteous suffer and the wicked prosper? This question is asked directly in Psalms and can be found echoed in many other places in the Tanakh, but it is addressed nowhere as forcefully as in the third book of the *Ketuvim,* the book of Job. Over the course of the book, the title figure is tormented by the loss of property, family, and health, despite his pious and humble nature.

Yet his faith remains unshaken. Even when his wife calls on him to reject God in his misery, Job resists. Eventually he is restored to his former prosperity and well-being. Yet when he *does* question the Almighty, the rebuke is swift and stunning: "Where were you when I laid the earth's foundations? . . . Have you ever commanded the day to break. . . . Would you impugn My justice? Would you condemn Me that you may be right?" At the heart of this book is the thought that to a mere human the ways of the Creator must remain inscrutable. The book doesn't really have a happy ending, despite the restoration of Job to *status quo ante.* But Job concludes that submission to the Divine Will is the only option really available to him.

SHIR HA-SHIRIM/ SONG OF SONGS

There are only two books of the Hebrew Scriptures that do not once mention the name of God. The first of them is the Song of Songs (also known in English as the Song of Solomon, because of the attribution of its authorship to the young king). The other is the Book of Esther. On Shabbat Pesakh, we read all of the Song of Songs, and the Sephardim also recite it after the Passover *seder* and on Friday afternoons just before the coming of Shabbat (to welcome the Sabbath Queen).

Song of Songs, the first of the *Five Megillot,* is quite simply a love song, an intensely erotic love song. Rabbi Akiba says in the Talmud that it is an allegory of the love of the Jews for Adonai. The Kabbalists drew heavily on the imagery of bride and groom in their mystical writings. Modern scholars believe it to be an anthology of love poetry written in the later Persian or early Greek periods.

RUTH

The book of Ruth is the second of the *Five Megillot,* and is read on Shavuot. The book tells the story of Ruth, a Moabite whose Hebrew husband has died, and her close relationship with her mother-in-law, Naomi. When a famine leaves the women (and Naomi's other Moabite daughter-in-law) destitute, and all their male kin dead, Naomi decides to return to Canaan. Ruth alone decides to go with her, "Whither thou goest, I will go." She becomes the most famous early convert to the Hebrew faith and her descendants will include King David.

LAMENTATIONS

The third of the *Megillot,* Lamentations, contains five elegies for the destruction of the Temple and the exile of the Israelites in Babylon. Each of its first four chapters is an acrostic, while the final chapter with its twenty-two verses is not. The book is traditionally recited on Tisha b'Av, the holiday memorializing the fall of the Temple.

KOHELET/ECCLESIASTES

The bleakly pessimistic and cynical book called Ecclesiastes (*Kohelet* in Hebrew after its putative author) is usually ascribed to an aging King Solomon. Its author decries the meaninglessness of the pursuit of wealth, wisdom, and pleasure. Interspersed with these dour observations are a series of other maxims that suggest this may be a compilation drawn from other Near Eastern wisdom literature of the time. One of the *Five Megillot,* Ecclesiastes is read on the Sabbath that falls during Sukkot, perhaps a reflection of the approach of winter.

ESTHER

The book of Esther is the last of the *Five Megillot* and the one most commonly referred to as a *megillah/scroll.* It recounts the tale of how the beautiful Esther and her brave uncle Mordecai outsmart the evil Haman, a royal counselor who wants King Ahashuerus to destroy all the Jews in Shushan (generally believed to be Persia). This is, of course, the story of Purim, and the book of Esther is read to raucous accompaniment on that holiday. Because the book does not mention the name of God, there was some opposition to its inclusion in the Tanakh when the Men of the Great Assembly were compiling the canon, but it managed to make it into the book, apparently after some debate.

DANIEL

The book of Daniel tells the story of its eponymous hero, a young Judean noble living in the Babylonian Exile. He and his three friends, Hananiah, Mishael, and Azariah, are brought to the court of Nebuchadnezzar who wants them to serve there. They resist attempts to be wooed from the Israelite faith. Daniel advances their position by successfully interpreting one of the king's dreams. But when the other three refuse to bow down to a golden idol, they are thrust into a fiery furnace; the flames do not harm them and they are restored to their previous positions at court by a chastened Nebuchadnezzar. These adventures continue, including the famous episode of Daniel in the lion's den; Daniel is cast into the den of a ferocious lion but, with the protection of God, emerges unscathed. The book concludes with a series of apocalyptic visions.

For textual reasons, the book of Daniel is thought by many modern scholars to be somewhat anomalous in its composition, at least partly of much later vintage than the rest of the Tanakh. In addition, only the beginning of the book (1:1 – 2:4, 8 – 12) is in Hebrew, the remainder is written in Aramaic. It also contains the first biblical reference to the idea of the resurrection of the dead at the coming of the Messianic age.

EZRA AND NEHEMIAH

Ezra and Nehemiah are the priest and governor, respectively, who shared power and authority over Judea after the return from the Babylonian Exile. At various times, this text has been a single book, then two separate books. Origen, one of the Church Fathers, divided them into two books, and the Latin translation, the Vulgate, followed his lead. Eventually, the Hebrew Bible adopted this structure as well. The books recount the history of the return from Exile and the rebuilding of the Temple in Jerusalem. The period covered runs from the declaration by Cyrus the Great that the Jews could return to Judea (538 B.C.E.) to the reign of Darius II (about 420 B.C.E.).

The history of the Babylonian Exile, encompassed in parts of II Kings, several of the books of the Prophets, and, perhaps most importantly, in Ezra and Nehemiah and the two books of Chronicles, is worth recounting at some length. After all, the Judeans were the only people in human history known to have been taken into captivity as an entire nation and yet to have survived with their religious and social identity intact. What kept them alive?

If one finds an answer to this question, it may unlock the secret of Jewish survival and success in the larger world-historical picture. From the destruction of the Temple in 586 B.C.E. to the present moment, more Jews have lived in *galut / exile* than in *Eretz Yisroel*. Even today, the vast majority of world Jewry lives in the Diaspora.

Ironically, the Judeans apparently thrived during the Babylonian Exile. When they were allowed to return to Judah, only ten percent did so; the remainder were comfortable enough in Babylonia to stay there. And the book of Ezra tells us that those who did return were able to make substantial financial gifts towards the restoration of the Temple. The Judeans were fortunate enough to be taken to a Babylonian empire that was flourishing, with an expanding economy that had ample room and need for the skills that they brought with them. Babylonia was the greatest power in Asia at this time, and Nebuchadnezzar was building a capital city to be remembered, with the famous Hanging Gardens as its centerpiece. Judean craftsmen were in demand. Even as slaves they were prized.

The next two generations of Judeans were raised in exile. Many assimilated easily into the Babylonian culture in which they grew up, but others resisted its blandishments. And throughout the period of Exile, the prophets sounded the note of warning, urging the Judeans to remain true to their religious beliefs, to live for the day on which the Temple would be restored. One need only read the somber words of these books to gain a sense of the longing for home and devastating sense of loss felt by many of the Judeans.

The Judeans faced a difficult question. If God had promised that the Davidic line would sit on the throne forever, if the Divine Presence dwelt within the Holy of Holies in the Temple, how was it possible that Nebuchadnezzar and his pagan armies had not only defeated Judah and deposed its rule, but had utterly destroyed Solomon's Temple?

For the prophets there was only one possible answer, the answer that they insistently repeated to the Judeans: you have betrayed the Covenant, worshipping pagan idols, participating in pagan rituals, and violating the commandments. One certainly didn't have to look very hard for evidence of such a betrayal. It was all around the Judeans, even propagated by their own rulers. There could be only one possible response, a return to Adonai's *mitzvot*.

But how could the Judeans retain the old practices of the Temple cult when the Temple lay in ashes in far-off Jerusalem? The answer lay in making prayer and study of sacred texts the central theme of Judean practice. One could not make sacrifices at a Temple that no longer existed, but one could go to the *bet midrash/house of study* and one could pray daily. Thus it was that the first Exile impelled the leaders of the Jewish people to reshape their religious practice, with the new shape gradually becoming something more recognizable to modern Jews.

Other captive peoples had taken their religions into exile with them. Yet those peoples disappeared, absorbed into their captors' cultures. What set the Judeans apart? First, as historian Richard Friedman notes, the pagan religious beliefs of the ancient Middle East were remarkably compatible with one another. To switch from Baal worship to Marduk worship or Zeus worship didn't require much of a cognitive leap—fundamentally they were all the same god(s), worshipped in very similar ways. Second, there was the insistent voice of the prophets, whose influence is not to be underestimated. Finally, the re-emergence of Hebrew texts was fortuitously timed to coincide with the last stages of the Exile. As we shall see momentarily, the key moment in the return of the Judeans to Jerusalem involves a renewal of the Covenant, enunciated in its most famous text.

The Exile would not last very long. Nebuchadnezzar's death precipitated Babylonia into a quick downward spiral and in 539 B.C.E. the Babylonian Empire went the way of the empires that had preceded it, conquered by a stronger power. The Persians, under Cyrus the Great, seized Babylonia. Cyrus issued a famous Edict of Liberation in which he urged the Judeans to return to Judah and rebuild the Temple.

As noted above, only a small percentage of the exiles followed Cyrus's promptings. Those who did found themselves in a land transformed by decades of war and neglect, without political autonomy, no Davidic king on the throne, ruins where their prosperous capital had once stood, before them the hard task of reconstruction and restoration.

The Judeans who returned to their homeland probably numbered in the vicinity of fifty thousand. They were led by a descendant of the House of David, Zerubabel. He served as the first head of the civil government of Judah in the return, with the High Priest Joshua the religious leader. When the Persians seemingly faltered in the aftermath of the suicide of Cyrus's son and successor, Cambyses II, the prophets Haggai and Zechariah declared Zerubabel God's anointed one, the king of a newly independent Judah; their dream of an autonomous Judah was premature (by about twenty-five hundred years) and Darius II, the new Persian ruler, crushed the rebellion easily.

Generally, though, Darius adhered to the Persian policy of allowing local priesthoods to control religious matters (an easy way to keep subject populations quiescent), and permitted the Judeans to go forward with plans for the restoration of the Temple in Jerusalem.

For the most part, the years following the return from the Exile were quiet ones, and the Second Commonwealth, as it was known, flourished. The Second Temple was completed and dedicated on Passover 516 B.C.E. A second wave of returning exiles arrived from Babylonia in the 450s. Among them was the scribe and priest Ezra. At the time of his arrival, 458 B.C.E., Nehemiah was the governor of Judah, appointed by the Persian emperor, Ataxerxes. Ezra carried with him two important documents: a letter from Ataxerxes empowering him to teach and enforce the laws of God before the Judeans, and a copy of the *"Torah* of Moses." It was this document—a version of the *Torah* very similar to the one we know today—that Ezra read aloud to the assembled people of Jerusalem during the fall festival that brought everyone to the capital city, with a translator repeating it in Aramaic, by then the language of daily life in the Holy Land. The reading was followed by a ceremony reaffirming the Covenant.

After all the years of suffering, the Judean people were enthralled to hear of their exalted heritage, their covenant with the Eternal One, the promises that had been made to their ancestors. Spontaneously, they demanded to be allowed to observe the holidays outlined in the sacred scroll.

Thus it was that the Jewish people re-embraced their religious heritage. Although that heritage would undergo many permutations in the centuries to come, they would never forsake it again and, it may be truly said, it was their faith that allowed the Jewish people to survive intact despite all the vicissitudes of their history.

A more immediate legacy of the reading of the *Torah* was the establishment, with the full knowledge of the Persians, of a theocratic state in Judah. This state, while hardly autonomous, was able to defend itself against its neighbors for many generations to come (thanks in no small part to a succession of larger powers that found it expedient to keep the Judean state intact). The state was ruled primarily by the High Priest and the wise old men of the *Knesset Hagadol / Great Assembly*.

I AND II CHRONICLES

The final two books of the Tanakh, I and II Chronicles, essentially offer a recap of the history of the House of David, the rise and fall of the First Temple, the Babylonian Exile and the return to Judea. Although they summarize earlier books, particularly II Samuel and Kings, the books of Chronicles add detail to our knowledge of the events of this period. On the other hand, the version of this history is also a sanitized one, omitting such embarrassing things as how David acquired Batshevah as a wife.

Chronicles brings the tale full circle. Like Genesis, it begins with Adam. Like Genesis, it ends with an anticipation of the return to *Eretz Yisroel*. The Temple may not be rebuilt at the moment the book closes, but the final words of the Tanakh, the decree of Cyrus, offer hope for the future: "Adonai God of Heaven has given me all the kingdoms of the earth, and has charged me with building a House in Jerusalem, which is in Judah. Any of you of all [God's] people, Adonai your God be with him and let him go up."

READiNG THE BOOK

No book in human history has engendered a richer and more varied interpretive literature than the Bible, and that statement is particularly true for the Tanakh. Contrary to what one might think, "fundamentalist" Judaism does not engage in a strict, literal reading of Hebrew Scripture. Although Orthodox Jews believe that the Bible is the Revealed Word of Adonai, dictated to Moses on Mount Sinai, and that even the Oral Law is God-given, they do not limit themselves to a reading of scripture as narrow or as literal as that practiced by fundamentalist Christians. Perhaps that's because they can read Hebrew and know how multilayered and ambiguous a text the Bible really is.

Jewish Bible commentators developed several methods of approaching the Torah as text. To get some sense of how varied their methods and interpretations can be, one need only look at a single page of *Mikraot Gedolot,* the Interpreters' Bible, a Jewish Bible printed with the texts of several leading medieval commentators alongside the scripture itself. On such a page, one will find the second-century C.E. Palestinian commentary of Onkelos; the eleventh-century French commentary of Rashi; a seventeenth-century Czech commentary on Rashi, the *Sifrei Chachamim/Book of Wisdom;* and the commentaries of the Rashbam and Ramban, twelfth-century French and thirteenth-century Spanish Jewish sages, respectively. On the facing page, you will encounter more Torah scholars of note: the eleventh-century Spanish philologist and rabbi, Abraham Ibn Ezra; the fifteenth-century Italian scholar Ovadia Sforno; the sixteenth-century Czech rabbi known as the Klei Yakar; and Rav Chaim ibn Atar's eighteenth-century Palestinian commentary, *Ohr Hachayim/Light of Life.* (The golden age of Torah commentary occurred during the medieval period. For profiles of some of the key Torah sages, see sidebar "Some Key Bible Commentators," p. 300.)

SOME KEY BIBLE COMMENTATORS

The American philosopher Walter Kaufmann once wrote, "A lack of clarity is almost indispensable to the survival of a book." He may have been thinking about the Bible. With its repeated narrative lines and often cryptic passages, the Tanakh has provided analysts with enough fodder to keep them grappling with it for over two millennia. For the Jews, commentary on the Bible has been an integral and essential pastime. The Talmud is nothing less than a massive series of Bible commentaries. (See Chapter 6, "The Rabbis Said: The Talmud and other Rabbinical Writings.) But there have been other equally distinguished thinkers who have devoted significant time and thought to the Tanakh.

Rashi

Rabbi Shelomo Yitzkhaki (1040–1105) is one of those extraordinary minds that humanity throws up periodically, a Torah scholar unequaled in the thoughtfulness of his commentaries, fluent in many languages, an accomplished poet, and a skilled philologist. Although he wrote commentaries to the Talmud and some 350 *responsa*, his best-known and most influential work is his commentary on the Torah. Any Jew who has had even a fleeting acquaintance with biblical commentary knows the phrase *khumash mit Rashi*, a copy of the Five Books of Moses that includes Rashi's commentaries.

Rashi lived in northern France in a period when that was a fairly comfortable environment for Jews until the coming of the First Crusade in 1095 with its wave of anti-Semitic violence in the Rhineland. Although he was not touched directly by the tragedies that befell these Jewish communities, he lost many friends and colleagues and some historians believe that these events may have hastened his death a decade later. Rashi had two daughters, Miriam and Jochebed, who married students of his; his grandsons, Samuel ben Meir, known as the Rashbam, and Jacob, known as Rabbenu Tam, were among the greatest Jewish scholars of their generation, following the path their grandfather had laid.

Rashi's biblical commentaries, which were the very first Hebrew books to be printed after the invention of movable type (even before the Bible itself!), are characterized by their reliance on *peshat/plain meaning* of the text. He writes a clear, concise, and readable Hebrew prose, drawing on a wide range of knowledge that includes the seeming trivia of agricultural life. He himself was a vintner as well as a rabbi, and he shows first-hand familiarity with the daily life of the ordinary farmer at many points in his Torah commentary. His considerable knowledge of Hebrew grammar is another strong point of the books.

At the same time, his writings are rich in *derash, midrashic* folklore and homilies that illustrate his points with charm and wit. This aspect of his writing is undoubtedly one of the attractions that has made his biblical commentaries a perennial favorite.

Abraham Ibn Ezra

Like Rashi, Abraham Ibn Ezra (c. 1092–1167) was a man of many talents, a poet, biblical commentator, grammarian and philologist, scientific writer and doctor. Although he was born in Spain, Ibn Ezra was widely traveled. At the age of fifty, he left his homeland to become a wandering scholar. He traveled to the Orient in hopes of finding his prodigal son, Isaac, who had converted to Islam. He lived variously in Italy, France, England, and eventually returned to his beloved Spain.

Among the great Bible commentators, Ibn Ezra's popularity is exceeded only by Rashi's. He is brief and concise, often darkly humorous. Ibn Ezra began his Bible commentaries while in Rome in 1140 and continued working on them for the remainder of his life. Like Rashi, he is primarily concerned with *peshat;* he draws heavily on his work in philology and grammar, even writing in the introduction to one of his books, "I will, to the utmost of my ability, try to understand grammatically every word and then do my best to explain it." A student of Torah, he held, must not only know Scripture, he must know grammar as well.

David Kimkhi

David Kimkhi (1160–1235) is the best-known of a distinguished French rabbinical family. His father was Joseph Kimkhi, a rabbi known as Rikam, a contemporary and friend of Ibn Ezra's and a translator of note. His oldest brother, Moses Kimkhi, known as Remak, was a pupil of their father, an author of commentaries on Proverbs, Ezra and Nehemiah, and Job, as well as a significant early Hebrew grammar.

But David, known as Radak, surpassed both his father and brother. His commentaries are found in virtually all *Mikra-ot Gedolot* and were widely translated during his lifetime. His work exercised considerable influence on Christian scholars in the Renaissance and may have even had some impact on the King James Version of the Bible.

More than either Rashi or Ibn Ezra, Kimkhi draws on contemporary events in the course of his commentaries, referring to the Crusades in several places. He draws extensively on the rabbinic literature of his predecessors as well as the philosophical writings of such sages as Saadiah Gaon and the great poets Shmuel Ha-Nagid and Ibn Gabirol. Unlike Rashi and Ibn Ezra, he can be a bit pedantic, repetitious, and even long-winded, but his interpretations of the Bible are essential reading for Torah scholars.

Nakhmanides

David Kimkhi was a synthesizer in both his biblical commentaries and his work on Hebrew grammar. The same may be said of his near contemporary from Spain, Moses ben Nakhman Gerondi, known as Nakhmanides or Ramban. Nakhmanides (1194–1270) was trained as a doctor but was also a prolific and powerful *halakhist,* so much so that in his native Spain he was known simply as "The Rabbi."

The respect he was accorded didn't end with the Jews of Spain either. He was a welcome figure at the court of King James I of Aragon as well. And when he was challenged to a disputation by the apostate Pablo Christiani and defeated the ex-Jew in a lengthy series of debates on theology at Barcelona, he was even rewarded by his patron. Unfortunately, the Dominican friars were rather less pleased, and Nakhmanides was forced into exile, although he was already seventy years old.

He eventually ended up in Palestine, where he became a pillar of the Jewish community, working steadily on his Bible commentaries. It was there that he died.

Nakhmanides, like Radak before him, was a staunch defender of Moses Maimonides; both men had tried to convince the French rabbinate to back down from their opposition to Maimonides's philosophical works, particularly *The Guide for the Perplexed.* (See the section on Maimonides, p. 415.) However, he did not share Maimonides' enthusiasm for philosophy as a guide to truth, even religious truth.

His differences with Maimonides are most apparent in his Bible commentaries, where he strenuously takes issue with the latter on many points. Nakhmanides is a strong fundamentalist in his thought, proclaiming Moses the author of Torah, as the recipient of Divine dictation. His commentaries range widely across many topics. He draws astutely on history and psychology and is perhaps the best of all the medieval commentators on finding the links between disparate *sidrot* and books within the Tanakh. At the same time, despite his apparent conservatism, Nakhmanides was a central figure in the mystical circle centered in Gerona (See Chapter 7).

As you can imagine, there are as many different Torah readings as there are Torah scholars. The pages of the *Mikra-ot Gedolot* barely scratch the surface. Because the commentators believed the Torah to be the Revealed Word of God, every single letter, even the ornamentations on the letters, was believed to have a meaning. One only needed a method with which to plumb the depths of the text—or four methods.

The sages of the Talmud wrote that every passage of Torah has seventy facets, a number that may reflect back to the seventy sages who made up the Sanhedrin, the holy court that interpreted the Torah in ancient Palestine. The medieval commentators recognized and practiced four principal methods of interpretation: *peshat,* the "plain sense" meaning of a passage; *derash,* the homiletical meaning (from which the word *midrash* is derived); *remez,* the allusive meaning; and *sod,* the hidden, mystical reading. Taken together, they form the acronym *PaRDeS,* actually a word of Persian origin meaning an area surrounded by a fence, used in the Talmud to mean an orchard or garden. (Taken into the Greek as *paradeisos,* the word also gave birth to the English word "paradise.")

PESHAT

The most basic way of reading the Bible is for its "plain sense" meaning, the meaning that is inherent in the text as we have it before us. *Peshat* draws on the context of the passage, its grammar, philology, historical content.

For example, Edward L. Greenstein draws on Rashi and his grandson Rashbam to show the distinction between a homiletic and a plain-sense reading of the passage from Genesis 49:7 in which Jacob says he "will divide" his sons Simon and Levi, "scatter them in Israel." Rashi writes: "I shall separate this one from that one so that Levi will not be in the number of the tribes—and they are indeed dispersed among the tribes." He believes that Jacob is punishing them for having banded together to do evil in the wake of the rape of Dinah and has separated them "like a grade school teacher imposing discipline," as Greenstein puts it. By contrast, Rashbam sees the passage in its most literal historical context: "For Levi was dispersed among the twelve tribes, as it is written in Joshua (Chapter 21)." In other words, that is the historical outcome that befell the tribe of Levi. And that's all there is to it.

At the same time, *peshat* undertakes a literary endeavor, by placing a passage in the larger context of the passages surrounding it and understanding the rhetorical devices that may be operating there. Or it may draw on linguistic knowledge to interpret it, as Ibn Ezra often does.

Peshat readings are broad enough to encompass metaphoric and figurative language. Thus the passage in Exodus that says "It shall be a sign upon your arm and a remembrance between your eyes," is understood by the Talmudic sages to refer to the wearing of the *tefillin* on the arm and head.

DERASH

Derash is a word derived from the verb *darash/to seek*. Used in the Bible, the verb means to ask of a prophet, rather like the ancient Greeks consulting the oracle at Delphi. As an interpretive technique, *derash* uses homily and parable to inquire of the text its latent meaning, as opposed to its "plain" meaning. Such a homily or parable is called a *midrash* (pl. *midrashim*), a word that we have seen often in this volume.

Biblical narrative is often elliptical, fragmented. *Midrash* is one way of filling in the gaps. The Bible served the rabbis as an ur-text to be elaborated on, filled out with more stories that refined the metaphors that the Bible itself was meant to be.

One of the most famous *midrashim* deals with the aftermath of the destruction of Pharaoh and the Egyptian army in the Reed Sea. The hosts of angels begin to sing as the last Egyptians disappear beneath the torrents and God rounds on them angrily, saying: "My children are dying and you sing!" This *midrash* underlines the delicate balance God walks throughout the Tanakh between stern judge and compassionate parent. (We will explore *midrashic* literature further in Chapter 6.)

REMEZ

Remez is the Hebrew for "hint," and as a method of Torah interpretation, it seeks the allegorical meaning of the text, focusing on the philosophical implications contained therein. The most obvious example of such a reading would be the statement by Talmudic sages that Song of Songs is in reality about the relationship between the people Israel and Adonai rather than the highly erotic love song it first appears to be.

SOD

There is a strong strain of mysticism in Judaism, best exemplified by Kabbalah (literally, "the tradition"), the mystical movement that arose in the twelfth century. Kabbalah would achieve its greatest flowering in Safed, in Palestine, in the sixteenth century, under the leadership of Isaac Luria (see the section "What Is Mysticism?" p. 360), but mysticism in Judaism dates all the way back to the beginning of the Common Era.

Central to Jewish mysticism is the idea that truth cannot be expressed solely in words. Words can only denote that which is perceived by the intellect and the senses. Truth, on the contrary, is beyond human sensory perception and cognition; it cannot be expressed by mere human language. The Bible is written in human language, but it is Divinely inspired. Therefore, the mystics reason, the words must contain Divine truth, but not when read in the way that humans normally read them. In some way, these Divine words must symbolize truth beyond words. Reading for denotation and connotation will not uncover that truth.

Instead, the mystics read the Bible as a sort of codebook, a dictionary of symbols to be deciphered by methods such as *gematria* and *notarikon*. As one mystical text puts it, "Many lights shine forth from each word and each letter."

Sod (literally, "mystery" or "secret"), the method of biblical interpretation that searched for mystical significance, became the special province of the Kabbalists who, more than other schools of Jewish mysticism, focused their attention largely on hermeneutics, the interpretation of texts (here, biblical texts).

We have already touched briefly on *Gematria* in Chapter 4, the system in which the letters of the Hebrew alphabet are assigned numerical values. Applied to reading Torah, it can be used to ferret out such meanings. For example, the Hebrew word *yihyeh* is composed of two *yod*s, each of which has a numerical value of ten, and two *heys*, each with a value of five. In Numbers 6:5, a passage delineating the ritual obligations of a Nazirite (one who has taken a particular vow of asceticism in the service of God), the phrase *kadosh yihyeh/he shall be holy* is thus interpreted as the reason that a Nazirite's vows last for thirty days (*yod* (10) + *hey* (5) + *yod* (10) + *hey* (5) = 30).

Another method of interpretation designed to reveal hidden meanings is that of the *notarikon,* a word derived from the Latin *notarius* or "shorthand writer." There are two types of *notarikon.* In the first, a word is understood as an acronym for its real meaning. For example, the first word of the Ten Commandments, *anokhi/I,* is actually an abbreviation for *"Ana Nafshi Ketavit Yahavit/I Myself wrote and gave [them],"* so there can be no doubt that the Decalogue is the word of the Almighty. In the second type of *notarikon,* a word may be broken up into other words. For example, the name Reuven becomes *re'u ven/see the son.*

As Gershom Scholem, the great historian of Jewish mysticism, wryly observes, "Explication the level of *sod,* of course, had limitless possibilities, a classic illustration of which is Nathan Spira's *Megillah Amukot* (1637), in which Moses's prayer to God in Deuteronomy (3:23ff.) is explained in 252 different ways."

Such is the multilayered complexity of Torah. We have discussed only four methods of reading the text; in fact, in the Talmud thirty-two hermeneutic tactics are enumerated.

WHO WROTE THE HEBREW BIBLE?

Jewish tradition has it that the Torah, the first five books of the Bible, were written by Moses, taking dictation from God. Yet Deuteronomy ends with Moses's death on Mount Nebo. Some Talmudic sages said that Joshua wrote the last eight verses of the book; others picturesquely describe Moses taking down God's words with tears in his eyes.

Not everyone's curiosity is so easily satisfied. Over the millennia since the Men of the Great Assembly finalized the process of the canonization, there have always been those who demurred when faced with this explanation. And both the internal evidence of the book—the repetition of episodes with significant changes, the vast differences in style among and even within passages—and archaeological evidence found in places like Qumran and the Cairo storehouse known as the *Genizah,* finished off that tradition.

Just as the process of canonization was a slow, historical evolution, so was our understanding of the composition of the Bible. Without going into great detail, one can say a few relatively certain things about the authors of the Tanakh. (For a comprehensive explanation of the process of the composition of the Torah, Richard Elliott Friedman's *Who Wrote the Bible?* is highly recommended as a thrilling intellectual detective story and an excellent introduction to historical study of ancient sacred texts.)

To take up the question of authorship for each of the books of the Hebrew Bible would easily double the length of this chapter. In recognition of the deserved primacy of the Torah, and because the story of its composition has been the most widely researched and written about, we will restrict ourselves to the identity of the author of the Five Books of Moses.

The Torah is probably the work of some four or five different authors, each of whom contributed a different point of view influenced by his or her own place in ancient Jewish society. First, there were the authors known as J and E; their initials refer to the most important clue that they were two different voices, that one called God *Yahweh,* the other *Elohim.* (Since the scholar who first enunciated this theory most effectively was Johann Gottfried Eichhorn, a German, the German spelling of *Yahweh,* with a J, was used to identify the *Yahwist* author.)

When one separates the E and J texts, it becomes apparent that they reflect the points of view of two different classes in the society of ancient Israel and Judea at the time after Solomon, but before the Assyrian destruction of Israel. One, E, was probably a Levite priest, while J may have been someone in the Judean court, which was involved in a power struggle with the Levite priests of Shiloh at that time. It is even possible that J was a woman, as Harold Bloom and others have suggested; certainly, as Friedman notes, the J stories are much more concerned with the feelings and problems of the women in them than is the case elsewhere in the Torah.

But, in fact, within the texts that had been attributed (by Eichhorn) to E were the works of yet another author, a member of the priestly caste who was responsible for the voluminous material regarding the role of the priesthood in Leviticus and Numbers (as well as many passages in Genesis and Exodus), who the scholars called P. And Deuteronomy was probably the product of yet another pair of writers, D_1 and D_2, at least one of whom had a stake in the reiteration of the law code and its relation to his own historical moment. When King Josiah died and the kingdom fell apart, further additions had to be made to take into account the impact of that catastrophe; in other words, someone had to reshape the earlier narrative so that the Jews of a much later period would see how the Deuteronomic laws could help them reconcile to their reduced state.

All of this makes the achievement of the person or persons who edited the Bible—the Redactor or R—all the more amazing. The book does not read seamlessly; if it did, then the scholars would never have discerned that there are four or five different voices in play here. But its overall structure is remarkable. We have already seen some of that literary architecture at work. Richard Friedman believes the Redactor may have been Ezra; certainly, as we have seen, Ezra was well-positioned for the task and, as the priestly power in a newly restored Jerusalem, had ample reason to restore the Torah. For Ezra, the public reading of the *"torah* of Moses" was the vehicle through which he would reunite the people of Judea and cement their devotion to the priestly line he represented.

Whatever the truth, ultimately what really matters, as Friedman himself observes, "is not only who wrote the Bible, but who reads it." Given the centrality of Torah study to subsequent Jewish history—as Chapter 6 will remind us—one answer to *that* question is, "The Jews do. Still."

NOTES

1. Pope John Paul II rejected the doctrine of supersessionism in a statement that was issued in 1990. However, other Christian denominations may disagree.

2. Besides the inclusion of some of the Apocrypha (see sidebar "The Apocrypha and Pseudepigrapha," p. 259), the most significant difference between the Hebrew and Christian Bibles occurs in the ordering of the books. Christian Bibles end with the Prophets, with Malachi the final book. The Hebrew Bible ends with Chronicles. The difference is not casual, but reflects two very different worldviews. Chronicles reaffirms

the Davidic line, the Jewish people's eternal mission, and their right to reclaim *Eretz Yisroel;* Malachi is a reminder of the coming of the Messianic Age, which Christians take as a prevision of the birth and death of Christ.

3. These alternate names are used primarily by the sages of the Talmud and some subsequent commentators. You will seldom if ever find them used elsewhere, and most non-Orthodox Jews will look at you in confusion if you refer to the books by them.

4. David Noel Freedman suggests the reason for this division was that Samuel, Kings, and Chronicles, each of which was divided in this manner, were among the longest books of the Hebrew Bible. When translated into Greek, a more prolix language than Hebrew, they must have strained the outer limits of what could be contained on a single scroll. So the resulting bifurcation was the result of practical necessity rather than some arcane theological argument.

5. The Christian versions of the Bible do not count the inscriptions that open many of the Psalms as verses themselves, so their verse count will differ slightly from this number.

CHAPTER 6

The Rabbis Said: The Talmud and Other Rabbinical Writings

The Bible is the cornerstone. The Talmud is the foundation. The edifice that they underpin is Rabbinic Judaism and from the middle of the First Millennium until the nineteenth century, that was the dominant kind of Judaism. We have already learned of the existence of such alternative Judaisms as Karaism (see p. 229), and the extent to which such modern movements as Reform, Conservative, and Reconstructionism (and even Orthodox) defined themselves—either directly or indirectly—by their departure from the guidelines and norms established by the sages of the Talmudic period and their successors. We have explored the norms—613 *mitzvot* and *halakhah*—themselves. But one cannot truly understand those norms and the lives that result from them without examining the Talmud and the major post-Talmudic writings that are the heart of Rabbinic Judaism.

The Talmud is unlike any other religious book ever compiled. It doesn't even *look* like any other religious book (except maybe the *Mikra-ot Gedolot*—the Commentator's Bible—with its garlands of Bible commentary laced around the text of the Tanakh, but that is a family resemblance of sorts). At first glance, the Talmud appears to be a chaotic amalgam of legal rulings, folktales, instructions for observance, dialogues between disparate religious figures (many of them not identified by name), maxims and sayings, even medical advice. Only after one begins to perceive the underlying structure does the Talmud begin to make a little sense. One could spend a lifetime studying it and never master its complexities.

Reduced to its simplest form, the Talmud consists of two parts. The first, the *Mishnah,* is an analysis, in Hebrew, of biblical law, of the *mitzvot,* as it emerges from the *praxis* of the rabbis. It is concise to the point of occasional incomprehensibility. The second part of the Talmud is *Gemara,* rabbinic commentaries, mostly in Aramaic, on Mishnah that attempt to elucidate that earlier work. Subsequent rabbinic literature consists primarily of, as you might expect, commentaries on the Talmud and the Torah.

In short, the key texts of Rabbinic Judaism constitute an elaborate debate—across generations, across millennia—about the nature of Jewish law, ritual, observance. In order to understand the form this debate took and why it took that form, one must look at the actual compilation of the Talmud. More than that, one must understand the historical forces that produced the debate and its product.

Every significant change in Jewish history that has occurred through the *Haskalah* and the Emancipation has produced a concomitant religious change. Although it pre-dated the destruction of the Second Temple, the synagogue became a central institution of Jewish worship life as a response to the tragedy of the destruction of the Temple and the bitterness of exile. The writing of the Mishnah and of the Gemara were the rabbis' answer to the destruction of the Temple, the creation of a Judaism based on guidelines and norms of behavior and practice that enabled the Jews to survive an even longer exile than the Babylonian one.

This historical context is worth keeping in mind as we explore the writing of the Talmud and subsequent key texts of Rabbinic Judaism.

ROOTS OF RABBINIC JUDAISM

When Ezra returned from the Babylonian Exile in the fifth century B.C.E. he held a public reading of the *"torah* of Moses" in Jerusalem. By doing so, and by encouraging the Israelite people to adhere to the lengthy code of laws offered in that scroll, he hoped to re-establish the nation of Israel on a firm footing. Ezra and Nehemiah (the political counterpart to Ezra's religious role) hoped to impress upon the people their deep roots of tradition and the powerful covenant that undergirded these roots. To make the impression stick, they would have to raise the Torah to the role of primary law text and ritual guide.

Although the teachings of the Torah were well-suited to this role in many ways, there were still ambiguities in its laws and many questions left unanswered. One should refrain from work on the Sabbath, yes. But what constitutes work? In the fall, the people were to dwell in booths for seven days. But what should the booths be made of, and what size should they be? We are instructed to "slaughter animals in the manner in which I have commanded you," but there are no other details given anywhere in the Torah. There were also problems of vocabulary; there were words whose meanings were unclear to the men who edited the Torah (primarily the names of some animals and plants).

To resolve these problems, it would be necessary to interpret the Torah, not merely read it. To that end, tradition says, Ezra convened a body of scholars (either 85 or 120 in number, depending on the source) that would be known as the *Knesset Ha-Gadol / Great Assembly.* The exact composition of the Great Assembly is not known, but in a period that extended roughly from 539 to 332 B.C.E., these men offered oral rulings on the Torah and its precepts. Among their greatest tasks was the establishment of the canon of the Hebrew Bible. (This version of the history of the period is the one favored by the sages of *Pirke Avot,* the tractate of Mishnah that discusses ethics, tracing an unbroken line of authority from Moses to their contemporaries. We do not actually know how much of this, if any, is historically accurate.)

The Men of the Great Assembly were not only interpreters of Torah; each was a rarity in those days, a man who could read and write. Hence, they were also known as the *soferim / scribes.* These men had the daunting task of bringing order to the rapidly accumulating body of oral law. Imagine what it would be like to codify and organize all of the case law handed down in the United States since the ratification of the Constitution in 1787; now imagine how much greater that task would be if almost all the decisions had been made orally, and before you could organize them you had to record them first. On a somewhat smaller scale, that was the task facing the *soferim.*

In Chapter 4 we discussed the process by which Oral Law became *halakhah.* But why were the Men of the Great Assembly working in an oral tradition in the first place? In large part, they believed that by recording the rulings of the rabbis and sages in writing, they would be undercutting the primacy of Written Law. At a time when their first task was the dissemination of the *"torah* of Moses," the Men of the Great Assembly were not inclined to draw attention away from the Pentateuch. Adding another book of written law might imply that it was the equal to the Written Law, the Torah.

Moreover, as the Oral Law (rightly) was seen as subject to further change, a malleable thing, to write it down would be to freeze it, to institutionalize it. The process of writing it down might have the effect of reducing the Oral Law to just another law code, rather than a vehicle for interpretation and a text for study and instruction.

The Men of the Great Assembly believed that there had been oral interpretation of Torah almost from the moment Moses came down from Mt. Sinai with the tablets in his hands. After all, was it not said that God had given the Oral Law to Moses on Sinai as well as the Torah, the Written Law? That the Almighty had whispered it into his ear by day, explained its meaning by night for forty days and nights? Were there not already *minhagim/customs* in place that were not specified in Torah but that were clearly extensions of it?

So for the time being the Oral Law was to remain oral. But this state of affairs could not last for very long. The return of many Jews from the Babylonian Exile meant an influx of men and women who were familiar with different practices developed far away from the ruins of the First Temple. Suddenly—but not for the last time—there were two variant forms of worship and practice in the Jewish community, those of the indigenous population of Palestine, and those brought back from Babylonia by a generation that had never seen the Temple when it stood. Moreover, the Israel and Judea to which they returned constituted a vastly diminished nation, with many holy sites no longer within its borders. Even the Second Temple was different, built to a different plan with different accoutrements. (One of the great enigmas of Jewish history is the disappearance of the Ark of the Covenant, which housed the tablets Moses received at Sinai, the central feature of the First Temple but absent from its successor.)

FROM THE PAIRS TO THE *TANNAIM*

After a series of weak leaders diminished the role of the Men of the Great Assembly in approximately 200 B.C.E., the power to make *halakhic* rulings passed to the heads of the Sanhedrin, the high court. The leaders were known as the *Zugot/Pairs*. The pairs—there would be five in succession—consisted of a *Nasi* and the *Av Bet Din,* the chairman and deputy chair of the Sanhedrin, the high court. Each of these pairs would add to the growing body of Oral Law, but none would add as distinctively as the last duo, Shammai (c. 50 B.C.E.–c. 30 C.E.) and Hillel (c. 70 B.C.E.–c. 10 C.E.).

One of the most famous stories in Jewish history concerns these two brilliant scholars and points up the difference in temperament between them (as well as underlying the importance of the "Golden Rule" in Judaism). A non-Jew came to Shammai, who was a builder by trade, and said to him, "Teach me as much Torah as I can learn while standing on one foot." Shammai was annoyed by this frivolous (not to say insulting) request and chased the man away with his measuring rod. The man then went to Hillel and made the same request. Hillel replied, " 'That which is hateful to you do not do to others.' That is all the Torah, the rest is commentary. Now go and study."

As might be expected, the *halakhic* rulings of Shammai and his followers, known as *Bet Shammai/the House (or School) of Shammai,* were usually more strict than those of Hillel and his followers, *Bet Hillel/the House (or School) of Hillel.* Shammai tended to rely on a very narrow and literal reading of *peshat/plain meaning* of Scripture.

Hillel, tradition says, developed his own methods for interpreting Torah that would serve as the basis for much of the Talmudic analysis of Torah in later generations. Based on seven principles (which Rabbi Ishmael would subsequently expand to 13; see sidebar "Thirteen Ways of Looking at the Torah," p. 315), Hillel's method was more flexible, allowing for both more and less restrictive *halakhic* rulings. The result was a veritable revolution in the interpretation of Torah.

The Sanhedrin was more than just the high court. Under the *zugot,* it also developed into a place of study, rabbinic learning, and discussion; it was not only a *bet din/house of judgment,* but also a *bet midrash/house of study.* In this way, it became the forerunner of the great academies, schools of Torah study from which would emerge the next generation of sages, the *Tannaim.* And it was these men, the *Tannaim,* who would finally set down the Oral Law in writing.

THIRTEEN WAYS OF LOOKING AT THE TORAH

Hillel posited seven rules of interpretation of Torah. Hillel did not invent these rules—the *soferim* had been using them for many years already—but he was the first to catalogue them as the basis for understanding the words of Scripture.

Rabbi Ishmael, the great teacher of the generation before the Bar Kokhba rebellion, developed these into thirteen rules. Eventually, Rabbi Eliezer ben Yose Ha-Galili would expand these further to thirty-two, but the thirteen *middot/measures* of Ishmael are so important a part of Jewish tradition today that the Orthodox include them in the weekday morning prayers. (Indeed, they were already present in the earliest known *siddur*, that of Amram Gaon.)

Here are Ishmael's thirteen *middot:*

1. *Kal Va-Khomer.* Inference from major to minor or minor to major; an *a fortiori* inference. A simple rule of logic, often framed in terms of leniency and strictness; i.e., if a more lenient case contains a certain stricter prohibition, then a stricter case must all the more; or if a strict case contains a certain leniency, then a lenient case certainly will as well. One of the most commonly offered examples is Moses' argument to God: "The Children of Israel have not listened to me, how then should Pharaoh hear me?" [Exodus 6:12]

   Rabbi Meir Zvi Bergman, a contemporary Orthodox *rosh yeshivah/head of yeshivah* in Israel, notes that the determinations of whether a case falls into the categories of stringent or lenient are "(a) logic; (b) the laws of Torah that pertain to the case." He offers examples of each, drawn from the Talmud. In the first, drawn from tractate Baba Kama, "If one is liable for the damages caused by his animal when it did not intend any harm, then, certainly, he should be liable for damages which the animal did intend to inflict." For the latter category, he cites tractate Kiddushin, "If a Jewish bondswoman, who cannot be acquired by an act of cohabitation, can be bought with money, then a wife, who may be acquired [for *kiddushin,* the first stage of marriage] through cohabitation, may certainly be acquired with money." (This example is true only in biblical law; the rabbis subsequently prohibited this practice.)

2. *Gezerah Shavah.* Drawing a conclusion by word analogy. An interpretative principle based in linguistics, *gezerah shavah* holds when two passages contain words that are similar or have identical connotations, the laws of the two passages are subject to the same regulations and applications. The contemporary scholar Rabbi Abraham Hirsch Rabinowitz offers the example of a famous debate between Hillel and the B'nai Bityra on whether it is permissible to bring the paschal lamb even on Shabbat. The question is settled by a *gezerah shavah:* the passage covering the daily offering says it is to be brought "*bemo'ado/in its due season,*" and this phrase recurs in the passage on the paschal lamb. Consequently, the rule governing the daily offering, which is not brought on the Sabbath, applies to the paschal lamb as well.

3. *Binyan Av.* In this interpretative principle, the meaning of a term is derived from one *(binyan av mi-katuv ekhad)* or two other texts *(binyan av mi-sheini ketivim)* and applied to a wider range of cases. In short, a law that occurs in one passage of Torah may be applied in other passages in which there is a structural similarity. Horowitz offers an example from Tractate Yebamot: "The school of R. Ishmael taught: Since the Torah mentions 'garments' in connection with several *mitzvot* without specifying their texture, and in one case the Torah specifies 'a woolen garment, or a linen garment'; wherever else 'garment' is mentioned it refers to a woolen or a linen garment."

4. *K'lal ufirat.* A generalization that is followed by a particular. One of the best-known examples of this principle is drawn from Leviticus 1:2, in which Jews are enjoined to bring an offering "*min habiheimah/of the beasts,*" a phrase that includes both wild and domestic animals, and "*min habakar u-min hatzon/from the herd and the flock,*" a phrase that suggests domestic animals only. The use of the more restrictive phrase after the generalization is taken to mean that wild animals are not to be brought for sacrifice.

5. *Perat uk'lal.* A particular followed by a generalization (an inversion of the previous principle). In such a case, the particular is

expanded by the more general term that follows it. When the Torah tells us that we must return lost articles to their rightful owners, it specifies "his ass . . . and his garment," then continues, "And you will do so with every lost thing of your brother's. . . ."

6. *K'lal u-ferat u-k'lal.* A general law, limited by a specific principle, then referred to once again in general terms. In such cases, the law must be interpreted according to the limitation presented by the specific case. Conversely, there is the case of the *Perat u-k'lal u-ferat,* a specification followed by a generalization followed by another specification. In such cases, the generalization is qualified by the specification.

    Rabbi Adin Steinsaltz (in the Reference Guide that accompanies his monumental English-language Talmud) offers the example of the money used to redeem the second tithe, described in Deuteronomy 14:26. The Torah says that the money must be spent on "whatever you desire—on cattle, sheep, wine, strong drink, or whatever you wish." Drawing from the details listed there, the Talmud says that the passage indicates that the money is to be spent on items that resemble the ones enumerated, that is, items that derive sustenance from the ground but do not themselves come from the ground, items that have undergone a process of growth or development.

7. *K'lal shehu tsarikh li-perat* or *Perat shehu tsarikh li-k'lal.* A general term that requires a specific term to clarify it, or a specific term that requires a generalization. Rashi explains the difference between this principle and *k'lal u-ferat* is that in the latter the general rule is understood and the specific is included to limit its application but in this case the specific is necessary because the general rule is unclear.

8. *Davar shehayah bi-k'lal v'yatsah min ha-k'lal li-lamed.* Something is included in a generalization, but was then singled out from the generalization in order to teach a specific lesson. Hence the exception that was offered is applied to the entire generalization (or else its inclusion would have been redundant). Attention is called to the specific instance because it teaches us something new. For example, the Torah states that all work is forbidden on the Sabbath. But it also specifically proscribes kindling a fire on the Sabbath. The Talmud takes this to mean that each category of work is prohibited independently; therefore, someone who per-

forms different kinds of forbidden work during Shabbat should be punished for each transgression.

9. *Davar shehayah bi-k'lal v'yatsah min ha-k'lal lit'on shehu k'iniyanu.* A case in which something is included in a generalization but is then singled out from the generalization in order to discuss a provision similar to the general category. In such cases, the specific instance usually exists in order to be more lenient than the generalization would have been.

For example, Rabbi Meir Zvi Bergman points out, within the discussion of skin diseases designated as *tza'arat/leprous afflictions*, in Leviticus 13, the Torah singles out two specific types of *tza'arah*. Ordinarily these would be treated under the general laws of *tza'arat* but because they receive separate attention here, they are considered to be exempted from two particular, stringent laws governing *tza'arat*, and are covered by the more lenient general regulations of *tza'arat*, even though they are not mentioned specifically in those general rules.

10. *Davar shehayah bi-k'lal v'yatsah min ha-k'lal min ha-k'lal lit'on to'an akhar shelo v'inyanu.* A case in which something is included in a generalization but is singled out to discuss a provision not similar to the general category. In this case, the specific instance is brought up because it carries its own set of laws that are different from the ones discussed in the generalization.

In the discussion of the laws of *tza'arat*, the Torah refers to "a man or woman [who] has an affliction of the head or the beard." As Rabbi Bergman explains:

Even these two afflictions of the skin are implied in the general laws . . . , the Torah nevertheless singles them out to tell us that they have neither the stringency of the general category, regarding which white hair in the affected area is a symptom of impurity, and here it is not, nor the leniency of the general category—that is, *tza'ara[t]* of the head and beard is indicated by the appearance of yellow-colored hair, while in other forms of *tza'ara[t]* it is not.

(Gateway to the Talmud)

11. *Davar shehayah bi-k'lal v'yatsah min ha-k'lal li-don ba-davar hekhadash.* A case in which something is included in a generalization but is singled out so that it will be treated as a new case. In such a passage, the principle of the generalization does not apply to this new case unless the Torah explicitly returns to the generalization. Steinsaltz points to the laws governing *sh'lamin/peace-offerings.* First the Torah discusses them generally. Then it sets forth specific laws of the *todah/offering of thanks,* a type of peace-offering. The Talmud concludes from this sequence that the laws of peace-offerings don't apply to the offering of thanks except where specified.

12. *Davar ha-lamed me'inyanu v'davar ha-lamed misofoh.* Interpretation of an obscure word or passage by inference from its context or from a subsequent statement in the passage. The classic example of this principle occurs in the Ten Commandments. Although "Thou shalt not steal" would seem to us a clear injunction against theft of property, the other crimes enumerated in this verse—murder and adultery—are punishable by death. Because more theft was not a capital crime, the rabbis inferred that the verb used here *(tignov)* specifies kidnapping, which is a capital offense.

13. *Shinei v'tuvim ha-mav'khishim zeh et zeh.* In a case in which two verses contradict each other, the meaning can only be determined by using a third text that reconciles them.

"O YOU SCRIBES AND PHARISEES!"

Who were the men who wrote the Talmud? They were members of that political/religious formation reviled by Jesus and his followers, the Pharisees. We have already encountered one group of their detractors, the Saduccees, in Chapter 4. The rule-based Judaism that developed in the post-biblical period, in the writing of the Mishnah and Gemara, was the product, in part, of thought often associated with the Pharisees. To better understand Rabbinic Judaism, it is necessary to understand them.

In truth, there are many open questions about the Pharisees. Trustworthy sources are hard to come by for this period. Much of what we know about them derives from highly colored accounts from Josephus, the Jewish-Roman historian who is our principal source on the "Jewish war" against Rome (including a vivid, if occasionally suspect, version of the death of the Jewish rebels at Masada); the Gospels of the New Testament; and the writings of the Church Fathers. Of course, none of these authors is objective: Josephus was a supporter of the Pharisees, perhaps a Pharisee himself; the authors of the Gospels and the Church Fathers were sworn enemies of the Pharisees.

This much seems clear. At some point during the period in which the Hasmonean dynasty ruled Palestine (approximately 164–63 B.C.E.), three distinct groups emerged within the Jewish community. The reason for the division was simple, as Dr. Albert I. Baumgarten, a contemporary Israeli scholar, explains.

If the period of the First Temple was one in which the central question of Jewish faith was whether to worship Adonai, the God of the Bible, alone, that question received a resounding answer with the Babylonian Exile: only Adonai was to be worshipped, and any pagan practices would be punished. "The Jews of the Second Temple period therefore were preoccupied with what can readily be understood as the next question in logical order," Baumgarten writes. "Once a commitment to the God of the Bible alone and to [the] Torah is made, the crucial matter becomes what interpretation of the Torah shall prevail." The lines within the Jewish community became sharply drawn around this issue as three groups emerged: the Saduccees, the Essenes, and the Pharisees.

These sects represented a small minority of the population of the Jewish world, probably no more than five percent in total, but their importance was far greater. As Baumgarten has written, they "set the tone for Jewish life as a whole," setting themselves apart as ones who alternated between denouncing the corruption and impurities of an increasingly decadent Hasmonean kingdom and setting new moral standards for the monarchy. As Baumgarten notes, the sects found boundaries of behavior, setting themselves apart from the general Jewish population in areas as diverse as food, dress, commerce, marriage, and worship.

Sectarian practice . . . indicates the sense of disapproval of the manner in which fellow Jews observed the laws of the Torah, making separation from those Jews to a greater or lesser extent inevitable. I suggest that this sense of inadequate stringency is part of the debate which had been taking place between Jews, virtually

since the return from the Babylonian exile, concerning the degree
of permitted contact with the surrounding nations.

The wars of the Maccabees, commemorated in the festival of
Hanukah, were wars against Hellenization and assimilation. With the
victory of the Hasmoneans who led those wars, it was probably
inevitable that these issues would continue to occupy the top drawer of
the Jewish psyche in a restored Jewish kingdom. And each of the sects
had their own position.

The Saduccees were a small elite group whose numbers included the
High Priest, who was in charge of the rites in the Temple in Jerusalem.
They believed in the Written Torah and only the Written Torah and, as
you might expect, believed in the primacy of the hereditary priestly
caste. The Essenes were a monastic group, possibly the sect that produced some, if not all, of the Dead Sea Scrolls. They rejected both the
other groups as corrupt and sought refuge from the daily world by
withdrawing from society, living in Essene homes, dressing differently,
and enforcing celibacy among their members.[1]

The Pharisees were the largest of the three formations; Josephus
puts their number at 6,000, although contemporary scholars believe
that figure to be inflated. They were apparently the only one of the
sects with a popular base. The Pharisees included in their ranks many of
the scribes, the men who copied the proceedings of the Sanhedrin and
the religious courts. They were deeply committed to the new interpretations of the Written Law being produced by those bodies. As a result,
they were the foremost exponents of the idea of the Oral Torah, which
would become the Talmud, as an adjunct to the Written Torah. In addition, the Pharisees brought the purity laws, previously applied only to
the priestly caste, into the Jewish home, creating an alternate center for
sanctity while the Temple still stood in Jerusalem.

Politically, the Pharisees were reformists, not particularly radical;
they had no great quarrel with the Roman authorities unless the
Romans openly abrogated Jewish law. But at the same time, they
dreamed openly of the day when Jewish autonomy would once more be
a reality in Palestine. The importance of the Pharisees cannot be
overemphasized: in the aftermath of the destruction of the Second
Temple, it is only through the efforts of the rabbis, the heirs of the
Pharisaic worldview, that Judaism was able to survive at all.

TRAGEDY, DISPERSION, AND THE WRITING OF THE MISHNAH

The first century of the Common Era would seem on the surface an unlikely time for an endeavor as demanding as the setting down of the Oral Law. In 70 C.E. the Romans would destroy the Second Temple. Anti-Jewish persecution under Emperor Hadrian would spark a violent uprising, led by Bar Kokhba in 135 C.E.; with the collapse of that rebellion, the Romans engaged in widespread repression and wholesale murder of the Jewish population. Legend says that they tortured and executed ten prominent rabbis, including Akiba, the greatest scholar of his generation. The growth of Diaspora communities in Babylon, Rome, Turkey, and elsewhere, combined with the destruction of the Temple and crushing of the anti-Roman rebellion, would spell an end to the primary role of the sages of Palestine, as scholars scattered throughout the Mediterranean.

Some Jews had hailed Bar Kokhba as the Messiah (or at least as the harbinger of the imminent Messianic Age). His utter and total defeat left little doubt that he was not going to deliver the Jews from Roman oppression. Perforce, Jewish leaders had to turn their attention to finding ways of preserving the integrity of Jewish identity and practice. With their people plunged from hope to despair, the *Tannaim* realized that they had to look to the past in order to secure the future.

The leadership of the Jewish people was almost completely obliterated. All that remained was a group of men who became known as the rabbis,[2] meaning masters or teachers. (The historical truth of this story is unclear; they may have been the moderate wing of the Pharisees.) Legend has it that while the Romans were besieging Jerusalem, Yokhanan ben Zakkai had his students, Eliezer ben Hyrcanus and Yehoshua ben Hananiah, smuggle him out of the city in a casket after spreading the rumor that the great sage had died. They brought him before Vespasian, then the Roman commander. Yokhanan hailed the Roman as the Emperor and King of Rome; Vespasian rebuked him for uttering a title that he did not hold, but Yokhanan replied that the Bible said that Jerusalem would fall only at the hands of a king. At that moment a messenger rode up to tell Vespasian that Nero had died and he was now Emperor of Rome. Vespasian offered to grant Yokhanan one request and the rabbi replied, "Give me [the town of] Yavneh and its sages."

They would prove to be leadership enough. As they had in times of crisis before, the religious leaders of the Jewish people turned their gaze inward and found strength in Torah. And as they had before, they adapted to a new situation. The synagogues had evolved as a response to the Babylonian Exile. Ezra had used the "scroll of Moses" as a rallying point for the Jewish masses.

Now the rabbis would turn their attention to the codification of Jewish law, shifting the focus of Judaism from Temple to Torah, to creating a Judaism whose invisible walls could not be breached by any intruder, no matter how heavily armed. Yokhanan ben Zakkai told Vespasian, "Give me Yavneh and its sages," and that would be all the army Judaism would need—or have—for the next eighteen hundred years.

In the period following the destruction of the Second Temple, the rabbis would establish the canon of the Tanakh, set the basic structure of the prayer service, and begin the lengthy process of codifying the Law, of creating the Oral Torah.

There had been collections of *halakhic* rulings in the past. Rabbi Meir had recorded and arranged the rulings of his mentor, Rabbi Akiba, in the second century C.E. *Tannaim* of earlier generations had also collected oral rulings, particularly those handed down in their own academies. But it was Judah Ha-Nasi (also known as Judah the Prince and Rabbi) who undertook the monumental task of creating a comprehensive book of *halakhah* up to his time, the Mishnah (from the Hebrew *shanah/to repeat,* "teaching by oral transmission").

Over a roughly twenty-year period between 200 and 220 C.E., Judah Ha-Nasi created a veritable constitution, an authoritative guide to Jewish law for judges and teachers to use. By doing so, he and the rabbis with whom he worked were asserting the continuing uniqueness of the Jewish people. At the same time, they were creating a written version of the law that would be impervious to the vagaries of oral transmission. The body of Oral Law had grown so great that no one could possibly recall all of it accurately. The existence of the Mishnah eliminated that problem.

But it did more. Not only did the Mishnah present a practical solution to a real-life problem—creating a manageable handbook of legal codes—it also sent a message to the Jewish people in a time of darkness. With its focus on the immutable nature of worship—the endless rhythms of the Jewish calendar, the unchanging problems of ritual cleanliness and impurity—the Mishnah presented Judaism as a faith and practice not bound by the fleeting passage of historical time.

Bar Kokhba is defeated? The new moon still will come this month and need to be welcomed on Rosh Khodesh. The Romans oppress us yet again? Spring still means Pesakh and summer Shavuot. Whether Jerusalem is in the hands of the Persians, the Greeks, the Romans, the Turks, Jews will still get married, give birth and be born, eat, work, and die, and the rituals that govern those realities must be themselves governed. Thus the Mishnah is a book of "an eternal present," as it has been phrased by Jacob Neusner.

The Mishnah, Neusner argues, is derived from the rabbis' reading of Aristotle and, like his ambitious writings on natural history, "aims at the hierarchical classification of all things." The operative word here is "things." Neusner observes that two-thirds of the tractates of Mishnah are philosophical rather than theological in intent and that "scarcely a line of Mishnah invokes the word 'God' or calls upon the active presence of God." This is, he argues, the profoundly radical nature of Mishnah, a nature that Gemara tried to rein in.

WHAT IS IN THE MISHNAH?

Essentially, the Mishnah is a collection of legal rulings and opinions, written in what has come to be known as Mishnaic Hebrew. Distinct from biblical Hebrew grammatically and, to some extent, in vocabulary, Mishnaic Hebrew has been proven by archaeological finds to have been the everyday language of the Hebrews of Judea at the time of Bar Kokhba. However, when the centers of rabbinic learning shifted to the Galilee, where Aramaic was the common tongue, Mishnaic Hebrew was destined to become a dead language and by the end of the *tannaitic* period it had.

The Mishnah is divided into six *sedarim/orders,* a structure that the *Tosefta* (a supplementary collection compiled anonymously in the same period) and both the Palestinian and Babylonian Talmuds will follow. (This order also gives Talmud one of its nicknames, *shas,* an acronym derived from *shishah sedarim/six orders.*) Each of the Orders, in turn, has between seven and twelve subdivisions called *masekhtot/tractates* (sing. *masekhet*), of which the Mishnah contains sixty-three. The tractates are divided into *per-*

akim/chapters, and the smallest units are designated as *mishnayot* (sing. *mishnah*) in the Babylonian Talmud or *halakhot* in the Palestinian Talmud. The tractates are given in order of length, beginning with the ones with the most chapters and continuing to those with the fewest.

Each of the six orders is named in a way that suggests one of its primary topics. The first order, *Zeraim/Seeds,* deals particularly with laws of agriculture. The second order, *Mo'ed/Appointed Seasons,* covers the laws governing the festivals, fast days, and the Sabbath. The third order, *Nashim/Women,* primarily is concerned with laws governing marriage, divorce, betrothal, and adultery (although this order also contains the tractates *Nedarim/Vows* and *Nazir,* which deals with the Nazirite vows of asceticism). The fourth order is *Nezikin/Damages,* and is largely concerned with what modern Anglo-American courts would call civil and criminal law, but also includes laws governing the treatment of idolators, and the most commonly read tractate of the Mishnah, the *[Pirke Avot/Sayings of the Fathers,]* a collection of ethical maxims. The fifth order, *Kedoshim/Holy Things,* covers such Temple-related matters as sacrifices, ritual slaughter, and the priesthood. The sixth and final order is *Tohorot/Purities,* and the majority of the tractates within it deal with issues of ritual purity and impurity.

WHAT'S IN THE MISHNAH AND THE TALMUD: PRIMARY SUBJECT MATTER OF THE TRACTATES AND WHERE THEY APPEAR

ORDER: ZERAIM (Seeds)

Berakhot—Prayers and benedictions (9 chapters in Mishnah; also in BT, PT, T*)

Pe'ah—Laws governing charity and gleanings (8 chapters; PT, T)

Demai—Doubtfully tithed produce (7 chapters; PT, T)

Kilayim—Seeds, trees, and animals (9 chapters; PT, T)

Shevi'it—Laws of the sabbatical year *(shemitah)* (10 chapters; PT, T)

Terumot—Contributions to the priests (11 chapters; PT, T)

Ma'aserot—Tithes for the Levites and the poor (5 chapters; PT, T)

* BT = Babylonian Talmud; PT = Palestinian Talmud; T = *Tosefta*

Ma'aser Sheni—Second tithe (5 chapters; PT, T)

Khalah—Dough offering to the priests (4 chapters; PT, T)

Orlah—Prohibition against harvesting trees for four years (3 chapters; PT, T)

Bikurin—Offering of first fruits (3 chapters; PT, T)

ORDER: MO'ED (Appointed Seasons)

Sabbath—Laws governing the Sabbath (24 chapters; BT, PT, T)

Eruvin—Laws establishing permissible limits (for carrying) on the Sabbath (10 chapters; BT, PT, T)

Pesakhim—Laws governing *khametz, matzah,* and the paschal sacrifice (10 chapters; BT, PT, T)

Shekalim—Laws governing the shekel donation to the Temple (8 chapters; PT, T)

Yoma—Yom Kippur sacrifices and fasting (8 chapters; BT, PT, T)

Sukkah—Laws governing the building of the *sukkah,* the Four Species, and festival of Sukkot (8 chapters; BT, PT, T)

Beitsah—General festival laws (5 chapters; BT, PT, T)

Rosh Hashanah—Fixing the date of the New Year, blowing of the *Shofar,* Rosh Hashanah prayers (4 chapters; BT, PT, T)

Ta'anit—Laws governing fast days (4 chapters; BT, PT, T)

Megillah—Laws governing Purim (4 chapters; BT, PT, T)

Mo'ed Katan—Laws governing *khol ha-mo'ed/intermediate festival days* (3 chapters; BT, PT, T)

Hagigah—Laws of the pilgrimage festivals (3 chapters; BT, PT, T)

ORDER: NASHIM (Women)

Yebamot—Levirate marriage, prohibited marriages (16 chapters; BT, PT, T)

Ketubot—Marriage contracts and agreements (13 chapters; BT, PT, T)

Nedarim—Laws governing vows (11 chapters; BT, PT, T)

Nazir—The Nazirite laws (9 chapters; BT, PT, T)

Sotah—Laws regarding adultery, war, and murder in which perpetrator is unknown (9 chapters; BT, PT, T)

Gittin—Divorce and the *get* (9 chapters; BT, PT, T)

Kiddushin—The marriage act, genealogy (4 chapters; BT, PT, T)

ORDER: NEZIKIN (Damages)

Baba Kama—Direct and indirect damages in civil law (10 chapters; BT, PT, T)

Baba Metzia—Losses, loans, work, wage contracts (10 chapters; BT, PT, T)

Baba Batra—Partnership, sales, promissory notes, inheritance (10 chapters; BT, PT, T)

Sanhedrin—Laws regarding the courts, criminal law, principles of faith (11 chapters; BT, PT, T)

Makot—Punishment by flagellation (3 chapters; BT, PT, T)

Shevuot—Oaths (8 chapters; BT, PT, T)

Eduyot—A collection of testimonies from the sages (8 chapters; T)

Avodah Zarah—Idolators (5 chapters; BT, PT, T)

Avot—Sayings "of the Fathers" (5 chapters, Mishnah only)

Horayot—Cases involving errors by the court and their correction (3 chapters; BT, PT, T)

ORDER: KEDOSHIM (Holy Things)

Zevahim—Laws of sacrifice (14 chapters; BT, T)

Menakhot—Meal offerings, *tefillin*, *tzitzit* (13 chapters; BT, T)

Khulin—Ritual slaughter and dietary laws (12 chapters; BT, T)

Bekhorot—Firstborn child, firstborn animals, defective animals (9 chapters; BT, T)

Arakhin—Valuation of Temple offerings and soil (9 chapters; BT, T)

Temurah—Substituting an animal offering (7 chapters; BT, T)

Keritot—Sins requiring expiation (6 chapters; BT, T)

Me'ilah—Sins of sacrilege against Temple property (6 chapters; BT, T)

Tamid—Daily sacrifices in the Temple (7 chapters; BT, T)

Midot—Measurements of the Temple (5 chapters, Mishnah only)

Kinim—Procedure in the event of mixing of sacrifices (3 chapters, Mishnah only)

ORDER: TOHOROT (Purities)

Kelim—Utensils and pollution (30 chapters; T)

Oholot—Laws governing the dead and ritual purity (18 chapters; T)

Nega'im—Leprosy (14 chapters; T)

Parah—Sacrifice of the red heifer, purification after contact with the dead (12 chapters; T)

Tohorot—Laws of purification (10 chapters; T)

Mikva'ot—Laws governing the *mikveh* (10 chapters; T)

Niddah—Menstruation and ritual impurity in women (10 chapters; BT, PT, T)

Makhshirin—Ways in which food becomes ritually unclean (6 chapters; T)

Zavim—Gonorrhea and purification (5 chapters; T)

Tevul Yom—Other types of ritual impurity (4 chapters; T)

Yadayim—Ritual uncleanliness of the hands (4 chapters; T)

Uktsin—Things that are susceptible to ritual uncleanliness (3 chapters; T)

Several things are immediately apparent from a survey of the six orders of the Mishnah. First, the structure of the book, despite some attempt at a systematic organization, is more than a bit haphazard. In part, the problem lies in Judah's decision to incorporate large sections of material intact from earlier sources; earlier collections often grouped rulings by their authors rather than subjects. For instance, in the middle of the Tractate Rosh Hashanah, we find a series of rulings from Yokhanan ben Zakkai that have nothing to do with the festival of the New Year. However, the structure also reveals the associative techniques that were often typical of the rabbinic mind at work; if the order *Nashim* includes betrothal and marriage, wouldn't it make sense to include other laws governing vows as well? After all, each of these kinds of vows—betrothal and marriage, legal and financial—involved what was considered in ancient times to be a transfer of title to property. On the other hand, within each tractate only one subject is pursued.

Second, the prominence given to issues relating to the Temple—virtually the entirety of *Kedoshim* and sections of all the other orders except *Nashim*—suggests that the *Tannaim* were committed to preserving Jewish continuity in the face of disaster. Perhaps the Temple had been destroyed more than 100 years ago, but they would carry on as if it were eternal, as sure as the turning of the earth. (Not every great Jewish thinker agreed with this focus on the long-defunct cultic rituals. Abraham Ibn Ezra, for one, decried scholars who devoted their time to the study of *halakhah* that had no practical relevance.)

Third, in its unusual focus on the quotidian—laws governing agriculture, criminal and civil law, rules governing the nuts and bolts of religious observance—the Mishnah is an elegant reminder of one of the governing principles of Judaism as a belief-system: that everything we do, no matter how mundane, has a spark of the holy within it. If we run through the areas of concern expressed in the tractates of the Mishnah, we can see how its worldview shaped Judaism.

HOW THE MISHNAH WORKS

The Hebrew prose of the Mishnah is terse and compact, orderly and repetitive, designed for easy memorization. In short, it reads like a law text. Professor Jacob Neusner characterizes it further as "small-minded, picayune, obvious, dull, routine—everything its age was not." But Neusner also explains that this seeming paradox was quite deliberate. The orderliness and routine of Mishnah represents an effort by Judah Ha-Nasi and his collaborators to resist the uncertainties of their age by reasserting verities of an older, more permanent vintage.

As noted above, within each tractate, a single subject provides the main focus of discussion. Thus, Tractate Nazir is concerned with the vows of the Nazirite, a member of an ascetic sect that pledged themselves to God (Samson being the most famous example): how long they are valid, what is prohibited to a Nazirite, when he may cut his hair, what sacrifices are required if he should be defiled, what the equivalent vows would be for a woman or slave wishing to become a Nazirite. Similarly, Tractate Avodah Zarah (Worship of Idols) discusses the practices of idol worshippers, warning Jews against protracted contact with them and advising how to purify utensils purchased from them. Even tractates that do not seem to belong in the order to which they are assigned pursue a single subject in its various ramifications. Although it may be unclear why it is the first tractate of the order *Zeraim* and, therefore, at least nominally concerned with agricultural matters, Tractate Berakhot (Blessings) maintains a single focus, the rules governing the recitation of the *Shema,* the eighteen Benedictions, and the *b'rakhot* over wine and food.

Where the tractates depart from their single topic, they often do so in order to follow a chain of associations that are not thematic. (Often the association is one chosen as an aid to memorization.) For example, in a passage from Tractate Sotah, which is concerned with adulterous women, there is a quote from Rabbi Yehoshua about immoral women; this quote is then followed by another from Yehoshua about those whose behavior threatens to bring destruction on the entire world.

There are exceptions. Tractate Eduyot, for example, compiles the teachings of later authorities, some one hundred of them, all of them supposedly taught on the day that Rabbi Eleazar ben Azariah was installed as the head of the Sanhedrin. In addition, the tractate includes forty examples of the dispute between the House of Shammai and the House of Hillel in which the results were actually the reverse of the usual, with the House of Shammai taking a more lenient position and the House of Hillel the more severe.

At least in theory, Mishnah parallels the Torah, discussing the 613 *mitzvot,* filling in the holes and interpreting the ambiguities. In practice, its commentary on Scripture takes different forms. There are tractates that do little more than paraphrase Scripture in order to clarify it, for example, the tractates in Mo'ed that deal with matters of ritual, particularly as it pertains to the observance of the festivals in the Temple. Other tractates take off from facts stated in the Torah, heading in directions that might have surprised, say, Moses. Neusner gives as an example Tractate Parah, which deals with the sacrifice of the red heifer. Because it occurs outside the Temple, the Torah would assume this sacrifice could not be conducted under circumstances of ritual purity, but the Mishnah actually not only assumes the opposite but demands circumstances of greater purity than could be found in the Temple, outlining the steps necessary to achieve such a state. Finally, there are tractates that deal with issues at best barely noted in the Torah. For example, the tractates governing marriage and divorce—Ketubot and Gittin, respectively—deal with issues that are covered in a few verses of Torah in passing; out of these few bricks, the rabbis erect a pair of multi-story buildings.

Nearly 150 sages are mentioned by name in the Mishnah, ranging chronologically from Hillel and Shammai to Judah Ha-Nasi himself. Wherever a difference of opinion is found on a specific ruling, Mishnah gives the minority view first, followed by the authoritative view, usually expressed "R. Judah says . . ." or "but the sages declare. . . ."

AN EXAMPLE FROM THE MISHNAH

In order to understand how this book works, let us examine a passage from Mishnah, in this case the opening of the first tractate, Berakhot. The Mishnah opens:

From what time do we recite the evening *Sh'ma?* From the hour that the priests enter to eat their *terumah* [the regular offering given to them in the days of the Temple] until the end of the first watch. These are the words of Rabbi Eliezer. And the sages say: until midnight. Rabban Gamaliel says: until the beginning of sunrise. It happened once that his sons returned from a celebration and said to him: We have not yet recited the *Sh'ma*. He said to them: If sunrise has not yet begun, you are obligated to recite it. And not in respect to this alone did they so decide, but wherever the sages said "until midnight" the obligation to perform the *mitzvot* applies until the sun comes up. If this is so, why did the sages say "until midnight"? To keep a man from transgression.

As we already know (from Chapter 1), we are obligated to recite the *Sh'ma* "when we lie down and when we rise up," that is, in the evening and the morning. We also know that the Jewish day begins with evening, as per Genesis ("And the evening and the morning were the first day"). So the Mishnah begins its exegesis of the Oral Law with the first thing that a Jew would do beginning the ritual day (if not the work day), reciting the evening *Sh'ma*.

This passage gives us three answers to the question: "From what time do we recite the [evening] *Sh'ma?*" Rabbi Eliezer, a *tanna,* says that one recites the evening *Sh'ma* from the time that the priests enter their houses to eat the *terumah* until the end of the first watch. The first watch—and the editors of the Mishnah assumed the reader would know—is when three small stars are visible in the night sky. In fact, in offering this answer to the question, Eliezer is merely restating an older practice dating to the days of the Temple.

The passage then offers a second answer, from the *Tannaim,* that one may recite the evening *Sh'ma* until midnight. This seems straightforward (particularly compared to Rabbi Eliezer's answer!). But Rabban

Gamaliel has a third answer, with a story to accompany it. Gamaliel, like Eliezer, is a second-generation *tanna,* the successor to Rabbi Yokhanan ben Zakkai as president of the Academy at Yavneh. In his story, Gamaliel shows how a certain leniency in a specific case—here toward his sons—allowed them to perform a *mitzvah* that Eliezer's more rigid version would have made them forgo.

But that brings us back to the final question asked in this passage: "Why did the sages say, 'until midnight'?" The answer now appears simple—so that a person does not run the risk of forgetting to say the evening *Sh'ma.* Yes, one may say it until sunrise, but the longer one postpones it, the greater the risk of not performing the *mitzvah.*

In this passage we find several important themes that will run throughout the Mishnah and subsequent works of Rabbinic Judaism. We see the relationship between holiness and time, the importance of the Temple cult, the tension between the rulings of the rabbis and the words of the Torah, the need to balance leniency and necessity, and the role of individual personalities in elaborating the Oral Law.

TOSEFTA AND *BARAITA*

The Mishnah was not the first compilation of *halakhic* rulings. It would not be the last. At approximately the same time that Judah Ha-Nasi and his collaborators were compiling the Mishnah, an unknown group was putting together another collection of rulings and maxims of the *Tannaim,* called the *Tosefta* (from the Hebrew meaning "addition" or "supplement").

The *Tosefta* follows the structure of the Mishnah fairly closely, containing the same six orders and all but three of the same tractates (it omits Tractates Tamid, Midot, and Kinim). The *Tosefta* includes a tractate not found in the Mishnah, *Avot* of Rabbi Nathan, which probably is meant to be a commentary on the Mishnaic tractate Avot. However, the *Tosefta* is four times as large as the Mishnah and, according to some scholars, less clearly written.

The materials on which the anonymous editor of the *Tosefta* drew are called *baraitot* (sing. *baraita*), from the Aramaic meaning "an external teaching." This term is used to designate any *tannaitic* statement not found in the Mishnah. It is also applied to writings from the next generation of sages, the *Amoraim,* that were intended to elucidate the Mishnah. While some *baraitot* may include *halakhic* rulings not found in Mishnah, others openly contradict the Mishnah. The latter are introduced with the Aramaic word *tanya / we have learned* or *tanu rabbanan / our rabbis taught.* Another oft-cited collection of *baraitot* is the *Midrash Halakhah.*

Neither the *Tosefta* nor other *baraitot* are considered authoritative for purposes of *halakhah.* Where they contradict Mishnah, the ruling of the latter is valid. However, they are useful tools, often elucidating matters on which the Mishnah is either unclear or silent. (Perhaps the closest equivalent in American jurisprudence is the function of a concurring opinion from a Supreme Court justice; the ruling is what matters but the opinion may elucidate that particular justice's thinking and may be invoked by someone deciding a future case.)

For purposes of comparison, here is the opening passage of Tractate Berakhot as it appears in the *Tosefta:*

[From what time may the evening *Sh'ma* be recited?] From the moment when people go in to partake of their meal on the eve of the Sabbath. Thus says Rabbi Meir. But the sages say: From the moment the priests have the right to eat their *terumah.* The sign for this is the appearance of the stars. And although it cannot be proved, this is what is meant in Nehemiah 4:15: "So we labored at the work, and half of them held the spears from the break of dawn till the stars came out."

GEMARA: THE TASK CONTINUES

In one sense, the rabbis' worst fears had come true. A law written down *is* frozen. The Mishnah would not change, but the times did. Thus, the task of interpretation continued. The only difference was that the interpretation was no longer of Scripture alone, but of Scripture and Mishnah (and of Scripture filtered through the rabbinic consciousness manifested in Mishnah).

The task was made somewhat more difficult by a new factor, the parallel development of rabbinic academies in Palestine and Babylonia. Once again the aftermath of Jewish dispersion was altering the nature of Judaism. With the death of Judah Ha-Nasi in 220 C.E., a new group of sages arose to meet this challenge. Significantly, they were given an Aramaic label, the *Amoraim* (sing. *amora*), meaning "speaker" or "interpreter," unlike *Tannaim,* which is Hebrew.

In truth there is little difference between the *Tannaim* and the *Amoraim* in methodology or ideology. The primary difference between them is chronological, with the completion of the Mishnah and the death of Judah serving as a reasonable breakpoint roughly in 220 C.E. There were five generations of *Tannaim;* there would be five generations of *Amoraim* in Palestine and seven in Babylonia.[3] (They would be followed, in turn, by the *Savoraim* and after them the *Geonim,* but those two bodies of scholars are post-Talmudic.)

A TIME LINE OF TALMUDIC SCHOLARS

Dates (approx.)	Group	Most Prominent Members
c. 350–200 B.C.E.	Men of the Great Assembly	Simeon Ha-Tzaddik
c. 200–First Century B.C.E.	The *Zugot/Pairs*	Yose b. Yoezer,
		Yose b. Yokhanan*
		Yehoshua b. Perakhya,
		Mattai
		Yehudah b. Tabbai,
		Simeon b. Shetakh
		Shemayah, Avtalyon
		Hillel, Shammai
First Century B.C.E.	*Tannaim,* First Generation	School of Hillel
		School of Shammai
		Rabban Gamaliel the Elder
		Hananiah
		Simeon b. Gamaliel I
		Yokhanan b. Zakkai
		Eliezer b. Jacob the Elder
		Haninah b. Dosa
c. 90–130 C.E.	*Tannaim,* Second Generation	
	Older Group	Rabban Gamaliel II
		Eliezer b. Hyrcanus
		Yehoshua b. Hananyah
		Yose the Priest
		Eleazar b. Azariah
	Younger Group	Ishmael b. Elisha
		Akiba b. Yosef
		Tarfon

* b. means "ben" (Hebrew) or "bar" (Aramaic), which translates as "son of."

		Simeon b. Azzai
		(called Ben Azzai)
		Simeon b. Zoma
		(called Ben Zoma)
		Elisha b. Abuyah
		(called *Akher/the Other*)
c. 130–160 C.E.	*Tannaim*, Third Generation	Students of Ishmael
		Students of Akiba:
		Meir
		Simeon Bar Yokhai
		Yose b. Halafta
		Yehudah b. Ilai
		Rabban Simeon b. Gamaliel II
Second Century C.E.	*Tannaim*, Fourth Generation	Rabbi and his contemporaries:
(Redaction of Mishnah, *Tosefta*)		Judah Ha-Nasi (called Rabbi)
		Simeon b. Yehuda
		Ahai b. Yosiah
		Dosa
		Eleazar b. Simeon (Bar Yokhai)
		Yose b. Meshulam
To 200 C.E.	*Tannaim*, Fifth Generation	Gamaliel III, son of Rabbi
		Hiyyah the Elder
		Bar Kaparah
		Rav Huna
c. 200 C.E.–Sixth Century		
(Redaction of *Halakhic Midrashim*, c. 300 C.E.; *Aggadic Midrashim*, Palestinian Talmud, c. 400 C.E.; Babylonian Talmud, c. 427–650 C.E.)		
	Amoraim, First Generation	
	Palestine:	Hanina
		Yannai
		Yehoshua b. Levi
	Babylonia:	Abba bar Abba
		Rav (Abba Arikha)
		Mar Samuel
	Amoraim, Second Generation	
	Palestine:	Yokhanan bar Napakha
		Simeon b. Lakish (called Resh Lakish)

Dates (approx.)	Group	Most Prominent Members
		Kahana
		Simlai
	Babylonia:	Huna
		Yehuda b. Yekhezkel
	Amoraim, Third Generation	
	Palestine:	Samuel bar Nakhman
		Abbahu
		Zera I
	Babylonia:	Hisda
		Rabba bar Nakhmani
	Amoraim, Fourth Generation	
	Palestine:	Haggai
		Hillel II
	Babylonia:	Abaye
		Raba
	Amoraim, Fifth Generation	
	Palestine:	Pinkhas
		Yehudah IV
	Babylonia:	Papa bar Hanan
		Huna son of Rab Yehoshua
	Amoraim, Sixth Generation	
	Babylonia:	Rabina I
		Huna bar Nathan
		Ashi
	Amoraim, Seventh Generation	
	Babylonia:	Yemar (at Sura)
		Yose
Sixth Century C.E.	*Savoraim,* Older Group	Sama bar Yehuda
		Akhai bar Rab Huna
		Rihumai
		Samuel bar R. Abbahu
	Savoraim, Younger Group	Aina
		Simona
		Rabbai

The book of commentary on Mishnah that resulted from their labors is called the Gemara. There is a double significance to this fact. First, like *amora, gemara* is Aramaic, not Hebrew; by 220 C.E., even Mishnaic Hebrew was no longer a widely spoken language, and Aramaic was the *lingua franca* of the Jewish world.

More important, *gemara* is the Aramaic word for "study," just as *talmud* is the Hebrew (and the combination of Mishnah and Gemara constitutes the book we know as the Talmud). What the rabbis and their disciples did in the academies in Palestine and Babylonia was both study and a kind of legislation. Herein lies another reason why so much of the Talmud is taken up with discussions and debates regarding the laws of the Temple and the cultic practices performed there; even if the Temple were not to be rebuilt within the foreseeable future, it was important that the rabbis understand and interpret the words of the Torah that governed it, with that knowledge as an end in itself—*Torah v'lishma / Torah for its own sake.*

In order to understand the process by which the Talmud was written, it is necessary to understand the academies of the time.

YAVNEH: THE FIRST GREAT ACADEMY

The first and most central of the Palestinian academies—indeed, the hub from which all the academies both in Israel and the Diaspora sprang —was at Yavneh. A small town about twenty-five miles west of Jerusalem, Yavneh already had been a minor gathering place for Torah scholars when the Temple was destroyed in 70 C.E. Then Yokhanan ben Zakkai asked Vespasian to grant it to him as a center for study.

Under Yokhanan's leadership, Yavneh flourished, taking on the role of the Sanhedrin, and spurring the founding and growth of a network of similar places of learning in *Eretz Yisroel*. However, with the collapse of the Bar Kokhba rebellion, many of the scholars were dispersed, some to Babylonia. The academy at Yavneh moved to Usha in Galilee in approximately 140 C.E., then to Sepphoris about sixty years later, where its head was Judah Ha-Nasi. One of the principal tasks performed there was the completion of the Mishnah. Eventually the academy would move once more, to Tiberias, where the Palestinian Talmud would be written and edited.

Babylonia had its own schools of Torah study, probably dating back to the last days of the Second Temple. Rav Shila and Abba bar Abba built the academy at Nehardea into a major center for Jewish thought about the same time that Judah Ha-Nasi was finishing the Mishnah, and they were in close contact with him. However, it would not be until Abba Arikha, known as Rav, founded the academy at Sura in approximately 220 C.E. that Babylonian Jewish study came into its own.

Significantly, Rav was ordained a rabbi by Judah himself. One could receive *semikhah / ordination by laying on of hands* only in Palestine (which is why the sages in the Palestinian Talmud are given the title "rabbi" but those of the Babylonian Talmud are known as "rav," the Aramaic word meaning "master" or "teacher"). Consequently, Rav's presence in Sura, aided in no small part by his reputation for scholarship and teaching ability, attracted more than 1,000 full-time students and revitalized Jewish learning in Babylonia. It was here that the Babylonian Talmud would be written and edited.

The Babylonian academies were modeled on their Palestinian counterparts. In both countries, the academy was not only a *bet midrash / house of study* and place where one could seek interpretations of law, but also a *bet din / house of judgment,* that is, a law court. Neither teachers nor students received pay; as a result, lectures took place in the early morning or at night so that all could work at other jobs. Needless to say, under such circumstances there were very few full-time students; much of the studying took place during a two-month period, the *yarhei kallah,* when students and teachers would gather at the academy for intensive study. The *yarhei kallah* was timed to coincide with the slower months of the agricultural calendar, as the bulk of the Jewish people were still tied to the land.

All sessions took place in a single lecture hall, with the *rosh yeshivah,* the President of the Academy, on a platform in front of the seated students. (In fact, the word *yeshiva* comes from the Hebrew word for "seated.") The greater the scholar the closer to the front he sat. The *rosh yeshivah* would open discussion of the *mishnah* for that day, often asking one of the sages seated before him to rise and lecture on it. Lively debate and discussion invariably followed, often veering from subject to subject.

The Gemara, the commentary on Mishnah that makes up the rest of the Talmud, is presented as the proceedings of the discussions of Jewish law and custom that would occur in the academies (although it might be more accurately characterized as an *ex post facto* re-creation). Where the Mishnah is a terse recounting of the results of such debates, the Gemara is a recapitulation of the give-and-take between the Torah sages of the time. Sages would speak from their platform for the general public, as well as their students, to hear; they would address their audience in Hebrew, with an assistant translating into Aramaic.

What kind of men were these teachers, these rabbis? There is much evidence in the Talmud itself, and it is not always flattering. With competing schools of thought battling for intellectual supremacy, there are occasional insults, bruised feelings, and hard words. There is the sage who dismisses another's argument, "Your teacher was a reed-cutter in a swamp." There are stories told by one school or rabbi to denigrate another, with no less stinging rejoinders from the victims of the first. There are hard-headed political wrangles. When Rabbi Akiba declared that Simon Bar Kokhba was indeed the "star out of Jacob," the messianic figure that was promised in the Tanakh, the Talmud tells us that his colleague Jokhanan ben Torta tartly replied, "Akiba, grass will grow out of your cheekbones and the Son of David will still not have come."

In other words, they were normal men, sometimes prone to envy or contempt for their colleagues. Yet the multiplicity of viewpoints given in Gemara, even when it leads to a definitive decision supporting one position over others, suggests a willingness to listen to and respect opposing ideas. Even the apostate—most prominently Rabbi Elisha ben Avuyah, who left Judaism and is referred to in the literature as *Acher/the Other*—is treated with some sympathy. That may also be the explanation for a phenomenon noted by Professor Richard Kalmin, that "even sources which are reported from a particular sage's point of view generally show no signs of polemical distortion in favor of the sage whose perspective they reflect."

The rabbis were men who worked for a living, often as simple laborers (yes, even as reed-cutters in a swamp). They were men with wives and children. They understood the day-to-day realities of life. Perhaps that is why, as contemporary scholar Samuel Lachs has written, "Some of the rabbis of the Talmudic era subscribed to a view of the world which starts with man rather than God and is reflected in their observations about the human condition."

SOME KEY FIGURES IN RABBINIC JUDAISM

Akiba (c. 45–135 C.E.) A figure of almost mythical stature, perhaps the most famous of the sages of the Mishnaic Era, a scion of the third generation of *Tannaim*. Akiba ben Joseph was a simple shepherd, an illiterate until he was in his forties when his wife Rachel encouraged him to leave home to study Torah. A pupil of Eliezer ben Hyrcanus and Joshua ben Hananiah, he quickly surpassed his masters. In a few years he had thousands of disciples himself, whom he brought to his home, telling them that they owed everything—as he himself did—to Rachel. Virtually all of the fourth-generation *Tannaim* were taught by Akiba at his academy at B'nei Barak. His interpretative methods were quite radical, drawing on such obscure details as the ornamentation of the letters of Torah. He was one of the most outspoken supporters of the Bar Kokhba rebellion, a position that cost him his life. It is said that as he was being tortured to death by the Romans, he uttered the *Sh'ma*, then said to his students, "All my life I didn't understand what it meant to 'say these words with all your heart.' Now I understand." And with his dying breath, he uttered the word *ekhad/one*.

Eliezer ben Hyrcanus (c. 40–c. 120 C.E.) Second-generation *Tanna*, a disciple of Yokhanan ben Zakkai; reportedly one of the two who smuggled Yokhanan to the Roman encampment in a casket during the siege of Jerusalem. A key figure in the establishment of *halakhah*, cited over three hundred times in the Mishnah. Known for his phenomenally retentive memory, a staunch conservative in matters of Jewish law. Left the Academy at Yavneh to establish his own at Lydda.

Hillel (c. 70 B.C.E.–c. 10 C.E.) Leader of the Pharisees at the time of Herod and the greatest sage of the Second Temple period. A descendant of the line of King David, he worked as a simple laborer while studying Talmud. He served as *Nasi*, the chair of the Sanhedrin, most memorably paired with Shammai as his deputy. A great teacher of Torah who urged that it be studied not for possible gain but for its own sake. His rules for the interpretation of Torah were the foundation for future biblical textual analysis (see the sidebar "Thirteen Ways of Looking at the Torah," p. 315). His stress on ethical conduct and the importance of community in the face of state power are principles that have lived on for two thousand years since his death.

Yokhanan ben Zakkai (first century C.E.) Probably best known as the founder of the Academy at Yavneh, a leader of the Pharisees and a pupil of Hillel. From about 30 C.E. he lived in Jerusalem, where he abolished the ordeal of the wife suspected of adultery and the rite of the Red Heifer. Called *Rabban*, the most exalted honorific bestowed on a sage, he was the chief nemesis of the Saduccees. (The story of his escape from the besieged Jerusalem is retold on page 322.) It was Yokhanan who prescribed *Tzedakah* as a substitute for the expiatory sacrifices brought to the now-destroyed Temple, thereby beginning the process of re-creating Judaism for the Diaspora.

Judah Ha-Nasi (c. 138–c. 220 C.E.) Head of the Jewish community in post-Temple Palestine, chief of the Sanhedrin and, perhaps most important, the sage who collected and codified the Mishnah. A son of Simeon ben Gamaliel II, he succeeded his father as head of the Sanhedrin. Immensely wealthy, Judah was also among the most powerful of the sages. As such he was one of the rare Jewish leaders to merit recognition even from the Romans; among his friends was the ruler Antoninus. He was a man of high culture as well, who permitted only Hebrew and Greek to be spoken in his household. The most important *halakhist* of his era, it is a measure of his importance that Judah is also known in Mishnah and subsequent texts simply as Rabbi—the Teacher.

Rav (c. 175–247 C.E.) Abba Arikha—Abba the Tall—an important Babylonian *Amora* of the first generation. Well-born, his uncle was the sage R. Khiya. He studied with his uncle and Judah Ha-Nasi, from whom he received ordination, and was in contact with many of the *Tannaim*. Upon his return to Babylonia, he first located at the academy at Nehardea, but in 219 C.E. founded his own academy at Sura. Rav was an expert in ritual law, and the Babylonian Talmud is full of his debates with his friend Samuel, who was the head of the academy at Nehardea.

Resh Lakish (c. 200–c. 275 C.E.) Simeon ben Lakish, a Palestinian *Amora* of the second generation, had a most unusual background for a Talmudic sage. In his youth, unable to find other work, he had worked as a Roman gladiator, and his strength is proverbial. Known as a skilled debater, his particular foil was Yokhanan bar Napakha, his own brother-in-law, whom he frequently bested in issues of *halakhah*. The two maintained a close relationship, though, and when Yokhanan founded the academy in Tiberias, Simeon joined him there. Resh Lakish was also an ardent proponent of Torah study and children's education.

Shammai (c. 50 B.C.E.–c. 30 C.E.) *Bet av din* of the Sanhedrin and, with Hillel, the last of the five *Zugot*, Shammai is best remembered for his debates with Hillel. A conservative on matters of *halakhah*, he favored a literal interpretation of *Tanakh/Hebrew Bible* and a stern line that is said to be a reflection of his rather dour, irascible personality. Yet one of his best-known statements, found in the *Pirke Avot/Sayings of the Fathers*, is "Greet everyone with a cheerful face."

Simeon bar Yokhai (second century C.E.) Fourth-generation *Tanna* and one of the foremost pupils of Akiba, teacher of Judah Ha-Nasi and staunch opponent of Roman rule, even after the defeat of Bar Kokhba. Marked for execution by the Romans, Simeon and his son, R. Eleazar, went into hiding, living in a cave for thirteen years, studying Torah there until the decree was revoked. Allegedly the author of the *Zohar*, one of the key works of Jewish mysticism (although, as we will see in the next chapter, his authorship is highly suspect). Known as a worker of miracles, his *yahrzeit* is celebrated by thousands who make a pilgrimage to Meron on Lag b'Omer to pray at his tomb.

HALAKHAH AND *AGGADAH*

What the sages would talk about fell into two categories, *halakhah* and *aggadah*. *Halakhah* we are already familiar with—it is the legal rulings and the reasoning behind them that govern Jewish practice. Mishnah consists largely of *halakhah,* as do another group of important rabbinic texts designated as *Midrash Halakhah / Study of Halakhah*.[4] These texts are devoted to the exegesis of legal rulings and the 613 *mitzvot* as derived from the Torah.

But there is much more than just *halakhah* in the Talmud. The other category of writings in the Talmud and other rabbinic texts is *aggadah / narration,* a term that takes in . . . well, anything that isn't *halakhah*. *Aggadah,* then, is anything found in rabbinic writings that isn't about legal discussions and decisions. In the Talmud, approximately a third of the text is *aggadic* in nature, comprising a wide-ranging compendium of ethical, folkloric, philosophical, historical, and theological writings. Although the Talmud is historically the first source of *aggadah,* the major source is the *midrashim* (see page 355).

How do these two components of the Talmud, of Rabbinic Judaism as a whole, interact? The great poet Hayim Nathan Bialik, who compiled one of the most comprehensive collections of *aggadic* folklore, the *Sefer Ha-Aggadah / Book of Tales* in the early part of this century, wrote:

Halakhah wears an angry frown; *Aggadah,* a broad smile. The one is the embodiment of the Attribute of Justice, iron-handed, rigorous and severe; the other is the embodiment of the Quality of Mercy, essentially lenient and indulgent, mild as a dove. The one promulgates coercive decrees and knows no compromise; the other, presumes only to suggest and is sympathetically cognizant of man's shortcomings . . . *Halakhah* represents the body, the actual deed; *Aggadah* represents the soul, the content, the fervent motive. . . .

Halakhah is the crystallization, the necessary and ultimate consummation of the *Aggadah;* whereas, *Aggadah* is the real content, as well as the soul, of *Halakhah*. . . . A living *Halakhah* is the embodiment of an *Aggadah* of the past and the seed of the future, and so it is also conversely; for the beginning and end of these two are indissolubly joined and linked with each other.

The ethical content of *aggadah*—and this material is always fundamentally didactic and moral in nature—informs the legal decisions of *halakhah*. And *halakhah* is the legal embodiment of the ethical worldview of *aggadah*.

But the Mishnah omits the bulk of *aggadic* material, focusing on the debates that led to the legal decisions it does record. Gemara, by contrast, includes much of this seemingly extraneous matter. But, of course, it is never really extraneous.

HOW THE GEMARA WORKS

As the architect Louis Sullivan said, form follows function. The style and content of the Gemara are a reflection of its purposes. Eliyahu Krupnick, a contemporary Orthodox rabbi and teacher of Talmud, has pointed to four reasons for the writing of the Gemara.

- The *Amoraim*, he writes, needed to explain the reasoning behind the laws compiled in the Mishnah; given the telegraphic style of the earlier book (probably designed as an aid to memorization when Mishnah was still orally transmitted), that need led to a more expansive style.

- Gemara is needed to resolve differences of opinion in *halakhic* matters between the *Tannaim* and *Amoraim*. As a consequence, Gemara records the arguments of both sides.

- The sages were still adjudicating cases. Their decisions and the reasoning behind them had to be recorded somewhere.

- The *Amoraim* were also beginning to collect the homiletical (i.e., sermon-based) literature and even some philosophical writings that found their way into the Gemara.

Obviously, the *Amoraim* decided to cast their redactors' nets wider than Judah Ha-Nasi did when he compiled the Mishnah, and the occasionally rambling and discursive style of Gemara is the result of that decision. Krupnick points to several ways in which Gemara fills in the gaps in Mishnah. It may offer explanations of a *mishnah* that differ from their apparent meaning, or refer to a passage regarding some specific situation where the older text does not specify one. Or a passage may be interpreted by inserting seemingly missing words that Rabbi X "relied upon the reader to understand as if they were written."

Just as the smallest basic unit of the Mishnah is a *mishnah,* basically a paragraph or so in length stating a single precept of the Law, the smallest basic unit of the Gemara is a *sugya/topic* (pl. *sugyot*). The way both Palestinian and Babylonian Talmuds are arranged is simple: a *mishnah,* followed by the *sugyot* that analyze it. The analysis takes the form of a question-and-answer, often attributed to the sage who authored it, with the discussion leading back to the biblical verse from which the law is derived. The *mishnah* may be compared to other *mishnayot* or to outside texts, *baraitot.* As we have seen, the rabbis' brand of logic was often associational so the discussion may seem to us to range far afield. Eventually, the discussion ends with a decision on what the law consists of, sometimes establishing a new principle of *halakhah*. Or it may end with the word *teku,* an acronym that means there is no solution to the problem and that it will be resolved by Elijah when he comes as the herald of the Messianic Age.

PALESTINIAN TALMUD VERSUS BABYLONIAN TALMUD

With two major centers of study in the Jewish world, Gemara developed on parallel tracks and the result was two separate (and not equal) books, the Palestinian Talmud, often called the Jerusalem Talmud (or *Talmud Yerushalmi* in Hebrew), and the Babylonian Talmud *(Talmud Bavli).* A brief comparison is in order.

The Palestinian Talmud, despite its provenance in *Eretz Yisroel,* is actually the less authoritative of the two works. It is only a third the length of its Babylonian counterpart. It does not contain Gemara on the last two orders of Mishnah, a sizable omission that scholars cannot account for. It does include Gemara on the entire order *Zeraim,* the agricultural laws, which the Babylonian Talmud omits. There is a logical reason for this state of affairs; the agricultural laws, by and large, apply almost entirely to farming in *Eretz Yisroel,* even without the existence of the Temple, so it is not surprising that the Palestinian sages gave them a weight that the Babylonian sages did not. After all, they had a practical daily usage in Palestine. (The Babylonian Talmud does include Gemara on Tractate *Berakhot,* the first tractate in *Zeraim;* since that tractate covers the laws of prayer, its importance even in Babylonia is obvious.)

The Gemara of the Palestinian Talmud is written in a dialect of Western Aramaic. Discussions are brief and concise. About a sixth of the work is *aggadic* in nature, no doubt because the academies in *Eretz Yisroel* were already compiling separate anthologies of *midrashim.*

The final redaction of the Palestinian Talmud was completed by 400 C.E. The primary spur to its completion, third-century rabbi Yokhanan bar Napakha, was dead long before its completion. The editing was done in the academies of Caesarea, Sepphoris, and Tiberias. But the political and social world of the Palestinian Jews was deteriorating. With the proclamation of Christianity as the official religion of the Roman Empire, the Jews suddenly found themselves an embattled minority in what was once their own land.

By contrast, when the Palestinian Talmud was essentially in its final form, the Babylonian sages were still debating Mishnah in their academies, particularly the academy of Sura. The Talmud that resulted from their debates was significantly different from its Palestinian counterpart. The Babylonian Talmud is written in Eastern Aramaic, with an admixture of New Hebrew. The Gemara is only about a third *halakhic* in content, and the debates are recorded in greater detail with more digressions and back-and-forth discussions. It is a massive work of some two-and-a-half million words in thirty-six tractates. The text of the Mishnah used in each of the two Talmuds differs, perhaps because the rabbis in Babylonia were more willing to question and even emend it, but the resulting variations do not have a significant impact on matters of law.

By the time the Babylonian Talmud was being completed, first under the supervision of Rav Ashi, who died in 425 C.E., then by his successors, the editors had incorporated much of the important *halakhic* material from the Palestinian work. The Babylonian Talmud was essentially completed by 500 C.E., although the next generation of scholars, the *Savoraim,* would continue to make minor changes in its text in the form of explanatory notes.

In the two hundred years that had elapsed between the editing of the two Talmuds, the weight of the Jewish world—in terms of population, prominence, and influence—had shifted to Babylonia. Gradually, the Babylonian Talmud came to assume a greater importance in matters of *halakhah* that reflected that shift. The next generation of post-Talmudic rabbis, the *Geonim,* who were headquartered in Babylonia, based their legal decisions, unsurprisingly, upon the Babylonian text; the Palestinian Talmud fell into disuse. Eventually, medieval scholars, Maimonides prominent among them, turned their attention to it; major Sephardic commentators have shown a particular interest in the Palestinian text. But the preeminence of the *Talmud Bavli* in matters of *halakhah* continues to be the rule today.

THE LATER COMMENTATORS

Copies of individual tractates and of the entire compilation began circulating to Jewish communities throughout the known world almost immediately. The Babylonian Talmud was barely completed before the next generation of Torah sages began to offer commentaries on it. Although it is, as Rabbi Adin Steinsaltz puts it, "the last book of source material in Jewish literature," because the works that follow are really extensions of it, the Talmud is anything but the last word.

The Talmud is not an easy text to digest. It calls for a degree of knowledge of Jewish law, and of Tanakh, that not every reader can claim. Moreover, the mixture of Hebrew and Aramaic rendered the text opaque to many of its contemporaries. And as Aramaic was gradually replaced as the common language of the Middle East by Arabic, the text became even more obscure to all but the most highly trained scholars.

Yet this was not what the rabbis had in mind. Did not one of the sages say, "The Torah speaks in the language of humans"? Thus it became necessary for commentaries on the Talmud to be developed.

The logical first place for such commentaries to be produced was the academies themselves. So the heads of the academies at Sura and Pumbedita—the two outstanding Babylonian academies of the immediate post-Talmudic period—found themselves engaged in Talmudic exegesis.

As had their predecessors, the *Geonim* would lecture on Talmud and Torah at the academies. But with the ever-widening dispersion of Jews throughout the world of the early medieval period, it soon became necessary for them to answer written requests for information and rulings as well. Thus the literature of rabbinic *responsa* began, a literature that continues to this day. Such correspondence represents the first recorded commentary on the Talmud, but the later *Geonim* also composed systematic writings on individual tractates. Still, the language of Talmud was fresh enough that the *Geonim* probably felt little need for a systematic and complete commentary on the massive work.

As the first millennium C.E. drew to a close, Babylonia was being displaced as the center of Jewish life, much as it was being overtaken by the rising power of the Muslim caliphs. The focus of Jewish scholarship was shifting to North Africa and the Iberian Peninsula (what would become Sephardic Jewry) on the one hand, and to Germany, Italy, and France (the populations that would evolve into Ashkenazi Jewry), on the other. These communities would form the loci for the next stage of Rabbinic Judaism. The sages who did this work were known as the *Rishonim*, literally, the "earlier ones" (a label used to distinguish them from the scholars who came after Joseph Caro, the *Akharonim/later ones*).

In eleventh-century Germany, Gershom ben Judah wrote a commentary on several tractates of the Babylonian Talmud. In North Africa at the same time, Hananel ben Khushi'el authored an extensive analysis and companion, often drawing on the Palestinian Talmud to make his points. Within the next century, the French scholar Rashi brought the light of his extraordinary mind to bear on the Babylonian Talmud, writing a commentary that covered all but a handful of tractates. As in his biblical commentary (see sidebar "Some Key Bible Commentators," p. 300), Rashi's Talmudic commentary is noted for its clarity, graceful and clear Hebrew prose, comprehensiveness, and breadth of vision. To call Rashi "one of the *Rishonim*" is like calling Beethoven "one of the Romantic composers."

Rashi's own followers, including his sons-in-law, Meir ben Samuel and Judah ben Nathan, and his grandson, Rabbenu Tam, authored the work known as the *Tosafot/Supplement* (not to be confused with the earlier *Tosefta*), an attempt to address questions that their master had left unanswered while presenting a single, integrated vision of the vastness of Talmud. Unlike Rashi's commentary, the *Tosafists* dealt with specific questions, difficulties and contradictions within the text, rather than the whole of Talmud, using their mentor's commentary as a jumping-off point, and often ending up with a totally different interpretation from his. The reasoning of the *Tosafists* is an excellent example of *pilpul,* a uniquely Talmudic brand of dialectics that sometimes seems like mere hairsplitting to the uninitiated (and even to some serious Talmud scholars!).

The *Rishonim* continued their work of Talmudic commentary up to the fifteenth century. The division between the *Rishonim* and the *Akharonim* is somewhat arbitrary, with Caro's *Shulkhan Arukh* as the breakpoint, the moment in the history of Rabbinic Judaism in which the focus of scholars seems to shift from commentary on the Talmud to the codification of the *halakhah* it encompassed. Needless to say, Talmudic commentary was still being written, indeed, is being written even today. As the outstanding Talmudic scholar Adin Steinsaltz says, "The Talmud has never been completed."

PROLIFERATION AND PERSECUTION

The first edition of the *Talmud Yerushalmi/Palestinian Talmud* began to circulate around 425 C.E. For the 1100 years between the redaction of the Talmud and the invention of movable type, scribes would copy the sacred texts by hand, a laborious process and one that led to a profusion of scribal errors, with unforeseen consequences (see p. 352). Copies of the Talmud were few and expensive. Scholars would scrimp on food and other necessities in order to buy even a single tractate. Few of the manuscript editions are still extant. The ones that do still exist are the survivors of a veritable war.

In the rather tortured history of freedom of expression in Europe, no written work has had a more tormented life than the Talmud. Throughout the Middle Ages and into the Renaissance, anti-Semites in positions of power and influence claimed that the Talmud was a base and pernicious work of blasphemy aimed against Christianity. Apostate

Jews who aided the Church in its attacks on Judaism invariably cited the Talmud as libeling Christ. And the Church, in an era in which its political power was at its height, took action.

In 1242 Pope Gregory IX ordered the burning of copies of the Talmud in Paris. Throughout the remainder of the thirteenth century, his successors would issue similar edicts. Thousands of copies of the Talmud were burned across Western Europe. On the Iberian Peninsula, the Church didn't call for the burning of the books, but insisted on censoring them, removing any statement that they took to be anti-Christian.

To some extent, the fortunes of the Jews were also influenced by divisions within the Christian world. For example, Pope Leo X permitted the printing of the Talmud in the early 1500s, but when the Counter-Reformation intensified, the book once again became a target and Pope Julius III ordered it burned in 1553. Pope Pius IV eased the ban in 1564, stating that the Talmud could once again be printed, but only if passages ostensibly attacking Christianity were excised; as a consequence, there was an edition printed in Basel, Switzerland, under the supervision of Catholic monks. That would not be enough to satisfy some—Clement II issued a papal bull in 1592 banning all study of the Talmud. There would be Talmud burnings as late as 1757 in Poland.

The burnings eventually stopped—at least until Hitler—but attacks on the Talmud continued. One of the most famous incidents occurred in Vienna, one of the most important breeding grounds of modern political anti-Semitism, in 1871. August Rohling, a professor of Hebrew literature in Prague and a Catholic canon, published a book, *Der Talmudjude/The Talmud Jew,* in which he alleged that the Jewish text referred to Christians as animals and advocated practicing fraud and deceit against them. Rabbi Joseph Bloch, a Viennese Jew, accused Rohling of being a forger and scoundrel who had knowingly falsified passages of Talmud. He said that Rohling was even unable to read the Aramaic text.

Rohling offered to testify before a Hungarian court that the Talmud did indeed contain the passages he had cited. That was exactly what Bloch had waited for; he accused Rohling of having perjured himself in a court of law and essentially dared the anti-Semite to sue him for libel. The affair would drag on until 1885 when Rohling was forced to publicly withdraw his suit, unable to face the challenge offered by Bloch, who had offered three thousand florins if the professor would translate even a single page of Talmud.[5]

Given the vehemence with which the Talmud has been attacked, it is ironic that the Jewish text was among the first books to be produced in quantity after the invention of movable type, and produced largely by Christian printers. Joshua and Gershom Soncino, Jewish printers in Italy, published some twenty-five tractates in the years between 1484 and 1519, but the first complete edition of Talmud (in this case, the Babylonian) was published by a Christian, Daniel Bomberg, in Venice in 1520. He printed the Palestinian Talmud as well shortly after. It was another Christian printer based in Venice, Marco Justiniani, who added to the third edition of the Babylonian Talmud several of the glosses that are now a standard part of any edition of the books.

The most famous edition of the Talmud is probably the one published in 1880 in Vilna, Lithuania, by "the Widow and Brothers Romm." The Vilna printers added several newly discovered commentaries of the medieval period, including those of Rabbenu Hananiel and Rabbenu Gershom. The Vilna Talmud was considered so definitive that almost all subsequent editions are based on it. A Talmud you buy today will replicate the pagination and page organization of the Vilna edition.

Despite the adversity it has faced, the Talmud survives. Even today it remains the basis for the training of Orthodox Jewish men, not only rabbis-to-be but every yeshiva student. In the yeshivot it is the study of Talmud rather than the study of the Bible that is of paramount importance, not only for the Talmud's role as the primary carrier of halakhah but for the method of thinking the book strives to inculcate in those who study it.

A PAGE OF TALMUD

Open any modern volume of Talmud (generally, each tractate occupies a single volume) to the first page. What you see is a daunting jigsaw puzzle, with multiple columns of text winding around one another in unpointed (that is, without the nikadot, the system of dots and dashes that constitute vowels) Hebrew and Aramaic, with marginal notes scattered seemingly at random. To the untrained eye there may not appear to be any pattern to this chaos, but in fact the Talmud is a highly ordered, if not easy, book.

Each tractate begins on page 2 (*bet,* the second letter of the Hebrew alphabet). As one saying has it, the reason for this practice is that one already knows a little Torah even before the book is opened, so no one is starting at page one. On the other hand, it is also said that by knowing that you have started on page 2, you must perforce realize that you can never know "all" the Talmud.

The explanation is simpler than that: because Talmud pages are actually counted in folios composed of two facing pages, page one is the title page, so the text proper begins on page 2. And because the Talmud's facing pages are not only contiguous to each other but also continuous across the page, pages are numbered 2a, 2b, 3a, 3b, et cetera. Moreover, the pages of Mishnah and Gemara are devised so that the page breaks are consistent for any edition, so if one wishes to cite a passage and refers to page 3a of Tractate *Berakhot,* the page breaks will fall in the same place in *any* edition of Talmud.

At the top center of the first page of a tractate is an ornately illuminated word. This is the first word of the Mishnah for that tractate, and the block of print that falls under it is the text of the first *mishnah,* paragraph, of the tractate from Mishnah. At the end of the *mishnah,* one sees the slightly enlarged Hebrew letters *gimmel-mem* (G-M), which indicates the beginning of the Gemara accompanying that passage of Mishnah. From here, the central column consists of discussion of the passage of Mishnah; it may run for many pages before it returns to the next paragraph of Mishnah.

But what of the other text surrounding the Mishnah and Gemara? The column nearest the gutter of the book, whether it is a recto or verso page, is always the commentary of Rashi. Just as Rashi wrote the single most important commentary on Torah (see sidebar "Some Key Bible Commentators," p. 300), he also is responsible for one of the most detailed and comprehensive commentaries on Talmud. Even the first printings of Talmud in the 1400s included Rashi's commentary. Rashi's writings will appear in a somewhat different typeface, a discursive type known as "Rashi script" (not because he wrote in it, but because it is the typeface traditionally chosen to set off his writings from other commentaries).

On the opposite side of the page, fittingly, are the *Tosafists,* the disciples of Rashi who wrote the *Tosafot.* The narrow columns of type that are found on the outside of pages in a printed Talmud contain an intricate list of cross-references; they cross-reference other passages of Talmud and medieval codes of Jewish law such as the *Shulkhan Arukh,* and Maimonides' *Mishneh Torah.* Also, here one may find keys to quotes from the Tanakh, and comments from later Talmudic scholars. These include the work of such distinguished rabbis as Joel Sirkes, seventeenth-century author of one of the most important commentaries on *halakhah,* and Elijah ben Solomon, better known as the Vilna Gaon, the eighteenth-century sage who led the opposition to the Hasidim.

MODERN TALMUDIC SCHOLARSHIP

As noted before, a passage of Gemara may end with no resolution to the questions posed, indicated by the word *teku,* the acronym that means that the problem will be resolved only by the prophet Elijah. But *"teku"* is not enough of an answer for some.

In the last half-century a new method of reading Talmud, the critical method, has evolved. Unlike the rabbis of the past, contemporary scholars using the critical method look at the process by which the Talmud was written, edited, and transmitted; the outside culture against which it was written; its relationship to comparable law-texts of other belief-systems of the period. Recognizing that the Talmud as we have it is the endpoint of a centuries-long process of accretion, selection, and redaction, the modern Talmud scholars try to reconstruct that process, correcting scribal errors and comparing variant texts to arrive at a deeper understanding of the thought processes of the sages.

Jonathan Fishburn, a contemporary English writer, describes the method as practiced by his Talmud teacher:

> He used facsimiles of manuscripts and old editions of the Talmud to reconstruct the correct text, indulging in a degree of literary detective work to identify the different threads. This experience of studying Talmud forced me to consider the complexities and processes of the written word as it evolves from a manuscript to a printed book. With the advent of printing, the Talmud became a fixed text, and so we are left with important questions which scholars continue to debate. What was the original text of the Talmud? How exactly did it evolve? What impact did this have on the final text?

This approach is markedly different from the yeshiva where the standard Vilna edition of the Talmud, published between 1880 and 1886, is used unquestioningly, and study is focused on the legal and philosophical concepts and issues.

—"Launching Into 'the Sea of Talmud':
A Personal Story"

Needless to say, the various approaches taken by scholars like David Halivni Weiss, Louis Ginsberg, and Shaul Lieberman, all of them yeshiva-trained, met with disapproval from the traditionalists in the rabbinate. Anyone who has read the early novels of Chaim Potok (particularly *In the Beginning, The Book of Light,* or *The Promise*) is familiar with the harsh reaction of the Orthodox rabbinate towards modern interpretive scholarship in the recent past.

What the Orthodox rabbis undoubtedly objected to was the implication that the sacred texts which were undergoing studies of their historicity were not Revealed Truth; after all, wasn't the Oral Law given to Moses at Sinai, just like the Written Law? How can one reconcile that belief with the notion that a passage of Mishnah may have been assembled from two different sources, thereby accounting for a discrepancy in wording? Ironically, as David Weiss Halivni, one of the leading practitioners of the critical method, has observed, the objections being raised in the yeshivot to the scientific study of sacred texts are more strident today than they were fifty years ago.

But a casual reading—even an in-depth reading—of Talmud leaves too many questions unanswered. So even the modern Talmudic scholars occasionally find themselves at the end of the day murmuring, *"Teku."*

HOW TO STUDY TALMUD

Judah Ha-Nasi taught that God studies Talmud three hours a day. Therefore, studying Talmud is merely one more example of *imitatio dei!* Judaism has always valorized intellectual activity—study of sacred texts—as an end in itself, and never more so than in Talmud study. As a way of understanding how Judaism took the shape it has, Talmud study is elucidating. Those who delight in mental acrobatics, in dialectical thinking, and in testing the powers of their mind will find Talmud study a pleasure in and of itself, if only as an opportunity to pit their own minds against some of the finest thinkers Judaism has produced. As Rav Moshe Taragin, a contemporary Talmud scholar, has written, "To learn Torah is to fully appreciate its quintessential infiniteness."

But where to begin?

Of course, one could enroll in a yeshiva, but that is a less than practical suggestion for most of us. One thing is certain, though: no one should begin to study Talmud alone. The vastness of the work is too great, its vocabulary and assumptions too removed from our normal intellectual practices, for the novice to do anything but get lost working alone. On top of these difficulties, unless you are highly fluent in Mishnaic Hebrew and Aramaic, you are going to be working from translations (albeit some very good ones).

But there is another, more important reason not to study Talmud alone.

The Talmud is a collection of dialogues, and it was meant to be studied in that way. As in the yeshiva, it is important for a would-be student of Talmud to get a *havruta* (from the Aramaic word for "fellowship"), a study partner. Talmud study is done aloud, with two partners batting ideas back and forth like a badminton birdie, reading aloud the text and not going forward until every nuance of every word has been explored.

The other essential component of Talmud study is to secure a teacher. Your own rabbi may be willing to work with you and your *havruta*. Many synagogues (particularly Conservative and Orthodox ones) offer classes. So do some local colleges.

Finally, there are numerous study aids on the market, glossaries, dictionaries, and guidebooks. A good Judaic bookstore can help you with these.

DAF YOMI

There is one other helpful hint for studying Talmud. As vast as the "sea of Talmud," as the sages called it, may be, you can swallow it easiest one sip at a time. That principle is the central thought behind the Daf Yomi movement.

Daf Yomi, which means "the daily page," had its beginnings with Meir Shapiro, a Polish rabbi who in 1923 organized students to study one page of Talmud each day. To study the entire Talmud Bavli took 2,711 days, about seven and a half years. In the ensuing decades, despite war, extermination, and dispersion, Jews around the world have soldiered on with daily Talmud study. In 1997, a global high-tech-fueled celebration was held to commemorate the completion of the seventh cycle of readings. More than seventy thousand people took part in the event, with gatherings at Madison Square Garden and the Nassau Coliseum, connected by satellite to similar groups as far away as Eugene, Oregon, and São Paulo, Brazil.

Since then, thousands of Jews have enthusiastically embarked on an eighth cycle of daily readings. Daf Yomi groups can be found in places as unlikely as Thailand, or you can find yourself a cyber-*havruta* through the Internet.

MIDRASH

Talmud is not the only example of the literature of Rabbinic Judaism. There is another rabbinic literature every bit as vast and rather more accessible to the modern reader, *Midrash* (from the Hebrew word meaning "study"). There are many types of Midrash, many collections of *midrashim* (the plural form). But most of them had their roots in the sermon. Indeed, the linguistic root of the Hebrew word for sermon, *derash,* is the same as the root of the word *midrash.* One who gives a sermon, delivers a homily, is a *darshan,* another word with the same root.

Midrash as a body of literature essentially is the interpretation of sacred texts, usually the Bible but also Mishnah. Of course, so is the Talmud. Because the purview of the *midrashim* even includes the Mishnah, there are *halakhic* and *aggadic midrashim,* just as there are both *halakhah* and *aggadah* in the Talmud. The evolution of these two distinct types of Midrash occurred during the *Tannaitic* period, with the *halakhic midrash* developing out of the academies and the *aggadic midrash* rising from the pulpit, from the sermons of rabbis.

As noted before, the language of the Bible is terse, almost taciturn at times. As a result many questions of *halakhah* are left unanswered. The Mishnah and Gemara address some of these. The evolving *halakhic midrashim* sought answers for others. These *Tannaitic* materials predate the writing of the Mishnah (although the key collections of *halakhic midrashim* were redacted around 300 C.E.), and many of them are cited in the *Tosefta*. It should be noted that some outstanding sages, most prominently Maimonides, rejected the use of midrash as a source of *halakhah;* they believed that *halakhah* must be derived from the Oral Law and that while midrash is important as a methodology for reconciling biblical text with legal doctrine, it does not represent actual evidence for *halakhic* rulings.

One important argument on the side of those who hold with Maimonides on this issue is that *halakhic midrashim* are predicated on the notion that everything in the Torah is accurate and concise and, therefore, significant. If there are no errors in transcription or redaction, then every word is there for a reason. Of course, as we have seen in Chapter 5, the compilation of the Torah was a long process that encompassed at least four, and probably more, authorial points of view. As a result, it is a bit hard for all but the most traditionally observant to accept the idea that the multiple repetitions and variant texts of legal rulings found in the Torah are there for a purpose. (Of course, as we shall see in the next chapter, for those who do believe that Torah is Revelation from Sinai, the word of God made manifest, even the ornamentation of the letters in a *sefer Torah* has significance.)

The primary collections of *halakhic midrashim* are the *Mekhilta de-Rabbi Yishmael/Method of Rabbi Ishmael,* which focuses on Exodus; *Sifra* on Leviticus; and *Sifre* on Numbers and Deuteronomy. While *Sifra* is almost exclusively *halakhic* in nature, *Mekhilta de-Rabbi Yishmael* is actually more than half *aggadic*, leading Jacob Neusner to suggest that the work is really an encyclopedic collection of commentaries on Exodus. It is, on the other hand, composed of the oldest *midrashic* materials of any of the collections, and is marked by the simplicity and straightforwardness of its interpretations.

Just as the legal language of the Bible is often elliptical, biblical narrative is even more so. It remains to be seen whether the nature of biblical narrative is a deliberately achieved effect, the result of ancient texts with passages missing, a problem created by linguistic changes that leave us uncertain of the meaning of many words, or a combination of all three. But it is clear that the Bible doesn't explain everything we may want to know about its stories. And as times change, the reader's relationship to the stories of the Tanakh change as well.

The result of such an evolutionary process, accompanied by the Bible's manner of telling a story, is that there are gaps and dislocations in our understanding of and relation to the sacred text. For the rabbis, the *aggadic midrash* was a way of addressing and easing those gaps and dislocations, sometimes by creating whole fables that give background and additional motivation to the sparse narratives of the Tanakh.

To that end, they created a rich and enduring literature that falls into three categories: exegetical, that is, explanatory (this group includes the *halakhic midrash* as well as the *aggadic*); homiletical, containing parables and moral lessons and resembling the sermons we hear in the synagogue today; and narrative, expanding on the storytelling of the Torah.

All three types of *midrash* utilize an array of literary tools in their attempts to elucidate the sacred texts of Judaism. They are rich in metaphor and allegory, clever wordplay, and densely arranged symbolism. For those seeking a simpler entry into the mind of Rabbinic Judaism, *midrash,* particularly *aggadic midrash,* is perhaps a more accessible doorway than the Talmud.

Of course, that doorway is not completely transparent. As Rabbi Eugene Mihaly observes, "Implicit in the midrashic exposition of a biblical text are a number of assumptions accepted without question by a second- or third-century audience, the context of the discourse—the thought patterns, canons of logic, literary forms, the psychology and the picture of reality current in the early centuries of the Christian Era." More than that, the rabbis were not concerned with elucidating the "original meaning" of the Bible. Narrative *midrash* is almost a recomposition of the stories found in the Tanakh, and the results can be surprising to modern readers.

The essential collections of *aggadic midrashim* date from the fourth to the sixth centuries C.E., a time of great crisis for Judaism, when the rising tide of Christianity in the Roman Empire threatened increased persecution for the Jews. *Genesis Rabbah, Leviticus Rabbah,* and *Lamentations Rabbah* are each focused on the interpretation of the book of Tanakh whose name they bear. *Pesikta de Rav Kahana* is a homiletical *midrash* on the festivals and the special Shabbatot.

SOME IMPORTANT MIDRASHIC TEXTS

The following is a brief list of key collections of *midrashim,* organized by chronology and type. English translations of virtually all of these are available today.

From "Midrash," *Back to the Sources: Reading the Classic Jewish Texts,* ed. Barry W. Holtz

Date	Exegetical	Homiletical	Narrative
Tannaitic	Mekhilta		
	Sifra		
	Sifre		
400–650 C.E.	Genesis Rabbah	Leviticus Rabbah	
	Lamentations Rabbah	Pesikta de Rav Kahana	
650–900 C.E.	Midrash Proverbs	Midrash Tanhuma	Pirkei de Rabbi Eliezer
	Ecclesiastes Rabbah	Deuteronomy Rabbah	Tanna Debe Eliahu
900–1000 C.E.	Midrash Psalms		
	Exodus Rabbah		
	Ruth Zuta		
	Lamentations Zuta		
1000–1200 C.E.	Midrash Aggadah		Sefer Ha-Yashar
	(by school of Rabbi Moshe Ha-Darshan)		

ÎLate anthologies of *Midrash* include:

Yalkut Shimoni

Midrash Ha-Gadol

Ein Yaakov

Midrash aggadah does not work by conventional means of literary interpretation as a modern reader would understand them. Often it takes its reading of Tanakh not from the text as read but by interpretations based on juxtaposition of events and commandments, sometimes even by interpreting individual words out of their original context. The resulting interpretation may actually be diametrically opposed to the meaning of the original passage, as in the case from *Lamentations Rabbah,* in which the opening verse of Lamentations, "Jerusalem has become like a widow," is read as an optimistic statement. Jerusalem has become "like a widow," not actually a widow. "Rather as a woman whose husband has gone abroad but who intends to return to her," the *midrash* says. In other cases, the rabbis strove to explain the many repetitions found in biblical narrative. Generally, it may be said that *midrash aggadah* is predicated on a principle first stated by Rabbi Akiba: "The juxtaposition of two sections of the Torah is meant to teach some lesson."

Or they may simply write new stories.

As an example, consider the numerous *midrashim* on the Jacob-Esau relationship, stories that make Esau into a murderer and the founder of the tribe of Edom, sworn enemies to the Israelites, an evil man who mocks his studious brother and implicitly rejects the faith of his father. To a modern sensibility, these seem like special pleading, perhaps downright dishonest attempts to absolve Jacob of his conniving in dealings with his brother and father. Many of these *midrashim* involve what seem to us to be obvious anachronisms, offering a portrait of Jacob as an earnest student of Torah, even though Torah doesn't exist yet!

But if we can study *midrash* on its own terms and in its own context, as Mihaly says, it "reveals to us the Jewish mind and soul in what is perhaps its most creative stage. . . ." If we put aside the suspicions we feel towards Jacob and the hindsight that we have and then read these *midrashim* in a different light, we see them as parables about the sort of person Jacob *should* be, about the values that Judaism extols—studiousness, commitment to Torah, and an abiding concern for the future of the Jewish people.

In that respect, *midrash,* like the Talmud, is part of a "book" that is never finished, one which continues to grow as we bring new historical understanding and new historical contexts to our own reading of the sacred texts. *Midrash* continued to be written after the great compilations of the rabbinic era. *Midrash* continue to be written today. Indeed, any time we gloss a biblical text ourselves, we are creating new *midrashim*.

NOTES

1. Baumgarten is of the belief that the Essenes were a separate group from the inhabitants of Qumran, the authors of the Dead Sea Scrolls, which would mean that there were four sects, rather than the three usually recognized by historians.

2. According to historian Peter Schafer, there are no documented instances of the use of the term "rabbi" prior to 70 C.E., so it may be inferred that the function filled by these Torah scholars was, in some fundamental way, a new one.

3. The numbering of the generations of the sages is not an exact science. *The Encyclopedia of Judaism* has eight generations of *Amoraim* in Babylonia; H. L. Strack has seven. Strack has five generations of *Tannaim,* but divides one of his generations into older and younger groups; Moses Mielziner numbers six generations of *Tannaim,* and only six generations of Babylonian *Amoraim.* (I have followed the 1996 revised edition of Strack, by Gunther Stemberger and Markus Bockmuehl, in the numbering.)

4. The works that are included under the rubric *Midrash Halakhah* are: *Mekhilta de-Rabbi Ishmael,* a *halakhic* commentary on Exodus; *Sifre Numbers; Sifre Deuteronomy; Mekhilta de-Rabbi Simeon; Sifra,* a *halakhic* commentary on Leviticus; *Sifre Zuta;* and *Midrash Tanna'im.*

5. You don't have to look back to the previous century, or even to the Nazis, to find such charlatans. To this day, there are anti-Semites who willfully distort the texts of the Talmud to proclaim it as evidence of Jewish anti-Christian thought and practice. One need only give an Internet search engine the word "talmud" in order to find them.

CHAPTER 7

Jewish Mysticism: Emanations of the Eternal

The rabbis took the hidden worlds of mysticism very seriously. So seriously that some sages would forbid the study of its mysteries to single men and those under forty. So seriously that when the Hasidic movement began to throw open the gates of mysticism to the ordinary Jew, the Vilna Gaon—at the time the most respected rabbi in all of Eastern European Jewry—would virtually declare war on its adherents.

They took it so seriously that the work of the mystics is the underpinning of almost all Orthodox Jewish thought, "the official theology of the Jewish people," as Rabbi Adin Steinsaltz has put it. Inasmuch as the mystical texts are the first attempt by Jewish writers to define and describe God, the primary work of theology, Steinsaltz is certainly right.

Is there a contradiction at work here? How can one reconcile the idea that the work of mysticism is both dangerous and yet at the heart of Jewish theology? Did the position taken by the Hasidim—that anyone could partake of the mysteries—represent a revolution, or was it a logical outgrowth of evolutionary change within Judaism itself?

Before we can answer those questions, there is a more basic one that must be addressed.

WHAT IS MYSTICISM?

The American College Dictionary defines mysticism as "the doctrine of an immediate spiritual intuition of truths believed to transcend ordinary understanding, or of a direct, intimate union of the soul with the

Divinity through contemplation and love." William Inge, a Protestant theologian, has written that "the complete union of the soul with God is the goal of all mysticism." William James, in his *Varieties of Religious Experience,* takes that notion a bit further. "The overcoming of the usual boundaries between the individual and the Absolute is the great mystic achievement."

Useful definitions, but they don't tell us how to achieve these goals. There are some things that are just very hard to convey with words, however intelligently chosen. For instance:

Define the color green.

Describe the sensation of being wet.

What does an apple taste like?

How does a rose smell?

Faced with such questions, it's not hard to grasp the limitations of human language.

Consider, then, how much more difficult it is to describe the ineffable, the infinitude of The Eternal. In the face of that dilemma many religious believers have thrown up their hands and answered with a more sophisticated version of "you'll know it when you experience it." Others, driven by the dictates of a rationalist philosophy (as we will see in the next chapter), choose to define God by negatives: "God is not . . . , nor does God. . . ." Accurate, perhaps, but hardly satisfying.

But if we cannot describe our experience of the Holy, perhaps we can at least allow others to share it, to experience it with us through meditation, ecstatic prayer, and other means. That impulse is one which underlies all religious mysticism.

In most faith traditions, the mystic strives for a total unity with the Almighty, achieved through the submersion of the ego in the worship experience. What she seeks is what some have called an "oceanic" feeling of dissolving into oneness with all Creation. At the very least, a mystic aims for an altered state of consciousness, a new kind of perception, or a new kind of understanding of what she perceives, a defamiliarization of the external world that allows her a glimpse, however fleeting, of the hidden nature of the Creation and the One Who Created all.

In Judaism, this striving is a minor element in some forms of ecstatic prayer (an effort to achieve a state of ecstasy and oneness with God through unusually intense prayer, a concept found in Hasidic Judaism, among other places). But what the Jewish mystic primarily aims for is something quite different from a state of personal elevation, nothing less than actually effecting an alteration in the nature of the Godhead itself. For the Jewish mystic, from the medieval period on, the human endeavor of *imitatio dei/imitation of God* means being an actual partner with the Creator in the repair of an unredeemed world. One performs the *mitzvot* in order to contribute to restoring balance in the Godhead itself, something that God cannot do alone. In this belief, Jewish mysticism sets itself apart from any of its Christian counterparts.

Mysticism is a highly sophisticated form of religious belief, often very cerebral and almost always elitist in nature, but it also posits a level of direct and intuitive spirituality that transcends the intellect. Mysticism hinges on the notion that God is immanent—inherently present, dwelling within in all creation—an idea that can take the form of pantheism, the belief that God is present in everything, or panentheism, that everything that was created is *in God,* a more common notion in Jewish mysticism. Finally, mysticism generally involves a highly ritualized set of practices, often ascetic in nature, designed to bring the mystic closer to the Divine. Not surprisingly, the rare strains of asceticism found in Jewish tradition generally turn up in communities of mystics such as the Ashkenazi Hasidim (see p. 368).

Gershom Scholem, the great scholar of Jewish mysticism, wrote, "There is no mysticism as such, there is only the mysticism of a particular religious system." The goals may be the same—an ecstatic union with the Creator, a deeper understanding of the Will of the Eternal One—but the methods used to achieve those ends will necessarily differ from faith tradition to faith tradition. What works for a Catholic will not work for a Buddhist, and so on.

The principal tool of the Jewish mystic is his access to the Torah, the Revealed Word of the Holy One. As a result, Jewish mysticism developed in two modes, as contemporary scholar Moshe Idel puts it, the moderate and the intensive. To the non-Jew, the intensive mode, which focuses on the study of techniques for reaching the heightened or altered states of consciousness described above, will seem the more familiar, resembling such non-Jewish disciplines as Yoga and Sufism.

By contrast, the moderate mode is usually based on textual study, a seeking of the *nistar/hidden* in the words of Torah that allows the mystic to reach "a position of influencing and contemplating the divine harmony," as Idel phrases it. If you have already read this far in the book, you can see why the moderate mode might seem to be more typically Jewish—achieving closeness to God by studying texts is about as typically Jewish an activity as one can imagine.

Essentially, the history of Jewish mysticism falls into five distinct periods:

1. the ancient, contemporaneous with the Talmudic period;

2. the early thinkers of the medieval period, who fall into two geographically distinct schools, the *Kabbalah* and the *Ashkenazi Hasidic* (not to be confused with the Hasidic movement that emerged in the eighteenth century);

3. the Kabbalah in thirteenth- through fifteenth-century Spain;

4. post-expulsion Kabbalah, centered in Safed around the charismatic figure of Isaac Luria (also known as Lurianic Kabbalah), in the sixteenth through eighteenth centuries; and

5. the modern schools that grew up around the Hasidic movement, its supporters and opponents from the eighteenth century to the present day.

Scholem once offered the observation that new schools of mysticism usually emerged in Judaism within two or three generations after a historical catastrophe. For example, the earliest mystical thought, like the compilation of Mishnah, can be seen as a response to the destruction of the Second Temple, while the emergence of the Hasidic movement in the 1700s may be accurately described as the aftermath of the terrible pogroms of the 1640s in the Ukraine. Jewish mysticism focuses largely on the idea that the actions of the faithful on earth can actually influence the Godhead by performing the *mitzvot;* it isn't hard to see why that notion would be appealing to a people who have been recently battered by mass murder and destruction.

Although it reached its first flowering in the medieval period, Jewish mystical thought dates back to the second century C.E., the era in which Judah Ha-Nasi was compiling the Mishnah, and possibly even earlier. Like the rest of Jewish thought (at least until the modern period, as we will see in Chapter 8), the various schools of mysticism believe that Tanakh is the source of all truth, the Revealed Word of God. So anyone who knows how to read the Bible can find the Truth.

Of course, there are numerous ways to read the Bible, a text as elliptical, freighted with multiple meanings, and sometimes as downright vague as any in world literature. As we already have seen, there are at least four ways—*peshat, derash, remez, sod*—that the rabbis have used to decipher the Tanakh, and Talmud and Midrash emerged as part of their efforts to clarify the obscure.

The question for the Jewish mystics too is "How do we read the Bible?" They proffer not one answer but a dialectic: mystical truth is derived from an esoteric symbol system embedded in the sacred text, but mystical truth can also come from dreams, visions, and revelations vouchsafed to a fortunate few. Over the course of its history, Jewish mysticism has been a battlefield of belief, veering toward the interpreters in one generation, then toward the visionaries in the next, in other words, between Idel's moderate and intensive modes. In fact, as Gershom Scholem observes, there is no such thing as *the* doctrine of Jewish mysticism. There are, rather, a profusion of Jewish mysticism*s*. (Which is about what you'd expect from a faith tradition that places so much stock in a work that speaks with as many voices and values as the Talmud.)

There is one other important thread running through all of the various Jewish mysticisms, setting them apart from their non-Jewish counterparts. Jewish mysticism was conceived by its practitioners as inseparable from Torah, Talmud, and Jewish ethics and ritual. No serious student of Jewish mysticism would tell you that you can master the esoteric teachings of Judaism until you have mastered the more basic and accessible ones. When the rabbis forbade the teaching of mystical texts to anyone under forty it was at least partly because none but the greatest Torah scholar under forty could claim to have achieved such mastery. (On the other hand, while deeply wedded to the rituals and traditions of Rabbinic Judaism, the mystics were not adverse to expanding on them. Many elements of our worship today were created by the kabbalists of Safed and the Ashkenazi Hasidim of the Rhineland.)

THE CHARIOT AND THE CHAMBERS: ANCIENT JEWISH MYSTICISM

Jewish mysticism proper may be said to have begun around the second century C.E. (although some of the early texts may be older) with the advent of two schools of thought, the *Merkavah/Chariot* and *Hekhalot/Chambers or Palaces*. Not surprisingly, both these mystical disciplines centered their work on the interpretation of Tanakh, choosing two particularly difficult and disturbing visions of the Godhead.

The *Merkavah* mystics focused their attention on the startling vision that opens the book of Ezekiel, in which the exiled and shackled prophet sees a manifestation from "the heavens," an astonishing tableau ringed with fire, of four winged creatures "like burning coals of fire," each with four faces, surrounding a heavenly chariot. (Obviously, Ezekiel's vision itself is evidence that there was some mystical strain in the Prophetic era, long before the period of the *Merkavah* mystics.[1]) The idea of the students of the Chariot was to re-create Ezekiel's experience and ascend in the Chariot to explore the heavens, or the Chambers of which Heaven was supposed to consist. The latter was the chief province of the *Hekhalot* mystics who, in works like *Hekhalot Rabbati/The Teaching of the Chambers,* expounded on the journey through these heavenly precincts.

The mystical writings that emerged from these two schools of thought are profoundly visionary in nature, clear examples of Idel's intensive mode, a search for the formula that would allow practitioners to make the same journey the Prophets had made. Jumping off from Ezekiel's vision or passages in the *Shir Ha-Shirim/Song of Songs,* they paint a vivid and imaginative picture of God's heavenly domain. In one of these works, *Shi'ur Komah/The Measurement of the Height,* the author actually describes the Creator in anthropomorphic terms, a humanlike creature of such gigantic dimensions as to occupy the whole cosmos: his neck is 130.8 million miles long, his fingers are each 150.3 million miles in length.

The mystics who engaged in such creative speculations are unknown to us, but their works are proverbially (and incorrectly) attributed to such prominent men as Akiba and Rabbi Ishmael, and there is a tradition that they were, in fact, members of Akiba's circle. Within the rabbinic literature, there is some justification for that view. The Mishnah,

Tosefta, and both Babylonian and Palestinian Talmuds all contain parallel passages in which it is explicitly stated that "it is forbidden to expound the Work of the Chariot before more than one" listener, passages in which Rabbi Akiba always figures prominently. Clearly, what Akiba and his colleagues were acknowledging is that a secret known by more than two people is not a secret, and a master must be sure of a pupil before giving him such highly charged information. Indeed, in each version of this proscription, the teachings are explicitly linked with two other topics that may be conveyed only under highly regulated circumstances: the secrets of Creation and the laws of incest.

The various emanations of the Almighty—the palaces, the chariot—were to be understood as aspects of the Godhead, as facets of the Creator, not as competing deities. The mystics were careful not to step away from the basic tenets of monotheism, and those who followed them maintained that same caution.

The work of the *Merkavah* mystics led to something of a cul-de-sac. The work of ascending into the Chariot or of passing through the Chambers of Heaven called upon a dizzyingly abstruse vocabulary of angelic names and obscure terms for the various portals to Paradise. Moreover, unlike the mystical literature that was to come, the *Merkavah* and *Hekhalot* literature had little to offer in the way of Jewish ethics, a key component in every other brand of Jewish mystical thought. For whatever reason, the ancient mystics reached the peak of their own influence in the fourth century C.E., and continued their works for another couple of centuries after that, but had little direct influence in Jewish mysticism or in Judaism in general. But they opened a door into a new kind of Jewish thought, and there are echoes of it in later writings.

THE MYSTERIES OF CREATION: *SEFER YETZIRAH*

Most of the *Merkavah* and *Hekhalot* literature concerned itself with Ezekiel's vision of the Chariot and the workings of the Heavenly Chambers or Palaces (when not dealing in outright magic, another of its substantial themes). But there are two contemporaneous works that are centered on cosmological questions that were of only passing interest to the mystics of the time. Each of them, *Beraita d'Ma'aseh Bereishit/Teaching on the Matter of Creation* and *Sefer Yetzirah/Book of Formation (or Cre-*

ation), delves into the workings of the Creation. The former is a detailed day-by-day recounting of the Creation including a description of the "upper worlds" in which the Creator resides. As such, it fits in fairly neatly with the other works of the Chariot and Chamber mystics.

Sefer Yetzirah is something altogether different, a Jewish text unlike any other written before, and a foundation stone for all the mystical thinkers who will come after. The book itself is shrouded in mystery, appropriately enough. No one knows who wrote it or when it was written. There are virtually no references to it in any of the ancient literatures we have discussed to this point. The book evinces no interest in the questions of cosmogony (the theory of the genesis of the universe itself) that fascinate its mystical predecessors. And the vocabulary of Hebrew and Aramaic in which it expresses its understanding of the mysteries of Creation bears no resemblance to what had come before.

There is something very appealing about the prospect of a lone scholar laboring in anonymity on a strange text whose terminology is utterly unique. That is precisely what we face in *Sefer Yetzirah*.

Gershom Scholem believed that the book contained interpolations from a later period but that it had been written sometime between the third and sixth centuries C.E. *Sefer Yetzirah* is actually a very short work, a mere sixteen hundred words even in the most complete version. The writing style is alternately terse and expansive, "at once pompous and laconic, ambiguous and oracular," Scholem calls it. And it is obscure in the extreme.

According to our anonymous author, the Creation was achieved through the manipulation of the ten numbers and twenty-two letters of the Hebrew alphabet, cumulatively what the book calls the "32 paths of hidden wisdom" of God. One term should jump out at anyone who has read later Jewish mystical writings. The ten numbers are referred to in *Sefer Yetzirah* as *sefirot,* the Hebrew word for ciphers, i.e., numbers. The importance of the number ten in the Creation is an old idea in Jewish thought. After all, God spoke ten times during the Creation, saying "Let there be . . ." and whatever he spoke came to be. The *Pirke Avot* even expresses this in the simple factual statement, "With ten sayings was the world Created."

But the author of *Sefer Yetzirah* intends something more. As Joseph Dan, one of the outstanding contemporary scholars of Jewish mysticism, dryly observes, the writer is not performing magic or engaging in mystical thought; he believes that he is engaged in scientific study, that if he can find the right combination of numbers and letters, he can re-create Creation itself.

The problem for readers of the *Sefer Yetzirah*—and not just for modern readers but for the medieval mystics who were enthralled by the book—is that the author's vocabulary and manner of expression are so personal, so *private* that the book is often totally opaque. At the end of the book, he writes of the *sefirot* cryptically: "Their end is connected to their beginning and their beginning to their end as a flame is connected to a coal, that the master is solitary and there is no second, and before one what do you count." What does this mean?

Like his predecessors of the *Ma'aseh Merkavah* and *Ma'aseh Hekhalot*, the author of *Sefer Yetzirah* offers a startlingly direct look at the nature of the Godhead, even if we aren't quite sure what it might be. All of these men partook of a visionary experience of some sort, something with an immediacy that would not appear in Jewish mysticism again until the rise of eighteenth-century Hasidism. These works may be a dead end historically, but they have a bold and sweeping power, a poetic intensity that makes them thrilling to read, if difficult to understand.

TEN *SEFIROT* TWICE OVER: EARLY KABBALAH AND THE ASHKENAZI HASIDIM

Jewish writers were writing commentaries on the *Sefer Yetzirah* as early as the tenth century. Despite its obscurity—or maybe *because* of it—the book had an impressive hold on both the emerging mystical and philosophical thought of the medieval period. It would provoke written responses from many as various and dissimilar as the rationalists Saadiah Gaon and Judah HaLevi (see Chapter 8) and the mystics of Gerona, Provence, and the Rhineland. And its ideas and terminology would reappear in vastly altered and more complex form in all the mystical writings to come.

Late in the Geonic period, compilations of the teachings of the *Hekhalot* and *Merkavah* literature were published. It was from the study of these texts, and the transitional *Sefer Yetzirah,* that the next wave of Jewish mysticism emerged. Again, two schools grew up alongside one another, emerging in the second half of the twelfth century in Western Europe.

Actually, to call Kabbalah (lit. "tradition," but implying something that has been handed down orally) and the Ashkenazi Hasidim (roughly, "the Pious Ones of Germany") "schools of thought" might be a bit misleading. In reality, each was composed of a group of solitary but like-minded scholars, working independently of one another (often unaware of each other's existence), but arriving at similar conclusions. The first movement to be called Kabbalah, the term most closely associated with Jewish mysticism today, arose primarily in northern Spain and southern France, mainly Provence. The primary thinkers of this group included the unknown author of the *Sefer Ha-Bahir,* Abraham ben David of Posquieres and his son, Isaac the Blind, and the *Iyun/Contemplation* circle, which produced numerous neo-Platonic mystical texts.

The Ashkenazi school consisted largely of the members of one German Jewish family, the Kalonymus family, centered in Worms and Spire. The central figures in this group were Samuel ben Kalonymus He-Hasid (the Pious), his son Judah He-Hasid, and Judah's disciple, Eleazar ben Judah of Worms. The Ashkenazi Hasidim collected and collated much of the pre-existing Jewish mystical literature. Were it not for their efforts, we would probably not have most of the *Hekhalot* and *Merkavah* texts that are extant today.

Undoubtedly influenced by the tragic persecution the Jews had undergone with the advent of the Crusades in the eleventh century, the Ashkenazi Hasidim took an unusually dark view of human behavior. Typical of their theories of sin and punishment is the position taken by Judah He-Hasid in his "Book of Angels," in which he wrote that every person will be punished by God not only for his own wrongdoing, but for sins caused by ideas implanted in his mind by angels of God. Judah's explanation for this seeming injustice is that each of us has a basic moral nature and that the angels merely fulfill that nature.

The Ashkenazi Hasidim were fascinated by demonology and what we would call the "supernatural." They believed in the existence of witchcraft and in astrology. But they considered such things to be part of the natural order, part of a world governed by God. There is no concept of Satan as the fount of all evil, and their studies of vampires and werewolves (yes, vampires and werewolves) were merely a way of gaining another insight into the workings of Adonai.

Inevitably, one must ask how Jewish mysticism managed to get from Palestine and Babylonia to the south of France and the Rhine Valley:

The answer, and not for the last time, is that it followed a trail of terror and Jewish blood. Jewish-Islamic relations in Palestine and Babylonia were fairly cordial in the early years of Islam, so cordial that Jewish mystics were exposed to and freely adapted meditation techniques from the Sufis, but when it became apparent to Mohammed and his followers that the Jews had no interest in converting to this new faith, some degree of friction ensued. With the rise of the fanatical Almohade movement, friction became outright persecution. The Almohade invaded Spain in 1145 determined to turn back the Christians' attempt at reconquest and to enforce intellectual conformity in Muslim-controlled communities. With the increasingly violent battles between Muslim and Christian monarchs for control of the Iberian Peninsula, the Jews would find themselves forced to flee back and forth between Spain, North Africa, and France. Once again, the tragedies of the here-and-now spurred an intense interest in the World-to-Come.

Sefer Yetzirah had provided a new framework for the exploration of the nature of the Almighty. The ten *sefirot / emanations* that were invoked by the anonymous author of that volume became transformed by the mystics of Provence and Gerona from a series of mathematical and linguistic per-mutations into a more complex set of attributes, powers, and energy flows. It is in another anonymous work, *Sefer Ha-Bahir / the Book of Brightness,* written sometime in the second half of the twelfth century, that this new version of the *sefirot* is first proposed under the rubric *Ma'amarot / Sayings,* an echo of *Pirke Avot's* description of the Creation.

Sefer Ha-Bahir is the earliest known work of Kabbalah. What sepa-rates the kabbalists from the previous mystics is their radical shift in focus. No longer are Jewish mystics concerned with riding the Chariot or exploring the Chambers. The goal of mysticism has changed from trying to ascend to heaven to something entirely different. Rather than seek the immediacy of the visionary experience, the kabbalists wanted to understand the sacred texts, to see meaning *behind* the words, to explore the nature of God rather than to pay a house call. The focus of Jewish mysticism would now be on the hermeneutical, that very Jewish activity of decoding sacred texts.

Sefir Ha-Bahir itself is a short, rather disorganized collection of *midrashim,* ethical sayings, and dialogues, attributed variously to a some-what mysterious figure named R. Nekhunya ben Ha-Kanah and to other sages, albeit fairly obscure ones whose names are drawn from later *midrash* collections. Historians of Jewish mysticism believe that the book is a mutilated version of a longer text, with passages that end abruptly, occasionally in mid-sentence. Its actual provenance is a subject of considerable speculation, although it is now generally believed that *Sefer Ha-Bahir* was compiled by some of the Provence kabbalists.

One of the most significant aspects of this strange book is the echoes it evokes of Gnosticism. The Gnostics were a group of early Christian sects that believed that the Creation and all that followed it were the result of a duality—in other words, that the Almighty was both Good *and* Evil. This belief system which bordered on the notion of two Gods was rejected by other Christians and the Gnostics were denounced as heretics.

But the Gnostic doctrine of "aeons," specific powers and emanations of God, found a new shape in Kabbalah, in an interpretation that fit more comfortably with Judaism's insistence on monotheism.[2] Nevertheless, the simple concept of a unified, omnipotent, omniscient Deity had been dealt a blow of sorts. Kabbalists offered a God whose unity consisted of a series of complex harmonies between oppositions, exchanges of Divine energy among attributes or emanations, body parts, and even genders.

But something else set the kabbalists apart from their Jewish predecessors. While such mystics as Rabbi Isaac the Blind firmly believed that their work was not intended for the masses (indeed, Isaac specifically forbade his students to spread the word of what they were doing), they also saw it as part of a continuum of Jewish practice. For example, Isaac utilized the names of the ten *sefirot* as a meditation to help instill proper *kavanah* during prayer. Prominent kabbalists in Spain could number the brilliant Nakhmanides as one of their circle; surely a scholar of Talmud and Torah of his stature would not be dabbling in texts that didn't have some connection to the sacred. Indeed Nakhmanides incorporated kabbalistic allusions into his commentary on the Pentateuch, admittedly in highly cryptic form. By these definitions, the mystical discipline (or disciplines) of Kabbalah was not outside the mainstream of Judaism.

KABBALAH IN SPAIN

The third stage of the development of Jewish mystical thought grew naturally out of the twelfth-century schools. The basic grounds on which European Jewish mysticism would stand had been prepared by the Ashkenazim under the leadership of Eleazar ben Judah of Worms (who wrote a key commentary on *Sefer Yetzirah*), and two Spanish groups; one, based in Gerona, was inspired by Isaac the Blind while the other, a more elite gathering, was led by Nakhmanides and centered in Barcelona. When the Ashkenazi group faded in the second half of the thirteenth century, the Spaniards came to the fore, incorporating their German brethren's thought into their own. Over the next two centuries, until the Jews were expelled from Spain in 1492, the Iberian nation would be the center of kabbalistic writing and thinking.

It may be said quite fairly that thirteenth-century Castille hosted the first Golden Age of Kabbalah. Any list of key figures in Jewish mysticism would have to include the Kohen brothers, Abraham Abulafia and Joseph Gikatilla. The influence of these men and a number of others, many of them anonymous, would come to influence Moses de Leon when he wrote what would prove to be the single most important text in Kabbalah, the *Zohar*.

They were a strangely assorted group, these Spanish Jewish mystics. Rabbis Jacob and Isaac ha-Kohen extolled a radical new brand of kabbalistic imagery with an unmistakable Gnostic bent; Rabbi Isaac posited an entire array of evil emanations, controlled by the sinister grouping of Asmodeus, Satan, and Lilith.

Abraham Abulafia pursued a very different line of inquiry. Influenced by the Ashkenazi Hasidim and the Sufis, he explored the possibilities of contemplative and ecstatic modes of prayer. Abulafia also wrote extensively on the use of kabbalistic doctrine to raise oneself to the level of prophecy. He was fascinated by the possibilities of permutations of the Hebrew letters in sacred texts, particularly the Torah. As Moshe Idel explains, "Torah was regarded by Abulafia as the most important text, reflecting the constitution of the intellectual world and being identical with the Active intellect and even to God Himself. On the other hand, Torah was interpreted in Abulafia's Kabbalah as an allegory to the psychological processes of the mystic, an approach different from the regular kabbalistic interpretation of this text as a symbolic corpus reflecting the divine intrasefirotic life." Intriguingly, Abulafia considered himself a follower of that arch-rationalist, Maimonides, and conceived his own work as the continuation of the Rambam's Aristotelian speculations in *The Guide for the Perplexed* (see Chapter 8).

Gikatilla, a disciple of Abulafia's, was particularly interested in the workings of the *sefirot*. His project was a complex synthesis of Abulafia's ecstatic Kabbalah, the conservatism of the Barcelona circle as embodied in the writings of Nakhmanides, and the poetic and intellectually rigorous work of a new figure on the scene, his own friend and protégé, Moses de Leon. It is de Leon who would reconfigure the entire world of Kabbalah— indeed, the entire world of traditional Jewish thought—with a mammoth and magnificent work, the *Zohar*. Ironically, de Leon would receive little credit for his achievement until the twentieth century.

SPLENDOR: THE *ZOHAR*

How important is *Sefer ha-Zohar/the Book of Splendor?* Rabbi Pinkhas of Koretz, a major figure in the first generation of the Hasidic movement (not to be confused with the medieval Ashkenazi Hasidim), wrote, "I thank God every day that I was not born before the *Zohar* was revealed, for it was the *Zohar* that sustained me in my faith as a Jew." Many other Orthodox Jews would agree with Pinkhas, even today. Michael Fishbane, a contemporary scholar, has written that the *Zohar* "pulses with the desire for God on every page," pinpointing part of its appeal. The *Zohar* has become one of the indispensable texts of traditional Judaism, alongside and nearly equal in stature to Mishnah and Gemara.

That de Leon did not receive credit for his work was in large part the result of his own design. When he began showing pieces of the manuscript to fellow kabbalists in the 1290s, he passed them off as ancient texts authored by the Talmudic sage Simeon bar Yokhai. Rabbi Simeon is best remembered for the thirteen years that he and his son spent living in a cave in Palestine, under threat of death from its Roman rulers. During that period of internal exile, the two men supposedly studied Torah and lived on next to nothing. But Simeon was rumored to have marvelous powers as well as a lightning intellect, and if you were going to pick a sage to claim as the author of a mysterious manuscript, he was a good choice.

Why did de Leon pass off his own writing (or that of a circle of kabbalists with him at the center, as some recent scholars claim) as the work of a second-century sage? Undoubtedly, the simplest answer is the correct one: having a distinguished provenance for the book would give it an authority that de Leon himself lacked. It also gave him an imaginative freedom that he might not otherwise have had, and the book soars with that sense of liberation.

Sefer ha-Zohar is written in Aramaic, a ploy that de Leon used to establish its ostensible authenticity as an ancient text. But the Aramaic he uses is full of anachronisms and awkward constructions that betray its medieval (and Latinate) origins. Moreover, as Scholem points out, many of its analyses of Torah are simply too lengthy to be *midrashim* from the classical period, and owe their underlying structure to medieval Jewish philosophy.

Despite those linguistic peculiarities, at first glance the *Zohar* appears to be yet another collection of *midrashim* on the weekly Torah readings, organized around the notion of a traveling party of scholars, led by Simeon bar Yokhai, making their way around Palestine, stopping periodically to discuss passages from holy texts. And that is, in fact, what the book consists of. But these *midrashim* are unlike any others written before. They are steeped in the vocabulary of Kabbalah, and interpret Torah in ways that are completely unlike, say, *Midrash Rabbah*.

The purpose of these interpretive speculations is quite different, too. As Fishbane says, "Recovering theosophical truths in the teachings of Torah, the mystics ascend exegetically into God." The *Zohar* reads Torah in a way that turns that sacred text into a complex set of codes and keys to a higher reality. Torah is seen not merely as sacred text, as law, myth, and narrative, as a statement of love of Adonai; for Simeon and his companions—and the readers who travel with them in the book's pages—Torah is part of the very essence of God, and to read Torah in their manner is to touch the wisdom and energy of the Eternal. Thus, Torah study becomes a form of elevated spirituality in itself, an intensification of the traditional importance of study of sacred text in Jewish practice.

Sefer ha-Zohar is the first work to fully enunciate an idea developing in mystical circles in Spain earlier that century, the Gnostic notion promoted by the Kohen brothers that there are a "left side" and a "right side" within the cosmos that are in constant struggle, with the former representing the satanic elements present within the Divine itself. The doctrine of the Ten *Sefirot* receives its most refined and fullest explication here as well. But what exactly are the *sefirot?*

THE TREE OF LIFE

If you have ever been witness to a solar eclipse, you know that it is highly inadvisable to watch it directly, that it could do serious permanent damage to your eyes. The only safe way to experience a solar eclipse is through smoked glass or some other filtering device.

To the Jewish mystic, direct exposure to the power of the Almighty was as unimaginable as looking directly at a solar eclipse. The infinitude of the Creator cannot be experienced directly or even comprehended by the limited minds of human beings. God is *Eyn Sof/Without End,* encompassing all there was, is, and ever will be. God is so transcendent that the true essence of the Almighty's existence cannot even be described.

Yet we are somehow sure of God's presence. How can *Eyn Sof* be manifested to us? Of course, the holy texts are one aspect of God's revelation. The *sefirot* (literally "numbers" but usually translated in kabbalistic literature as "emanations") are another. We experience God in many forms through the *sefirot,* which act as sort of filters—a smoked glass, if you will—between us and God. Another translation of *sefirot* is "channels"; it may help to think of the *sefirot* as the "channels" that allow us to focus on and hear the "radio signals" of the All Powerful mixed in among the static of everyday life. The emanations, then, are the ways in which God is able to interact with the sensual world, the world we inhabit.

There are ten *sefirot,* linked in a complex figure that some have called the "Tree of Life," significantly a phrase also often used to refer to the Torah. They are *Keter/Crown, Hokhmah/Wisdom, Binah/Understanding, Hesed/Lovingkindness, Gevurah/Might, Tiferet/Beauty, Hod/Splendor, Netzakh/Victory, Yesod/Foundation,* and *Malkhut/Sovereignty.*[3] Each of them represents one aspect of the Godhead, a facet of the powers of the All Powerful. Each is also identified with a part of the body or aspects of the human personality, a color, and one of the Names of the Holy One.

The relationship of the *sefirot* looks something like this:

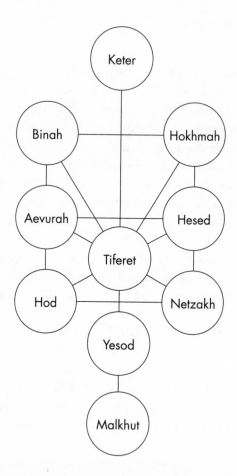

As you can see from the diagram, the attributes of God are highly interdependent, with each one linked to several others. (According to the kabbalists of Safed, whom we will encounter shortly, each of the ten *sefirot* contains within it all of the others.) By understanding their interrelationship, we can understand in some small way the process of The Creation itself.

In the Beginning—and Always—is the *Eyn Sof,* that Infinitude from which everything comes, including the *sefirot.*

- ***Keter/Crown*** (occasionally called *Keter Elyon/the Supreme Crown*) represents the first stirrings of Will within the Godhead, a primal impulse that precedes even thought but which is essential for any action to take place. It is also called *Ayin/Nothingness,* for it was out of the infinite void that the Almighty created. When a Jew seeks a oneness with God through ecstatic prayer or meditation, it is to this state of Nothingness, the annihilation of all ego, that she aspires.

The name of God associated with *Keter* is *"Ehyeh,"* which is what God says when Moses asks who speaks from the burning bush: *"Ehyeh asher ehyeh / I am what I will be."* In some kabbalistic texts, this *sefirah* is associated with the point at the tip of the letter *yod* in the Tetragrammaton (the four-letter name of God which is never spoken, but which is spelled *yud-hey-vav-hey* in Hebrew). The body part associated with *Keter* is "aura," the space directly above the head; *Keter* has no color.

- *Hokhmah / Wisdom* represents the first impulse to Create as it arose in the Creator. It is "primordial *Torah,*" absolute and Divine wisdom, the flash of intuition or inspiration that precedes conscious thought. In another sense, *Hokhmah* is the "sperm" that will impregnate *Binah / Understanding* as the first step in the Creative process. (One aspect of the Infinitude is that God, although without gender, encompasses both male and female attributes.)

  The name of God associated with *Hokhmah* is *Yah,* or the *yod* in the Tetragrammaton. The body part associated with *Hokhmah* is the right hemisphere of the brain. *Hokhmah*'s color is blue.

- *Binah / Understanding* represents the point at which the Divine inspiration begins to take on a definite form. Some refer to *Hokhmah* as the contemplative and synthetic element of Divine Thought; by contrast, *Binah* is seen as analytic and distinguishing. The uppermost female element of the *sefirot, Binah* is the womb into which the "sperm" of *Hokhmah* was deposited. From that union, the lower seven *sefirot* were born. To put it differently, *Binah,* which is also translated as "insight" or "discernment," is the point at which the flash of intuition is refined into a conscious thought.

  Binah is associated with the letter *hey* in the Tetragrammaton, and with the name of God *Elohim*. In the body, *Binah* is usually associated with either the left hemisphere of the brain or the forehead. *Binah*'s color is green.

- *Hesed / Lovingkindness* represents the generous, benevolent side of God, the quality of unconditional Divine Love. *Hesed* is often translated in this context as "love," "compassion," or "grace."

Hesed is associated with the Divine name *El* or *El Elyon/Supreme God*. It corresponds to the right arm. *Hesed*'s color is white.

- *Gevurah/Might* (also called *Din/Judgment*) counterbalances *Hesed*. It is the side of God most familiar to those with a superficial understanding of the Hebrew Bible, the wrathful Divinity of awful punishments. Without *Gevurah*, the world would be so overwhelmed by God's love that it would be reabsorbed into the Divine; without *Hesed*, God's judgment would unleash forces of destruction on the world. It must be noted that the seeds of the *Sitra Akhra/Other Side* are found in *Gevurah*, as well; *Sefer ha-Zohar* teaches that an excess of *Gevurah* is the source of Ultimate Evil. It is the balance of Justice and Mercy, evoked repeatedly in Tanakh, Talmud, and Midrash, that is the key to the world's thriving. And that balance, necessary in the Divine realm, is also essential in human endeavor.

  Gevurah is associated with *Elohim* as the name of God. It corresponds to the left arm. *Gevurah*'s color is red.

- *Tiferet/Beauty* (also translated as "glory") is found in the middle of the "tree" of *sefirot*, a balancing force between *Hesed* and *Gevurah*, in fact, their offspring. This balance is essential to the proper running of the universe. *Tiferet* is the *sefirah* that unites the upper nine powers. It is considered the primary "male" attribute of God. (In some versions of the *sefirot*, this attribute is called *Rakhamim/Mercy*.)

  Often associated with the Written Torah, *Tiferet* corresponds to the Tetragrammaton itself; in some systems, it is associated with the *vav* of the Tetragrammaton. The torso is the body part that corresponds to *Tiferet*. *Tiferet*'s color is purple.

- *Netzakh/Victory* and *Hod/Splendor* are counterparts to one another. They may be seen as more earthly versions of *Hesed* and *Gevurah*, respectively; the former represents God's active grace and benevolence in the world, the latter the manner in which the judgment of the Deity is dispensed on earth. *Hod* is also associated with the power of prophecy.

  Netzakh and *Hod* are associated with the Divine names *YHVH Tsva'ot/Lord of Hosts* and *Elohim Tsva'ot/God of Hosts*, respectively. *Netzakh* corresponds to the right leg, *Hod* the left, but they are also often linked to the left and right kidneys (sources of advice in Talmudic lore), the testicles or the female breasts (sources of fertility and nurturing sustenance, respectively). *Netzakh*'s color is light pink, *Hod*'s dark pink.

- *Yesod/Foundation* is the channel that unites the other two middle figures of the "tree." In other words, it is the means by which *Tiferet,* the male principle of the Divine, impregnates *Shekhinah* or *Malkhut,* the female embodiment of the Divine. *Yesod* is the way in which Divine Creativity and Fertility are visited upon all creation.

  Yesod is associated with the phallus and is, therefore, closely linked with the *mitzvah* of circumcision. *Yesod*'s color is orange, and the names of God it corresponds to are *El Hai/The Living God, El Shaddai/God Almighty,* and the point at the bottom tip of the *vav* in the Tetragrammaton.

- *Malkhut/Sovereignty* is the culmination and synthesis of all the attributes of God, the recipient of all the forces in play in the delicate balance of the *sefirot,* the quality that links the Eternal Sovereign to the "real" world. *Malkhut* is perhaps more familiarly known as the *Shekhinah,* the Divine Presence, God's immanent and female aspect, the way in which we experience the Divine. When the Jewish people are in exile, the *Shekhinah* travels with them; when their exile ends with the coming of the Messiah, the *Shekhinah*'s wanderings will end as well.

  In some kabbalistic systems, *Malkhut* corresponds to the feet but in others it is said to be associated with the mouth. *Malkhut* is associated with the name *Adonai/Our Lord* or the final *hey* of the Tetragrammaton. *Malkhut*'s colors are blue and black.

As you can see from the diagram and the description of the *sefirot,* the left side of the "tree" corresponds to attributes of power and justice, the attributes that characterize *Gevurah.* This is seen by the kabbalists as the feminine side of God, representing the fear and awe of God, the principles of separation and distinction. By contrast, the right side, the masculine side, represents qualities of unity, harmony, and benevolence, the attributes that characterize *Hesed.* But the world can only survive if it is founded on a balance between the two.

It is in the search for that balance that the human role in Creation comes into play. The *sefirot* have a purpose and we are an integral part of that purpose. Our behavior in the lower world, our world, affects the upper world (or worlds, as Luria's followers would have it) of the Divinity. Only when the ideal balance of justice and mercy, of God's transcendent and immanent qualities, is achieved can there be peace and fulfillment. And that, the kabbalists teach, can only be brought about through human actions—through self-mastery, through prayer and meditation and the fulfillment of the *mitzvot*. Thus, the kabbalistic idea comes back to the basic teachings of the sacred texts.

Reading even brief summaries of the *sefirot* and their interrelationships one can see that the kabbalists provided Judaism with a richer theology than had been available before. The picture of the nature of the Deity given in the *Zohar* and subsequent works of Kabbalah is vastly more complex than the one offered in Tanakh or the rabbinic literature (although *midrash* approaches it in its literary imaginativeness, albeit without the systematic completeness of Kabbalah). More than that, the kabbalists fill in the seeming gaps in the story of the Creation and do so with a "psychological" portrait of God that anticipates the work of people like William James. They also invested their notions of God with a startling eroticism, which is undoubtedly one of the reasons that they insisted that only married men study Kabbalah; in a world of premarital chastity, who else could hope to understand these matters?

But what does this complex set of concepts mean to an ordinary Jew?

Simply put, this densely worked out systematic theology offered a reason for performing the *mitzvot*—*tikkun olam*—and an explanation for the way the world is. In the teachings of Isaac Luria and his circle in the sixteenth century, that reason and that explanation reached their fullest flower. And, as is so often the case in Jewish history, the genius will arise from the ashes of persecution.

THE STAR OF DAVID

The six-pointed star, composed of two interlocking equilateral triangles, is one of the most familiar symbols of Judaism. Such stars can be found in many Near Eastern civilizations, long before there was a Jewish people. And this star was used ornamentally by Christians and Muslims as late as the medieval period. Like its five-pointed counterpart, the pentagram, the hexagram was believed to have magical powers and both were used interchangeably by Arab mystics well into the sixteenth century.

In fact, the first written association of the magic of the hexagram with King David occurs in the Koran. The earliest known reference to the term *Magen David/Shield of David* in kabbalistic circles occurs in a book by the grandson of Nakhmanides entitled *Sefer Ha-Gevul*, written in the early fourteenth century. Supposedly composed of two triangles made of lines of text containing the magical secret names of God, the symbol was purported to have great protective powers, hence its Hebrew name.

This magical symbol became more commonly used as an indicator of Jewish content when it was adopted as a printers' mark by Jewish printing houses based in Prague, Italy, and Holland (the latter two being centers of the Sephardic Diaspora after 1492). By the nineteenth century, the "Star of David" had become a standard Jewish symbol, an attempt to imitate Christian use of the cross. By then its roots in mysticism had been long forgotten.

THE LION SPEAKS: LURIANIC KABBALAH

In 1492 the Jews of Spain were expelled by royal decree; five years later the Jews of Portugal faced a similar fate. It is hard to underestimate the impact of this disruption. Iberian Jewry had lived in comparative peace with its Muslim and Christian neighbors for hundreds of years. These were the most stable and prosperous Jewish communities since the glory days of Judah and Israel. Suddenly, they were swept into exile like every Jewish community in history before them. The Sephardic Jews who were forced to leave the Iberian peninsula could carry little in the way of concrete riches, but the treasure of intellectual achievement they took with them was immense.

In no field was this truer than in the realm of Jewish mysticism. And the results of that involuntary exodus could be seen almost immediately. By the sixteenth century, the *Zohar* was an integral part of Jewish religious thought, and kabbalistic thinking was becoming part of the mainstream, spurred by the dispersion of its principal adherents. New intellectual centers sprang up in Italy, Turkey, and, most of all, Safed in Palestine. It was in Safed that Moses Cordovero authored a definitive commentary on the *Zohar*. It was in Safed that Joseph Caro authored the *Shulkhan Arukh*, the definitive code of Jewish law. And it was in Safed that the single most influential thinker in all of medieval Jewish mysticism emerged, Rabbi Isaac Luria (1534–1572), also known by the acronym *Ari / the Lion*.

Safed was, and is, a small town in the Galilee, an unlikely place to serve as a locus for some of the finest Jewish minds of the sixteenth century. But through a complicated series of circumstances, that is precisely what it was. Luria himself is a mysterious figure. No one knows how he came to Safed or where he came from. Moses Cordovero had already established himself there, writing his many important kabbalistic works, and Joseph Caro had also settled in Safed before Luria arrived.

Luria left no writings. He taught his esoteric thought to a dozen or so followers before his death at thirty-eight in an epidemic. Rabbi Hayim Vital, his amanuensis, recorded his ideas and, in turn, taught them to a select few, in keeping with Luria's wishes that they not be disseminated to the masses. But by the seventeenth century, Luria's ideas and the unique vocabulary in which they were expressed had not only spread throughout European Jewry; they had become a central pillar of traditional Jewish thought, a position they occupy to this day.

Scholem argues that Luria and his followers devised a religious ideology that was a direct response to the afflictions of the Jewish people of the time. The exile of the Iberian Jewry was no less a tragedy than the destruction of the Temple in 70 C.E. An answer was needed to the question of the existence of evil in the world—the sort of evil that had forced thousands of Jews to convert to Christianity at swordpoint, killed countless thousands of other Jews, and finally driven the Iberian Jews into exile.

The key concepts in Lurianic Kabbalah are the *tzimtzum / contraction* and the "shattering of the vessels." Luria posits a story of creation in which Creation is essentially a negative act in which the *Eyn Sof* must bring into being an empty space in which Creation can occur. The Almighty was everywhere—only by contracting into itself, like a man inhaling in order to let someone pass in a narrow corridor, could the Godhead create an empty space, the *tehiru* (Aramaic for "empty"), in which the Creation could occur. God retracts a part of the Eternal being into the Godhead itself in order to allow such a space to exist, a sort of exile. So Creation begins with a Divine exile.

After the *tzimtzum,* a stream of Divine light flowed from the Godhead into the empty space the Almighty had created, taking the shape of the *sefirot* and *Adam Kadmon/Primal Man*. The light flowed from *Adam Kadmon,* out of his eyes, nose, mouth, creating the vessels that were eternal shapes of the *sefirot*. But the vessels were too fragile to contain such a powerful—Divine—light. The upper three vessels were damaged, the lower seven were shattered and fell. Thus the *tehiru* became divided into the upper and lower worlds, a product of the *shevirah/shattering*. And so evil came into the world, through a violent separation between those elements that had taken part in the act of creation and others that had willfully resisted, contributing to the shattering of the vessels. The elements that had fought against the creation, were the nascent powers of evil but, because they opposed creation they lack the power to survive; they need access to the Divine light, and continue to exist in the world only to the extent that they can gather the holy sparks that fell when the *shevirah* took place.

Joseph Dan has noted that the genius of Lurianic Kabbalah is the way in which it unites Jewish mysticism and Jewish ethics. That unification occurs here, in the conception of the way in which mankind can undo the damage done in the Creation, can repair the *shevirah*. Think back to Chapter 4 and the idea of *tikkun olam,* of repairing the world. For Luria and his followers, *tikkun* had a very specific meaning. Every time that a human performs a *mitzvah,* she raises one of the holy sparks out of the hands of the forces of evil and restores it to the upper world. Conversely, every time that a human sins, a divine spark plunges down. The day will come, if all do their part, when the entire remaining supply of Divine Light will be restored to the upper world; without access to the Divine Light, evil will be unable to survive and will crumble away to dust.

For Luria and his followers, the commandment *tikkun olam/repair the world* takes on a highly specific meaning in which it is through Jewish ritual life that we contribute to the reversal of the shattering of the vessels, ward off the powers of evil, and pave the way of Redemption. Ethical behavior, following the *mitzvot,* no matter how seemingly trivial, takes on a new, cosmic significance. Forget to say the blessing over bread? You have contributed to universal evil. Put up a *mezuzah* on the door of your new house? You have helped to redeem the entire world.

Clearly, the act of repairing the world is arrogated to the Jewish people exclusively in this system. At first, God was hoping that Adam would be a perfect human being and therefore would complete the redemption by himself, but Adam's sin shook down more of the sparks. When God chose the Jewish nation and they heard the Revelation at Sinai, it became their task to restore the world.

The responsibility placed on the Jewish people is a collective one; under Luria's terms, the Jewish people should be seen as a fighting army under siege. No days off, no respite, a hard battle to live by the Commandments and to repair the world. If one falters, others must take up his burden. Consequently, Lurianic thinking combines a radical understanding of God and Creation with a profoundly conservative attitude towards Jewish observance. But it also reanimates the daily routine of observing the *mitzvot,* giving them a new and more intense significance than ever before.

One can easily see how appealing this notion—that merely by fulfilling the *mitzvot* one could do battle against evil—must have been to the persecuted, weary Jews of Luria's time. What cannot have been foreseen is the direction it would take under the pressures of the next wave of severe anti-Semitic violence in a different part of the world. The next major wave of Jewish mysticism would come from a self-proclaimed messiah who would eventually convert to Islam, shaking the Jewish world to its roots.

THE FALSE MESSIAH: SHABBATEANISM

A desperate people will believe in anyone who claims to help them. In the 1660s, the Ashkenazi Jews of Poland and Ukraine were a desperate people. In 1648 the Cossack chieftain Bogdan Chmielnicki and his "Black Hundreds" massacred between one hundred and two hundred thousand Jews. In 1655, the Russo-Swedish War led to more pogroms aimed at the Jews of Poland, hitting areas untouched by the Cossacks. Those tragedies were not sufficient to explain the extraordinary events that occurred afterwards, but they certainly are not to be discounted.

No, the hysteria that swept the Jewish world from the Maghreb through Palestine to Poland and Ukraine, a hysteria that touched the Christian world too, was in no small part the direct outgrowth of the rapid spread of Lurianic Kabbalah. If a Jew named Shabbetai Tzvi had not immersed himself in Kabbalah as an adolescent, it might never have occurred to him that he was the Messiah. Which would have spared everyone a great deal of anguish, even Shabbetai Tzvi himself.

He was born in Smyrna on Tisha b'Av in 1626. Tradition has it that the Messiah will be born on this most mournful of Jewish holidays. (Was he really born on Tisha b'Av or did someone alter the records to make his messianic status more convincing? No one knows.) His father, Mordecai Tzvi, was a successful businessman, an agent for foreign traders. Shabbetai Tzvi's brothers would grow up to become wealthy merchants. Even as a pampered youth, his own gifts were quite apparent; he was ordained as a *khakham,* a member of the contemporary rabbinic elite, at the age of eighteen. He was a deeply pious ascetic, tormented by his adolescent sexual impulses, but seemingly destined for great things.

But at age twenty-two he suffered what today might be characterized as a nervous breakdown. Scholem suggests—and the behavior patterns that mark the remainder of Tzvi's life tend to confirm—that the young man was a manic-depressive. Throughout his adult life he would suffer violent swings between deep depressions when he would withdraw from society, and periods of "illumination," during which he would receive messages confirming his exalted status and would offer startling and grand pronouncements, advising all and sundry of his monumental plans.

In his twenties, Tzvi began to wander through the Mediterranean, acquiring a wife (who rumors say may have been a prostitute), expounding a variant of Lurianic Kabbalah, and informing those who would listen that he was the Messiah. He spent several years in Greece, particularly in the burgeoning Jewish community of Salonika, where he stirred up trouble by performing a wedding ceremony for himself, under the bridal canopy with a Torah scroll. On many occasions to come, he would commit outrageous blasphemies when in the grips of an "illumination."

Sometime in 1665, Shabbetai Tzvi heard of a miraculous kabbalistic scholar in Gaza who had the power to rid him of his abnormal states of mind. Nathan of Gaza was a brilliant, if eccentric, 20-year-old with his own distinctive spin on Lurianic Kabbalah and an apparent talent for magical healing. Nathan had not met Tzvi (although their paths may have crossed briefly in Jerusalem a few years earlier), but in a vision he proclaimed the older man the true Messiah. If Shabbetai Tzvi was looking for someone to cure him of his manic episodes, he definitely was coming to the wrong man when he went to Gaza; their meeting resulted in the birth of a full-fledged movement. Over the next several years, one man's mania would become a global hysteria.

Nathan was, as Scholem notes, the first man to confirm Shabbetai Tzvi's own belief in his role as the Messiah. Legend has it that when the two celebrated Shavuot together with the most prominent rabbis of Gaza, Nathan went into a trance and revealed his guest's exalted status, to the amazement of all assembled. On May 31, 1665, Shabbetai Tzvi proclaimed himself the Messiah in Gaza, and the entire Jewish community there was swept into a frenzy.

The news traveled quickly and within weeks, the Jewish communities of Palestine were sharply divided between those who supported his claims and those who opposed them. Nathan was very active on his behalf and his followers were vehement, threatening violence against unbelievers. Lines of communications between Palestine and the oriental Jewish communities were strong, and news of the new Messiah spread quickly throughout the Mediterranean basin.

Nathan preached a new variation on Lurianic Kabbalah, one specially suited to the rise of Shabbateanism. Where Luria and his followers said that it was the work of every Jew to perform *mitzvot* and raise the holy sparks, Nathan wrote that there were some sparks so deeply in the hands of evil that no ordinary Jew could effect a change in their status. Only the Messiah, a bearer of Divine powers, could release them and redeem the world. Thus, his version of Kabbalah placed responsibility for the most difficult work of *tikkun olam* not on Jewish practice but on support of, and belief in, a messianic figure. (As we will see shortly, this belief would have a far-reaching effect long after both Nathan and Shabbetai Tzvi were dead.)

Nathan prophesied that Shabbetai Tzvi would go to Constantinople and there the Sultan of Turkey would voluntarily surrender his throne to the new Messiah. With this vision of his new role in history in mind, Shabbetai Tzvi now set off for Turkey, with his followers behind him in ever-increasing numbers.

Given the peremptory nature and brutal dispatch of Turkish justice in this period, it is fascinating to observe the restraint with which the Sultan handled his bizarre visitor. He listened to Shabbetai Tzvi attentively, discussed his proposal that he abdicate, and offered him the hospitality of the palace while a decision was being reached. Essentially, the "Messiah" was placed under house arrest, although he lived quite comfortably. Eventually, after considerable debate in the Turkish court, Shabbetai Tzvi was given the choice of converting to Islam or being put to death. He chose Islam.

By the time he converted in 1666, Shabbetai Tzvi's followers could be found all over Eastern and Western Europe, as well as the Middle East and North Africa. The idea of the Messiah's arrival found particularly fertile ground in the ravaged Jewish communities of Poland and Ukraine.[4] News of his conversion to Islam was shattering in its effect in such communities.

Not that Nathan and the other faithful didn't have an explanation. This maneuver was a necessary part of the Messianic plan, they explained. Before he could free the holy sparks, the Messiah would have to partake of all that was forbidden, perhaps even to turn his back on Judaism itself for a time. Given that Shabbetai Tzvi was one who often prayed blasphemously, "Blessed is He who permits the forbidden," there is a certain twisted logic to this position.

But the damage to the movement was irreparable. Many Shabbateans would follow their leader into Islam, some of them continuing to practice an idiosyncratic kabbalistic brand of Jewish ritual in secret (much like the *conversos,* those secret Jews who had converted at swordpoint in the Iberian peninsula two centuries earlier). But the movement's momentum was severely blunted and, with Shabbetai Tzvi's death on Yom Kippur 1676, it was essentially spent—but not quite.

Shabbateanism became a secret sin, a part of one's past that was best forgotten. Several prominent figures in the Jewish world managed to have their own involvement in the movement suppressed. But a list of those whose writings included deeply veiled echoes of Nathan of Gaza and Shabbetai Tzvi includes some important Jewish thinkers, most prominently the Italian scholar and rabbi Moses Chaim Luzzato and the German kabbalist Jonathan Eybeschutz. Shabbatean groups would persist into the nineteenth century, and another band of messianic heretics led by Jacob Frank would have a similar if considerably smaller impact in the eighteenth century, helped by their involvement in leadership of the French Revolution.

More important, the idea of the individual possessed of special powers and a unique relationship to the Divinity was now established in some Jewish thinking, particularly in kabbalistic circles. It was an idea that was not without an obvious appeal to the still embattled Jews of

Eastern Europe. None too surprisingly, it would be in Poland and western Russia that the next and most popular manifestation of Jewish mysticism would take place.

And this one would last.

HASIDIC MYSTICISM

Like the Shabbatean movement, the emergence of Hasidism in the mid-eighteenth century is a direct outgrowth of the success of Lurianic Kabbalah. By now, mysticism had moved to the center of Jewish religious thought, so it is not surprising to find that both the Hasids and their principal detractors, the *Mitnagdim/Opponents* (see Chapter 9, page 461), both espoused some version of Lurianic thought. For the Hasidic *rebbes* (who were not necessarily ordained rabbis) the doctrine of faith in a charismatic leader of great mystical powers, a *tzadik,* became a primary pillar. For the Mitnagdim, this represented nothing less than a return to the terrible errors of the Shabbatean movement. Regardless, both sets of antagonists—their battle moving to center stage in Jewish belief at the same time that the Enlightenment led to many who might have opposed both groups leaving the circle of faith—shared a deeply rooted mysticism. Thus it was that Jewish mysticism became a core value in what we think of today as Orthodox Judaism, not in spite of the catastrophe of Shabbateanism, but almost as a direct result of it.

Given their profound distaste for one another today, it is ironic to reflect that the birth of both Hasidism and Reform were the product of lay leaders who were dissatisfied with the strictures of traditional Judaism as it was practiced in the eighteenth century. In a sense, the founders of Reform and the early Hasidic *rebbes* both chose to go over the heads of the rabbinate to appeal to the people. Of course, what they were appealing for differed quite a bit.

Contemporary Hasidism traces its roots to a single Polish folk preacher and itinerant healer, Israel ben Eliezer, called the *Baal Shem Tov/Master of the Good Name,* or the *Besht* for short. The Baal Shem Tov was probably born in 1700. Sometime in the 1730s, he began to gather around him a following of similarly pious Jews, who would come to call themselves the Hasidim, "the pious ones."

Before his death in 1760, the Besht had incurred the wrath of the Vilna Gaon and some of the most important scholars in traditional

Judaism. What could this simple man have done that would engender furious opposition from such learned antagonists? He told his followers that the way to oneness with God didn't necessarily flow through the world of sacred texts and scholarship but that oneness with the Divine was open to any Jew, no matter how unlettered.

At the heart of Hasidic practice were some rather straightforward ideas. The Baal Shem Tov and the first generations of Hasidic *rebbes* placed a high value on *devekut* (becoming attached to God), on the annihilation of the self through ecstatic worship, on *kavanah/intention and focus* as an absolute necessity in prayer. But where *kavanah* meant a knowledge of the intricacies of the *sefirot* to a kabbalist, for the Hasid it signified a sincere involvement of the heart in prayer. Clearly, on some level the Mitnagdim saw this anti-intellectualism as a direct threat. How could unlettered peasants possibly engage in serious study of sacred texts? It was said that the Besht himself was particularly fond of the prayer of a poor shepherd who said, "Dear God, though I keep cattle and sheep for others for pay, for You I would keep them for nothing because I love You."

The Hasidim were also relentlessly anti-ascetic. Even the perpetually depressed Rabbi Nakhman of Braztlav, the Besht's great-grandson, counseled his followers, "It is forbidden to despair. Never give up hope!" Worship should be accomplished with joy, with music and dance. The Mitnagdim were appalled by the spectacle of Hasidic worship, of men turning cartwheels and shaking uncontrollably in their prayers, singing and shouting and clapping their hands.

As Herbert Weiner says in his book *9½ Mystics: The Kabbalah Today,* ecstatic prayer as practiced by the Baal Shem Tov and his followers goes beyond merely allowing the illiterate to partake of the joy of worship. The Besht, he writes, "was a mystic, even an ecstatic . . . he emphasized the hidden truths over the revealed aspects of Torah." (And it is this aspect of Hasidism that is conspicuously absent from Martin Buber's writings on the movement, as noted in Chapter 8.)

Perhaps that is the key to what Gershom Scholem told Weiner: "The method which Hasidism used for finding joy and meaning was 'to extract, I may even say distill, the perpetual life of God out of life as it is. This extracting must be an act of abstraction. It is not the fleeting here and now that is to be enjoyed, but the everlasting unity and presence of Transcendence.'"

At the same time that he acknowledged the "unity and presence of Transcendence," the Hasid still found the Divine Presence immanent—inhering—in everything. Among the most controversial positions espoused by the first generations of Hasidim, they believed that the immanence of God in everything meant that even great evil or pollution had a spark of the divine hidden somewhere within it. The Hasidim took this to mean that one must not only redeem and raise the holy sparks from the hand of evil but that it was imperative to correct and uplift the evil itself. As Dov Baer, the *Maggid/Preacher* of Mezeritch, the Besht's successor as leader of the rapidly expanding Hasidic flock, explained it, since the evil once resided in the Godhead itself, it must have been good at its origin; if we can return it to the source, it will not only be cleansed of its evilness but its force will be added to the goodness of the Divine. For the Mitnagdim, this veered dangerously close to the Shabbatean and Frankist heresy of "redemption through sin," fighting evil by becoming one with it. At the very least, such exposure to the forbidden put one at considerable risk.

Then there was the matter of the role of the *tzadik/wise (or just) man*. The idea that a Hasid could not by himself achieve the fullest potential of oneness with God without help from a divinely inspired source—his *rebbe*—echoed Nathan of Gaza. It reminded the Mitnagdim of the Shabbateans more than they were comfortable with. The *tzadik* or *rebbe* or *admor* (an acronym from *adoneinu, moreinu, ve-rabeinu/our master, our teacher, our rabbi*), whatever his designation, is able to intercede with the Almighty on behalf of his Hasidim. He serves not only as a spiritual advisor, but counsels his charges in material matters too, everything from choosing a bride to making investments. In fact, this particular element of Hasidic thought did not gain currency until late in the eighteenth century, around the time that the second and third generation Hasidic masters were emerging from under the great shadow cast by the Besht and the Maggid. As the "courts" of the various local *rebbes* became established and the movement grew, hereditary dynasties began to form. (Intriguingly, although his son was a rabbi, the Besht did not pass the reins to him but, rather, to Dov Baer, undoubtedly out of recognition of the latter's brilliance.)

The Hasidic doctrine of the *tzadik* differs in key elements from the Shabbatean notion of the Messiah. The *tzadik* is empowered to speak on behalf of only his own Hasidim, and only during his own lifetime. He seldom is called upon to act in cosmic and messianic matters but almost exclusively in questions of daily life and of redemption and sin. Still, the echoes of Nathan and Shabbetai Tzvi were certainly there.

Despite those echoes, the Hasidic belief that, as the Torah said, "there is no place that is empty of [God]" would lead Hasidism not only back into the fold, but to a position of unprecedented conservatism within Orthodoxy.

The Besht taught that one could show devotion to the Almighty in *everything* one did. There is a famous story about a Hasid who traveled hundreds of miles to worship with a particular *rebbe;* when asked why, he said, "I wanted to see how he ties his shoes." Driven by their concern with even the tiniest of quotidian details, Hasidic Jews, even today, follow *halakhah* with a determination and even rigidity that is unparalleled in the Jewish world. Regardless of which branch of Hasidism one belongs to, the strict adherence to even the most minute details of *halakhah* is essential.

Ironically, as Joseph Dan observes, rather than becoming a force for heresy, the Hasidim have become perhaps the most conservative, traditional force in all of Orthodox Judaism, the most vocal in their denunciation of any deviation from their version of Jewish tradition, no matter who the transgressor might be.

SOME OTHER KEY FIGURES IN JEWISH MYSTICISM

Abraham Abulafia (c. 1240–1291) was the founder and chief proponent of what has been called the "prophetic" school of Kabbalah, which believed that an adherent could achieve a spiritual state in which prophecy is possible by extended meditations on the letters of the Hebrew alphabet. A prolific author whose works include three treatises on Maimonides's *A Guide for the Perplexed,* Abulafia conceived the notion that he had been chosen to convert Pope Nicholas III to Judaism. Fortunately for Abulafia, Nicholas died suddenly, thereby obviating the need to burn the Spanish Jew at the stake for his presumption. Abulafia is perhaps the first kabbalist to write extensively on the importance of meditation and contemplative prayer in the achievement of a state of ecstasy.

Elia Benamozegh (1823–1900), an Italian rabbi of Moroccan extraction based in Livorno, was one of the few Jewish thinkers to promote the importance of Kabbalah in an era dominated by rationalists. His writings include a five-volume commentary on the Psalms, another five-volume work on the Torah, lengthy *halakhic* and apologetic writings, and even a book on the relationship between Kabbalah and Spinoza.

Moses Cordovero (1522–1570), a Sephardic rabbi who was a key member of the Safed circle, was a contemporary of Joseph Caro and Solomon Alkabetz and teacher of Isaac Luria. Cordovero's theological writings are an outgrowth of his readings of the *Zohar*, elaborating on the nature of the *sefirot* and the transcendent nature of God.

Nathan of Gaza (c. 1643–1680) was the chief ideologist of Shabbateanism. Born Abraham Nathan ben Elisha Hayim Ashkenazi, he was the son of Jews who had emigrated from Poland. Nathan's father was a well-regarded rabbi with a strong background in Kabbalah. Nathan was a brilliant student who began studying Kabbalah at the age of twenty. He immersed himself in the ascetic teachings of the followers of the Ari and began to have visions, including one in which he discovered that Shabbetai Tzvi was the Messiah. It is often speculated that Nathan, much the more intellectually capable of the two, was the moving force behind Shabbateanism. Certainly, Nathan was one of the few who remained loyal to the vision of the movement even after Tzvi converted to Islam. He would continue to visit with the failed Messiah until the latter's death, defending the apostasy and continuing to write mystical texts grounded in the ideas of Shabbateanism.

Hayim Vital (1542–1620) was the source of most of what we know about Lurianic Kabbalah. Isaac Luria did not write down his ideas, perhaps because he died so young. But Hayim Vital, a member of his circle of intimates, did. Vital, who was born in Safed and studied with Moses Alsheikh and Moses Cordovero, was not a particularly originial thinker in his own right. But he was a prolific writer who recorded and passed on the teachings of Luria. His most significant work, *Eytz Khayim/The Tree of Life,* is the first systematic exposition of Lurianic Kabbalah and, because of his closeness to Luria, one of the most authentic.

KABBALAH IN THE TWENTIETH CENTURY

What became of the mystical flames that burned in the hearts of the Hasidim? As we will see in Chapter 9, Hasidism continued to carry that flame in some form, but it became weakened by the insularity of the

Hasidic communities, the decay of the dynastic courts as weak leaders followed strong, and the emigration of young Hasids to America, where many gradually abandoned their old-world ways. Eventually, European Hasidism was extinguished by the more tangible and destructive flames of the Holocaust. Countless Hasidic communities were obliterated by the Nazis. The primary killing grounds were right in the heart of the Hasidic base—Poland, Lithuania, Ukraine. Others met only slightly less grisly fates in the Gulag. (Strangely enough, it is in America that Hasidism began to thrive once more, ironic given the effect that the United States had on a previous generation of Orthodox Jews. But this is getting ahead of the story.)

However, the Jews had not abandoned the Kabbalah. Hardly. Lurianic Kabbalah, in particular, was now firmly embedded in traditional Jewish practice. But there was something a bit stagnant about the state of kabbalistic thought in the period between the rise of the Hasidim and the end of the nineteenth century. With the advent of the *Haskalah,* the Jewish Enlightenment, Orthodoxy's fight was against rationalism, secularism and assimilation, and all energies seemed directed there, rather than toward further explorations of Kabbalah.

That is why it is so surprising that one of the few original thinkers in the field of Jewish mysticism to emerge in the early twentieth century would turn out to be an Orthodox rabbi, with strong hereditary ties to both the Hasidic and Mitnagdic camps, who believed in Darwin, vegetarianism and secular education, who mingled willingly with the secular Jews of the early Zionist movement and who espoused his own brand of religious Zionism. His name was Abraham Isaac Kook.

RABBI KOOK

Kook was born in 1865 in Latvia and received a traditional Orthodox education. In 1904, after several years serving as a rabbi in Eastern Europe, he settled in Palestine, eventually being appointed the chief rabbi of Jaffa. The First World War began while he was in Switzerland for a conference, leaving him stranded in Europe, unable to return to the Middle East. He found a safe haven and a pulpit in London and was there at the time of the Balfour Declaration, with which England recognized the right of the Jewish people to a homeland in Palestine. Kook was one of the rare Orthodox rabbis who applauded that development.

With the end of the war, he returned to *Eretz Yisroel* and was supposed to accept an appointment as the first Ashkenazi Chief Rabbi of Palestine. Then Kook gave the secular Zionists working the land a halakhic dispensation from the strictures of the *shemitah*—the biblical ordinance that declared the land must be allowed to lie fallow every seven years, and that the produce of that year may not be eaten by Jews—arguing that *shemitah* was impractical in a nascent economy. The Orthodox rabbinate, already unhappy with his favorable attitude to Zionism, were infuriated and resisted his appointment. He would not assume the position of Chief Rabbi until 1921.

Kook did not endear himself to the heavyweight *halakhists* of Jerusalem with his pronouncements in favor of secular studies, with the fact that the yeshiva he founded, *Mercaz Ha-Rav,* taught secular as well as religious courses (and still does today), or with his observation that *halakhah* by itself was an arid and eventually stagnant phenomenon, "unless we add to it from the vast domain of Kabbalah, . . . the domain of pure faith which stems from within the soul and emanates from the source of life."

They were even more unhappy with his support for the Zionist movement. That aspect of his career will be examined in Chapter 9, but it is important to note here that Kook, virtually alone among prominent Orthodox rabbis, either Hasidic or Mitnagdic, was well disposed towards the Zionist project. Indeed, it was intimately linked to his mystical thinking.

For Kook, the return of Jews to Zion, whether they were secular or religious Jews, was not only an event of world-historical significance but also a step on the path to redemption.

> *Eretz Yisroel* is not something apart from the soul of the Jewish people; it is no mere national possession, serving as a means of unifying our people and buttressing its material or even its spiritual survival. . . . What *Eretz Yisroel* means to the Jew can be felt only through the Spirit of Adonai which is in our people as a whole, through the spiritual cast of the Jewish soul, which radiates its characteristic influence in every healthy emotion. . . . The hope for the Redemption is the force that sustains Judaism in the Diaspora; the Judaism of *Eretz Yisroel* is the very Redemption.
> — *The Essential Writings of Abraham Isaac Kook*

Intriguingly, Kook's respect (dare I say affection) for the secular Zionist, those sweaty, muscular men and women who were literally building a new Jewish nation with their bare hands, had its roots in his understanding of Kabbalah. He recalled the disastrous shattering of the vessels that was part of the Lurianic story of Creation and argued that the vessels must be strengthened to prevent their shattering again in the time of the Redemption, the coming of the Messianic Age.

Kook brought to his analysis of the place of the secular a perspective hitherto unique among the rabbis of the Hasidic and Mitnagdic movements. Rather than do battle with secularists, as the Orthodox had done when the *Haskalah* began in the late eighteenth century, he sought to analyze the phenomenon of secularism, to see it as separate from, and yet intertwined with, the holy. In his magnum opus, *Orot HaKodesh / Lights of Holiness,* Kook writes:

> There is a world of the secular, and a world of the holy, worlds of secularity and worlds of holiness. These worlds contradict each other. Obviously the contradiction between them is relative: Man, in his limited comprehension, is unable to harmonize secularity and holiness, and is unable to neutralize their contradictions. They are, however, reconciled in the higher world, in the place of the holy of holies.

Yet there is, he writes in a passage just before this one, "nothing totally secular in this world," but all the dimensions of holiness "are secular in comparison to the exalted light of holiness that emanates from the *Eyn Sof.*" This is a fascinating new spin on Lurianic Kabbalah, one that seems to take the modern world as it comes, to recognize that, as the great Hasidic rabbi Nakhman of Bratzlav once taught, all the great discoveries of science are but manifestations of the Will of the Almighty.

GERSHOM SCHOLEM AND THE STUDY OF MYSTICISM

In the middle of the nineteenth century, German Jews with a rationalist cast of mind founded what they called the *"Wissenschaft des Judentums / Science of Judaism,"* an attempt to submit Judaism to the rigors of such academic disciplines as philology, history, and literary criticism. Part of the *Haskalah* and closely allied with the nascent Reform movement, the *Wissenschaft* thinkers were engaged in spirited apologetics, arguing for the long and proud history of their people. One of the elements of that history of which they were less than proud was Jewish mysticism. Historians like Leopold Zunz and key founding members of the Reform movement like Abraham Geiger and the Conservative movement's Zecharias Frankel were dismissive of Kabbalah and its forebears and openly contemptuous of Hasidism, which embarrassed them with what they felt was its boisterousness, credulity, and superstition.

This was the state of things when a young graduate student named Gershom Scholem decided to write a thesis on Jewish mysticism.

Scholem (1897–1982) tells a story about his early research that sums up the position of mysticism in Judaic studies in Weimar Germany. He was directed to a prominent rabbi who was considered an expert on Kabbalah. Scholem visited the rabbi in his home, saw the many books, and asked the rabbi about them. He replied, "This trash? Why would I waste my time reading nonsense like this?"

That conversation, Scholem always said, made him realize that this was a neglected field in which a dedicated scholar could make a mark. He explained his interest in Jewish mysticism to Herbert Weiner, "I've done my research in this history of the Kabbalah simply because I loved Judaism and wanted to show that mysticism was a legitimate part of this Judaism. Not some strange flower, but an indigenous growth."

Scholem was a staunch Zionist, and would emigrate to Palestine in the 1920s. The growing tide of Zionist feeling of the period was, he has written, a partial spur to the revival of interest in Kabbalah among scholars who saw mysticism as one more aspect of Jewish expression, another facet of Jewish nationhood. In fact, the major center for the study of Jewish mysticism in this period was founded in 1925 at Hebrew University in Jerusalem. Perhaps a more significant turning point in the growth of interest in Jewish mysticism, though, was the series of lectures that Scholem gave at the Jewish Institute of Religion in New York City in 1938, subsequently collected and published as *Major Trends in Jewish Mysticism,* a brilliant and remarkably comprehensive introduction to the history and ideas of the Jewish mystics.

The success of Scholem's project—almost single-handedly reviving interest in mysticism as a subject for study—reclaimed an important part of the Jewish religious heritage. In a 1972 essay on Kabbalah for the *Encyclopedia Judaica,* Scholem observed that the academic study of Jewish mysticism was still in its comparative infancy. In the nearly thirty years since, it has emerged as a formidable branch of Judaic studies and produced some of the most significant works in Jewish historiography of the second half of the twentieth century, and it may be truly said that the scholars who have done this work are the sons and daughters of Scholem.

ZALMAN SCHACHTER-SHALOMI AND THE JEWISH RENEWAL MOVEMENT

But scholars of Kabbalah are not necessarily kabbalists. (Scholem probably wasn't, although he was less than forthcoming when asked directly.) Hasidim and Mitnagdim continued to include in their worship heavy doses of Lurianic Kabbalah, but outside of those traditional communities, mysticism had fallen out of favor in the post-Holocaust world. Scholem himself was skeptical of the possibilities of a revival of mysticism in Jewish belief. He noted in a 1962 lecture that two centuries had passed since the two most recent significant developments in Jewish mysticism, the birth of Hasidism and the founding of a mystical center for Sephardic Jews in Palestine. Without a wholehearted acceptance of the basic elements of the faith, Scholem argued, a concomitant belief in the mystical elements was at best unlikely, if not impossible.

In the past, Jewish longings in the face of terrible catastrophe had found symbolic expression in new forms of mysticism. Surely the worst violence ever visited upon the Jewish people—the Shoah—would engender such new symbolic forms. Or had the success of the Zionist project—the founding of the State of Israel—short-circuited this particular historical pattern, replacing mysticism with a new political reality?

Even now, more than a half-century after the liberation of the death camps, more than a half-century after the founding of a Jewish state, it is hard to give a definitive answer to that question. If you had asked the same question in 1542, fifty years after the expulsion from Spain, the answer might have been only slightly clearer.

But certain trends are certainly emerging. With the liberal wing of American Judaism—Reform, Reconstructionism, the "left" wing of Conservative—openly embracing and seeking a return to more traditional spirituality and practice, there is a renewed interest in the mystical elements of Judaism. Some of that interest comes from the New Age movement with its constant search for the latest enlightenment flavor of the month, spurred on by very public flirtation with Kabbalah by celebrities like Madonna and Roseanne. But much of the new fascination derives from the work of Scholem and his successors whose studies have served as a powerful reminder of the continued relevance of mysticism throughout Diaspora Jewish history.

And for many, that relevance consists of finding new expression in the unification of mysticism with worship, as it did in the nascent Hasidic movement more than two centuries earlier.

Perhaps the best example of contemporary Jews seeking new meaning in Kabbalah is the slow but steady growth of the Jewish Renewal Movement. Jewish Renewal represents the coming together of numerous trends in the Jewish-American community that began in the late 1960s and early 1970s. Jews who were involved in the liberation struggles of women, African-Americans, gays and lesbians, in the ecology and anti-war movements, began to seek specifically Jewish ways of addressing the political and social issues that concerned them. As blacks and Latinos began to seek manifestations of pride in their heritage, Jewish student radicals began a similar quest. At the same time, as we saw in Chapter 1, a process of respiritualization was beginning in both Reform and Reconstructionist Judaism, a process not unlike that which led to the birth of the Hasidic movement; similarly, within Conservative Judaism, the rising tide of the *Havurah* movement (see Chapter 1, p. 65) heralded a new orientation towards a more intimate and personally satisfying worship practice.

Essentially, these various trends found their fullest expression in the work of several Philadelphia-based thinkers and groups, coming in part out of the Reconstructionist Rabbinical College, which is located there. Arthur Waskow, a prominent '60s radical who became a focal point for those trying to unite their political commitment to their religious identity, published a seminal work, *Godwrestling*, in which he began to grapple with the paradoxes that seemed to inhere in that combination.

In 1979, Waskow would found a magazine, *Menorah*, which attempted to explore these issues further. (Six years later, renamed *New Menorah*, it would become the publication of the Jewish Renewal Movement.) Around the same time that Waskow was getting *Menorah* off the ground, Rabbi Zalman Schachter-Shalomi relocated to the City of Brotherly Love.

Schachter-Shalomi is an unusual figure, to say the least, a bit reminiscent of Abraham Kook. Unlike Kook, Schachter-Shalomi, who was born in 1924 in Vienna, received both a traditional Jewish education and a secular one as well. Forced to flee by the Nazis, Schachter-Shalomi and his family spent much of 1940 in an internment camp in France before coming to the United States. He received his rabbinical education at the Lubavitcher Hasidic yeshiva in Brooklyn and was highly regarded by the Lubavitcher *rebbe* himself.

But a lively, questing mind steeped in Kabbalah took him beyond the Hasidic movement. He was one of the members of *Havurat Shalom* in its first years in Boston (see p. 65). He has prayed in groups with Native American shamans, imams, Buddhist monks, and Catholic priests. He describes himself as "a Jewish practitioner of generic religion," one who is concerned with making God's presence in daily life a vivid reality.

"Western religions are suffering from having become oververbalized and underexperienced," Schachter-Shalomi has written. "It is in the nature of the situation that people will turn away from something that is not satisfying to them." As a result, he found many young Jews turning to Eastern disciplines. Yet they would come to him saying that, say, Transcendental Meditation was too foreign. They would ask him, "Can you give me a Jewish mantra?"

Jewish Renewal draws heavily on Kabbalah, returning to elements of Jewish mysticism that are not unlike those of the Eastern disciplines that so many disaffected youth turned to in the 1960s and '70s. But these mystical elements have always been part of Judaism. Meditation has been a constant in Judaism since the *Merkavah* mystics (see sidebar "Meditation," p. 400). Chanting has been part of Jewish worship for millennia. What is different about Jewish Renewal is its commitment to an integrated program that unites diverse political concerns with overtly mystical beliefs in an explicitly Jewish way. To put it simply, here is a movement that is trying to combine the spiritual fervor of early Hasidism with the social justice concerns of Reform Judaism, and is willing to utilize Yoga or chanting mantras or any other means to achieve that synthesis.

MEDITATION

Meditation has been a part of Jewish mystical practice since the days of the *Merkavah* and *Hekhalot* mystics; indeed, the key element in the work of those mystics was meditating on the mysteries of the Chariot or the Palaces. Some would argue that the Jewish practice of meditation is more ancient than that, that it was through meditation that the prophets achieved a state of prophecy (a position taken in several mystical texts from the medieval period and later). The term *Hitbonenut/meditation* first appears in kabbalistic writings in the thirteenth century.

Unlike Christian mystics, the kabbalists made no distinction between contemplation and meditation. To them, contemplation was an intellectual process of exploring a single subject in great depth; to achieve that end, they believed it was necessary to arrest the thought processes, thereby closing out other subjects so as not to be distracted from that single subject. By contrast, the earlier mystics conceived of meditation as an actual visual process, of "seeing" the Chariot and the Palaces so that one could understand the workings of the upper world.

Until recently, Jewish meditation has been known only to those who were raised in the Hasidic and Mitnagdic traditions. That began to change in the 1970s when a physicist turned Orthodox rabbi named Aryeh Kaplan wrote his trilogy of books on meditation: *Jewish Meditation, Meditation and the Bible, Meditation and Kabbalah.* Kaplan could hardly be credited with inventing Jewish meditation, but his books marked the first time since the early days of Hasidism that a Jewish writer chose to discuss this subject with a lay readership. Since Kaplan, there has been a flood of books on Jewish meditation, both historical and practical. For more information, see Kaplan's three titles; *The Practice of Kabbalah* by Rabbi Steven Fisdel, a protégé of Reb Zalman Shachter-Shalomi; *The Way of the Flame* by Avram Davis; or any of several books by Rabbi David Cooper.

It remains to be seen how lasting the impact of Jewish Renewal will be. At present its impact, like that of Reconstructionism, one of its forebears, is certainly disproportionate to the number of those publicly pledged to it. Then again, the same might be said of Kabbalah, which began as an elitist element within the Jewish world and became the basis for Hasidism, one of the most popular forms of Jewish belief, eventually inflecting almost all Jewish practice.

THE LASTING INFLUENCE OF JEWISH MYSTICISM

Jewish mysticism has influenced both ritual and liturgy. Consider the elements that go into observing the Sabbath. The rituals of *kabbalat shabbat/welcoming the Sabbath* derive heavily from the practices of the sages of Safed. *L'kha Dodi* was written by Solomon Alkabetz, one of the Safed mystics. Many of the rituals associated with the Sabbath, although rabbinic in origin, took on new meanings with the advent of the Lurianic Kabbalah. The ritual handwashing is rabbinic, but the passing of the vessel of water from left hand to right so as to wash the right hand first is kabbalistic, a reflection of the priority of *Hesed* over *Gevurah* on the Sabbath. The emphasis on the importance of conjugal relations during the Sabbath is another kabbalistic innovation. The influence of Kabbalah can be felt in the observance of the festivals, too. The practice of welcoming the *ushpizin,* the invisible guests from the greatness of the Jewish past, into the *sukkah* is kabbalistic in origin. The all-night study session before Shavuot is a Lurianic innovation as well.

But the ultimate marker of the influence of mysticism in Judaism is not necessarily the specific changes in ritual or liturgy that it brought about. Rather, it is the philosophical shift that underlies Jewish belief. As Scholem observes, as early as the thirteenth century, rabbis were interpreting *halakhah* in kabbalistic terms, divining mystical explanations for the *mitzvot*. The symbols of Kabbalah have permeated traditional Jewish religious thought quite completely and between 1500 and 1800, kabbalistic thought was the true theology of Judaism. Kabbalistic motifs can be found in virtually every prayer book issued in the seventeenth and eighteenth centuries. The idea of the interrelationship between the upper and lower worlds, affected by the prayers Jews utter, is a constant in traditional Judaism throughout this period and beyond. And the popular works of the *musar* movement, a nineteenth-century Orthodox movement concerned with ethics and ethical behavior, are full of kabbalistic imagery and ideas, imagery and ideas that still can be found in the twentieth century in the writings of Rabbi Kook, among others.

Ultimately, one may reject the mystical streak in Jewish thought and practice, preferring to concentrate on the no less significant rationalistic elements, but there is no evading an historical reality best enunciated by Gershom Scholem, who wrote of Kabbalah, "It has been one of the most powerful forces ever to affect the inner development of Judaism, both horizontally and in depth."

HOW TO STUDY KABBALAH

The contemporary Talmudic scholar Adin Steinsaltz has said that "Kabbalah is the official theology of the Jewish people." Certainly since 1492 there is more than a grain of truth in that statement, at least as far as the Orthodox are concerned. The urge to explore Jewish mysticism is understandable.

Today, there is an army of charlatans peddling some version of Kabbalah as a New Age remedy for what ails you spiritually. A few rules of thumb should guide anyone wishing to study Jewish mysticism seriously:

1. It is extremely difficult to fully absorb the writings of the great Jewish mystical thinkers without a solid grounding in Tanakh and Talmud. Therefore, do not pay heed to anyone who claims to be able to teach you Kabbalah in an hour, in a series of workshops lasting a total of a few hours, in a week, in a month, or a year. The study of Jewish mysticism is like the study of Torah, it is the work of a lifetime.

2. The Torah was written in Hebrew. Much of the Kabbalah was written in Hebrew or Aramaic. As we have seen, many of its Divine secrets are predicated on the mysteries of the Hebrew alphabet, the hidden names of God and such. Kabbalah in translation loses much of its meaning.

3. Kabbalah had a vogue among Christian mystics in the medieval period, as well as the circles of the Hermetic thinkers. Their works, while having validity of their own (to the extent that any of these texts have validity), ultimately owe little to Jewish theology and usually involve significant distortions of Kabbalah in the interest of fitting its round peg into the square hole of Christian theology.

4. The last caution I will offer on this subject grows out of the first three. Beware of anyone who tells you he can teach you the secrets of "practical" Kabbalah, how to effect this-that-and-the-other magical transformation through the teachings of the Jewish mystics. While there is a branch of Kabbalah that deals in "practical" applications, it is a minor element within the Jewish tradition. Even

> if such applications are actually possible, it was never the intention
> of the kabbalists that they be put into the hands of the unschooled
> and unready (or, to be brutally honest, the non-Jew).

The serious study of Kabbalah begins with the works of the great historians of Kabbalah, with the likes of Gershom Scholem, Moshe Idel, Adin
Steinsaltz, and Joseph Dan. Anyone who is interested in the theological
thinking that the kabbalists brought to Judaism should begin by reading
these men and their like. After that, as with the study of Talmud, one
should find a teacher, one who makes no outsized claims for himself or
for the texts.

NOTES

1. In fact, Paul, in the Second Epistle to Corinthians, Chapter 12, suggests the existence of a mystical strain among some of the Pharisees as well, which would clearly date
the *Merkavah* and *Hekhalot* mystics earlier than the second century C.E.

2. Not so coincidentally, the Cathars, a Gnostic group that underwent serious persecution at the hands of the Church, were based in Provence.

3. Several of the *sefirot* have other names. *Keter* is often called *Ayin*, a reference to the
Divine nothingness within which the Almighty is concealed from us. *Gevurah* is also
referred to as *Din/Judgment, Tiferet* as *Rakhamim/Mercy,* and *Malkhut* as *Shekhinah/Divine
Presence.*

4. For a particularly vivid portrait of the effect of Shabbateanism on the Polish Jews,
read Isaac Bashevis Singer's early novel, *Satan in Goray*.

CHAPTER 8

The Philosophers: The Continuing Evolution of Jewish Thought

Up to now, we have been following the development of Judaism in a roughly chronological order from the days of the Torah to this century. However, there was a parallel set of developments within Judaism that took place outside the synagogue and the academies. Serving as a rationalistic counterweight to the mystics, and dating from just before the destruction of the Second Temple to the present, this phenomenon is the evolution of Jewish philosophy. To follow the philosophers' path, it is necessary to take a step back to the early days of Rabbinic Judaism, the same period in which the first Jewish mystics were producing their work.

Rabbinic Judaism, as we have seen, continued to evolve throughout the Talmudic period and beyond. Like a palimpsest, rabbinic thought was layered commentary upon commentary. But, despite the process of evolution of rabbinic thought in its response to pressures from the outside world, there was a sense in which its development took place in a vacuum. The rabbis would undoubtedly have been content to continue their dialogue across time and space with one another without ever confronting the non-Jewish world around them (except in the somewhat hostile terms of Talmud tractate Avodah Zarah, which is dedicated to relations with idolaters).

The dispersion of Jews throughout the known world shattered the hermetic seal that enveloped Jewish thought. As a result, Jewish thinkers—many of them dedicated to Rabbinic Judaism—were forced to deal with non-Jewish thought in a direct way. The result was Jewish philosophy, a sort of parallel development alongside Rabbinic Judaism for most of its history that veered away from (and, later, back towards) the words and beliefs of the rabbinical writings.

Had Judaism remained securely ensconced in ancient Israel, with limited contact with non-Jews (and that contact highly circumscribed by rabbinic strictures), it would have stayed an isolated phenomenon. It is futile to speculate what path Judaism would have taken had that happened, but the likelihood is that it would have eventually stagnated, turned inward and sectarian, and gone the way of the other belief-systems of its contemporaries.

RABBIS VERSUS PHILOSOPHERS

From the time of the Babylonian Exile to the present, there have always been more Jews in the Diaspora than living in *Eretz Yisroel*. Rabbinic Judaism is one response to the pressures of living in the Diaspora. Jewish mysticism is another. Jewish philosophy may rightly be said to be a third.

Without the contact between the Jews and Hellenistic civilization, Philo would not have read Plato. Without the contact of the Jews with medieval Christianity and Islam, Maimonides would not have read Aristotle. Without the dispersion of the Jews in Europe, which led to the fight for emancipation, Mendelssohn would not have read his German contemporaries. Without the Jewish Enlightenment, Buber and Rosenzweig would not have read Kierkegaard.

The exposure to non-Jewish thought was precisely what the rabbis found objectionable about philosophy. At the heart of the tension between rabbinic thought and Jewish philosophical writing is the degree to which the latter represents exposure to and incorporation of non-Jewish thought, the unwanted fruit of the Diaspora. (While we may find the rabbinic rejection of the non-Jewish world less than laudable, given the high degree of hostility and downright violence that often accompanied such contacts, it is understandable.) This disdain for outside thought goes a long way in explaining the considerable hostility of many rabbis to Maimonides' *Guide for the Perplexed,* even though Maimonides was a rabbi himself, author of the *Mishneh Torah,* a compendious commentary on *halakhah,* and of the Thirteen Principles of Faith, a statement of Jewish belief so concise and compelling that it was incorporated into the weekday morning service.

Is such a thing as Jewish philosophy even possible? Philosophy by its very nature encourages the challenging of all received truths, while religion cannot abide such a lack of faith. Obviously, the goal of the Jewish philosophers who remained both Jews and philosophers was to solve that paradox, to reconcile Judaism and philosophy, balancing critical thought and religious belief in one package. It is a poignant historical irony that even those thinkers who seemed to stray the farthest from Rabbinic Judaism often were serious believers. The movement of Jewish thought in the twentieth century has been back towards a sort of post-modernist Rabbinic Judaism, as personified by Emmanuel Levinas, a French philosopher who found some of his most interesting ideas in repeated confrontations with the Talmud. Hence, Jewish thought has come full circle, returning to sacred texts once more.

Franz Rosenzweig, one of the most perceptive and original thinkers of the first part of this century, says, "The biblical literature of antiquity may be seen as the source and foundation of everything that is living in Judaism, its encyclopedic expression may be found in the Talmudic and rabbinic writing of later times, its sublimity may be discovered in the works of the philosophers."

As Ernest Rubinstein, a contemporary scholar, notes, "Judaism has incorporated strains of philosophical spirituality since its biblical days." Rubinstein offers as two examples the books of Ecclesiastes and Job, texts that reflect on the relationship between man and Maker in ways quite different from the Pentateuch. In the remainder of this chapter, we will consider an array of philosophers whose meditations on the relationship between man and God are central to their work.[1]

PHILO JUDAEUS (20 B.C.E.–50 C.E.)

We know remarkably little about the life of Philo (also called Philo Judaeus—"Philo the Jew"). We do know that Philo was the scion of a rich and politically connected family in Alexandria, Egypt. He was a contemporary of Jesus and Paul, and alive at the time of the Second Temple. Of this information, the most pertinent fact is that his roots were in the Jewish community of Alexandria. Alexandria had become one of the crown jewels of the Diaspora as the Common Era began. The Jewish community was large, the product of a steady stream of emigration to Egypt that had begun during Hasmonean rule in Palestine. As was the case throughout the Hellenistic world, the Jews formed a community governed by its own members, subject to its own laws and leaders. As a result of this arrangement, the Jewish community was able to observe *halakhah* and, although there was no comparable national Jewish leadership, the sheer size and wealth of the Alexandrian community made it the first among Egyptian Jewish groupings.

Alexandria had a thriving economy and sophisticated culture and was among the most important cities of the Mediterranean basin until the rise of Rome. As an intellectual center and a mercantile center, it would have been an appealing place to displaced Jews and, not surprisingly given its many attractions, it became home to a variety of Jewish apostasies drawn to Hellenism. On the whole, Alexandrian Jews had found a comfortable niche, balanced between their Jewishness and the Greco-Roman institutions of the city.

That balance found its voice in Philo's writings. He wrote exclusively in Greek, and probably read the Torah in the Septuagint, the Greek translation. (We do not know if he understood any Hebrew at all.) Yet he wrote in praise of the synagogues as "schools of prudence," and says that he himself traveled to Jerusalem "to sacrifice and pray." He is at home in the turbulent waters of Greek philosophy that whirled around Alexandria, quoting from the Stoics and Pythagoreans with ease and owing a sizable intellectual debt to Plato. But Philo is first and always a Jew. The bulk of his formidable output is dedicated to biblical exegesis, almost all of it centered on the Torah, the first five books of the Bible.

Philo attempted a synthesis of the two primary influences in his life and thought: Platonism and Judaism. His efforts to adapt Plato's teachings to other, later influences such as Christianity and Judaism represent an important bridge between Platonism and neo-Platonism. That bridge would be more traveled by Christian thinkers than Jewish ones (Plotinus comes to mind), and it would be Philo's influence on early Christian theology that would result in the preservation of his writings through the medieval period. Ironically, his influence on Jewish thought would be negligible for some time as a result of the near-destruction of the Jewish community of Alexandria in a rebellion in 115–117 C.E.

From this point onward, major Jewish thinkers would write either in Semitic languages or in the tongues of modern Europe.

It would be misleading to suggest that Philo produced a consistent and coherent philosophy in his writings. That was not, strictly speaking, his intention. His primary concern was broader and of necessity more diversified: to reconcile Torah and philosophy (still a Greek institution at the time). In fact, it is Philo's contention that much of the wisdom of the Greeks is derived from Jewish teachings.

Philo reads Scripture allegorically, with a result that is immediately recognizable as a sort of *midrash*. In this respect he fits squarely in the Jewish literary tradition of using *midrash* "as his preferred medium" of interpreting Torah, notes Naomi Cohen, an Israeli Philo scholar. Given that in Philo's day *midrash* was the most generally accepted form of Jewish public discourse, this should come as no surprise.

Philo's brand of *midrash* makes for a comfortable blend with the Plato who constructed the allegory of the cave. Of course there were times when the blend was a bit awkward: in order to apply the Platonic four virtues—prudence, courage, self-control, justice—in a Jewish context, Philo identifies them with the legendary four rivers that flowed from the Garden of Eden. (And although he accepts the four virtues as consonant with Judaism, he also adds to them the more traditionally Jewish virtues of compassion, repentance, and piety.)

Of course, Philo derived from Plato more than just a taste for a literary device. Rather, the Jew takes from the Greek the idea that the natural world, the material world, is but an inferior copy of the ideal world. For Philo, as for his predecessor, there is a distinction to be made between the higher, spiritual realm and the lower, material world. Truth can only be attained in the former, a realm that is native to the mind of God, the Ultimate, the Thinker of divine thought.

But Philo then departs significantly from Plato, borrowing from the Stoics the concept of the *Logos/the Word*. The Stoics held that the *Logos* was the chief organizing principle of the world, but Philo puts a specifically Jewish spin on that notion. It is by the *Logos* that God created the world out of nothingness; as the liturgy says, "God spoke and the world came to be." As Genesis recounts the creation, God says nothing more than "Let there be light," and there *is* light. God performs the work of creation in the voice of the *Logos,* as the center of all reason.

It isn't hard to see why Philo was so attractive to the early Church

Fathers. The Gospel According to John opens, "In the beginning was the Word, and the Word was with God, and the Word was God." All that Christian thinkers had to do was add that Jesus was the bearer of the *Logos*.

It is Philo's conception of the *Logos* as part of God—precisely the idea that made him appealing to the early Christians—that separates him from Rabbinic Judaism. The *Logos* is the means by which man approaches God in Philo's thinking. But as any cursory reading of Mishnah and Gemara will prove, for the rabbis, one approaches God through the Torah and *halakhah*.

(N.B.: The quotations that follow are taken from *Selections*, ed. Hans Lowy.)

FROM THE WRITINGS OF PHILO

[J]ust as Plato said, the Creator is the greatest and best of causes, while the world is the most beautiful of created things.

Truth will properly blame those who without discrimination shun all concern with the life of the State, and say that they despise the acquisition of good repute and pleasure. They are only making grand pretensions, and they do not really despise these things. They go about in torn raiment and with solemn visage, and live the life of penury and hardship as a bait, to make people believe they are lovers of good conduct, temperance, and self-control. Therefore, be drunk in a sober manner.

God welcomes genuine service, and that is the service of a soul that offers the bare and simple sacrifice of truth but from false service, the mere display of material wealth, he turns away.

SAADIAH GAON (882 C.E.–942 C.E.)

In the first five centuries of the Common Era, the greatest minds of the Jewish community were occupied with the creation of the Mishnah and Gemara, the foundations of Rabbinic Judaism. It would be another four centuries before a major thinker emerged in the field of Jewish philosophy and, unsurprisingly, he was an integral part of the institutions that had produced Rabbinic Judaism.

Saadiah ben Joseph al-Fayyumi was not merely one of the finest scholars of the Geonic period; he was a Gaon, the head of the academy at Sura, a communal leader who repeatedly found himself embroiled in political controversies within the Jewish community, more often than not emerging victorious.

Saadiah was born in Pithom, in the Fayyum district of Upper Egypt, of humble origins; his many opponents would throw in his face the fact that he was the son of a manual laborer, no doubt forgetting that some of the greatest Talmudic sages were sons of workers and workers themselves. Not much is known of his early years, but he authored a Hebrew dictionary at the age of twenty and three years later issued an effective polemic against the Karaites, the sect that opposed Rabbinic Judaism (see page 229).

As a young man Saadiah migrated to Palestine, settling in Tiberias, where he emerged as a powerful figure who did not shy away from conflict. Aaron ben Meir, a leading Palestinian rabbi, sought to reclaim for his rabbinate the right to set the ritual calendar, a duty that had long since passed to the more robust academies of Babylonia. Saadiah's battle with the older ben Meir began in 921 and would last for two more years, during which time the younger man would move to Babylonia; eventually, Saadiah prevailed and the balance of power in the Jewish world shifted to the Diaspora.

Saadiah's great intelligence was recognized within the Jewish world. Upon his arrival in Babylonia in 922, he was granted the title of *aluf/prince,* in recognition of his erudition, and appointed head of the academy at Pumbedita. In 928 C.E., when discussions concerning the failing academy at Sura resulted in his name being brought up, he was appointed to the post of *gaon* of Sura by David ben Zakkai, the political head of the Jewish community in Babylonia. Eventually ben Zakkai and Saadiah had a falling-out, a row that lasted seven years, with Saadiah coming out on top.

Saadiah Gaon is among the first rabbis to write "books" as we understand that term, and he was a prolific author, although few of his works have survived. He compiled a Hebrew rhyming dictionary, a listing and explication of words that appear only once in the Bible, a grammar text, many liturgical poems, and a volume on the study of the Talmud. His translation of the Bible into Arabic is used by Yemenite Jews to this day. He compiled one of the earliest prayer books and a forerunner of the modern Passover *Haggadah*. He was also the first to write books on *halakhah* in Arabic, which had by now replaced Aramaic and Hebrew as the *lingua franca* of Diaspora Judaism.

The first great Jewish thinker of the medieval period, Saadiah was concerned with refuting the ideas of competing faiths rather than embracing a combination of Greek philosophy and Torah thought. The pagan belief systems of Philo's time had given way to Judaism's "off-spring," the monotheisms of Christianity and Islam. The major centers of Jewish thought were now found in Palestine and Babylonia, surrounded by the rising tide of Arab Islamic conquest.

Saadiah's major philosophical work, *The Book of Beliefs and Opinions*, suggests how much the world in which the Jews lived had changed since the time of Philo. The principal influence on Saadiah's thought is the Arabic *kalam/school* known as the Mutazilite. The Mutazilite *kalam* held that rational argument was a vital component of religious belief and that Greek philosophy (particularly Aristotle) was a useful tool in such matters.

Written in 933, *The Book of Beliefs and Opinions*, the earliest example of medieval Jewish thought to have survived to the present, utilizes these tools for the specific purpose of refuting the claims of Christianity and Islam in the realm of monotheism and the no less vigorous arguments of the Zoroastrians, whose conception of a deity was dualistic. Writing in Arabic, Saadiah offers a spirited polemic that spends as much time battling opposing views as it does in expounding those of its author.

Saadiah, like Philo, is not concerned with the erection of a systematic and coherent philosophical worldview (although his writing style is quite systematic in itself). Rather, he sets out to find rational proofs for the beliefs of Rabbinic Judaism, for the Oral and Written Torah. Saadiah is, in effect, the first Jewish philosopher to present systematic formal proofs of the existence of God, something that the rabbis had previously taken for granted.

There are, Saadiah argues, four sources of knowledge: sense-experience; intuition of self-evident truths (for example, lying is wrong, telling the truth is good); logical inference; and growing out of these three, reliable tradition. It is the last of these that places us squarely in the mainstream of Jewish thought.

For Saadiah, "reliable tradition" is transmitted to us from others.

(Our ability to trust their reports is the basis of human society. Hence the emphasis on lying and truth.) For the Jew, reliable tradition has a special meaning; the heart of Judaism is the transmission of the Oral and Written Torah, of God's revelations as passed on by the Patriarchs and the prophets. The Torah's origins are divine in nature, which makes it unique among human traditions.

Needless to say, Saadiah's view of human knowledge only passes muster if he can prove the existence of God, of a Supreme Being who created the world, in whom resides absolute truth. Saadiah argued for a Deity who is alive, powerful, and wise, who created the world *ex nihilo*, who pre-existed the world, a Being who is separate from the world. That Creator is one, a unity, not a plurality—in distinction from Christianity's Trinity and Zoroastrianism's dual gods.

Like the Arab thinkers who came before him (and Maimonides, among others, after him), Saadiah argues that if God has a plurality of attributes, this implies that the Creator is composite in nature. Therefore, we can only understand the various supposed attributes of "Godness" as implications imposed on God by our limited understanding of the Almighty's nature, rather than actual attributes of the Deity. The only reason we anthropomorphize God is that we lack both the comprehension to delineate God's true nature and the language with which to express it. God is the cause of all corporeal existence, yet is not corporeal, for if the Creator were corporeal there would have to be something that caused God to come into being.

Saadiah anticipates Maimonides in his discussion of Creation, arguing that God created the world not from any necessity but out of free will. And he harkens back to Akiba in his reliance on what philosophers have come to call "the argument from design" for the existence of God: all the parts of the world fit together in a skillful pattern; all levels of creation fit and reflect this design; it is impossible to expect that such elegant results can be anything but the product of a skilled artisan, a Supreme Being with a plan. Ergo, someone must have created the world and everything in it, someone who must have pre-existed the world in order to have created it. All the facets of God that were enumerated above can be derived logically from this single fact.

Much of the worldview that Saadiah erects proceeds, in turn, from the argument from design. It is reasonable to give thanks to one's Creator, therefore humans should follow the commandments as an expression of gratitude. At the same time, the commandments were given to the people Israel by God so that humanity should lead a fulfilling life. For Saadiah, observing the *mitzvot* is a form of self-actualization as well as a way of thanking God for the bounty of Creation.

He believes that the *mitzvot* fall into two categories: those that can be understood by human reason and those that cannot. Reason tells us that it is bad to murder because in the end it would lead to the extinction of humanity. Reason tells us that we do not like to be insulted, therefore it is reasonable that we should be prohibited from insulting God by taking Adonai's name in vain.

On the other hand, Saadiah readily acknowledges, there is a body of *mitzvot* that seemingly have no rational basis. Here, too, he says, reason can help us to understand the commandments. It is entirely reasonable that a man give some unnecessary employment to a poor man so that he may be able to pay him, thereby conferring some benefit upon him. Similarly, it is reasonable that God should give humankind the ceremonial laws that seem to be without any basis in human reason, because they allow us to confer honor on God by observing them.

But the existence of *mitzvot* that defy our rational powers suggests one other key component of Saadiah's philosophy: the role of Revelation. Without Revelation, humanity cannot arrive at true understanding of the 613 commandments. Nor can we do so without reason. In Saadiah's thinking, the two are inextricably linked, mutually necessary and unable to refute each other. Without Revelation, reason would reduce the rationally derived laws to a set of abstract concepts with naught but general significance. Without reason, we can never hope to understand the basis of all the laws.

Jewish law—the *taryag mitzvot/613 commandments*—is true and valid for all time, Saadiah argues. We have free will and can abrogate the commandments, but God punishes those who do and rewards those who observe the *mitzvot*. Why, then, he asks, do the wicked prosper?

The answer lies in his concept of the duality of body and soul. Each human has a soul, a pure, luminous substance that can only achieve fulfillment through physical embodiment, i.e., it cannot act on its own. There is more suffering than happiness in the world, so it is necessary that the soul be immortal so that we can receive our appropriate reward in the World to Come. (Saadiah also believes that the body is immortal in the sense that God can and will re-create it in the Messianic Age, resurrecting the dead.) According to Saadiah's understanding of the problem of good and evil and just rewards, even the wicked have some good in them, so in order for them to receive the full measure of punishment in the World to Come, they are rewarded for the good now; the good suffer now for the little evil they have within them, but will prosper in the Next World.

Saadiah had the great historical advantage of coming along after the Talmud was compiled, during a fertile period in the writing of Talmud commentary and *midrashim*. He was granted the perspective necessary to unite the previous Jewish sacred literature into a philosophical system. More than that, the range of his learning was vast, from philology to philosophy, from grammar to Torah and Talmud. Even Maimonides, who had numerous disagreements with Saadiah's writings, readily acknowledges his centrality: "Were it not for Saadiah, the Torah might have disappeared from the midst of the Jewish people." And Saadiah's worldview will live on, most notably in the writings of Maimonides' opponents.

(N.B.: The quotations that follow are taken from *The Book of Beliefs and Opinions*.)

FROM THE WRITINGS OF SAADIAH GAON

[God] is above and beyond any form or likeness or evaluation or conception or association, as it was said, "To whom then will ye liken God?"

We must immediately accept the teachings of religion, together with all its implications, because they are confirmed by the evidence of our sense. They have also been handed down by reliable tradition. . . . However we are also commanded by God to take time in making rational inquiries and arrive at the truth of religion by logical argument. We must not abandon our attempts until we have found convincing arguments and are forced to believe the revelation of God from the evidence of our own eyes and ears.

Little children do not lie until they are taught to do so.

> Though we speak of the "Creator" we must not construe the term in a corporeal sense. A physical agent must himself move, . . . needs materials, time, space and tools. All this is far removed from God.
>
> Blessed are they who pay good for good to Adonai, and good for evil to men.

MAIMONIDES (c. 1135 c.e. – 1204 c.e.)

He is one of the giants of Jewish thought, either inside or outside the circle of faith. He wrote the definitive study of the 613 *mitzvot,* some of the most incisive commentaries on Talmud and Torah, and the most distinguished work of explicitly Jewish philosophy until this century. And he was an important and highly regarded physician and Jewish communal leader.

Moses ben Maimon, called Maimonides (the Greek equivalent of ben Maimon, meaning "son of Maimon" in both languages), is a towering figure in Judaism, indeed in medieval philosophy. More than just a philosopher, though, he is revered in the Orthodox world as one of the greatest arbiters of *halakhah,* author of the voluminous legal code, the *Mishneh Torah.*

Maimonides (who is also often called Rambam, an acronym for Rabbi Moses ben Maimon) was born in Cordoba, Spain, the son of that city's *dayan / rabbinical judge.* His was a well-to-do family of scholars, and the boy was educated by his father until he reached the age of a *bar mitzvah.* Although relations between the Jewish community and Spain's Muslim rulers were fairly cordial, in 1148 the family was forced to flee Cordoba, one step ahead of the rise to power of the fanatical Almohade Dynasty. For the next eight or nine years, they wandered through Spain, probably undergoing a false conversion to Islam as a safeguard against further persecution. Maimonides settled in Fez, Morocco, in 1160. It was there that he received his training in medicine. Eventually settling in Cairo, Maimonides became the court physician of the great Muslim leader, Saladin,[2] and a highly respected leader of the Jewish community there. It was in Cairo that he would die, holding both these honored positions up to the time of his death. Most of his important writing was done while he lived in Cairo. He is buried in Israel in Tiberias, and pilgrims still go to his grave every day.

Maimonides' writings fall essentially into two groups, the *halakhic* and the philosophical. The writings on *halakhah* include his *Commentary to the Mishnah,* written when he was still a young man and including his famous "13 Principles of the Jewish Faith" (see sidebar below); numerous pastoral letters and *responsa,* written in answer to queries from Jewish communities throughout the Mediterranean at a time when these communities were under a variety of pressures ranging from forced conversions to false messiahs; the *Sefer Ha-Mitzvot / Book of the Commandments,* enumerating and explaining the 613 commandments; and the *Mishneh Torah* (also known as *Yad Ha-Khazakah / the Mighty Hand*), a monumental, comprehensive, and systematic code of Jewish law, organized and written in a clear, lucid style.

13 PRINCIPLES OF THE JEWISH FAITH

1. I believe with perfect faith that God is the Creator and Ruler of all things. He alone has made, does make, and will make all things.
2. I believe with perfect faith that God is One. There is no unity that is in any way like His. He alone is our God—He was, He is, and He will be.
3. I believe with perfect faith that God does not have a body. Physical concepts do not apply to Him. There is nothing whatsoever that resembles Him at all.
4. I believe with perfect faith that God is first and last.
5. I believe with perfect faith that it is only proper to pray to God. One may not pray to anyone or anything else.
6. I believe with perfect faith that all the words of the prophets are true.
7. I believe with perfect faith that the prophecy of Moses is absolutely true. He was the chief of all prophets, both before and after him.
8. I believe with perfect faith that the entire Torah that we now have is that which was given to Moses.
9. I believe with perfect faith that this Torah will not be changed, and that there will never be another given by God.
10. I believe with perfect faith that God knows all of man's deeds and

thoughts. It is thus written (Psalm 33:15), "He has molded every heart together, He understands what each one does."

11. I believe with perfect faith that God rewards those who keep His commandments, and punishes those who transgress Him.

12. I believe with perfect faith in the coming of the Messiah. No matter how long it takes, I will await his coming every day.

13. I believe with perfect faith that the dead will be brought back to life when God wills it to happen.

Within the context of the *halakhic* writings, Maimonides often discusses philosophy, but these books are clearly written for a different audience from that at which the philosophical writings were aimed. Written in a pellucid Hebrew, the *halakhic* works are designed for a readership of practicing Jews—not necessarily learned but deeply committed to Judaism. These readers are not troubled by the apparent contradictions between *halakhah* and Aristotelian rationalism. By contrast, the potential readers of Maimonides' major philosophical work, *The Guide for the Perplexed,* were severely vexed by that contradiction.

Written in Arabic, the *Guide* is addressed to non-Jews and Jews who find themselves in an intellectual dilemma brought on by attacks on Judaism by the neo-Aristotelian Arab philosophers of the period. A key purpose of this work is to allow its Jewish readers to reconcile Aristotle and Torah, to adhere to the faith of their ancestors while still embracing the rationalism that a man of science, like Maimonides, embraced willingly.

Maimonides was, indeed, a man of science. Young men of Sephardic origins were encouraged to balance Torah study with the sciences in this age, and, as a trained physician, he was typical in that respect. Undoubtedly, it was his background in the natural sciences that led to his affinity for Aristotle, the great naturalist of classical philosophy, the cataloguer and taxonomist of nature, the apostle of close observation. (It should be pointed out, however, that his knowledge of Aristotle was heavily influenced by the Muslim Aristotelians Avicenna and al-Farabi.) In the *Guide,* Maimonides attempts to apply a rationalism that has its roots firmly in the real world to matters of metaphysics and religion. The result is work written in the language of philosophy rather than Torah, one that assumes a knowledge both of the Aristotelian vocabulary and the vocabulary of Torah and Talmud.

At the heart of the *Guide* is Maimonides' conception of God. When we say that "God is one" every day, what do we mean by that statement? For many Jewish philosophers—Maimonides chief among them—this is the central question of Jewish philosophy. He argues that God is a perfect unity, not admitting of any plurality. God does not have parts, either literally or figuratively—no arms or legs, no back or front, no end or beginning. (One of the alternate names for God in Jewish discourse is *Ein Sof/Without End.*)

That also means that, in Aristotelian terms, one cannot actually say "God is . . ." and proceed to enumerate God's attributes. To describe the Eternal One in such a sentence is to admit of a division between subject and predicate, in other words, a plurality. (Maimonides writes in Chapter 50 of the *Guide,* "Those who believe that God is One and that He has many attributes declare the Unity with their lips and assume the plurality in their thoughts.") Therefore, he concludes, one cannot discuss God in terms of positive attributes. On the other hand, one *can* describe what God is *not.* God is not corporeal, does not occupy space, experiences neither generation nor corruption (in their Aristotelian sense of birth, decay, and death). For obvious reasons, Maimonides' conception of the Supreme Being is usually characterized as "negative theology," that is, defining by the accumulation of negatives. Maimonides writes, "All we understand is the fact that [God] exists, that [God] is a being to whom none of Adonai's creatures is similar, who has nothing in common with them, who does not include plurality, who is never too feeble to produce other beings and whose relation to the universe is that of a steersman to a boat; and even this is not a real relation, a real simile, but serves only to convey to us the idea that God rules the universe, that it is [God] that gives it duration and preserves its necessary arrangement."

But what of all the anthropomorphic terms that we encounter in Jewish sacred texts? What of "Adonai's rod and staff . . ." or the Creator who "reaches out a hand . . ."? There are thousands of passages like this in the Torah, in the Talmud, in Midrash, in our liturgy. Maimonides' response is that these are allegorical passages, designed to ease the transition of the Jewish people from idolatry to monotheism. Even the famous description of man's creation *b'tselem Elohim/in the image of God* is meant metaphorically; God created out of free will and we are granted the ability to reason and a free will of our own. But there is no "family resemblance."

The way that we come to know God and the world is through a combination of revelation and reason. Prophecy, for example, is not merely a gift from God processed through the human imagination. According to Maimonides, prophecy also requires perfection of wisdom and morality as well as a developed imagination. And that gift from God is passed through the mediation of the Active Intellect (a "rational emanation" of the presence of the Almighty in the world), so reason must always play a part.

Indeed, reason must play a role in the love of God, Maimonides holds. It is in large part through the intellect that we attain religious and spiritual goals. By the same token, he says, the sacred writings of Judaism are truthful and do not require us to accept anything that cannot be proven by reason. Where they appear otherwise, we are to read them as allegory. For this reason, study of Torah is one way of achieving greater knowledge of God, engaging the intellect in the search. Faith and reason are not enemies but, in Maimonides' thought, essential to each other if we are to understand God.

But, above all else, the purpose of Mosaic law is to lead the Jewish people away from the practice of idolatry, from paganism. The ritual sacrifices prescribed in the Torah represent a stopgap, a way station between the paganism that the people Israel had left behind, and a truly ethical and rational monotheism.

As much as he prizes reason, Maimonides believes that a Jewish life must combine the intellect with moral action, a synthesis of the Aristotelian life of the mind and the Jewish daily phenomenon of the act. That was the life Maimonides himself led; he did charity work among the poor as a physician, was a dedicated leader of the Jewish community, and wrote on both Jewish law and philosophy. This practice is echoed later in the medieval period by Christian writers like Thomas Aquinas.

Jewish thinkers of his time were divided on Maimonides. His detractors, who could be quite violent in their denunciations, were infuriated by his apparent rejection of the resurrection of the dead in the Messianic Age, his insistence on the intellect as a component of prophecy, his reliance on Aristotelian concepts and vocabulary. To many he was a heretic, despite his erudition in Mishnah and seeming commitment to traditional Judaism in practice.

In 1230, twenty-six years after his death, some authorities tried to place a ban on the study of *The Guide for the Perplexed* and on sections of Maimonides' legal writings. The battle raged with particular ferocity in France for several more years until both pro- and anti-Maimonideans were shocked into a common position by a group of Dominican inquisitors who burned copies of Maimonides' writings. This was too much for either side to bear and for a time the battle subsided. At the end of the thirteenth century, it began to heat up again when a group of anti-Maimonidean rabbis issued an edict prohibiting anyone under the age of twenty-five from studying Greek philosophy. But the worst of the conflict came to an abrupt end when most of France's Jews were expelled in 1306 C.E., giving the community something much more pressing to worry about.

Today, Maimonides is the one exponent of medieval Jewish philosophy whose works are widely taught outside the Jewish world; his attempts to unite Aristotle and Torah had a profound influence on his Christian contemporaries. Within the Jewish world, Maimonides is still among the most frequently cited authorities on *halakhic* matters, even by those who would never consider reading *The Guide for the Perplexed*, and his ethical writings inform Jewish thought to this day.

(N.B.: The quotations that follow are taken from *The Ethical Writings of Maimonides*.)

FROM THE WRITINGS OF MAIMONIDES

The numerous evils to which an individual person is exposed are due to the defects existing in the person themselves. We complain and seek relief of our own faults; we suffer from the evils which we, by our own free will, inflict on ourselves. Why then ascribe them to God, who has no part in them?

It is improper to consider personal danger when the public welfare is at stake.

If you build a synagogue, let it be more beautiful than your house. When you feed the hungry, clothe the naked, or devote anything to a holy purpose, it must be from your finest.

Free will is granted to every man. If he wishes to direct himself toward the good way and become righteous, the will to do so is in his hand; and if he wishes to direct himself toward the bad way and become wicked, the will to do so is likewise in his hand. Thus it is written in the Torah, "Behold, the man is become as one of us, knowing good and evil" (Gen. 3:22)—that is to say, the human species has become unique in the world in that it can know of itself, by its own wit and reflection, what is good and what is evil, and in that it can do whatever it wishes.

JUDAH HaLEVI (1075 c.e.–1141 c.e.)

When Maimonides was born circa 1135, Judah HaLevi had only six more years to live. HaLevi really is of the generation before Rambam, but the central thrust of his philosophical work is to refute the attachment of the likes of Saadiah and Maimonides to reason and philosophy.

Judah HaLevi was born in Spain, probably in Tudela. He received the education of the well-brought-up Sephardic gentleman, a combination of Jewish learning and secular studies, with a strong scientific and mathematical component to go with the Torah. As a result, he was well-versed in medicine (and, like Maimonides, would have a successful practice as a doctor), Arabic, Hebrew, and philosophy.

It was an uncomfortable time to be a Jew in Spain. The Iberian peninsula had been under Muslim rule but the Christian kings and queens to the north had decided to reconquer Spain and Portugal in the name of their religion. The Muslim response to the *reconquista* was no less definite, with the fanatical Almoravides counter-attacking from the south in the 1080s and the Almohades repeating that effort some sixty years later. Those two assaults neatly bracket Judah's life span.

Under both the Muslim and Christian rulers, Spanish Jewry enjoyed a precarious existence. Both sides cultivated the wealthy intelligentsia who lived within their lands, but poor Jews fared badly under Muslim and Christian alike. By birth and, one suspects, temperament, Judah belonged to the former group. He was a successful merchant as well as a doctor. As a young man, his behavior and interests were a reflection of that security.

In his twenties, Judah traveled in literary circles. He also began to practice medicine in Toledo. But he continued to write poetry, most of it either about love or in praise of wealthy patrons.

It is not hard to imagine what changed that focus in his writing. As the *reconquista* raged across Iberia, Judah watched one after another Jewish community going up in flames. His poetry found a new subject, elegies for dead friends, and he came to understand that whichever side finally won control of the peninsula, it could only be bad for the Jews, caught between the hammer of Christianity and the anvil of Islam. His poetry took on a new, anguished tone of longing for the East and *Eretz Yisroel*.

The upheavals took on a form that would be familiar throughout Jewish history, with false messiahs emerging in the embattled communities, attracting desperate followers with nothing left to lose. Perhaps it was in this vein that Judah himself, at the age of sixty, threw off his old life, abandoning his wife, children, and home, and set out for the Holy Land. He got as far as Alexandria, where he was delayed for several months. Although legend has it that he was trampled to death by an Arab horseman as he stopped to recite one of his poems of longing for Jerusalem outside the walls of the holy city, the reality is more mundane. He apparently died somewhere in Egypt of natural causes.

At the center of a body of writing that includes over 800 poems, Judah left one work of philosophy, a volume written in Arabic under the title *Kitab al-Khukka waal-Dalil fi Nasr el-Din al-Dhalil / The Book of Argument and Proof in Defense of the Despised Faith*. It is better known by the Hebrew title, *Sefer Ha-Kuzari / The Book of the Khazars*. The "despised faith" in question is, of course, Judaism, and Judah takes as the starting point for his discourse an historical fact: in the ninth century, the central Asian tribe known as the Khazars collectively converted to Judaism. HaLevi imagines a lengthy series of dialogues in which the king of the Khazars questions an Aristotelian philosopher and scholars of Christianity and Islam about their belief systems. After listening to the latter two deride Judaism despite their acknowledgment that their faiths are its offspring, he decides to speak with a rabbi. The bulk of the book consists of that dialogue.

For HaLevi, Aristotelianism is only valid when applied to mathematics and the sciences; in psychology or metaphysics it is ineffective. In fact, he argues through his rabbi mouthpiece that logic and reason are not convincing arguments at all when offered in defense of the existence of the God of Judaism. Rather, he believes that it is the past experience of the Jews that demonstrates their special relationship with

God. The Jews are God's chosen people, and Adonai watches over them. The evidence is not rational—it is direct and empirical—and the God of the Jews is not the God of the philosophers. The Egyptians and Jews who saw the deliverance of the Hebrews from bondage in Egypt are witnesses to that covenant.

At the center of the argument is the role of prophecy, which HaLevi interprets very differently from Maimonides. For HaLevi, prophecy is distinctly different from reason. It is the product of revelation, derived from God and more evidence of the relationship between the Almighty and the Jewish people. Only to the Jewish people has it been given to prophesy, HaLevi says. Prophecy sets the Jews apart from other peoples, and validates God's choice of Israel. A convert will be equal to a born Jew in all other things, HaLevi's rabbi cautions the king of the Khazars, but he will be denied the gift of prophecy.

Nor can one advance to prophecy through philosophy, through rationality alone. One can only do so through Torah, through the adherence to the *mitzvot,* immersion in Hebrew, the sacred tongue, and a turning towards the East and *Eretz Yisroel* (an ironic statement coming from a man writing in Arabic in Spain!).

For HaLevi the term "Jewish philosopher" is an oxymoron, an insupportable contradiction in terms, and *The Book of the Khazars* is an oddity—a work of beautifully crafted philosophical logic written to dynamite philosophy. Despite that seeming contradiction, HaLevi tried valiantly to live his dream, hoping for the coming of the Messianic Age that would deliver the Jewish people back to Jerusalem. At the close of the book, the rabbi is preparing to leave for the Holy Land, just as Judah HaLevi himself would, not long after he completed *Sefer Ha-Kuzari.*

(N.B.: The quotations that follow are taken from *The Book of the Khazars.*)

FROM THE WRITINGS OF JUDAH HaLEVI

The pious man is comparable to a prince in that he is obeyed by his senses, and his mental as well as his physical faculties, which govern corporeally, as it is written: "He that ruleth his spirit [is better] than he that taketh a city." [Proverbs 16:32] He is fit to rule because were he the prince of a country he would be as just [to his people] as he is to his body and soul.

An individual who prays but for himself is like one who retires alone into his house, refusing to assist his fellow citizens in the repair of their walls. His expenditure is as great as his risk. But he who joins the majority spends little, yet remains in safety, because one replaces the defects of the other. The city is in the best possible condition, all its inhabitants enjoying its prosperity with but little expenditure, which all share alike.

Man can approach God only by doing His commands.

They attribute to Him mercy, although this is surely nothing but a weakness of the soul, . . . which cannot be applied to God. . . . He has no sympathy with one nor anger with another.

The blessing of one prayer lasts until the time of the next, just as the strength derived from the morning meal lasts until supper. The further [the pious man's] soul is removed from the time of prayer, the more it is darkened by coming into contact with worldly matters. The more so, as necessity brings it into the company of youths, women or wicked people; when one hears unbecoming and soul-darkening words and songs which exercise an attraction for his soul which he is unable to master. During prayer he purges his soul from all that passed over it, and prepares it for the future.

When we are worthy and have good deeds to our credit, God gives us our reward; and when we have nothing of our own, God blesses us for the sake of His love, for He is good.

Preparing for a pleasure doubles the enjoyment. This advantage has he who recites a benediction with devotion.

BARUCH SPINOZA (1632 C.E.–1677 C.E.)

With Baruch Spinoza, Jewish philosophy moved into the modern era. He was the first Jewish philosopher who did not believe that the Oral and Written Torah were Revealed Truth, given to Moses at Mt. Sinai. He was the first Jewish philosopher to accept the heliocentric model of the solar system, which had serious ramifications for the reading of Torah: how could the sun stand still at Gibeon if it never moved in the first place; what does it mean for the earth to no longer be at the center of the universe? In accepting the heliocentric solar system, one accepts the larger dictates of science, a universe based on necessary laws of nature, not a God-governed contingency.

In his own system of thought Spinoza strayed farther from the traditional path than Maimonides, so much so that he would be excommunicated. He is also by far the most significant philosopher to emerge from a Jewish community prior to the twentieth century, one whose influence far outstrips that of Maimonides.

Baruch Spinoza's ancestors were Portuguese Jews who were forced to convert to Christianity in the late 1490s. His father fled Portugal and settled in the Netherlands, probably in 1622. Like thousands of others, Spinoza's father had fled to Dutch soil to escape the persecutions that still continued in the waning years of the Inquisition, and to practice his religion in public rather than under cover of darkness. At the time, the Netherlands was a fairly tolerant country, with a steady influx of Jewish refugees from the Iberian peninsula. But the Dutch and the Spanish would be at war intermittently throughout the first half of the seventeenth century, and the position of the new Dutch Jews was thought a precarious one.

Born in Amsterdam, Spinoza was given a traditional Jewish education. An outstanding student, he became deeply immersed in the works of the medieval Jewish philosophers. He also became familiar with the works of more contemporary philosophers, particularly René Descartes, and began to travel increasingly in Christian circles. Prior to his father's death, Baruch had been the dutiful son and observant Jew; Michael Spinoza's death in 1654 probably allowed a change in behavior for his erudite son.

Many of Spinoza's supposedly heretical views can be found in the works of the Jewish mystics and even in those of other Jewish philosophers. It was his behavior, rather than his writings, that jeopardized his standing among Amsterdam's Jewish community. The Dutch were a notably tolerant people, but given the political situation, the transplanted Sephardim of Amsterdam felt their presence in the city was not entirely welcome. To have in their midst a figure of controversy, which Spinoza became almost from the first moment he began writing on philosophy, undoubtedly stirred feelings of unease.

There were two other factors that contributed to the excommunication of Baruch Spinoza. First, the Sephardic community had already been grappling with a series of "heresies" in recent months, the most prominent of them committed by a Spanish doctor, Juan de Prado, who questioned key tenets of Judaism such as the precedence of Mosaic law. A generation earlier, Uriel da Costa was expelled from the Amsterdam community for denying the immorality of the soul.

The second factor was the undeniable tensions between Christian and Jew that were exacerbated significantly when an ostensible Jew like da Costa was accused of heterodox behavior. Whether Spinoza learned his heterodoxies inside or outside the Jewish fold, his decision to express them in public—and in the company of Christians at that—cannot have been well received in the city's synagogues.

On July 27, 1656, Baruch Spinoza was excommunicated by the Amsterdam Jewish community, cut off from *Am Yisroel/the People Israel* forever. Spinoza apparently accepted the judgment with little rancor. This was, as Ben-Shlomo writes, the end of Spinoza's life as a Jew—or was it?[3]

Emil Fackenheim has written that Spinoza and Franz Rosenzweig (see p. 433) are the "only two modern Jewish philosophers of the first rank [who] considered their Jewish identity as a philosophical issue." Spinoza, it must be noted, chose not to embrace Christianity after his excommunication. He became an unchurched "free" man.

As a free man, he also became the center of a circle of like-minded intellectuals. Earning his living as a lens grinder, Spinoza published only one book in his own name, an analysis of Descartes' philosophy, in 1663. His second book, the *Tractatus Theologico-Politicus,* published anonymously in 1670, stirred a new firestorm of controversy, but also won to his side many followers and admirers. In the future, he would write and speak for the benefit of those in his circle but never in public. The *Tractatus* was denounced by the Church Council of Amsterdam as a "work forged in Hell by a renegade Jew and the Devil," and was officially banned by the Church authorities, and Spinoza would undoubtedly have found himself in trouble with them had he not died at forty-five of tuberculosis, aggravated greatly by his lens-grinding work. In addition to the two books published in his lifetime, Spinoza left several works that emerged posthumously, most notably his *Ethics.*

What could this most modest of men, this seeker of tranquillity, possibly have believed and written to engender such obloquy from Christian and Jew alike? More than previous Jewish philosophers, Spinoza offered a political philosophy, the component of his work that is easiest to comprehend. The purpose of religion, he believed, is to provide humanity with a framework for ethical action (a very Jewish concept). Philosophy, on the other hand, is concerned with the search for truth. Philosophers should not be constrained by religious beliefs, nor should the state be able to legislate belief. Such an attempt is a violation of the social contract, which Spinoza, like Hobbes and Descartes before him and the *philosophes* after, believed is at the heart of human society.

As for his own system of belief, Spinoza proposed a unity of God and nature: God and nature are one, everything in the world exists within the mind of God. God or Nature, whichever you prefer, the world is the product of a single, infinite, and self-caused Substance. God is totally immanent—not transcendent—and all the interconnections within the divine system are logical connections. Nothing is contingent in these connections; each and all are necessary.

Inasmuch as his system is monistic, predicated on a unity of one God in one universe, Spinoza's system is logically consistent with Judaism. Hegel calls it "monotheism raised to the plane of thought." (It was precisely this concern for unity that led Spinoza finally to reject Descartes.) Likewise, his concern with religion as a framework for ethical behavior is reminiscent of the traditional Jewish elevation of act over thought. Some thinkers consider Spinoza's thought to be the purest distillation of Jewish thought, the philosophical system that brings Judaism into the modern era.

Spinoza would not agree. The *Tractatus* specifically speaks of the contradictions between his thought and Judaism. He explicitly rejects the Maimonidean effort to unite faith and reason. As for the affinities some detect between Spinoza and Jewish mysticism, he once said that Kabbalah is foolishness.

Spinoza's system of belief is rationalistic and deductive. He develops it in the manner of a mathematician proving geometric theorems. This method is entirely appropriate for someone who believes that the supreme ambition of a good person is the "intellectual love of God."

Is the result a bloodless rationalism? The intensity with which Spinoza expresses this complex system of belief belies the accusation. And one of the greatest strengths guiding his thought was his personality; the seeming detachment with which he approached these large questions, combined with his self-effacing nature, make him a philosopher's philosopher. The key figures of German idealism—Lessing, Herder, Goethe—proceeded from his thought. In his rationalism, his defense of freedom of thought, and his pantheism, he anticipated the *philosophes*. In *The History of Philosophy,* Hegel writes, "Thought must begin by placing itself at the standpoint of Spinozism; to be a follower of Spinoza is the essential commencement of all philosophy."

(N.B.: The quotations that follow are taken from *The Ethics,* as excerpted in *The Philosophy of Spinoza.*)

FROM THE WRITINGS OF BARUCH SPINOZA

God is absolutely the first cause.

If this be denied, conceive, if it be possible, that God does not exist. Then it follows that His essence does not involve existence. But this is absurd. Therefore God necessarily exists.

Nature has no particular goal in view, and final causes are mere human figments.

Man is a social animal. . . . Men can provide for their wants much more easily by mutual help, and only by uniting their forces can they escape from the dangers that beset them.

If we live according to the guidance of reason, we shall desire for others the good which we seek for ourselves.

MOSES MENDELSSOHN (1729 C.E.–1786 C.E.)

If we accept the rule of science, as Spinoza urged, what happens to Revelation? Moses Mendelssohn is a pivotal figure in the history of Jewish thought because he was the first to face that and related questions. He is also the first significant post-Spinoza Jewish philosopher, an Orthodox Jew who extolled the *Haskalah/Jewish Enlightenment,* a friend of Christians who remained an observant traditional Jew, yet whose thought undermined the foundations of Orthodoxy as surely as Kant would undermine the foundations of Mendelssohn's thought. He was also the first Jewish thinker of note to emerge from Germany, the culture that played a significant role in the thought of virtually every subsequent Jewish philosopher of importance.

Moses Mendelssohn was born in Dessau, the son of a Torah scribe. He received a traditional Orthodox upbringing and education, studying with Rabbi David Frankel. When Frankel was named chief rabbi of Berlin in 1743, his star pupil followed him to the capital. There, the fourteen-year-old boy eked out a meager living working as a copyist and private tutor. The boy's physical limitations were numerous. He suffered from a nervous disorder, was a stutterer, and had a severe curvature of the spine that resulted in a hunched back. He was exceedingly short and, to be frank, homely. But he was possessed of a lightning intellect, a personal warmth and charm, modesty and integrity that overcame any shortcomings his body might have imposed.

In Berlin, Mendelssohn studied secular subjects under the tutelage of several excellent Jewish scholars. He quickly mastered High German, Italian, French, Latin, Greek, English, mathematics, and philosophy. It was also in this period that he met the German playwright and poet Gotthold Lessing. Thus began a lifelong friendship between two dissimilar men, one Jewish, the other Christian, brought together by a passion for the life of the mind and a deep respect and affection for one another.

With Lessing's encouragement and assistance, he published his first writings. Mendelssohn would not need Lessing's help for very long. He quickly established himself as a writer and literary critic; in 1763 he was awarded the first prize of the Prussian Royal Academy for his treatise, "On Evidence in the Metaphysical Sciences." That same year he received an even rarer honor, being granted the "right of residence" in Berlin by Frederick the Great. Although the Prussian ruler was notably liberal for this era, even toward his Jewish subjects, it was highly unusual for such a residency permit to be given.[4]

Mendelssohn clearly enjoyed a privileged status granted to very few European Jews in the eighteenth century. That status, bestowed on a man who continued to comport himself as an Orthodox Jew, pointed up the uncomfortable duality that faced him in Frederick's Prussia (and anywhere else in Europe, for that matter), a duality that has characterized the position of Diaspora Jews throughout the modern era, albeit with the lines drawn less sharply today. On the one hand, Mendelssohn was permitted to practice his faith, to maintain his Jewish identity, and to enjoy a degree of acceptance in the salons and even some public acclaim. But he was never allowed to forget who and what he was, or that all the success could be swept away with the stroke of a monarch's pen, that he was, as Mendelssohn himself ruefully noted, "a member of an oppressed race."

This painful contradiction was brought home to Mendelssohn forcefully in 1769 by a turn of events that would cause him to shift the focus of his philosophical endeavors for the rest of his life.

Ironically, it began with another seeming honor. An acquaintance named Johann Caspar Lavater, a young Calvinist clergyman, so admired Mendelssohn that he dedicated his German translation of a religious tract to the older man. Unfortunately, he also included in its introduction a public challenge to Mendelssohn: read the treatise and refute it publicly or convert to Christianity. Whatever motivated the young pastor, Mendelssohn would not be drawn into a public quarrel; he published a quietly dignified reply, restating his commitment to Judaism and his pride in his Jewish identity.

But the incident reminded Mendelssohn of the metaphorical tightrope he walked. From this point on, the focus of his life's work shifted to questions of Jewish identity, emancipation, and belief. Emil Fackenheim writes that despite the sensation caused by the Lavater affair, "it would be a tempest in a teapot were it not for one important result: it occasioned the first work in modern Jewish philosophy." (Of course, Spinoza's adherents would disagree with that last statement.)

That work, *Jerusalem,* was completed and published in 1783. It presents Mendelssohn's major statement on Jewish identity and Christian-Jewish relations. It is an elegantly written and compassion-stirring argument for tolerance of religious differences on all sides.

Putting Judaism in the context of the European Enlightenment, Mendelssohn breaks sharply with Maimonides and other medieval Jewish thinkers, arguing that if religion is based on reason (as the neo-Aristotelians believed) then it serves no purpose, for revelation cannot disclose any truths not already available to the rational, questing mind. Judaism is not "revealed religion" but "revealed law," the product of doctrines of religious reason that require no proof or revelation to be intelligible. What distinguishes the Jew from the non-Jew is not a revelation of reason but a unique body of Mosaic law, an historical fact that is attested to by the six hundred thousand men, women, and children of the Hebrew people present at Sinai. Therefore, Jews can only achieve fulfillment by adhering to the laws of Moses. The God of reason and the God of Sinai are unified in the observance of *halakhah* (an interesting forerunner to the ideas of Rabbi Soloveitchik; see p. 449). It is the sheer *daily-ness* of these observances that brings Jews closer to eternal truths.

Jerusalem is also a plea for religious tolerance. The knowledge of Truth is an indispensable part of human happiness, Mendelssohn says, so truth must be accessible to all, regardless of creed or nation. No religion, not even Judaism, can be the only path to God's truths. Therefore, freedom of thought and tolerance for other systems of thought are a prerequisite to happiness. As he observes, "According to the tenets of Judaism, all inhabitants of the earth have a claim to salvation, and the means to attain it are as widespread as mankind itself, as liberally dispensed as the means of satisfying one's hunger and other natural assets."

At the same time, Mendelssohn argues in both this work and his later writings, Diaspora Jews must integrate themselves into the cultures that host them:

> Even now, no better advice than this can be given to the House of Jacob: Adopt the mores and constitution of the country in which you find yourself, but be steadfast in upholding the religion of your fathers, too. Bear both burdens as well as you can.

After all, isn't that the task Moses Mendelssohn had taken on himself?

Mendelssohn would spend the remainder of his life trying to reconcile the two sides of his existence. He became a dedicated and public battler for the rights of German Jews, an activist within the community itself. At the same time, he worked for the modernization of German Jewish culture, translating the Bible into High German, thereby providing the Jews with a lesson in High German and the Germans with an introduction to Jewish belief.

His writings do not constitute an original system of thought; they are a reflection of the rationalist liberalism of the Enlightenment salons in which he was an honored guest. But he triggered the Jewish Enlightenment, the *Haskalah,* with his passionate double emphasis on the modernization of Jewish culture paired with the emancipation of Diaspora Jewry. As such the *Haskalah* became something Mendelssohn never intended, a most formidable assault on the edifice of Rabbinic Judaism. Combined with the beginnings of emancipation for Europe's Jews and the concomitant temptations of assimilation, that assault was more devastating for traditional Judaism than Mendelssohn could have dreamed, resulting in the rise of the Reform movement and its eventual offspring, the advent of secular Judaism and, in our time, a splintering of *Am Yisroel / the Jewish people* into several different cultures.

The most spectacular sign of what Mendelssohn—who remained a practicing Orthodox Jew up to his death at the age of fifty-seven—had triggered occurred within his own family. His grandson, Felix, the composer, whose fame would outstrip his own, was baptized a Christian.

(N.B.: The quotations that follow are taken from *Jerusalem*.)

FROM THE WRITINGS OF MOSES MENDELSSOHN

Each conception of spiritual beauty is a glimpse at God.

God punishes the sinner not according to His own infinity but according to the sinner's frailty.

If you take mankind as a whole, you will not find that there is constant progress in its development that brings it ever nearer to perfection. On the contrary, we see constant fluctuations; mankind as a whole has never yet taken any step forward without soon and with redoubled speed sliding back to its previous position.

All commandments of the divine law are addressed to man's will, to his capacity to act. In fact, the original Hebrew term [*emunah*] that is usually translated as "faith" means, in most cases, merely "trust," confidence or firm reliance on pledge and promise. . . . Whenever the text refers to eternal verities, it does not use the term "believe" but "understand" and "know". . . .

As I see it, Judaism has from its inception consisted of both doctrines and laws, convictions and actions. The doctrines of Judaism were never tied to phrases or formulations which had to remain unchanged for all men and times, throughout all revolutions of language, morality, ways of life, and circumstance.

The ultimate purpose of the written and the unwritten laws prescribing actions as well as rules of life is public and private salvation.

FRANZ ROSENZWEIG (1886 C.E.–1929 C.E.)

Mendelssohn opened the doors of German Protestant society to Jewish intellectuals, and they would remain open until 1933 and the rise to power of Adolf Hitler. Mendelssohn chose to remain outside those doors in a meaningful way; his grandson Felix chose otherwise. Franz Rosenzweig, arguably the most important and original Jewish thinker of the twentieth century, walked a similar path to Felix Mendelssohn, but turned back at the very threshold of the Church. The drama of his decision to return to the circle of the faith of his forefathers provides a moving metaphor for the existential dilemma of modern Judaism; in the wake of the Emancipation and the Enlightenment, we are all "Jews by choice." And the instant of Rosenzweig's own choice reverberates throughout his writings, giving them a power that mitigates their extreme difficulty.

Franz Rosenzweig was born in Kassel, Germany. His family were wealthy, highly cultured, and thoroughly assimilated Jews who maintained their Jewishness mainly as a protest against anti-Semitism. Such Jews would have been unimaginable before Moses Mendelssohn. The family attended synagogue on the High Holy Days and virtually at no other time; Rosenzweig would not even be aware of Sabbath observances until he was in college.

On the other hand, at least one member of the family called the boy's attention to his Jewish identity. His uncle, Adam Rosenzweig, told the six-year-old Franz on his first day of school, "My boy, you are going among people for the first time today; remember as long as you live you are a Jew."

That attitude was atypical in the Rosenzweig family. Several of Franz's relatives converted to Christianity, including his cousin and close friend Hans Ehrenburg, who was baptized in 1909.

An excellent student, Franz entered the University of Gottingen with an eye towards medical studies (apparently at his father's urging), but transferred twice, ending up at Freiburg. To his father's dismay, he was losing interest in medical studies and wanted to focus his attention on history and philosophy instead.

It was at Freiburg in 1910 that Franz went to a conference of philosophy and history graduate students along with his cousins Hans and Rudolf Ehrenburg. It was there that he met another key figure in his life, Eugen Rosenstock-Huessy, a distant cousin who would become a lifelong friend. Rosenstock-Huessy, like Hans Ehrenburg, had converted from Judaism to Christianity. Over the next several years he would encourage Rosenzweig to follow suit. On a summer evening in 1913, the two converted cousins engaged Franz in a dialogue that culminated in their convincing Rosenzweig to give serious consideration to a similar path.

But Franz's intellectual integrity was too great for him to simply abandon the faith of his ancestors and jump into the waters of Christianity. He decided that if he were to come to Christianity it would have to be "as a Jew," rather than as a pagan. He told no one of his decision, but for Rosh Hashanah went home to Kassel, where he read deeply in the Gospels. Then, on Yom Kippur, the most solemn of Jewish holidays, he went to an Orthodox synagogue in Berlin, convinced that he would leave it ready to become a Christian.

But a most unexpected turn of events befell Franz Rosenzweig on Yom Kippur, 1913. He never explained exactly what happened to him during the services, but as he stood in prayer surrounded by other Jews, total strangers, he had the sensation that he truly stood before God as an individual. He suddenly realized that the faith which provided him with the orientation to the outside world that he sought in religion was Judaism.

What Rosenzweig came to understand was that while Rosenstock-Huessy was telling him that one could only reach the Father through his Son, Jesus, he knew that as a Jew he needed no one to intercede for him with the Eternal One. As a Jew he stood before God in an unmediated relationship.

Now his path seemed clear. He stayed in Berlin and began studying the history and religion of Judaism. He became a student of Herman Cohen, the brilliant neo-Kantian Jewish philosopher, and studied at the *Lehranstalt fur die Wissenschaft des Judentums / Institute for the Scientific Study of Judaism,* the foremost educational and research institution of its kind in the world, learning Hebrew, Arabic, and Talmud. And he became acquainted with Martin Buber, another young Jewish scholar and philosopher-in-the-making with whom he would enjoy a lifelong friendship and fruitful collaboration.

The outbreak of World War I interrupted Rosenzweig's program of study. He enlisted in the army and found himself assigned to the field artillery. He continued working on his dissertation, "Hegel and the State," and began to work on the book that would be his magnum opus, *The Star of Redemption. Star*'s early sections were written under the most unusual circumstance; Franz would jot them down on postcards and mail them home to his mother or friends, who slowly assembled the contents into a draft of what would eventually become his book. At this time, he also became interested in creating a program of Jewish education, and wrote several essays on the subject.

In the summer of 1920, Rosenzweig was given an opportunity to put his theories of Jewish learning into practice. He was appointed head of *Das Freie Jüdische Lehrhaus/the Free House of Jewish Learning* in Frankfurt-am-Main. The "free" school offered no degrees, had no entrance exams, and encouraged its students to engage in free inquiry. There really was no fixed abode for the Lehrhaus; seminars and classes met all over the city. Rosenzweig assembled a formidable group of instructors. He put together a faculty that represented a wide range of Jewish viewpoints of the day. Rosenzweig also encouraged Martin Buber to teach at the Lehrhaus; although Buber was developing a reputation among both Jewish and Christian scholars, he was not yet comfortable with the idea of delivering lectures, but did lead some small seminars on Hasidism.

As 1921 began, Rosenzweig was on the threshold of real public acclaim. His lectures on German Idealism were well-received and *The Star of Redemption* was published. His publisher was worried that the book's appeal was limited by its extreme difficulty, so he asked Franz for another text that would present his ideas in a more accessible fashion. The result was *Understanding the Sick and the Healthy,* an attack on German Idealism—particularly Hegel—that offered an extended metaphor of a sick and paralyzed patient who cannot be treated by the "old thinking," but who is cured by the "new thinking" extolled by Rosenzweig.

It would turn out to be a tragically ironic literary device. A few months after it was completed, Rosenzweig began having problems with his motor functions. He was diagnosed with amytrophic lateral sclerosis (known commonly as "Lou Gehrig's disease"), a degenerative neuromuscular disease that involves the gradual loss of all muscle function. Within a year, Rosenzweig would be confined to bed. Gradually he would lose the use of his limbs, the ability to hold his head up or to swallow. The slow paralysis would affect his speech as well and soon his wife, Edith, would have to interpret for him with even close friends.

Yet Rosenzweig was undaunted by his illness. Indeed, he entered into a period of feverish literary activity. When it became impossible for him to type any longer, he was given a specially constructed typewriter that allowed him to pick out letters on a steel plate which would transfer them to the page. Eventually, he would need Edith's help even to use this device. Finally, he would be forced to give Edith "dictation" which would consist of her pointing to the letters of the alphabet on a board, with Franz blinking his eyes to indicate yes or no for each letter.

In this laborious manner, Rosenzweig carried out his part in an ambitious collaboration with Buber on a radical new translation of the Hebrew Bible into German (see the sidebar "Rosenzweig and Buber Translate Torah," below) and a collection of essays describing their work, a series of translations of the poetry of Judah HaLevi, accompanied by stunningly erudite commentary on both the poetry and the translation process, and numerous essays and even music reviews. Finally, in December 1929 Rosenzweig's body gave out completely. He received a traditional Jewish burial, with Buber reading Psalm 73 rather than delivering a eulogy.

ROSENZWEIG AND BUBER TRANSLATE TORAH

The principles underlying the translation of the Hebrew Bible into German by Franz Rosenzweig and Martin Buber are interesting for what they tell us about the attitudes of these two men toward sacred texts. It was their stated belief that the role of the translator in such a work is not to smooth over the difficulties presented by the process of translation; rather, they envisioned their task as *creating* difficulties, expanding the distance between reader and text! It is imperative that the experience of reading the Bible in one's own tongue—a seemingly familiar text with a larger-than-life importance—should serve as a vivid reminder of the original in all its estrangement. Consequently, the Buber-Rosenzweig translation emphasizes re-creating the sound values and repetitions of the Hebrew as much as, if not more than, the literal meaning.

In a 1926 essay written shortly after embarking on the project, Buber wrote:

> This book has since its beginning encountered one generation after another. Confrontation and reconciliation with it have taken place in every generation. Sometimes it is met with obedience and offered dominion; sometimes, with offense and rebellion. But each generation engages it vitally, and faces it in the realm of reality. Even where people have said "no" to it, that "no" has only validated the book's claim upon them—they have borne witness to it even in refusing themselves to it.

Four years later he would add:

> The special obligation to create a new version of the Bible, which came alive in our time and led to our undertaking, resulted from the discovery that the passage of time had largely turned the Bible into a palimpsest. The original traits of the Bible, the original meaning and words, had been overlaid by a familiar abstraction, in origin partly theological and partly literary.
>
> — *Scripture and Translation*

For the non-German reader who wishes to get a sense of what the Buber-Rosenzweig Hebrew Bible is like, a reading of Everett Fox's *The Five Books of Moses* is recommended. Fox has attempted a translation of the Torah into English based on the principles that guided his German predecessors, and the result is a formidable achievement, quite unlike any other Torah translation available in English today.

Given the dramatic story of his life and death, the philosophy of Franz Rosenzweig might seem almost superfluous. But *The Star of Redemption* is, despite its abstruseness, one of the most important works of Jewish philosophy. As Michael Oppenheim has written, "*The Star* reflects Rosenzweig's comprehensive definition of the nature of Jewish philosophy. He discusses our understanding and experience of the human being, the world, and God. His examination includes elements of all the classical segments of philosophy; an ethics, aesthetics, epistemology, metaphysics, and logic, as well as a critique of philosophy from the perspective of Jewish categories." In addition, the book deals with questions of Judaism vs. Christianity, Judaism vs. paganism, the nature of truth, and the meaning of life in the face of death, all seen from a specifically Jewish perspective.

This lengthy agenda would be hard work for readers under any circumstances, but what renders the book more difficult for even the most philosophically sophisticated reader is that it is written in the private language of the author's circle. As Rosenzweig scholar Robert Gibbs remarks ruefully, "He draws on various philosophical and theological vocabularies, denoting clusters of concepts by the use of a single word or phrase. . . . Rosenzweig's analyses are thus so cryptic that, unless one already knows the result, it is often virtually impossible to follow his line of reasoning."

The heart of the book may be said to reside in its title; the "star of redemption" of which Rosenzweig speaks is the *Magen David/Shield of David,* the familiar six-pointed Jewish star, composed of two interlocking triangles. Each of the points of those triangles represents a part of a tripartite relationship on which reality rests. In the upper triangle, we find God, the World, and Man; the lower triangle represents Creation, Revelation, and Redemption. God makes the World through Creation. God chooses Man through Revelation. Man, moved by God, redeems the world. Place these two triangular relationships one upon the other and you have the Star of Redemption.

What makes Rosenzweig's thought so radical, Ernest Rubinstein observes, is that "he recasts these seeming subject-object relationships — in Creation, God is subject, world object; in Revelation, God is subject, man object; in Redemption man and God are subject, world object — in much more equal and mutual terms." Thus it is not so much that God creates the world but that the Creator's need to be providential and the world's need to be cared for "meet" in creation. There is a complex dialectic of active and passive at work in Rosenzweig's conception of this process; God's prior need to be providential has a passive quality, while the world's passive need to be cared for has an active element to it. That dialectic becomes even more pronounced in the Revelation, where God shows a vulnerability in the love of Creator for humanity and humanity, in turn, actually helps sustain God's love by complying to the Almighty's command, "Love me!"

Revelation is an ongoing process, according to Rosenzweig, a process of God making the Eternal manifest to the individual who seeks. *Halakhah* and Torah must speak to the individual, who then can open his or her heart to the Divine teachings in a love relationship. But this can only happen over time.

Rosenzweig is the first Jewish philosopher to consider Christianity as an equally legitimate belief system. Each of the two faiths has its origins in the encounter with the Divine. Rosenzweig speaks of the doctrine of the Two Covenants: Christianity is the Judaism of the non-Jew, with the potential to bring the entire world into a relationship with God, a relationship that is already directly experienced by the believing Jew and constituted in Judaism. Judaism cannot take on the role of embracing the rest of the world, a role left to Christianity, because to do so would threaten the intensity of the God-Israel relationship. Ideally, he hopes, each of the two faiths can recognize the integrity of the other, giving understanding and not asking for change. (Still, he sees Christianity as historically dependent on Judaism in a way that is irreversible and not reciprocal.) No other faiths have a role comparable to that of these two.

Rosenzweig places a great deal of emphasis on the manner in which the relationship between human beings reflects the Divine love between human and Eternal. In that respect, he seconds Buber (see p. 440) and anticipates the focus of Emmanuel Levinas on ethical obligations towards the Other. The chain of relationships that results—human to God, God to human, human to human—makes it possible for us to break through the isolation of life with its inescapable ending in death, giving it meaning.

As Oppenheim notes in a 1993 essay on Rosenzweig and Levinas, neither of them fits the classic existentialist paradigm of basing notions of authenticity on the encounter with death (although *Star* opens with a brief discussion of the fact of death as an argument against the inauthenticity of idealism). But it would be hard to imagine a more extraordinary model for how one faces death than the determination and courage with which Franz Rosenzweig lived each day of his ongoing struggle with the inevitable over the last seven years of his life.

(N.B.: The quotations that follow are taken from Nahum Glatzer's *Franz Rosenzweig: His Life and Thought*.)

FROM THE WRITINGS OF FRANZ ROSENZWEIG

The Bible is a parable of man's advance to the family, to the tribe, to a nation with a national ideal, to a nation with a universal ideal.

None of us has solid ground under his feet; each of us is only held up by the neighborly hands grasping him by the scruff, with the result that we are each held up by the next man, and often, indeed most of the time, hold each other up mutually.

A people's entry into universal history is marked by the moment at which it makes the Bible its own in a translation.

The river of life . . . flows from birth to death. Day follows day with wearisome monotony. Only the holidays twine themselves together to form the circle of the year. Only through the holidays does life experience the eternity of the river that returns to its sources. Then life becomes eternal.

To be a Jew means to be in exile.

MARTIN BUBER (1878 C.E.–1965 C.E.)

Franz Rosenzweig initiated a chain of twentieth-century Jewish thinkers to which each subsequent Jewish philosopher is linked. However, the link was not solely forged by intellectual debt to Rosenzweig—although his influence is inescapable. There were connections of a more personal nature as well, a passing of authority as direct as the one cited in the first verse of *Pirke Avot*. The torch of Jewish existentialism was handed from Rosenzweig to Buber, his longtime friend and collaborator, from Buber to Heschel, who replaced him as head of the Lehrhaus, then to Levinas and Fackenheim.[5] Several generations of rabbinical students at Jewish Theological Seminary studied under Heschel, and their number includes some of the finest thinkers in American Judaism. Today the torch is borne aloft by younger scholars such as the group that styles itself the "Postmodern Jewish Philosophy Network."

But first there was Buber, playing Aaron to Rosenzweig's Moses.

Thanks in no small part to his longevity, prolificacy, and the comparative accessibility of his writing, Buber's reputation far surpassed that of his friend during the former's lifetime. Today, however, it would be hard to find a Jewish philosopher who would valorize Buber's thought over Rosenzweig's.

Few educated Jews outside the academy have read Rosenzweig (an understandable omission given the daunting opacity of his major work). On the other hand, it is common to hear rabbis quote Buber regularly, invoking his dialogical principle, the idea of the I-Thou relationship, even his progressive positions on Jewish-Christian and Palestinian-Israeli relations. His stature among Christian theologians is, if anything, greater.

Although born in Vienna, Buber was raised by his grandfather, Solomon Buber, in Lvov, Poland. This circumstance guaranteed that the boy would receive a first-class Jewish education, for Solomon was a well-known Midrash scholar who gave the boy the benefit of his many years of study and passed on a love of Bible, Talmud, and Judaism. In his early twenties, Buber experienced a (short-lived) crisis of faith and began reading Kant and Nietzsche. He returned to Vienna as a student at the university there, then continued his studies in Leipzig, Berlin, and Zurich. It was in Zurich that he became a protégé of Theodor Herzl, the father of political Zionism.

The young Buber was one of the rising stars of the nascent Zionist movement, but he had significant differences with Herzl, eventually breaking with him over the political content of Zionism. Buber would come to advocate a cultural version of Jewish nationalism, a position to which he would adhere in one form or another for the rest of his life. (For more information on Herzl and the various forms and evolution of the Zionist movement, see p. 480.) Eventually, he would become one of a group of "cultural Zionists" who in 1916 founded their own publication, *Der Jude / The Jew,* with Buber as its editor. The group advocated a humanist-based socialist version of Zionism that Buber called "Hebrew Humanism." As early as the turn of the century, Buber espoused the cause of a bi-national state of Palestine, shared equitably between Jew and Arab "in which both peoples will have the possibility of free development." He would hold to that position his entire adult life, even after he moved to Palestine, where such a position was certain to win him enemies.

Sometime in 1903 Buber made a literary discovery that would alter his life and thinking; he came across the tales of Rabbi Nakhman of Bratzlav, great-grandson of the Baal Shem Tov, and a great and unique Hasidic leader in his own right. Buber wrote literary adaptations of Nakhman's beautiful, cryptic stories, and was deeply touched by their mysterious visions of devotion to Adonai. He began to explore the Hasidic movement more deeply, and eventually would translate two more volumes of Hasidic tales, returning this time to the simplicity of the originals.

More important than their literary influence on Buber, the Hasidic masters' writings fascinated him with the directness with which they approached and related to the Eternal One. He would return to the subject of Hasidism repeatedly in his writings (even taking the lives of the first generation of Hasidic rabbis as the subject of his only novel, *For the Sake of Heaven*). The unmediated relationship between Hasid and Creator as depicted in their writings undoubtedly helped shape the key insight of Buber's philosophy, the "dialogical principle," most tellingly enunciated in *I and Thou,* his most famous work. Other scholars of Hasidism, most prominently the premier historian of Jewish mysticism, Gershom Scholem, would belittle Buber's reading of Hasidism as being more a restatement of his own particular philosophy than an accurate explanation of the Hasidic worldview, but Buber's importance in drawing attention to Hasidism is indisputable. Before Buber, the Hasidim were dismissed as superstitious peasants who believed in miracle-working "wonder rabbis," the sort of simple men who were the butt of jokes in Yiddish short stories. After Buber, the Hasidim were taken seriously as the pietistic movement they were.

In the 1920s Buber became a close friend and collaborator with Franz Rosenzweig. He offered seminars on Hasidism at Rosenzweig's *Lehrhaus,* and would eventually take over some of Rosenzweig's classes when his friend's illness left him homebound.

It was also in this period, in 1923, that Buber wrote and published his pivotal work, a slender volume entitled *I and Thou,* in which he first enunciated the idea of the relationship between human and human, between human and God, as one of dialogue. To a certain extent, every one of Buber's many subsequent books and essays is a development of and variation on this idea. Two years later, the first parts of his joint translation of the Hebrew Bible with Rosenzweig appeared.

Buber's academic career was also blossoming. He was lecturing on religion and philosophy at the University of Frankfurt, and would be made a professor of religion there in 1930. He would hold the professorship for only three years, though; in January 1933 the Nazi Party took power and shortly after universities were required to dismiss their Jewish faculty members. In the face of the rising brutality of Nazi conduct towards the Jews, Buber did the one thing he knew how to do: he taught Jews about Judaism. He traveled throughout Germany lecturing and teaching to Jewish groups, urging them to maintain their Jewishness in the face of the coming oppression. Finally, in 1938 it was impossible for Buber to continue any longer. He appointed a young scholar named Abraham Joshua Heschel as his successor at the *Lehrhaus,* and emigrated to Palestine, where he received an appointment as professor of social philosophy at Hebrew University. He would remain in that position for the next twenty-seven years, until his death at the age of eighty-seven in Jerusalem.

In *I and Thou,* Buber offers a new version of the classic Jewish understanding of the relationship between God and humanity. There are, Buber believed, two types of fundamental relationships, I-It and I-Thou, and we each experience both types over the course of a day, over the course of our lives.

The more common of the two is the I-It relationship, the way that we experience the world most of the time, as a relationship between ourselves and a world of objects, the things that surround us. In an I-It relationship, the two terms of the relationship are not equals or partners; for the I, the It is an instrumentality at best, an inanimate object at worst. There is nothing inherently wrong with the I-It relationship; both modes are essential to life, Buber says. The I-It relationship makes possible the acquisition of knowledge of the world, for example.

The I-Thou relationship is fundamentally different. An I-Thou relationship engages two subjects, standing alongside one another in dialogue. In an I-Thou relationship, the two terms undergo dialogue in which there is manifested mutuality, openness, directness, and human sympathy. Such qualities are essential to the formation of human values. One can understand an I-Thou relationship only by experiencing it. And one experiences it with the innermost core of one's being.

The tragic aspect of modern society, Buber argues, is that gradually the I-It relationship has edged the I-Thou towards oblivion, that I-It relationships are displacing the I-Thou, with the result that our lives are increasingly unfulfilled.

The road to restoring the balance between these two modes is through the Eternal Thou, God. In all relationships but one, there come moments in which a Thou becomes an It, a dialogue between thinking subjects becomes a monologue of subject and object. But God is the exception to this process: God is the Eternal Thou, the Thou which can never become an It, the ground upon which all Thous are unified, upon which the relationship with a particular Thou is made possible. "Every particular Thou is a glimpse through to the Eternal Thou," he writes. "[B]y means of every particular Thou the primary word addresses the eternal Thou. Through this mediation of the Thou of all beings fulfilment, and non-fulfilment, of relations comes to them: the inborn Thou is realized in each relation and consummated in one. It is consummated only in the direct relation with the Thou that by its nature cannot become an It."

Revelation consists of the meeting with the Eternal Thou and the recognitions that accompany that dialogue. Revelation is not something finite, something that happened to 600,000 Jews at Sinai and about which we can only read and wonder; Revelation can happen to us any-time we can reach a dialogue with the Eternal Thou. Revelation is not—as the standard interpretation of the miracles of Sinai would have it—God "revealing" some inner, secret truth to humanity. In fact, Buber says, Revelation has no objective content. Revelation is the com-ing "face to face" with the Eternal Thou and thereby reaffirming the meaningfulness of life. What has been "revealed" is God's Presence in our lives. To follow this line of reasoning to its logical conclusion, Buber offers, we must realize that the *mitzvot* are not themselves the content of Revelation. What they are is the human response to Revela-tion, an attempt to objectify the Divine Presence in a constant form.

Buber applies the "dialogical principle" to virtually every aspect of his writings. His social and religious philosophy grows out of the idea of dialogue between humans, of trying to maintain an I-Thou relationship with other humans. The Bible, as he analyzes it in numerous essays and books of exegesis, is nothing less than the record of an ongoing dia-logue between God and the people Israel. Thus every generation is required to make its own dialogue with God. The laws are not to be taken as immutable, for they are nothing more than the objectified form of that dialogue. (Needless to say, this vision of a flexible *halakhah* did not win Buber any supporters among the Orthodox, and even Rosenzweig had his differences with this notion.)

Finally, Buber, whose thought has had considerable resonance for Christian theologians, argued strongly for an ongoing Jewish-Christian dialogue. Like his friend and collaborator Rosenzweig, Buber believed that both faiths retained a validity in the eyes of the Eternal. He argues that no other faith has invested so much in his concept of God as the Jews, but he refers to Jesus as "my brother," a great Jewish teacher. The problem with Christianity, Buber says, arises not from the teachings of Jesus, but from the dogmatic faith in Christ propagated by Paul and his successors. Christianity is least true to Jesus' vision when the Paulines are in ascent. Finally, Buber admits that while Jesus is a great teacher and a great historical figure, as a Jew he cannot accept Jesus as the Messiah. The world remains yet unredeemed, but a close and brotherly dialogue between Jew and Christian, based on mutual respect for one another's faiths, is a necessary step towards its redemption. The next thinker we consider, Abraham Joshua Heschel, will extend the chain of belief further, and his own innovations in Jewish-Christian dialogue will be one of his many contributions.

(N.B.: The quotations that follow are taken from *The Way of Response*.)

FROM THE WRITINGS OF MARTIN BUBER

Only he who learns to love men one by one reaches, in his relation to heaven, God as the God of all the world. He who does not love the world can only refer, in his relationship to God, to an equally solitary God or to the God of his own soul. For he learns to love the God of the universe who loves His world, only in the measure in which he himself learns to love the world.

In all the seriousness of truth, hear this: without It man cannot live. But he who lives with It alone is not a man.

How powerful is the unbroken world of It, and how delicate are the appearances of the Thou!

The extended lines of relations meet in the eternal Thou.

> Every particular Thou is a glimpse through to the eternal Thou; by means of every particular Thou the primary word addresses the eternal Thou.
>
> There is a purpose to creation; there is a purpose to the human race, one we have not made up ourselves, or agreed to among ourselves; we have not decided that henceforward this, that, or the other shall serve as the purpose of our existence. No. The purpose itself revealed its face to us and we have gazed upon it.
>
> God wills to need man for the work of completing His creation; in this sentence is to be grasped the foundation of the Jewish doctrine of redemption. But that God wills this means that this "needing" becomes working reality: in history as it takes place, God waits for man.

ABRAHAM JOSHUA HESCHEL (1907 C.E.–1972 C.E.)

There is a Hebrew word commonly used in Ashkenazi circles, *yikhus*. It means, more or less, one's pedigree, the amount of honor that accrues to you from previous generations of your family. Abraham Joshua Heschel had *yikhus* to spare, on both sides of his family. On his mother's side of the family he was a descendant of Levi Yitzkhok of Berdichev and Pinkhas of Koretz, central figures in the first generation of Hasidic rabbis. His father was Rabbi Moses Mordecai Heschel, and through Moses Mordecai, he could trace his family back through Rabbi Israel of Ruzhyn, Abraham Joshua Heschel of Opatov, and the great Rabbi Dov Baer of Mezeritch, the Baal Shem Tov's hand-picked successor. In short, Heschel's rabbinical pedigree went back almost to the Baal Shem Tov himself.

Heschel's intellectual credentials were equally impressive. That he underwent a traditional yeshiva education as a young man is not surprising; he received intensive training in Hasidic thought and in the mystical writings known as Kabbalah. This last is indicative of how well regarded the young Abraham was as a student, for Kabbalah was not taught to many in the Eastern European Jewish schools. Heschel also received a top-notch secular education, culminating in a doctorate in philosophy from the University of Berlin, earned with a dissertation on that favorite subject of earlier Jewish philosophers, prophecy. Even before he was granted his degree from Berlin or his rabbinical ordination from the prestigious *Hochschule für die Wissenschaft des Judentums,* Heschel was lecturing on Talmud at the *Hochschule*. It was while teaching there in 1937 that he was approached by Martin Buber who asked him to serve as Buber's successor as director of the *Lehrhaus* in Frankfurt, that beacon of progressive Judaism founded by Franz Rosenzweig.

Three weeks before Heschel had completed his orals for his doctorate, the Nazis had come to power in Germany. The two professors who had passed his dissertation, both of them Jews, had been stripped of their teaching posts by 1935. The only way that Heschel was able to get his dissertation published—then a requirement from degree-granting German universities—was through the intervention of the Polish consulate, who helped him secure the imprint of the Polish Academy of Sciences in Kracow.

Heschel tried desperately to find a teaching position outside Germany as well. He accepted Buber's offer, but it must have been clear to both men that the days of *Lehrhaus*—and of German Jewry—were numbered. In October 1938 the Polish-born Heschel, along with all other Jews holding Polish passports, was arrested and deported to the Polish border. Heschel was taken in by his family in Warsaw. For the next ten months he would teach in the Polish capital, all the while knowing that Poland—and her Jews in particular—were doomed to fall in the face of a German onslaught. He spent the entire ten months trying to find a position outside of Europe, and six weeks before the German invasion, he succeeded. Heschel left Warsaw for the United States to teach at the Reform movement's rabbinical school, Hebrew Union College, in Cincinnati. His mother and two of his sisters were murdered in the death camps. He never returned to Germany, Austria, or Poland.

Heschel taught at HUC for nearly the rest of the war, accepting a full professorship in 1945 at Jewish Theological Seminary, the primary rabbinical school of the Conservative movement. He would remain there until his death. He wrote and published widely, and as a theologian and philosopher touched on every subject of Jewish interest. He also distinguished himself with a record of public activism that bore vivid personal testimony to his philosophy: he was one of the most visible Jewish leaders in the civil rights movement (a personal friend of Dr. Martin Luther King, he walked in the front row at the Selma march) and an early and trenchant opponent of the Vietnam War.

Heschel's conception of religion, particularly of Judaism, is suggested by the titles of two of his most important books: *Man Is Not Alone* and *God in Search of Man*. In a sense, his philosophy of religion is the logical next step after Buber's "dialogical principle," with humanity called into being by God, its meaning and purpose being derived from a relationship with the Almighty. The result is a dialectical interaction between Creator and created. Both are transformed by the relationship, by the power of this meeting. Heschel himself acknowledged the centrality of this concept to his thought, calling it an "absolute presupposition."

Man and woman must transcend their petty, egocentric interests and respond to the Creator with love and devotion. This is the first step towards finding answers to the existential question of alienation that is at the core of humanity in modern society.

At the same time, we must maintain our sense of wonder, of the awe-inspiring mystery of natural existence; this feeling is not inherently Jewish, but is a prerequisite for religious belief, for faith. Heschel is particularly eloquent in his consideration of prayer and the inability of the individual to articulate what he or she feels in the face of this sense of wonder. Revelation is nothing less than the sense of awe we feel when we become aware of being confronted by God in one of these moments of wonder and mystery.

Echoing the kabbalists, Heschel holds that God is moved and affected by our actions (which is, undoubtedly, one of the reasons why the social action component of Judaism resonated so powerfully in Heschel's life and work). Heschel calls this openness of the Eternal to our actions "Divine pathos," and he argues that the Bible itself gives us the best evidence for its reality, depicting Adonai as a caring, moral figure.

The center of much of God's caring is the people Israel. The drama of Jewish history, Heschel says, is the repeated efforts of the Jewish people—often unsuccessful—to respond to their perceptions of God's will. Judaism is nothing less than an ongoing, living relationship with the Creator, and the *halakhah* an attempt to satisfy one term of the relationship. The holy deed, the *mitzvah,* is the uniquely Jewish expression of the human soul responding to the Eternal.[6]

Finally, Heschel expressed the rich tapestry of his ideas in a prose style that reads more like great poetry than anything else. It would not be much of a stretch to argue that Abraham Joshua Heschel, besides articulating a unique and startlingly clear vision of Judaism, is also one of the finest prose stylists Judaism has ever produced.

(N.B.: The quotations that follow are taken from *I Asked for Wonder* and *Quest for God*.)

FROM THE WRITINGS OF ABRAHAM JOSHUA HESCHEL

Faith is real only when it is not one-sided but reciprocal. Man can rely on God, if God can rely on man. To have faith means to justify God's faith in man. Faith is awareness of divine mutuality and companionship, a form of communion between God and man.

The universe is not a waif and life is not a derelict. Man is neither the lord of the universe nor even the master of his own destiny. Our life is not our own property but a possession of God. And it is this divine ownership that makes life a sacred thing.

God is hiding in the world.

Our task is to let the divine emerge from our deeds.

Prayer is a way to master what is inferior in us, to discern between the signal and the trivial, between the vital and the futile, by taking counsel with what we know about the will of God, by seeking our fate in proportion to God.

There are no proofs for the existence of the God of Abraham. There are only witnesses. The greatness of the prophet lies not only in the ideas he expressed, but also in the moments he experienced. The prophet is a witness, and his words a testimony.

JOSEPH SOLOVEITCHIK (1903 C.E.–1993 C.E.)

Like Abraham Joshua Heschel, Joseph Dov Soloveitchik was the product of a long and distinguished line of Orthodox rabbis. Unlike Heschel, Soloveitchik never left the Orthodox fold. On the contrary, by the time of his death, he had become the single most forceful exponent of modern centrist Orthodoxy in the United States and probably the entire world. Yet his thought fits comfortably within the same niche of "Jewish existentialism" as Heschel's, Buber's, and Rosenzweig's.

The biggest difference between Soloveitchik and the other three is that he remained a working rabbi as well as an educator, grappling with the day-to-day realities of ordinary Jews to forge a philosophy that unites Kierkegaard and *halakhah* with intellectual elegance. As head of the Seminary at Yeshiva University, he ordained some two thousand Orthodox rabbis—an entire generation of American Orthodox rabbis—and served as *the* authority on Jewish law for the vast majority of America's Orthodox Jews (even those rightists who today denigrate his contribution).

Joseph Soloveitchik was born in Purzhany, Belarus. He was named for his great-grandfather, Joseph Baer Soloveitchik, who published widely on Talmud and Torah, and who served as a prominent *rosh yeshiva/head of the yeshiva* in nineteenth-century Lithuania. The two Josephs are a pair among a distinguished family of Lithuanian rabbis. The first Joseph was actually trained by his grand-uncle, Isaac, son of the founder of the Volozhin yeshiva. Joseph Baer's son Khayim was famed as the "Brisker rabbi," a scholar whose tenure as rabbi in the city of Brisk included the creation of a new, more scientific method of Talmud study, one that drew heavily on Maimonides' *Mishneh Torah,* and called for a critical independence previously unencouraged. His grandson, Joseph Dov, would develop the "Brisker method" even further. Khayim's sons, Moses and Isaac Zev, both became prominent rabbis, Moses chairing the Talmud faculty at Yeshiva University's Rabbi Isaac Elkhanan Theological Seminary (where Joseph would teach for decades), and Isaac succeeding their father as Brisker rabbi.

This was the heritage that fell upon the shoulders of Joseph and his youngest brother Aaron, who also would become a prominent Orthodox rabbi, based in Chicago for most of his career. Until he was in his twenties, Joseph would study Talmud almost exclusively, mastering the difficult "Brisker method" while still a young man. Working with private tutors he earned the equivalent of a high school diploma then went on to the University of Berlin in 1925. There he majored in philosophy and earned a doctorate in 1931. The following year he emigrated to the United States, settling in Boston. In the U.S., Soloveitchik founded the Maimonides School, the first Orthodox Jewish day school in New England, and served as rabbi of Boston's Orthodox community until 1941, when he was invited to teach at Yeshiva University's theological seminary. He remained a member of the YU faculty until his retirement was forced by ill health in 1985.

Soloveitchik was almost compulsively modest, a perfectionist who seldom could be persuaded to publish his work. His most prominent venue was the annual lecture he gave at the convention of the Rabbinical Council of America, the largest Orthodox rabbinical group in the United States. There he would sit at a table with little more than a book of Talmud, a reference work or two, and a glass of milk, and discourse for anywhere from two to five hours to an audience of his colleagues who were held in rapt attention. His public lectures outside the RCA drew large crowds who were similarly responsive. In his lifetime, Soloveitchik's output consisted of only three slender books, totaling less than 500 pages, each of them an important milestone in Jewish philosophy, *Halakhic Man, The Halakhic Mind,* and *The Lonely Man of Faith.*

What set Soloveitchik apart from his colleagues—and dismayed many of the ultra-Orthodox rabbinate—was his willingness to consider *halakhah* in the light of modern philosophical thought, mostly that of non-Jews, which no doubt multiplied the unease of his colleagues. In a sense, his philosophical work is the logical outgrowth of a world in which it is possible to be a Jew and yet not be governed by *halakhah,* a world in which *halakhah* is an option that one actually chooses. Soloveitchik speaks directly from the traditions of Rabbinic Judaism with unquestioned *halakhic* authority. But he does so drawing on Plato, Kant, and Kierkegaard.

Soloveitchik takes us back to the first Jewish authority, the Torah, and the two parallel accounts of the Creation found in the first two chapters of *Bereishit.* Why are there two accounts of Creation? The question has intrigued rabbinical authorities since the Talmudic period. For Soloveitchik, the two Creations suggest the two types of man: the Adam of Genesis 1, created "in the image" of Adonai, destined to dominate the earth, subduing nature and mastering its laws; the other, emerging in the following chapter, open to the wonder, awe, and mystery of Creation, a questioning, metaphysically concerned man. As Soloveitchik puts it, the second Adam is not concerned with the world, but with its sources, seeking to commune with God by asking those questions. Hence, he breaks humanity into two kinds, the objective-scientific and the subjective-religious. (Of course, these categories are meant to be suggestive; he doesn't believe that there are literally two types of people, etc.)

The first Adam, the scientific creature, seeks for himself the dignity and majesty that should accompany dominion over the natural world. For this, he requires human society, and it is for him that God creates Eve. He lives comfortably in social interaction with other human beings and lives to pursue his technical and biological quests.

By contrast, the second Adam, *homo religiosus* as Soloveitchik designates him at one point, lives not for dignity but for redemption. As Adam I is a social creature, Adam II is an ontological one and, because redemption takes place in the space between human and Creator, a solitary one, "the lonely man of faith," as Soloveitchik phrases it.

It is a key historical irony for Soloveitchik that the technological mastery of Adam I has left humanity increasingly alienated from itself, filled with what the existentialists would call "anxiety," and ever more alone. Of course, each of us contains both Adams, seeking dignity and respect from other humans but turning to God to be redeemed, to be rescued from our loneliness and sense of lack of purpose. When two isolated individuals come together through a shared commitment to seeking God and redemption, the result is a relationship with three units, I-Thou-God. Thus, in such a "covenantal community," the Eternal is always the third, unnamed partner.

Like Buber, Soloveitchik believes in the centrality of dialogue in such relationships. But there is a most important corollary, one that none of the other Jewish existentialists emphasizes as much, the role of *halakhah*. For Soloveitchik *halakhah* is the means by which humans can turn abstract and ill-defined subjective religious feelings into positive moral actions. *Halakhic* man is the partner of God, that partnership solidified by his willingness to submit himself entirely to God's will, by allowing *halakhah* to become the expression of God's omnipresence, the role of the Almighty in every facet of everyday life.

Soloveitchik's thought brings us back to our discussion of the significance that Judaism places on even the most mundane of daily activities, washing, eating, sleeping. *Halakhah* invests each of these and many more with a sense of holiness and of God's immanence in the material world. As Soloveitchik might put it, observance of *halakhah* truly cements our partnership with God in a covenantal relationship, making our goal one with that of the Creator.

(N.B.: The quotations that follow are taken from *The Halakhic Mind* and *Halakhic Man*.)

FROM THE WRITINGS OF JOSEPH SOLOVEITCHIK

Who is qualified to engage God in the prayer colloquy? Clearly, the person who is ready to cleanse himself of imperfection and evil. Any kind of injustice, corruption, cruelty, or the like desecrates the very essence of the prayer adventure, since it encases man in an ugly little world into which God is unwilling to enter. If man craves to meet God in prayer, then he must purge himself of all that separates him from God.

The Shabbat as a living entity, as a queen, was revealed to me by my mother; it is a part of *torat imekha/the teachings of my mother*. The fathers knew much about the Sabbath; the mothers lived the Sabbath, experienced her presence, and perceived her beauty and splendor. The fathers taught generations how to observe the Sabbath; mothers taught generations how to greet the Sabbath and how to enjoy her twenty-four-hour presence.

Halakhic man's ideal is to subject reality to the yoke of the Halakhah. However, as long as this desire cannot be implemented, halakhic man does not despair, nor does he reflect at all concerning the clash of the real and the ideal, the opposition which exists between the theoretical Halakhah and the actual deed, between law and life. He goes his own way and does not kick against his lot and fate.

EMMANUEL LEVINAS (1906 C.E.–1995 C.E.)

Emmanuel Levinas closes the circle of Western philosophy, returning it to its roots in ancient Greece, in Plato and Aristotle, by arguing that the core of philosophical thought is ethical thought. In a much-quoted formulation, he states, "Ethics is first philosophy." At the same time, he recapitulates and refines many themes encountered earlier in this chapter, drawing on his own inventive interpretations of several of the philosophers previously discussed (most notably Rosenzweig, with whom he has pronounced affinities).

Levinas was born in Kaunas, Lithuania, where his father owned a bookstore. During his childhood, the family lived the desperately peripatetic existence that has afflicted many European Jews in this century. His parents were practicing Jews, and Levinas learned Hebrew and Russian as a boy, graduating from the Russian lycée in Kaunas after the family's return there. An avid reader, he immersed himself in the great nineteenth-century Russians, and Dostoevsky's novels would have a particular resonance for his philosophical work later. He was also fluent in German, a language upon which he would draw heavily in the future.

In 1923, the young Emmanuel went to the University of Strasbourg, where he received a degree in philosophy; it was there that he began a lifelong friendship with the French novelist and essayist Maurice Blanchot. It was also there that he discovered the writings of Edmund Husserl, the father of phenomenology (and, coincidentally, a Jew). Levinas spent the 1928–29 academic year at the University of Freiburg where he met and became friends with Martin Heidegger, perhaps *the* pivotal figure in twentieth-century philosophy. Levinas never suspected that Heidegger would eagerly throw in with the Nazis in 1933, being appointed rector of the University by Hitler. In a 1981 interview, he looked back on his long discussions with Heidegger with a rueful nostalgia: "I always try to recapture the atmosphere of those readings, when 1933 was still unthinkable." Elsewhere he would say that although there were Germans who could be forgiven for the Holocaust, he could never forgive Heidegger.

But the influence of the German philosopher on Levinas' thought was profound, and his own French-language book on phenomenology, dealing primarily with Husserl and Heidegger, would be a watershed work, introducing Sartre and other post–World War II French intellectuals to this important school of thought.

The war was a turning point in Levinas' life and career. Before it, he did little work in philosophy itself; after, he would establish himself as a key figure in French thought. Levinas had become a French citizen when he passed his doctorate. Thus it was that in 1939 he was an officer in the French army. When France fell, he was taken prisoner; because of his rank, he was fortunate enough to be treated as a prisoner of war rather than a Jewish prisoner, and spent virtually the entire war as a POW. It was in this captivity that he wrote his first complete book of philosophy, *De l'existence à l'existant* (published in English as *Existence and the Existant*, although that translation loses the movement of the title which literally means "From Existence to the Existant"). Given the circumstances of its composition, it is appropriate that the book represents a deliberate and complete reversal of Heidegger, moving from the ontological—the study of being—to the ontic, being itself. While Levinas was a prisoner of the Germans, his wife and young daughter were being hidden in a monastery. The rest of his family was not so fortunate. Everyone who still lived in Lithuania was murdered in the Nazi death camps.

The post-war French intellectual world was a maelstrom of new thought, spearheaded by the existentialists and phenomenologists, sparked by the likes of Jean-Paul Sartre, Simone de Beauvoir, and Maurice Merleau-Ponty. In this atmosphere, a Jewish teacher attracted little attention, although Levinas was well known as an interpreter of Husserl and Heidegger to the French intelligentsia. This state of affairs didn't really change substantially until 1961, the year in which Levinas published a breakthrough work, *Totality and Infinity*. It was also the year in which he was finally invited to teach at a major French university. He would remain in the French university system until his retirement in 1976. With retirement, Levinas turned his attention to his writing and produced numerous volumes, many of which sold in France at levels unheard of in the United States for serious works of philosophy.

Like his first major influences, Husserl and Heidegger, Levinas' philosophical writings are difficult and highly technical. Yet the ideas are compelling and can be seen as a logical development from Rosenzweig and Buber.

At the heart of Levinas' thought is the concept of Otherness, the Other, and the obligation each human has towards the Other. Significantly, that obligation is ethical in nature and for Levinas the heart of philosophy is ethics. Where Buber emphasizes the voice as the vehicle of the dialogical principle and Rosenzweig the body as a primary physical manifestation, for Levinas the key to ethics is the literally face-to-face encounter with the Other. Levinas' philosophy, then, is grounded first and foremost in the relations *among* human beings. By seeing the face of another we are forced to acknowledge our involvement with the Other. "I cannot disentangle myself from the society of the Other, even when I consider the Being of the existent [i.e., the free subject] he is." Seeing the face of the Other calls up in us the generous desire to do good for the Other. More than that, as Levinas writes in one of the most famous passages in his work, it involves a recognition of a shared humanity and a shared mortality; hence, to see the face of the Other is to be forcibly reminded of the edict, "Thou shall not kill."

What Levinas has done is to reverse the trend of modern philosophy, turning his back on Descartes and virtually everyone who follows him by stating boldly "ethics precedes ontology." Ethical thought comes before any study of the nature of being. Knowledge can only come after we have achieved an ethical relationship, and the first insight of the "thinking I" of the Cartesian *cogito* must be the understanding of our common ground with the Other.

Although Levinas generally considered his Talmudic writings as separate and distinct from his philosophical works, the same themes run through both literatures.[7] His last published book, *New Talmudic Readings,* closes with the statement, "Ontology [is] open to the responsibility for the other." More than that, it is not a great leap to see the intensely ethical bent of his philosophical writings as being of a piece with the key teachings of Judaism. Levinas himself invokes the oft-quoted passages from Torah about the responsibility of the Jew to the "stranger among you," to the widow, the orphan, the poor. Plainly, what Emmanuel Levinas achieves is to unite some of the philosophical advances of the twentieth century with four thousand years of Jewish teaching. In that, he has truly brought us full circle.

(N.B.: The quotations that follow are taken from *Ethics and Infinity, Difficult Freedom,* and *In the Time of Nations.*)

FROM THE WRITINGS OF EMMANUEL LEVINAS

I am always more Responsible than the Other, because I am also Responsible for his Responsibility, and when he is Responsible for my Responsibility, then still I am Responsible for the Responsibility the Other has for my Responsibility: *ein ladavar sof/and this will never end.*

I cannot disentangle myself from the society of the Other, even when I consider the Being of the existent he is.

Morality begins when freedom, instead of being justified by itself, feels itself to be arbitrary and violent.

Since the end of the [Second World War], bloodshed has not ceased.

Racism, imperialism and exploitation remain ruthless. . . . But at least the victims know whither to lift their dying gaze. . . . What was unique between 1940 and 1945 was the abandonment. One always dies alone, and everywhere hapless people know despair. . . . But who will say the loneliness of the victims who died in a world put into question by Hitler's triumphs, in which lies were not even necessary to Evil, certain of its excellence? Who will say the loneliness of those who thought themselves dying at the same time as Justice, at a time when judgments between good and evil found no criterion but in the hidden recesses of subjective conscience, no sign from without?

NOTES

1. Because the focus of this chapter is on those Jewish philosophers whose thought has a direct bearing on issues of the relations between man and God, of spirituality and of Jewish identity, I have omitted several important thinkers who are, of course, Jewish. Karl Marx, Sigmund Freud, Henri Bergson, Walter Benjamin, Theodor Adorno, Ernst Bloch, Ernst Cassirer, Edmund Husserl, Hannah Arendt, and Jacques Derrida (among others) are regrettably but necessarily absent.

2. Maimonides was considered a great physician in his time. Legend has it that Richard the Lion-Hearted asked him to serve in his court. He is also famed for the oath for doctors that is traditionally attributed to him. Actually, the authorship of the oath post-dates Maimonides by several centuries.

3. Spinoza marked his departure from Judaism by changing his name from Baruch to Benedictus—"blessed" in Hebrew, then in Latin.

4. Frederick's toleration had its limits. When the Royal Academy elected Mendelssohn to its ranks in 1771, the king declined to ratify the appointment as was the custom.

5. Even Joseph Soloveitchik, whose intellectual provenance is quite different, can be linked to this chain of modern Jewish thought (see p. 449).

6. Heschel, it should be noted, remained a practicing, observant Jew throughout his entire life, regardless of where he lived or for what denomination he taught. One of the most brilliant of the superb essays in the recent collection of his work, *Moral Grandeur and Spiritual Audacity,* is a speech on *halakhah* that he delivered at a convention of the Reform rabbinate's Central Conference of American Rabbis.

7. In these Talmudic analyses he applied his own methods and thought to Rabbinic Judaism; interestingly, he considered these separate from his philosophical works and even used a different publisher for them. They are notably less opaque than the technical philosophy.

CHAPTER 9

Beyond the Rabbis: How Judaism Got Where It Is Today

As Michael Oppenheim has noted, every philosopher is the product of his or her own history, class, ethnicity, race. It is an indicator of the nature of Jewish history that almost every one of the philosophers discussed in Chapter 8 was pummeled in some way by events that befell his Jewish community. Philo traveled to Rome to appeal to Caligula on behalf of Alexandria's Jews. Maimonides and Judah HaLevi were caught up in the whirlwind of the Crusades and the battle between Christian and Muslim for control of the Iberian peninsula. Spinoza's family fled Spain and the Inquisition, with long-term ramifications that would have an impact on him over a century later. Mendelssohn was able to live in Berlin only at the sufferance of the authorities. Buber, Heschel, Soloveitchik, and Levinas were all touched directly by the Holocaust. It is impossible to conceive of Jewish philosophy, indeed, of Jewish thought of any kind, apart from the extraordinary drama of Jewish history.

More than that, it is impossible to understand Judaism today without understanding where Judaism has been in the past three hundred years. From the state of the State of Israel to the Reform movement's new-found traditionalism, from the divisions within Conservative Judaism to the resurgence of interest in Yiddish, the headlines in this morning's newspaper have their roots in events that have happened to Jews over the past three centuries.

Every significant change in Jewish history that occurred through the *Haskalah / the Jewish Enlightenment* and the Emancipation—the series of sweeping political changes that gave Western European Jews full citizenship—produced a concomitant religious change. Although it existed before the destruction of the Temple, the synagogue became a central institution of Jewish worship life as a response to the tragedy of the destruction of the Second Temple and the bitterness of exile. The writing of the Mishnah and Gemara were the rabbinate's answer to the destruction of the Temple, the creation of a normative Judaism that enabled the Jews to survive an even longer exile than the Babylonians. The influence of Kabbalah was spread by the expulsion of the Iberian Jews. The rise of the most potent (and catastrophic) messianic movement, Shabbateanism, was a response to the pogroms of the 1600s. And the splitting off of new denominations in Judaism grew out of the Emancipation.

However, with Emancipation and the changes in the fabric of Jewish society wrought by the *Haskalah,* a very important shift occurred, a shift in how Jewishness itself was defined. One of the most important results of the *Haskalah*—one entirely unforeseen and unintended by Moses Mendelssohn, a traditionally observant Jew—was that Jewish identity became uncoupled from Jewish belief. For the first time since the Jews were a nomadic tribal group wandering the stony deserts around Palestine, one could be a Jew without believing in the God of Abraham, Isaac, and Jacob. This was a cognitive break that created a new phenomenon: the secular Jew.

The result was a subtle change in the formula stated above, a sort of corollary to Jacob Neusner's observation "that the Judaic religious tradition is shaped by the historical life of the Jewish people." From now on, in addition to changes in religious reality, every change in Jewish history would produce a change in the *political* reality of the Jews.

And every political event would precipitate a new crisis of Jewish identity. The Dreyfus Affair (see p. 484) helped give birth to Zionism, a force that was fueled by every pogrom that would take place in Czarist Russia and, even more intensely, by the fires of the Nazi inferno that consumed six million Jews. The Holocaust forced a serious reevaluation process in Jewish theology and philosophy, but the impact of the new thinking wrought by the Shoah[1] trickled down to the ordinary Jew gradually; the primary impact of the Holocaust took place on the political ground first, in the final victory of Zionism, the founding of the State of Israel. That political change, in turn, would have enormous ramifications for the concept of Jewish identity.

In the twisted mirrors of hatred, one can see these principles of Jewish history played out on a grand scale. If Jewish identity changed, then its enemies would respond in kind. The nature of European anti-Semitism changed after the Emancipation, shifting its aim from a religion to politics and "race."

It should be remembered that before the *Haskalah,* the multiplicity and permanence of the divisions within the modern Jewish world— Orthodox, Reform, Conservative, Reconstructionist, secular, and so on—would have been inconceivable. A Jewish thinker would have lacked both the means and *the need* to formulate the questions that Jews face today. There have always been divisions within the Jewish people. Dating back to the rivalry between Joseph and his brothers, Jews have pitted themselves against one another for as many reasons as there are Jews. Judaism has never been a monolith. The Karaites, the Samaritans, the Essenes, Sadducees, and Pharisees differed from accepted wisdom on matters of religious law. Sephardic and Ashkenazi Jews differed in practice as a result of centuries of parallel development in different parts of the Western world.

But for a period of some 1500 years, the basic choices were Rabbinic Judaism or exclusion. There was no such thing as "orthodox" because that's what everyone was. You were a traditionally observant Jew of some sort or you were an apostate. With the rise of the Hasidim and their conflict with the Mitnagdim, the effects of the Enlightenment on Western Europe's Jews, the rise of secular brands of Jewish identity and the modern denominations of Judaism, everything changed again. A whole new range of choices evolved and Judaism has not been the same since.

THE JEWS IN THE EAST

At the beginning of the eighteenth century, at the birth of the Baal Shem Tov, the overwhelming majority of Eastern European Jews lived in rural areas, scattered through Poland, Ukraine, Lithuania, and Russia. They lived in relative poverty, as farmers, timbermen, carters, peddlers. The small towns in which they lived, called *shtetlakh* (Yiddish;

sing. *shtetl*), are vaguely familiar to us from the stories of Sholem Aleichem or the romanticized version presented in *Fiddler on the Roof*. The *shtetl* would have a *shokhet/ritual slaughterer*, a rabbi, maybe a *kheyder* where the boys would learn a bare minimum of Torah, a *bet midrash* where the townspeople could *daven*. And the town was almost completely Jewish. Everyone spoke Yiddish; some were also fluent in Russian or Polish (depending on where the village was located).

By and large, the Jews were protected by the Polish nobility and the Crown, who needed their organizational skills; Jews served in such unpleasant capacities as estate agents and managers or tax collectors. The Polish Jews enjoyed (if that is the word) considerable political autonomy. The Jewish community was essentially self-governing. Originally, the Jewish community was governed locally by the *kahal,* a community authority that was responsible for almost every aspect of local Jewish life. Eventually, a larger *kahal* was created to govern the "Four Lands," the major provinces of which Poland was composed — Great Poland, Little Poland, Lithuania, and Volhynia. This Council of the Four Lands served as an intermediary between the Jews and the Polish court. The system might have worked, too, had Poland itself not been slipping into chaos.

Although sixteenth-century Poland had been among the most powerful kingdoms in Eastern Europe, it had fallen from that exalted status in less than two hundred years thanks to a decadent Saxon nobility. The Jews had fared little better, attacked first by the Cossacks, then caught between the hammer of Russian soldiers and the anvil of Polish nationalist outrage during the Russo-Swedish War. Add to that the bitter enmity towards the Jews expressed constantly by the Catholic Church in Poland, and it is not hard to see why Polish Jews were desperate. By the time the French Revolution broke out in Western Europe, Poland had been repeatedly partitioned by the greater powers that surrounded her. The Council of Four Lands proved utterly unable to defend the Jews against such outside threats as the Cossacks and the Russians, or the internal anti-Semitism of peasants and Church.

SWORN ENEMIES: HASIDIM AND MITNAGDIM

This was the situation into which the Hasidic movement was born. The theological implications of that birth are discussed in Chapter 7, but the political and social ramifications are no less significant.

There are two diametrically opposed schools of thought on the rise of the Hasidim and their staunch opponents, the Mitnagdim. In the past, historians believed that the Hasidim were rebels against the established but decaying order of the Jewish communities of Volhynia, Ukraine, and Poland, simple men who appealed directly to the semi-literate and illiterate Jews who worked the land and who held the dirtiest jobs in the *shtetlakh,* the blacksmiths and woodcutters, the peddlers and junkmen. By contrast, the Mitnagdim were an intellectual elite, close to the ruling class of the Jewish world, men of great learning who felt threatened by the popularity of the Hasidim among the lower classes. They were enraged by the idea that Talmud Torah was less important than *kavanah* and by Hasidic attempts to spread Kabbalah to the ordinary Jew in the street.

In the past two decades, however, historians have begun to reevaluate that model for these historical developments. They have questioned the degree to which the Hasidim were rebels and the alleged compliance of the Mitnagdim with the wealthy and powerful (such as they were) of East European Jewry. There probably is no single answer.

Hasidism was founded by the Baal Shem Tov, the Master of the Good Name, the *Besht* for short, in the mid-eighteenth century. Born in an era before Social Security numbers and birth certificates, Israel Ben Eliezer, the Besht, is a figure shrouded in some mystery. Some later detractors of Hasidism suggested that he was a mythical figure. Recent findings have not only confirmed his existence but have given some credence to the hagiographical work written by his followers after his death, *Shivhei ha-Besht / In Praise of the Baal Shem Tov.*

Ben Eliezer was born in the village of Okup, in the Carpathian Mountains, sometime between 1698 and 1700. He earned his living either as a schoolteacher or a kosher slaughterer (depending on the source). By all accounts, hostile or favorable, the Besht was a simple and pious man; he was not an outstanding student when young, preferring to go off into the forest to meditate.

According to Hasidic legend, the Besht was thirty-six years old[2] when he revealed his mission to the circle of men with whom he prayed, his *havurah kedisha / holy company.* Before that time he had been one of many men called *ba'alei shem / masters of the name,* itinerant healers and herbalists, peddlers of amulets and would-be magicians. But his new message, of *devekut / cleaving to God, hitlahavut / ecstatic prayer,* and the consciousness of the presence of the Almighty in all things, won him followers far beyond those of an ordinary *baal shem,* as his new name indicated.

There were, at the time, other groups of itinerant mystics, other circles like that surrounding the Besht, but his quickly became the dominant one and the others either joined with him or faded into obscurity. The Hasidic movement grew with surprising rapidity, not with the wildfire intensity of Shabbateanism, but with its own steadier flame.

The comparison is not made casually. To the great Talmud scholars of Vilna, the preeminent center of Jewish learning in all of Eastern Europe, Hasidism must have looked frighteningly like Shabbateanism *redux.* Here was a movement that formed its own breakaway houses of worship, *shteiblakh* (Yiddish; sing. *shteibl*), where they prayed with their own prayer book that incorporated Sephardic rituals derived from Lurianic Kabbalah, where they proclaimed the special powers of their leaders, their miracle-working "wonder rabbis," where worship was so unbridled in enthusiasm that men turned cartwheels during the *Amidah!*

And this was a movement that was growing quickly. As it swept north towards Vilna itself, a confrontation was inevitable.

Is it any wonder that the Vilna Gaon, the foremost Talmudic scholar of the era, probably the greatest living authority on *halakhah,* issued an edict of excommunication against the Hasidim in 1772? To have incurred the wrath of the Vilna Gaon, one must have done something formidably wrong.

In the edict of excommunication, Hasidic worship practice was roundly condemned: "In their recitation of the 18 Benedictions [the *Amidah*] they roar in abominable words in the vernacular and they behave in a crazed manner and say that their thoughts wander in all the worlds. They belittle the study of Torah and repeatedly claim that one should not study much, nor deeply regret one's transgressions."

These men who opposed the Hasidim, who denounced them with such vehemence and bitterness, would come to be known as the *Mitnagdim / Opponents.* Their foremost spokesman was Elijah ben Solomon Zalman, the Gaon of Vilna. The original *Geonim* were the men who had codified much of Jewish law after the Talmud was edited and they actually were chosen community leaders with considerable power. By the time Elijah was born in 1720 C.E. it had been some six centuries since the *Geonim* had been either political or religious leaders. It is a mark of how respected he was that he bore the honorific Gaon.

It was a respect he had earned. The Vilna Gaon was one of the great child prodigies of Talmud Torah, the study of Torah. He gave a sermon in the great synagogue of Vilna before his seventh birthday, and had mastered all of the Tanakh and Talmud, along with the learned commentaries, by the time he was nine. His learning was proverbial; unlike most of his contemporaries, he knew the Palestinian Talmud as well as the Babylonian. He was conversant with the whole range of extant *midrashic* materials and was also a devoted student of Kabbalah. He was also comfortable in numerous secular fields, writing Hebrew books on mathematics, astronomy, and biology.

It is likely, as Rabbi Elijah J. Schochet, author of *The Hasidic Movement and the Gaon of Vilna,* has said, that the anti-Hasidic "edicts may have reflected fears of future developments even more than condemnations for present practices." The Vilna Gaon not only issued the excommunication edict in 1772 and called for the burning of all books of the Besht's teachings, he followed it with a ban nine years later on intermarrying or doing business with Hasidim.

One issue that troubled the Mitnagdim was the fact that the Hasidim favored specially honed knifes for ritual slaughtering. Was it because of the separatism implicit in that choice, because their knives might not be *halakhically* acceptable, or because it meant that followers of the Hasidic movement would not be paying monies to the *kahal* for taxes and fees on kosher slaughtering? The rising influence of a Hasidic rabbi meant an explicit decrease in the power of the local rabbi appointed by the *kahal,* and an implicit rebuke against the *kahal.* Given that the local authorities were responsible for the distribution of tax monies, there was more at stake here than how one *davened* the *Amidah*.

In the past two decades, however, some experts in the field have come to believe that the class issues were not so clear-cut. Yaacov Hasdai has observed that the social criticism found in Mitnagdic literature of the period is actually more trenchant and broad-based than any expressed by the Hasidim of the time, including strong opposition to the workings of the *kahal*. Moshe Rosman has found records in Poland previously unavailable to scholars that reveal that the Besht lived rent-free in a house owned by the Jewish community of Miedzyboz, which suggests that he may have had a more cordial relationship with the ruling elite than previously believed.

Two hundred years after the fact, the larger truth is a bit murky, but the events themselves are quite clear. The 1772 excommunication decree was an act of war, and the Hasids were quick to respond, declaring that the Vilna Gaon was excommunicated. He rejected an offer of a truce from leading Hasidic rebbes. After his death in 1797, matters became even more heated. Economic sanctions were invoked by both sides and vicious and scurrilous attacks were issued in print.

In the meantime, there had been one significant change in the political situation that had a terrible impact on the Jewish community. Poland had been partitioned once again, and the Jews found themselves now under the yoke of the Russian Tsar. Leaders of both the Hasidim and the Mitnagdim denounced one another to the Russian police. In 1804, the Tsar acted to settle the dispute once and for all, issuing an "edict of tolerance" that allowed the Hasidim to carry on their activities without further interference from their opponents. Of course, this statute served the Tsar's purpose of undermining whatever authority remained in the hands of the Mitnagdic forces.

Gradually, the heat of the argument began to cool. Shneur Zalman, who founded the Hasidic dynasty today known as Lubavitch (after the town in which it was centered), believed in a Hasidism that placed great value on Torah learning. Known as *Chabad* (an acronym derived from *Chokhmah/Wisdom, Bina/Insight, Da'at/Knowledge*), it remains one of the largest and most influential of Hasidic groups. Just as the *Chabad* (or Lubavitcher) Hasidim placed greater value on Talmud Torah, Hasidim in general moderated the most outrageous excesses of the early days.

The once-antagonistic movements would now evolve on more or less parallel tracks. The Vilna Gaon would leave a legacy of great Lithuanian Talmudists, scholars who would use his "critical" method of reading Talmud, a method that analyzed textual questions, shifting the emphasis of Jewish learning almost exclusively to the Talmud. (Among his ideological descendants was Rabbi Hayim Soloveitchik, whose grandsons included Joseph Soloveitchik.) Other followers of the Mitnagdic position would develop teachings based on ethical thought, called *Musar*. Spearheaded by Rabbi Israel Lipkin, known as the Salanter (for his hometown of Salant), the *Musar* movement became something of a middle ground between Mitnagdic and Hasidic thought. Salanter and his followers encouraged a constant study of ethics, combined with self-examination and text study, and urged Jews to be active in the daily life of the community.

The Hasidic movement continued to grow, too. But the rise of dynastic lines of *rebbes* led to bitter rivalries, the exaltation of the skills of one's own *rebbe* to the detriment of others, and battles over succession. Still, there were men of great talents who kept the original ideals of the Besht alive, prominent among them his great-grandson, Rabbi Nakhman of Bratzlav (1772 C.E.–1810 C.E.).

The survival of some dynasties and death of others seems to be a matter of luck or Divine choice. Some *tzadikim* died childless, with no obvious heirs. Others suffered a different kind of loss as their children abandoned Hasidism for the blandishments of the New World and a secular life. In the second half of this century, another darker fate befell many of the lines of succession: fully half of Europe's Hasidim were murdered in the Nazi death camps.

The Mitnagdim didn't fare much better when the Nazis came along. Many prominent *roshei yeshivot/heads of yeshivas* emigrated from Lithuania to the United States in the 1930s, establishing Lithuanian-style yeshivot in exotic locales like Brooklyn and Baltimore. But many others died in Auschwitz and Treblinka and Sobibor.

Those who survived from either group were faced with the difficult task of rebuilding after the war. Most found a haven in the United States or the nascent State of Israel. Today there are about a dozen different groups of Hasidim functioning as before in one of those two countries, most prominently the Lubavitch, Bobover, Satmar, and Gerer Hasids. There are Mitnagdic enclaves in both the U.S. and Israel as well, with a thriving Lithuanian-style yeshiva in Jerusalem.

All that was in the future. A catalyst for peace between the warring factions had to make itself felt first. What finally would unite the Hasidim and Mitnagdim was not an act propagated by an outside authority. No "edict of toleration" or moderation of behavior by either camp could do that. It required a new common enemy, a wind out of the west called the Enlightenment.

"WHY DO THEY DRESS LIKE THAT?"

Today, Hasidic men stand out in a crowd. Their mode of dress is instantly distinctive. Black suits with long black coats or a black caftan, white shirts—coat and shirt buttoned right over left, that is, the reverse of conventional men's clothing—white socks, often black knickers, sometimes a *shtreiml*, a round, fur-trimmed hat, a black silk *gartel/girdle* around his waist, and always a beard (as prescribed in the Torah). Their instant visibility has long been a source of derision or outright hostility among non-Hasidic Jews.

To the Hasid, this mode of dress proclaims him a servant of God. His clothing is a constant reminder to the outside world and to himself of his chosen religious discipline, his separateness. Avraham Yaakov Finkel, a Hasidic Jew himself and the author of several books on Hasidism, explains, "His long coat covers his body and de-emphasizes his physicality, especially his organs of digestion and reproduction. The gartel, the black silk belt he wears around his waist during prayer, separates his heart and mind from his animal functions. He buttons his coat and shirt in the reverse manner, from right to left, and wears white socks to remind himself that he is different and is not 'following the customs of the nations' (Leviticus 20:23). His clothes are his badge of honor; they tell him that his conduct should reflect honor on God's name." In some cases, the clothing also has a mystical significance; for example, the *shtreiml* worn by the Satmar Hasidim has 13 tails in it, for the 13 attributes of God's mercy.

At the same time, this mode of dress—based in part on that of the Polish aristocracy of the eighteenth century—hearkens back some three hundred years to the birth of Hasidism in the *shtetlakh* of Poland and Ukraine.

ENLIGHTENMENT AND EMANCIPATION

For the Jews of Eastern Europe, hardship was a way of life, but they had a degree of freedom of movement unknown to their brethren in the West. That would change. With the annexation of most of Poland, Catherine the Great acquired one million Polish Jewish subjects that she didn't want; for three centuries Russia had explicitly excluded Jews.

Beginning in 1795 Catherine's new Jewish subjects were confined to the Pale of Settlement, a rectangular piece of land that essentially consisted of the newly annexed Polish territories. In time, a few successful Jews would be allowed to live outside the Pale of Settlement, but they would require written permission to do so and would need to keep their papers on them at all times, a system that anticipated the bureaucratic racism of Nazi Germany and South African apartheid.

For the Jews of Western Europe, such indignities were familiar and unwanted companions. All over Western Europe during the Middle Ages and the Renaissance, the Jews were set apart by laws that forced them to wear distinctive clothing, hats, or yellow badges, and to live in walled enclaves called ghettoes, under strict curfews that were enforced by the locking-in of the residents at night and on Sundays. They were barred from owning land and from many occupations. Feared as the people who "killed Christ," and who denied Christ's divinity, they were the victims of expulsion from England, Spain, and Portugal, of violent riots in Germany and France, of suspicion everywhere. Nowhere were they citizens. At best they were non-Europeans, reluctantly and grudgingly accepted; at worst they were seen as avatars of the Antichrist.

There was one redeeming feature to this gruesome treatment. The Jewish community was forced to be self-reliant by a society in which every hand was turned against it, allowed to be self-governing because nobody else wanted any part of them. At the beginning of the eighteenth century, there were 400,000 Jews in Western Europe, segregated from non-Jewish society, kept in by the walls of the ghettos, but with complete autonomy within their own realm, with their own social service system, educational system, police, courts, leadership, and institutions.

This, briefly, was the state of Jewish affairs at the dawn of mercantilism, the socio-economic force that would produce the Enlightenment in the West, the birth of democratic societies from the violent labor pains of revolution in America and France, and the totally unlooked-for Emancipation of the Jews in Western Europe. It is important to remember that although no other group was subjected to the array of persecutions visited on the Jews, the very concept of *individual* freedom was in its infancy.

European society before the French Revolution was by and large organized around "corporate" bodies that received privileges in exchange for payment of a fee—the medieval craftsmen's guilds, for example—and "estates" like the Church, manors, universities, towns, and commercial and financial companies. Many religious or ethnic groups were included in this system, including the Jews. The rights of individuals were moot; it was the rights of groups that were safeguarded.

The system was a mixed blessing. Hemmed in on all sides by restrictive laws, Jews could hold only those jobs permitted them by Christian rulers guided by a hostile Christian clergy. But the Jewish community was cohesive and had no problems with continuity. Intermarriage? Unheard of. Conversion? Only at swordpoint during periodic outbreaks of anti-Jewish violence. If a Jew had to wear a yellow badge or a conical hat, had to pay a tax to leave the ghetto by day and to reenter by night, that was the price—quite literally—of doing business in a Christian world.

There were always a few fortunate Jews whose business acumen— usually in banking, one of the fields open to Jews because the Church disdained it as being beneath a Christian—would raise them to a slightly more exalted level. These *Hofjuden/Court Jews* were welcomed by local monarchs, relied upon for loans and financial advice. But they were a tiny handful of individual Jews, no matter how powerful they might become.

Then the Enlightenment came along, spawning revolutions in philosophy and politics, and nothing was the same again. The Enlightenment led to the end of the corporate system, an anachronism ill-suited to a world in which capital and people moved quickly.

How would all this change affect the Jews? In a word, Emancipation. The emancipation of the Jews did not happen all at once. It's not as if someone decided, on the day the French mobs stormed the Bastille, "Hey, as long as we're freeing people, let's liberate the Jews!" Rather, it was a gradual process that occurred at different speeds all over Western Europe. The Sephardim were highly successful in seventeenth-century Holland, where Jewish businessmen quickly became an integral part of the Dutch East India Company. On the other hand, the Venice ghetto would not be closed down officially until 1867.

The French Revolution spelled a definitive end to the corporate system. Within a year of its success, the National Assembly had voted to grant citizenship to the Sephardic Jews of France. On September 28,

1791, the Jews of France who took the oath of citizenship and renounced all previous communal privileges could be citizens. There would be continuing battles for Emancipation in other European countries, but for all intents and purposes this battle had been won. What had the Jews won with Emancipation? Freedom or something more ambiguous?

The walls of the ghetto had kept the Jews in. But they also kept the Christians out. An English travel writer described an event in the Venice ghetto that seems typical; the seventeenth-century poet and diplomat Sir Henry Wotton decided to proselytize on behalf of Christianity in the ghetto and found himself surrounded by Jews who pummeled him soundly and threw him out. No surprise, then, that there were even Jewish leaders who had applauded the erection of the ghetto, seeing it as a safe haven.

For the first time in their history, the Jews were now declared citizens of the nations that were their homes in the Diaspora. They had the same duties and rights as non-Jews. They were expected to become integrated into the society around them. The situation presented entirely new dilemmas, and in addressing them, both Jews and non-Jews were entering an unknown territory.

Emancipation really meant that Jews were to be granted new rights as individuals. They no longer had to wear distinctive clothing. They were no longer confined to the ghettoes. Gradually, in the few extant democracies of Western Europe, Jewish men were granted the franchise.

Previously the Jews had had rights as a group, as members of a group. These rights had helped to preserve the solidarity, the cohesiveness of the Jewish community under constant pressure from their non-Jewish neighbors. Those rights no longer existed.

In their place was an avalanche of problems stemming from one question: Could the Jews maintain their identity as Jews while becoming members of a civil society? That was the Jewish Question.

THE JEWISH QUESTION

Strictly speaking there really were two sets of Jewish questions, one for non-Jews and one for Jews. For the non-Jews the question could be framed, "What do we do with these people? How do we fit them in and where do we draw the line?" For the Jews, the question was, "How do we relate to a civil society dominated by non-Jews? Can we negotiate the terrain between being Jewish and being French, English, German?" These questions had not been asked before because the separation between Jews and non-Jews had hitherto been so rigid, and seemingly permanent.

To the non-Jew, the Jews appeared to be a separate nation with their own communal leaders (both laymen and rabbis), customs, holidays, courts, and laws. How much of that would have to go? Should the Jews get their rights and then be encouraged to adjust to the non-Jewish world, or vice versa? What was it that set the Jews apart anyway?

To the non-Jew of the time, there appeared to be four possible explanations:

1. The Jew is a victim of his environment, of the ghettoes, massacres, restrictive laws, of persecution. He is brighter than most and a capable businessman; treat him fairly and he will make a valuable contribution to society.

2. The Jew is a victim of Judaism. If you can wean him away from the Jewish traditions, from nasty habits like money-lending and speaking Hebrew, get him involved in farming, give him a secular education, he can be a useful addition to society.

3. The Jew is taking jobs and money from good Christians. Expel him and everything will be all right.

4. Science has proven that the Jew is racially inferior. There's nothing we can do to integrate him into civilized society.

These were the non-Jews' answers to the *Judenfrage/Jewish Question*, three of them quite hostile. Is it any wonder that Hitler and his minions referred to the planned extermination of Europe's Jews as "the Final Solution" to the question?

It is hard to discern where all the animus the Enlightenment thinkers bore towards the Jews came from. Voltaire, Diderot, and Montesquieu all derided the Jews, either openly in the first two cases or in unpublished works in the last. For Voltaire, the greatest proponent of free thought and anti-clericalism of his era, disdaining the Jews undoubtedly went hand-in-hand with disdaining the Church; after all, wasn't Christianity the offspring of Judaism? If one rejects revelation in favor of human reason, then isn't the revelation at Mount Sinai to be as disdained as the Sermon on the Mount?

But even the *defenders* of Jewish rights did so in terms that were little short of derisory. Consider this passage by Christian Dohm from an essay in defense of equal rights for Jews written in 1781: "[T]hey have a strong tendency to be on the lookout for every sort of gain and they love usury. . . . These defects are made worse in many of them by their self-imposed isolation which is based on their religious laws and on rabbinic sophistry."

What all these writers have in common, what all four answers to the Jewish Question have in common (besides the assumption that the Jews couldn't continue *status quo*), is that they represent a definite break with the terms of past debates about the Jews. They had moved from the religious anti-Judaism of the Church Fathers and the medieval period to something altogether different, a phenomenon that would not have a name until the 1870s when one of its enthusiastic practitioners, Wilfred Marr, called it anti-Semitism.

For the Jews, the Jewish Question presented a whole new set of issues and a challenge to traditional Jewish religious ideas. In the past, *halakhah* had united the Jewish people. Indeed, it had marked them off from other peoples in ways that were immediately apparent. Jews dressed differently even when the secular laws didn't require them to. They couldn't eat with non-Jews because of their dietary laws. They didn't work on Saturdays, but would work on Sundays.

The Jews found themselves in an unfamiliar position. With Emancipation, with the privileging of individual rights over the prerogatives of the group, Jews—individual Jews, not THE Jews—could make their own choices, indeed, *had* to make their own choices. Religion would become a matter of individual conscience, of choice rather than birth. (As one pundit has observed, "We are all 'Jews by choice' today.")

A primary assumption of philo-Semitic non-Jews regarding the Emancipation was that the Jews would integrate themselves into the societies in which they lived. That meant that Jews now had to choose *how* Jewish they should be: should they abandon their communal, cultural, national, religious identities and blend in? Should they embrace the universalist ideals of the Enlightenment and turn their backs on the particularism of their forefathers and mothers? Give up the idea of Chosen-ness? Did the Jews still have a historic mission to serve as "a light unto the nations"? As Jews were they responsible for fellow Jews in other lands? If so, what of the claim by Jew-haters that the Jews possessed "dual loyalties" and couldn't be trusted to defend the interests of the homeland before those of world Jewry? In the same vein, what happened to the idea of a return to a Jewish homeland in Palestine? What happened to those elements of Judaism—dress, dietary laws, language—that set the Jews apart from their neighbors?

The answers to those questions found expression in two different battlegrounds, the religious and the secular, with the birth of Reform Judaism and the responses it engendered as the manifestation of the religious, and the *Haskalah,* with its own diverse set of offspring, the secular. And in each case, it was the Orthodox Jews—as they were now being called—who offered a vehement counterpoint, calling for the Jewish people to turn their backs on the temptations of Emancipation, assimilation, and, as they saw it, disintegration.

SWORN ENEMIES: REFORM AND ORTHODOX

While the first major schism within traditional Judaism occurred in Eastern Europe, the next challenge came from the West and was precipitated, ironically, by a traditionally observant Jew. Moses Mendelssohn never intended to undermine traditional Judaism (see pp. 428–33); he remained what we would call an Orthodox Jew until his death in 1786. Whether he knew it or not, he had set the stage for the Reform movement to challenge Orthodoxy from within the family, never more so than when he translated the Tanakh into German.

This is the paradox that Mendelssohn embodied, a paradox enacted by the translation of Torah into the vernacular. To read Torah in the vernacular was to acknowledge implicitly that one was now divided between competing identities, Jewish and German (or French or English or American).

Reform Judaism was one response to that paradox, an attempt to remake the old ways to fit a radically changed world. The first stirrings of what would eventually become Reform took place in the late 1790s when several radical thinkers who felt that traditional Judaism was insufficiently responsive to the changed circumstances of the German

Jewish community attacked the established Jewish leadership. In 1810, Israel Jacobson, a layman, acted on their ideas. (It's interesting to note that the original impetus for Reform came not from the rabbinate but from laypeople, indicative of a seismic shift that took place in the German Jewish community, with the rabbinate no longer lawmakers and judges but, like their Protestant counterparts, "clergymen.") Jacobson opened a chapel—complete with choir and organ—at a private school he had founded in Seesen, a town in Westphalia in the Harz Mountains. Sermons were delivered in German. Services were shorter and people prayed in unison or not at all. Significantly, Jacobson invited local Christian leaders to attend the dedication and first service and they were suitably impressed. Five years later, Friedlander instituted similar services in Berlin but the local government banned them after 1817 in response to the local Orthodox rabbinate, a last gasp of Orthodox power.

The following year, 1818, saw the dedication of the first actual Reform synagogue, the Hamburg Temple. The founders chose October 18 for this solemn occasion. It was not a Jewish festival day; it was the anniversary of the famous German victory in the Battle of Leipzig. By the choice of date and name, the Reformers were sending a clear message. Germany—not Zion—was their home. They were good German patriots, celebrating a great day in German history. They no longer looked to the Temple in Jerusalem—they had their own "temple" right in Hamburg. (Incidentally, that is why Orthodox congregations are never named "Temple So-and-so.") They wanted to emulate their Christian neighbors. Services were conducted in German. Prayer books opened from the left, unlike a Hebrew *siddur* which opens from right to left. There was a mixed-gender choir and an organ.

How did traditional Jews respond? The *bet din,* the rabbinic court in Hamburg, was infuriated. They denounced the Reformers as ignorant of Jewish law and claimed that praying in the vernacular and the use of musical instruments were strictly proscribed. In their responsum, the rabbis wrote, "[T]hese people have no religion at all. All they want to do is to show off before the Christians as being more learned than other Jews."

The response of the Reformers was swift and erudite. The wonderful irony here is that they wrote in Hebrew—demonstrating their knowledge of the *lashon kodesh/holy tongue*—to justify praying in German. Conversions out of Judaism—one of the many unlooked-for "benefits" of the Emancipation—were increasing rapidly all over Germany, but Jews were coming to the Hamburg Temple in defiance of that trend, the Reformers said.

Reform began to stake out positions that were increasingly radical and deliberately conceived as a rebuke to traditional Jews. In 1842, the Society of Friends of Reform was founded in Frankfurt with a platform that explicitly rejected the validity of the Talmud. Another Frankfurt-based group, founded three years later, held its services on Sundays, entirely in German, and the men didn't cover their heads. The same year, a Reform group in Berlin rejected Hebrew, head-covering for men, and the blowing of the *shofar.*

New battle lines were being drawn.

SWORN ENEMIES: THE RABBIS AND THE *HASKALAH*

The Orthodox rabbis had anticipated something like this. From the outset, they had been opposed to Emancipation, believing that exposure to mainstream non-Jewish culture would introduce temptations to many Jews. They were even more ill-disposed towards the *Haskalah,* the Jewish Enlightenment. Even though Moses Mendelssohn was an observant Jew, the rabbis banned the reading of his German translation of the Torah. With a sudden and explosive rise in conversions to Christianity affecting the German-Jewish community, the empirical case for the rabbis' position couldn't have been much stronger, although some of those conversions were at best reluctant.

But the rabbis were swimming against the tide of history. Mendelssohn had established the first of what would eventually be many Jewish schools in which secular subjects were taught alongside religious ones. His followers and other *maskilim* (adherents of the *Haskalah*) would follow suit.

An eclectic movement, the *Haskalah* did not speak with one voice, but when it did, the voice resembled that of Moses Mendelssohn. Like Mendelssohn, the *maskilim* believed in rationalism, rejected supernaturalism in religion, yet by and large remained committed to some kind of Jewish identity. The forms that such identity took varied widely (and sometimes wildly), and eventually led to a series of splits within its adherents.

The more moderate *maskilim* embraced the notion that the Jewish people could find new meaning through Hebrew literature—not the sacred texts of old, but a new secularized Hebrew literature that reflected the interests and concerns of contemporary German and Austrian Jewry. For the first time in perhaps a thousand years, new texts were being produced in Hebrew by poets, journalists, and essayists.

Despite their religious conservatism, what the German Hebrew *maskilim* envisioned was a revival of Hebrew as a language for a Jewish intellectual elite, with German as the language of everyday life. The Hebrew texts they favored were secular. They were fascinated by German literature, and that fascination would be even stronger when the *Haskalah* finally took root in Eastern Europe, particularly in Russia. As Jacob Raisin wrote in 1913, "Germany was to the Jewish world during the early *Haskalah* movement what France was to Europe during the Renaissance."

The Russian town of Shklov became a lively center of Hebrew *Haskalah* literature. Rav Judah Leyb Margoliot published *Bet Midot/House of Measures* in Shklov in the 1780s; this volume was an introduction to medieval Jewish philosophy that focused on its rationalist strain, omitting any mention of mysticism. Naftali Hirtz Schulman, another Shklov-based writer, wrote a 1797 Hebrew edition of *Hope of Israel*, a seventeenth-century volume on the discovery of America, written by a Dutch rabbi, Manasseh ben Israel; as Professor David Fishman notes, "No Hebrew book ever printed in Poland or Russia was as replete with citations of Gentile literature and as skimpy on rabbinical material." Russian Jews had to open their eyes to an entire world of non-Jewish literature and learning. (The first modern drama composed in Hebrew, *War Against Peace* by Hayim Avraham Katz, was also published in Shklov in 1797.)

The *Haskalah* began to suffer divisions as it moved eastward. There were, it seemed, as many ways to be an emancipated Jew as there were ways to be a religious one. In a world in which rationalists were challenging the wisdom and power of religion, secularism was the rising tide; in the Jewish world, most of the new ways of being a Jew were secular ways.

The most prominent example of a secular movement fueled by the energies and blood of Jews was the multifaceted socialist movement. Of course, Karl Marx himself was an apostate, a baptized Jew, as were significant figures in the Russian Revolution, most notably Leon Trotsky (born Lev Davidovich Bronstein). But there were also Jewish socialists who insisted on retaining their Jewish identity even as they rejected their Jewish religious training.

Their numbers overlapped with that of another devoutly secular group, the Yiddishists, men and women who embraced the use of Yiddish, one of the many languages created by Jews in the Diaspora, as a vehicle for the expression of a Jewish identity that retained only an oblique relationship to religion. But the Yiddishists would be left behind by history, the victims of the success of another brand of post-Emancipation Jewish thought, Zionism.

YIDDISH: THE "MOTHER TONGUE"

As a people in seemingly perpetual exile, the Jews have had to learn new languages wherever they have landed. Understandably, they also developed dialects that addressed specifically Jewish circumstances, composed of borrowed vocabulary from their non-Jewish neighbors blended with the Semitic languages of their forebears. (The written versions of these dialects would use the Hebrew alphabet.) One finds a wealth of folk and fine literature in Ladino (a Judeo-Spanish that has its roots in the Iberian peninsula but which spread throughout the Sephardic world after the Expulsion in 1492; see sidebar "Ladino," p. 480), Judeo-Persian, Judeo-Greek, and others.

But no Diaspora-born Jewish language made a greater impact on the Jewish world or on non-Jews than Yiddish. Yiddish can claim with some justice to be one of the most widespread languages spoken on this planet, a language that was heard from Argentina to Armenia, from Los Angeles to London. Yiddish words and phrases pepper contemporary English. The works of the great Yiddish writers are read in translation all over the world. And a group of Yiddish writers and ideologues tried to make the language, affectionately known to its speakers as the *mame-loshen/mother tongue*, into the *lingua franca* of the East European *maskilim*.

Historians trace the roots of Yiddish back as far as the ninth century, when the language first began to evolve in southern Germany as a specifically Jewish variant of Middle High German. There was a vital Yiddish literature long before the *Haskalah*. Although Yiddish texts of the early medieval period have not survived, there is evidence of Yiddish literature as early as the thirteenth century. The earliest Yiddish texts are glosses on biblical texts and *midrashim*. The earliest known printed Yiddish book is a Hebrew-Yiddish concordance of the Tanakh, published in Krakow in 1534. Within a decade, there were Yiddish versions of the Pentateuch being published in Germany and a *Taytsh-Khumesh*, a Yiddish version of the Torah that also included the *Five Megillot* and Rashi's commentary, appeared in Cremona, Italy, in 1560.

Yiddish was the language of the Jew in the street and versions of sacred texts published in Yiddish made them accessible to the ordinary, unscholarly man and woman. For Jewish women, who were discouraged from learning Hebrew (when not prohibited outright), Yiddish glosses on Torah became a passageway into the holy. The most famous of these, *Tzena Urena*, is a full-fledged biblical commentary that has remained in print constantly since the sixteenth century, having been issued in over two hundred different editions.

Yiddish also became the chosen language of daily life for the Hasidim and the *Musar* movement (see p. 466). One did not use the *lashon hakodesh* for anything but prayer and meditation; its homelier Germanic counterpart was acceptable for more mundane matters.

The fact that it was a language favored in literature written mostly for women (and for men who had no Hebrew) undoubtedly contributed to the low regard in which Yiddish was held by Jewish intellectuals at the outset of the *Haskalah*. German *maskilim* were appalled by the idea that they would be identified with this gutter "jargon," they who spoke and wrote fluently in modern German, who had mastered the intricacies of Hebrew. It is one of the ironies of the history of the *Haskalah* that the German *maskilim* rejected Yiddish, leaving it for some of the East European *maskilim* to champion. (Of course, for many of the East European *maskilim*, Yiddish was supposed to be the rising tide that would lift Jewish boats intellectually; after that, it could be discarded as an unnecessary reminder of the ghetto.) The result of this development was that Yiddish developed a sophisticated secular literature in Russia, Ukraine, and Poland while it nearly disappeared in Germany (with the added result that the medieval Yiddish classics produced in Germany were surpassed in fame by German Hebrew literature).

In Eastern Europe, Yiddish became the language of the *Haskalah* and it produced a vibrant literature that depicted the life of the *shtetl* vividly, without sugar-coating the poverty, ignorance, bigotry, and superstition that one could find there in abundance. The Eastern *maskilim* enlivened Yiddish with new admixtures drawn from their Slavic environment, and a passionate disdain for their religious Yiddish-speaking counterparts, the Hasidim and Mitnagdim. The three giants of modern Yiddish literature, Mendele Mokher Sforim, Sholem Aleichem, and Yitzhak Leib Peretz, nurtured several generations of fine poets, novelists, short-story writers, essayists, journalists, and playwrights. Had the vast Yiddish-speaking and -reading populations of Russia, Ukraine, and Poland not been decimated by Hitler and Stalin, had their American equivalents not gradually abandoned the *mame-loshen* for American English, this literary renaissance might have continued unabated to this day.

Although the secular Yiddishists are probably not too thrilled to admit it, Yiddish remains the daily language of the Hasidim and Mitnagdim even today. They do not speak Hebrew except in prayer and, like their forebears, are essentially bilingual, using the language of their present place of residence when necessary and Yiddish among themselves. They may not be producing literature of the caliber of Sholem Aleichem or Isaac Bashevis Singer, but they *are* daily users of the *mame-loshen*, and their children undoubtedly will continue to be the same.

There are two other hopeful signs for the future of the Yiddish language. First, there has been a steady and rapid growth of interest in Yiddish in the universities, both in the U.S. and elsewhere around the globe. Granted, university programs in Yiddish are unlikely to provide a new generation of speakers and writers; Columbia, Fordham, and NYU have been teaching Latin for years with no noticeable increase in the number of Latin speakers on the New York City subways. However, we can count on such programs at the very least to guarantee some effort to preserve the literary heritage that already exists.

But there also is a very real movement among circles of politically progressive secular Jews who grew up in Yiddish-speaking households to revive spoken Yiddish in their own homes and with like-minded friends. It would be rash to make predictions; it should be remembered that when Eliezer Ben-Yehuda and his wife Deborah decided in the 1880s that their children would be raised speaking Hebrew, their oldest was the first child raised in a Hebrew-speaking household in something like a millennium. Who would have predicted that from little Itamar Ben-Avi would come an entire modern nation speaking Hebrew?

LADINO

Ladino (sometimes called Judeo-Spanish) is a Romance language still spoken by Sephardic Jews in the Balkans, Greece, Turkey, Israel, and the Maghreb. Like Yiddish, Ladino's pool of speakers was devastated by the Holocaust; Jewish communities in Greece and the Balkans were decimated by the Nazis. (These were substantial Jewish enclaves before the Holocaust; the Jewish-dominated port of Salonika, Greece, would close down on Saturdays.)

Ladino offers some interesting insights into the evolution of the language from which it was derived, in this case Spanish. Much as Yiddish does for German, Ladino preserves words and grammatical usages that have been lost in modern Spanish. The language is written in Hebrew characters (also like Yiddish). Ladino words turn up in the writings of Joseph Caro, and it is very likely that it was the day-to-day spoken language of the kabbalists of Safed.

THE ZIONISTS

The Jewish past is littered with the dreams of visionaries like the Yiddishists, trampled underfoot by the march of history, which usually wears jackboots. But not all visionaries fail. Theodor Herzl wrote of the budding Zionist movement, "If you will it, it is no dream." His vision would not become a reality during his lifetime, but it would become a reality.

The roots of the idea of Jewish nationhood are buried deep in the rich soil of Torah and the first gardeners to tend it predate Herzl by a century. As such, they were of a piece with the *zeitgeist* of nineteenth-century Europe as much as any element in their Jewish heritage.

The nineteenth century was a time of great nationalist upheavals. The revolutions of 1848, Garibaldi's valiant efforts in Italy, numerous uprisings against the Ottoman Empire that led romantic figures like Lord Byron to die fighting for freedom in Greece—this was the atmosphere of the time. Jewish thinkers were hardly immune to it.

One could argue with some truth that Zionism—the idea of an independent, autonomous Jewish nation-state located in Palestine—really goes back to the time of Moses as he trekked through the wilderness with six hundred thousand Jews, slowly approaching a land promised to them by God. But whatever the merits of those claims, the ancient nation of Israel had foundered badly, divided, and died over centuries. The remnants of that nation were now wandering again, cast into *galut/exile*. By the nineteenth century, many Jews were inured to the state of things, but with the *Haskalah* and the nationalist fervor seizing Europe, new possibilities began to present themselves. Writers like Peretz Smolenskin were turning Hebrew back into a viable literary language, and the *maskilim* were insisting on the value of Jewish history and culture. Eliezer Ben-Yehuda was beginning to reinvent Hebrew as a modern language.

ELIEZER BEN-YEHUDA

Ben-Yehuda is often and rightly called the "father of Modern Hebrew." Born Eliezer Yitzhak Perelman in Lithuania in 1858, he studied medicine in Paris until felled by the tuberculosis that was to plague him his entire life. Abandoning medicine and seeking a warm, dry climate, he accepted a place in Palestine in the teachers' program of the Alliance Israelite Universelle, a French-Jewish educational group that ran schools throughout North Africa and the Middle East that gave birth to several generations of Jewish educators, intellectuals, and administrators.

By 1880 Ben-Yehuda was a vocal and visible advocate for the teaching of Hebrew and its adaptation as the official language of instruction in all the Jewish schools in Palestine. It was a position not calculated to endear him to the Orthodox rabbis of *Eretz Yisroel* for whom Hebrew was *lashon kodesh/the sacred tongue*, only to be used for prayer and meditation. They would attempt to have him removed from his post and the country and he would spend a year in jail over false charges they lodged against him.

In 1881 Ben-Yehuda married a childhood friend, Deborah Jonas. The couple settled in Jaffa, speaking only Hebrew at home. When their son, Ben-Zion (later Itamar Ben-Avi), was born, they raised him speaking Hebrew exclusively at home as well; thus, the Ben-Yehudas were the first Hebrew-speaking household in Palestine in perhaps a thousand years and Ben-Zion was the first Modern Hebrew–speaking child.

Ben-Yehuda was a tireless proselytizer for the Hebrew language. In addition to teaching in the Alliance's Jerusalem school, he founded two Hebrew-language journals and wrote prolifically for them. After Deborah died in 1891, he married her sister, Hemdah, who also became a productive Hebrew translator and writer.

In 1890 Ben-Yehuda and a group of colleagues founded the organization Va'ad Ha-Lashon, which would eventually evolve into the Hebrew Academy; this institution serves much the same function for the Hebrew language as the Academie Française does for French, certifying new words for inclusion in the standard Hebrew dictionaries. It may be in the field of lexicography that Ben-Yehuda made his most lasting contribution. His most ambitious project, completed after his death by his son, was a massive, seventeen-volume dictionary of Modern Hebrew, the definitive work of its kind, and still the basis of Modern Hebrew as spoken in Israel.

Ben-Yehuda's achievement is nothing short of remarkable. Working virtually alone, he revived a "dead" language that had not been spoken outside of a synagogue for centuries. He created a new Hebrew vocabulary adapted to the needs of the modern world, literally inventing new words for technologies and phenomena that had been unknown in the time of the Bible. More than that, by his tremendous energy he managed to make this revitalized language the coin of the realm in a Jewish world that had long since abandoned its everyday use.

The first advocates of Jewish nationalism were both Orthodox rabbis. In fact, Zevi Hirsch Kalischer, one of the two, was a student of the great Akiva Eiger and a staunch and vocal opponent of Reform Judaism, while Judah Alkalai was a Sephardic rabbi with a secure grounding in Kabbalah. Each of them arrived independently at the idea that the Jewish people must prepare for the arrival of the Messianic Age by actively working for a Jewish home in Palestine. The third forerunner of the Zionist movement was a socialist, Moses Hess, a close friend of Karl Marx. (Indeed, the phrase "religion is the opiate of the masses" from *The Communist Manifesto* was Hess's contribution to his friend's famous book.) Hess, however, watched with interest as Garibaldi and other Italian nationalists fought to unify their country; and he was not oblivious to the rampant anti-Semitism growing in post-Emancipation Germany. He returned to his Jewish roots to espouse a new kind of socialism, a Jewish nationalism that would create a socialist state in Palestine.

Hess was not the only Jew who was disturbed by the new waves of anti-Semitism. Leon Pinsker could have told him that things were a lot worse in Russia than they were in Germany. Born in 1821 in what was then Russian Poland, Pinsker had believed, like many *maskilim,* that if Jews were given their full political rights, the Jewish Question would be resolved peaceably. The wave of anti-Jewish riots that swept Russia in 1881 disabused him of any further notions along those lines. The following year he published his book *Auto-Emancipation,* calling for a renewed national consciousness among the Jewish people and a struggle for an independent Jewish homeland.

The ideas were in place. Men and women were acting on them. In the wake of the 1881 pogroms, young Russian Jews were leaving for Palestine. In Kharkov, Russia, an organization called BILU *(Bet Ya'akov Lechu Venelkhah/O House of Jacob, Let Us Go Up)* was formed in 1882, inspired by Pinsker's book; its members left for Palestine, the first Jews to "make *aliyah,*" to emigrate permanently to *Eretz Yisroel.* Two years later, another organization, *Hovevei Yisroel/Lovers of Israel,* was founded in Odessa for the same purpose.

All that was missing was a charismatic leader who would work untiringly for the Zionist cause. Such a leader was about to emerge from the most unlikely place.

HERZL AND HIS SUCCESSORS

He was as totally assimilated as any nineteenth-century Jew could be without actually converting. He was a failed playwright and a successful journalist. In short, Theodor Herzl was an unlikely candidate to lead world Jewry back to the Promised Land.

Herzl's story has become so well-known that it becomes difficult to separate fact from legend, and he was never adverse to embellishing his role. He was born to a well-to-do Jewish family in Budapest in 1860. Herzl was raised squarely in the traditions of the *Haskalah;* his family belonged to the city's Liberal Temple and young Theodor celebrated his *bar mitzvah* there. He received an excellent secular education and when the family moved to Vienna, he entered the university in the Austrian capital. Herzl pursued a law degree there and completed it in 1884.

Although he experienced some anti-Semitism at the University of
Vienna, Herzl would remain a Jew, albeit a comfortably assimilated
one. When his first son was born in 1891, he didn't bother to have the
boy circumcised.

Herzl was one of those people who go through life convinced that they
are destined for greatness. He had no idea in what forum he would
achieve that status, but he was convinced it would come. Uninterested in
the law, he began a career as a journalist shortly after receiving his
degree, writing plays (of no particular merit) on the side. As a journalist
he had a certain gift and by 1894 was the Paris correspondent of Vienna's
Neue Freie Presse. It was there that Herzl would cover a story that changed
his life, or so the story goes, the trial of Captain Alfred Dreyfus.

Dreyfus was another assimilated Jew, so assimilated that he had risen
to a position of some sensitivity in the French Army. His elevated position combined with his Jewishness to make him a perfect fall guy for a
fellow officer who was spying for the Germans. Tried for espionage and
treason, Dreyfus was found guilty on less than compelling evidence and
sentenced to life imprisonment in the penal colony at Devil's Island.

It is impossible to overestimate the significance of the Dreyfus Affair
in French life in the 1890s. The matter would drag on for several years
as evidence was uncovered that Dreyfus had been framed. The French
Army and the French courts refused to pardon him even in the face of a
confession from the actual perpetrator. Eventually, with popular novelist Emile Zola (a non-Jew) championing his cause, Dreyfus would be
released from prison.

The French people were split violently over the case and the Dreyfus
Affair echoed through French politics, through the Nazi occupation and
after, virtually up to the present. It exposed a deep seam of anti-
Semitism beneath the surface of "Liberty, Equality, Fraternity."

Covering the case for his newspaper, Herzl was initially convinced of
Dreyfus' guilt, but he was appalled by the mobs in the streets calling
"Death to the Jews!" as Dreyfus was stripped of the symbols of his military rank. When the Vienna municipal elections ended with the self-
proclaimed anti-Semite Karl Lüger elected on a platform of Jew-
baiting, Herzl began to rethink his position on the Jewish Question.

Did Herzl dash from the humiliation of Dreyfus to his desk to begin
writing what would become *Die Judenstadt / The Jewish State*? So the legend goes. There is nothing in his meticulously kept diaries to suggest

the impact of the trial in his mind was quite so immediate, but it is indisputably true that the one event followed shortly after the other. *The Jewish State* is a disappointing read. For all the historical importance of the book, it is dry, even dull. The Israeli writer and translator Hillel Halkin has observed that "large sections of it read more like a stock market prospectus than a call for national independence." Which is deliberate, as Halkin himself admits.

Herzl was a man of the world, a sophisticated political correspondent. He knew that the idea he was advancing would seem quixotic at best, insane at worst, unless it was presented in the most coolly dispassionate tones. The heart of *The Jewish State* essentially *is* a stock prospectus, as Herzl explains how the creation of "The Jewish Company" will make it possible to raise funds to buy land and resettle millions of Jews somewhere on earth in a Jewish homeland.

There is one significant difference between *The Jewish State* and, say, *Auto-Emancipation*. Herzl would make it happen. Herzl had finally found his cause, the vehicle that would bring him the fame he craved. And he seized it with both hands and all his might.

Whatever shortcomings Herzl may have had as a writer, he was a tremendously energetic wheeler-dealer and, by sheer force of will, an organizer. He began his campaign by contacting the wealthy and powerful, Baron de Hirsch and Baron Rothschild, neither of whom showed any interest in his project. Their rebuffs did not slow him down. He lobbied and wooed supporters, gathered important contacts from sympathizers, and worked his way up the ranks of the nobility, from the Grand Duke of Baden to the Sultan of the Ottoman Empire.

Herzl was a master of gamesmanship, and he would need to be. As David J. Goldberg wryly observes:

> To Germans he implied that the proposed Jewish territory would become an outpost of Berlin; to the British, that it would seek colonial status; to the Turks, that Jewish capital would alleviate their chronic economic situation; to the Jewish bankers, that it only required their loans for everything to fall into place.
> —*To the Promised Land: A History of Zionist Thought*

Perhaps, as Goldberg surmises, Herzl was making it up as he went along, lurching from one outpost of power to another with nothing more calculated than desperation guiding him. But his handling of the Jewish world suggests a shrewder mind at work, for this would be his toughest sell: to pull together a fractious and divided people for a founding meeting that would create a vehicle to make the Zionist dream a reality.

Herzl called the First Zionist Congress for 1897 in response to the pointed rejection of his plans by Edmond de Rothschild. If class wasn't interested, perhaps mass was. If he couldn't appeal to the richest Jews, maybe he could rally the poorer ones—there certainly were more of them.

Herzl contacted Zionists of every political stripe from all over Russia and Europe, often personally. And they came. On August 29, 1897, the First Zionist Congress convened, with 250 delegates attending from 24 different nations. Herzl was acclaimed as a hero, the last time he would enjoy such unalloyed triumph. Future Zionist Congresses—and they would be held every year until the founding of the State in 1948— would be more contentious and Herzl himself would be on the receiving end of the acrimony on more than one occasion. But the Zionist movement was suddenly more than just the writings of a few obscure Jews in pamphlets or ill-distributed books. Herzl would not live to see the creation of a Jewish homeland; he died only two months after his forty-fourth birthday. But his efforts laid the foundation of the Jewish State, just as he had triumphantly proclaimed in his diary: "At Basel I founded the Jewish State. If I said this out loud today, I would be answered by universal laughter. Perhaps in five years, and certainly in fifty, everyone will know it." He was only off by one year.

The First Congress was relatively uncontentious, with the delegates suitably awed at Herzl's success in making the Congress happen at all, but there were rumblings of dissent almost immediately. In the aftermath of the First Zionist Congress, Herzl had written, "At Basel I founded the Jewish State." Asher Ginsburg—better known by his pen name *Ahad Ha'am/One of the People*—wrote, "At Basel I sat solitary among friends, like a mourner at a wedding feast."

It would be hard to imagine two more dissimilar men working for the same goal than Theodor Herzl and Asher Ginsburg. Where Herzl was grandiloquent, melodramatic, narcissistic, Ginsburg was spare, austere, stern. Herzl, with his deep, sad eyes and luxurious beard, cut a dramatic figure; Ginsburg, bald, with a neatly trimmed goatee and mustache and pince-nez glasses, looked like a bad-tempered schoolmaster. Herzl craved followers and the spotlight; Ginsburg hated expressions of fealty from those who orbited in his powerful gravitational field, and turned down repeated offers of positions of power. Even their prose was notably different. Herzl wrote a soaring, almost bombastic German, Ginsburg a coolly lucid Hebrew.

But what really led Ahad Ha'am to break with Herzl from the very outset of the modern Zionist movement was a complete lack of congruence between the two men's ideas of what such a movement should aspire to. Herzl was the avatar of what quickly became known as "political Zionism," a movement dedicated to working the diplomatic channels and financial world to secure a Jewish State, a homeland that would be a political entity as well as (or instead of, depending on who one asked) a religious one.

Ahad Ha'am was the first and foremost spokesman for "cultural Zionism." Raised in a Hasidic household, he had discovered for himself the fascination of secular studies, and his youthful reading of the French positivist Comte and others had shattered his religious faith. But he remained deeply committed to Jewish peoplehood and to finding a synthesis between Jewish thought and European philosophy and literature. Thus, when the young Ginsburg joined *Hovevei Zion* he quickly became a critic of its settlement-building agenda, positing in its place a search for Jewish cultural regeneration and the revival of Hebrew. For Ahad Ha'am, a Jewish homeland would exist as a beacon to Diaspora Judaism, a center of explicitly Jewish cultural life that would reinforce Jewish values in the Diaspora.

Ahad Ha'am was no activist. He was not a programmatic thinker. The men and women who espoused socialist and Marxist versions of Zionism were the exact opposite. Nakhman Syrkin and Dov Ber Borochov believed that capitalism's inexorable growth in Europe and Russia would drive the Jews into a choice between the misery of the urban proletariat and periodic pogroms or an exodus to Palestine. Once in Palestine, they could construct a socialist state, a society in which a Jewish proletariat led the class struggle with a goal of the liberation not only of world Jewry but of the working classes everywhere. The socialist-Zionist movement split into many smaller groupings, some openly Marxist, others social-democratic in nature. The largest impact of the Socialist Zionist formations came in the youth groups they spawned,

Hashomer Hatz'air and *Hekhalutz* most prominently, and the active role that these teenagers and young adults would take in the practical building of Jewish settlements in Palestine and the Diaspora. The *kibbutz* movement, one of the best known manifestations of socialist thought in Israeli politics, owes its beginnings in large part to these men and women, and the contemporary Labor Party is their descendant (albeit an apple that has fallen far from the socialist tree).

At the other end of the political spectrum from the Socialists, there emerged another dynamic and occasionally quixotic Zionist writer and thinker, Vladimir Jabotinsky. Jabotinsky called for a reevaluation of the basic premises of Zionism in the early 1920s, thereby giving a name to his movement, Revisionist Zionism. The movement's goals were harshly militaristic, a drumbeating counterpoint to the moderate Chaim Weizmann, who had risen to leadership of the World Zionist Organization after Herzl's death. Jabotinsky called for continuous pressure on Great Britain, which controlled Palestine after World War I and had offered nebulous support of the idea of a Jewish homeland in the famous Balfour Declaration (see Appendix 1). To that end the Revisionists supported mass illegal immigration of Jews to Palestine. At the same time, the Revisionists had the clearest, if most sanguinary, solution to a question that few Zionist leaders had faced, the presence of Arab settlers on the land the Zionists wished to claim as their own. One can trace a straight line from Jabotinsky to the terrorist and guerrilla groups that fought against British mandatory rule in Palestine in the 1940s and from those groups to the Likud Party of today. Menachem Begin, Likud's first elected prime minister, was a disciple of Jabotinsky's, as were several other Likud leaders of his generation.

Among the Orthodox leadership, Zionism was looked upon with dismay as another form of the secularism pioneered by the *Haskalah*. Most of the rabbinate believed it was impermissible to do anything to hasten the Messianic Age.

But not every Orthodox rabbi rejected Zionism. A group of Orthodox rabbis who supported the work of the World Zionist Organization formed their own group, *Mizrakhi / Eastern* (but also an acronym for "spiritual center"), in 1905, under the leadership of a Lithuanian *rosh yeshiva,* Rabbi Isaac Jacob Reines. The Mizrakhi movement saw the establishment of a Jewish state as a vehicle for enhancing the observance of Torah through the creation of a Jewish society dwelling in the

Holy Land. Mizrakhi was an active participant in subsequent Zionist Congresses and trained its members for agricultural work in the settlements in Palestine, even creating its own settlements in the Beit She'an Valley.

And then there was Rabbi Abraham Kook (see pp. 393–95). For Kook (as for Hegel and Marx, both of whom he had probably read), the movement of history is a movement towards perfection and enlightenment, and the recognition of the Jewish people that they have a tie to the Land of Israel that transcends the merely political, the recognition of the non-Jewish world that there is a valid Jewish claim to national restoration in Palestine, is one key element in the eschatology. For that reason, Kook believed that the secular Zionist settlers were doing the work intended by the Almighty, the One who serves as Guarantor of the relationship between the Land and the People. Of course, Kook would have added, Zionism must have some Jewish religious content or it is merely another empty form of secular nationalism. But if the relationship of Land and People were brought to fruition, it would herald the beginning of a universal spiritual awakening.

As we can see, Zionism, which began its life as a Jewish variant on the various national awakenings of the mid-nineteenth century and simultaneously as a response to the Jewish Question, quickly transmuted into *several* responses to the Jewish Question.

But there was another response to the Jewish Question, one that came from the non-Jewish world. And that response would have its own set of brutal repercussions for the Jews.

THE EVOLUTION OF ANTI-SEMITISM

In 1171 the Jews of Blois, France, were accused of having crucified a Christian child during Passover. Supposedly they then threw the corpse into the Loire. This is the first known instance of the accusation of ritual murder on the Continent. The accusation that Jews use the blood of Christian children in making *matzot* is an old one, known as the "blood libel." In this case, the ruler of the region, Theobald V (known, in one of those ironies that make medieval history such a delightful field of study, as Theobald the Good), had all the Jews of Blois imprisoned. Eventually, over thirty Jewish men and women of Blois were burned to death.

We could list dozens, indeed hundreds more such incidents from the medieval period. And it isn't hard to find the impetus for them. The charge was made from pulpits throughout Europe: the Jews killed Jesus, rejecting him as the Messiah and Son of God.

This, in short, was religious anti-Semitism, the kind that had existed since the ascension of the Christians from sect to official religion of the Roman Empire. It might be more accurate to call it anti-Judaism or Judaeophobia, as some historians now prefer, because it was not based on a rejection of the Jews as a racial or national group but on a rejection of the religious principles by which they lived.

The Emancipation altered all that. It didn't eliminate religious anti-Semitism, of course; you can still find instances of that phenomenon today. What it did was create a new type of anti-Jewish feeling, one that ultimately would prove deadlier and more pernicious.

What had happened was quite simply that as the Jews became citizens of the European nation-states, they found themselves opposed by a new kind of hatred, racial anti-Semitism. Racial anti-Semitism, unlike religious anti-Semitism, did not offer even the minimal escape of conversion. Jews were not hated for what they believed, but for what they were believed to be. (Of course, conversion, whatever other psychical and emotional traumas it exerted, offered a threadbare shield; instead of being persecuted for denying Christ, you could now be tortured by the Inquisition because you were a "secret Judaizer.")

There was a certain ingenuity to racial anti-Semitism, too. It allowed the anti-Christian Enlightenment thinker like Voltaire to reject Judaism because it had spawned Christianity, but it never superseded the religious anti-Semite's agenda of attacking the Jews for not accepting Christ. It merely extended it.

Your "race" was immutable, hard-wired into your body and mind by your genes. Once a Jew, always a Jew. The new "scientific" racism delighted in the categorizing of body-types and racial characteristics. Jews were red-haired, hook-nosed, with bad eyes, bad posture, bad feet; they were physically weak and cowardly, undersized with abnormally small cranial cavities. Of course, they were also shrewd, cunning, dishonest, lazy, and oversexed. And they were coming for Gentile women, for whom they lusted.

Racial anti-Semitism in the nineteenth century reached a sort of apex of achievement in the hands of the composer Richard Wagner. Wagner's theories of the racial inferiority and evil of the Jews would provide the basis for the writings of Houston Chamberlain, a brilliant but utterly deranged Englishman who latched onto Adolf Hitler's rising star in Germany in the late 1920s, and for Hitler himself.

It must be understood that one of the more pervasive and reactionary outgrowths of the nationalist movements of the mid-nineteenth century was a new emphasis on blood purity as a function of nationhood, a throwback to the notions of the Spanish monarchs of the Expulsion era. Wagner articulates this idea with great power in both his writings and his operas. To him, the "Jewish race" was an enemy of the purity of humanity, an enemy to be quarantined and avoided.

Economic collapse has always fed suspicion of Jews. In the 1870s a depression in Central Europe became the rallying event for a new wave of anti-Semitic propaganda. It provided fresh fuel for the founders of mass-based movements like the German Christian-Social Party, headed by Adolf Stoecker, a Lutheran preacher. It is important to remember that by the 1870s Emancipation had reached almost all of Western Europe; Jews were now competing for jobs in fields formerly barred to them.

Nowhere was this more clear than in Vienna, where a small Jewish minority, about eight percent of the city's population, was becoming highly visible in medicine, law, literature, and journalism. Thus it was that in 1897 Vienna elected Karl Lueger its mayor, the first man (but not the last) democratically elected to public office in Europe on an explicitly anti-Semitic platform. Vienna was a hotbed of organized anti-Semitism. It was in Vienna that a young would-be painter named Hitler first encountered the anti-Semitic literature that would fire his imagination and drive him for the rest of his life.

There is a vast literature on Adolf Hitler and the Third Reich. The Nazis' ideology was driven by the ideas of racial purity, the mystique of blood and land, and the anti-Semitism that characterized the writings of Wagner, Comte de Gobineau, and Chamberlain, the avatars of "scientific" racism. What Hitler accomplished—the murder of six million of Europe's eleven million Jews—was unprecedented in human history, even in the history of organized Jew-killing.

That cataclysm made it necessary for even the most devout Jews to reconsider the basis of their faith.

SIFTING THROUGH THE ASHES

Judaism is a belief system based on certain key ideas: there is one God who created the world *ex nihilo;* God is omnipotent, omniscient, omnipresent; God is just and merciful; God made a covenant with the Jews, choosing them to be "a light unto the nations." At the heart of Judaism (and of most monotheistic religion) is the idea of theodicy, a term coined by the German philosopher Liebniz, meaning the "justification of God," that is, the explanation or justification of the relationship between God and evil.

The possibilities of theodicy are a running theme in modern Jewish thought. Even modernist thinkers like Buber, Heschel, and Rosenzweig engage with this issue in some fashion. But in the aftermath of the *Shoah* it takes on a new urgency.

The history of the Jewish people is filled with martyrs, men and women who died because of their religious convictions, who died *kiddush hashem/sanctifying the Holy Name*. What sets the *Shoah* apart from those other martyrdoms, from the victims of the Crusaders, of the Inquisitors, of rampaging Cossacks? Indeed, a very few Jewish theologians argue that the *Shoah* is merely more of the same, but there are significant differences.

First, the victims of the Nazis were not killed because they believed in Judaism. They were killed because one of their four grandparents was a Jew (and not necessarily a religious Jew at that); this was how Nazi racial laws defined Jewishness. Moreover, unlike many Jewish martyrs of the past, the Jews who died in the death camps, who were killed on the plains of the Ukraine and in the forests of Poland, were never given the choice of conversion to save their lives. Secular, Reform, Mitnagdic, Hasidic, all were killed regardless of what kind of Jews they thought they were. Finally, the Nazis made a particular point of targeting Jewish children for murder.

The *Shoah* was not the first genocide in modern history. But it is the first and, to date, only example of genocide committed by a cultured, industrialized Western nation against its own citizens and neighbors. It is the first and, to date, only example of a nation setting a genocidal task for itself and pursuing it by a methodical and highly technical process of extermination. The industrial scale and manner in which the *Shoah* was conducted is unprecedented.

And because it was perpetrated by the nation of Beethoven and Goethe, the *Shoah* represented a cognitive break in our understanding of what constitutes "Western civilization." For Jews, that break was even more wrenching. In the wake of the *Shoah,* Martin Buber found himself in a rare state of confusion. In a 1958 essay, Buber asked,

> Can one still speak to God after Oswiecim [the Polish town in which the Auschwitz death camp was situated] and Auschwitz? Can one still, as an individual and as a people, enter into a dialogue relationship with Him? Dare we commend to the survivors of Oswiecim, the Jobs of the gas chambers, "Call to Him for He is kind, for His mercy endureth forever"?

What possible justification or explanation can lead us to accept the idea of an omnipotent God, a just and compassionate God, who permits the erection and operation of the six death camps—Auschwitz, Belzec, Chelmno, Maidanek, Sobibor, Treblinka—whose *only* purpose was to kill Jews? Certain other excruciating questions must follow from this one. What is the meaning of Chosenness if this is the fate of the Chosen People? What good is the Covenant under such circumstances?

Steven T. Katz, a prominent historian of the *Shoah,* has enumerated nine basic responses to the *Shoah* in Jewish thought:

1. The Holocaust is like all other tragedies. While it raises once again the question of theodicy, it does not significantly alter the problem.

2. The *Shoah,* like the destruction of the Temple and other national catastrophes, was punishment for the sins of the Jewish people, who had forgotten the *mitzvot.*

3. As stated in Isaiah 53, the Jewish people are the "suffering servant" of all mankind, suffering in atonement for the sins of others.

4. Like the binding of Isaac, the *Shoah* is a test of our faith in God.

5. The *Shoah* is an example of *hester panim/the hiding of the face* of God, an occasion on which God is absent from human history.

6. God is dead. If there really was a just and powerful God, the *Shoah*

could not have taken place. Therefore, God is either dead or never existed.

7. God does not act in human history; God gave humanity free will. Radical evil of the sort manifested by the Nazis is the price we pay for freedom. The *Shoah* is the work of men, evil men, not of God.

8. The *Shoah* is an act of revelation in which a new, 614th Commandment was voiced: You shall not grant Hitler a posthumous victory; you must survive.

9. The *Shoah* is an inscrutable mystery, transcending human understanding. Like all God's mysteries it demands of us faith and silence.

These are not, of course, the only responses. Moreover, they are usually stated in a more nuanced manner, often in combination with one another. The *Shoah* itself was a multifaceted and complex event (or series of events); it demands an equally complex explanation, if an explanation is possible.

Some post-*Shoah* theologians, notably Eliezer Berkovits and Ignaz Maybaum among others, argue that the *Shoah*, for all its technologized terrors, is merely a more extreme version of many ghastly things that have befallen the Jews throughout history. And the questions of theodicy that it raises are not as dissimilar from past Jewish reactions to catastrophe as one might think. If the Holocaust is *not* unique, then those questions are merely intensified versions of old ones.

Much has been written about the sustaining effects of Jewish ritual in the death camps. David Weiss Halivni, a leading Jewish scholar and an Auschwitz survivor, recounts the experience of finding a scrap of a page of Talmud in Auschwitz, and the eagerness with which he and fellow prisoners would pore over it. Emil Fackenheim, a contemporary philosopher and a survivor of the Sachsenhausen concentration camp, has said that the knowledge that there were many in the death camps who took terrible risks to perform basic religious duties had a formative effect on the development of his thought in this area (expressed as #8 above).

Their experiences suggest that ritual can be an anchor, a structure that provides comfort, allowing us to find meaning in our daily lives, even under the most dire circumstances. Prayer allows us to believe there is a world beyond our fingertips, beyond our sensory impressions, a world of the Infinite. And it situates us in the history of the Jewish people and in their present. When we celebrate a Passover *seder,* we do not do so alone; whether we are conscious of it or not, millions of Jewish men and women around the world will sit down that same evening to celebrate the liberation from slavery. The Jews of the Warsaw Ghetto held their own *seders* on the night that they began their final uprising against the Nazis on Passover eve 1943.

When we pray, we might hear the voices of those Jews in 1943, not only of those who died but also those who survived, who produced astonishingly high birth rates in the displaced persons camps after the war, who had come back from the brink, determined to create new life. We cannot evade death. But we can face it in ways that give our life meaning.

EXILES' RETURN

Even if the *Shoah* is an unprecedented event in human and Jewish history, it would be hard not to acknowledge that another no less real break in Jewish history occurred three years later, with the founding of the State of Israel. This, too, was a rupture in Jewish history, albeit a positive one, that is truly unique, a restoration of Jewish sovereignty for the first time since the assassination of Gedaliah 2,500 years earlier. An autonomous Jewish state, secured by force of Jewish arms, proclaiming the Law of Return and urging the Ingathering of the Exiles—in terms of Jewish eschatology, this political event should have vast theological ramifications.

Yet, strangely, it has engendered nothing like the amount of theological speculation and discussion brought about by the Holocaust. There are, I think, several reasons for this surprising gap. (One could argue, with some degree of accuracy, that the existence of a Jewish homeland is entirely consistent with previous theological thought and that the absence of a decisive break is entirely appropriate. But this position overlooks the profound changes in the relationship between Diaspora Jews and Israeli Jews, and between newly empowered Jews in a sovereign, explicitly Jewish state and a predominantly non-Jewish world.)

First, the slow emergence of the truth about the *Shoah* overwhelmed anything else that crossed the radar screens of prominent Jewish theologians. Quite understandably, a tragedy of this magnitude dwarfed any event that came on its heels. The extensive literature on the theological implications of the *Shoah* is ample testimony to that fact.

Second, the antipathy that most of the Orthodox felt toward the Zionist project colored their reactions to its apparent success. As a result, a lot of important theologians simply remained silent. Conversely, the largely secular nature of the Zionist movement all but guaranteed that the Zionists themselves would not provide a theological reaction to the creation of the Jewish State. (One theologian who might have had something useful to say about this remarkable turn of events was Abraham Kook, but he died fifteen years before the State of Israel became a reality.)

There are two possible explanations for the relative lack of discussion of the theological ramifications of the founding of the State of Israel, one historical, the other psychological.

It is important to remember that the continued survival of the State of Israel was an open question for nearly twenty years, from the 1948 War of Independence to the Six-Day War in 1967. Surrounded by hostile neighbors and seemingly without help from outside the region, the Jewish State was faced with overwhelming odds from its birth. Until the spectacular victory of 1967, one could not be sure that there would *be* a State of Israel from one day to the next. With the obvious exception of the Israelis themselves, many Jews tend to forget that on the eve of the Six-Day War the consensus was that Israel would be swept into the sea by the Arabs in a total war.

With that victory came a new set of issues and responsibilities, new territory, and the gradual emergence of a Palestinian nationalist movement. As a result, attentions were turned to other questions. There has never been a time in which Jews have been able to relax where Israel is concerned. That sense of insecurity is felt keenly throughout the Jewish world, particularly after the dangerous fiasco of the 1973 Yom Kippur War, when Israeli defenses were unready and nearly overwhelmed. Even with the small successes of the peace process, from the Camp David accords with Egypt up to the Wye River Agreement, the focus of Jewish pundits has been on the specifics of the process itself.

The Jews have been schooled by history to expect the worst. Jewish pessimism is proverbial, the source of countless jokes. Our most eloquent philosophical and theological writings are responses to disaster—the two destructions of the Temple, pogroms, blood libels, the Expulsion from Iberia, the *Shoah*. In the introduction to his book *Conflicting Visions: Spiritual Possibilities of Modern Israel,* Rabbi David Hartman recalls a conversation with Rabbi Joseph Soloveitchik in the euphoric aftermath of the Six-Day War. Hartman writes, "For Soloveitchik, one does not change the direction of Jewish spirituality just because of an overwhelming experience. One must build from sobriety, from careful appreciation of complexity, and not allow oneself to be swept along by the enthusiasm of events."

Rabbi Hartman, head of the Shalom Hartman Institute for Advanced Jewish Studies in Jerusalem, has written eloquently and thoughtfully on the divisions within the Jewish world and within Israeli society, and on the theological implications of an autonomous Jewish state in the contemporary world. Hartman is a Modern Orthodox rabbi, one of Joseph Soloveitchik's many students, who made *aliyah* from New York in 1971.

As might be expected from a protégé of one of the outstanding *halakhists* of this century, Hartman is concerned with the tension between the demands of *halakhah* and the practical necessities of running a modern nation-state. As a result, he says, the existence of a Jewish state actually broadens the "range of *halakhic* concerns to encompass all aspects of life."

As Hartman writes in *Conflicting Visions,* "[T]he rejection of the traditional posture of waiting for messianic redemption can *itself* be seen as a further elaboration and intensification of the spirit of covenantal responsibility found in the biblical and, above all, in the rabbinic tradition." In a formulation that echoes Abraham Kook, he says that the secular Zionists who built the State of Israel opened the way for the restoration of a Jewish nationalism that was not dependent on supernatural intervention, by eliminating the need to wait for the God of history to intervene. If God's design was for humanity to have free will, then surely there is room for this victory for the Jewish people.

Hartman brings the classic progressivism of American democracy to his work in Israel. He argues for such American ideas as electoral democracy, separation of church and state, tolerance of religious pluralism both within the Jewish community and in relation to the non-Jews within Israel's borders. These ideas are not of themselves new, of course, but espoused by an Orthodox rabbi in Israel, they take on a very different heft.

One recent development, of which the Hartman Institute has been an active part, suggests that change within Israel may come in unexpected ways. There is a growing movement among secular Israeli Jews seeking Jewish literacy, studying Torah and Talmud. At a time when secular-Orthodox tensions in Israel have never been more pronounced or more volatile, secularists are "seeking their place in Judaism rather than opt[ing] for a 'post-Jewish' Israeli identity," Yossi Klein Halevi wrote in *Jerusalem Report* at the end of 1996. The product of this loosely-knit "Jewish empowerment movement," as it is sometimes called, is a small wave of secular Israeli Jews who are striving to define themselves through a Jewishly rooted secular identity, an identity that has knowledge of Jewish texts and history as a key component.

Rabbi Hartman's son, Rabbi Donniel Hartman, bubbled with the enthusiasm of youth when asked about this movement: "Of course we're going to change the country. It will take at least a generation but we're going to win." Needless to say, that remains to be seen, but if it happens, Donniel's father's deepest wish will have become a reality.

FEMINISM REMAKES JEWISH THEOLOGY

Perhaps the most fruitful development in Jewish thought in the second half of the twentieth century is the rise of an explicitly feminist theology. As is so often the case in Jewish history, the impetus for this development came from events outside the Jewish world, but were given a distinctly Jewish spin by thinkers inside the Tabernacle. On the most obvious level, the fact that more than half of the students today entering the rabbinical seminaries of the Reform, Reconstructionist, and Conservative movements in the United States are women is testimony to the power of those ideas. But beyond the practical ramifications of a specifically Jewish feminist movement, there has been a considerable theological impact as well.

Some of the changes are self-evident. Liturgy is being adjusted to reflect the idea that God is neither male nor female—or both male and female. Jewish women are rediscovering all-but-forgotten elements of worship like the ceremonies for Rosh Khodesh, and creating new ones like the *brit habat*. Women's *tefillah* groups are innovating constantly and the movement is growing. But there are other, subtler and more far-reaching changes.

To understand the impact of feminist thought on all streams of Judaism, it is necessary to go back to the early chapters of this book and recall the situation of women in traditional Jewish practice.

Although Judaism has always placed great value on the role of women in the home, in the public arena they have been pushed to the margins. Literally. Recall the arrangement of a traditional synagogue: the women sit either in the balcony or behind the *mekhitzah*, the partition, curtain, or screen that separates them from the men. Generally, their view of the service is at best partial, at worst nonexistent. Everything important happens in the men's section; the sacred Scrolls of the Law are kept in the men's section; the reading table is in the men's section. (With the rise of the denominations, that changed. But the role of women in the public sphere changed more slowly than the seating arrangements did.)

The response of Orthodox pre-feminist women to this marginalization was to develop rituals of their own, centered in the home. Although there are only three positive commandments that are designated for women—lighting Sabbath candles, taking *khallah*, the laws of *niddah*, that is, ritual purity before and after menstruation (and two of these can be performed by men)—women have throughout the years devised ways of making the ordinary household chore a sacred ritual as well. Lisa Keele points to the extra effort made by observant women in cleaning their houses of *khametz* before Pesakh as an example of transforming and heightening the quotidian in the name of the *mitzvot*.

But these tasks, like women in an Orthodox *shul*, are invisible to men. And that didn't change, even in the Reform and Conservative worlds, for a very long time.

Women's feelings of enforced inferiority in the Jewish world were very real and were provoked not only by their place (or lack thereof) in the sanctuary but also by the disdain shown for educating Jewish women in their religion. Jewish women were discouraged from learning Hebrew, studying Talmud and Torah throughout the entire medieval and early modern period, even into this century in many communities. Although that all began to change slowly in the 1950s in the Reform and Conservative movements, the pace of the changes was altered considerably with the rise of a new feminist movement in the United States at the end of the '60s. A concerted effort by young Jewish women to take a more active role in worship and education came out of the *Havurah* movement. The Reform movement ordained its first woman rabbi, Sally Preisand, in 1972, the Reconstructionists two years after. *Lilith,* a high-quality Jewish feminist magazine, began publication in 1976; on its cover was a picture of a woman wearing *tefillin* and a *tallit*. Nine years after that, the Conservative movement, amid considerable controversy and rancor, ordained its first woman rabbis.

Even within Orthodoxy, the ripples are felt. Orthodox Jewish women are attending college, receiving advanced degrees, and participating in the workforce, even as they claim no affinity with feminism. Today, women attend lectures on Jewish religious topics alongside men. Women are being trained as *poskot*, female *halakhic* decisors, in areas of *kashrut, niddah,* and the Sabbath. Orthodox Jewish women are training in women's yeshivot here and in Israel, studying Talmud as men have for a thousand years. And an annual Conference on Feminism and Orthodoxy has been held in New York two years running with sell-out attendance.

Will the Orthodox eventually ordain women as rabbis? Orthodox feminist Blu Greenberg believes it is inevitable. "Learning is the road to ordination, and you can't close the last gate of the path," she told the Jewish Telegraphic Agency (JTA) in 1995.

The active presence of women in Judaism is reshaping our theology and worship. Women have begun to move center stage in Judaism in profound ways. Rivka Haut, co-founder of the Women's Tefillah Network, told JTA, "In the tefillah movement we are looking less to rabbis and are figuring out the [*halakhot*] involved by ourselves, creating new rituals and even writing new prayers. This is happening without rabbinic approval."

Life-cycle events traditionally have focused on the male experience, from circumcision to the days after death, when a woman cannot be counted toward a traditional *minyan* to say *Kaddish* for a family member. That is changing. Women are writing new prayers and devising new rituals for the act of giving birth, previously marked only by a woman *bentsching gomel* (saying the prayer for having come through a life-threatening experience). Sociologist Sylvia Barack Fishman writes:

Contemporary Jewish feminism has turned a systematic spotlight on the religious souls of Jewish women. Jewish feminism has gone back to the biblical, rabbinic, and historical wellsprings of Judaism to rediscover, reemphasize, and reinterpret women's roles in the development of Judaism as a religion, an ethical system, and a culture. It has opened the doors of classical Jewish learning to women of all ages. It has worked toward reinvesting major female life-cycle events with formal, Jewishly significant spiritual import. It has rediscovered old prayers and created new ones both to transcend the patriarchal attitudes and to give expression to female Jewish spirituality, and it has moved women into more public positions in prayer services themselves.

—*A Breath of Life: Feminism in the American Jewish Community*

Jewish feminism has also altered the perspective from which many men read Jewish texts. God the avenging Father is now tempered by the other aspects of the Divine. It takes a feminist to remind Jewish men of the passage from *Genesis Rabbah* in which it is explicitly stated that God created Adam as an androgynous being, "as it is written, 'Male and female [God] created them . . . and . . . called their name Adam'" And Jewish women have reminded us powerfully of the restorative and nurturing powers of immersion in the *mikveh*.

At a time when American Jews are concerned with their survival in an era of assimilation, the new commitment to Judaism evinced by Jewish feminists should be a cause for rejoicing. As Fishman has written, "Jewish feminists, rather than walking away from Jewish traditions and following powerful tides of assimilation, seek out a more complete relationship with their spiritual heritage." In that respect, they may be one of the groups that saves American Jewry from itself.

THE TEMPTATIONS OF ASSIMILATION

After the 1990 National Jewish Population Survey, conducted for United Jewish Appeal, was released, dire warnings were being issued throughout Jewish America. An intermarriage rate of 52%? Birth-rate well below the replacement level? Could this mean the end of American Jewry?

Jerusalem Report columnist Ze'ev Chafets (a transplanted Detroiter, by the way) was less worried. The basic thrust of his column on the subject was, "so what?" The center of the Jewish world has shifted many times before in Jewish history—Palestine, Babylonia, Spain, Germany, America. If it shifts to Israel in the near future, that's as it should be.

There is something to be said for Chafets's cavalier attitude. He's certainly right about the way that the gravitational field of the Jewish world has moved around over the millennia. And if American Jewry disappeared because of assimilation, it would be a nice change of pace from defeat in war, forcible expulsion, and genocide, the causes of the other sea-changes.

But there are reasons not to be as pessimistic as some who have read the 1990 study and its 1993 follow-up. The American glass may not be half-full, but it isn't draining any faster than before. In 1993 UJA released another survey, the 1991 New York Jewish Population Study, which suggested some possible areas of progress. That report said, "We have consistently underestimated the extent to which we have created a set of American Jewish experiences . . . [that are] not merely a holdover from the immigrant experience but . . . reflect unique aspects of American Jewish identity." Experiences such as *bar/bat mitzvah,* Jewish summer camps, youth group memberships, college activities like Hillel, trips to Israel—these activities are open to men and women equally and are voluntary. Their growth cannot help but be a hopeful sign. More than that, as a general return to spirituality in American society takes place, Jews are an active part of it.

America (and to a slightly lesser extent England) may indeed represent a positive answer to the Jewish Question in the Diaspora. A democracy whose system includes sufficient checks and balances to protect a minority against the "tyranny of the majority," to use de Tocqueville's apt phrase, the United States is also a pluralistic society in which Otherness is accepted, if grudgingly at times, and diversity is tolerated and occasionally even celebrated. This is the Enlightenment ideal come to life, albeit in frequently flawed form. (For example, once the Jews were accepted as "white" people, they were allowed considerably more leeway than African-Americans, and that remains the case today.)

The resurgence of ethnicity in American social and political life since the 1960s has certainly affected Jewish-Americans. The renewed focus on spirituality in Reform and Reconstructionist congregations, accompanied by a significant new interest in such matters in non-Jewish America as well, has given new life to many synagogues (and something new to argue about, the life's blood of the Jewish experience).

Although there have been Jews in America since 1654, there has only been a significant Jewish presence since the wave of Russian immigrants that began in 1881. There have been Jews in *Eretz Yisroel* for nearly 4,000 years, but an independent Jewish state there for just over 50 years. Look back over the history recounted in this book. The monarchical period in ancient Israel lasted over 500 years. The writing and editing of the Talmud took more than four centuries. The Jews lived in the Diaspora for two millennia before the modern State of Israel was founded.

Jewish history works in long cycles. It is much too early to offer "final" conclusions about the state of American Jewry, the nature of modern Israel, or the future of the Jewish people, in the Diaspora or not. The playing-out of the forces that have affected four thousand years of Jewish history continues. Rav Soloveitchik's warning to David Hartman is a point well-taken.

It is not given to mere humans to foresee the future. Who would have predicted that a tiny people, never more than a single-digit percentage of the earth's population, would survive for four millennia, would completely alter the way that humanity envisioned its relationship with nature, re-shape ethics in a way that would last as long as they did? Who would have foreseen that this nation would endure the worst atrocities that could be visited upon it and emerge intact, even—some might say—triumphant? It doesn't pay to make predictions about the Jews.

One of Judaism's great strengths has always been its adaptive powers, a combination of an almost Darwinian survival instinct and a certain flexibility regarding the culture of its neighbors. We cease to be nomads and settle in Canaan? Build the Temple as a place to honor the One God. The Temple is destroyed? Build synagogues and substitute prayer for sacrifice. We achieve political emancipation? Start working to create a Jewish nation-state.

Jewish practice, ritual, and thought have always been inflected by events, shaped by history even when they have consciously sought to stand apart from its flow. That process will continue. Judaism remains a vibrant, living faith espoused by a small but dedicated portion of the world's population. As long as Jews can continue to find meaning in their rites, their celebrations, their observances, or reshape them to give them meaning, that will remain the case.

NOTES

1. When writing about the murder of six million Jews by the Nazis and their minions, nomenclature is very important. Many Jewish writers are not entirely comfortable with the use of the word Holocaust, from the Greek meaning "burnt offering," because it is heavily freighted with Christian symbolism and because they reject the idea that these people were an "offering" to anyone or anything. *Shoah,* the Hebrew word meaning "whirlwind," is, they feel, preferable. But with the frequency of its usage, "Holocaust" becomes inevitable.

Likewise, use of the word "exterminated" when discussing the *Shoah* plays into the Nazis' propaganda message, that the Jews were a form of vermin to be wiped out like cockroaches. "Murdered" fits the reality better.

2. The number 36 has great mystical significance in Jewish lore. Twice 18, the number that corresponds to *khai/life,* it is also the number of the hidden righteous men on whom the world's safety depends, the *lamed-vavniks (lamed-vav* being the Hebrew letters that signify the number 36).

Some Key Documents
of Contemporary
Jewish Belief

REFORM JUDAISM

The Pittsburgh Platform, 1885

Convening at the call of Kaufmann Kohler of New York, Reform rabbis from around the United States met from November 16 through November 19, 1885, with Isaac Mayer Wise presiding. The meeting was declared the continuation of the Philadelphia Conference of 1869, which was the continuation of the German Conference of 1841 to 1846. The rabbis adopted the following seminal text:

1. We recognize in every religion an attempt to grasp the Infinite, and in every mode, source or book of revelation held sacred in any religious system the consciousness of the indwelling of God in man. We hold that Judaism presents the highest conception of the God-idea as taught in our Holy Scriptures and developed and spiritualized by the Jewish teachers, in accordance with the moral and philosophical progress of their respective ages. We maintain that Judaism preserved and defended amid continual struggles and trials and under enforced isolation, this God-idea as the central religious truth for the human race.

2. We recognize in the Bible the record of the consecration of the Jewish people to its mission as the priest of the one God, and value it as the most potent instrument of religious and moral instruction. We hold that the modern discoveries of scientific researches in the domain of nature and history are not antagonistic to the doctrines of Judaism, the Bible reflecting the primitive ideas of its own age, and at times clothing its conception of divine Providence and Justice dealing with men in miraculous narratives.

3. We recognize in the Mosaic legislation a system of training the Jewish people for its mission during its national life in Palestine, and today we accept as binding only its moral laws, and maintain only such ceremonies as elevate and sanctify our lives, but reject all such as are not adapted to the views and habits of modern civilization.

4. We hold that all such Mosaic and rabbinical laws as regulate diet, priestly purity, and dress originated in ages and under the influence of ideas entirely foreign to our present mental and spiritual state. They fail to impress the modern Jew with a spirit of priestly holiness; their observance in our days is apt rather to obstruct than to further modern spiritual elevation.

5. We recognize, in the modern era of universal culture of heart and intellect, the approaching of the realization of Israel's great Messianic hope for the establishment of the kingdom of truth, justice, and peace among all men. We consider ourselves no longer a nation, but a religious community, and therefore expect neither a return to Palestine, nor a sacrificial worship under the sons of Aaron, nor the restoration of any of the laws concerning the Jewish state.

6. We recognize in Judaism a progressive religion, ever striving to be in accord with the postulates of reason. We are convinced of the utmost necessity of preserving the historical identity with our great past. Christianity and Islam, being daughter religions of Judaism, we appreciate their providential mission, to aid in the spreading of monotheistic and moral truth. We acknowledge that the spirit of broad humanity of our age is our ally in the fulfillment of our mission, and therefore we extend the hand of fellowship to all who cooperate with us in the establishment of the reign of truth and righteousness among men.

7. We reassert the doctrine of Judaism that the soul is immortal, grounding the belief on the divine nature of human spirit, which for-

ever finds bliss in righteousness and misery in wickedness. We reject as ideas not rooted in Judaism, the beliefs both in bodily resurrection and in Gehenna and Eden (Hell and Paradise) as abodes for everlasting punishment and reward.

8. In full accordance with the spirit of the Mosaic legislation, which strives to regulate the relations between rich and poor, we deem it our duty to participate in the great task of modern times, to solve, on the basis of justice and righteousness, the problems presented by the contrasts and evils of the present organization of society.

The Columbus Platform, 1937
(published as "The Columbus Platform: The Guiding Principles of Reform Judaism")

In view of the changes that have taken place in the modern world and the consequent need of stating anew the teachings of Reform Judaism, the Central Conference of American Rabbis makes the following declaration of principles. It presents them not as a fixed creed but as a guide for the progressive elements of Jewry.

A. Judaism and Its Foundations

1. Nature of Judaism. Judaism is the historical religious experience of the Jewish people. Though growing out of Jewish life, its message is universal, aiming at the union and perfection of mankind under the sovereignty of God. Reform Judaism recognizes the principle of progressive development in religion and consciously applies this principle to spiritual as well as to cultural and social life. Judaism welcomes all truth, whether written in the pages of scripture or deciphered from the records of nature. The new discoveries of science, while replacing the older scientific views underlying our sacred literature, do not conflict with the essential spirit of religion as manifested in the consecration of man's will, heart and mind to the service of God and of humanity.

2. God. The heart of Judaism and its chief contribution to religion is the doctrine of the One, living God, who rules the world through law and love. In Him all existence has its creative source and mankind its ideal of conduct. Though transcending time and space, He is the indwelling Presence of the world. We worship Him as the Lord of the universe and as our merciful Father.

3. Man. Judaism affirms that man is created in the Divine image. His spirit is immortal. He is an active co-worker with God. As a child of God, he is endowed with moral freedom and is charged with the responsibility of overcoming evil and striving after ideal ends.

4. Torah. God reveals Himself not only in the majesty, beauty and orderliness of nature, but also in the vision and moral striving of the human spirit. Revelation is a continuous process, confined to no one group and to no one age. Yet the people of Israel, through its prophets and sages, achieved unique insight in the realm of religious truth. The Torah, both written and oral, enshrines Israel's ever-growing consciousness of God and of the moral law. It preserves the historical precedents, sanctions and norms of Jewish life, and seeks to mould it in the patterns of goodness and of holiness. Being products of historical processes, certain of its laws have lost their binding force with the passing of the conditions that called them forth. But as a depository of permanent spiritual ideals, the Torah remains the dynamic source of the life of Israel. Each age has the obligation to adapt the teachings of the Torah to its basic needs in consonance with the genius of Judaism.

5. Israel. Judaism is the soul of which Israel is the body. Living in all parts of the world, Israel has been held together by the ties of a common history, and above all, by the heritage of faith. Though we recognize in the group loyalty of Jews who have become estranged from our religious tradition, a bond which still unites them with us, we maintain that it is by its religion and for its religion that the Jewish people has lived. The non-Jew who accepts our faith is welcomed as a full member of the Jewish community. In all lands where our people live, they assume and seek to share loyally the full duties and responsibilities of citizenship and to create seats of Jewish knowledge and religion. In the rehabilitation of Palestine, the land hallowed by memories and hopes, we behold the promise of renewed life for many of our brethren. We affirm the obligation of all Jewry to aid in its upbuilding as a Jewish homeland by endeavoring to make it not only a haven of refuge for the oppressed but also a center of Jewish culture and spiritual life. Throughout the ages it has been Israel's mission to witness to the Divine in the face of every form of paganism and materialism. We regard it as our historic task to cooperate with all men in the establishment of the kingdom of God, of universal brotherhood, Justice, truth and peace on earth. This is our Messianic goal.

B. Ethics

6. Ethics and Religion. In Judaism religion and morality blend into an indissoluble unity. Seeking God means to strive after holiness, righteousness and goodness. The love of God is incomplete without the love of one's fellowmen. Judaism emphasizes the kinship of the human race, the sanctity and worth of human life and personality and the right of the individual to freedom and to the pursuit of his chosen vocation. Justice to all, irrespective of race, sect or class, is the inalienable right and the inescapable obligation of all. The state and organized government exist in order to further these ends.

7. Social Justice. Judaism seeks the attainment of a just society by the application of its teachings to the economic order, to industry and commerce, and to national and international affairs. It aims at the elimination of man-made misery and suffering, of poverty and degradation, of tyranny and slavery, of social inequality and prejudice, of ill-will and strife. It advocates the promotion of harmonious relations between warring classes on the basis of equity and justice, and the creation of conditions under which human personality may flourish. It pleads for the safeguarding of childhood against exploitation. It champions the cause of all who work and of their right to an adequate standard of living, as prior to the rights of property. Judaism emphasizes the duty of charity, and strives for a social order which will protect men against the material disabilities of old age, sickness and unemployment.

8. Peace. Judaism, from the days of the prophets, has proclaimed to mankind the ideal of universal peace. The spiritual and physical disarmament of all nations has been one of its essential teachings. It abhors all violence and relies upon moral education, love and sympathy to secure human progress. It regards justice as the foundation of the well-being of nations and the condition of enduring peace. It urges organized international action for disarmament, collective security and world peace.

C. Religious Practice

9. The Religious Life. Jewish life is marked by consecration to these ideals of Judaism. It calls for faithful participation in the life of the

Jewish community as it finds expression in home, synagogue and school and in all other agencies that enrich Jewish life and promote its welfare. The Home has been and must continue to be a stronghold of Jewish life, hallowed by the spirit of love and reverence, by moral discipline and religious observance and worship. The Synagogue is the oldest and most democratic institution in Jewish life. It is the prime communal agency by which Judaism is fostered and preserved. It links the Jews of each community and unites them with all Israel. The perpetuation of Judaism as a living force depends upon religious knowledge and upon the Education of each new generation in our rich cultural and spiritual heritage.

Prayer is the voice of religion, the language of faith and aspiration. It directs man's heart and mind Godward, voices the needs and hopes of the community and reaches out after goals which invest life with supreme value. To deepen the spiritual life of our people, we must cultivate the traditional habit of communion with God through prayer in both home and synagogue.

Judaism as a way of life requires in addition to its moral and spiritual demands, the reservation of the Sabbath, festivals and Holy Days, the retention and development of such customs, symbols and ceremonies as possess inspirational value, the cultivation of distinctive forms of religious art and music and the use of Hebrew, together with the vernacular, in our worship and instruction.

These timeless aims and ideals of our faith we present anew to a confused and troubled world. We call upon our fellow Jews to rededicate themselves to them, and, in harmony with all men, hopefully and courageously to continue Israel's eternal quest after God and His kingdom.

A Centenary Perspective, 1976
(adopted at San Francisco, 1976)

The Central Conference of American Rabbis has on special occasions described the spiritual state of Reform Judaism. The centenaries of the founding of the Union of American Hebrew Congregations and the Hebrew Union College–Jewish Institute of Religion seem an appropriate time for another such effort. We therefore record our sense of the unity of our movement today.

One Hundred Years: What We Have Taught

We celebrate the role of Reform Judaism in North America, the growth of our movement on this free ground, the great contributions of our membership to the dreams and achievements of this society. We also feel great satisfaction at how much of our pioneering conception of Judaism has been accepted by the Household of Israel. It now seems self-evident to most Jews: that our tradition should interact with modern culture; that its forms ought to reflect a contemporary esthetic; that its scholarship needs to be conducted by modern, critical methods; and that change has been and must continue to be a fundamental reality in Jewish life. Moreover, though some still disagree, substantial numbers have also accepted our teachings: that the ethics of universalism implicit in traditional Judaism must be an explicit part of our Jewish duty; that women have full rights to practice Judaism; and that Jewish obligation begins with the informed will of every individual. Most modern Jews, within their various religious movements, are embracing Reform Jewish perspectives. We see this past century as having confirmed the essential wisdom of our movement.

One Hundred Years: What We Have Learned

Obviously, much else has changed in the past century. We continue to probe the extraordinary events of the past generation, seeking to understand their meaning and to incorporate their significance in our lives. The Holocaust shattered our easy optimism about humanity and its inevitable progress. The State of Israel, through its many accomplishments, raised our sense of the Jews as a people to new heights of aspiration and devotion. The widespread threats to freedom, the problems inherent in the explosion of new knowledge and of ever more powerful technologies, and the spiritual emptiness of much of Western culture have taught us to be less dependent on the values of our society and to reassert what remains perennially valid in Judaism's teaching.

We have learned that the survival of the Jewish people is of highest priority and that in carrying out our Jewish responsibilities we help move humanity toward its messianic fulfillment.

Diversity Within Unity, the Hallmark of Reform

Reform Jews respond to change in various ways according to the Reform principle of the autonomy of the individual. However, Reform Judaism does more than tolerate diversity; it engenders it. In our uncertain historical situation we must expect to have far greater diversity than previous generations knew. How we shall live with diversity without stifling dissent and without paralyzing our ability to take positive action will test our character and our principles. We stand open to any position thoughtfully and conscientiously advocated in the spirit of Reform Jewish belief. While we may differ in our interpretation and application of the ideas enunciated here, we accept such differences as precious and see in them Judaism's best hope for confronting whatever the future holds for us. Yet in all our diversity we perceive a certain unity and we shall not allow our differences in some particulars to obscure what binds us together.

1. God—The affirmation of God has always been essential to our people's will to survive. In our struggle through the centuries to preserve our faith we have experienced and conceived of God in many ways. The trials of our own time and the challenges of modern culture have made steady belief and clear understanding difficult for some. Nevertheless, we ground our lives, personally and communally, on God's reality and remain open to new experiences and conceptions of the Divine. Amid the mystery we call life, we affirm that human beings, created in God's image, share in God's eternality despite the mystery we call death.

2. The People Israel—The Jewish people and Judaism defy precise definition because both are in the process of becoming. Jews, by birth or conversion, constitute an uncommon union of faith and peoplehood. Born as Hebrews in the ancient Near East, we are bound together like all ethnic groups by language, land, history, culture, and institutions. But the people of Israel is unique because of its involvement with God and its resulting perception of the human condition. Throughout our long history our people has been inseparable from its religion with its messianic hope that humanity will be redeemed.

3. Torah—Torah results from the relationship between God and the Jewish people. The records of our earliest confrontations are uniquely important to us. Lawgivers and prophets, historians and poets gave us a heritage whose study is a religious imperative and whose practice is our chief means to holiness. Rabbis and teachers, philosophers and mystics, gifted Jews in every age amplified the Torah tradition. For millennia, the creation of Torah has not ceased and Jewish creativity in our time is adding to the chain of tradition.

4. Our Religious Obligations: Religious Practice—Judaism emphasizes action rather than creed as the primary expression of a religious life, the means by which we strive to achieve universal justice and peace. Reform Judaism shares this emphasis on duty and obligation. Our founders stressed that the Jew's ethical responsibilities, personal and social, are enjoined by God. The past century has taught us that the claims made upon us may begin with our ethical obligations but they extend to many other aspects of Jewish living, including: creating a Jewish home centered on family devotion; lifelong study; private prayer and public worship; daily religious observance; keeping the Sabbath and the holy days; celebrating the major events of life; involvement with the synagogues and community; and other activities which promote the survival of the Jewish people and enhance its existence. Within each area of Jewish observance Reform Jews are called upon to confront the claims of Jewish tradition, however differently perceived, and to exercise their individual autonomy, choosing and creating on the basis of commitment and knowledge.

5. Our Obligations: The State of Israel and the Diaspora— We are privileged to live in an extraordinary time, one in which a third Jewish commonwealth has been established in our people's ancient homeland. We are bound to that land and to the newly reborn State of Israel by innumerable religious and ethnic ties. We have been enriched by its culture and ennobled by its indomitable spirit. We see it providing unique opportunities for Jewish self-expression. We have both a stake and a responsibility in building the State of Israel, assuring its security, and defining its Jewish character. We encourage aliyah for those who wish to find maximum personal fulfillment in the cause of Zion. We demand that Reform Judaism be unconditionally legitimized in the State of Israel.

At the same time that we consider the State of Israel vital to the welfare of Judaism everywhere, we reaffirm the mandate of our tradition to create strong Jewish communities wherever we live. A genuine Jewish life is possible in any land, each community developing its own particular character and determining its Jewish responsibilities. The foundation of Jewish community life is the synagogue. It leads us beyond itself to cooperate with other Jews, to share their concerns, and to assume leadership in communal affairs. We are therefore committed to the full democratization of the Jewish community and to its hallowing in terms of Jewish values.

The State of Israel and the Diaspora, in fruitful dialogue, can show how a people transcends nationalism even as it affirms it, thereby setting an example for humanity which remains largely concerned with dangerously parochial goals.

6. Our Obligations: Survival and Service—Early Reform Jews, newly admitted to general society and seeing in this the evidence of a growing universalism, regularly spoke of Jewish purpose in terms of Jewry's service to humanity. In recent years we have become freshly conscious of the virtues of pluralism and the values of particularism. The Jewish people in its unique way of life validates its own worth while working toward the fulfillment of its messianic expectations. Until the recent past our obligations to the Jewish people and to all humanity seemed congruent. At times now these two imperatives appear to conflict. We know of no simple way to resolve such tensions. We must, however, confront them without abandoning either of our commitments. A universal concern for humanity unaccompanied by a devotion to our particular people is self-destructive; a passion for our people without involvement in humankind contradicts what the prophets have meant to us. Judaism calls us simultaneously to universal and particular obligations.

Hope: Our Jewish Obligation

Previous generations of Reform Jews had unbound confidence in humanity's potential for good. We have lived through terrible tragedy and been compelled to reappropriate our tradition's realism about the human capacity for evil. Yet our people has always refused to despair. The survivors of the Holocaust, being granted life, seized it, nurtured it, and, rising above catastrophe, showed humankind that the human spirit is indomitable. The State of Israel, established and maintained by the Jewish will to live, demonstrates what a united people can accomplish in history. The existence of the Jew is an argument against despair; Jewish survival is warrant for human hope.

We remain God's witness that history is not meaningless. We affirm that with God's help people are not powerless to affect their destiny. We dedicate ourselves, as did the generations of Jews who went before us, to work and wait for that day when "They shall not hurt or destroy in all My holy mountain for the earth shall be full of the knowledge of the Lord as the waters cover the sea."

The Doral Country Club Resolution, 1997
100th Anniversary of the Zionist Movement

Adopted by the 108th Annual Convention of the Central Conference of American Rabbis, June, 1997:

WHEREAS 1997 marks the 100th anniversary since Theodor Herzl convened the first World Zionist Congress, which adopted the Basel Program and established the Zionist movement, and

WHEREAS, the Zionist Movement is one of the most successful movements of national liberation of modern times, transforming a millennial dream into a political reality, restoring an ancient people to its ancestral homeland and creating a model society based on Jewish value and morality, and

WHEREAS, the 50th anniversary of Israel as a sovereign Jewish State which will be celebrated in 1998 can only be understood in the context of the accomplishments of the Zionist Movement, and

WHEREAS, among the founders of the Zionist organization were American Reform Rabbis, Rabbis Judah L. Magnes, Abba Hillel Silver and Stephen S. Wise, and

WHEREAS, our movement has explicitly rejected the anti-Zionist stances held prior to World War I, specifically endorsing Zionist aims: calling for a Jewish National Home in the 1937 Guiding Principles, joining in the 1942 Baltimore Platform's call for a Jewish state, and subscribing to the Jerusalem Programme, and

WHEREAS, throughout most of the Zionist century our institutional undertakings have supported Zionist activity, from our affiliation with the Jewish Agency in 1929 to the establishment of the Jerusalem campus of HUC–JIR, the establishment of the year study program for rabbinical and cantorial students, to the creation of Progressive congregations and schools in Israel. The Reform kibbutzim and mitzpim, and the Progressive youth movement, Tzofei Telem, and the founding of

ARZA, demonstrating through these activities our deep commitment to the goals of Zionism,

THEREFORE, BE IT RESOLVED, that the CCAR promote and encourage congregational and community celebrations of the centennial of modern Zionism, and the 50th anniversary of the State of Israel, and

BE IT FURTHER RESOLVED, that this celebration be a catalyst for educating the Jewish community about the history of Zionism and its relevance for the future, to develop new support for the Zionist movement and to educate about Zionism's role in the establishment of the State of Israel whose 50th anniversary will be celebrated next year.

CONSERVATIVE JUDAISM

On Changes in Judaism
Zecharias Frankel

Maintaining the integrity of Judaism simultaneously with progress, this is the essential problem of the present. Can we deny the difficulty of a satisfactory solution? Where is the point where the two apparent contraries can meet? What ought to be our point of departure in the attempt to reconcile essential Judaism and progress and what type of opposition may we expect to encounter? How can we assure rest for the soul so that it shall not be torn apart or be numbed by severe doubts while searching for the warm ray of faith, and yet allot to reason its right, and enable it to lend strength and lucidity to the religious feeling which springs from the emotions? The opposing elements which so seldom are in balance must be united and this is our task. . . .

Judaism is a religion which has a direct influence on life's activity. It is a religion of action, demanding the performance of precepts which either directly aim at ennobling man or, by reminding man of the divine, strengthen his feelings of dependence on God. And because of this trait neither pure abstract contemplation nor dark mysticism; could ever strike root in Judaism. This, in turn, guaranteed that the lofty religious ideas were maintained in their purity, with the result that even today the divine light shines in Judaism.

By emphasizing religious activity, Judaism is completely tied to life and becomes the property of every individual Jew. A religion of pure ideas belongs primarily to the theologians; the masses who are not adapted to such conceptions concern themselves little with the particulars of such religions because they have little relationship to life. On the other hand, a religion of action is always present, demanding practice in activity and an expression of will, and its demands are reflected in the manifold life of the individual, with the result that the faith becomes the common property of every follower. Thus we have reached the starting point for the consideration of the current parties in Judaism. The viewpoint of the Orthodox party is clear. It has grown up in pious activity; to it the performance of precepts is inseparable from faith, for to it, the two are closely and inwardly connected. Were it to tear itself away from observance and give up the precepts, then it would find itself estranged from its own self and feel as though plunged into an abyss. Given this viewpoint, the direction and emphasis of the Orthodox party is clear. Where else, save in the combination of faith and meticulous observance of the precepts, can it find that complete satisfaction which it has enjoyed in the heritage of the fathers? When it will reject that which it has so long kept holy and inviolable? No—that is unthinkable.

Against this party there has arisen of late another one [Reform] which finds its aim in the opposite direction. This party sees salvation in overcoming the past, in carrying progress to the limit, in rejecting religious forms and returning merely to the simple original idea. In fact, we can hardly call it a party in Judaism, though its adherents still bear the name Jew, and are considered as such in social and political life, and do not belong to another faith. They do not, however, belong wholly to Judaism, for by limiting Judaism to some principles of faith, they place themselves partly outside the limits of Judaism. We will now turn to a third party which has arisen from the first party, and not only stands within the bound of Judaism, but is also filled with real zeal for its preservation and endeavours to hand it over to the descendants and make it the common good of all times.

This party bases itself upon rational faith and recognizes that the task of Judaism is religious action, but it demands that this action shall not be empty of spirit and that it shall not become merely mechanical, expressing itself mainly in the form. It has also reached the view that religious activity itself must be brought up to a higher level through giving weight to the many meanings with which it should be endowed.

Furthermore, it holds that we must omit certain unimportant actions which are not inherently connected either with the high ideas or with the religious forms delineated by the revealed laws.

We must, it feels, take into consideration the opposition between faith and conditions of the time. True faith, due to its divine nature, is above time, and just as the nobler part of man is not subjected to time, so does faith rise above all time, and the word which issued from the mouth of God is rooted in eternity. But time has a force and might which must be taken account of. There is then created a dualism in which faith and time face each other, and man chooses either to live beyond time or to be subjected to it. It is in this situation that the Jew finds himself today; he cannot escape the influence of the conditions of the time and yet when the demands of faith bring him to opposition with the spirit of the time, it is hoped that he will heed its call—find the power to resist the blandishments of the times. This third party, then, declares that Judaism must be saved for all time. It affirms both the divine value and historical basis of Judaism, and therefore believes that by introducing some changes it may achieve some agreement with the concepts and conditions of the time.

In order to have a conception of what changes should and can be introduced, we must ask ourselves the question—does Judaism allow any changes in any of its religious forms? Does it consider all of them immutable, or can they be altered? Without entering into the citation of authorities pro and con, we may point out that Judaism does indeed allow changes. The early teachers, by interpretation, changed the literal meaning of the Scriptures; later scholars that of the Mishnah and the post-talmudic scholars that of the Talmud. All these interpretations were not intended as speculation. They addressed themselves to life precepts. Thanks to such studies, Judaism achieved stabilization and avoided estrangement from the conditions of the time in various periods. . . . [The rabbis] established a rule which was intended as a guardian and protector against undue changes. It reads as follows: That which was adopted by the entire community of Israel and was accepted by the people and became a part of its life, can not be changed by any authority.

In this fundamental statement there lies a living truth. Through it there speaks a profound view of Judaism which can serve for all times as a formula for needed changes and can be employed both against destructive reform and against stagnation.

This fundamental statement helps to make clear to us what changes in Judaism are justified and how they can be realized. True, Judaism demands religious activity, but the people is not altogether mere clay to be molded by the will of theologians and scholars. In religious activities, as in those of ordinary life, it decides for itself. This right was conceded by Judaism to the people. At such times as an earlier religious ordinance was not accepted by the entire community of Israel, it was given up. Consequently, when a new ordinance was about to be enacted it was necessary to see whether it would find acceptance by the people. When the people allows certain practices to fall into disuse, then the practices cease to exist. There is in such cases no danger for faith. A people used to activity will not hurt itself and will not destroy its practices. Its own sense of religiosity warns against it. Only those practices from which it is entirely estranged and which yield it no satisfaction will be abandoned and will thus die of themselves. On the whole there is always a great fund of faith and religious activity to afford security against negation and destruction.

We have, then, reached a decisive point in regard to moderate changes, namely, that they must come from the people and that the will of the entire community must decide. Still, this rule alone may accomplish little. The whole community is a heavy unharmonious body and its will is difficult to recognize. It comes to expression only after many years. We must find a way to carry on such changes in the proper manner, and this can be done by the help of the scholars. Judaism has no priests as representatives of faith nor does it require special spiritual sanctimoniousness in its spokesmen. The power to represent it is not the share of any one family, nor does it pass from father to son. Knowledge and mastery of the law supply the sanctity, and these can be attained by everybody. In Jewish life, spiritual and intellectual ability ultimately took the place of the former priesthood which, even in early times, was limited in its function primarily to the sacrificial cult. Even in early days, Judaism recognized the will of the people as a great force and because of this recognition a great religious activity came into being. But this activity, in turn was translated into a living force by the teachers of the people through the use of original ordinances and through interpretation of the Scriptures. At times these actions of the sages lightened the amount of observance; at times they increased it. That the results of the studies and research of the teachers found acceptance among the people proves, on the one hand, that the teachers knew the character of their time, and, on the other hand, that the people had confidence in them and that they considered them true representatives of their faith. Should Jewish theologians and scholars of our time succeed in acquiring such a confidence, then they will attain influence with the introduction of whatever changes may be necessary. The will of the community of Israel will then find its representatives and knowledge will be its proper exercise.

The scholars thus have an important duty in order to make their work effective. It is to guard the sense of piety of the people and to raise their spirit to the height of the great ideas. For this they need the confidence of the people. Opposition to the views of the people, such as some reformers display, is unholy and fruitless. The teacher thereby loses the power to make the essence of faith effective, for in place of that confidence which is the basis in correct relations between teacher and community there comes mistrust and an unwillingness to follow. The truths of faith must be brought nearer to the people so that they may learn to understand the divine content within them and thus come to understand the spiritual nature and inner worth of the forms which embody these truths. Once the people are saturated with an awareness of the essential truths and the forms which embody them, a firm ground will have been established for adhering to Jewish practices. And if the people then cease to practice some unimportant customs and forms of observances it will not be a matter of great concern. And it will not, as recent changes have, lead some Jews into shock and hopelessness. They will no longer see all such changes as leading to the disappearance of our faith and language, as their pusillanimity leads them to believe, the end of the existence of Judaism.

The Ideal Conservative Jew:
Eight Behavioral Expectations
Rabbi Jerome M. Epstein, Executive Vice President,
The United Synagogue of Conservative Judaism

It is my deepest conviction that the American synagogue's most important task is to train Jews to live Jewish lives. This has not always been
the synagogue's role. The early synagogue—as an extension of and a
replacement for the Temple of Jerusalem—was, in the main, a focus
for Jewish communal ritual expression. Indeed, in Israel today, the self-
defined function of most synagogues is to serve as a house of prayer.
While a few congregations in Israel might offer an occasional study
group, the focus remains on ritual expression.

The role of the Conservative synagogue in North America, on the
other hand, has evolved beyond that point. Today, the concept of a syna-
gogue-center created by Mordecai Kaplan nearly 70 years ago is taken for
granted. While the synagogue continues to serve as a house of prayer, it
does more—much more. The modern congregation is a place for study,
Jewish celebration, social action, social events, counseling and the fulfillment of communal needs. Our challenge today is to focus all of these
toward our prime objective: the conservation of Jewish life.

In the Torah portion this morning, we read: "And Abram took Sarai,
his wife, and Lot their brother's son, and all their sustenance which
they had gathered and the souls that they had created in Haran." Com-
menting on this verse, Rabbi Leazar observed in the name of Rabbi Jose
Ben Zimra: "If all the nations assembled to create one insect they could
not endow it with life." Yet we read that Abram was "creating souls."
How does a human being create "souls"? Says Rabbi Leazar: "He who
brings a person near to God it is as though he had created him."

The real task today for the Conservative synagogue is to create Jewish souls. Like Abram, we are called—"lech lecha"—go and take
responsibility for building a community. Like Abram, we are called—
"lech lecha"—to bring people closer to God. In order to meet this
challenge, we must face our task with a sense of direction. We must
have an image of the soul of the Conservative Jew we are trying to create. For without that image clearly imbedded in our sense of mission,
we cannot succeed.

For years, the architects of the Conservative Movement were reluctant to articulate a self-definition. Our congregants often complained, and rightly so, that there was no statement as to what Conservative Judaism was and is. In recent years, with a sense of pride and self-confidence, several major statements defining Conservative Judaism have been published. Individual books written by scholars such as Dr. Elliot Dorff and Dr. Neil Gillman grappled with theological and philosophical approaches to Conservative Judaism. Emet V'Emunah, the statement of ideological principles of Conservative Judaism, was developed by a broad-based panel representing academics, pulpit rabbis and committed lay people. At our last Biennial Convention, Dr. Ismar Schorsch articulated what he believed to be the core values of Conservative Judaism.

As important as ideology, beliefs and values are, the foundation of Judaism is personal behavior; the way Jews, as individuals, live their lives. It is not so much what we believe, but rather what we do, that defines us as Jews. A member of one of our congregations recently described the Orthodox, Conservative and Reform Movements as "crazy, hazy and lazy." While I am not certain which description went with which Movement, most Jews think of the Conservative Movement as "hazy."

If the synagogue is to create Jewish souls, we must have a definition of the behaviors that define a Conservative Jew. Obviously, some Jews will disagree. Or some may decide that rather than meeting the expectations, or working to grow toward them, they will instead leave the Movement. Our goal must be to educate, persuade and inspire our members so that we may prevent rejection of what we stand for.

Without defining Conservative Jewish living, there is no target towards which to strive. It is not sufficient to articulate the ideology of our Movement. Our constituency is entitled to know what Conservative Judaism teaches about the way they should live their lives. For if Judaism does not affect the way Jews live, it is meaningless. If Conservative Judaism does not shape the life of Conservative Jews, it will render itself irrelevant.

I am not proposing standards. I am not proposing directives. We will only stimulate the uncommitted if we welcome them with openness and warmth. But we must recognize, first, that our congregants have a right to know what we expect of them as part of our Movement, and, second, that we have an obligation to share our expectations. The time has come to admit that a large number of Conservative Jews do not yet live the values of our ideology. There is no shame in not having reached our goal. There is only shame in not doing everything possible to achieve it.

Today, I wish to set before you eight proposed behavioral expectations toward which each Conservative Jew should strive. They are concrete. They are specific. It is my hope that The United Synagogue—as the association of Conservative synagogues—will boldly articulate behavioral expectations so that we can, as did Abram, create Jewish souls.

First, the ideal Conservative Jew must support a Conservative synagogue by participating in its activities. Judaism is a communal religion. While a Jew can be a Jew by himself, the Conservative Jew will enrich Jewish living through the synagogue. Although one can pray by herself, our ideal is prayer in a minyan. Shabbat and Yom Tov are enriched in community.

It is hard to be a Jew alone. Jewish life is strengthened through the support of community members. And, thus, we err in recruiting congregational members without explicitly sharing our "expectation" of their active participation. We dare not be satisfied with placing names on our congregational rolls. If we go no further, affiliation is only self-serving. It inflates our corporate ego, permitting us to boast of increased size or growth. But is that really our goal?

Enrolling new members also permits us to increase our budget. Yet if the increased budget does not enable us to affect more people in the context of the synagogue mission, to what avail are the additional resources? Without participation, membership is meaningless. Our congregations exist to strengthen Jewish life. Affiliation is merely a first step. After affiliation, Conservative Jews must commit time and energy to participate in the synagogue to create a sense of community through common activity.

Just as family implies interdependence, so too does congregation. But unless we tell those who join our Conservative synagogues that we expect their participation and commitment, we may never get it.

Second, the ideal Conservative Jew will study—as a Conservative Jew—a minimum of one hour per week. Our approach to study is distinct. We study texts critically. We bring to bear the knowledge we have amassed from other disciplines to enable us to understand the text as it was intended. At the same time, we approach the text with a bias to preserve our sacred traditions. Jewish learning is an imperative.

Solomon Schechter, in his formulation of the concept of Klal Yisrael, could not conceive of a community in which Jews were not learning. The concept of Klal Yisrael, in which each Jew has a stake in the decision-making process of the community and in charting its destiny, assumes participation by individuals who are committed to study the issues involved. Without appropriate learning, decisions are made in ignorance. By studying Jewish texts at least one hour a week, the Conservative Jew will become acquainted with the sources. Over the course of a lifetime, that foundation will expand. Unless such a commitment is made, however, Jewish growth is impossible.

We are the "people of the Book." But most Conservative Jews don't read "the Book." We have no right to claim that Torah is a core value if we do not study it. Conservative Jews have a right to know, therefore, that they are expected to study as Conservative Jews.

Jewish learning is important—Jewish knowledge is essential. But, as our sages are quick to point out, Jewish learning holds a revered position because it guides Jewish behavior. To the Conservative Jew, learning is the goal, but only to the degree that it has an effect on the student. Thus, the third behavioral expectation for the Conservative Jews is that Jewish learning will guide behavior—even when it conflicts with personal feeling or inclination. Most of us are creatures of habit. Many of us react to situations by instinct. Often, we make choices based upon our personal needs, desires, and interests.

Our struggle is to utilize Jewish values and ideology as we live our lives. There are times when we will discover ethical standards that conflict with the choices we would like to make. At times, we will become aware of moral imperatives that contradict that which we choose to do. The Conservative Jew seeks to integrate Jewish learning with his or her daily life.

Fourth, the Conservative Jew will increase personal Jewish living out of commitment and as a result of thought by adding a minimum of three new mitzvot each year. Conservative Judaism is unique in its approach to halakhah and mitzvot. For Reform Jews, halakhah is not binding. For Orthodox Jews, halakhah is not evolving. For Conservative Jews, halakhah is both evolving and binding. We have been fairly effective in educating congregants as to the evolving nature of halakhah. We have not yet met our goal of educating them as to its binding nature. It is to this task that we must devote ourselves.

We have made a wonderful statement that our Movement accepts people where they are. This position is both laudable and appropriate. But accepting people where they are does not imply that synagogues are exempt from urging congregants to continually grow in their Jewish living. We have been successful in conveying the message of our openness to people who are not yet committed to full Jewish living. We have not yet succeeded in transmitting the expectation that their commitment will grow.

Each Conservative Jew may be at a different rung on the personal ladder of Jewish fulfillment. Our challenge is to convincingly and sensitively explain to Conservative Jews that while we embrace them at whatever point they are in their personal journey, to be a Conservative Jew is to think about Jewish life and to come to conclusions about where one chooses to grow in the broad field of Jewish living. While we have attempted to educate our congregants about kashrut and Shabbat, we must become more passionate in urging the adoption of these focal points in their personal life. We must articulate our expectation that each Conservative Jew should choose a minimum of three new mitzvot each year to enrich his or her life.

The Conservative Jew has a vision that extends beyond the Jewish world; to a community in which most individuals are not Jewish. In many ways, the broad community enriches us. But we have responsibilities, as well. We must take from the community as willing recipients. And we must give to that community in return. Jewish values extend one's concern beyond himself to the entire world that God created.

The fifth behavioral expectation, therefore, is that a Conservative Jew will employ the value of Tikkun Olam to help in the world's continual repair. We are God's partners in safeguarding that which He created. A Conservative Jew does not just believe in repairing the world; she does something about it. She works towards that goal. A Conservative Jew does not only believe in equal rights; he struggles to personally ensure them. The Conservative Jew is not only pained by human suffering; he does something to relieve it.

As I mentioned earlier, one of the most prominent values of Conservative Judaism relates to Klal Yisrael. For Solomon Schechter, Klal Yisrael was the "collective conscience" of the community. It was and continues to be the corporate identity of our Jewish community. Thus, the sixth behavioral expectation is that in making a decision about Jewish behavior, the Conservative Jew considers the effect that decision will have on Klal Yisrael.

When Reform Judaism chose to advocate patrilineal descent, they, in effect, catalyzed a schism in the Jewish community. We must avoid taking such actions. When a Conservative Jew makes a decision about Jewish education with no regard for the standards of the Movement, he in fact weakens the intent of all other Conservative Jews to strengthen Jewish education. The Conservative Jewish parent who permits her teenager to interdate is taking an action that affects the entire Jewish community.

As Conservative Jews, we must realize that we are part of Klal Yisrael. What we do impacts not only on our own lives and our families, but also on the community in which we live. Klal Yisrael is not only a value—it is a behavioral expectation that must govern the way the Conservative Jew lives his life.

Since its inception, the Conservative Movement has believed in, and helped to further, the cause of Zionism. Although, by his own claim, Solomon Schechter was not an official expounder of this philosophy, he openly expressed his allegiance to it. The preamble to The United Synagogue Constitution, written in 1913, expresses hopes for Israel's restoration. What does this mean to the Conservative Jew? Believing that Israel is important and having warm feelings about the country, whether emotional or intellectual, does not have any practical consequences. While we can be proud of the large numbers of young people from our congregations who participate in USY Israel Pilgrimage, we have not begun to capture the imagination of the largest percentage of our membership.

Conservative Jews must know that they are expected to increase their ties to Israel in concrete ways: through working to ensure Israel's welfare; through articulating the importance of Israel to the Jewish, as well as the non-Jewish, community; through political action for Israel; through joining Mercaz; through financial support; through short visits to Israel, leading to extended visits; and finally, through aliyah. Israel must be more than a lofty ideal and catalyst for emotional feelings. The Conservative Jew must increase his or her concrete ties to Israel.

While, for most of us, Hebrew is a foreign language, the architects of our Movement regarded Hebrew as essential. "The maintenance of the traditional character of the liturgy with Hebrew as the language of prayer" was one of the purposes of The United Synagogue, as articulated in the preamble to our constitution. Indeed, Hebrew is chanted in most of our congregations. Still, if most Conservative Jews do not understand Hebrew, it cannot be the language of prayer. How can one pray in a language that one does not minimally understand?

It is imperative that we not only maintain Hebrew in our services but that we also express the expectation that Conservative Jews will increase their knowledge of Hebrew. One doesn't have to be a linguist in order to learn to read Hebrew. One does not have to become a Hebrew scholar in order to become increasingly familiar with the terminology of the prayerbook. Even without a working knowledge of fluent Hebrew, one can develop the resources to understand basic concepts.

These eight expectations of Conservative Jews are indeed "great expectations." Sadly, they will not be readily accepted by our constituency, since they fly in the face of the erroneous assumption that Conservative Jews may select what they want to observe and discard what they choose to reject. It is our challenge to correct this belief. Indeed, this is our mandate.

We, as Conservative Jews, are a people with a mission. Our mission, like that of Abram, is the creation of souls—Jewish souls. This is no easy task. It will require us to diligently and conscientiously set forth a program that will affect the behaviors of those who identify themselves as Conservative Jews. We have a vision. We have a mission. It is this commitment that will enable us truly to create Jewish souls.

May we be blessed in our work!

The Ideal Conservative Jew:
Eight Behavioral Expectations

1. The ideal Conservative Jew supports a Conservative synagogue by participating in its activities.

2. The ideal Conservative Jew studies as a Conservative Jew a minimum of one hour per week.

3. The ideal Conservative Jew employs learned Jewish values to guide behavior even when it conflicts with personal feeling or inclination.

4. The ideal Conservative Jew increases personal Jewish living out of commitment and as a result of thought, by adding a minimum of three new mitzvot a year.

5. The ideal Conservative Jew employs the values of tikun olam to help in the world's continual repair.

6. The ideal Conservative Jew makes decisions about Jewish behavior only after considering the effect these decisions will have on Klal Yisrael.

7. The ideal Conservative Jew increases ties and connections to Israel.

8. The ideal Conservative Jew studies to increase his or her knowledge of Hebrew.

RECONSTRUCTIONISM

Who Is a Reconstructionist Jew?

A Reconstructionist Jew has strong commitments both to tradition and to the search for contemporary meaning. Reconstructionists encourage all Jews to enhance their own lives by reclaiming our shared heritage and becoming active participants in the building of the Jewish future.

The Evolving Religious Civilization of the Jewish People

Reconstructionists define Judaism as the evolving religious civilization of the Jewish people. By "evolving" we mean that Judaism has changed over the centuries of its existence. The faith of the ancient Israelites in the days of Solomon's Temple was not the same as that of the early rabbis. And neither of those faiths was the same as that of our more recent European ancestors. Each generation of Jews has subtly reshaped the faith and traditions of the Jewish people. Reconstructionist Jews seek to nurture this evolution. We see it as the lifeblood of Judaism, the power that allows Judaism to continue as a dynamic tradition in every age. By "religious" we mean that Judaism is the means by which we conduct our search for ultimate meaning in life. God is the source of meaning. We struggle, to be sure, with doubts and uncertainties. Reconstructionists affirm that struggle; we believe it is the duty of all Jews to question and to study in order to find unique paths to the divine. We believe in a God who inhabits this world and especially the human heart. God is the source of our generosity, sensitivity and concern for the world around us. God is also the power within us that urges us toward self-fulfillment and ethical behavior. We find God when we look for meaning in the world, when we are motivated toward study and when we work to realize the goals of morality and social justice. By "civilization" we mean that Judaism is more than a religion. The Jewish people share historical memory and historical destiny. Judaism includes a commitment to our ancient homeland and language. We share a love for Jewish culture, Jewish morality and Jewish philosophy. We are heirs to a rich legacy of literary and artistic achievement, of laughter and tears, a legacy which continues to grow in our day. By "the Jewish people" we mean that all Jews, whether by birth or by choice, are members of the extended Jewish family. We recognize a diversity of Jewish religious ideology and practice and seek to join with other Jews in accepting that diversity while working toward a shared vision of Jewish peoplehood. The Reconstructionist philosophy affirms the uniqueness of the Jewish people and its heritage among the peoples of the world. However, our affirmation of Judaism's uniqueness implies no sense of superiority over others. Reconstructionists believe that all peoples are called to the service of righteousness, and we welcome dialogue with people of good will from all traditions.

The Past Has a Vote, Not a Veto

The starting point of Reconstructionism is our quest to understand the historical and spiritual experience of the Jewish people. We believe "the past has a vote." Therefore we struggle to hear the voices of our ancestors and listen to their claim on us. What did this custom or that idea mean to them? How did they see the presence of God in it? How can we retain or regain its importance in our own lives? We believe "the past does not have a veto." Therefore we struggle to hear our own voices as distinct from theirs.

What might this custom or that idea mean to us today? What might we borrow from this custom to create a new tradition that is more significant for us today? When a particular Jewish value or custom is found wanting, it is our obligation as Jews to find a means to reconstruct it—to find new meanings in old forms or to develop more meaningful, innovative practices. A vital, contemporary Judaism must respond fully to the changes in modern Jewish history: the Holocaust, renewed Jewish statehood, new and different family structures, the evolving relationships of men and women, as well as the role of religion in a universe threatened by both ecological and nuclear disaster. Only a combination of searching, questioning, and self understanding within the Jewish tradition will create a Judaism that speaks convincingly to the contemporary Jew.

What Makes a Reconstructionist Jewish Community Unique?

Orthodox Judaism has about it a seriousness and level of devotion that are truly admirable. We seek to retain that seriousness. Unlike Orthodoxy, Reconstructionism does not view Judaism as a total and immutable revelation from God to Moses at Sinai that is essentially unchanged through all generations.

We see Judaism as the ever-evolving product of history, an ongoing attempt to forge a society based on holy values. Conservative Judaism has made significant contributions to Jewish life in the realms of education and scholarship. While we support this effort, Reconstructionism diverges from Conservative Judaism in terms of priorities. We believe that the basic tenets of Judaism need to be re-examined and re-stated for our age. We see this as a more pressing priority than the particulars of Jewish law. Jews need to know why they should be Jewish at all before they worry about how to change details of observance. Concerning observance, we differ specifically on the issue of how far one may go in amending Jewish law and who has the right to be involved in that process. We believe that rabbis and scholars should work together with committed lay members of the Jewish community formulating guides to Jewish practice for our time. These guides should reflect a desire to protect and preserve tradition as well as an openness to creativity and evolution as we face a new age in Jewish society.

Reform Judaism emphasizes the centrality of the prophetic tradition and insists that standards of ethical monotheism be applied universally. We Reconstructionists affirm this emphasis and share in its commitment. Reconstructionism differs from Reform Judaism, however, concerning how much of the tradition needs to be preserved. Reconstructionists encourage Jews to give honest consideration to a wider range of traditional practice. We believe that Judaism is more than ethical monotheism. Judaism is the historic, unique and most satisfying way by which the Jewish people can find ongoing meaning in the great moments in our history and the special moments in our individual lives. Through Judaism, we dedicate ourselves to universal spiritual values that transcend any one individual, society or nation.

Israel: The Cradle of Jewish Civilization in Partnership with the Diaspora

Recognizing Judaism as the civilization of the Jewish people, Reconstructionists affirm the attachment of our people to the Land of Israel—the site of our origins and the focus of our hope through the millennia. From its inception, Reconstructionism has been a Zionist movement. We are firmly committed to the building of the State of Israel and the establishment of a just and humane Jewish society there. We consider the Jewish national rebirth centered in Israel to be the greatest accomplishment of the Jewish people in our century and encourage all Jews to develop their ties with the State of Israel. We emphasize the importance of visiting Israel, and we commend those Jews who commit their lives, through aliyah, to the rebuilding of our people's homeland. While our support for Israel is unconditional, a variety of opinion exists within the Reconstructionist movement with regard to specific policies of the Israeli government. We are united in supporting efforts by the World Union for Progressive Judaism (with which we are affiliated) and others who work to strengthen religious freedom in Israel and to make Israel a religious home for all Jews. At the same time, we believe that Diaspora communities, particularly those as strong as the ones in North America, are important centers of Jewish learning and cultural growth. Israel alone serves as a laboratory for the creation of a fully Jewish society. But where Jews thrive as citizens in multi-ethnic societies, Jewish ideals can be integrated with the highest values of contemporary civilization in unique and important ways. We look forward, as Israel matures as a society and achieves peace and stability, to a more properly balanced relationship between Israel and the Diaspora. We believe that through mutual respect and cultural exchange, these two forms of Jewish living can enrich one another.

Living in Two Civilizations: A Commitment to Social Justice and Personal Ethics

Jews who now find themselves in democratic societies live primarily in a secular civilization—governed by non-Jewish legislatures and courts, speaking non-Jewish languages, singing popular music, working in secular environments with non-Jews, learning in non-Jewish schools, and structuring their lives according to accepted Western values. Reconstructionists call upon Jews to embrace this open, democratic society—not only because its structural pluralism does not require the abandonment of Judaism, but also because American ideals at their best coincide with Jewish ideals as they ought to be developed and reconstructed. We have much to gain by incorporating contemporary mores into the Jewish civilization—with regard to the role of women, respect for individual liberties, and acceptance of cultural pluralism. Just as we seek to democratize the Jewish community, so also do we recognize the need to bring the insights of Jewish tradition to bear upon the issues that secular society confronts.

Religious values coupled with ethical action have always influenced the evolution of North American society. The voice of Jewish tradition has been prominent among those seeking social reform. In recent years, the role of religion in society has been enhanced by the leading role that clergy and religiously committed individuals have taken in movements for racial justice, the elimination of poverty, and the pursuit of peace. Reconstructionists support these efforts and participate actively in using religious tradition as a positive force for social change. We believe that Jews today are heirs to the prophets as well as to many generations of rabbis. We applaud the application of prophetic values of justice and compassion to all segments of our society. At the same time, we do not maintain that authentic Jews must adopt one political view to the exclusion of all others. Rather, we suggest that both the Jewish community and secular society have much to gain when committed Jews study their tradition in order to apply its insights to contemporary issues. Within the realm of social action, the Reconstructionist movement works actively in several areas including international conflict resolution, hunger and civil rights. It has committed itself in particular to issues concerned with the environment. As we Jews concern ourselves with the spiritual and cultural legacy that we leave to future generations, we must also commit ourselves fully to such legacies as clean air, pure water and unpolluted soil. The Reconstructionist movement through Shomrei Adamah, Guardians of the Earth, works closely with other groups concerned with the environmental future. Personal as well as social ethics are an integral feature of Reconstructionist Judaism. We affirm the centrality of ethical behavior in our lives and insist that traditional religious behavior, when not accompanied by the highest ethical standards, becomes a desecration of Judaism. We challenge our own communities to reach for the highest application of ethical standards.

Belonging to a Democratic Jewish Community in a Post-Halakhic Age

If halakhah is defined as the Jewish process of celebrating, creating and transmitting tradition, Reconstructionist Jewish communities would certainly fit within the framework of halakhah. But if halakhah has the meaning of a rigid body of law, changeable only under very rarefied circumstances, most Jewish people, including Reconstructionists, no longer accept its binding authority. While Reconstructionists are lovers of tradition and support community celebration of the Jewish sacred year and life-cycle events, we also believe that the face of the Jewish community is changing and that individuals have the right to adapt Jewish tradition to new circumstances. Reconstructionist communities challenge Jews to participate fully in our shared Jewish civilization. From building a sukkah to appreciating Jewish music, from caring for the Jewish young and old to leading Torah study—community members should experience Jewish civilization in our day as fully as they experience secular civilization. Judaism will continue to be a dynamic civilization only if we choose to participate, create and transmit vitality to future generations. Reconstructionist rabbis work in partnership with committed lay people to formulate guidelines that serve as Jewish touchstones for our times. These guidelines are presented and democratically considered in Reconstructionist communities as standards for enhancing the Jewish life of the individual and the community rather than as binding laws.

The Reconstructionist Vision of the Jewish Future

We Reconstructionists envision a maximalist liberal Judaism. This means Jewish life that is engaged in study, worship and action and yet is completely supportive of a Jew's full participation in secular life.

We hope for a Judaism that serves as a rich source of spiritual self-expression and moral challenge in the way we conduct our lives. We dream of a Jewish people that will overcome divisions and realize its commitment to the single goal of transforming the world into one where all people are respected as bearers of the divine image. We picture an Israel at peace and a Jewish people, in both Israel and the Diaspora, that will have the dedication, knowledge, and prosperity to develop an ever richer tradition to hand down to future generations. Like all Jews, Reconstructionists are firm believers in the future. It is our dedication to the future, characterized by commitment and creativity, by the faithful heart joined to the open mind, that makes us proud of the Reconstructionist contribution to the ever-evolving heritage of the Jewish people.

ORTHODOXY

*The Orthodox Jewish Congregational Union of America**

A convention of Orthodox Congregations met in New York, Wednesday, June 8, 1898. A resolution favoring Zionism was adopted. The principles of the convention adopted are as follows:

The Conference of delegates from Jewish congregations in the United States and the Dominion of Canada is convened to advance the interests of positive, Biblical, Rabbinical and Historical Judaism.

We are assembled not as a synod and therefore we have no legislative authority to amend religious questions, but as a representative body, which by organization and cooperation will endeavor to advance the interests of Judaism in America.

We favor the convening of a Jewish Synod specifically authorized by

---

* Founding statement of what would become the Orthodox Union, the leading body of Modern Orthodox congregations in the United States.

congregations to meet, to be composed of men who must be certified Rabbis, and

a. Elders in official positions (Cf. Numbers 9:16)

b. Men of wisdom and understanding and known amongst us (Cf. Deuteronomy 1:13)

c. Able men, God-fearing men, men of truth, hating profit (Cf. Exodus 18:21).

We believe in the Divine revelation of the Bible, and we declare that the prophets in no way discountenanced ceremonial duty but only condemned the personal life of those who observed ceremonial law but disregarded the moral. Ceremonial law is not optative; it is obligatory.

We affirm our adherence to the acknowledged cores of our Rabbis and the thirteen principles of Maimonides.

We believe that in our dispersion we are to be united with our brethren of alien faith in all that devolves upon men as citizens, but that religiously, in rites, ceremonies, ideals and doctrines, we are separate, and must remain separate in accordance with the Divine declaration: "I have separated you from the nations to be Mine."

And further, to prevent misunderstanding concerning Judaism, we reaffirm our belief in the coming of a personal Messiah and we protest against the admission of proselytes into the fold of Judaism without *milah* [circumcision] and *tevilah* [immersion in the *mikveh*].

We protest against intermarriage between Jew and Gentile; we protest against the idea that we are merely a religious sect and maintain that we are a nation, though temporarily without a national home, and

Furthermore, that the restoration to Zion is the legitimate aspiration of scattered Israel, in no way conflicting with our loyalty to the land in which we dwell or may dwell at any time.

Founding Program of Agudat Israel
(May 1912)

The purpose of Agudat Israel is the solution of the respective tasks facing the Jewish collectivity, in the spirit of the Torah. In accordance with this purpose, it sets itself the following goals: (1) the organization, concentration and unification of dispersed parts of Orthodox Jewry, especially of the Jews in Eastern and Western Europe; (2) the generous promotion of

Torah studies, and of Jewish education in general, in countries where this promotion is needed; (3) the improvement of economic conditions of the Jewish masses, not only in Palestine, but wherever they suffer want; (4) the organization and promotion of emergency aid in cases of necessity; (5) the advancement of a press and literature in the Jewish spirit; (6) a representative forum of all Jews adhering to the Torah; this forum will parry the attacks directed against the Torah and its adherents.

Against this work of unifying Orthodox Jewry, a stock objection is raised in a part of the national Jewish press which states that Agudat Israel lacks a clear program. In this respect, Agudat Israel is unfavorably compared with Zionism.

This much is correct: Zionism has not only set up a general program, but is fortunate enough to be able to outline the way in which it hopes to find a definite solution to all Jewish problems. The "national home secured by public law," for which the first battle was fought in Basle, is considered to be the panacea for all national ailments. It is only for this means, transformed into an end, that the Zionists are ready to mobilize and organize their forces.

Agudat Israel, on the other hand—or so they claim—has no program of redemption. And an organization without a program, it is held, is tantamount to an organization without a clear purpose suspended in midair without a foundation and without a supporting pillar.

It can be argued that the general task of Orthodox Jewry has from ancient times been clearly and programmatically defined, and that for its propagation there is no need for any other base than that which has supported and united us through centuries of suffering. New currents and movements must be based on newly created foundations. The work of unification on behalf of Orthodox Jewry does not derive from any new and revolutionary idea. It only wishes to unify, collect and conserve on the basis of our ancient program.

ZIONISM

The Basel Program
Passed by the First Zionist Congress (1897)

The aim of Zionism is to create for the Jewish people a home in Palestine secured by public law.

The Congress contemplates the following means to the attainment of this end:

1. The promotion, on suitable lines, of the colonization of Palestine by Jewish agricultural and industrial workers.

2. The organization and binding together of the whole Jewry by means of appropriate institutions, local and international in accordance with the laws of each country.

3. The strengthening and fostering of Jewish national sentiment and consciousness.

4. Preparatory steps towards obtaining government consent, where necessary, to the attainment of the aim of Zionism.

The Balfour Declaration

During the First World War, British policy became gradually committed to the idea of establishing a Jewish home in Palestine (Eretz Yisrael). After discussions in the British Cabinet, and consultation with Zionist leaders, the decision was made known in the form of a letter by Arthur James Lord Balfour to Lord Rothschild. The letter represents the first political recognition of Zionist aims by a Great Power.

Foreign Office
November 2nd, 1917

Dear Lord Rothschild,

I have much pleasure in conveying to you, on behalf of His Majesty's Government, the following declaration of sympathy with Jewish Zionist aspirations which has been submitted to, and approved by, the Cabinet.

His Majesty's Government views with favour the establishment in Palestine of a national home for the Jewish people, and will use their best endeavours to facilitate the achievement of this object, it being clearly understood that nothing shall be done which may prejudice the civil and religious rights of existing non-Jewish communities in Palestine, or the rights and political status enjoyed by Jews in any other country.

I should be grateful if you would bring this declaration to the knowledge of the Zionist Federation.

Yours sincerely,
Arthur James Balfour

Declaration of Israel's Independence, 1948
Issued at Tel Aviv on May 14, 1948 (5th of Iyar, 5708)

The land of Israel was the birthplace of the Jewish people. Here their spiritual, religious and national identity was formed. Here they achieved independence and created a culture of national and universal significance. Here they wrote and gave the Bible to the world.

Exiled from Palestine, the Jewish people remained faithful to it in all the countries of their dispersion, never ceasing to pray and hope for their return and the restoration of their national freedom.

Impelled by this historic association, Jews strove throughout the centuries to go back to the land of their fathers and regain their statehood. In recent decades they returned in masses. They reclaimed the wilderness, revived their language, built cities and villages and established a vigorous and ever-growing community with its own economic and cultural life. They sought peace yet were ever prepared to defend themselves. They brought the blessing of progress to all inhabitants of the country.

In the year 1897 the First Zionist Congress, inspired by Theodor Herzl's vision of the Jewish State, proclaimed the right of the Jewish people to national revival in their own country.

This right was acknowledged by the Balfour Declaration of November 2, 1917, and re-affirmed by the Mandate of the League of Nations, which gave explicit international recognition to the historic connection of the Jewish people with Palestine and their right to reconstitute their National Home.

The Nazi holocaust, which engulfed millions of Jews in Europe, proved anew the urgency of the re-establishment of the Jewish state, which would solve the problem of Jewish homelessness by opening the gates to all Jews and lifting the Jewish people to equality in the family of nations. The survivors of the European catastrophe, as well as Jews from other lands, proclaiming their right to a life of dignity, freedom and labor, and undeterred by hazards, hardships and obstacles, have tried unceasingly to enter Palestine.

In the Second World War the Jewish people in Palestine made a full contribution in the struggle of the freedom-loving nations against the Nazi evil. The sacrifices of their soldiers and the efforts of their workers gained them title to rank with the peoples who founded the United Nations.

On November 29, 1947, the General Assembly of the United Nations adopted a Resolution for the establishment of an independent Jewish State in Palestine, and called upon the inhabitants of the country to take such steps as may be necessary on their part to put the plan into effect. This recognition by the United Nations of the right of the Jewish people to establish their independent State may not be revoked. It is, moreover, the self-evident right of the Jewish people to be a nation, as all other nations, in its own sovereign State.

ACCORDINGLY, WE, the members of the National Council, representing the Jewish people in Palestine and the Zionist movement of the world, met together in solemn assembly today, the day of the termination of the British mandate for Palestine, by virtue of the natural and historic right of the Jewish people and of the Resolution of the General Assembly of the United Nations,

HEREBY PROCLAIM the establishment of the Jewish State in Palestine, to be called ISRAEL.

WE HEREBY DECLARE that as from the termination of the Mandate at midnight, this night of the 14th and 15th May, 1948, and until the setting up of the duly elected bodies of the State in accordance with a Constitution, to be drawn up by a Constituent Assembly not later than the first day of October, 1948, the present National Council shall act as the provisional administration, shall constitute the Provisional Government of the State of Israel.

THE STATE OF ISRAEL will be open to the immigration of Jews from all countries of their dispersion; will promote the development of the country for the benefit of all its inhabitants; will be based on the precepts of liberty, justice and peace taught by the Hebrew Prophets; will uphold the full social and political equality of all its citizens, without distinction of race, creed or sex; will guarantee full freedom of conscience, worship, education and culture; will safeguard the sanctity and inviolability of the shrines and Holy Places of all religions; and will dedicate itself to the principles of the Charter of the United Nations.

THE STATE OF ISRAEL will be ready to cooperate with the organs and representatives of the United Nations in the implementation of the Resolution of the Assembly of November 29, 1947, and will take steps to bring about the Economic Union over the whole of Palestine. We appeal to the United Nations to assist the Jewish people in the building of its State and to admit Israel into the family of nations. In the midst of wanton aggression, we yet call upon the Arab inhabitants of the State of Israel to return to the ways of peace and play their part in the development of the State, with full and equal citizenship and due representation in its bodies and institutions—provisional or permanent.

We offer peace and unity to all the neighboring states and their peoples, and invite them to cooperate with the independent Jewish nation for the common good of all. Our call goes out to the Jewish people all over the world to rally to our side in the task of immigration and development and to stand by us in the great struggle for the fulfillment of the dream of generations—the redemption of Israel.

With trust in Almighty God, we set our hand to this Declaration, at this Session of the Provisional State Council, in the city of Tel Aviv, on this Sabbath eve, the fifth of Iyar, 5708, the fourteenth day of May, 1948.

A Time Line of Major Events

c. 1850–1700 B.C.E.	Abraham & Sarah, Isaac & Ishmael; origin of traditions of the "Abrahamic covenant," traditions of Jacob/Israel and the Twelve Patriarchs
c. 1300–1200 B.C.E.	Mosaic period (Israel); Exodus from Egypt; Torah given at Sinai, entry into Canaan (c. 1250–1200)
c. 1200–1000 B.C.E.	Judges rule in Israel
c. 1000–587 B.C.E.	Monarchical period in Israel; Saul (c. 1030–1010); David, making Jerusalem his capital (c. 1010–970); Solomon, and building of the First Temple (c. 970–931)
c. 931 B.C.E.	Secession of Northern Kingdom (Israel) from Southern Kingdom (Judah)
c. 750–720 B.C.E.	Amos, Hosea, and Isaiah prophesy
722–720 B.C.E.	Assyrians invade and conquer Israel; Northern Kingdom destroyed (Ten Lost Tribes)
640 B.C.E.	Reign of Josiah begins; prophecies of Zephaniah
c. 626 B.C.E.	Jeremiah is called to prophesy
612 B.C.E.	Nineveh is destroyed by Babylonians and Medes
597 B.C.E.	Ezekiel taken in captivity to Babylonia
586 B.C.E.	Destruction of the First Temple
568–538 B.C.E.	Babylonian Exile

c. 550 B.C.E.	"Second Isaiah" prophesies
539 B.C.E.	Babylonian Empire falls to Persians
520–515 B.C.E.	Second Temple built
c. 520 B.C.E.	Prophecies of Haggai, Zechariah
Fifth Century B.C.E.	Oldest known example of a *ketubah*
c. 450–400 B.C.E.	Ezra returns to Judah with the *"torah of Moses,"* and with Nehemiah begins reform of Judaism in the spirit of the Torah; Torah begins to gain recognition as Scripture
c. 400 B.C.E.	Beginnings of group prayer as a Jewish phenomenon
c. 350–200 B.C.E.	Men of the Great Assembly
Third Century B.C.E.	Rise of the Sadducees
	Septuagint; Greek translation of Hebrew Bible
c. 200 B.C.E.	*Nevi'im/Prophets* recognized by some as Scripture; weekly readings of *haftarot* become the norm
c. 200–First Century B.C.E.	The *Zugot/Pairs*
Second Century B.C.E.	Idea of resurrection of the dead gains currency in Jewish circles for the first time
165–163 B.C.E.	Maccabees fight against Syrian rulers of Palestine (events commemorated by Hanukah)
First Century B.C.E.	Tannaim, First Generation
	Rabbi Simeon ben Shetakh establishes the first schools and orders parents to send their children to them
c. 20 B.C.E.	Philo Judaeus born
38 C.E.	Philo goes with Alexandrian delegation to Rome
c. 50 C.E.	Philo dies
c. 50–125 C.E.	Christian Testament writings
70 C.E.	Second Temple destroyed on the 9th of Av
c. 90–130 C.E.	Tannaim, Second Generation

c. 90–150 C.E.	*Ketuvim/Writings* discussed and accepted as sacred scripture; canonization of Hebrew Bible is essentially complete
First Century C.E.	Prayer service begins to evolve towards its present structure; Rabbi Joseph ben Gamla, the High Priest of the Second Temple, arranges for towns to have their own teachers
c. 130–160 C.E.	Tannaim, Third Generation
135 C.E.	Bar Kokhba rebellion defeated at Betar by Romans on 9th of Av
c. 135 C.E.	Roman governors ban circumcision
Second Century C.E.	Onkelos authors commentary on Torah; Tannaim, Fourth Generation; redaction of Mishnah, *Tosefta, Merkavah,* and *Hekhalot* texts written
c. 200–Sixth Century C.E.	Amoraim
c. 220 C.E.	Judah Ha-Nasi (Judah the Prince, also known as Rabbi) dies
Third–Sixth Centuries C.E.	*Sefir Yetzirah* written sometime in this period
Third Century C.E.	Rabbi Simlai states that there are 613 commandments given by God in the Torah
c. 300	Redaction of Halakhic Midrashim
315	Christianity is proclaimed official religion of the Roman Empire; proselytizing for Judaism is punishable by death
353	Non-Jews who convert to Judaism in Roman Empire forfeit all their goods to the State
358	Rabbi Hillel II introduces permanent fixed ritual calendar
c. 400	Redaction of *Aggadic Midrashim;* Palestinian Talmud
c. 427–650	Redaction of Babylonian Talmud

Sixth Century C.E.	Savoraim
Eighth Century C.E.	Rise of the Karaites; king of the Khazars and his entire people convert to Judaism
Ninth–Tenth Centuries C.E.	Masoretic text, with vowel markings and cantillation, becomes the accepted version of Hebrew Bible
Ninth Century C.E.	*Seder Rav Amram Gaon*
882	Saadiah Gaon born in Egypt
922	Saadiah Gaon arrives in Pumbedita and is named head of the academy there; in six years he will be named *gaon*
Tenth Century C.E.	Saadiah Gaon writes his *siddur;* earliest commentaries on *Sefer Yetzirah*
933	Saadiah writes the *Book of Beliefs and Opinions*
942	Saadiah Gaon dies
c. 1000	Rabbenu Gershom rules that a wife may not be divorced without her consent
Eleventh Century C.E.	*Makhzor Vitry*
1040–1105	Rashi (Rabbi Shelomo Yitzkhaki)
1075	Judah HaLevi born in Spain
c. 1092–1167	Abraham ibn Ezra
1096	First Crusade, massive anti-Jewish violence in France and Germany
1138	Moses ben Maimon, called Maimonides, born in Spain
c. 1141	Judah HaLevi dies
1145	Almohade invasion of Spain
c. 1150	Rabbi Jacob Tam issues ruling that allows for some exceptions to Rabbenu Tam's decree on divorce
1160–1235	Radak (Rabbi David Kimkhi)

1165	Maimonides publishes *Mishneh Torah,* a monumental compendium of Jewish law
Late Twelfth Century C.E.	Ashkenazi Hasidim, early kabbalists in Spain; *Sefer Ha-Bahir* written
1180	Maimonides named court physician to Saladin
1190	Jews of York, England, massacred on 9th of Av
1194–1270	Nakhmanides (Rabbi Moses ben Nakhman)
Thirteenth Century C.E.	*Maoz Tzur* composed
1204	Maimonides dies
1230	Some rabbinic authorities argue for a ban on Maimonides' *Guide for the Perplexed*
Late Thirteenth Century C.E.	Rise of kabbalistic circles in Gerona and Barcelona
c. 1290	De Leon writes *Sefer Ha-Zohar*
c. 1400	First known examples of *bar mitzvah* ceremony
1492	Jews expelled from Spain
1497	Jews expelled from Portugal
1534	Isaac Luria (the Ari) born
c. 1540	Solomon ben Moses Ha-Levi Alkabetz writes *L'kha Dodi*
c. 1555	Joseph Caro completes the *Shulkhan Arukh,* definitive code of Jewish law
1565	Joseph Caro publishes *Shulkhan Arukh*
c. 1622	Spinoza family settles in the Netherlands
1632	Baruch Spinoza born in Amsterdam
1648	Cossack "Black Hundreds" massacre over 100,000 Jews in Ukraine, Poland
1655	Russo-Swedish War; thousands of Jews massacred in Poland
1656	Spinoza is excommunicated
1663	Spinoza publishes book on Descartes

1665	Shabbateanism spreads across Middle East, Eastern and Western Europe
1670	Spinoza writes *Tractatus Theologico-Politicus*
1677	Spinoza dies
1700–1760	Israel Baal Shem Tov, founder of Hasidism
1729	Moses Mendelssohn born in Germany
1754	Mendelssohn's first published works
1763	Mendelssohn wins prize from Prussian Royal Academy for his essay, "On Evidence in the Metaphysical Sciences"; is granted "right of residence" in Berlin by Frederick the Great
1772	Mitnagdim issue order of excommunication against Hasidim
1783	Mendelssohn publishes *Jerusalem*
1786	Mendelssohn dies
1789	Jews granted full legal equality in United States
1791	Jews granted full legal equality in France
1796	Jews granted full legal equality in the Netherlands
Nineteenth Century C.E.	Reform movement experiments with abridged services for children
1810	Israel Jacobson opens his synagogue (beginnings of Reform), introduces confirmation ceremony
1818	Hamburg Temple founded October 18, denounced by *bet din*
1832	Jews granted full legal equality in Canada
1842	Society of Friends of Reform founded in Frankfurt
1856	Jews granted full legal equality in Great Britain
1857	Isaac Mayer Wise publishes *Minhag America*
1861	Jews granted full legal equality in Italy
1865	Birth of Abraham Isaac Kook

1867	Jews granted full legal equality in Hapsburg Empire
1871	Jews granted full legal equality in Germany
1874	Jews granted full legal equality in Switzerland
1875	Union of American Hebrew Congregations (Reform) established; Hebrew Union College (Reform) opens in Cincinnati
1878	Martin Buber is born in Vienna; Jews granted full legal equality in Bulgaria; Jews granted full legal equality in Serbia
1881	BILU, Jewish youth group, established in Russia; they will send first settlers to Palestine the following year
1882	Pinsker publishes *Auto-Emancipation*
1885	Pittsburgh Platform (Reform) rejects *halakhah* as binding upon contemporary Jews
1886	Jewish Theological Seminary (JTS; Conservative) founded; Franz Rosenzweig is born in Germany
1895	*Union Prayer Book* (Reform)
1896	Herzl publishes *The Jewish State*
1897	First Zionist Congress leads to founding of World Zionist Organization
1898	Founding of Orthodox Union in U.S.
1901	Theodor Herzl names Buber editor of official Zionist journal, *Die Welt*
1902	Solomon Schechter becomes head of Jewish Theological Seminary
1903	Buber stumbles across the tales of Rabbi Nakhman of Bratzlav; Joseph Dov Soloveitchik is born in Belarus; Kishinev pogrom—49 Russian Jews killed

1904–14	Second *Aliyah*
1905	Unsuccessful revolution in Russia
1906	Emmanuel Levinas born in Lithuania
1907	Abraham Joshua Heschel born in Lithuania
1908	Jews granted full legal equality in Ottoman Empire; Czernowitz conference of Yiddishists
1910	Jews granted full legal equality in Spain
1913	Contemplating conversion to Christianity, Rosenzweig attends Yom Kippur services and resolves to remain a Jew
1915	Rosenzweig enlists in German Army, begins writing *Star of Redemption* on postcards he sends home from the front
1917	Balfour Declaration; Russian Revolution in February overthrows Romanovs; second Russian Revolution in October—Bolsheviks overthrow Kerensky's Provisional Government; Jews granted full legal equality in Russia in the wake of Bolshevik victory
1920	Rosenzweig is appointed head of the *Lehrhaus* in Frankfurt; begins lifelong friendship with Martin Buber
1921	*Star of Redemption* is published; Abraham Kook appointed Chief Rabbi of Palestine
1922	Mordecai Kaplan, opens his synagogue, the Society for the Advancement of Judaism; his daughter, Judith Kaplan, is first girl to undergo *bat mitzvah* ceremony
1923	Buber's *I and Thou* is published
1925	First sections of Buber-Rosenzweig translation of Torah are published
1928–29	Levinas in Freiburg, studies with Husserl and Cassirer and befriends Heidegger
1929	Rosenzweig dies after long struggle with amytrophic lateral sclerosis
1932	Soloveitchik emigrates to U.S., settling in Boston
1933	Adolf Hitler named Reichschancellor; Hitler names Heidegger Rector of University of Freiburg
1937	Buber appoints Abraham Joshua Heschel head of the *Lehrhaus* and emigrates to Palestine; Columbus Platform (Reform)
1938	Heschel is deported to Poland by the Nazis;

	Gershom Scholem lectures on Jewish mysticism at Jewish Institute of Religion, New York City
1939	Heschel leaves the Continent, first for London, then New York, where he will spend the remainder of his life; Levinas, an officer in the French Army, is taken prisoner by Germans; a POW for virtually the whole war, he writes *De l'existence a l'existant* in captivity
1941	Soloveitchik appointed to faculty at Yeshiva University's rabbinical seminary; by the time of his retirement in 1985, he will ordain over 2,000 rabbis
1942	Deportations from Warsaw to death camp at Treblinka begin on 9th of Av
1945	*Kol Haneshama* (Reconstructionist) published; a group of Orthodox rabbis condemn and publicly burn it; Heschel appointed to faculty of Jewish Theological Seminary
1948	War of Independence; Israel declares its independence (commemorated by Yom Ha-Atzma-ut)
1950	Knesset passes the Law of Return
1951	Knesset, Israeli Parliament, establishes Yom ha-Shoah
1961	Levinas publishes *Totality and Infinity*
1965	Martin Buber dies
1967	Jerusalem re-united by Israeli victory in Six-Day War (commemorated by Yom Yerushalayim); Reconstructionist Rabbinical College opens in Philadelphia; First *havurah* founded in Denver
1972	Abraham Joshua Heschel dies; Reform movement ordains its first woman rabbi; Beit Chayim Chadashim, first gay and lesbian synagogue, founded in Los Angeles
1974	Reconstructionist movement ordains its first woman rabbis
1975	*Gates of Prayer* (Reform)
1979	Arthur Waskow founds *Menorah,* which will become official publication of Jewish Renewal Movement
1980	World Congress of Gay and Lesbian Jewish Organizations founded
1983	Reform movement recognizes as Jewish the children of inter-

marriages between male Jew and female non-Jew in cases in
which the children are raised in the Jewish faith

1984   Star of David, organization for adopted Jewish children,
founded; Conservative movement ordains its first female
rabbis

1993   Joseph Soloveitchik dies

1996   Emmanuel Levinas dies

Where the Jews Are Today

(N.B.: The following statistics, derived from the *Information Please Almanac* [New York: Simon & Schuster, 1998,] are rough approximations.)

Jewish population of the world (0.2%)	13,866,000
Africa	165,000
Asia (incl. former Soviet Central Asian Republics)	4,257,000
Latin America	1,084,000
North America	5,836,000
Europe	2,432,000
Oceania	92,000

Jewish population of the United States	
1900	1,500,000 (2.4%)
1970	6,700,000 (3.2%)
1990	5,535,000 (2.2%)
1995	5,518,000 (2.1%)
2000 (proj.)	5,500,000 (2.0%)

Jewish population in other countries (from U.S. Census International Database; year given is most recent data available; needless to say, figures for Iran and Iraq, for example, are long since outdated; for countries not represented below, data was not available)

Australia (1991)	74,167
Bahamas (1970)	477
Brazil (1980)	91,795
Canada (1991)	318,070

Egypt (1986)	794
Finland (1985)	994
Germany (1970)	31,700
Gibraltar (1981)	589
Hong Kong (1977)	500
Iran (1976)	62,258
Iraq (1965)	3,187
Ireland (1981)	2,127
Israel (1983)	3,349,997
Macau (1970)	13
Mexico (1990)	57,918
Portugal (1970)	1,300
South Africa (1991)	67,654
Switzerland (1980)	18,330
Turkey (1965)	38,267

Here is another set of numbers, ostensibly more recent, drawn from the web pages of Virtual Jerusalem (http://www.virtualjerusalem.com /communities/wjcbook/chartmap.htm):

United States	5,800,000
Israel	4,600,000
France	600,000
Russia	550,000
Ukraine	400,000
Canada	360,000
United Kingdom	300,000
Argentina	250,000
Brazil	130,000
South Africa	106,000
Australia	100,000
Hungary	80,000
Belarus	60,000
Germany	60,000
Mexico	40,700
Belgium	40,000
Italy	35,000
Uzbekistan	35,000

Venezuela	35,000
Uruguay	32,500
Azerbaijan	30,000
Moldova	30,000
Netherlands	30,000
Iran	25,000
Turkey	25,000
Sweden	18,000
Switzerland	18,000
Georgia	17,000
Chile	15,000
Kazakhstan	15,000
Latvia	15,000
Romania	14,000
Spain	14,000
Austria	10,000
Denmark	8,000
Poland	8,000
Morocco	7,500
Hawaii, USA	7,000
Panama	7,000
Czech Republic	6,000
India	6,000
Lithuania	6,000
Slovakia	6,000
Colombia	5,650
Greece	5,000
New Zealand	5,000
Kyrgyzstan	4,500
Bulgaria	3,000
Estonia	3,000
Peru	3,000
Puerto Rico	3,000
Costa Rica	2,500
Hong Kong	2,500
Yugoslavia	2,500
Croatia	2,000
Japan	2,000

Tunisia	2,000
Tajikistan	1,800
Norway	1,500
Guatemala	1,200
Finland	1,200
Paraguay	1,200
Turkmenistan	1,200
Cuba	1,000
Ecuador	1,000
Ireland	1,000
Monaco	1,000
Zimbabwe	925
Portugal	900
Yemen	800
Bosnia-Herzegovina	600
Gibraltar	600
Luxembourg	600
Ethiopia	500
Kenya	400
Netherlands Antilles	400
US Virgin Islands	400
Bolivia	380
Zaire	320
Jamaica	300
Singapore	300
Dominican Republic	250
Philippines	250
Syria	250
Thailand	250
Armenia	200
Bahamas	200
Suriname	200
South Korea	150
El Salvador	120
Iraq	120

Cities with the largest Jewish population in the Diaspora
(from Virtual Jerusalem)

New York, USA	750,000
Miami, USA	535,000
Los Angeles, USA	490,000
Paris, France	350,000
Philadelphia, USA	350,000
Chicago, USA	248,000
San Francisco, USA	210,000
Boston, USA	208,000
London, UK	200,000
Moscow, Russia	200,000
Buenos Aires, Argentina	180,000
Toronto, Canada	175,000
Washington, DC, USA	165,000
Kiev, Ukraine	110,000
Montreal, Canada	100,000
St. Petersburg, Russia	100,000

Jewish Holidays, 1999–2006

Jewish Year Secular Year	5760 1999–2000	5761 2000–1	5762 2001–2	5763 2002–3	5764 2003–4	5765 2004–5	5766 2005–6
Rosh Hashanah	9/11–12	9/30–10/1	9/18–19	9/7–8	9/27–28	9/16–17	10/4–5
Yom Kippur	9/20	10/9	9/27	9/16	10/6	9/25	10/13
Sukkot	9/25–26	10/14–15	10/2–3	9/21–22	10/11–12	9/30–10/1	10/18–19
Shemini Atzeret– Simkhat Torah	10/2–3	10/21–22	10/9–10	9/28–29	10/18–19	10/6–7	10/25–26
Hanukah	12/4–11	12/22–29	12/10–17	11/30–12/7	12/20–27	12/9–15	12/26–1/2
Purim	3/2	3/21	3/9	2/26	3/18	3/25	3/14
Pesakh	4/20–27	4/8–15	3/28–4/4	4/17–24	4/6–13	4/24–5/1	4/13–20
Shavuot	6/9–10	5/28–29	5/17–18	6/6–7	5/25–26	6/13–14	6/2–3
Tisha b'Av	8/10	7/29	7/18	8/7	7/27	8/14	8/3

How Do I Know It's Kosher?

An Orthodox Union Kosher Primer

The Hebrew word *kosher* means fit or proper. As it relates to dietary (kosher) laws, it means that a given product is permitted and acceptable.

The sources for the laws of Kashruth are of biblical origin and expounded in rabbinic legislation, through which the rabbis interpreted, refined, or added preventative measures to the biblical regulations. These laws are codified in the Shulkhan Arukh (Code of Jewish Law), and are discussed in the ancient, medieval, and contemporary writings of the rabbis.

The laws of Kashruth are complex and extensive. The intention of this guide is to acquaint the reader with some of the fundamentals of Kashruth and provide an insight into their practical application. Given the complex nature of the laws of Kashruth, one should consult an Orthodox rabbi when a question involving Kashruth arises.

Though an ancillary hygienic benefit has been attributed to the observance of Kashruth, their ultimate purpose and rationale is simply to conform to the Divine Will as expressed in the Torah.

Not too long ago most food products were made in the family kitchen, or in a small factory or store in the community. It was easy to find out if the product in question was reliably kosher. If rabbinical supervision was required, it was attended to by the rabbi of the community, who was known to all. Today, industrialization, transcontinental shipping, and mass production have created a situation where most of the foods we eat are treated, processed, cooked, canned, or boxed commercially in industrial settings which are likely to be located hundreds or thousands of miles away from home. Furthermore, it is often impossible to tell from the label what ingredients or processes have actually been used. This last assumption is based on the following facts:

A. The law does not always require listing ingredients or all ingredients used, especially when used in relatively small amounts or in amounts less than the law requires to be listed on the package.
B. The consumer has no way of knowing if the ingredients listed are derived from non-kosher animals or other non-kosher sources, or if the machinery used was not kosher because it was also used to process non-kosher products.
C. The technical name of the ingredients printed on the label may not be adequate to inform the consumer of what is actually being used, and if it is or is not kosher. (See our Guide to Common Food Ingredients.)
D. The use of general ingredient terms such as "spices," "flavors," is as good as no information at all.

Because we all have the tendency to take for granted that certain products are kosher even if they don't carry reliable Kashruth supervision, the consumer is urged to be mindful that:

A. Because of the complicated and intricate nature of food production, foods which we consider "obviously kosher" may not be kosher at all, and may require rabbinic supervision and approval.
B. Some ingredients which we might believe are simple, such as "chocolate flavor," might be made up of over 30 separate ingredients.
C. Before eating ask yourself, "Is there a Kashruth problem?"

KOSHER AND NON-KOSHER MEAT, POULTRY, AND FISH

Meat: The Torah (in Leviticus I, 1) lists the characteristics of permitted mammals and fish, and enumerates the forbidden fowl. The only mammals permitted are those which chew their cud (ruminants) and are cloven-hoofed.

Poultry: The Torah does not enumerate specific characteristics to distinguish permitted from forbidden birds. Instead, it enumerates 24 forbidden species of fowl. The Shulkhan Arukh states that we may eat only those birds for which there is an established tradition that the bird is kosher. In the United States, the only poultry prepared for the kosher market are chicken, turkey, duck, and geese.

Fish: The Torah establishes two criteria in determining kosher fish. They must have fins and skin of the fish (cycloid and ctenoid). All shellfish are prohibited. Unlike meat and poultry, fish requires no special preparation. One however should not eat fish with meat. Filleted or ground fish should not be purchased unless one is assured that it comes from a kosher fish. Processed and smoked fish products require rabbinic supervision, as do all processed foods.

KOSHER SLAUGHTERING

The processing of kosher meats and poultry requires that the animal be slaughtered in the manner prescribed by the Torah (Shekhita).

A. Shekhita: Only a trained kosher slaughterer (shokhet) whose piety and expertise have been attested to by rabbinic authorities is qualified to slaughter an animal. The trachea and esophagus of the animal are severed with a special razor-sharp, perfectly smooth blade causing instantaneous death with no pain to the animal.

B. Bedika: After the animal has been properly slaughtered, a trained inspector (bodek) inspects the internal organs for any physiological abnormalities that may render the animal non-kosher (treif). The lungs in particular must be examined to determine that there are no adhesions (sirkhot) which may be indicative of a puncture in the lungs. If an adhesion is found, the bodek must examine it carefully to determine its Kashruth status.

C. Glatt Kosher: Though not all adhesions will necessarily render an animal treif, some Jewish communities or individuals only eat of an animal that has been found to be free of all adhesions. "Glatt" literally means smooth, indicating that the meat comes from an animal whose lung has been found to be free of all adhesions. Of late "glatt kosher" has come to be used more broadly as a consumer phrase meaning kosher without question.

D. Nikkur: There are special cutting procedures for beef, veal and lamb, called "Nikkur" in Hebrew. Many blood vessels, nerves, and lobes of fat are forbidden and must be removed before, a costly and time-consuming procedure.

E. Koshering: The Torah forbids the eating of the blood of an animal. The two methods of extracting blood from meat are salting and broiling. Meat once ground cannot be made kosher, nor may meat be placed in hot water before it has been "koshered."

1. Salting: The meat must first be soaked for a half hour in cool (not ice) water in a utensil designated only for that purpose. After allowing for excess water to drip off, the meat is thoroughly salted so that every surface is covered with salt. Only coarse salt should be used. In processing poultry both the inside and outside of the slaughtered bird must be salted. All inside parts must be removed before the koshering process begins.

Each part must be soaked and salted separately. If the meat had been sliced with a knife during the salting process, the surface of the cut must be soaked and salted as well. The salted meat is then left for an hour on an inclined or perforated surface to allow the blood to flow down freely. The cavity of poultry should be placed open side down. After the salting the meat must be thoroughly soaked and washed to remove all salt.

According to rabbinic law, meat must be koshered within 72 hours after slaughter so as not to permit the blood to congeal. If meat has been thoroughly soaked or rinsed, an additional seventy-two hours is granted for the salting process.

2. Broiling: An alternate means of "koshering" meat is through broiling. Because of the preponderance of blood in the liver, it can only be koshered through broiling. The liver must first be thoroughly washed to remove all surface blood. It is then salted slightly on all sides. The liver is then broiled on a perforated grate over an open fire which draws out the internal blood. The liver must be broiled on both sides until the outer surface appears to be dry and brown. At this point it is permissible. When koshering a whole liver, slits must be made in the liver prior to broiling. After broiling, the liver is rinsed off. Separate utensils should be used for the koshering of liver.

F. The Kosher Butcher: Koshering and nikkur are usually the responsibility of the kosher butcher who must be a trained and reliable professional, as well as a man of integrity under strict Kashruth supervision.

G. Packaging: From the time of slaughter, kosher meat and poultry must be properly tagged and labeled until it reaches the consumer. This requirement dictates that rabbinic supervision be maintained until the meat reaches the consumer. In the processing of fowl, a metal tag called a plumba, bearing the kosher certification, serves as an identifying seal.

H. Caterers, Restaurants, Resorts: Caterers, restaurants, and hotels should be supervised by a reputable Orthodox rabbinic authority. It cannot be assumed that Kashruth is maintained simply because a kosher impression is created by an advertisement or by a statement, "we serve a kosher clientele." Too often, "vegetarian" or "dairy" restaurants are assumed to be kosher and beyond the need for supervision. Unfortunately this is a prevalent misconception. For example, sea squab and sturgeon are non-kosher fish popular in many such eateries. Fish, baked goods, cheese shortening, oil, eggs, margarine, dressings, and condiments are among the many foodstuffs requiring supervision in "vegetarian" and "dairy" restaurants. Even those food items that are kosher in their raw states could be rendered non-kosher when prepared on equipment used for non-kosher food. In these restaurants, as in all other food-serving establishments, reputable Kashruth supervision is the best guarantee of Kashruth.

MEAT AND MILK IN THE KOSHER KITCHEN

The Torah forbids cooking meat and milk together in any form, eating such cooked products, or deriving benefit from them. As a safeguard, the rabbis extended this prohibition to disallow the eating of meat and dairy products at the same meal or preparing them on the same utensils. One must wait up to six hours after eating meat products before any dairy products may be eaten. However, meat may be eaten following dairy products with the one exception of hard cheese (6 months old or more), which also requires up to a six-hour interval. Prior to eating meat after dairy, the mouth must be rinsed.

A. Utensils: The kosher kitchen must have two separate sets of utensils, one for meat and poultry and the other for dairy foods. There must be separate, distinct sets of pots, pans, plates, and silverware.

B. Washing Dishes: In a sink used for both meat and milk dishes and products, dishes and utensils must be placed or washed on a rack. Separate racks are to be used for meat and dairy use. When soaking dishes, a competent rabbinic authority must be consulted.

EGGS

The eggs or animal by-product of non-kosher birds or fish are not kosher. Caviar, therefore, must come from a kosher fish and this requires reliable supervision. Eggs of kosher fowl which contain a bloodspot must be discarded, and therefore eggs should be checked before use. Commercial egg products also require supervision.

BAKERIES, BAKED GOODS, BREAD, ROLLS, PASTRIES, AND BAGELS

A. Shortening and Oils: The display of the label has undergone strict changes due to government regulations. Not only must the label specify the type of shortening, i.e. vegetable or animal, but it must declare the actual source as well. Thus, it is commonplace to mention cottonseed oil, lard, coconut oil, and the like. The result of this explicit label display is that the consumer can easily detect what is blatantly non-kosher. However, the kosher status of a product containing vegetable shortening of any type can only be verified by reliable kosher certification. The reason for this is that manufacturers of vegetable shortening often process animal fats on equipment common to their vegetable product [and although it] may be a pure one, *halakhically* it is rendered non-kosher due to its processing on non-kosher equipment.

B. Emulsifiers: Emulsifiers are complex substances that are used in all types of food production. They can perform a number of critical functions, among them allowing two ingredients to mix together which ordinarily could not. These materials are listed on the ingredient label as polysorbates, mono- and diglycerides, sorbitanonostearate, etc. These products are produced from both animal and vegetable sources and thus require careful supervision and controls. The special qualities of these products, acting as surfactants, making oil and water soluble, enable them to be invaluable basic components in many food items, such as margarine, shortenings, cream fillings and toppings, coffee creamers, whiteners, prepared cake mixes, doughnuts, and puddings. It must be emphasized that ice cream, frozen desserts, instant mashed potatoes, peanut butter, snack-pack foods, and many breakfast cereals also contain diglycerides and require Kashruth certification.

A product whose ingredients list "emulsifiers" or "emulsifier added" indicates the use of glycerides and requires Kashruth certification. Many chocolates and candies contain such glyceride emulsifiers.

C. Bread, Rolls, Challah, Bagels, and Bialys: These basic household staples present several Kashruth problems and require Kashruth certification.

D. Breads: Many breads are made with oils and shortenings. Basic ingredients of specially prepared dough mixes and dough conditioners are shortenings and diglycerides. In bakeries, pans and troughs in which the dough is placed to rise are coated with grease or divider oils which may be non-kosher. These oils often do not appear on the label: only specially prepared kosher pan grease may be used.

E. Dairy Breads: It is rabbinically prohibited to bake bread with dairy ingredients. Since bread is normally eaten at all meals, the rabbis were concerned that one might inadvertently eat dairy bread with a meat meal. There are two exceptions—if the bread is baked in an unusual shape or design indicating that it is dairy, or if the loaf is so small that it would be consumed at one meal.

F. Cake, Pastries, and Doughnuts: These products should be considered non-kosher unless certified kosher. The shortenings and other ingredients universally used in the manufacture of these items have an extremely high diglyceride content and require expert supervision.

Lard-based shortenings are often used in pie and other crust preparations because of lard's unique flaking quality.

G. Fillings and Cremes: All fillings, cremes, and fudge bases must be certified kosher because they may contain fats, emulsifiers, and gelatin stabilizers.

H. Flavors: A critical sector of the food industry are manufacturers of flavors. Flavors, whether artificial or natural, are components of nearly every product. Flavor production is highly complex and uses raw materials from every imaginable source. In addition, the flavor industry utilizes grape- and wine-derived ingredients in a wide array of products. For this reason, any product containing flavors requires accurate supervision and control.

I. The "Taking" of Khallah: The Torah requires that a portion of every batter of dough prepared for baking be set aside as "khallah." The khallah portion taken may be of any size and is to be burned. This ritual is obligated only when the dough is of Jewish ownership and is made from the flour of five grains: wheat, oats, rye, spelt, and barley. When the flour used is a blend with other types of flour, e.g. corn, rice, etc., a rabbinic authority is to be consulted.

J. If this *mitzvah* has not been performed in the bakery, it may be performed in the home by placing all the baked goods in one room, breaking open all sealed packages, and removing and burning a small piece from one of the loaves. When some of the loaves are of wheat flour and some of the loaves are of rye (or one of the five previously listed grains), khallah must then be taken from the loaf of each type. When one bakes at home and has used a minimum of 2 lbs. 10 oz. of flour in the making of dough, khallah is to be taken from the dough before baking. In this case no blessing is recited.

When a minimum of 4 lbs. 15⅓ oz. of flour is used, the blessing is recited before performing the *mitzvah*.

DAIRY PRODUCTS

A. Cholov Yisroel: A rabbinic law requires that there be supervision during the milking process to ensure that the source of the milk is from a kosher animal. Following the opinion of many rabbinic authorities, OU policy considers that in the United States, the Department of Agriculture's regulations and controls are sufficiently stringent to ensure that only cow's milk is sold commercially. These government requirements fulfill the rabbinical requirement for supervision.

B. Cheese: All cheeses require Kashruth certification, including hard cheeses (Swiss, cheddar, etc.) and soft cheeses (cottage, farmer, pot, and cream cheese). Rennet, processed from the stomachs of unweaned calves, is used in the production of cheese as a curdling and coagulating ingredient, and is also used in the production of sour cream, buttermilk, and some varieties of yogurt and yogurt-type desserts. The use of a non-kosher coagulant renders the product non-kosher.

C. Cheese and dairy products made under OU supervision are processed with kosher-approved animal or microbial rennet. Kosher animal rennet is derived from the stomachs of kosher slaughtered calves and is specially prepared for use in kosher cheese production. Microbial rennet is derived solely from vegetable and plant sources and is produced under OU certification.

D. Sherbets: According to government standards, any product labeled "sherbet" or "fruit sherbet" must contain milk and is, therefore, not pareve. Water ices should not be considered pareve unless endorsed OU pareve on the label.

E. Margarine: Margarine usually contains glycerides and therefore requires rabbinic certification. Margarine often contains up to 12% dairy ingredients. Unless the margarine is marked pareve, it should be considered dairy.

NATURAL AND HEALTH FOODS

With the proliferation of natural and health food products in the United States, some clarification is in order with regards to their Kashruth status. It should be noted that many of these products are natural but nevertheless non-kosher. Products containing pure vegetable oils could be problematic as many oil manufacturers produce animal tallow on the same equipment. Natural flavors could contain polysorbates, grape derivatives, beaver extracts, etc., all of which are natural but require supervision or are non-kosher.

Even if a product is sold in a natural or health food store, it requires supervision if it contains questionable ingredients.

WINES AND GRAPE PRODUCTS

All grape wines or brandies must be prepared under strict Orthodox rabbinic supervision. Once the wine has been cooked, no restrictions are attached to its handling. Grape jam is often produced from grape pulp and juice and may not be used. OU-certified grape jam is produced from ground whole grapes and no juice is extracted from or added to the product. This is not a wine product and is permitted.

Grape jelly is produced from grape juice and can be used only when produced from kosher grape juice under proper supervision.

Natural and artificial grape flavors may not be used unless kosher-endorsed. Many grape flavors contain natural grape extracts and are labeled artificial or imitation because other flavoring additives are used in the formula.

Liqueurs, even though not possessing a wine base, nevertheless require supervision because of the flavorings used in these products.

TRAVELING KOSHER

For the businessman or tourist traveling across the United States, kosher certified products are available just about everywhere, even in the smallest groceries in the most remote towns. However, it is much more difficult to obtain reliably kosher certified products in most foreign countries. A traveler bringing along frozen (TV) dinners which must be reheated in a non-kosher oven must completely cover the frozen package with two layers of aluminum foil.

When traveling by plane, train, or ship, kosher meals should be ordered in advance. These meals are also heated in non-kosher ovens. The employees of the carrier are instructed to heat these meals exactly the way they receive them, totally wrapped in double foil with the caterer's seal and the rabbinic certification seal intact. The traveler can ascertain by the intact seals that the dinners have not been tampered with. Any dinner which is not so sealed should not be eaten. The kosher certification only applies to the food in the sealed package.

Any other food (rolls, wines or liqueurs, cheeses, and coffee creamers) or snacks served loose by the carrier are not included in the kosher endorsement.

The following glossary owes a great deal to one assembled by Professor Robert Kraft of the University of Pennsylvania, which can be found at numerous websites. As was my practice in the main text of the book, I have used Sephardic pronunciations and my own system of transliteration.

Adon Olam   "Eternal Ruler," title of hymn that is part of the morning service and is recited before bedtime.

Adonai   "Our Lord," one of the commonly used names for the Deity.

Aggadah   (lit. "telling") Non-*halakhic* matter in Talmud and Midrash; includes folklore, legend, theology/theosophy, scriptural interpretations, biography, etc.; also spelled haggadah, not to be confused, however, with the text of the Passover Seder, which is also called "the Haggadah."

Agunah   (pl. *agunot;* lit. "one who is chained") An abandoned woman who has not been given a divorce decree ("get") from her husband. She cannot remarry under Jewish law, even if her husband is presumed (but not proven) dead.

Ahavah Rabbah   Prayer in morning version of the *Sh'ma* and its blessings, giving thanks to God for the gift of the *mitzvot* and the Torah.

Akeidah   (lit. "binding") Biblical account of God's command to Abraham to offer his son Isaac as a sacrifice, found in Genesis 22.

Akharonim   (lit. "the later ones") Refers to rabbinical authorities who followed the Rishonim, dated usually from the sixteenth century on (although some sources date them as early as the twelfth century).

Alef-Bet   The Hebrew alphabet. The name is derived from the first two letters of the alef-bet.

Aleinu   Closing prayer of every service, proclaiming God's sovereignty.

Aliyah   (lit. "going up," "ascending") (1) Term used when a Jew is called to say a blessing before and after the Torah is read. (2) Permanent emigration to Israel. Literal meaning is "going up" or ascension; thus, emigrating to Israel is seen as a spiritual ascension. One who "makes" aliyah is an *oleh,* pl. *olim.*

Am Yisroel   (lit. "the people Israel") Usually used to refer to the Jewish people (the descendants of Jacob, also called Israel).

Amidah   The silent prayer recited, while standing, morning and evening that contains eighteen (actually nineteen) blessings. Also called *Shemoneh Esrei / 18 [Benedictions]* and *Ha-Tefilah / The Prayer.*

amora   (lit. "speaker") Rabbinic Jewish teachers of the 3rd and 4th centuries C.E. who produced the Gemara for the Babylonian and Palestinian Talmuds. (pl. *amoraim*)

Amudah   Reading desk at the front (or center) of sanctuary at which the Torah will be read.

Aninut   The period of mourning between the time of death and the time of burial.

Apocrypha   (adj. apocryphal) From the Greek, meaning "to hide" or "to uncover." It is used in a technical sense to refer to certain Jewish books written in the Hellenistic-Roman period that came to be included in the Old Greek Jewish scriptures (and thus in the Eastern Christian biblical canon) and in the Latin Vulgate Roman Catholic canon, but not in the Jewish or Protestant biblical canons.

Aramaic   Semitic language, closely related to Hebrew, in which key Jewish texts, most notably the Babylonian and Palestinian Talmuds, were written. Once the *lingua franca* of the Jewish world, it is no longer spoken.

Arbah Minim   (lit. "four species") Branches and fruit—myrtle, palm, willow, and citron—used to fulfill the commandment to "rejoice before Adonai" during Sukkot. The *lulav* and *etrog.*

Ark   An acronym of *aron hakodesh.* The word has no connection with Noah's Ark, which is "teyvat" in Hebrew.

Aron Hakodesh   (lit. "holy chest") Holy Ark, usually found at the front of sanctuary, containing two or more Torah scrolls.

Arvit   Evening service (more often called *ma'ariv*).

Ashkenazi   The term now used for Jews who derive from northern Europe and who generally follow the customs originating in medieval German Judaism, as distinct from Sephardic Jews, whose distinctive roots are traced back to Spain and the Mediterranean. Originally the designation Ashkenaz referred to a people and country bordering on Armenia and the upper Euphrates; in medieval times, it came to refer to the Jewish area of settlement in northwest Europe (northern France and western Germany). By extension, it now refers to Jews of northern and eastern European background (including Russia) with their distinctive liturgical practices or religious and social customs.

Ashrei Song of praise to God drawn from Psalm 145.

Atonement In Judaism, atonement (Hebrew, *kaparah*), or reconciliation between God and humanity, is achieved by the process of teshuvah/repentance, seeking forgiveness and making amends with our fellow human beings.

Aufruf The groom's aliyah on the Shabbat before his wedding.

Avelut The year of mourning after the burial of a parent.

Ba'al kriah (lit. "master of the reading") One who reads or chants aloud from the Torah during services.

Ba'al Teshuvah (lit. "one who has returned") A formerly non-observant Jew who returns to Jewish practice (in a traditionally observant manner, it is implied).

Bamidbar (lit. "in the desert") The fourth book of the Torah, the Book of Numbers.

Bar Aramaic word meaning "son."

Baraita Any teaching of the tannaitic period not included in the Mishnah. Tosefta is the best known collection of *baraitot,* but these teachings can be found scattered throughout both the Babylonian and Palestinian Talmuds.

Barekhu (lit. "Blessed are You") The call to worship that begins the service proper.

Bar Mitzvah (pl. *B'nai mitzvot;* lit. "son of the commandment") A boy who has achieved the age of 13 and is consequently obligated to observe the commandments. Also, a ceremony marking the fact that a boy has achieved this age.

Barukh She'amar "Blessed is He who spoke," prayer of praise to the Creator that is part of the first section of the morning service.

Bat Mitzvah   (pl. *B'not mitzvot;* lit. "daughter of the commandment") A girl who has achieved the age of 12 and is consequently obligated to observe the commandments. Also, a ceremony marking the fact that a girl has achieved this age.

Bavli   Shorthand term for the Babylonian Talmud.

B.C.E.   Before the Common (or Christian) Era.

Ben   (Hebrew, "son," "son of"; Aramaic "bar," "ibn") Used frequently in "patronymics" (naming by identity of father); Rabbi Akiba ben Joseph means Akiba son of Joseph.

Bentsch   (Yiddish) To bless, to recite a blessing.

Bentsch gomel   To recite the blessing thanking God for seeing one safely through a life-threatening event.

Bereshit   Hebrew name for the Book of Genesis, taken from the opening word of the book.

Bet Din   (lit. "house of judgment") A rabbinical court made up of three rabbis who resolve business disputes under Jewish law and determine whether a prospective convert is ready for conversion.

Bet Knesset   (lit. "house of assembly") A synagogue.

Bet Midrash   (lit. "house of study") A place set aside for study of sacred texts such as the Torah and the Talmud, generally a part of the synagogue or attached to it.

Bimah   Place at front of synagogue from which service is led, i.e., the pulpit.

Binah   Intuition, understanding, intelligence. Also, in kabbalistic thought, one of the Ten Sephirot.

Birkat Ha-Mazon   (lit. "blessing of the food") Grace after meals.

Blood libel   The accusation often leveled against Jews that they kill Christian children to use their blood in various religious rituals (usually for baking *matzah*).

B'nai Yisrael   The Children of Israel.

B'rakhah   (pl. *b'rakhot*) A blessing. A prayer beginning with the phrase "barukh atah . . ." (blessed art Thou . . .).

Brit   (lit. "covenant") Used in Judaism especially for the special relationship believed to exist between God and the Jewish people.

Brit Habat   Naming ceremony for newborns, usually for female children (who do not undergo a *brit milah*).

Brit Milah   (lit. "covenant of circumcision") The ritual circumcision of a male child before the age of 8 days or of a male convert to Judaism. Frequently referred to as a bris.

B'tzelem Elohim   In the image of God.

Canaanites   Ancient tribes that lived in Canaan before the Israelites came.

Cantor   (from Latin, one who sings) In Judaism, a reciter and chanter/singer of liturgical materials in the synagogue; also used similarly in Christian contexts (choir leader, etc.). Also called *hazan.*

CCAR   Central Conference of American Rabbis, organization of the Reform rabbinate.

C.E.   Common (or Christian) Era. Preferable to A.D., "Anno Domini," Latin for "Year of Our Lord," because of its implication that Christ is the Son of God, a concept which Jews and Muslims (among others) reject.

Chabad   Acronym (C[k]hokhmah/Wisdom, Binah/Insight, Da'at/Knowledge) used to designate the Lubavitcher Hasidim.

Commandments   According to rabbinic Jewish tradition, there are 613 religious commandments referred to in the Torah (and elaborated upon by the rabbinic sages). Of these, 248 are positive commandments and 365 are negative. The numbers respectively symbolize the fact that divine service must be expressed through all one's bodily parts during all the days of the year. In general, a mitzvah refers to any act of religious duty or obligation; more colloquially, a mitzvah refers to a "good deed."

Confirmation   A ceremony found in both the Christian religion and in some branches of the Jewish religion. A sacrament of the Catholic Church, it marks the admission of the person to full membership in the church (takes place between ages 7–14). A rite of passage in Judaism, confirmation usually marks the end of formal religious school training (age 15–16), and traditionally occurs around the time of Shavuot.

Conservative Judaism   A modern development in Judaism, reacting to early Jewish Reform movements in an attempt to retain clearer links to classical Jewish law while at the same time adapting it to modern situations. Its scholarly center in the U.S. is the Jewish Theological Seminary in New York.

Counting of the Omer   The counting of the days between Passover and Shavuot. In Hebrew, *Sefirat ha-Omer*.

Daf Yomi   "The daily page," a program of studying Talmud, one page a day, a cycle that takes approximately seven years to complete.

Daven   (Yiddish, "to pray") Pray. Contrary to occasional misuse, this does not refer to the rocking back and forth that one may see among praying Jews in traditional synagogues.

Days of Awe   Ten days from Rosh Hashanah to Yom Kippur, a time for introspection and considering the sins of the previous year.

Decalogue   A Greek term referring to the Ten Commandments *(aseret hadibrot)* received by Moses on Mount Sinai according to Jewish scriptures (Exodus 20:1–17; Deuteronomy 5:1–21).

Deuteronomy   From the Greek meaning "second [telling] of the Law," fifth and final book of the Pentateuch.

Devarim   The Book of Deuteronomy.

Devekut   "Cleaving" to God, aspiring to oneness with the Divine through meditative or ecstatic prayer; key concept in Hasidic prayer.

Diaspora   (Hebrew, *galut*) The dispersion of Jews throughout the world after the fall of the Second Temple (70 C.E.). Refers to all Jews living outside of Israel. Also known as the "Exile."

Elohim, El   Hebrew general terms for deity.

Emancipation   In Jewish history, the nineteenth-century movement/ events that led to Jews being granted full civil status in European societies.

Eretz Yisrael   (Hebrew, "land of Israel") In Jewish thought, the special term for the Palestinian area believed to have been promised to the Jewish people by God in the ancient covenant.

Erev   Erev means "evening," usually the evening before a holiday, e.g., Erev Shabbat is Friday evening, Erev Rosh Hashanah is the evening before the day of Rosh Hashanah.

Eruv   A boundary within which it is permissible to carry on Shabbat or the festivals.

Essenes   The name of a Jewish subgroup in the first century C.E. according to Josephus, Philo, and other sources.

Etrog   A citron; "the fruit of goodly trees" (Leviticus 23:40) carried in procession in the synagogue with the *lulav* during the festival of Sukkot (Feast of Tabernacles).

Exilarch   (Aramaic, *resh galuta,* "head of the exile") A term used in early Rabbinic Judaism for the head of the Jewish community in exile in Babylonia. The exilarch was depicted as an imperial dignitary, a member of the council of state, living in semi-royal fashion, who appointed communal officers and judges and was a descendant of the House of David.

Exodus   (from Greek, "to exit or go out") Refers to the event of the Israelites leaving Egypt (*see also Passover*) and to the biblical book that tells of that event. Hebrew name of the book is *Shemot/The Names*.

Eyn sof   (Hebrew, "without limit") In Jewish kabbalism, a designation for the divine—"the unlimited one."

Eyshet Khayil   "A woman of virtue," ode derived from Proverbs 31, often sung by a husband to his wife at Shabbat evening dinner.

Eytz Khayim   (lit. "tree of life") (1) Hymn that is sung/recited as Torah is returned to the Ark at the end of *Seder Kri'at ha-Torah.* (2) The wooden spindles on which the Torah scroll is mounted.

First Temple   Built in Jerusalem by Solomon, destroyed by the Babylonians in 586 B.C.E., it housed the Ark of the Covenant, and was the site of all the most important rites of pre–Rabbinic Judaism.

Fleishig   (Yiddish, "meat") Used to describe kosher foods that contain meat or meat by-products, and therefore cannot be eaten with dairy.

Four Species   Fruit and branches used to fulfill the commandment to "rejoice before the L-rd" during Sukkot.

Gabbai   Lay person who assists prayer leader during Torah reading, calling to the *bimah* those who have *aliyot.*

Galut (Hebrew, "exile") The term refers to the various expulsions of Jews from the ancestral homeland. Over time, it came to express the broader notion of Jewish homelessness and state of being aliens. Thus, colloquially, "to be in *galut*" means to live in the Diaspora and also to be in a state of physical and even spiritual alienation.

Gaon (pl. *Geonim;* adj. *geonic;* Hebrew, "eminence, excellence") A title given to the Jewish head of the Babylonian academy and then to distinguished Talmudic scholars in the sixth to twelfth centuries.

Gelilah Act of dressing the Torah scroll after the reading from it at a service. One who performs this honor is called the *golel.*

Gemara (Hebrew, "completion") Popularly applied to the Jewish Talmud as a whole, to discussions by rabbinic teachers on Mishnah, and to decisions reached in these discussions. In a more restricted sense, the work of the generations of the *amoraim* in "completing" Mishnah to produce the Talmuds.

Gematria An interpretative device in Rabbinic Judaism which focuses on the numerical value of each word.

Gemilut khasadim Deeds of lovingkindness, one of the three pillars on which the rabbis said the world rests.

Genizah (Hebrew, "hiding") A hiding place or storeroom, usually connected with a Jewish synagogue, for worn-out holy books. The most famous is the Cairo Genizah, which contained books and documents that provide source material for Jewish communities living under Islamic rule from about the ninth through the twelfth centuries. It was discovered at the end of the nineteenth century.

Get (pl. *gittin*) Decree of divorce.

Gezerah (pl. *gezerot*) A law instituted by the rabbis to prevent people from unintentionally violating commandments.

Gnostic, Gnosticism Derived from Greek gnosis, "knowledge." Refers to various systems of belief characterized by a dualistic view of reality—the God who created the material, phenomenal world is different from (often antithetical to) the ultimate (hidden) God of pure spirit. Possession of secret gnosis frees a person from the evil material world and gives access to the spiritual world. Gnostic thought had a great impact on the eastern Mediterranean world in the second to fourth century C.E., often in a Christian form.

Goy Hebrew word for nation or people ("goy kadosh," a Holy People/Nation); Yiddish word for non-Jew. Sometimes seen as a pejorative, although negative meaning is derived from the context, and not from the word itself.

Gragger   A noisemaker used to blot out the name of Haman during the reading of the Megillah on Purim.

Hadassah   Jewish women's Zionist organization in the United States.

Haftarah   (pl. *haftarot*) Specific section of the biblical prophets read in synagogue services immediately after the corresponding Torah (Pentateuch) section called the *parashah*.

Hagbah   The act of holding the Torah scroll aloft for the entire congregation to see (open wide enough for four columns of writing to be visible). The one who performs this honor is the magbiah.

Haggadah   The liturgical manual used in the Jewish Passover Seder.

Hakafah   (pl. *hakafot*) Procession around the sanctuary with the Torah scrolls.

Hakham   (pl. *hakhamim* or *hakhmim;* "the wise") A Jewish title given to pre–70 C.E. proto-rabbinic sages/scholars and post–70 C.E. rabbinic scholars.

Halakhah   Any normative Jewish law, custom, practice, or rite—or the entire complex. *Halakhah* is law established or custom ratified by authoritative rabbinic jurists and teachers. Colloquially, if something is deemed halakhic, it is considered proper and normative behavior.

Halitzah   A ceremony related to the Levirate law of marriage, which frees the widow to marry someone other than her husband's brother. In this ceremony the widow removes a shoe from her brother-in-law's foot, which is symbolic of removing his possessive right over her.

Hallel   Psalms 113–118, recited at end of morning services at festivals.

Hamentaschen   (lit. "Haman's pockets") Triangular, fruit-filled cookies traditionally served or given as gifts during Purim.

Hanukah   (lit. "dedication") An eight-day holiday celebrating the rededication of the Temple in Jerusalem to more traditional modes of Jewish worship by Judah the Maccabee around 164 B.C.E.

HaShem   (lit. "The Name") Used by traditionally observant Jews so as to not actually utter one of the names of God.

Hashkiveinu   Evening prayer thanking God for protecting us while we sleep.

Hasidim, Hasidism   (sing. *hasid;* Hebrew, "pious ones") The term may refer to Jews in various periods: (1) a group that resisted the policies of Antiochus Epiphanes in the second century B.C.E. at the start of the Maccabean revolt; (2) pietists in the thirteenth century, known as the Ashkenazi Hasidim, much involved in mysticism of the period; (3) followers of the movement of Hasidism founded in the first half of the eighteenth century by Israel Baal Shem Tov.

Haskalah   Jewish rationalistic "enlightenment" in eighteenth- and nineteenth-century Europe.

Hasmoneans   Descendants of Hashmon, a Jewish family that included the Maccabees and the high priests and kings who ruled Judea from 142 to 63 B.C.E.

Havdalah   (Hebrew, "separation") The Jewish ceremony using wine, spices, and candles at the conclusion of the Sabbath. Smelling the spices signifies the hope for a fragrant week; the light signifies the hope for a week of brightness and joy. Brief group of prayers that mark the end of a festival.

Havruta   A study partner, or the practice of studying (usually Talmud) with a partner.

Havurah   (lit. "fellowship" or "companionship") A small worship circle, usually egalitarian in nature, led by lay people rather than a rabbi.

Hecksher   Insignia placed on food designating the approval of a kosher certifying body.

hermeneutics   Principles of interpretation (from the Greek "to interpret, translate"). The term is often used with reference to the study of Jewish and Christian scriptures.

Hofjuden   (German) "Court Jews," that select few who, by dint of their superior intellect or—more often—financial skills, were welcome among the crowned heads of Christian Europe before the Emancipation.

Hoshanah Rabba   (lit. "great hosanna") The seventh day of Sukkot, on which seven circuits are made around the synagogue reciting a prayer with the refrain, "Hoshah nah!" ("Please save us!").

HUC-JIR   Hebrew Union College–Jewish Institute of Religion, the rabbinical seminary of the American Reform movement.

Israel   A name given to the Jewish patriarch Jacob by God (Genesis 32:38). In Jewish biblical times, this name refers to the northern tribes (as distinct from Judea, the southern tribes), but also to the entire nation. Historically, Jews have continued to regard themselves as the true continuation of the ancient Israelite national-religious community. The term thus has a strong cultural sense. In modern times, it also refers to the political state of Israel.

Jehovah   Mechanical attempt to represent the special name for deity, YHWH, the Tetragrammaton.

JTS   Jewish Theological Seminary, rabbinical seminary of the Conservative movement in the United States. (The west coast equivalent is the University of Judaism in Los Angeles.)

Judenfrage   (German) The "Jewish Question," how was non-Jewish society to deal with the newly emancipated Jews?

Kabbalah   A system of Jewish theosophy and mysticism.

Kabbalat Shabbat   Opening section of Shabbat evening service, "welcoming the Sabbath."

Kaddish   Prayer that extols the greatness of God. Best known as the mourners' prayer, Kaddish is said at other times during Jewish liturgy; the shortened version, the *khatsi (half) Kaddish,* occurs as a punctuation at various points in the liturgy to separate sections.

Kaddish D'Rabbanan   *Kaddish* prayer extolling our teachers, recited after learning in a group (which includes sections of the morning service that are considered Torah study).

Kahal   (Hebrew, "congregation, gathering") Used to refer to the corporate Jewish community of medieval Europe.

Kapparah   Ritual of atonement performed just before Yom Kippur, involving the swinging of a live chicken (now often replaced by a handkerchief containing money) as a surrogate for one's sins.

Karaism, Karaites   Derived from Hebrew "kara," meaning "a reader of Scripture." Group that arose in opposition to Rabbinism in the eighth century C.E., and emphasized the written scriptures while criticizing the rabbinic use of "oral law."

Kashrut   Dietary laws.

Kavanah   (lit. "intention" or "direction") The focus and concentration that is essential to meaningful prayer.

Kedushah   Prayer proclaiming God's holiness, recited on Sabbath and festivals.

Kehillah   (Hebrew, "community") Jewish sense of community, in a particular sense, within the larger *knesset Israel*.

Ketubah   Religious marriage certificate.

Ketuvim   (Hebrew, "writings") The third and last division of the Jewish Bible (TaNaKh), including large poetic and epigrammatic works such as Psalms and Proverbs and Job as well as a miscellany of other writings (Song of Songs, Ruth, Lamentations, Ecclesiastes/Kohelet, Esther, Daniel, Ezra-Nehemiah, Chronicles).

Kevah   Fixed, as in prayers that have been written down and whose order is specified in the prayer book.

Khag Sameakh   Hebrew greeting on a festival, meaning "happy holiday." (The Yiddish equivalent is "Gut Yuntif.")

Khai   (lit. "living or life") Life. Word often used as a design on jewelry and other ornaments. Donations to charity are often made in multiples of 18, the numerical value of the word; hence, double Khai would be 36.

Khallah   A sweet, eggy, yellow bread, usually braided, which is served on Sabbath and holidays. The ritual of "taking *khallah*" consists of the removal and burning of a small portion of dough when baking bread, and gives its name to this bread.

Khannukat Ha-Bayit   (lit. "dedication of the house") A brief ceremony dedicating a Jewish household, during which the *mezuzah* is affixed to the doorposts.

Kharoset   A mixture of fruit, wine, and nuts eaten at the Passover seder to symbolize mortar used by the Jewish slaves in Egypt.

Khatsi Kaddish   "Half-kaddish," omitting the final three verses, recited at several points in liturgy as a separation between sections of the worship service.

Khelev   The fat surrounding organs, as distinguished from the fat surrounding muscles. Forbidden to be eaten under the laws of Kashrut.

Khevra Kaddisha (lit. "holy society") A burial society, an organization devoted to caring for the dead.

Kheyder (lit. "room") The one-room Hebrew school commonly found in small villages throughout Eastern Europe in the nineteenth and early twentieth centuries.

Khillul Ha-Shem (lit. "profanation of the Name") Causing G-d or Judaism to come into disrespect, or causing a person to violate a commandment.

Khol Ha-Mo'ed The intermediate days of Passover and Sukkot, when work is permitted.

Khumash (lit. "five") A compilation of the first five books of the Bible and readings from the prophets, organized in the order of the weekly Torah portions.

Khuppah The wedding canopy, symbolic of the groom's home, under which the nisuin portion of the wedding ceremony is performed.

Kibbutz A communal settlement in modern Israel.

Kiddush Prayer of sanctification, recited over wine sanctifying the Sabbath or a holiday.

Kiddush Ha-Shem (lit. "sanctification of The Name [of God]") One who dies a Jewish martyr is said to have died "*kiddush Ha-Shem.*"

Kiddushin (Hebrew, "consecration") Denotes betrothal for marriage, signifying the sanctity of the relationship.

kippah A headcovering worn for worship, religious study, meals, or at any other time; also called *yarmulke*.

Kittel The white robes in which the dead are buried, worn by some during Yom Kippur services.

K'lal Yisroel The community of Israel, that is, the Jewish people.

Knesset (lit. "assembly") The legislative branch of the present-day Israeli government.

Knesset Ha-Gadol "The Great Assembly," the main spiritual and legislative body of the post-prophetic era, numbering 85 or 120 sages (depending on the source). Institutionalized many important liturgical practices (reading of Torah on Shabbat, festivals, Mondays, and Thursdays; recitation of the Amidah two times daily; blessings before meals, etc.) and the foundations of *halakhah.*

Knesset Israel "Assembly of Israel," or the Jewish people as a whole.

Kohein (pl. *kohanim*) The priestly caste in ancient Palestine. In a traditional congregation, a kohein will be given the first *aliyah* when the Torah is read.

Kol Nidre   Hymn sung during the Yom Kippur evening service, absolving Jews of all vows made in the previous year to God.

Kosher   (Hebrew, "proper" or "ritually correct") *Kashrut* refers to ritually correct Jewish dietary practices. Traditional Jewish dietary laws are based on biblical legislation. Only land animals that chew the cud and have split hooves (sheep, beef; not pigs, camels) are permitted and must be slaughtered in a special way. Further, meat products may not be eaten with milk products or immediately thereafter. Of sea creatures, only those (fish) having fins and scales are permitted. Fowl is considered a meat food and also has to be slaughtered in a special manner *(shekhitah)*.

K'riah   (lit. "tearing") The tearing of one's clothes upon hearing of the death of a close relative.

Ladino   The colloquial language of Sephardic Jews, based primarily on Spanish, with words taken from Hebrew, Arabic and other languages, and written in the Hebrew alphabet.

Lamed-vavniks   (Yiddish, "one of the 36") According to one legend, the fate of the human race rests on the shoulders of the 36 truly righteous ones of each generation. Those who are of that select group are thus designated by the Hebrew letters for the number 36, lamed-vav, and colloquially called *"lamed-vavniks."*

Lashon Hara   (lit. "evil language") Encompasses all forms of forbidden speech (gossip, slander, lying, etc.).

Lashon kodesh   (lit. "the holy tongue") Hebrew.

Latkes   Potato pancakes traditionally eaten during Hanukah.

Law of Return   Israeli law that permits Jews to make *aliyah* to Israel, receiving automatic citizenship.

L'Chaim   (lit. "To Life") Used as a toast.

Levirate marriage   From *levir* for *yabam,* brother-in-law; a biblical system of marriage in which the *levir* marries his brother's widow (Deuteronomy 25:5–10).

Levite   A descendant of the tribe of Levi, dedicated to the service of the *kohanim,* the priestly caste. In a traditional synagogue, a Levite will be given the second *aliyah* when the Torah is read.

Liberal Jews When used in the United States it means an adherent to any of the non-Orthodox streams of Judaism. In the United Kingdom, refers to member of the British equivalent of Reform Judaism in the United States.

Liberal Judaism British denomination similar to Reform Judaism in the United States.

Liturgy (adj. liturgical) Rites of public worship, usually institutionalized in relation to temple, synagogue, church, kaba, or mosque locations and traditions, but also in other formalized observances.

L'Khah Dodi Hymn welcoming the Sabbath Bride during Kabbalat Shabbat, an acrostic that spells the name of its composer, sixteenth-century mystic Solomon Alkabetz.

L'Shanah Tovah Tikateivu Greeting said between Rosh Hashanah and Yom Kippur, "May you be written [in the Book of Life] for a good year."

Lulav The interwoven branches of palm, willow, and myrtle used in the Sukkot celebration.

Ma'ariv Evening service.

Machzor The High Holy Day prayer book (as distinct from the *siddur,* the Shabbat and daily prayer book). Also may refer to prayer book for some festivals.

Maftir The "concluder," one who has the final *aliyah* during the Torah reading.

Magen Avot (Hebrew, "shield of our fathers") Brief prayer, "the essence of Tefillah," recited at the end of the Sabbath evening Amidah.

Magen David (Hebrew, "shield of David") The distinctive six-pointed Jewish star, used especially since the seventeenth century.

Maggid (Hebrew, "a speaker") A kabbalistic notion of how the holy spirit is mediated to the mystic; later meant a preacher among the eighteenth-century Hasidim (as Dov Baer, the Maggid of Mezritch).

Mah Tovu Hymn that begins morning services, five verses from Numbers and Psalms, beginning "Mah tovu ohalekha Ya'akov mishkenotkha Yisrael/How lovely are your tents, O Jacob, your dwelling places, O Israel."

Mame-loshn (Yiddish, "the mother tongue") Yiddish.

Mamzer   (lit. "bastard") The child of a marriage that is prohibited and invalid under Jewish law, such as an incestuous union.

Marranos   An old Spanish term meaning "swine," used to execrate medieval Spanish Jews who converted to Christianity but secretly kept their Judaism.

Maskilim   (Hebrew, "the enlightened ones") Eighteenth- and nineteenth-century Jews who engaged in secular rationalistic studies and facilitated the acculturation of Jews to Western society; adherents of the *Haskalah*.

Masoretes, Masoretic text   Derived from *masorah*, meaning "tradition"; the Masoretes were the rabbis in ninth-century Palestine who sought to preserve the traditional text of the Bible (hence called the Masoretic text), which is still used in contemporary synagogues. The Masoretes were scholars who encouraged Bible study and attempted to achieve uniformity by establishing rules for correcting the text in matters of spelling, grammar, and pronunciation.

Matzah   Jewish unleavened bread used at Passover.

Mazel Tov   Means congratulations and good luck in Hebrew and Yiddish.

Megillah   (lit. "scroll," pl. *megillot*) Refers to one of the five scrolls read on special holidays: Sukkot—*Kohelet/Ecclesiastes;* Purim—*Esther;* Pesakh—*Shir ha-Shirim/Song of Songs;* Shavuot—*Ruth;* Tisha b'Av—*Eikhah/Lamentations.*

Mekhitzah   The wall or curtain separating men from women during religious services in a traditionally observant synagogue.

Melakhah   Work, any of the categories of labor forbidden on the Sabbath.

Menorah   A candelabrum. Usually refers to the nine-branched candelabrum used to hold the Hanukah candles (more properly called a *hanukiyah*). Can also refer to the seven-branched candelabrum used in the Temple.

merkavah   (Hebrew, "chariot") The "chariot vision" was an integral element of the first school of Jewish mysticism, drawn from the Book of Ezekiel, signifying a mystical vision of divinity.

Messiah   (lit. "anointed one") Ancient priests and kings (and sometimes prophets) of Israel were anointed with oil. In early Judaism, the term came to mean a royal descendant of the dynasty of David who would restore the united kingdom of Israel and Judah and usher in an age of peace, justice, and plenty; the redeemer figure. The concept developed in many directions over the centuries. The Messianic Age was believed by some Jews to be a time of perfection of human institutions; others believed it to be a time of radical new beginnings, a new heaven and earth, after divine judgment and destruction. The title came to be applied to Jesus/Joshua of Nazareth by his followers, who were soon called "Christians" in Greek and Latin usage (from the Greek word for anointed one, "christos"). Jesus is also "Messiah" in Islam (e.g., Quran 3:45).

Mezuzah (pl. *mezuzot;* Hebrew "doorpost") A parchment scroll with selected Torah verses (Deuteronomy 6:4–9; 11:13–21) placed in a container and affixed to the exterior doorposts (at the right side of the entrance) of Jewish homes (see Deuteronomy 6:1–4), and sometimes also to interior doorposts of rooms. The word *shaddai* (almighty) or the letter *shin* usually is inscribed on the container.

Midrash (pl. *midrashim*) From Hebrew darash, "to inquire," whence it comes to mean "exposition" (of scripture). Refers to the "commentary" literature developed in classical Judaism that attempts to interpret Jewish scriptures in a thorough manner. Literary Midrash may focus either on *halakhah,* directing the Jew to specific patterns of religious practice, or on *aggadah,* dealing with theological ideas, ethical teachings, popular philosophy, imaginative exposition, legend, allegory, animal fables, etc.—that is, whatever is not *halakhah.*

Mi Khamokha Hymn, "who is like You," proclaiming the wonders that God has done for the people Israel.

Mikra-ot Gedolot The Commentators' Bible, a single volume that incorporates the text of the entire *khumash* and the commentaries on it authored by numerous important medieval and early modern rabbis, including Rashi, Ibn Ezra, and others.

Mikvah A ritual bath used for spiritual purification. It is used primarily in conversion rituals and after a woman's menstrual cycles, but many Hasidim immerse themselves in the mikvah regularly for general spiritual purification.

Milchig (Yiddish, "dairy") Used to describe kosher foods that contain dairy products and therefore cannot be eaten with meat.

Minhag (pl. *minhagim*) Custom that evolved for worthy religious reasons and has continued long enough to become a binding religious practice. The word is also used more loosely to describe any customary religious practice.

Minkhah   Afternoon service.

Minyan   A prayer quorum of ten Jews over the age of 13; in traditional congregations, only men are counted toward a minyan.

Mi shebeirakh   Prayer for the well-being of one who is ill, has just given birth, or is about to be circumcised. Requested by an individual and read following the blessing after reading of Torah.

Mishnah   (Hebrew, "teaching") The digest of the recommended Jewish oral *halakhah* as it existed at the end of the second century and was collated, edited, and revised by Rabbi Judah Ha-Nasi. The work is the authoritative legal tradition of the early sages and is the basis of the legal discussions of the Talmud.

Mishpatim   Judgments.

Mitnaged   (pl. *mitnagdim*, "opposer[s]") Traditionalist and rationalistic Jewish opponents of eighteenth-century Jewish Hasidism.

Mitzvah   (pl. *mitzvot*) Obligation or commandment. Colloquially, a good deed.

Modern Orthodox   A branch of Orthodox Judaism found primarily in the U.S. Believers in *halakhah* and traditionally observant, they also accept the importance of secular study, modern dress, etc.

Mohel   A specialist who performs a circumcision at a Brit.

Motzi   The blessing over bread recited before eating.

Musaf   "Additional" service that follows immediately after *shakharit* on Sabbath and festivals.

Musar   Nineteenth-century Orthodox movement, headed by Rabbi Israel Salanter, that espoused a renewed focus on ethics.

Mystic, mysticism   (adj. mystical; from Greek for "initiant" into religious "mysteries") A vaguely used term to indicate certain types of behavior or perspective that goes beyond the rational in the quest of what is considered to be the ultimate in religious experience (often described as union or direct communion with Deity).

Nasi   (lit. "prince") The presiding officer of the Sanhedrin, serving in tandem with the Av Bet Din.

Navi (pl. *nevi'im*) A prophet. "Nevi'im" became a designation for a section of the TaNaKh encompassing the books of the prophets.

Nazir, Nazirite Member of an ascetic sect within Judaism who took vows of abstinence from alcohol, did not cut their hair, and were not permitted to come into contact with the dead. Their vows could last anywhere from a brief time to an entire life. Samson is the most famous Nazirite.

Nei'ilah (lit. "locking") The final service of Yom Kippur, when the Gates of Heaven are closed (hence the Hebrew name).

Ner Tamid "Eternal light" that hangs in front of the Ark in a synagogue.

Nevelah (lit. "a carcass") A dead animal that was neither slain by another animal as prey nor killed by a ritual slaughterer. May not be eaten by an observant Jew. One who touches it contracts ritual impurity.

Niddah Laws of ritual purity governing menstruation.

Nisim b'khol yom Morning prayers that thank God for ability to distinguish day from night, the strength to rise in the morning, for clothing, freedom, the earth itself, and the people Israel.

Nisuin (lit. "elevation") The second part of the two-part Jewish marriage process, after which the bride and groom begin to live together as husband and wife.

Omer The sheaf of grain offering brought to the temple during Passover, on Nisan 16; thus also the name of the seven-week period between Passover and Shavuot.

Oral Law In traditional Pharisaic/rabbinic thought, God reveals instructions for living through both the written scriptures—the Pentateuch—and through a parallel process of orally transmitted traditions. Critics of this approach within Judaism include Sadducees and Karaites.

Orthodox The most traditionally observant stream of Judaism.

OU Orthodox Union, the largest umbrella group of Modern Orthodox congregations in the United States, also the largest kosher certifying body in the world (their hecksher is a capital U inside an O).

Palestine   (Greek form representing "Philistines," for the seacoast population encountered by early geographers) An ancient designation for the
area between Syria (to the north) and Egypt (to the south), between
the Mediterranean Sea and the River Jordan; roughly, modern Israel.

Parashah   (Hebrew, "section") Prescribed weekly section of biblical
Torah (Pentateuch) read in synagogue liturgy on an annual cycle.

Pareve   (Yiddish, "neutral") Used to describe kosher foods that contain
neither meat nor dairy and therefore can be eaten with either. Fish is
considered pareve for purposes of kashrut.

Parokhet   The curtain (as distinguished from the doors) in front of the
Aron Hakodesh.

Passover   *(Pesakh)* The major Jewish spring holiday (with agricultural
aspects) also known as *khag hamatzot* (festival of unleavened bread)
commemorating the Exodus or deliverance of the Hebrew people
from Egypt (see Exodus 12–13). The festival lasts eight days, during
which Jews refrain from eating all leavened foods and products. A
special ritual meal (called the Seder) is prepared the first two nights,
and a traditional narrative (called the *Haggadah*), supplemented by
hymns and songs, marks the event.

Pentateuch   (from Greek for "five books/scrolls") The five books
attributed to Moses: Genesis/Bereishit, Exodus/Shemot, Leviti-
cus/Vayikra, Numbers/Bamidbar, and Deuteronomy/Devarim;
known in Jewish tradition as *Torat Mosheh* (the teaching of Moses), or
simply the Torah.

Peshat   Interpretative method of reading Torah based on the "plain"
meaning of a text.

Pharisees   *(perushim,* lit. "separatists") The name given to a group or
movement in early Judaism, the origin and nature of which is
unclear. Many scholars identify them with the later sages and rabbis
who taught the oral and written law; others see them as a complex
of pietistic and zealous separatists, distinct from the proto-rabbis.
According to Josephus, the Pharisees believed in the immortality
of souls and resurrection of the dead, in a balance between predesti-
nation and free will, in angels as active divine agents, and in authoritative oral law. In the early Christian materials, Pharisees are often
depicted as leading opponents of Jesus/Joshua and his followers,
and are often linked with "scribes" but distinguished from the Sadducees.

Phylacteries   (Greek for "protectors").

Pidyon Ha-Ben   Ceremony for the redemption of the firstborn son.

Pikuakh nefesh   The principle that saving a life takes precedence over almost all other ritual obligations and overrides all other prohibitions except idolatry, murder, and immoral behavior.

Pilpul   Dialectical rational method of studying Jewish oral law as codified in the Talmud, usually identified with the Tosafists.

Pirke Avot   A Tractate of Mishnah that deals with ethical and moral behavior; traditionally read and studied during the summer.

Piyyutim   Medieval Jewish synagogue hymns and poems added to standard prayers of the liturgy.

Pogrom   From the Russian word for "devastation"; an unprovoked attack or series of attacks upon a Jewish community.

Pseudepigrapha   (adj. pseudepigraphical), from pseudos, "deceit, untruth," and epigraphe, "writing, inscription." A name given to a number of intertestamental apocryphal writings that are implausibly attributed to an ancient worthy such as Adam/Eve, Enoch, Abraham, Moses, Isaiah, Ezra, etc.

P'sukei D'zimrah   "Songs of Praise," drawn from Psalms and I Chronicles 16:8–36, recited in the morning service before the *Sh'ma* and its blessings.

Purim   Festival commemorating the deliverance of Jews in Persia as described in the Book of Esther.

Pushke   A box in the home or the synagogue used to collect money for donation to charity.

Qumran or Khirbet Qumran   The site near the northwest corner of the Dead Sea in modern Israel (west bank) where the main bulk of the Jewish "Dead Sea Scrolls" were discovered around 1946. The "Qumran community" that apparently produced the scrolls seems to have flourished from the third century B.C.E. to the first century C.E., and is usually identified with the Jewish Essenes, or a group like them.

Rabbi   (lit. "my teacher" or "my master") Ordained expert in Jewish worship and law. An authorized teacher of the classical Jewish tradition after the fall of the Second Temple in 70 C.E. The role of the rabbi has changed considerably throughout the centuries. Traditionally, rabbis serve as the legal and spiritual guides of their congregations and communities. The title is conferred after considerable study of traditional Jewish sources. This conferral and its responsibilities is central to the chain of tradition in Judaism.

Rabbinic Judaism   A general term encompassing all movements of Judaism descended from Pharisaic Judaism.

Rabbinical Assembly   Organization of the Conservative rabbinate in the United States.

Rebbe   The title of the spiritual leader of the Hasidim.

Rebbetzin   (Yiddish) The wife of a rabbi.

Reconstructionist Judaism   Founded by Mordecai M. Kaplan (1881– 1982), this represents a recent development in American Judaism, and attempts to focus on Judaism as a civilization and culture constantly adapting to ensure survival in a natural social process. The central academic institution is the Reconstructionist Rabbinical College in the Philadelphia suburbs.

Redactor   An editor, especially with reference to ancient books such as the Jewish and Christian scriptures.

Reform Judaism   Modern movement originating in eighteenth-century Europe that attempts to see Judaism as a rational religion adaptable to modern needs and sensitivities. The ancient traditions and laws are historical relics that need have no binding power over modern Jews. The central academic institution of American Reform Judaism is the Hebrew Union College in Cincinnati and New York, and it is represented also by the Central Conference of American Rabbis.

Responsa   Also called *teshuvot*, from *sheelot uteshuvot* (questions and answers); answers to questions on *halakhah* and observances, given by Jewish scholars on topics addressed to them. They originated during the geonic period, and are still used as a means of modern updating and revision of *halakhah*.

Revelation   A general term for self-disclosure of the divine (God reveals to humans), which is often considered to be focused in the revealed scriptures.

Rishonim   (lit. "the early ones") Generally used to refer to rabbinic authorities codifying Jewish law between the completion of the Talmud and the publication of the Shulkhan Arukh.

Rosh Hashanah (Hebrew, "head of the year") Jewish New Year celebration in the fall of the year, the month of Tishri.

Rosh Khodesh (Hebrew, "head of the month") The New Moon Festival.

Rosh Yeshiva Head of a Talmudic academy.

RRC Reconstructionist Rabbinical College, rabbinical seminary of the Reconstructionist movement in the United States.

Sabbath The seventh day of the week (Hebrew, *shabbat*), recalling the completion of the creation and the Exodus from Egypt. It is a day symbolic of new beginnings and one dedicated to God, a most holy day of rest. The commandment of rest is found in the Bible and has been elaborated by the rabbis. It is a special duty to study Torah on the Sabbath and to be joyful. Sabbaths near major festivals are known by special names.

Sadducees Sect of the Second Temple period, allied with the priestly caste in opposition to the Pharisees.

Samaritans Another of the numerous subgroups in early Judaism and residents of the district of Samaria north of Jerusalem and Judah in what is now Israel. They are said to have recognized only the Pentateuch as scripture and Mt. Gerizim as the sacred center rather than Jerusalem. There was ongoing hostility between Samaritans and Judeans. Samaritan communities exist to the present.

Sanhedrin (from Greek for "assembly" [of persons seated together]) A legislative and judicial body from the period of early Judaism and into rabbinic times. Traditionally composed of 71 members.

Savoraim (lit. "explainers") Scholars and heads of the Babylonian academies in the period between the *amoraim* and the geonim, roughly the sixth to seventh centuries C.E.

Second Temple Rebuilt after the Babylonian Exile, the Temple stood in Jerusalem until it was destroyed by the Romans in 70 C.E.

Seder (lit. "order") The ritual dinner held on the first two nights of Passover.

Seder Kri'at ha-Torah Service for the reading of the Torah.

Sefer K'ritut (lit. "scroll or book of cutting off"). A writ of divorce. Also called a *get*.

Sefer Torah (pl. *sifrei Torah*) A Torah scroll.

Sefira (pl. *sefirot;* Hebrew, "counting, number") In Kabbalah, the *sefirot* are the primary emanations or manifestations of deity that together make up the fullness (pleroma) of the godhead.

Selikhot Penitential prayers traditionally read at midnight before Rosh Hashanah.

Sephardim The designation Sepharad in biblical times refers to a colony of exiles from Jerusalem (Obadiah 20), possibly in or near Sardis; in the medieval period, Sephardi(c) Jews are those descended from those who lived in Spain and Portugal (the Iberian peninsula) before the Expulsion of 1492. As a cultural designation, the term refers to the complex associated with Jews of this region and its related diaspora in the Balkans and Middle East (especially in Islamic countries). The term is used in contradistinction to Ashkenazi, but it does not refer, thereby, to all Jews of non-Ashkenazi origin.

Septuagint Strictly speaking, refers to the ancient Greek translation of the Hebrew Pentateuch, probably made during the reign of Ptolemy II, Greek ruler of Egypt around 250 B.C.E. Subsequently, Greek translations of other portions of the Jewish scriptures came to be added to the corpus, and the term Septuagint was applied to the entire collection. Such collections served as the "scriptures" for Greek-speaking Jews and Christians.

Se'udat Havra'ah (lit. "the meal of condolence") The first meal that a family eats after the burial of a relative, prepared by a neighbor.

Se'udat sh'lishit (lit. "third meal") The Shabbat afternoon meal, traditionally a time for spirited Torah discussion and singing of *z'mirot*.

Shabbat (Hebrew) The Jewish Sabbath, beginning at sundown Friday night and ending at sundown the following evening. (In Ashkenazi pronunciation, it is transliterated as Shabbos, in Yiddish usually as Shabbes.)

Shabbat Shalom A greeting given on Shabbat, meaning "[may you have] the peace of the Sabbath."

Shabbateanism A messianic movement begun in the seventeenth century by Shabbetai Tzvi (1626–1676), who ultimately converted to Islam.

Shakharit Morning service.

Shalakh Manos (lit. "sending out portions") The custom of sending gifts of food or candy to friends during Purim.

Shaliakh Tzibur "Messenger of the community." The lay leader of a service (not an ordained rabbi or cantor).

Shalom bayit (lit. "Peace of the house") The principle that domestic tranquillity should be undisturbed as much as possible.

Shamas (lit. "servant") (1) The candle that is used to light other Hanukah candles; (2) the janitor or caretaker of a synagogue.

Shavuot (Hebrew, "weeks") Observed fifty days from the day the first sheaf of grain was offered to the priests; also known as Festival of First Fruits. Holiday celebrates the giving of the Torah at Sinai.

Sheitel Wig worn by traditionally observant Orthodox women after marriage.

Shekhinah Jewish term for the divine presence; the Holy Spirit. In Kabbalah it often took on the aspect of the feminine element in deity.

Shekhitah Kosher ritual slaughtering.

Shem HaMeforash "The Forbidden Name," the Tetragrammaton.

Shemini Atzeret (the Eighth Day of Assembly) Festival that immediately follows the seven-day festival of Sukkot (Tabernacles).

Shemitah The "Sabbatical Year" mandated in Leviticus 25:2, during which time land is supposed to lie fallow. Trade in produce that grows that year is forbidden.

Shemoneh esreh (Hebrew, "eighteen") The main section of Jewish prayers recited in a standing position and containing 19 (yes!) "benedictions": praise to (1) God of the fathers/patriarchs, (2) God's power and (3) holiness; prayers for (4) knowledge, (5) repentance, (6) forgiveness, (7) redemption, (8) healing sick persons, (9) agricultural prosperity, (10) ingathering the diaspora, (11) righteous judgment, (12) punishment of wicked and heretics *[birkat haminim]*, (13) reward of pious, (14) rebuilding Jerusalem, (15) restoration of royal house of David, (16) acceptance of prayers, (17) thanks to God, (18) restoration of Temple worship, and (19) peace.

Shemot (lit. "Names") The Book of Exodus.

Sheol Place of departed dead in (some) ancient Israel thought, without reference to punishments and rewards.

Shevah B'rakhot "Seven Blessings," recited during the wedding ceremony.

Shivah   (Hebrew, "seven") Seven days of mourning after the burial of a close relative (as in, "to sit shiva").

Shloshim   (Hebrew, "thirty") An intermediate stage of thirty days of mourning, which includes the *shivah* period.

Sh'ma   (Hebrew, "hear") Title of the fundamental, monotheistic statement of Judaism, found in Deuteronomy 6:4 ("Hear, O Israel, the LORD is our God, the LORD is One"; *Shema Yisrael YHWH elohenu YHWH ehad*). This statement avers the unity of God and is recited daily in the liturgy (along with Deuteronomy 6:5–9, 11:13–21; Numbers 15:37–41; and other passages), and customarily before sleep at night. This proclamation also climaxes special liturgies (like Yom Kippur), and is central to the confession before death and the ritual of martyrdom. The *Shema* is inscribed on the *mezuzah* and the *tefillin*. In public services, it is recited in unison.

Shoah   (Hebrew, lit. "whirlwind") The Holocaust.

Shofar   Ram's horn sounded at Rosh Hashanah morning worship and at the conclusion of Yom Kippur, as well as other times in that period during the fall.

Shokhet   A kosher ritual slaughterer.

Shomrim   (lit. "guards, keepers") People who sit with a body between the time of death and burial.

Shteibel   (Yiddish, pl. *"shteiblakh"*) A small synagogue, often a storefront and little else.

Shtetl   (Yiddish, pl. *"shtetlakh"*) A small Eastern European village, usually predominantly Jewish.

Shtreimel   Fur-trimmed round hat worn by some Hasidic men.

Shuklin   Swaying or rocking during prayer.

Shul   Yiddish for synagogue.

Shulkhan Arukh   (lit. "the prepared table") Sixteenth-century compilation of Jewish ritual laws, put together by Joseph Caro, considered authoritative by most traditionally observant Jews.

Siddur   Prayer book.

Siddur   (Hebrew, "to order") Jewish prayer book used for all days except special holidays.

Sidra   (pl. *sidrot*) Section of the Torah read during a particular week.

Simkhat Torah   (Hebrew, "rejoicing with the Torah") A festival which celebrates the conclusion of the annual reading cycle of the Torah.

Six-Day War   Conflict in June 1967 in which Israeli forces routed their Arab attackers, seizing the Sinai Peninsula, the Suez Canal, the Golan Heights, and the West Bank of the Jordan, including the entire city of Jerusalem.

S'khakh   (lit. "covering") Material used for the roof of a *sukkah*.

S'mikhah   Rabbinic ordination.

Sofer   (pl. *sopherim,* "scribe") Used as a general designation for scholars and copyists in both Talmudic and later literature; a "scholastic," a learned researcher whose vocation was the study and teaching of the tradition. In early times the *sofer* was the scholar. By the first century C.E. he was no longer a real scholar but a functionary and teacher of children. Today it usually refers to one who writes a Torah scroll.

Sukkah   (lit. "booth") The temporary dwellings Jews traditionally live in during the holiday of Sukkot.

Sukkot   (Hebrew, "booths, tabernacles") Seven-day fall festival beginning on Tishri 15 commemorating the *sukkot* where Israel lived in the wilderness after the Exodus; also known as Khag Ha'asif, the Festival of Ingathering (of the harvest).

Synagogue   (Greek for "gathering"). The central institution of Jewish communal worship and study since antiquity, and by extension, a term used for the place of gathering. The structure of such buildings has changed, though in all cases the ark containing the Torah scrolls faces the ancient Temple site in Jerusalem.

Takanah   (pl. *takanot*) A law instituted by the rabbis and not derived from any biblical commandment.

Takhanun   Prayer of supplication, requesting grace and forgiveness from God, recited daily in morning service, except on Shabbat, festivals, and joyous occasions like weddings.

Tallit   A large, four-cornered shawl with fringes and special knots at the extremities, worn during Jewish morning prayers. The fringes, according to the Bible (Numbers 15:38–39), remind the worshiper of God's commandments. It is traditional for the male to be buried in his *tallit,* but with its fringes cut off.

Tallit Katan   (lit. "small *tallit*") A four-cornered, poncho-like garment worn under a shirt to fulfill the commandment to put *tzitzit* (fringes) on the corners of our garments.

Talmud   (Hebrew, "study" or "learning") Rabbinic Judaism produced two Talmuds: the one known as "Babylonian" is the most famous in the western world, and was completed around the fifth century C.E.; the other, known as the "Palestinian" or "Jerusalem" Talmud, was edited perhaps in the early fourth century C.E. Both have as their common core the Mishnah collection of the *tannaim,* to which are added commentary and discussion (Gemara) by the teachers *(amoraim)* of the respective locales. Gemara thus has also become a colloquial, generic term for the Talmud and its study.

TaNaKh (Tanakh)   A relatively modern acronym for the Jewish Bible, made up of the names of the three parts Torah (Pentateuch or Law), Nevi'im (Prophets), and Ketuvim (Writings).

Tanna   (Hebrew, "repeater, reciter"; adj. tannaitic, pl. *tannaim*) A Jewish sage from the period of Hillel (around the turn of the era) to the compilation of the Mishnah (200 C.E.), distinguished from later *amoraim. Tannaim* were primarily scholars and teachers. The Mishnah, *Tosefta,* and *halakhic midrashim* were among their literary achievements.

Targum   (Hebrew, "translation, interpretation") Generally used to designate Aramaic translations of the Jewish scriptures (in a sense, Greek Targums).

Taryag mitzvot (or Taryag)   The 613 *mitzvot* prescribed in the Torah.

Tashlikh   The Hebrew word means "to send, to cast out." This is the special ceremony on Rosh Hashanah afternoon in which Jews symbolically cast their sins (in the form of bread crumbs) into a body of flowing water.

Tefillah   Prayer. The *Amidah,* the standing prayer, is often referred to as *Ha-Tefillah,* "The Prayer."

Tefillin   Usually translated as "phylacteries." Box-like appurtenances that accompany prayer, worn by adult males (and now some females as well) at the weekday morning services. The boxes have leather thongs attached and contain scriptural excerpts. One box (with four sections) is placed on the head, the other (with one section) is placed (customarily) on the left arm, near the heart. The biblical passages emphasize the unity of God and the duty to love God and be mindful of him with "all one's heart and mind" (e.g. Exodus 13:1−10, 11−16; Deuteronomy 6:4−9, 11:13−21).

Temple   In the ancient world, temples were the centers of outward religious life, places at which public religious observances were normally conducted by the priestly professionals. In traditional Judaism, the only legitimate Temple was the one in Jerusalem, built first by King Solomon around 950 B.C.E., destroyed by Babylonian king Nebuchadnezzar around 587–586 B.C.E., and rebuilt about seventy years later. It was destroyed by the Romans in 70 C.E. The site of the ancient Jewish Temple is now occupied, in part, by the golden domed "Dome of the Rock" Mosque. In recent times, "temple" has come to be used synonymously with synagogue in some Jewish usage (but never by Orthodox Jews, for whom the only "temple" is the Temple in Jerusalem).

Teshuvah   The Hebrew word for "repentance," which literally means "turning"—away from sin, towards the good. It is the central goal of the days between Rosh Hashanah and Yom Kippur.

Tetragrammaton   (Greek for "four-lettered [name]") The four-letter "forbidden name" of God.

Theology   The study of God and the relations between God and the universe.

Theosophy   Study of the nature of the Godhead.

Tisha B'Av   The ninth of the Hebrew month Av. A twenty-five-hour fast day that commemorates the destruction of both First and Second Temples.

Torah   (Hebrew, "teaching, instruction") In general, Torah refers to study of the whole gamut of Jewish tradition or to some aspect thereof. In its special sense, "the Torah" refers to the "five books of Moses" in the Hebrew scriptures. In the Koran, incidentally, "Torah" is the main term by which Jewish scripture is identified.

Tosafists   Generation of Talmudic interpreters after Rashi. Best-known as exponents of *pilpul,* hair-splitting dialectical exegesis of Talmud.

Tosefta   (Hebrew, "supplement" pl. *Tosafot*) Tannaitic supplements to the Mishnah. Called *baraita* (extraneous material) in the Talmud.

Treif   (lit. "torn") Food that is not kosher.

tzaddik   (Hebrew, "righteous one") A general term for a righteous person in Jewish tradition. More specifically, the spiritual leader of the modern Hasidim, popularly known as *rebbe*.

Tzedakah   (Hebrew, "righteousness," "justice") Term in Judaism usually applied to deeds of charity and philanthropy.

Tzizit   (Hebrew, "fringes").

UAHC   Union of American Hebrew Congregations, umbrella organization of Reform congregations in the United States.

United Synagogue   Umbrella organization of Conservative congregations in the United States.

UTJ   Union for Traditional Judaism, umbrella organization of Traditional congregations in the United States.

V'shamru   Hymn enjoining us to keep the Sabbath, recited or sung during evening Sabbath service just prior to the *Amidah.*

Yad   (lit. "hand") Hand-shaped pointer used while reading from Torah scrolls.

Yahrzeit   (Yiddish, "anniversary") The anniversary of the death of a close relative.

Yamim Nor'aim   Days of Awe. Hebrew name for the High Holy Days (Rosh Hashanah, Yom Kippur, and the ten-day period that separates them).

Yeshiva   (pl. *yeshivot;* from the Hebrew meaning "seated") A Jewish rabbinic academy of higher learning.

Yetzer Hara   The inclination to do evil.

Yetzer Hatov   The inclination to do good.

YHWH (Yahweh)   The sacred name of God in Jewish scriptures and tradition; also known as the tetragrammaton. Since Hebrew was written without vowels in ancient times, the four consonants YHWH contain no clue to their original pronunciation. They are generally rendered "Yahweh" in contemporary scholarship. In traditional Judaism, the name is not pronounced, but Adonai ("Our Lord") or something similar is substituted. In most English versions of the Bible the tetragrammaton is represented by "LORD" (or less frequently, "Jehovah").

Yiddish   (from German "Juedisch" or Jewish) The vernacular of Ashke-nazic Jews; it is a combination of several languages, especially Hebrew and German, written in Hebrew script.

Yigdal   (from Hebrew to be great; thence "Great is he") A hymn/chant/poem from eleventh century or earlier, frequently found at the beginning or end of the Jewish prayer book *(siddur)*.

Yishtabakh   Last of the *P'sukei D'zimrah,* recited in morning service.

Yizkor   (lit. "remembrance") Memorial service for the dead that takes place on Yom Kippur and certain other festivals. Also the name of the prayer memorializing the dead that occurs in that service.

Yom Ha-Atzma-ut   Israeli Independence Day.

Yom Ha-Shoah   Holocaust Remembrance Day.

Yom Ha-Zikkaron   Israeli Memorial Day.

Yom Kippur   (Hebrew "Day of Atonement") Annual day of fasting and atonement, occurring in the fall on Tishri 10 (just after Rosh Hashanah); the most solemn and important occasion of the religious year.

Yom Yerushalayim   Holiday celebrating the reunification of Jerusalem in the hands of the modern state of Israel.

Yotzer   "Giver of light," prayer recited in morning service as part of the *Sh'ma* and its blessings, thanking God for the gift of light.

Zealot   (Greek for "to be enthusiastic") A general term for one who exhibits great enthusiasm and dedication to a cause. Specifically, a member of an early Jewish group or perspective that advocated Jew-ish independence from Rome.

Zion, Zionism   Zion is an ancient Hebrew designation for Jerusalem, but already in biblical times it began to symbolize the national homeland (see, e.g., Psalms 137:1–6). In this latter sense it served as a focus for Jewish national-religious hopes of renewal over the centuries. Ancient hopes and attachments to Zion gave rise to Zionist longings and movements since antiquity, culminating in the modern national liberation movement of that name. The Zion-ist cause helped the Jews return to Palestine in this century and found the state of Israel in 1948. The goal of Zionism is the poli-tical and spiritual renewal of the Jewish people in its ancestral home-land.

Z'mirot   Shabbat table songs.

Zohar   "Book of Splendor"; the chief literary work of the kabbalists. The author of the main part of the *Zohar* was Moses de Leon (twelfth century) in Spain, but it is pseudepigraphically ascribed to the Palestinian tanna Simeon bar Yohai (second century C.E.).

The Jews are called the "People of the Book," and you never know how true that epithet is until you've written a book about Jews. Roland Barthes wrote, "In order to speak one must seek support from other texts." When you write about Judaism, you have plenty of texts from which to choose. Needless to say, I have drawn on many other texts in writing *Essential Judaism,* and this is the place to acknowledge those debts and to steer readers to books that treat the many topics I have skimmed over in greater depth and with greater erudition. This is truly a Golden Age of Judaic studies, with important new books coming out every year on virtually every topic relating to the Jewish people. Add to that the Internet, CD-ROMs, videotape, and "media not yet invented," as the contracts say, and you can find the answer to almost any question on Judaism.

On a project like this, there are always books and websites that one keeps coming back to. Certain absolutely indispensable volumes have been on my desk or in my mind regardless of what chapter I was work-ing on. As someone who haunts used bookstores, thrift shops, garage sales, and the like, I found myself running across many obscure but highly useful books on Judaism, so some of the titles below may not be easily found outside of a library, but these are the books that "support" this book. Titles marked with an asterisk (*) are particularly good for beginners.

GENERAL

Amsel, Nachum. *The Jewish Encyclopedia of Moral and Ethical Issues.* Northvale, NJ: Jason Aronson, 1996.

Ben-Sasson, H. H., ed. *A History of the Jewish People.* Cambridge, MA: Harvard Univ. Press, 1976.

*Birnbaum, Philip. *A Book of Jewish Concepts.* New York: Hebrew Pub-lishing Company, 1964.

*Buxbaum, Yitzhak. *Jewish Spiritual Practices*. Northvale, NJ: Jason Aronson, 1990.

Cohen, Arthur A., and Paul Mendes-Flohr. *Contemporary Jewish Thought*. New York: Free Press, 1987.

Donin, Rabbi Hayim Halevy. *To Be a Jew*. New York: Basic Books, 1972.

Frankel, Ellen, and Betsy Platkin Teutsch. *The Encyclopedia of Jewish Symbols*. Northvale, NJ: Jason Aronson, 1992.

Gordis, Daniel. *God Was Not in the Fire: The Search for a Spiritual Judaism*. New York: Scribner's, 1995.

Helmreich, William. *Wake Up, Wake Up to Do the Work of the Creator*. New York: Bantam Books, 1976.

Holtz, Barry W., ed. *Back to the Sources: Reading the Classic Jewish Texts*. New York: Summit Books, 1984.

*Lutske, Harvey. *The Book of Jewish Customs*. Northvale, NJ: Jason Aronson, 1995.

Mendes-Flohr, Paul and Jehuda Reinharz, eds. *The Jew in the Modern World: A Documentary History*. 2nd ed. Oxford: Oxford Univ. Press, 1995.

Nulman, Macy. *The Encyclopedia of Jewish Prayer*. Northvale, NJ: Jason Aronson, 1996.

————. *Encyclopedia Judaica*. Jerusalem: Keter, 1971.

————. *The Encyclopedia of the Sayings of the Jewish People*. Northvale, NJ: Jason Aronson, 1997.

Olitzky, Kerry M., and Ronald H. Isaacs. *A Glossary of Jewish Life*. Northvale, NJ: Jason Aronson, 1996.

*Syme, Daniel B. *The Jewish Home: A Guide for Jewish Living*. Northvale, NJ: Jason Aronson, 1988–89.

*Wigoder, Geoffrey, and R. J. Zwi Werblowsky, eds. *The Encyclopedia of the Jewish Religion*. New York: Adama Books, 1986.

PRAYER AND LITURGY

The following prayer books were referred to repeatedly in the writing of this chapter and in numerous other places in this book:

The Artscroll Siddur (Brooklyn, NY: Mesorah, 1984).

Gates of Prayer (New York: Central Conference of American Rabbis, 1975).

Gates of Repentance (New York: Central Conference of American Rabbis, 1984).

The Metsudah Siddur (New York: Metsudah Publications, 1982).

Siddur Sim Shalom (New York: The Rabbinical Assembly and United Synagogue of Conservative Judaism, 1989).

*Barth, Rabbi Samuel. *All You Want to Know About Sabbath Services: A Guide for the Perplexed.* West Orange, NJ: Behrman House, 1995.

Bettan, Israel. "Affirmation and Study." In *Shaarei Binah: Gates of Understanding,* edited by Lawrence A. Hoffman. New York: Central Conference of American Rabbis, Union of American Hebrew Congregations, 1977.

Borowitz, Eugene. "The Individual and the Community in Jewish Prayer." In *Shaarei Binah: Gates of Understanding,* edited by Lawrence A. Hoffman. New York: Central Conference of American Rabbis, Union of American Hebrew Congregations, 1977.

Chofetz Chayim, The (Rabbi Israel Meir HaKohen), gathered and arranged by Rabbi David Zaretsky, translated by Yishai Tobin. *The Chafetz Chaim on the Siddur.* Jerusalem: Hamesorah Publications, 1981.

Cohen, Samuel S. "Three Paths to the Holy." In *Shaarei Binah: Gates of Understanding,* ed. by Lawrence A. Hoffman. New York: Central Conference of American Rabbis, Union of American Hebrew Congregations, 1977.

Donin, Rabbi Hayim Halevi. *To Pray As a Jew: A Guide to the Prayer Book and the Synagogue Service.* New York: Basic Books, 1980.

Edelman, Marsha Bryant. "Some Thoughts on Identity and Jewish Music." *Sh'ma,* October 4, 1996.

Eisenberg, Philip Arian and Azriel. *The Story of the Prayer Book.* Bridgeport, CT: Hartmore Press, 1971.

Emanuel, Rabbi Moshe Shlom. *Tefillin: The Inside Story.* Southfield, MI: Targum Press, 1995.

Friedlander, Daniel H. "The Role of Jewish Communal Singing." *Sh'ma,* October 4, 1996.

*Garfiel, Evelyn. *Service of the Heart: A Guide to the Jewish Prayer Book.* No. Hollywood, CA: Wilshire Books, 1958.

*Hammer, Reuven. *Entering Jewish Prayer: A Guide to Personal Devotion and the Worship Service.* New York: Schocken Books, 1994.

Heschel, Abraham Joshua. *The Quest for God: Studies in Prayer and Symbolism.* New York: Crossroad Publishing Co., 1954.

Hoffman, Rabbi Lawrence A. "The Liturgical Message." In *Shaarei Binah: Gates of Understanding,* edited by Lawrence A. Hoffman. New York: Central Conference of American Rabbis, Union of American Hebrew Congregations, 1977.

———. *The Art of Public Prayer: Not for Clergy Only.* Washington, DC: The Pastoral Press, 1988.

———. *Beyond the Text: A Holistic Approach to Liturgy.* Bloomington, IN: Indiana University Press, 1987.

*———. *My People's Prayer Book. Vol. 1: The Sh'ma and Its Blessings.* Woodstock, VT: Jewish Lights Publishing, 1997.

*———. *My People's Prayer Book. Vol. 2: The Amidah.* Woodstock, VT: Jewish Lights Publishing, 1998.

Kirzner, Yitzchok, with Lisa Aiken. *The Art of Jewish Prayer.* Northvale, NJ: Jason Aronson, 1991.

Kohn, Joshua. *The Synagogue in Jewish Life.* New York: Ktav Publishing, 1973.

Lazar, Matthew. "We Are the Music Makers." *Sh'ma.* October 4, 1996.

Loeb, Laurence D. "More Thoughts on Identity and Jewish Music." *Sh'ma,* October 4, 1996.

Mintz, Alan. "Prayer and the Prayerbook." In *Back to the Sources: Reading the Classic Jewish Texts,* edited by Barry W. Holtz. New York: Summit Books, 1984.

Munk, Rabbi Dr. Elie. *The World of Prayer,* 2 vols. Spring Valley, NY: Feldheim Publishers, 1963.

Petuchowski, Jacob. "Some Basic Features of Jewish Liturgy." In *Shaarei Binah: Gates of Understanding,* edited by Lawrence A. Hoffman. New York: Central Conference of American Rabbis, Union of American Hebrew Congregations, 1977.

*Posner, Raphael, Uri Kaploun, and Shalom Cohen, eds. *Jewish Liturgy: Prayer and Synagogue Service Through the Ages.* New York: Leon Amiel, 1975.

Scherman, Rabbi Nosson. *Kaddish: The Kaddish Prayer.* Brooklyn, NY: Mesorah Publications, 1991.

Scherman, Rabbi Nosson, and Rabbi Meir Zlotowitz. *Shema Yisroel: The Three Portions of the Shema.* Brooklyn, NY: Mesorah Publications, 1982.

Siegel, Eliezer, Notes and course materials at http://acs.
ucalgary.ca/~elsegal/Courses.html. Univ. of Calgary.

Slonimsky, Henry. "Prayer and a Growing God." In *Shaarei Binah: Gates
of Understanding,* edited by Lawrence A. Hoffman. New York: Central Conference of American Rabbis, Union of American Hebrew
Congregations, 1977.

THE FESTIVALS

Agnon, S. Y. *Days of Awe.* New York: Schocken Books, 1965.

————. *Present at Sinai: The Giving of the Law,* translated by Michael
Swirsky. Philadelphia: Jewish Publication Society, 1994.

Chofetz Chayim, The (Rabbi Israel Meir HaKohen), *The Chafetz Chaim
on the Days of Awe,* edited by Rabbi David Zaretsky, translated by
Yishai Tobin. Jerusalem: Hamesorah Publications, 1981.

————. *The Chafetz Chaim on the Sabbath and Festival Days,* edited by
Rabbi David Zaretsky, translated by Yishai Tobin. Jerusalem: Hamesorah Publications, 1981.

Culi, Rabbi Yaakov, and Rabbi Yitzhak Bakhor, Agruiti. *MeAm Lo'ez: The
Story of Tisha b'Av,* translated by Rabbi Aryeh Kaplan. New York:
Moznaim Publishing Co., 1981.

Dresner, Samuel H. *The Sabbath.* New York: The Burning Bush Press,
1970.

Gershon, Stuart Weinberg. *Kol Nidre: Its Origin, Development and Significance.* Northvale, NJ: Jason Aronson, 1994.

*Goodman, Philip. *Rejoice in Thy Festival: A Treasury of Wisdom, Wit and
Humor for the Sabbath and Jewish Holidays.* New York: Bloch Publishing
Co., 1956.

*Heschel, Abraham Joshua. *The Sabbath: Its Meaning for Modern Man.*
New York: Farrar, Straus and Giroux, 1951.

Kandel, Peter, ed. *Gates of the Seasons: A Guide to the Jewish Year.* New
York: Central Conference of American Rabbis, 1983.

Katz, Rabbi Mordechai. *Menucha v'Simcha: A Guide to the Basic Laws of
Shabbos and Yom Tov.* Spring Valley, NY: Feldheim Publishers, 1982.

*Klein, Isaac. *A Guide to Jewish Religious Practice.* New York: Jewish
Theological Seminary of America, 1979.

Peli, Pinchas H. *Shabbat Shalom: A Renewed Encounter with the Sabbath.*
Washington, DC: B'nai B'rith Books, 1988.

*Raphael, Chaim. *Festival Days: A History of Jewish Celebrations.* New York: Grove Weidenfeld, 1991.

Rubinstein, Ernest. "Ecclesiastes and Sukkot" (unpublished paper).

Schneerson, Rabbi Menachem M. *Timeless Patterns in Time: Chassidic Insights into the Cycle of the Jewish Year,* 2 vols. Adapted by Rabbi Eliyahu Touger, translated by Uri Kaploun. Brooklyn, NY: Kehot Publication Society, 1994.

*Waskow, Arthur. *Seasons of Our Joy: A Handbook of Jewish Festivals.* New York: Summit Books, 1982.

LIFE CYCLE

Bial, Morrison David. *Liberal Judaism at Home: the Practices of Modern Reform Judaism.* New York: UAHC Press, 1971.

Boteach, Shmuel. *Kosher Sex.* New York: Doubleday, 1998.

————. "Letter to a Jewish Feminist" (Oxford, UK: self-distributed e-mail, February 8, 1995). oxford-judaism@shamash.org.

————. "Should Couples Use Physical Closeness to Mend Arguments?" (Oxford, UK: self-distributed e-mail, May 17, 1995). oxford-judaism@shamash.org.

Breitowitz, Rabbi Yitzchok. "Physician-Assisted Suicide: A Halachic Approach." In *Jewish Law: Examining Jewish Issues and Secular Law* (1997). Website at http://www.jlaw.com.

————. "The Right to Die: A Halachic Approach." In *Jewish Law: Examining Jewish Issues and Secular Law.* 1997. www.jlaw.com.

————. "The Sanctity of Life and Jewish Abortion," address given at Silver Spring Jewish Center, July 9, 1995, in *Jewish Law: Examining Jewish Issues and Secular Law.* 1997. www.jlaw.com.

Central Conference of American Rabbis. "Agunot," in *New American Reform Responsa.* New York: CCAR, October 1988.

————. "Divorce (Get)," in *American Reform Responsa.* New York: CCAR, 1946.

————. "On the Treatment of the Terminally Ill." Responsa 5754.14. New York: CCAR, 1994.

————. "When Is Abortion Permitted?" In *Contemporary American Reform Responsa.* New York: CCAR, January 1985.

Cohen, Deborah Nussbaum. "Orthodox Caucus Calls Repackaged Prenuptial Agreement Vital." Jewish Telegraphic Agency. New York: 1995.

―――. "The Plight of the Agunah: Blackmail, Bitterness and Betrayal Escalate As Women Struggle for Jewish Divorce." Jewish Telegraphic Agency. New York: 1996.

*Diamant, Anita, with Howard Cooper. *Living a Jewish Life*. New York: HarperCollins, 1991.

Feinstein, Blema. "What Does the Torah Say About Aging?" *Midstream,* August–September 1996.

Gilman, Sander. *Jews in Today's German Culture*. New York, 1995.

Glaser, Gabrielle. "What Do You Mean I'm Not a Jew?" *Washington Post Weekly Edition*. April 28, 1997.

Klagsbrun, Francine. "The Anguish of a Chained Woman." *Jewish Week,* October 11, 1996.

Maslin, Simon J., ed. *Gates of Mitzvah: A Guide to the Jewish Life Cycle.* New York: Central Conference of American Rabbis, 1979.

McClain, Ellen Jaffe. "Converts: Reminding Us What Being Jewish Is All About." *Moment,* August 1996.

Plaskow, Judith. "The Year of the Agunah." *Tikkun,* September–October 1993.

Raphael, Simcha Paull. *Jewish Views of the Afterlife*. Northvale, NJ: Jason Aronson, 1994.

Robinson, George. "To Be or Not to Be: A Jewish Answer to Dr. Death." *Manhattan Jewish Sentinel,* September 8, 1993.

Ross, Tamar. "Can the Demand for Change in the Status of Women Be Halakhically Legitimated?" *Judaism: A Quarterly Journal of Jewish Life and Thought,* Fall 1993.

*Schauss, Hayyim. *The Lifetime of a Jew, Throughout the Ages of Jewish History*. New York: UAHC Press, 1950.

Shenhav, Sharon. "Trapped." *Jerusalem Report,* May 15, 1997.

*Sonsino, Rifat, and Daniel B. Syme. *What Happens After I Die: Jewish Views of Life After Death*. New York: UAHC Press, 1990.

Stein, Jacob. "Between Mercy and Murder." *Manhattan Jewish Sentinel,* January 17, 1997.

THE *MITZVOT*

Berkovitz, Eliezer. *Crisis and Faith*. New York: Sanhedrin Press, 1976.

Buber, Martin. *Israel and the World*. New York: Schocken Books, 1948.

Chill, Abraham. *The Mitzvot: The Commandments and Their Rationale.* Jerusalem: Keter, 1974.

Chofetz Chayim, The (Rabbi Israel Meir HaKohen). *Ahavath Chesed: The Love of Kindness as Required by God,* translated by Leonard Oschry. Spring Valley, NY: Feldheim Publishers, 1976.

————. *The Concise Book of Mitzvoth: The Commandments Which Can Be Observed Today.* Spring Valley, NY: Feldheim Publishers, 1990.

*Dosick, Rabbi Wayne. *Living Judaism: The Complete Guide to Jewish Belief, Tradition and Practice.* San Francisco: HarperCollins, 1994.

Ganzfried, Rabbi Solomon. *Kitzur Shulchan Aruch: Code of Jewish Law,* rev. ed., translated by Hyman E. Goldin. New York: Hebrew Publishing Company, 1961.

Greenstein, Edward L. "Biblical Law." In *Back to the Sources: Reading the Classic Jewish Texts,* edited by Barry W. Holtz. New York: Summit Books, 1984.

Heschel, Abraham Joshua. "Towards an Understanding of Halacha." In *Moral Grandeur and Spiritual Audacity,* edited by Susanna Heschel. New York: Farrar, Straus and Giroux, 1996.

Isaacs, Ronald H. *Mitzvot: A Sourcebook for the 613 Commandments.* Northvale, NJ: Jason Aronson, 1996.

Jacob, Walter, ed. *Liberal Judaism and Halakhah: A Symposium in Honor of Solomon B. Freehof's 95th Birthday.* Pittsburgh, PA: Rodef Sholom Press, 1988.

Kellner, Rabbi Menachem Marc, ed. *Contemporary Jewish Ethics.* New York: Sanhedrin Press, 1988.

Lauterbach, Jacob Z. "The Ethics of Halakah," in *Rabbinic Essays.* Cincinnati: Hebrew Union College Press, 1951.

Rosenberg, Shalom. *Good and Evil in Jewish Thought,* translated by John Glucker. Tel Aviv: MOD Books, 1989.

THE BIBLE

Alter, Robert. *The Art of Biblical Narrative.* New York: Basic Books, 1981.

Bickerman, Elias. *From Ezra to the Last of the Maccabees: Foundations of Post-Biblical Judaism.* New York: Schocken Books, 1962.

Bonchek, Avigdor. *Studying the Torah: A Guide to In-Depth Interpretation.* Northvale, NJ: Jason Aronson, 1996.

*Freedman, David Noel. *The Unity of the Hebrew Bible*. Ann Arbor, MI: Univ. of Michigan Press, 1991.

*Friedman, Richard Elliott. *Who Wrote the Bible?* New York: Summit Books, 1987.

Greenstein, Edward L. "Biblical Law." In *Back to the Sources: Reading the Classic Jewish Texts,* edited by Barry W. Holtz. New York: Summit Books, 1984.

————. "Medieval Bible Commentaries." In *Back to the Sources: Reading the Classic Jewish Texts*, edited by Barry W. Holtz. New York: Summit Books, 1984.

Isaacs, Ronald H. *The Jewish Bible Almanac*. Northvale, NJ: Jason Aronson, 1997.

Katz, Rabbi Mordechai. *Ulmode Ul'Lamed: From the Teachings of Our Sages* . . . Spring Valley, NY: Feldheim Publishers, 1978.

Levenson, Jon D. *Sinai and Zion: An Entry Into the Jewish Bible*. New York: HarperCollins, 1985.

Lichtenstein, Murray H. "Biblical Poetry." In *Back to the Sources: Reading the Classic Jewish Texts,* edited by Barry W. Holtz. New York: Summit Books, 1984.

*Mihaly, Eugene. *A Song to Creation: A Dialogue with Text*. Cincinnati: Hebrew Union College Press, 1975.

Orlinsky, Harry M. *Ancient Israel,* 2nd ed. Ithaca, NY: Cornell Univ. Press, 1960.

Rosenberg, Joel. "Biblical Narrative." In *Back to the Sources: Reading the Classic Jewish Texts,* edited by Barry W. Holtz. New York: Summit Books, 1984.

THE TALMUD AND OTHER RABBINIC WRITINGS

Abrams, Judith Z. *The Talmud for Beginners. Vol. I, Prayer.* Northvale, NJ: Jason Aronson, 1991.

*Adler, Morris. *The World of the Talmud*. New York: Schocken Books, 1963.

Baumgarten, Albert I. "Ancient Jewish Sectarianism," in *Judaism,* Fall 1998.

Bergman, Rabbi Meir Zvi. *Gateway to the Talmud*. Translated by Rabbi Nesanel Kasnet. Brooklyn, NY: Mesorah Publications, 1985.

Bialik, Hayim Nakhman. "Halakhah and Aggadah." In *Modern Jewish Thought,* edited by Nahum Glatzer. New York: Schocken Books, 1977.

Carmell, Aryeh. *Aiding Torah Study.* Spring Valley, NY: Feldheim Publishers, 1988.

Chevlen, Eric M. "Discovering the Talmud," in *First Things,* August–September 1998.

Cohen, Deborah Nussbaum. "Celebrating the Study of Talmud: Thousands Find a 'Spiritual Uplift.' " Jewish Telegraphic Agency. New York: September 29, 1997.

Feldman, Louis H. *Jew and Gentile in the Ancient World: Attitudes and Interactions from Alexander to Justinian.* Princeton, NJ: Princeton Univ. Press, 1993.

Fishburn, Jonathan. "Launching Into 'the Sea of Talmud': A Personal Story." *The Jewish Quarterly,* Autumn 1998.

Glatzer, Nahum. *Hammer on the Rock: A Midrash Anthology.* New York: Schocken Books, 1962.

Goldenberg, Robert. "Talmud." In *Back to the Sources: Reading the Classic Jewish Texts,* edited by Barry W. Holtz. New York: Summit Books, 1984.

Holtz, Barry W. "Midrash." In *Back to the Sources: Reading the Classic Jewish Texts,* edited by Barry W. Holtz. New York: Summit Books, 1984.

Kalmin, Richard. *Sages, Stories, Authors and Editors in Rabbinic Babylon.* Providence, RI: Brown Univ. Press, 1994.

*Katz, Michael, and Gershon Schwartz. *Swimming in the Sea of Talmud.* Philadelphia: Jewish Publication Society, 1997.

Kolatch, Alfred J. *Who's Who in the Talmud.* New York: Jonathan David, 1964.

Krupnick, Eliyahu. *The Gateway to Learning: A Systematic Introduction to the Study of Talmud,* rev. ed. Spring Valley, NY: Feldheim Publishers, 1998.

*Lehrman, S. M. *The World of Midrash.* New York: Thomas Yoseloff, 1961.

Neusner, Jacob. *Ancient Israel After Catastrophe: The Religious Worldview of the Mishnah.* Charlottesville, VA: Univ. Press of Virginia, 1983.

———. *Invitation to the Talmud: A Teaching Book.* New York: Harper and Row, rev. ed., 1984.

———. *The Midrash: An Introduction.* Northvale, NJ: Jason Aronson, 1990.

Ochs, Peter. "From Peshat to Derash and Back Again: Talmud for Modern Religious Jews," in *Judaism,* Summer 1997.

Rabinowitz, Abraham Hirsch. *The Study of Talmud: Understanding the Halachic Mind.* Northvale, NJ: Jason Aronson, 1996.

Resnick, Henry. "Conversations with the Talmud," at New York Kollel website at www.huc.edu/kollel/talmud.

*Schwartz, Howard. *Reimagining the Bible: The Storytelling of the Rabbis.* Oxford: Oxford Univ. Press, 1998.

Shinan, Avigdor. *The World of Aggadah,* translated by John Glucker. Tel Aviv: MOD Books, 1990.

Siegel, Eliezer. "A Page of Talmud"; website at http://www.acs.ucalgary.ca/~elsegal/TalmudPage.html.

*Steinsaltz, Adin. *The Essential Talmud.* New York: Basic Books, 1976.

————. *The Talmud: A Reference Guide.* New York: Random House, 1989.

Strack, H. L., and Günter Stëmberger. *An Introduction to the Talmud and Midrash,* translated and edited by Markus Bockmuehl. Minneapolis: Fortress Press, 1992.

JEWISH MYSTICISM

*Ariel, David. *The Mystic Quest: An Introduction to Jewish Mysticism.* New York: Schocken Books, 1988.

Ben-Shlomo, Yosef, translated by Shmuel Himelstein. *Poetry of Being: Lectures on the Philosophy of Rabbi Kook.* Tel Aviv: MOD Books, 1990.

Dan, Joseph. *The Ancient Jewish Mysticism,* translated by Shmuel Himelstein. Tel Aviv: MOD Books, 1993.

————. "An Interview with Joseph Dan," from Jason Aronson, Inc. Website at www.aronson.com/Judaica.

————. Introduction to *The Early Kabbalah.* New York: Paulist Press, 1986.

————. *Jewish Mysticism and Jewish Ethics.* Northvale, NJ: Jason Aronson, 1996.

————. *Jewish Mysticism, Vol. 1: Late Antiquity.* Northvale, NJ: Jason Aronson, 1998.

————. *Jewish Mysticism, Vol. 2: The Middle Ages.* Northvale, NJ: Jason Aronson, 1998.

Davis, Dr. Avram, and Manuela Dunn Mascetti. *Judaic Mysticism.* New York: Hyperion, 1997.

Fine, Lawrence. "Kabbalistic Texts." In *Back to the Sources: Reading the*

Classic Jewish Texts, edited by Barry W. Holtz. New York: Summit Books, 1984.

Fishbane, Michael. "The Book of Zohar and Exegetical Spirituality." In *The Exegetical Imagination: On Jewish Thought and Theology.* Cambridge, MA: Harvard Univ. Press, 1998.

Green, Arthur. "Teachings of the Hasidic Masters." In *Back to the Sources: Reading the Classic Jewish Texts,* edited by Barry W. Holtz. New York: Summit Books, 1984.

Idel, Moshe. *Kabbalah: New Perspectives.* New Haven, CT: Yale Univ. Press, 1988.

*Jacobs, Louis. *Hasidic Prayer.* New York: Schocken Books, 1973.

*Kaplan, Aryeh. *Jewish Meditation.* New York: Schocken Books, 1985.

————. *The Light Beyond: Adventures in Hassidic Thought.* New York: Moznaim, 1981.

Scholem, Gershom. *Kabbalah.* New York: Meridian Books, 1974.

————. *Major Trends in Jewish Mysticism.* New York: Schocken Books, 1941.

————. *The Messianic Idea in Judaism and Other Essays on Jewish Spirituality.* New York: Schocken Books, 1971.

————. *On the Kabbalah and Its Symbolism.* New York: Schocken Books, 1965.

————. *On the Mystical Shape of the Godhead: Basic Concepts in the Kabbalah,* translated by Joachim Neugroschel. New York: Schocken Books, 1991.

————. *On the Possibility of Jewish Mysticism in Our Time and Other Essays,* edited by Avraham Shapira, translated by Jonathan Chipman. Philadelphia: Jewish Publication Society, 1997.

————. *Shabbetai Sevi: The Mystical Messiah, 1627–1676.* Princeton, NJ: Princeton Univ. Press, 1973.

Weiner, Herbert. *9 ½ Mystics: The Kabbalah Today.* New York: Collier Books, rev. ed., 1992.

JEWISH PHILOSOPHY

Atterton, Peter, webmaster for "An Emmanuel Levinas Web Page," website at http://pw1.netcom.com/~cyberink/lev.html.

Beavers, Anthony. "Emmanuel Levinas and the Prophetic Voice of Post-modernity," lecture written and delivered in 1993; website may be found at www.evansville.edu/~tbu/trip/prophet.htm.

Ben-Shlomo, Yosef. *Lectures on the Philosophy of Spinoza,* translated by Shmuel Himelstein. Tel Aviv: MOD Books, 1989.

Buber, Martin. *I and Thou,* translated by Walter Kaufman. New York: Scribners, 1970.

————. *The Way of Response: Martin Buber, Selections from His Writings,* edited by Nahum N. Glatzer. New York: Schocken Books, 1966.

Buber, Martin, and Franz Rosenzweig. *Scripture and Translation,* translated by Lawrence Rosenwald and Everett Fox. Bloomington, IN: Indiana Univ. Press, 1994.

Cohen, Naomi. *Philo Judaeus: His Universe of Discourse.* Frankfurt: Peter Lang, 1995.

Cohn-Sherbok, Dan. *Fifty Key Jewish Thinkers.* London: Routledge, 1997.

Committee of Public Safety. " 'My Place in the Sun,' Reflections on the Thought of Emmanuel Levinas," in *Diacritics.* Baltimore, MD, 1996.

Epstein, Rabbi Dr. Isidore. "Maimonides," in *Jewish Philosophy and Philosophers,* edited by Raymond Goldwater. London: Hillel Foundation, 1962.

Fackenheim, Emil. *Jewish Philosophers and Jewish Philosophy,* edited by Michael L. Morgan. Bloomington, IN: Indiana Univ. Press, 1996.

Gibbs, Robert. *Correlations in Rosenzweig and Levinas.* Princeton, NJ: Princeton Univ. Press, 1992.

Glatzer, Nahum. *Franz Rosenzweig, His Life and His Thought.* New York: Schocken Books, 1953.

HaLevi, Judah, translated by Hartwig Hirschfeld. *The Kuzari: An Argument for the Faith of Israel.* New York: Schocken Books, 1964.

Heschel, Abraham Joshua. *God in Search of Man: A Philosophy of Judaism.* New York: Farrar, Straus and Giroux, 1955.

————. *I Asked for Wonder: A Spiritual Anthology,* edited by Samuel H. Dresner. New York: Crossroad, 1984.

————. *Maimonides: The Life and Times of the Great Medieval Jewish Thinker.* New York: Doubleday, 1982.

————. *Man Is Not Alone: A Philosophy of Religion.* New York: Farrar, Straus and Giroux, 1951.

————. *Moral Grandeur and Spiritual Audacity,* edited by Susanna Heschel. New York: Farrar, Straus and Giroux, 1996.

————. *The Quest for God: Studies in Prayer and Symbolism.* New York: Crossroad Publishing Co., 1954.

Husik, Jacob. *A History of Medieval Jewish Philosophy.* New York: Jewish Publication Society, 1930.

*Katz, Steven T. *Jewish Philosophers.* New York: Bloch Publishing Co., 1975.

Kraft, Robert A. "Philo and the Sabbath Crisis: Alexandrian Jewish Politics and the Dating of Philo's Works." In *Ioudaios* (website at ftp.lehigh.edu /pub/listserv/ioudaios-l /Articles/sabbath).

Lechte, John. "Emmanuel Levinas." In *Fifty Key Contemporary Thinkers.* London: Routledge, 1997.

Leibowitz, Yeshayahu, translated by John Glucker. *The Faith of Maimonides.* Tel Aviv: MOD Books, 1989.

Levinas, Emmanuel. *Difficult Freedom: Essays on Judaism,* translated by Seán Hand. Baltimore, MD: Johns Hopkins Univ. Press, 1990.

————. *Entre Nous: Thinking-of-the-Other,* translated by Michael B. Smith and Barbara Harshav. New York: Columbia Univ. Press, 1998.

————. *Ethics and Infinity: Conversations with Philippe Nemo,* translated by Richard A. Cohen. Pittsburgh, PA: Duquesne Univ. Press, 1985.

————. *In the Time of the Nations,* translated by Michael B. Smith. Bloomington, IN: Indiana Univ. Press, 1994.

————. *Nine Talmudic Readings,* translated by Annette Aronowicz. Bloomington, IN: Indiana Univ. Press, 1990.

————. *Outside the Subject,* translated by Michael B. Smith. Palo Alto, CA: Stanford Univ. Press, 1994.

————. *Proper Names,* translated by Michael B. Smith. Palo Alto, CA: Stanford Univ. Press, 1996.

Loewe, Raphael. "Philo and Judaism in Alexandria." In *Jewish Philosophy and Philosophers,* edited by Raymond Goldwater. London: Hillel Foundation, 1962.

Maimonides (Moses ben Maimon). *Ethical Writings of Maimonides,* edited by Raymond L. Weiss with Charles Butterworth. New York: Dover Publications, 1975.

Martin, Bernard. *Great 20th Century Jewish Philosophers: Shestov, Rosenzweig, Buber.* New York: Macmillan, 1970.

Maybaum, Rabbi Dr. Ignaz. "Franz Rosenzweig and the Existentialist Philosophers," in *Jewish Philosophy and Philosophers,* edited by Raymond Goldwater. London: Hillel Foundation, 1962.

Mosès, Stéphane. *System and Revelation: The Philosophy of Franz Rosenzweig,* translated by Catherine Thianyi. Detroit, MI: Wayne State Univ. Press, 1992.

Oppenheim, Michael. *Mutual Upholding: Fashioning Jewish Philosophy Through Letters.* New York: Peter Lang, 1992.

————. "Franz Rosenzweig and Emmanuel Levinas: A Midrash or Thought-Experiment." *Judaism,* Spring 1993.

Philo. *Philosophia Judaica: Selections,* edited by Hans Lewy. Oxford: Phaidon Press, 1946.

Raphael, David Daiches. "Spinoza." In *Jewish Philosophy and Philosophers,* edited by Raymond Goldwater. London: Hillel Foundation, 1962.

Rosenstock-Huessy, Eugen, and Franz Rosenzweig. *Judaism Despite Christianity.* New York: Schocken Books, 1969.

Rosner, Fred. *Maimonides' Introduction to His Commentary on the Mishnah.* Northvale, NJ: Jason Aronson, 1995.

Roth, Leon. "Is There a Jewish Philosophy?" In *Jewish Philosophy and Philosophers,* edited by Raymond Goldwater. London: Hillel Foundation, 1962.

Rubinstein, Ernest. "The Spirituality of Philosophical Judaism." *Studies in Formative Spirituality,* February 1987.

Saadiah Gaon. *The Book of Beliefs and Opinions,* translated by Samuel Rosenblatt. New Haven, CT: Yale Univ. Press, 1948.

Samuelson, Norbert M. "Medieval Jewish Philosophy." In *Back to the Sources: Reading the Classic Jewish Texts,* edited by Barry W. Holtz. New York: Summit Books, 1984.

Seeskin, Kenneth. *Maimonides: A Guide for Today's Perplexed.* West Orange, NJ: Berhman House, 1991.

Seland, Torrey. "Philo and the Clubs and Associations of Alexandria," in *Ioudaios* (website at ftp.lehigh.edu/pub/listserv/ioudaios-l/Articles/tsphilo).

————. "What Do We Know About Philo, His Authorship, and His Addresses?" (website at www.hivolda.no/asf/kkf/philopag.html).

Soloveitchik, Rabbi Joseph B. *Halakhic Man,* translated by Lawrence Kaplan. Philadelphia: Jewish Publication Society, 1983.

————. *The Halakhic Mind: An Essay on Jewish Tradition and Modern Thought.* New York: Free Press, 1986.

————. *The Lonely Man of Faith.* New York: Doubleday, 1965.

————. *Reflections of the Rav: Lessons in Jewish Thought,* adapted by

Rabbi Abraham R. Besdin. Jerusalem: Department for Torah Education and Culture, World Zionist Organization, 1979.

Spinoza, Baruch. *The Philosophy of Spinoza, Selected from His Chief Works,* edited by Joseph Ratner. New York: Modern Library, 1927.

Steinfels, Peter. "Emmanuel Levinas, 90, French Ethical Philosopher." *The New York Times.* New York: December 27, 1995.

Vermes, Pamela. *Buber.* New York: Grove Press, 1988.

BEYOND THE RABBIS

Academy for the Advancement of Science and Technology. "The Yiddish Homepage," website at http://www.bergen.org/AAST/Projects/Yiddish/English/index.html.

Ahad Ha'Am (Asher Ginsberg). *The Selected Essays of Ahad Ha'Am,* translated and edited by Leon Simon. New York: Atheneum Books, 1981.

Baron, Salo W. "The Modern Age." In *Great Ages and Ideas of the Jewish People,* edited by Leo W. Schwarz. New York: Modern Library, 1956.

*Beller, Steven. *Herzl.* New York: Grove Press, 1991.

Berkovitz, Eliezer. *Faith After the Holocaust.* New York: KTAV, 1973.

Bottomore, Tom, ed. *A Dictionary of Marxist Thought.* Cambridge, MA: Harvard Univ. Press, 1983.

Braiterman, Zachary. *(God) After Auschwitz: Tradition and Change in Post-Holocaust Jewish Thought.* Princeton, NJ: Princeton Univ. Press, 1998.

Brown, Dee. *Bury My Heart at Wounded Knee: An Indian History of the American West.* New York: Holt, Rinehart and Winston, 1971.

Cohen, Deborah Nussbaum. "Successful conference spawns new Orthodox feminist alliance." Jewish Telegraphic Agency (New York: July 3, 1997).

————. "Women carving new place in Orthodox Judaism." Jewish Telegraphic Agency (New York: September 1, 1995).

Cohen, Israel. *Vilna.* Philadelphia: Jewish Publication Society, 1992.

*Cohn-Sherbok, Dan. *Holocaust Theology.* London: Lamp Press, 1989.

*Cohn-Sherbok, Lavinia and Dan. *A Short History of Judaism.* Oxford: Oneworld, 1994.

*————. *A Short Reader in Judaism.* Oxford: Oneworld, 1996.

*Comay, Joan. *The Diaspora Story: The Epic of the Jewish People Among the Nations.* New York: Random House, 1980.

Elon, Amos. "Israel and the End of Zionism." *New York Review of Books,* December 19, 1996.

Etkes, Emanuel. "Hasidism as a Movement—The First Stage." In *Hasidism: Continuity or Innovation?,* edited by Bezalel Safran. Cambridge, MA: Harvard Center for Jewish Studies, 1988.

Fackenheim, Emil. "The Zionist Imperative." *First Things,* February 1995.

————. *God's Presence in History: Jewish Affirmations and Philosophical Reflections.* New York: Harper and Row, 1970.

————. *Mending the World: Foundations of Post-Holocaust Jewish Thought.* Bloomington, IN: Indiana Univ. Press, 1994.

Fein, Richard J. *The Dance of Leah: Discovering Yiddish in America.* Rutherford, NJ: Fairleigh Dickinson Univ. Press, 1986.

Fishman, David. *Russia's First Modern Jews: The Jews of Shklov.* New York: New York Univ. Press, 1995.

Fishman, Sylvia Barack. *A Breath of Life: Feminism in the American Jewish Community.* New York: The Free Press, 1993.

Fogel, Rabbi Yehezkel, ed., translated by Edward Levin. *I Will Be Sanctified: Religious Responses to the Holocaust.* Northvale, NJ: Jason Aronson, 1998.

Fuchs, Nancy. *Our Share of Night, Our Share of Morning: Parenting as a Spiritual Journey.* San Francisco: HarperCollins, 1996.

Gilman, Sander L., and Zipes, Jack, eds. *Yale Companion to Jewish Writing and Thought in German Culture, 1096–1996.* New Haven, CT: Yale Univ. Press, 1997.

*Goldberg, David J. *To the Promised Land: A History of Zionist Thought.* New York: Penguin Books, 1996.

Goldsmith, Emanuel S. *Modern Yiddish Culture: The Story of the Yiddish Language Movement.* New York: Fordham Univ. Press, 1997.

Gorny, Yosef. *From Rosh Pina and Degania to Demona: A History of Constructive Zionism,* translated by John Glucker. Tel Aviv: MOD Books, 1989.

Green, Arthur. "Teachings of the Hasidic Masters." In *Back to the Sources: Reading the Classic Jewish Texts,* edited by Barry W. Holtz. New York: Summit Books, 1984.

Halevi, Yossi Klein. "Zionism, Phase II." *Jerusalem Report,* December 26, 1996.

Halivni, David. "Holocaust Questions." *Judaism,* Fall 1997.

Halkin, Hillel. "Foundering Father: Herzl's 'Jewish State' at 100." *The Forward,* September 9, 1996.

Harshav, Benjamin. *The Meaning of Yiddish.* Berkeley, CA: Univ. of California Press, 1990.

Hartman, David. *Conflicting Visions: Spiritual Possibilities of Modern Israel.* New York: Schocken Books, 1990.

Hasdai, Yaacov. "The Origins of the Conflict Between Hasidim and Mitnagdim." In *Hasidism: Continuity or Innovation?,* edited by Bezalel Safran. Cambridge, MA: Harvard Center for Jewish Studies, 1988.

Herzl, Theodor. *The Jews' State,* translated by Henk Overbeg. Northvale, NJ: Jason Aronson, 1997.

*Heschel, Abraham Joshua. *The Earth Is the Lord's: The Inner World of the Jew in Eastern Europe.* New York: Farrar, Straus and Giroux, 1949.

Horowitz, Elliott. " 'The Vengeance of the Jews Was Stronger Than Their Avarice': Modern Historians and the Persian Conquest of Jerusalem in 614," *Jewish Social Studies,* vol. 4, no. 2.

Jacobs, Louis. *Hasidic Prayer.* New York: Schocken, 1973.

Katz, Jacob Marcus, ed. *The Jew in the Medieval World: A Sourcebook, 315–1791.* New York: Athenaeum, 1978.

Katz, Steven T. *Post-Holocaust Dialogues: Critical Studies in Modern Jewish Thought.* New York: New York Univ. Press, 1983.

Keele, Lisa. "Hidden Worship: The Religious Rituals of Orthodox Jewish Women." *Women in Judaism: A Multidisciplinary Journal,* 1997; website at http://www.utoronto.ca/wjudaism/journal/index.html.

Kook, Rabbi Abraham Isaac. *Orot,* translated by Bezalel Naor. Northvale, NJ: Jason Aronson Inc., 1993.

Laqueur, Walter. *A History of Zionism.* New York: Schocken Books, 1989.

Mayer, Michael A. *The Origins of the Modern Jew: Jewish Identity and European Culture in Germany, 1749–1824.* Detroit: Wayne State Univ. Press, 1967.

Mintz, Rabbi Adam. "The Still Quiet Voice: The Process of Transformation in Judaism," sermon delivered at Lincoln Square Synagogue, March 1, 1997. (At Lincoln Square Synagogue website: http://www.lss.org/ser1ii.html)

Painton, Frederick. "A Century Late, the Truth Arrives: The French

Army Concedes That Alfred Dreyfus Was Innocent." *Time,* September 25, 1995.

Rabinowicz, Tzvi M., ed. *The Encyclopedia of Hasidism.* Northvale, NJ: Jason Aronson, 1996.

Raisin, Jacob. *The Haskalah Movement in Russia.* Philadelphia: Jewish Publication Society, 1913.

Robinson, George. "Population Study Offers Glimmer of Hope: Are We Creating a 'Uniquely American' Jewish Experience?" *Manhattan Jewish Sentinel,* October 20, 1993.

*Sachar, Howard M. *The Course of Modern Jewish History,* rev. ed. New York: Vintage Books, 1990.

Sacks, Jonathan. *Crisis and Covenant: Jewish Thought After the Holocaust.* Manchester: Manchester Univ. Press, 1992.

Shepard, Richard F., and Vicki Gold Levi. *Live and Be Well: A Celebration of Yiddish Culture in America.* New York: Ballantine Books, 1982.

Shimoni, Gideon. *The Zionist Ideology.* Hanover, NH: Brandeis Univ. Press/University Press of New England, 1995.

Shluker, Zelda. "Orthodoxy, Meet Feminism." *Hadassah Magazine,* March 1997.

Siegel, Rachel Josefowitz. " 'I Don't Know Enough': Jewish Women's Learned Ignorance." *Women in Judaism: A Multidisciplinary Journal,* Fall 1997; website at http://www.utoronto.ca/wjudaism/journal/index.html.

Streit, Noah, and Daniel Ehrenreich. "Second Conference on Feminism and Orthodoxy: Over 2,000 people in attendance." *Yeshiva University Commentator,* vol. 62, no. 8.

Trainin Blank, Barbara. "An Orthodox Feminist on a Role: Portrait of Blu Greenberg." *Hadassah Magazine,* February 1998.

Wigoder, Geoffrey, ed. *The New Encyclopedia of Zionism and Israel.* Madison, NJ: Fairleigh Dickinson Univ. Press, 1994.

Wistrich, Robert S. *Antisemitism: The Longest Hatred.* New York: Pantheon Books, 1991.

Yovel, Yirmiyahu. "Sublimity and Ressentiment: Hegel, Nietzsche, and the Jews." *Jewish Social Studies,* vol. 3, no. 3.

INDEX